CONTENTS

VERA BRITTAIN

Diary of the Thirties

1932–1939

CHRONICLE OF FRIENDSHIP

Edited by Alan Bishop

LONDON
VICTOR GOLLANCZ LTD
1986

First published in Great Britain 1986
by Victor Gollancz Ltd,
14 Henrietta Street, London WC2E 8QJ

Vera Brittain's diary © the literary executors for the
Vera Brittain Estate, 1986; compilation and editorial matter
© Alan Bishop, 1986

British Library Cataloguing in Publication Data
Brittain, Vera
    Chronicle of friendship: diary of the Thirties,
    1932–1939.
    1. Brittain, Vera—Biography
    2. Authors, English—20th century—Biography
    I. Title   II. Bishop, A. G.
    828'.91209   PR6003.R385Z/

ISBN 0-575-03602-8

Photoset in Great Britain by
Rowland Phototypesetting Ltd, Bury St Edmunds, Suffolk
and printed by St Edmundsbury Press, Bury St Edmunds, Suffolk
Illustrations originated and printed by Thomas Campone, Southampton

LIST OF ILLUSTRATIONS

following page 192

ACKNOWLEDGMENTS

The text of Vera Brittain's diary (1932–39), "A Perfect Day" and most of the illustrations are published with the permission of the William Ready Division of Archives and Research Collections, McMaster University Library, Hamilton, Ontario, Canada.

I am greatly indebted to several colleagues at McMaster: to Graham Hill (University Librarian) and members of the Library staff including Charlotte Stewart, Bruce Whiteman, Renu Barrett, Linda Stewart, Margaret Foley and Dr Kathy Garay (Research Collections), Narendar Passi, Liz Bayley, Merike Koger and Richard Harkin (Reference), and Dennis Driscoll (Music); to Manon Ames (Humanities Word-Processing Centre); and to Dr Fred Bottley for his extensive research assistance in indexing and in collecting information for use in annotation.

I also acknowledge with gratitude the support of the Social Sciences and Humanities Research Council of Canada through a Research Grant which greatly assisted my editorial work.

The quotations, in my Introduction, from *O Dreams, O Destinations* by Phyllis Bentley are reprinted by permission of A. D. Peters & Co. Ltd.

Finally: I wish to thank Paul Berry (Vera Brittain's Joint Literary Executor) for his continuously generous help; Vera Brittain's children John Brittain-Catlin and Shirley Williams for their thoughtful consideration of the text and help with the illustrations; Geoffrey Handley-Taylor (Joint Literary Executor); Livia Gollancz and her staff; my wife and children.

ALAN BISHOP

INTRODUCTION

WHEN VERA BRITTAIN began this diary in 1932, she had not kept a continuous "reflective record" for about fifteen years. Her very detailed and moving diary of the First World War (published in 1981 under her own title *Chronicle of Youth*) had petered out in 1917, as she struggled to keep her grip on life in the midst of extreme personal loss and the suffering of the hideously-wounded soldiers she was nursing. During the intervening years she had twice kept travel diaries (in 1924 and 1925)—a practice she was to continue, when travelling abroad, for the rest of her life. But these were primarily a journalist's "working notes", preserving facts and impressions, and recording interviews, for likely future use in articles or reviews.

The diary she began in 1932 was quite different in nature. As her brief Foreword makes clear, it was intended to be a counterpart and sequel to *Chronicle of Youth*: a second full, continuous, personal record of her daily life, against the background of national and international events. But the life itself, she believed, would be strikingly different from that of the young VAD from Buxton: "Contrast between old life in Buxton before War & in hospitals during war with my present existence could hardly be greater." That was to reckon without Crass Casualty. The new diary in fact traces a pattern increasingly, and ironically, reminiscent of the old: begun in optimism, centred on personal relationships and literary preoccupations, it was to record, harrowingly, the death of her closest friend and the destructiveness of a second Great War.

This diary runs from 1932 to the end of 1945, though with considerably more variation than its predecessor, and with larger gaps (she had now so much less time to keep a diary, and so many more responsibilities). In her frustration she burst out (on 11 December 1936) "The trouble with all momentous periods of my life—whether due to public or private events or to a mixture of the two—is that I never have time while they are going on either to take things in properly, or adequately record them." But that was overstating a typical diarists' dilemma. For much of the time, despite extreme pressure on her time and energy, Vera Brittain managed to keep an impressively full and valuable record—even if, on occasion, it had to be composed a few days afterwards or in hasty note-form. Some years are very much better represented than others, however: 1932 comes close to being a day-by-day record, while 1934 contains little more than her journey to the United States, and 1938 has only four brief entries.

Containing over 300,000 words in all, the 1932–1945 diary is too long to print, even in a necessarily abridged form, as a single volume. But the onset of the Second World War during 1939 divides it, thematically and by word-count, into two almost equal sections. So the present volume, *Chronicle of Friendship*, contains Vera Brittain's "reflective record" of the thirties, and its sequel (to be entitled *Chronicle of Experience*—the three *Chronicles* paralleling her three *Testaments*) will contain her record of the Second World War. Although the two sections of the complete diary —1932–39, and 1939–45—are of course closely linked by many continuities, they are also separated by a number of shifts: from uneasy peace to total war; from the primacy of private to the urgency of public concerns; from feminist to pacifist priorities in Brittain's journalism and political activity. In addition, Vera Brittain's friendship with Winifred Holtby binds the 1932–39 volume into a unity: it begins as Holtby's fatal illness takes hold, reaches its climax in her death, and follows the aftermath, for Brittain, to a resolution as she completes the biography *Testament of Friendship* just before the outbreak of war.

Proportionately less of the text (no more than a quarter) has been omitted from the edition of this diary than was necessary (and desirable) for *Chronicle of Youth*; and every attempt has been made to retain all passages of personal or historical interest and importance (in particular, the long account of Winifred Holtby's final illness and death, and all references to contemporary international events, have been printed with little excision). Material from *Chronicle of Friendship* appears in three of the four books Vera Brittain wrote during the thirties—*Honourable Estate* (published in 1936), *Thrice a Stranger* (1938) and *Testament of Friendship* (1940)—as well as in *Testament of Experience* (1957), her "Autobiographical Story of the Years 1925–50"; but duplication was neither frequent nor extensive enough to become a reason for omitting passages. As in *Chronicle of Youth*, I have not indicated excisions, partly to accord with Brittain's own practice, partly because I believe that such indications in the text distract readers while giving them information of little value and no precision. The full text of the diary can be consulted in the seventeen notebooks D14 to D30 of the Vera Brittain Archive, McMaster University Library.

This edition also retains the other editorial principles established in *Chronicle of Youth*. Spelling errors and obvious slips of the pen have been corrected silently; square brackets indicate an added word or uncertain reading; punctuation and paragraphing have been altered occasionally to make the sense immediately clear and to ensure untroubled reading; entry-headings have been standardised and some conventions adjusted to accord with present practice. But otherwise I have attempted to preserve features (such as casual alternations of "and" and "&") native to the informality and fluidity of a diary.

The Notes comment very briefly on the relation between the diary-entries and the major events of Brittain's life in each year; they explain any abbreviation that, on first occurrence, might be expected to puzzle readers;

and they aim to enlighten any obscurities, to identify quotations and to provide additional information in connection with the diary's more important references to people, organisations or events. (But perfection, though striven for, has not been attained: in particular, because the range of reference is so wide, it has not been possible in the time available to annotate all individuals mentioned in the diary, and for this lack editorial apologies are offered.) The Notes are keyed to page numbers of the text, and are indicated, not in the text itself (where typographical marks would distract some readers), but whenever possible in the Index; so it is suggested that readers use the Index to find out both where references occur in the text and whether (and where) a relevant note has been provided.

II

As a very personal account of the thirties—a period which continues to attract the fascinated attention of historians, critics and general readers —Vera Brittain's diary often recalls two lively social histories compiled as the period ended: *The Thirties* by Malcolm Muggeridge and *The Long Week-end* by Robert Graves and Alan Hodge (both published in 1940). Her account is not, of course, a broad survey, the product of retrospection, research and synthesis. It is the record of a very perceptive observer living a busy and varied life—an observer who was, moreover, a trained historian, a practising journalist and autobiographer, and a committed social and political activist. Written in the very flux of daily experience, her diary breathes life into history, returns the past to its present, allows us to *feel* what it was like to be alive during the thirties.

Consider, for instance, her vivid, succinct description of George V's Silver Jubilee celebrations in May 1935. Graves and Hodge recalled, at some length, that "royal and popular fête" as the Depression waned; Muggeridge recalled the "enormous, and often spontaneous, enthusiasm" of the crowds. Brittain plunges us into the streets: "King's Road, Chelsea, one vast patriotic shriek like the rest of London . . . Several people faint during the morning—mostly men, including two soldiers . . . Procession comes at last—just King & Queen going at a swift trot. Queen in silver cloak & pink turban" (that gimlet eye for women's clothing!) "—bowing & doing her duty as usual, conscientiously but not graciously. King looked tired & rather bored . . ." (He was to die within a few months.) At such moments she is the eye and pen of her compatriots. But then she also turns that glittering coin over, to see what is behind its crowned profile:

Children played all afternoon at soldiers & Kings & Queens; demanded war stories & wanted to see my war medals. I'm afraid these official ceremonies with all their troops don't exactly help to educate the youngest generation in the way of peace!

The rueful tone here matches a counterpointed crowd-scene: the May Day Demonstration just before the Jubilee; "usual British crowd" with its "air of patience & respectability rather than rebellion or daring. Usual facility for turning everything into a picnic (as for a long time it did the war) . . ."

The war, the War. Memories of 1914–18 are always near the surface of her mind; and on another, sadder Royal Occasion—the Abdication of Edward VIII in December 1936—her clamorous, impassioned support is for a beleaguered and betrayed member of the "war generation".

> . . . I said that I, like King Edward VIII, belonged to a generation which had seen almost more history than any generation could bear & was still only on the early side of middle age . . . I pointed out that at least one factor in this crisis was the profound and unbridgeable gulf between the attitude of the older generation towards morals & that of the war generation.

Later in its middle age, that generation was to experience the second catastrophe which many of its members, like Vera Brittain and Winifred Holtby, had worked so hard to prevent. At first, in this diary, Brittain seems overwhelmingly preoccupied with re-living the First World War —in 1932 and 1933 she was struggling to complete her retrospective *Testament of Youth*, that "vehement protest against war" begun in 1929, the year before her daughter Shirley was born. When it was done, and in the hands of her publishers, she went on holiday to recover from the strain and pain of its writing—and chose to tour the battlefields of the Somme; standing, on the nineteenth anniversary of the outbreak of the Great War, beside the grave of the fiancé killed in 1915:

> Had forgotten that Roland's grave is the first one comes upon when entering from the side path. Don't know why they put his age as 19 when he was really 20. . . . Put on his grave, against the words "Never Goodbye" just under the edge of the grass, the two withered roses—pink from the Leightons' garden, red from mine—that I brought from London. All around the cemetery the harvest was being gathered into sheaves, and the air was filled with the smell of mown grass and hay.

A moving ceremony of communion with the precious dead of her generation. But if she was looking back, in remembrance, she was also looking ahead, in apprehension. She carried with her to the Somme a copy of Beverley Nichols' just-published *Cry Havoc!*, a best-seller which, like *Testament of Youth*, warned of the danger and horror of another world war. At Étaples, just before returning to England, she and Holtby signed the Visitors' Book at the huge military cemetery near where she had nursed in 1917: "And below our names I wrote the words: 'No More War!' "

In the spring of 1936, a few months after Winifred Holtby's death, Brittain and her husband, the political scientist and academic George

(Gordon) Catlin, spent several weeks observing the state of Germany and France. In the election posters facing them as they crossed the border, Nazism lowers upon them. She visits a pleasant middle-class home to hear the broadcast of a speech by Hitler, and finds that the mother and her two teen-aged children are "all very keen Nazis, especially the boy". She is in the audience to hear Goering: "Speech terrifying, like the letting loose of some enormous imprisoned force . . . No possibility of thought, reason, consideration here—only of crass emotion on the largest possible scale." And Hitler himself: "A man in the prime of life . . . Voice anything but falsetto . . . though it begins to crack and shrill when he gets emotional . . . Did not strike me as wily diplomatist but religious maniac." Everyone tells her that "the last thing Germany wants is war", but everywhere there is hatred. She is taken to a Jewish café, and is racked by its "collective sense of humiliation . . . Marked admixture of classes who would normally not talk to each other driven together by common misfortune. . . . I felt as if I were among a gathering of Girondins under the Terror . . ." Crossing into France, she feels intense relief at escaping the "consciousness of being watched & supervised in Germany; letters opened, conversations listened to, telephone calls noted."

Six months later she became a pacifist. Like many intellectuals of her generation, she believed that Fascism and Nazism were in large measure a consequence of the Versailles Treaty of 1919, for whose punitive clauses she blamed Allied (and particularly French) vindictiveness. She and Holtby had worked hard, from 1921 when they left Oxford and took a flat in London, in support of the League of Nations, that white hope of international reconciliation and progress. But in the thirties the League lapsed into irrelevance as the Dictators trampled its good intentions; and the British League of Nations Union, which had been strongly anti-war in the twenties, sidled towards acceptance of rearmament for "collective security". Even before she visited Germany in 1936, Brittain had come very close to pacifism: "I fear War more than Fascism; anyhow I am sure that you can't use Satan to cast out Satan, that Fascism which sprang from colossal injustice will only grow stronger if the injustice is rammed home . . ." Now, under the charismatic influence of Canon Dick Sheppard and of Bertrand Russell's *Which Way to Peace?*, she took the decision that had come to seem inevitable, and early in 1937 agreed to become a member and Sponsor of the Peace Pledge Union, Sheppard's new and vigorous peace movement. This decision changed the pattern of her life as she devoted more and more of her time and energy to committee meetings, speeches and articles in the pacifist cause.

War, she knew, would hurt the working class more than the middle and upper classes. She and Holtby had become socialists in the mid-twenties, after seeing the misery of London slums while campaigning for the election of a Liberal M.P., Sir Percy Harris. And now, ten years later, another election campaign—her husband's, as Labour candidate for the working-class division of Sunderland—showed her even worse poverty and despair, in the wake of the Depression:

> . . . terrible slums, & crowded rooms with indescribably filthy bedding. In one house saw family of man & woman with nine children all living in two rooms—man an ex-serviceman who had never had a job since the War; woman looked very ill, shapeless & entirely overwhelmed by life. Children only semi-clothed. . . . Realised as so often what an expensive luxury cleanliness is. Have never seen such terrible housing before—not even in Glasgow.

This knowledge of the "other England" was an important, if intermittent, factor in the social and political activities recorded in Brittain's diary. But her own lifestyle in the thirties was the comfortable compromise common in literary and left-wing circles (and especially common in Chelsea, a fashionable neighbourhood both respectable and mildly bohemian). The Brittain–Catlin–Holtby ménage of wife, often-absent husband, and female friend provoked some whispers, according to Brittain, but its unconventionality was firmly supported by middle-class aspirations and expectations. The household ran on four servants: housekeeper, maid, nurse (or, later, governess), manservant. Cocktail parties, dinners, plays, dances, exhibitions, walks in Battersea Park, shopping expeditions, visits to the Babies' Club, to the dentist, to her parents—Vera Brittain's daily round must have been very like that of most of her friends and neighbours. But the range of her additional commitments was certainly far greater.

During the thirties, Brittain continued her work for women's rights. She had become a firm feminist when a schoolgirl, under the influence of Olive Schreiner's *Woman and Labour*, and in the twenties had devoted much of her energy and time to lecturing, journalism and committee-work for the cause. Increasingly in the thirties, however, direct feminist activism gave way to the urgent need to work for peace, and expressed itself more indirectly, in support for several reforming movements. Like Schreiner, Brittain believed strongly in the mutual support and the essential unity of all liberating social and political change, and so in a responsibility to support them all whenever practicable. And her responsibilities as a mother of two small children naturally increased her interest in several movements pressing for social and educational reform—Birth Control, Babies' Clubs, Nursery Schools, New Education; to these, as her diary indicates, she gave considerable practical support.

Yet, however deep her commitment to social and political reform, she was always conscious that her primary professional responsibility was to fulfil herself as a writer. When a schoolgirl eleven years old she had written several "novels"; she had been strongly influenced by the example of George Eliot and other women writers; she had published two novels in the early twenties; she was a respected journalist. Now she must write major works that would be widely influential and admired. Nothing else, she knew, could satisfy her, ultimately. So when any serious conflict occurred between her writing and her other commitments, it was always resolved in favour of her writing. To her fellow P.P.U. Sponsors she explained "what I thought function of writers in the movement should be"—"what we needed most was not to be always activising but to go away quietly & do a little thinking . . ."

She also recognised that she could more effectively bring about social change through her writing than through direct social action. When, for instance, she learned that her housekeeper's mother had just endured a twelve-hour labour, she sent eggs and fruit, but reflected that

> . . . [I] never have been philanthropically-minded or felt that philanthropy is any good. What it *does* is to make me more politically-minded than I can bear—seeing that I'm really a writer and it's no use trying to be otherwise—& I feel we all ought to put everything aside until a doctor and anaesthetics are available for *every* maternity case in the country. The moral for me, I suppose, is to go on urging it in books, articles & speeches until enough people care sufficiently to get something done.

Her expertise and popularity as a platform-speaker gave her much satisfaction. Her talks were meticulously prepared and effectively delivered, and comments in her diary (immodest comments on occasion, but also self-critical) show clearly that her numerous addresses to organisations large or small, on tour or locally, were usually very well received. She was a professional, and proud of it. But that achievement was small beer compared with her literary ambitions:

> Kept on wondering, as so often, why the very measure of my indifference to lecturing seems to make me so successful as a lecturer, whereas I care so much more about books & succeed so much more hardly. Lecturing is of course a trivial art compared with writing, but I get quite irritated with myself when I find my college-educated brain selecting the right facts & presenting them lucidly, my well-developed voice rendering them audibly, & my possibly instinctive clothes sense enabling me to make a pleasant appearance.

During the thirties, Vera Brittain wrote her three most important and successful books: the autobiography *Testament of Youth*, the novel *Honourable Estate*, and the biography *Testament of Friendship*. For long periods her absorption in them was so extreme that other events (except her domestic responsibilities, as wife and mother) were pushed to the very periphery of her consciousness. Her diary records important stages in the composition of each of the three books (in the case of *Honourable Estate*, even the evolution of a climactic passage). It also details other aspects of a professional writer's daily life: relations with publishers (including Victor Gollancz and Harold Macmillan) and with literary agents, for instance; literary functions and literary gossip. Vera Brittain got to know, as acquaintances, several of the "lions" of her time, among them H. G. Wells, Rebecca West, J. B. Priestley, Naomi Mitchison, E. M. Delafield, St John Ervine, Cecil Roberts, Louis Golding; and her record of London literary life, especially in 1932 and 1933 (when she was completing *Testament of Youth* and then enjoying its enormous success) is of considerable interest.

But not only were most of her acquaintances writers: most of her friends were too. This is a diary of the thirties, and a writer's diary; it is also a chronicle of friendship and friendships, of close relationships that gave Vera Brittain intense pain, and pleasure.

III

Several close relationships thread this diary—apart from those between Vera Brittain and her two children, John and Shirley. Three are with women: Winifred Holtby, Phyllis Bentley and Storm Jameson, fellow writers from the North of England (they were born and grew up in Yorkshire). Three are with men: her father Thomas Brittain, her husband Gordon Catlin, and her American publisher George Brett. They are complex relationships, all of them, but of greatly varying intensity and longevity.

Brittain's friendship with Phyllis Bentley was the shortest, beginning and ending in 1932 (though the two women managed a quiet acquaint-anceship in later years, largely because of their mutual admiration of Winifred Holtby, through whom they came to know each other). In her autobiography *"O Dreams, O Destinations"* (1962), Bentley recalls the "ill-fated" friendship in considerable detail—a friendship that "had a profound effect, for good and ill, upon my life". Her account, which closely matches Brittain's, is generous in shouldering blame for failure: "In 1932 . . . I was thoroughly provincial," she says, "simple, naive, credulous" and, like her fellow-Yorkshiremen, "both blunt and reserved".

> Accordingly, I felt thoroughly inferior to Vera in all social matters. Vera was beautiful; she had a husband, two children and an Oxford degree; she was admirably dressed, spoke and wrote fluent, pointed, expressive Oxford English and knew hosts of people in literary London. I admitted my inferiority gladly and gladly learned from her; I was deeply grateful for all her many kindnesses, and respected her opinion.

It is easy to see, in comparing the two accounts, that Brittain did not suspect, torn as she was between respect and envy, how much she intimidated her shy guest. And it is in retrospect that Bentley recognises what a rebuke she must have represented to the ambitious Brittain—"I, gawky self-righteous little provincial, with all my difficulties apparently over and my long book safely published." The turning-point came quickly, in that unexpected argument which hurt them both deeply and which both describe in detail.

A discussion on the difference between the creative and the critical mind developed into an argument, in which Vera said I wrote dully and was not a conscious artist. I was ready to concede the first contention, but passionately rejected the second, which dismissed all my long years of struggle to learn my craft. Freud has explained why we forget, so it is not surprising that I did not at the time record, and when I first wrote this passage could not recall, what retort I made to this second accusation. But now I remember: I questioned what part conscious artistry could play in an autobiography, the material of which must be factual. Vera naturally rejected this fallacy with indignation, and a hot quarrel was the result. I thought I must leave the house and during the afternoon made private arrangements to do so. I have often wondered whether such a departure would have worked out better for Vera and myself than a continued association. But in the evening, through Winifred, we were reconciled.

Still, the wounds festered, in spite of the "very happy month" that followed. The final dispute, at the end of 1932, had its immediate cause in Brittain's illness; but at a deeper level the friendship was destroyed, Bentley comments, by "severe private tensions" on both sides, and she is both perceptive and sympathetic in describing the "prolonged strain" that Brittain was experiencing throughout their time together:

In 1932 she had been engaged for many years in planning, and for almost three years in writing, through every kind of harassment and interruption, the poignant and classic *Testament of Youth* which afterwards brought her fame. If anyone thinks it a small matter to manage a household, give birth to a child, nurse two children through chicken-pox, mumps and whooping-cough, and provide ever-ready counsel, escort and help to ageing parents, while writing a long and emotionally painful book, let him try it. (I say *him*, for alas too many women are all too familiar with similar tasks.) Such a situation brings frustration to an almost unbearable pitch.

One can only regret that the friendship perished, for in so many ways Bentley and Brittain were complementary personalities—"Vera has a great ability to state abstract ideas directly," Bentley notes, "while I must always express them in terms of fiction"—and might have influenced each other to mutual advantage. Bentley's summing-up is sober; regretful but appreciative. Yes, there was serious damage: "my new-found confidence, caused by literary success, was destroyed and I became more diffident personally . . . while a large (perhaps too grandiose) brother-of-man novel I was planning perished." (And she also attributes to the failure of the friendship her decision to abandon pacifism: "I found I could not turn the other cheek in our argument . . . I cannot believe that a procedure which does not work in private life can be valid in public affairs.") But there were also beneficial results: "contact with these two brilliant young women was extraordinarily stimulating", and "the introduction to the literary world both in 1932 and at later dates opened for me new horizons and opportunities. I also learned a great deal of valuable social know-how during my residence in Glebe Place."

Brittain's friendship with Margaret Storm Jameson, which also began in 1932, developed more slowly—no doubt in part because, even when Jameson, her husband Guy Chapman and her son by a previous marriage moved to London, both women had so many interests and responsibilities that meetings could not be frequent or long. In the late thirties, the friendship was strengthened by their common pacifism and concern about totalitarian persecution on the Continent, and they worked in harmonious partnership within the P.P.U. and P.E.N. But this friendship—which seems never to have been as deep as its predecessor—was also doomed to disintegrate in acrimony. The causes were complex, but one was Jameson's recantation of her pacifism—she was one of several prominent pacifists (including Bertrand Russell) to recant in the face of Hitler's unwavering evil.

With her husband, Brittain created a strong relationship of mutual freedom and tolerance. Like any marriage, it had its moments of anger and exasperation; but their "semi-detached" marriage—which had come into practical force in 1926 when she returned from the United States (after a year at Cornell University, where Catlin taught Political Science) so as to resume her career as a journalist—survived the strain of frequent separation. Not a mere marriage of convenience, it yet allowed the two partners to maintain separate careers, as well as a secure family-life for themselves and their children. It was a fulfilment of feminist aspirations, as Brittain recognised. Marrying Catlin without romantic passion—after the death of her first and great love, Roland Leighton, during the First World War—she was grateful to him for his calm dependability, his forbearance, his warm concern for her and for their children.

> I seem to be lucky over Gordon; most women writers seem either to have husbands who put upon them, like Delafield, or whom they have divorced, like Lady R., or else to be like Phyllis tormented with a sense of frustration because they haven't had sex experience at all. Companionate marriage is a partial solution but it doesn't meet the desire for children which physiologically-normal women like Phyllis do feel. Probably the only solution—and a slow one—is the education of men to the point where they really do give and take, really can be companions to women & feel as strong a sense of obligation to be unselfish and responsible as most women feel.

George P. Brett, Jr, President of the Macmillan Company of New York, came into Vera Brittain's life in June 1933 (shortly before her diary-entries begin that year): passing through London on their way to the Continent, he and his wife Isabel met the author of the big book, *Testament of Youth*, that his firm was soon to publish. Brittain must have been impressed by him from the first—Phyllis Bentley calls him "debonair"; he was handsome, intelligent, strong-willed, an exact contemporary who had been injured while fighting with the American forces in the Argonne Forest during the final days of the First World War. She got to know him well during her American lecture tour of 1934: on 21 September, the day of her arrival, he is "Brett"; two days later, at his country "shack" in Connecticut, he is "George Brett, whom I find attractive". The following June, when she and her friend Archie Macdonell throw a literary party for the Bretts in London, she is in love with "George".

By then she was in the later stages of writing *Honourable Estate*, and greatly enjoyed discussing her novel with him; arguing with him when he said it was too long, getting him to vet her American dialogue (for her heroine, Ruth Alleyndene, a young VAD nursing in France, falls deeply in love with a handsome American soldier, Eugene Meury, who is later killed in action—and who is clearly an amalgam of Roland Leighton and George Brett). Her diary drapes the progress of Brittain's infatuation, ecstatic, painful, in a series of resonant quotations.

But there can be no resolution of this romantic impasse: both are married, and it is unclear whether Brett recognises, or wants to recognise, her feeling for him: "he was sorry he couldn't manage another half-hour for tea but would 'phone in the morning. It may have meant a great deal or absolutely nothing." She weeps in her misery, but stoically sees the Bretts off on their transatlantic liner, wearing a "black dress, hat & cloak, & a button-hole of pink carnations & roses"—"(Had previously sent Isabel a garden basket of pink carnations & lilies-of-the-valley to boat.)" (Throughout her life, flowers were a precious joy to Brittain; her notebooks contain many pressed flowers memorialising emotional moments.)

So it is over, though she will keep in touch with him, see him again, talk to the dying Winifred Holtby about the comfort of his memory during the period of her Father's death. On her next American lecture tour, in September 1937, she

> Felt shy after not seeing him for over a year & I think he did too though he never shows it. I thought he looked, not older, but thinner, from strain of greater responsibilities & family troubles since his father's death.

The tone now is affectionate, sympathetic, calm: she has safely come through a romantic admiration of great depth and has transmuted it into enduring friendship.

Her own father's death in August 1935, by apparent suicide, was a great shock to Vera Brittain. In girlhood her relations with him had often been stormy. His pet-name for her then, and to the last, was "Jack" (or "John"): to this she responded with ambiguities of anger and love; and his running challenge to her, as mere female in a man's world, is at the root of her early, intense feminism and the fierce ambition that took her to Oxford and on to fame and success. Even in 1934 the best-selling author of *Testament of Youth* would pounce aggressively on a suspected sexist slight from her father: "he said: 'The lad's a credit to his father!' and I laughed & said 'But what about his mother?' "

That the aggression is tempered by humour, however, is a measure of the friendship between them in later years. Thomas Brittain had retired from his directorship of the family paper-mills in 1915, far too early for a man of proud vitality. His daughter's grief at the premature end of a half-wasted life—"a grief", she wrote in *Testament of Experience*, "which surprised me by its depth"—was a poignant tribute, not only to a loved father, but to a relationship, continuously influential in her life, which had modulated over the years from antagonism to affection.

Of the sixteen-year friendship between Vera Brittain and Winifred Holtby which dominates this diary, much has already been written—and much will be written in the future. As Paul Berry, their Literary Executor, has said in his fine Introduction to *Testament of a Generation,* their selected journalism, "It was obvious to all who knew them that it was a friendship of rare nobility." To us, fifty years after the untimely death of Winifred Holtby, that "rare nobility" is even more obvious, thanks to some of the social changes for which they fought so determinedly (especially those associated with the feminist movement); and it is possible, now, for us to assess the relationship in the terms Vera Brittain proposed when she wrote *Testament of Friendship*:

> From the days of Homer the friendships of men have enjoyed glory and acclamation, but the friendships of women, in spite of Ruth and Naomi, have usually been not merely unsung, but mocked, belittled and falsely interpreted. I hope that Winifred's story may do something to destroy these tarnished interpretations, and show its readers that loyalty and affection between women is a noble relationship which, far from impoverishing, actually enhances the love of a girl for her lover, of a wife for a husband, of a mother for her children.

What this diary shows very clearly, I think, is that the nobility of their friendship was no effusion of ethereal exaltations: it was built of human solidities, the daily imperfect workings of the mind and the body. They talked a lot about sex, for instance, and were often "ribald" in conversation. And Holtby was quite capable of saying to Brittain (not entirely with tongue in cheek, one surmises) "You've been the most important person in too many people's lives, you little bitch!"

Winifred Holtby was greatly loved for just that vitality, warmth, openness and honesty. You could trust her, utterly. She did not delude herself or others by shuffling sugar-encrusted images. And she gave herself unstintingly to the causes in which she believed, like the long fight against racial oppression in South Africa. Many took advantage of her generosity of spirit—there is no more moving moment in the diary, for me, than Brittain's own *mea culpa* as, writing *Testament of Friendship*, she meditates on the implications of Holtby's closest relationships: "wrote first draft of the Epilogue, being inspired to do so by all the evidences of exploitation (particularly by Lady R., her mother & me) in W.'s letters." Yet Holtby *wanted* to be exploited, to serve—surely intuiting this as the quintessence of friendship—and her relationship with Brittain was also a very practical working partnership between two ambitious writers. Just as Holtby encouraged, cajoled, forced Brittain towards the completion of her master-piece, *Testament of Youth*, so Brittain put aside her own half-completed novel after Holtby's death and worked furiously at *South Riding*, revising its text and overcoming Mrs Holtby's objections to early and complete publi-cation.

Theirs was "a complementary friendship of opposites" (to borrow Paul Berry's phrase). They were physically and temperamentally very different: Brittain small, dark, volatile; Holtby tall, fair, calmer. (The contrast between temperaments is neatly pointed when Brittain and Phyllis Bent-ley, exhausted by the emotional turmoil of their quarrel and reconciliation, find "Winifred, calm, tactful, never surprised by anything, ... sitting placidly in the window-seat reading the *New Statesman*"!) Yet, for all the contrasting characteristics, Brittain and Holtby held firmly in common their literary ambitions, academic training and values—those moral, social and political values that made them recognise service to the com-munity, and to humanity, as an obligation. They came to understand each other so well that they could correct each others' proofs without hesitation; indeed, they found themselves in "telepathic" communication, so that (Brittain wrote in an article later) Holtby would often write reporting "a knowledge of my thoughts at a given moment, or answer my enquiries before she could possibly have received the letter which made them." Yet it was in no way a limiting or exclusive friendship: both had other close friends, and wide circles of acquaintances and colleagues, and lived their lives as independently of each other as they wished.

Above all, it was a *joyous* friendship. This diary certainly conveys that joy, but intermittently since, as it opens, Holtby is already seriously ill. So I have chosen to end this Introduction—and to preface the diary text that follows—with a brief "duologue" found among Vera Brittain's papers. Written in July 1931, a few months before *Chronicle of Friendship* begins, it presents, with sprightly malicious humour, a typical day in their lives, when their great friendship was poised in radiance.

IV

A Perfect Day, or, The Superiority Complex
(A Duologue: July 26th, 1931)
by Vera Brittain

9 a.m.

V.B.   Hallo, W.! I thought you must have *had* your breakfast or something. We're nearly finished.

W.H.   Oh, *no*! I've only been finishing my letters. Since I got up I've done
ten letters and finished my S. African Report. Anyway it doesn't
matter my being late because I'm always so much quicker than
you.

V.B.   Could I have *The Times*—or the *Herald*?

W.H.   Well, won't it do if you see them at lunch-time? I want to take them
upstairs for my *Time and Tide* Notes. I've got four to do by eleven
o'clock.

V.B.   All right. Will you be in for lunch?

W.H.   Oh, *no*. I shall be out for lunch, *and* supper, and I don't think I can
get back for tea. I've got to go to the office and write a leader before
lunch; then I'm lunching with Miss West to talk book-reviews, and
at three o'clock I've *got* to go to a Kenya Committee and shall
probably have to cut tea because if I don't stay to the end and see
the motion through myself it's sure to be lost. I shall just have time
to dash home and change before dining at the House of Commons.

V.B.   I see. Who are you dining with to-night?

W.H.   Oh, nobody special—only the Prime Minister, and Mr Baldwin,
and Lady Astor, and Sir Oswald Mosley and Mr Lloyd George.

*

10.30 a.m.

W.H.   (entering study) Goodbye, darling, I'm just off.

V.B.   Right-O. Got your Notes written?

W.H.   Oh dear, yes! And two book reviews and a *Manchester Guardian*
article and my story for the *Radio Times* as well. How much book
have you written this morning?

V.B.   Not a word. I took John with me to the Bank after breakfast, and
ever since then I've been struggling with these beastly accounts.

W.H.   I can't think *how* you take so long over your accounts. When I did
them last week they didn't seem to make any difference.

V.B.   I've always been so hopeless at figures.

W.H.   Oh, so was *I* at school—everybody is—but the housekeeping in
this household is so extraordinarily simple. Why, when you were
away, I'd seen Amy, and taken John for a walk, and been to the
Bank, and done the accounts, and paid the books for the week, and

written fifty-seven letters and five *Time and Tide* Notes, all by half-past ten. But of course it *does* make a difference my getting up when I'm called, and always being so quick over my bath and dressing, and then having so little breakfast . . .

V.B. Yes, I know. Shall I see you at all this evening?

W.H. Well, I *may* have a moment to look in after I've changed, but you see I shan't have more than seven minutes all told to get my bath and wave my hair and get into my evening things.

V.B. Right-O. See you after dinner then.

*

11.30 p.m.

V.B. Hallo? That you, W.?

W.H. Yes—just got back. What are you doing?

V.B. Only trying to fix my fountain-pen. Something's gone wrong with it.

W.H. Give it to me. Let me have it. If there's anything wrong with it I'm sure I can put it right.

V.B. Did you get your leader done all right?

W.H. Oh, yes. I had to re-write it three times, but I got it done, and four Notes and a short story as well.

V.B. How did your Committee go off?

W.H. Oh, it was as boring as ever, but it *was* a good thing I went, because it was entirely due to my speech that the motion went through, N. and M. and D. would *never* have pushed it by themselves.

V.B. And what about the dinner at the House?

W.H. Oh, they were all there. After dinner Lord Cecil and Mr Henderson and Susan Lawrence joined us to talk disarmament, and then we all went along to the Bull-in-the-Basement in Piccadilly to have cocktails and discuss the new South African Franchise Bill with Smuts and Lord Lugard. What have you been doing all day? Been out?

V.B. Oh, no, I haven't been out. I've just been doing the usual things. Did a short review this morning; this afternoon had to shop and take John to have his hair cut, then had the children again after tea; had to give Nurse a row about the bathroom after supper and finish Gordon's and my accounts. But I've just got on to my book and been doing it since about half-past nine.

W.H. What a *rotten* day! You *must* be tired. Why don't you go to bed?

V.B. I shall soon—I *am* rather tired; hauling the children round is so fatiguing. But you go to bed first—you must be *dead*; you've been running round all day.

W.H. Oh, *I'm* not tired. I'm not going to bed for *ages* yet! I've got to finish my review for the *Daily News*, and write an article for the *Evening*

Standard, and do six Notes for *Time and Tide* before *I* go to bed! You
go now and I'll turn on your bath for you!

*

Epilogue. Scene, any day, any time.
A. (a Somervillian)   Whatever's happened to V.B. lately? She's so quiet
—seems to be suffering from an inferiority complex.
B. (another Somervillian)   Can't imagine. Can't think why she doesn't
write more. Why don't you ask W.H.? She's lived with her for ages and
Knows All About Her.

*

Finis!

(On receiving this, Winifred Holtby, who was holidaying in France with
Lady Rhondda, founder and editor of *Time and Tide*, wrote: "Lady R. and I
rocked with laughter over the delicious dialogue. Lady R. says Brilliant,
and why don't you do something of that kind publishable? The only thing
she says is exaggerated is your meekness! I agree!")

ALAN BISHOP

1932

FOREWORD   *19 Glebe Place, Chelsea, London*
Decided, after nearly 15 years, to start keeping this again. Life too interesting now for its events to remain unchronicled; always doing exciting work and meeting worth-while people. Contrast between old life in Buxton before War & in hospitals during war with my present existence could hardly be greater. Have meant vaguely for some time to resume keeping of this record but was induced to come to point by Phyllis Bentley when she stayed with me in the spring of this year.

A bad year for journalism—writing world still in depths of slump—few demands from editors—& what is asked for paid at lower rates than hitherto. But am getting on with second half of my Autobiography "Testament of Youth" which I have been working on since November 1929.

I am 38; John Edward and Shirley are growing fast from babies into children & already the formative years of my life seem very far away—yet I feel that all my achievements that matter belong to the future and will one day come to pass.

Friday January 1st
Uneventful New Year's Day. Supper with Rebecca & Henry last night at Orchard Court; G. B. Stern, Pamela Frankau & Anthony there.

Tuesday January 5th
Winifred supposed to be sufficiently recovered from her blood-pressure etc. to leave nursing home & start convalescing. Took her down to Miss Chattell's convalescent home at Sidmouth. Stayed myself at Faulkner Hotel. W. on top of cliff. Faulkner Hotel on Esplanade at bottom. Comfortable journey; got her down without mishap.

Wednesday January 6th–Friday January 15th   Sidmouth
Winifred happy; appeared to be recovering. Huge gales & roaring seas; rather alarming at night as my hotel right on top of sea. St John Ervines came over to tea one afternoon. Had it in W.'s sitting room. Mrs St J. E.'s conversation as catty as usual. St John working on his biography of General Booth. Returned home on 15th, leaving W. down there; found Gordon quite happy, children well & actually nothing having gone wrong in absence.

Tuesday January 19th   London
Rebecca West & Henry to dinner. The Mitchisons supposed to be coming too, but Naomi got 'flu & couldn't. Brailsford also ill but Clare turned up.

Dinner very successful; Rebecca very handsome in green dress; Gordon obviously pleased with whole affair. After dinner Vernon Bartlett, Joan Temple, Henrietta Leslie & Dr Schutze came in; also Randolph Hughes. Rebecca very friendly all evening; I told her about my autobiography & Randall's remark recently over luncheon: "I shouldn't have thought that anything in your life was worth recording." She was much amused & when Henry in usual rather blundering way showed tactless tendency to agree with Randall, turned on him & said: "You mean she's not a Field-Marshal? But it's the psychological sort of autobiography that succeeds nowadays—not the old dull kind."

Wednesday January 20th
Women's peace petition started on its road to Geneva by Lord Cecil. Send-off ceremony at 55 Gower Street (H.Q. of W.I.L.). Don't know why I went as it was great waste of time.

Friday January 22nd
Saw French Exhibition with Gordon, who wanted to go; suppose it was good, but hate exhibitions & never remember a thing about them after-wards. At 8.0 an L.N.U. meeting in Chelsea Town Hall; Ellen Wilkinson & Duff Cooper speaking. The latter very sincere & popular, but Ellen hit out hard about honesty & sincerity, & shocked complacent Conservative audience. Wrote a note afterwards to congratulate her on brave speech.

Monday January 25th
C. E. M. Joad to tea—with grizzled beard looks about 55 instead of 40. Discussed youthful political organisations & projected letter to *The Times* about sun-bathing, which I agreed to sign in conjunction with Shaw, Naomi Mitchison & various others of the Sex Reform Congress people.

Tuesday January 26th
Evening reception for G. & me by Brentford & Chiswick Labour Party; cold supper in a cold schoolroom—ham, salad, a chilly pudding. G. & I made short speeches; it was a kind of send-off for his departure to U.S.

Wednesday January 27th
Gordon left for America—sailing in *Bremen*. Saw him off at Waterloo at very early hour; he looked most charming as he said goodbye—hatless curly head, eyes very blue.

   Parents' meeting at nursery school in evening; Miss Neville, the psychologist, on difficulties of growing up.

Thursday January 28th
Winifred came back from Sidmouth; John & I met her at Waterloo. Before she came he & I watched the revolving advertisements outside the

platform; one of Punch (whom he knows as "Punchinello, little fellow") much intrigued him. He saw W. before I did. She seemed cheerful & much better.

Friday January 29th
Dined at 27 Markham Street with Junior Council to hear Basil Blackwell talking on books. B. only moderately friendly to me when I met him before dinner but gave quite good talk. Left early and went on to Ellen Wilkinson's "Bloomsbury Squash" at 36 Great James Street. Very pleasant. Talked to the Horrabins & several people whose names I didn't grasp. Ellen very agreeable.

Wednesday February 3rd
Attended for first time at Marie Stopes' Executive Committee as member. Must go warily or shall have pressure put on me to undertake various non-literary jobs.
  Dropped in afterwards at Paul & Millicent Bloomfield's cocktail party; disappointing & dull; knew nobody there. Dreadful squash in tiny Westbourne Street rooms.

Friday February 5th
W. taken ill again with bad headache & high blood-pressure. Forbidden to go to Monks Risborough for week or ten days.

Sunday February 7th
John started chickenpox. Foresaw complicated and harassing time with both him & W. in bed.

Friday February 12th
Winifred well enough to leave & go down to Monks Risborough. J.'s chickenpox not very bad but need to isolate & amuse him very tiresome. Felt thoroughly ill myself with bad 'flu cold & so much nursing and housework.

Monday February 15th
Had to cancel lecture to London School of Economics Labour Club on "Youth Morals To-day and Yesterday" owing to influenza & quarantine.

Tuesday February 16th
Started chickenpox myself. Decided to get in trained nurse.

Wednesday February 18th–end February
Chickenpox. Dismal wretched world. Kind elderly nurse; got good rest in bed. J. getting better; Shirley had one or two spots & we don't really know whether it was chickenpox or not. Whole household peevish & disgruntled;

weather very cold. Nothing to record; no alleviations but Winifred's letters from Monks R.

Tuesday March 8th

Monica Whately came to supper; said she'd had c.p. & didn't fear infection. First contact with outside world again; very pleasant. Yesterday wrote to tell Winifred about Rebecca West's new persecution mania over Patrick Thompson; she rang me up on Sunday & talked for ¼ of an hour about his having published a scurrilous faked interview with her in her own stamping-ground, the N.Y. *Herald-Tribune*. She asked me to tell her all I knew about him; I thought it rather strange that as a Director of *Time and Tide* she didn't know far more about him than I.

Thursday March 10th

After supper Henrietta Leslie (who has had c.p. twice & also isn't afraid of it) came in to spend the evening with me. She talked about her new book *Naomi's Child*, & also mentioned (which was news to me) that she had been unhappily married and divorced when very young. I had to steer rather judiciously round the subject of *Naomi's Child* because Jarrold's sent me the proofs with a request for a "puff" which they could publish. And as I don't think the book very good I have no intention of sending the puff.

Friday March 11th

Monica took me down to Monks Risborough in her car for the day to see Winifred. It was a bitter cold day with a heavy wind. I didn't much like Winifred's cottage in spite of the amiability of Mrs Calcroft; thought it dark & a little cold & at the bottom of a hill instead of the top. Monks Risborough too bleak for me and too full of highbrows; I don't care much for downs & high winds & bare woods, nor for little villas all on top of each other painted in highbrow colours. Winifred looked pale & obviously under the weather but was cheerful & talkative; can't remember what we discussed. Monica & I ran into a snowstorm coming back & in the dark could hardly see but she's a magnificent driver & we weathered it successfully. Being still more or less convalescent, I felt rather weary by the end of the day.

Monday March 14th

Spring-cleaning problem simplified as Aunt Florence has offered to have John & Shirley at Guildford for ten days. J. passed as free from chickenpox by Dr Gray; also myself.

Tuesday March 15th

Three rooms & bathroom fumigated; children & self washed hair & had Lysol baths; house full of choking smell of formalin & strips of sticky plaster; no work.

Gordon looking with envious eyes on C. K. Webster's Chair of Internat. Relations at Aberystwyth—free next autumn bec. C.K.W. has been appointed to London. I cabled advising him to seek good offices of Morgan Jones.

Thursday March 17th
Felt worlds better after spending afternoon in West End—first time for weeks; went to Baird Lewis & was measured for a two-piece and 2 hats. Reading Graves' postscript to *Goodbye to All That—But It Still Goes On* —results of publishing a frank autobiography seem to be terrifying.

Saturday March 19th
Dentist in morning; lunched in town & went to Academy Theatre to see *Kameradschaft*—Pabst's great film-epic of the mines on the Franco-German border. Lovely thing—far more anti-war than any amount of direct propaganda. When the German rescuers arrive at the gate of the burning French mine & waiting French women cry in astonishment "Les Allemands!" I began to cry, & remained with tears running down my cheeks all through the performance.

Monday March 21st
Monica came here for a night & I went down to Monks Ris. to spend to-night & to-morrow with Winifred. She was entirely in bed, blood-pressure being up. Cold & wet again.

Tuesday March 22nd   Monks Risborough
Talked to Winifred all day. Discussed *Kameradschaft*, wireless programmes; also a forthcoming novel called *Inheritance* by Phyllis Bentley, who was here to tea one afternoon last year. W. said she spent a year over this novel though her previous books haven't been specially successful; when at last in great trepidation she sent it to Gollancz he *telegraphed* that he thought it "magnificent". Wish something of this kind could one day happen to "Testament of Youth". Left W. by late train & got home to find everything all right for once.

Wednesday March 23rd   London
Dentist, fittings, took children to Babies' Club. Went on to a cocktail party given by Hilda Reid at her cousin's in the King's Road, to celebrate publication of *Two Soldiers & a Lady*. Met no one I knew.

Monday March 28th
Easter Monday. What a long week-end it has seemed with no letters from Winifred. Have had the usual "days off" to cope with—Amy on Friday, Dorothy on Saturday, Nurse to-day—and have had the children constantly on my hands. But have also used comp. postlessness of these days to

get on with some work—did article "I Denounce Domesticity" for the *Quiver* on Friday (2,000 words) & between Sat. & this evening wrote 27 pages of "Testament of Youth" (beginning of the France chapter). Result, swollen forefinger & neuritis in right shoulder.

Lady Rhondda off to rest cure in Alsace after bad heart attack in Wales.

Wednesday March 30th
Took John to see Helen Mayo—he was a wee bit frightened but she managed to look at his teeth & said he had a perfect set. Also bought him a tricycle at Hamley's & took him to tea at Marshall's—both these things caused great joy.

Thursday March 31st
Made various appointments for W. with Dr Gray to see specialists etc. next week.

When reading *Evening Standard* over supper saw a *marvellous* review by J. B. Priestley of Phyllis Bentley's novel *Inheritance*, which was apparently published to-day; the review was entitled "A Young Novelist Arrives" & should make the book's fortune; it begins "A promise has been fulfilled," & goes on praising the book & writer to the skies; incidentally makes it sound most interesting & dramatic. Cut out the review & sent it to W., who is most anxious for the book to succeed because she stayed with P.B. when she was doing her Extension lectures in Halifax. Liked her very much & also thinks she has had a grey life, tragic through negation, & needs & deserves compensation by success.

Friday April 1st
Sent Winifred a belated & very mixed Easter present—handkerchiefs, asparagus, salted almonds, dates etc. Clare telephoned, very anxious for W. to see her own doctor, Obermer, & not Halls Dally, who she says is a fool.

Winifred wrote that Phyllis Bentley has sent her a copy of *Inheritance* —*three* editions sold before publication. Looks like a real success—perhaps *will* be the reward for what W. calls "the mouldiest life".

Sunday April 3rd
In *Observer* saw magnificent review (the leading one of the week) of P.B.'s book by Robert Bell—called "The Story of a Mill"—emphasised the capital-and-labour aspect of it. She is certainly "made" as a writer. Decided to write to her & did so, even though I don't really know her & haven't yet read the book—but feel I have, because W. wrote yesterday saying *she* had finished it & thought it "magnificent. Strong, human, abounding in human characters, passionate, rich, *really* something worth

praising." Mentioned my own "Testament of Youth" to P.B. She mayn't be interested—but on the other hand she may; and Gollancz is her publisher.

News also appeared in the *Observer* today of Edward Marjoribanks, M.P. for Eastbourne, & author of the Marshall-Hall biography, having been "Found Shot" at Lord Hailsham's place in Sussex. Obvious suicide—such evidence as the papers publish point to his having been in midst of nervous breakdown. He was our decorative contemporary at Oxford (Christ Church).

Monday April 4th

Had fitting of new blue frock & coat, & bought Father leather notecase for birthday present. W. wrote enclosing a most contemptuous review of *Inheritance* by Rebecca in last Friday's *Daily Telegraph*; it calls the book "conventionally conceived", "sedative" & "negative", & [argues] that Phyllis "will never be without fervent acclamation because she writes just the sort of books that male authors like female authors to write". W. says all this is *most* unfair; that for some reason Rebecca obviously dislikes P.B.'s work, & had a sarcastic reference to an earlier book *Trio* in *Ending in Earnest*. Whence, however, this obvious sex prejudice? P.B.'s book sounds much more the kind that men like to write themselves.

Wednesday April 6th

Father's 68th birthday. At midday met Winifred & Clare in Halls Dally's consulting room—C. had W. up by car. Dr Gray met us there. Halls Dally thought W.'s condition fairly serious but she didn't seem to mind much, thinking him a fool, & was delighted (also Dr G.) that he suggested handing her over to Obermer. She came back here to lunch & tea & I took her to the nursing home about 6.0 for three days' tests.

Very fine reviews of *Inheritance* in both *M.G.* & *Punch* (I saw latter in Dally's room; described the book as "a fine performance difficult to overpraise"). W. brought her copy up & I began to read it; got thrilled almost at once; it reminded me of *Clayhanger* & also *The Mill on Floss* & stood the comparison extremely well. A short but very friendly note came this morning from P.B. acknowledging my letter of congratulation.

Thursday April 7th

Dentist in morning; children in afternoon. Reading *Inheritance* on & off all day. Found myself still reading it—& crying over it—at 2 a.m. Discussed with W. at nursing home the possibility of inviting P.B. to stay with me—I feel, especially as she's had such a grey life, that she ought to get some enjoyment out of her success as well as capitalise it with editors—& also that I'd like to have a hand in it. W. seemed a little surprised—as P.B. is *her* friend not mine—but thought she might like to come.

Friday April 8th
J.'s school broke up. Monica came to tea. Wrote to P.B. asking if she'd care to come & stay with me for a week next month. Do hope she does; she's obviously very intelligent & sincere & compassionate & I shall so much enjoy her companionship after all these lonely weeks. Her book is great; it holds me fast.

Saturday April 9th
Took children to Guildford in morning; Aunt F. sent car for them. Lunched with her & Miss Street. Back by train; found ground floor already dismantled.

Monday April 11th
Started spring-cleaning. Dining room & day nursery being painted yellow. Got letter from P.B. to say she would like to come & stay round about May 11th when Gollancz has an At Home (to which I, being tarred with the *T. & T.* brush, am *not* invited though she seems to take for granted I am). Seems pleased because it's so convenient—tho' like W. just a little surprised.

Tuesday April 12th–Saturday April 16th
Spring-cleaning. All well with children. Saturday night dined with the Ernest Davies' at Ormond Gate; met the young man (didn't catch name) from London School of Economics who is helping Sir W. Beveridge with the Family Life Questionnaires.

Monday April 18th
Photographed for Press by Elisabeth Ivimey. Took children as well.

Tuesday April 19th
Winifred definitely gave up staying at Monks Risborough & went back to Courtfield Gardens for various tests etc. for several weeks. Clare took her direct there & I went round in the afternoon.

Wednesday April 20th
Dined with Henrietta Leslie to meet Roger Pippett. Was tired after so much spring-cleaning & felt too sleepy to shine. Discovered from the conversation that Pippett had given Jarrold's a puff for *Naomi's Child*. As I had written to them only a day or two ago definitely refusing to "puff" the books of my friends I felt rather awkward, tho' I don't think Henrietta would really feel unfriendly for it. We discussed *Inheritance*; Pippett had reviewed it—not so very well—for the *Daily Herald* and thought it too long, but agreed that Rebecca was most unfair.

Thursday April 21st
Cleaning almost done. Children came back from Guildford, both looking well. Aunt F. stayed to lunch.

Friday April 22nd
John's school began again. Dr Nelson quite pleased with his general condition.

Saturday April 23rd
Fifteen years since Geoffrey Thurlow was killed in action at the battle of the Scarpe.

Sunday April 24th
After supper went around to Dr Waller at 5 Cheyne Gardens to discuss wording of the Babies' Club Annual General Report. Sat beside Lady Jones (Enid Bagnold).

Monday April 25th–Saturday April 30th
Uneventful. Working hard to finish France chapter of "Testament of Youth" before Phyllis Bentley comes on May 6th. Sent out invitations for a party I have decided to give for her on May 9th.

Monday May 2nd
Babies' Club Committee. New Dr Gibbens introduced; young, pleasant-looking, slightly bumptious but will grow out of it; obviously able. Reluctantly agreed to make short speech on Babies' Club movement to Maternity & Child Welfare Conference in July.

Wednesday May 4th
Went to British Museum to look at account of Asiago Battle in *Observer* of June 16th 1918, & found it closed for cleaning. Taxied to *Observer* office & asked to see this number; some reluctance at letting me see one so far back, which instantly disappeared when I said I'd been at Somerville with Viola Garvin & wrote down my name.

In afternoon saw *Femina-Vie Heureuse* Prize presented to Stella Benson for *Tobit Transplanted* & Northcliffe Prize to M. Jean Schlumberger by Harold Nicolson. Amabel Williams-Ellis in Chair. All very urbane & gracious— v. different from last year (Noel Coward presenting to Richard Hughes). Talked to Naomi afterwards.

Parents' meeting in evening at John's school; parents gently but firmly hauled over the coals by Natalie Davies for various small forms of inconsiderateness.

Thursday May 5th
Finished "Between the Sandhills & the Sea" (Chapter VIII, France) of

"Testament of Youth"; can now give myself up to making Phyllis Bentley
not only be a success but feel one.

Friday May 6th
Had early lunch & went off to King's Cross to meet Phyllis by the 1.55 from
various parts of Yorkshire (Winifred's familiar train). As the Halifax
portion was right at the back I feared I might miss her, & also was not
entirely convinced that I should recognise her again, but in the end I met
her without difficulty. She was wearing a tweedy brown coat and hat and
pince-nez and looked just as school-mistressy as I expected but somehow
less irretrievably plain than I seemed to remember; not quite the "embit-
tered spinster" of last year but as if something had gone all through her &
warmed her up, even though it hadn't yet exactly made her unbend. Hair
was going grey though—too grey for 37; it wasn't last year. W. said it's the
effect of writing *Inheritance* all in a year—certainly a performance in
will-power alone.

She came up to me with that mixture of stiff shyness & determined
downrightness which I know now as the Yorkshire manner & said: "It *is*
you, isn't it?" I agreed that it was, & we went round together to *John O'
London's* to pick up her review books. We began to thaw even in the taxi and
much to my surprise (I had meant to do it but not so soon) I found myself
telling her about "Testament of Youth" & *Time & Tide*'s quarrel with
Gollancz over reviews & advertisements, & being listened to sympathetically. (A woman "bestseller" surely very different from a man here; can't
imagine a man wanting to talk about any book but his own for at least three
months.) Over tea we thawed still more & discussed Lady Rhondda &
Time & Tide.

After she had unpacked (in Winifred's room) we had early dinner &
went to see Robert Nichols' play *Wings Over Europe* at the Globe. About
young scientist who discovered how to control the energy in the atom &
was murdered only just in time to prevent him from exploding the universe
because the British Cabinet wouldn't carry out his idea of a millennium.

Saturday May 7th
Phyllis went to see Winifred in the morning at Courtfield Gardens; W. told
me afterwards she seemed very puzzled as to why I had asked her to stay,
and W. repeated my own remark that it was "a daimon".

In evening we went to dinner at the Criterion & on to *The Miracle* at the
Lyceum. At dinner I tried to explain a little to Phyllis by saying how I loved
people to get on. Found the "mime" of *The Miracle* rather trying before the
end & longed for speech, but thought both Lady Diana Cooper & Tilly
Losch quite as lovely as the criticisms said they were.

Sunday May 8th
Did gardening & then took children to Oakwood Court while Phyllis spent

the day with friends in Highgate. She finished her *John O' London* review in the morning—works with a kind of dynamic "I won't waste time" resolution which gets things done. After she had come in & gone to bed *Daily Dispatch* rang me up & wanted by to-morrow afternoon an article answering Margaret Kornitzer's book *The Modern Woman & Herself*. (I haven't read it but this didn't seem to matter as the Editor gave me a résumé.)

Had just finished call when Amy came up very tearful because she thought Dorothy's young man had insulted her, & anyhow it was nearly 11 so I had to go down & turn him out. This didn't predispose my thoughts towards the article but I drafted out about ⅔ of it before going to bed about 1 a.m.

Monday May 9th

Woke up with a headache through hardly having slept owing to the rumpus in the kitchen. Headache not improved by fact that it poured with heavy rain all day & that I had to finish *Daily Dispatch* article "Libelling Modern Woman" by 3.0. I did this, then raced out for half an hour in rain & came back to help maids prepare for party. (Phyllis out all day; didn't come in till just before dinner.) Felt quite pleasantly hopeful about party as of the 30 people I asked, 29 accepted—interested, I suppose, to meet Phyllis but perhaps partly because of me too, as both the previous parties here have been good.

Mother & Aunt Lillie turned up to help with the food just after dinner & Phyllis to my delight appeared looking really nice in a very pretty black & silver dress that revealed to me the fact that she had a quite beautiful figure. After the oranges and greens of the previous days, & Winifred's remarks about her clothes being terribly provincial & all hung about with beads & things, it was a pleasant surprise; also her face seemed better looking as on Saturday I hinted gently how becoming her horn-rimmed spectacles were, & she thereafter abandoned the pince-nez & stopped looking like a school-mistress. She looked animated too and happily expectant, like a pleased child.

Cecil Roberts came first, somewhat before the others, then Monica, & then, in quick succession, David & Mrs Higham, Henrietta Leslie & Dr Schutze, Ernest & Natalie Davies, the Miss Isitts, Miss Davison of the *Week-end Review*, Miss West of *T. & T.*, Clare & Brailsford, the Scott-Jameses, the Horrabins & Ellen Wilkinson. Everyone *very* agreeable to Phyllis; I managed to get her introduced to them all & yet gave her a fair time for conversation with each. Ernest Davies suggested she should contribute a monthly article to the *New Clarion* when it comes out in June; Miss Davison talked to her for some time; & Clare & Ellen Wilkinson teased her very pleasantly about being a celebrity; "What does it feel like to have everybody talking about you?" asked Ellen; Phyllis blushed & protested that they weren't but Ellen went on "I hear your name & about your book wherever I go." Meanwhile Mrs Scott-James and I stood by the mantelpiece watching. V.S.J. (who had only seen Phyllis once before—an interview at V.S.J.'s house, when P. was apparently very plain & bustling & dogmatic) said very quietly: "What *has* happened to Phyllis Bentley? She's *quite* different. And she's got such a becoming frock on." I said, "Yes, isn't she different from last year. She's been getting more animated & self-confident ever since she came. It's great fun watching someone turn into a celebrity under your eyes." And V.S.J. remarked thoughtfully: "Yes—it's very pleasant, isn't it. Success *does* alter people. I'm ever so glad."

Finally, very late as usual, Naomi Mitchison turned up. I introduced Phyllis (dragged her away from conversing with Miss Davison with the query: "Do you want to meet Naomi Mitchison?" to which P. replied with great emphasis: "Yes, I *do*") but for the moment Naomi didn't take much notice as she was talking earnestly to Brailsford whom she had always wanted to meet. But when I came back from seeking out everybody else (they all left together in a kind of rush, as people do) I found Phyllis & Naomi sitting on either side of the dining-room fire (we had turned the newly decorated dining-room and nursery into one & it looked charming) all alone. I brought sandwiches & drinkables (the maids were clearing up down below & then went to bed) & we sat there talking together about half an hour, Naomi in her lovely deep voice discussing her children—schools —books—the difference between buggers & lechers—the *Femina-Vie* prize. Phyllis sat rather silent but very intent & interested. Finally Naomi went & I took her out to her car.

I came back to find Phyllis standing by the table looking radiant & yet for some reason deeply moved. Quite suddenly she said: "I'm so happy! I've never been so happy as this in my life before. I've never enjoyed a party so much as this party." And I said: "It isn't often that one sees a dream coming true, is it? I've enjoyed it immensely too—seeing it come true & watching your success." She went on: "At least I've done one worth-while thing—written one good book. Of course I believed in it myself, but . . ." "Now you realise that other people believe [in] it too," I finished for her; "Well, it's a very enviable feeling—& it's made you quite different. Last year you had an inferiority complex; this year it's gone."

"I was very unhappy", she said, "when you saw me last year. *Trio* hadn't succeeded and I'd just been ill, & I was only starting *Inheritance* & felt I'd never finish it . . ." "But all that's over now," I said. "You've deserved your success & you've a right to enjoy it—if only *I* could say the same—but then again I'm nothing but a competent journalist . . ." But she took my arm & interrupted me. "Oh, don't talk nonsense! You're tired & you've got a headache; you won't feel like that in the morning." But I knew I should—and always shall—unless "Testament of Youth" succeeds.

As we went up the stairs she said again "Thank you—I do thank you" in her unadorned direct way, & I felt that the party really had been worth-while.

Tuesday May 10th
In afternoon went to Annual General Meeting of Babies' Club. Phyllis & I went to Vaudeville in evening to see *Vile Bodies*—very amusing but we were both rather tired & didn't talk much.

In afternoon looked at Lyceum Club & Women's Service Hostel; P. obviously not much taken with either so I invited her back to Glebe Place when she returns to town.

Wednesday May 11th
Very crowded day. Took Phyllis to the Marie Stopes Annual Luncheon at the Criterion; introduced her to Marie Stopes. Canon Percy Dearmer spoke at the lunch; fine head; whole manner rather too intense & fanatical. Phyllis sat beside the (elderly male) representative of the *Star* who put in a paragraph about her afterwards. Tea at home & then both of us dropped in for a few minutes to Lady Harris's cocktail party in Hertford Street; Percy was there & we were introduced to Mrs Hobman, who had just published a book & told us she was not "famous like us". Otherwise we knew no one. Don't know whether the pictures on the walls (by Lady H. in her role of "Jesus Chutney") or the people at the party were the more wonderful.

Played with the children after tea & went to bed early while Phyllis went to dinner with the J. B. Priestleys & afterwards on with them to the Gollancz At Home to which I was *not* invited. I was still awake when she came back about 2.0 a.m. & she gave a most amusing account of the whole proceedings. At the Priestleys were one or two relatives (Mrs P. still upstairs with the last baby) and the L. A. G. Strongs. J. B. Priestley himself was just back from the production of *Dangerous Corner* at Glasgow; very full of it & himself; usually treats Phyllis in an informal friendly fashion as one native of Yorkshire to another, but all through dinner was grand & formal & a little drunk & wouldn't meet her eye.

At the party Mrs Gollancz came up & congratulated Phyllis—escorted her around—introduced her to people & lionised her generally; P. said it was *very* different from last year when she was just ignored & left to go around by herself (which I saw, being there on that occasion; in fact she went around part of the time with me). She was introduced to Rose Macaulay & the Norman Collins'; saw Louis Golding, but only at a distance.

Thursday May 12th
Quiet day—Phyllis very tired after strenuousness of preceding day—also seems the kind of person with whom excitement goes all inside & turns to exhaustion. She had to broadcast just before tea; came back extremely pale so I put her to bed early.

Winifred came round at tea-time; the doctors are going to let her come back from the nursing home on Saturday; have found enough what is the matter with her to continue the treatment at home.

Friday May 13th

In morning started drafting *Quiver* article on changes in work & leisure while Phyllis went to *Everyman* & arranged to answer their attack on her book & the long novel—also to the *New Statesman*, where Ellis Roberts definitely arranged for her to do novel reviews for a time in place of Viola Meynell.

We had tea together & then I went to St Pancras—she asked me to—to see her off. She looked very ill & pale & unhappily could only get a bad seat in a smoking carriage all the way to Halifax owing to the Whit Week-end crowds. She tried to thank me again for the week, and I to tell her why I had asked her, but the crowds were too thick & she too tired for much intimate conversation. I did feel sorry she had nowhere more comfortable to sit & rest in for the long journey home. As I went out of the station I saw several copies of *Inheritance* on the book-stall with a small paper placard "A Great Novel: 5th Edition" fixed above them. Dropped around to nursing home to see Winifred on my way home but found she had gone out to tea & dinner with Stella Benson; very sorry not to see her.

Saturday May 14th

W. came back from nursing home with all her belongings; both of us very pleased; talked for ages about Gordon, Phyllis & various other attractive topics.

Sunday May 15th

Whit Sunday. Children to Oakwood Court. Went on with *Quiver* article.

Monday May 16th

Finished *Quiver* article. Charming note from Phyllis saying she *was* ill all the way back to Halifax but had arrived alive & happy, & that I had altered her prospects & whole outlook on life. It ended with the words "Yours affectionately" scratched out & the phrase inserted: "No, I think I'd rather say: Yours with love."

Whit Monday. Gardened a good deal with children.

Tuesday May 17th

Started Chapter IX of "Testament of Youth"—"This Loneliest Hour" —period between leaving France and the Armistice. Sorted out the notes. Wrote to P.B.

Wednesday May 18th

Went down to Oxford to lunch with Pa Catlin. Not so bad as I expected;

doctor had pronounced him quite well & Mrs Wood was very agreeable. Day started warm & ended with pouring rain. In morning walked all way from station to Summertown; all Oxford sweet with the smell of wall-flowers & lilac.

Friday May 20th
Lunched at Parnell's Club with Miss Styer to meet Mrs Ensor of New Education Fellowship & discussed publicity for their summer conference at Nice. Went to dentist; returned to Glebe Place to find that Phyllis & her mother had been here, to leave P.'s box. Phyllis returned later for tea & I helped her unpack her box before she went on to Highgate friends for the week-end.

Sunday May 22nd
Children to Oakwood Court. Phyllis came back after supper, to occupy Gordon's room until his return. Felt very pleased to have her there.

Monday May 23rd
Went on with Chapter IX. Long talk in W.'s room after supper between W., Phyllis & me, all about ourselves. P. referred yet again to our rapid talk (W.'s & mine) as "brilliant conversation". Said she thought I ought to feel utterly fulfilled, being so pretty & having such a "gift for life". I explained why I never could unless I wrote a really great book, & talked about the War which I had told her something of last week. She repeated what she told me then, that she had never been anyone's mistress & that the scenes from *Inheritance* which seemed to show sex experience were all imagined.

Tuesday May 24th
Went to tea given by Mme André Rieder for Spanish Ambassador at American Women's Club. Wore new blue things—coldish day—and took Phyllis. Pethick-Lawrences there & Maude Royden but everything rather dull; too much speechifying & everyone felt constrained. Met a French woman journalist who apparently knew of me & my works & said she had never thought of me as such a young woman. Suppose she took me for about 27.
  Week-end Review sent me the Romieu book on George Eliot to review; 400 words.

Thursday May 26th
After dinner Phyllis & I went to coffee with Miss Davison (*Week-end Review*) in Barkston Gardens flat (top floor flat; very agreeable). No one else there except a non-highbrow married sister as makeweight—P. said afterwards that Miss D. very skilfully drew me out & made me reveal my inside knowledge (such as it is) of the Suffragette movement but I really wasn't aware of the process.

Friday May 27th

W. out to lunch with Lady Rhondda & afterwards to a committee where Norman Leys was—she brought him back to supper but I had to have mine early owing to making speech at Wellgarth Rd. Phyllis sat with me while I had it. Went up to Golders Green in pouring rain & talked to rows of indifferent girls at the Training School about the Babies' Club movement. Coffee afterwards with Miss Talbot & the Matron. Returned (still in pouring rain) to find P. & W. both gone to bed.

Saturday May 28th

Phyllis out to lunch with Lady R.—went off looking nice in dark blue & red. Cicely Hamilton dropped in to tea, just come back from France; we talked about the French, war memorials & the War. P., back from lunch & rather tired, lay on W.'s divan in her dressing gown & listened; then went out to a sherry party at Charles Morgan & Hilda Vaughan's flat; taken there by Macmillan's London agent.

Sunday May 29th

Dispute over lunch about respective merit of critical & creative qualities in literature (already discussed with some animation by Phyllis & myself a day or two before in relation to the place in literature of Rebecca West) and the relation of both to inspiration & sincerity. For some reason or other it developed into a furious argument & ended in a row, with Phyllis & I both losing our tempers. I told her that she put *everything* in her novels & called that creative, & she said in retaliation (though she hasn't read anything of mine except my articles) that my over-critical non-creativeness was the great difference between her & myself. This struck hard because I'd been struggling all morning with a particularly vile part of Chap. IX, and I suddenly felt so near tears I had to get up & pretend to play with John. I said loudly to Winifred on the stairs that P. was "damned superior" & then P. came to my bedroom & tried to apologise for being horrid about my book, but I wouldn't have it & took John off to Oakwood Court without showing her the way to Queen's Gate, which I'd promised to do.

Just before supper, when I'd put J. to bed and Winifred & I were just going to the post, Phyllis came in; Winifred asked her to come with us but I remarked supper was just ready & I suppose conveyed without meaning to that we didn't want her. Anyhow we'd hardly finished our soup when Phyllis got up with her eyes full of tears, said she wouldn't stay for any more, & went off upstairs. Tried to persuade W. to go & fetch her back but she said that obviously *I* must, so I went up to find her in Gordon's room. She let me come in & I found her sitting in the arm-chair, crying quite hard; she began saying she'd been so happy with us but now she'd hurt me about my work & it was all dreadful; none of her personal relations ever did go right & she just couldn't stay if we were going to be cold & distant. I felt terribly sorry because she was obviously feeling it all so dreadfully whereas

I had only been superficially annoyed by a too-acute & rather unfair criticism. Also I felt awkward because I don't really understand Yorkshire people (except Winifred now) nor how far one can go towards intimacy with them, but I sat beside her on the arm of the chair & took her hand & said I'd really only lost my temper & one shouldn't discuss a book one's actually working on.

Then she cried more than ever & all the repressed misery of her past life burst out in a flood—how grey, how negative it had been, how women hadn't loved her nor men married her; how writing had been the only thing & she was still defenceless against even a mere remark which suggested she might not have even that. I told her that *Inheritance* had settled that question for ever & she must try to believe that she was an established success & I at least had been interested & intuitively attracted by her even before she came. I also said I did understand the greyness & frustration & sorrow because though I hadn't had that particular grief I'd had others, & she said: "Yes, I could tell you about it because you *are* acquainted with grief." And she said she would try to believe that she was successful, & able to be loved & that it wasn't too late for her life to have a flowering time; "You see," she said, "I can't put beauty and charm & happiness into my books because I've never known them." And I insisted—and believe —that through her own achievement she is just at the beginning of knowing them & that they will come into the next books she writes.

So at last she stopped crying and I persuaded her to come down to supper; Winifred, calm, tactful, never surprised by anything, was sitting placidly in the window-seat reading the *New Statesman*. After supper we talked in the dark in my study till Winifred went to bed. Before going myself I showed Phyllis my poem "The Superfluous Woman" & I think persuaded her that I had felt like that—so much as she does—in 1920. Anyhow, she kissed me & said "Goodnight, my dear" & I began to feel as if I had known her always.

Tuesday May 31st
After dinner Phyllis & I went to J. B. Priestley's new play *Dangerous Corner* at the Lyric. Full of suspense & psychology; we both thought it good. After we got home drank hot milk & sat for ages talking in my bedroom.

Wednesday June 1st
In morning Louis Golding—who has been intrigued by idea of Phyllis for ages as he is magnanimously but definitely jealous of her best-selling era having so swiftly succeeded his own—rang up ostensibly to ask W. to dinner to-night but really (since he must have known W. would have to refuse) to ask her if she thought he could ask Phyllis at the last moment like that. W. told him to try & called Phyllis who went to the telephone very cheerily & said: "Well, Mr *Magnolia Street*, what do you want of me?" She accepted the invitation to dinner, & agreed, after spending afternoon

reading books for her *New Statesman* review, to meet me for tea at Ridgeway's & together buy a red evening dress & a black velvet evening cloak.

After lunch Mother & I went to the Academy—terribly dull; half an hour afterwards I couldn't remember a thing about it except Richard Sickert's picture of the raising of Lazarus—and then had tea with P. at Ridgeway's. Quest for frocks very successful; after one or two boss shots we went to Marshall's & got a beautiful dress in Persian red & a black velvet evening cloak with white fur collar. Brought the garments back & she dressed herself up in them; W. & I made her make up her lips & did up her eyebrows for her; the result was to make her face look really interesting & the frock showed up her nice figure to perfection.

Was in bed but not asleep when Mr Grayson, one of the publishing firm, brought her back in his car. Dinner had been both ornate & funny; the Norman Collinses & L.A.G. Strongs were there. It started with prawns —in their shells, with eyes & whiskers—& afterwards for 2 solid hours Louis read the company letters he had received about *Magnolia Street*, including a proposal of marriage. (Phyllis, needless to say, doesn't even show her letters, let alone read them aloud.) The evening ended with his saying to her: "We best-sellers count each other's thousands so jealously, don't we?" and her replying with equanimity "Well, I don't need to count yours because I know they're exactly double mine!" *Inheritance* now in its 18th thousand; *Magnolia Street* in its 38th.

Thursday June 2nd
Just before lunch finished Part II of "Testament of Youth"—ending with my walking up Whitehall on Armistice Day. Nine chapters finished—in 2½ years. It seems so strange that I have thought about little else but the War for eighteen years—and now, perhaps, shall never write of it again. Only Part III—three chapters—to do now.

Phyllis broadcasting in afternoon. All tired & went to bed early.

Friday June 3rd
Felt miserable all day with attack of colo-cystitis. Felt dull & empty after finishing Part II. Phyllis working hard on *New Statesman* review. After tea went to see *Kameradschaft* again at the Boltons cinema, with her, W. & Cicely Hamilton. C.H. came back with us to supper.

Sunday June 5th
Garden party at Dr Stella Churchill's. Went alone; talked to Barbara Drake, Dr Churchill, Mrs Rubinstein, & various people from G.'s constituency.

After supper had long talk with Phyllis over study fire about effects of war & how they deprived worth-while things in the present of their value. She said two memorable things: 1) "Jesus was a great psychologist. He was thinking of people like you when he said: 'From him that hath not shall be taken away even that which he hath.' " 2) After I had said that no one was left who remembered the War for me, and even John belonged to Gordon & not to Roland, she said: "But it's biologically true, isn't it, that the essential part of him was within you in the days when you were with your brother & your lover—and so in a way he belongs to them too." She seemed much moved & spoke of people like her father and youngest brother, whose lives had been thrown away in their life-time, without their having to die. Again kissed me goodnight & called me "my dear".

Monday June 6th
In morning wrote review of Romieus' book on George Eliot for *Week-end Review*.

Phyllis & Winifred & I went to tea with Louis Golding. *Very* interesting, the reactions of the two best-sellers to each other; I sat between them & poured out (W. very silent & tired) and at first had hard work to break the ice, but succeeded in the end. Couldn't help finding Louis a lovable creature though he *did* try to deprive her of credit at every turn—saying that the success of *Magnolia Street* had helped to sell *Inheritance*, & that the *Daily Dispatch* had serialised the latter because it couldn't get the former! Phyllis took it all very philosophically & didn't seem to mind. Louis showed us his collection of cherubs, his "roof-garden" & all over the 13 Cambridge St. maisonette, but he *didn't* read us letters about *Magnolia St* though he talked of them. Did say that success had taken him out of his depth, made him lose all sense of perspective, etc. He made Phyllis cut the cake as if it were a wedding cake—then called her "Phyllis"—she said she preferred it, but went on calling him "Mr Golding" till we teased her out of it. After tea she & Louis discussed financial rewards of success; he told us he'd made an arrangement with his English & American agents to be paid £750 a year salary on either side for 4 years & in that time to write 3 novels—could still make more than this, of course, if royalties amounted to more. He told Phyllis that—even though she doesn't know what will happen in U.S., where *Inheritance* won't be pub. till September, she ought to be able to bargain for £400 a year from either side—but she told us afterwards that she couldn't possibly write well on such terms or want to tie herself to 3 novels in 4 years.

Before we left Louis presented her with a signed & inscribed copy of *The Miracle Boy*. She shook hands very graciously, said "Thank you, Louis", & promised to send him a signed copy of *Inheritance*.

Only just over an hour later Phyllis & Louis & I all met again at the Lyceum Club for the Annual Authors' Braid dinner. We made a little group in a corner & Cecil Roberts joined us. Louis gave me a cocktail; Phyllis wouldn't. At dinner tho' not a guest found myself at "High Table" opposite Phyllis & Cecil Roberts, who sat together; Agnes Grozier Herbertson Chairman (very "refained") with Louis Golding & Dr Cronin on either side of her. Cecil Roberts, Phyllis & Dr Cronin (& eventually

Louis, who had pretended he didn't want to, but in the end discoursed longer than anyone else!) all spoke on the subject of the evening, "Sources of Inspiration". Phyllis obviously nervous at making her first London speech but did very well—spoke with great assurance & even a little over-dogmatically—homely metaphors, Hardy & Arnold Bennett all brought in,—but she looked very nice in the black dress with her lips painted. Everyone lionised her a good deal. Louis at the end of evening asked when he was going to see her again—& Cecil Roberts fixed a day for her & me to go down together for the day to his home at Henley.

Tuesday June 7th
Mr Catlin & the Harbards came to tea to see the children. Terrible afternoon; they stayed two hours & I felt I could scream with boredom. When the children did come in they encouraged them to tear up paper & walk all over the window-seat (which I never let them do) & simply made them riotous.

Phyllis out all day with Dorothy Whipple; called on Gollancz to get a First Edition of *Inheritance* for Louis Golding & Victor told her that he sold 400 copies of *Inheritance* last week & was probably publishing a seventh edition.

She & I went to dine at P.E.N. Club in evening, chiefly to take Dorothy Whipple; usual crowd of obscure "thirsters". Ernest Raymond was Chairman; Phyllis, who had been completely ignored at a P.E.N. dinner last year before she wrote *Inheritance*, was carefully selected by Mrs Dawson Scott to sit next him. Phyllis wore the red dress & looked nice. She & Ernest Raymond disagreed about absolutely everything; I sat beside her & listened. After dinner got into dull group with Nora Heald & the Editor of *Vogue* so broke away & joined Phyllis, Bradda Field & Dorothy Whipple.

Wednesday June 8th
In bed all day with colo-cystitis pain. Chiefly slept.

Thursday June 9th
Sat in garden all day; worked mildly. Phyllis lunched with Bradda Field at Institute of Journalists' dinner. Found it dull.

Friday June 10th
Still feeling rather mouldy. But at 1.15 went to Boulestin's to lunch with Lady Rhondda (first time of meeting her since all the row over Winifred last November). Thought she looked pale & was obviously thinner; prolonged illness has changed her a good deal. Others there were E. M. Delafield, Professor Cullis, Miss Head, Jean Lyon, Miss Pearn, Miss Maudsley. Told Delafield (truthfully) that I had spent the whole of yesterday afternoon & evening reading *Thank Heaven Fasting*. We all talked of the *T. & T.* party & clothes we were getting for it. Lady R. said she

thought the author had replaced the actress (who after all could always be seen for the price of a seat) as the object of star-gazing, & someone else said the only pity was that actresses had lovely clothes & knew how to wear them, while most authors didn't. So Lady R. suggested that Delafield & I ought to start a "School of Dress for Authors", and Miss Head continued by saying that some people certainly had the "cosmetic urge" more than others, & that at such a school we should have to decide who should be allowed to indulge theirs & who not. Professor Cullis said that once at Agay she had asked Delafield if she should make up, & Delafield had said mournfully: "No; I'm afraid it wouldn't do any good." Delafield protested a) that she hadn't said it, b) that if she [had], it really meant that Professor Cullis's face was too superior to be improved; no one of course believed her. Miss Pearn spoke of Rose Macaulay & said she was a tremendous party fan; Lady Rhondda remarked she'd never have thought it, but Miss Pearn insisted that Rose *would* go to parties instead of getting on with her work, & she (Miss P.) had even tried mild remonstrance over tête-à-tête meals.

Wondered if the remark about School of Dress for Authors had been telepathic when I got back for tea to find that Phyllis had gone off to Marshall's to get black frock & hat for party. She came in just before supper having bought them & apparently very pleased with herself.

Long discussion after supper until quite late about sex & sex experience, my reaction to matrimony & theirs to virginity. We all seemed to imagine we were highly sexed, but this is almost certainly only true of Winifred. Phyllis repeated that—despite Witt & Amy in *Inheritance*—she had never been anyone's mistress, but had always wished for sex experience & still did.

Saturday June 11th
Very hot & lovely. Another day mostly in garden. Over showing me her hat (which *was* very becoming) after tea, Phyllis said that my life & its late flowering after much frustration had given her (& would give to other people similarly circumstanced) the hope that hers too after such long aridity might flower. She said she felt dimly that she was just beginning to lay hold on it for the first time—to dare to feel that happiness & life might be for her after all, though she had always assumed they never would be & she was only an onlooker & interpreter. Certainly success is an emotional experience—& all the desire to buy & use cosmetics which she has suddenly shown does seem to point to some very positive development.

After dinner P. & I had long talk in my bedroom about the exasperations which interrupt the writing of long books, & how they may be overcome & perhaps in the end even contribute to the richness of one's material.

Sunday June 12th
Nurse had day off; children on my hands. Winifred & Phyllis helped to look after them in morning; W. & I took them to Oakwood Court in afternoon.

Shirley very pretty; said "Dinner" quite plainly. In afternoon Phyllis went up to play tennis with the Priestleys; came back after supper much pleased with the day, having been the only woman playing with 3 men. Said Priestley wasn't much good but hit so hard that when he did get the ball in the only thing to do was to get out of the way. Hilda Reid came in to supper; brought "Yo-yo" which she manipulated very skilfully.

Wrote a few notes for book—part about International Relations.

Monday June 13th

Spent day with Cecil Roberts at Henley. Phyllis & I left by 10.30 bus for Oxford; he met us at Henley at the bus stop & took us to his cottage in his car. Before lunch showed us round. Beautifully fine—a little dull at first but later sun came out & glorified all the woods. Cottage really exquisite & garden even better—dated from 1620. He bought it cheap, completely modernised it inside, put up sun platform & made the circular garden even more exquisite. Lupins, borage, irises, lilies-of-the-valley, laburnum & rhododendron all in full bloom. Cottage had circular plan inside too, & all furniture was just right. He obviously loves the place as he has never loved an individual.

Over lunch told us of a quarrel he was having with a film company over the scenario of his novel *Bargain Basement*. I got on to the subject of lectures in America & he promised Phyllis an introduction to Lee Keedick; lucky he heard her at the Lyceum the other evening. Obviously he is trying to make her an *amende honorable* for his bad review of *Inheritance*, not (for these are his values) so much for having misjudged a good book as having failed to "spot" a winner. After lunch took us in car for drive through woods to see new cottage he had bought—met old couple (82 & 80) who inhabit it; he is allowing them to remain there for rest of their lives. Later when cottage becomes his it has great possibilities—gorgeous views; Windsor Castle visible on fine days. Stopped for few minutes on way back to pick laburnum. Then till tea he showed us diary of Sir Alfred Fripp, whose Life he is writing—very interesting, but terse, inarticulate & rather unobservant; v. different from a writer's diary. Was touched to notice constant recurrence of phrase "dined together alone"; apparently he loved his wife very much.

A married couple came to tea—non-literary; man an Army officer of some kind. Wife just a wife, but had been reading *Inheritance*. Cecil Roberts told 2 good film stories over tea: 1) Galsworthy went to a trade film show to see one of his own books filmed; after 2½ hours of strange films went round & said to manager: "Look here, when's my film coming on? I can't waste any more time here." Manager, amazed, replied: "But, Mr Galsworthy, it finished an hour ago." 2) Sir Philip Gibbs, asked if he ever went to see the films of his own books, replied: "Oh, yes, I always go to the film of my last novel to get the plot for my next." He also said that Sir P. Gibbs when staying with him had taken 3 whole days to read from cover to cover an

ordinary length novel which he (C.R.) could read in half an hour.
Mentioned himself & Phyllis to his friends as "best-sellers", "which," he
added, "the general public takes to mean that we can't write".

He took us back to the bus stop in his car & we got home for supper about
8.0. After hasty meal rushed off to Chiswick to speak to Women's Section
meeting at Hardie House; only about 15 there; gave speech about International Peace & my reasons for becoming Socialist which I made up for
last Election & didn't use; managed to be quite moving & impressive in
spite of extreme sleepiness & absolutely no preparation.

Tuesday June 14th
Quiet day. Hot & bright; strong breeze. Phyllis went down to Fisherton-
de-la-Mare, in Wiltshire, to stay two days with Helen Ashton. In morning
sorted own letters to W.H. in garden. After lunch bought two hats—one
white with veil, one blue; neither expensive. Gardened with John after tea.
Made notes for book; Winifred helped me to remember events at Oxford.
Three adorable & expensive pairs of stockings came from Gordon.

Wednesday June 15th
The 14th anniversary of Edward's death on the Asiago Plateau. The
family's In Memoriam notice & mine both in *The Times* as usual. Miss
Thurlow sent me, as before, pink & red & white carnations. Mother came
round just after lunch to bring me a cream cheese which Mrs Fowler had
sent. Had hair washed. In evening Peggy Smith asked me if I would
propose the toast "Literature & World Peace" for Priestley to reply to at
the L.N.U. dinner to-morrow; said I would.

Phyllis returned just before 11 p.m.; had found Helen Ashton & husband rather depressing, as husband is always a bore & H.A. was having a
kind of nervous breakdown bec. her book *Bricks & Mortar* wasn't a success.
She got Phyllis to read the 1st typescript of her new one & P. said it wasn't
good either; nothing but a collection of short stories about a house.

Thursday June 16th
Hot lovely day; sat in garden in morning & rather idly made up speech for
evening. Phyllis rather glum & depressed bec. of hers although she had
letter from Gollancz saying *Inheritance* going into 7th Edit. (20,000).

At tea-time dressed up in black maroon with cape & tiny black, white
and red bow, & white hat with little veil; hat cheap but effective—Phyllis
expensively but somewhat stiffly dressed in black & white garments from
Marshall's—and went off to the Dorchester for the *Time & Tide* reception.
E. M. Delafield & Rebecca were receiving with Lady Rhondda; Rebecca
dropped her eyes & looked rather embarrassed when Phyllis came up &
Phyllis most annoyingly looked embarrassed too—so further efforts on my
part were useless & as Rebecca was receiving there was no time. She looked
charming & very young in a blue flowered dress & blue hat; had gone

much thinner. Delafield most cleverly & effectively dressed in a saffron-coloured "smock" frock—very *chic* & yet *"Provincial Lady*-ish".

Phyllis very soon met L. A. G. Strong & went off to tea with him so I detached myself & had tea upstairs with Naomi, Stella Benson, Miss Davison of the *Week-end Review*, Ernest Rhys of *Everyman*, & Winifred & Mrs Holtby. We who were "celebrities" all wore labels, & after tea Louis Golding who had exchanged his with Rose Macaulay tried to make me change with L. A. G. Strong but the latter wouldn't.

Looked vainly for Mother & Aunt Florence & eventually found them in Ballroom waiting for speeches. Didn't like the Dorchester on the whole —rooms too dark for bright summer day; ceilings too low & seemed to be pressing down on one.

Just before speeches began found Phyllis again; we didn't go on platform but sat at back with Eleanor Farjeon & listened to speeches. Subject was, as usual, respective merits of dailies & weeklies. Professor Cullis, as Chairman, was supposed to draw names from hat & "celebrities" to respond without preparation but neither process was quite as impromptu as it appeared. Laski began the performance & Rebecca West followed —afterwards Stephen Gwynn, Rose Macaulay, E. M. Delafield, Louis Golding, Ellen Wilkinson, Wyndham Lewis & Norman Angell. All excellent; Rose far better than usual, Delafield full of delicious malice. Had a word with Rebecca afterwards; she told Winifred to tell me that she (W.) & I reminded her of "our Press photographers' impressions of the fashions at Ascot".

When it was all over Phyllis & Hilda Reid & I walked on to Pinoli's for the L.N.U. dinner. There Phyllis introduced me to J. B. Priestley & he sat between her & me at dinner. At first glance I saw a broad, shortish, very pale & slightly bloated-looking Yorkshireman, speaking with a Yorkshire accent far broader & more definite than Phyllis; very blue eyes rather bloodshot but twinkling; altogether he looked younger than I remembered from seeing him at the Gollancz party last year. He began dinner by saying: "Now, you're one of the people who dislike me, aren't you?" & after that we got on very well. I told him I'd only reviewed *The Good Companions* & that well, but when I got home remembered *Farthing Hall* & the disagreeable review I gave it; had forgotten it was Priestley's as well as Walpole's. We discussed the Yorkshire character; he swore Yorkshire people were no more alike than the individuals of any other group & said that the resemblances between him & Phyllis were purely superficial. I couldn't talk to him as much as I wished as Mr Penman, the very dull Chairman, kept on talking to me about his quite uninteresting visits to Italy & elsewhere. But at one point Priestley suddenly turned to me and said: "Would you rather your daughter went off with a chimney-sweep, knowing he'd make her unhappy & the whole thing would smash up, or have nothing happen to her at all?" Don't know why he asked this, & a month ago I might have been uncertain how to answer, but after having

Phyllis in the house for some weeks I knew just what I thought & answered: "I'd rather she went off with the chimney-sweep. If she had one kind of experience, even though it went wrong she might still believe that life would bring her another, but if nothing ever happened she'd cease to believe anything would happen & get a dreadful inferiority complex." Priestley said he agreed. He talked a good deal to Hilda about plays. Phyllis obviously wanted to talk to him badly but with characteristic masochism turned to the Frenchman next her & left Priestley to me.

When the time for speeches came I spoke first, beginning with story told by *Evening Standard* of Keynes telling an American that the only parallel to the present depression was called the Dark Ages & lasted for 500 years. Went on to toast of literature & world peace, showing how literature was compatible with war in early civilisation but function became quite different when civilisations had developed to such a point that war got out of control & threatened foundations of society itself. Quoted *The Dynasts* & *Inheritance*, also referred to Priestley's work & to that of the War writers. Quite a good speech of the more serious type, which I took some trouble to prepare. Priestley in reply made a very perverse speech, rambling, obviously unprepared, & witty in places; he made a point of contradicting most things I had said, maintained that the interchange of literature had no effect on international relations at all, & made fun of various national characteristics to rather greater extent than the numerous foreigners present really liked.

After he had spoken Philippa Fawcett in usual pale & deprecating manner proposed toast of the guests, & Phyllis replied to it with the rather stiff, assured manner & slightly harsh emphatic voice which after hearing it twice I now feel sure is her normal method of speaking—efficiency & knowledge but no grace or charm; much better suited to lecturing than to after-dinner speaking. Priestley left at this point as the curtain to the Second Act of *Dangerous Corner* was being changed, & the evening petered out with various foreign guests—of whom much the wittiest was the representative of Soviet Russia—making five-minute speeches in reply to the toast.

Found Winifred awake & talked to her for some time. Phyllis came up to my room to say goodnight, kissed me twice & said she did wish she wasn't going away.

Friday June 17th
Winifred's poem "Promenade Concert", written in memory of Edward last summer, in *Time & Tide* to-day; queer it should go in this week.

Charming letter from Gordon; thinks *Europa* gets in Sunday night. Mentioned among other things that Hugh Walpole had given me a "boost" in an article in the *Herald-Tribune*. Can't believe this possible after H.W.'s article in the *Week-end Review* calling Winifred & myself the "Miss Beale & Miss Buss of contemporary literature". Either the reference is sarcastic or G. has got mixed up & it is not Hugh Walpole. Had article "Standing Up for Ourselves" in *M. Guardian*; also received cheque from *Gd Housekeeping* for "One-Roomitis".

After breakfast we got on to subject of Phyllis's inhibitions again; I told her that when people obviously sought her out she must make some gesture of response or they in their turn would drift into the inferiority complex that is in everybody & think themselves not wanted. She said she'd do her best but after such long loneliness & restraint it was possible that gestures & caresses which were a tremendous effort to her meant hardly anything to the other person. She got back again on to her childhood, & how she sought other girls out & they wouldn't be friends, & was made afraid by being forced, before it was discovered that she was short-sighted, to jump & dive into space when she couldn't see where she was going or what she was doing—and thence on to the awful humiliation of going to dances when young & being snubbed or despised and anyhow not danced with by men. (Personally I think that somehow this tyranny of dances in provincial towns should be stopped; seems to account for more youthful misery & inferiority complexes in intelligent women than anything else.) She ended by crying again & asking how she could possibly be expected to make gestures of seeking towards anyone at all after a girlhood like this. I went on insisting that it wasn't too late for some kind of happiness, some sort of flowering time to come, if only she could overcome the conviction—so deeply rooted in young bitter experience—that happiness was not for her.

For rest of morning helped her pack up & looked over notes for my speech at the Conference on the Family. Saw Phyllis off to Charing Cross for a week-end at Hythe & then went to the Conference on "The Family in a Changing Society" at Friends' House. Was purposely a little late & arrived at end of speech by the American woman, Mrs Sidonie Gruenberg; Ellen Wilkinson & Naomi Mitchison were already there. As second chief speaker I had to speak almost at once; talked on usual topic of changing position of married women, denunciation of present wasteful domesticity; need for most women both to marry & to make their special contribution of whatever kind to politics, art, literature, social service etc. For some reason I kept the audience laughing all the time though I *meant* it to be a serious speech. Ellen Wilkinson spoke with her usual animation on the position of the "ordinary" married woman made uncomfortable by the way in which professional women, married like Naomi & me, or unmarried like herself, insisted on stirring things up. Naomi gave a somewhat vague paper on changes in the family, and greatly scandalised that congregation of good social workers by seriously suggesting that children at co-educational schools should be taught amongst other things "to sleep together beautifully". After I had replied to one or two criticisms of my speech made by a very foolish woman doctor, Naomi & I left together; she took me home in her car but wouldn't come in for tea as she was feeling sick & thought she might be pregnant again.

After dinner Winifred & I for about 2 hours discussed Phyllis, her dark, intense misery & the tragedy & grief of frustration, & whether there was anything we could do to help her, warm her, soften her, make her happier & more attractive. I felt deeply oppressed by the greyness & the negativeness of her present life, of which the needs & the sorrows seem incapable of alleviation by literary success (and even this in a way is limited; various distinguished readers of *Inheritance*, such as Lady Rhondda, don't like it—not that Lady R. is any judge of literature).

When W. had gone to sleep & I went down for my bath I heard strange noises in the basement & went down to find Amy looking for Dorothy (it was just about midnight) & discovered her in the kitchen sitting in the dark crying after a quarrel with her young man (who had no business to be here this evening anyway, as it isn't his night here or one of D.'s nights out). I told D. that as I wasn't always spying in the kitchen she really might try to show me she could be trusted, & she said perhaps she'd better give me notice, but I told her it was after midnight & she wasn't to be so silly. She was so upset I really couldn't be very angry.

And afterwards I thought a good deal about the various forms of unhappiness, & how strange it was that within the same day I should have under my roof the successful & extremely intelligent woman novelist of 37 crying bitterly because (it amounts to that) she hadn't had a man, & at the other end of the intellectual scale the little housemaid of 20 crying just as bitterly because she had. I decided that on the whole it was probably far more bearable to be Dorothy, and, thinking of Phyllis, wrote a new paragraph which I should like to see added to the Litany:

> That it may please thee to strengthen & comfort all those that are lonely and sick at heart; for the frustrated who vainly desired experience, for the desolate who longed to give & receive love & were repudiated by their fellows, for the barren women who hoped to share in the pain & dignity of birth and were denied the fulfilment of children, for those who suffer from a sense of inferiority & believe themselves despised & rejected of men, we beseech thee to hear us, O Lord.

Saturday June 18th

Saw by this morning's *Times* that the *Europa* gets in on Thursday at 10.30 a.m. Lovely warm day with strong breeze, spent mostly in garden working. Mother came in after tea; also Monica, with Miss Foot & Edna Rankin, to tell me all about the machinations & interrelations of the Labour Women's Conference at Brighton last week. They wouldn't let Dora Russell be a delegate & Susan Lawrence was a quite devastating Chairman.

Winifred had tea with Violet Scott-James, who said she was sure Phyllis's dark intensity meant genius of some kind; they compared her with George Eliot. Got a charming note to-night from J. B. Priestley acknowledging mine, written yesterday, to correct statement that I'd never given

him a bad review; said he remembered *Farthing Hall* but that now it
"obviously didn't matter", & that he had liked meeting me. Mother said
my speech at the L.N.U. dinner was much the best of any.

After she had gone John and I made a bonfire of old sticks & rubbish;
great excitement; got a spark in his face & cried a little but on the whole
enjoyed it.

Sunday June 19th
Took children in morning; Oakwood Court for tea. Afternoon became cold
and windy. Working on Notes for Chapter IX. Uneventful. Shirley fell
down about 10 times & kept on cutting her knees & scratching her poor
little face.

Monday June 20th
Gordon came back from U.S.A. *Europa* supposed to arrive at 10.30 a.m.;
actually didn't get in till 2.30 p.m. After ringing Norddeutscher Lloyd
Agency at intervals all day, went to Waterloo at 7.0 & train eventually
came in at 7.35. Put on best new blue. G. looked well & good-looking. Four
of his small packages were missing but we eventually discovered them in
the Lost Property Office & got back for supper about 8.15.

G. had had uneventful voyage; no one special in the Tourist class; dull
smooth weather. In midst of supper Phyllis arrived back from Hythe for
her luggage; hadn't had supper so joined us & stayed for coffee &
conversation afterwards. Told me while packing up evening-dresses that
her mother had been bullying her about the money made by *Inheritance*;
wanted P. to "invest" it & for the two of them to live on next to nothing &
manage with one maid, P. doing a large share of the housework. As P.'s
work & ability to earn largely depends on their having adequate domestic
help she naturally protested against this absurd short-sighted economy,
but it had involved her in argument & depression & made her feel poor
after she'd been feeling happy & well-to-do here.

G. showed us the Hugh Walpole article which mentions W. & myself
(also concludes with paragraph about Phyllis, rating *Inheritance* lower than
her other books but saying she is one of "the finest novelists we have and I
am glad that she has come into her own"; reference to W. & me obviously
intended to be a sarcastic allusion to our "fair" criticism).

After Phyllis had gone off with her belongings to Crosby Hall, we all
helped G. unpack & got more or less straight by midnight. Stayed with him
in his room till 2 a.m.

Tuesday June 21st
G. saw the children properly at breakfast; Shirley apt to mix him with
Father & refer to him as "Danad". Took Phyllis's letters round to Crosby
Hall after breakfast; found her rather depressed but she was immediately
cheered by my appearance, & by a letter I brought from Peters, enclosing

one from his American agent saying that Macmillan's are going to spend $5,000 (£1,000) on advertising *Inheritance* in America & are appointing a special publicity agent to work on it 2 months before publication in September & 2 months after. They also ask if P. can be got out for a short lecture tour; say they can guarantee practically the whole of her travelling & hotel expenses if she'll come. She went off at once to see Peters about it; came into lunch delighted with her interview & said Peters talked of arranging a visit to America in September.

After lunch we discussed Dorothy's affairs—W. talked to her when she did her room to-day & discovered that she was secretly married to the saxophonist 2 months ago & now thinks she is expecting a baby. Hence the tears of the other night. We are getting Dr Gray to see her. Amy knows her parents & the young man's parents, so it seems probable that the marriage is real & not pretence. D. is only keeping it from her mother bec. she is more or less illiterate & the brothers will read the letter aloud & make trouble; as soon as we go on holiday next month Dorothy will go up there with Amy & break the news at home. So till then there is nothing to be done. Phyllis & Gordon were there when we discussed it, & when I was upstairs changing my dress Phyllis remarked to Winifred: "Well, sometimes it does seem as if we frustrated spinsters had the best of it after all!"

We all four had tea in the garden after I had been to the produce sale at the Babies' Club & bought various oddments, including some sweet peas for Phyllis's room at Crosby Hall. After tea went (G. & P. & I) to Hilda's sherry party at 46 Tedworth Square; placid as usual, only a few people & no one introduced to anyone else. Saw Hilda's study; pleasant, looks on garden.

Wednesday June 22nd
Gordon went off to Oxford by early train. Letters which I took to Phyllis at Crosby Hall included an invitation to dinner from Priestley to meet Hugh Walpole. She came in later for lunch which we had alone together; we discussed chiefly Rebecca West and her early dramatic criticisms in *Time & Tide*.

Had early tea with Phyllis & Winifred, & went off to the Marie Stopes Committee; she wasn't there but her husband H. V. Roe conducted a vigorous anti-National Birth Control Association campaign on the ground that they were perpetually "stealing the credit" from Marie Stopes, & therefore the C.B.C. must break off relations with them. I set my face steadily against this—not only because I know & like Mrs How-Martyn & the rest of the N.B.C.A., but because I have no patience with societies which are working for the same objects continually quarrelling with each other on the ground that one or the other of them gets more credit, instead of just carrying on with the work. Rival organisations always do quarrel, of course, & always will, but I won't be associated with it; as a writer, working in detachment, I am far more interested in getting certain things done than in the particular societies that are doing them, and if the C.B.C. insists on quarrelling with the N.B.C.A., I shall just resign from the Committee.

Parents' meeting at the nursery school in evening; a discussion on parents' reports & on the teaching of reading; presentation to Miss Thomson on leaving; Mrs Davies did it with obvious emotion.

Thursday June 23rd

Winifred's 34th birthday. Gave her a dressing-gown of thin peach-coloured satin. Phyllis came round during breakfast to tell us about the Gollancz dinner-party which she went to last night; very thrilled, seems so surprised & delighted that she loves parties here though she hates them in Halifax; I tried to explain this by describing the utterly different basis of London literary parties from the snobbishness, exhibitionism, conventionality or mere propinquity which provokes the giving of parties in the provinces. Phyllis sat next to Ellis Roberts, who was very affable; obviously liked her *New Statesman* review & made it clear that he was sending her more books to do. Other people there included Rose Macaulay, Stella Benson, Louis Golding, Norman Collins & the Harold Rubinsteins; only a small group which included Phyllis were invited to dinner & the others came in afterwards. They finished by playing charades, in the first scene of which Ernest Milton was the Rector of Stiffkey with Rose Macaulay as his provincial wife & one of Sylvia Lynd's daughters as "Barbara". Another scene represented the L. of N. at Geneva, with Louis as President & Alan Thomas of the L.N.U.—who writes detective stories—as the French President.

Walked back with P. to Crosby Hall, where we conversed for half an hour; spent rest of day in garden with W., looking after the children & doing notes for "Testament"; found to my horror that I had left out all mention of feminism during the War & had to go back & put in the granting of the vote to women over 30 in Jan.–Feb. 1918. After supper W. & I discussed ourselves & Phyllis; sat in garden till 9 p.m. Lovely warm day.

Friday June 24th

At breakfast parcel from Benn's turned out to be a copy of *Carr* which Phyllis had sent me. I could see after looking at it for a few moments that it is obviously an extremely good if not actually a great book—the biography of an ordinary man, of the same large-scale type as *Inheritance*.

Went round to Crosby Hall to thank her for it and we discussed the reasons why it hadn't sold and resulted chiefly in a rather belated *succès d'estime* among the critics; I talked my usual philosophy about "staying the course" (a type of grit which is, I am sure, quite as often the explanation of success as actual intellectual endowment—though of course it would be useless if the latter didn't exist), but it is also quite evident that Benn's didn't understand Phyllis's work & the art of selling it & that Gollancz is precisely the right publisher for her. She said that she had so clearly realised how much of an advance it had been on her previous work that its comparative failure nearly broke her heart, but I said that this would be atoned for now; it would be republished in a Uniform Edition & read & appreciated; & that after the appearance of *Inheritance* in America, *Carr* and the other earlier books would be published & achieve success there just as the early work of Sinclair Lewis did here. We talked a little of our respective careers & how hers has made such obvious big strides at intervals while I have never had periods of tremendous advance & yet seemed to have had a measure of success and to be generally known. I said my work was just a trickle, but she compared it to putting up a building by laying quantities of smooth carefully-polished stones upon one another, while her building went up in the form of large slabs finished on the ground & only erected at intervals.

Worked in garden all afternoon. G. came back from Oxford for tea; went down to jamboree at Chiswick in evening. After supper went to Miss West's At Home in Taviton Street. Small affair but quite pretty flat. Talked to James Laver & Ellen Wilkinson all the time; she is off to India in August, travelling "native" all the way; wants to work back via Afghanistan to India. Found the party a little dull because I was tired, and left early. The young Hungarian who does factotum for *T. & T.* said he had been lunching with Rebecca, who had told him she was tired of criticism & was now going to devote herself to novels.

Saturday June 25th   Rye
Phyllis came to lunch; she & W. stood on steps to see Gordon & me off to Rye. Hot journey down but quite tolerable. Old Hope & Anchor as pleasant as usual; warm welcome from Miss Bellhouse. Choice of two nicest rooms given us—I suppose as tribute to wedding anniversary. After tea went for walk over Rye Hill. Whole country perfect in June; large hayfields in full bloom of grass & flowers; cutting must have just begun & the whole world smelt of new-mown hay. G. & I sat on a log on the summit of the hill near Lady Warrender's house & talked of his political plans.

Sunday June 26th
Walk to Camber in morning over Marsh—warm & scented; full of rare birds & flowers; larks singing joyously in sunshine. Sea beach beyond Camber black with cars but we found a quiet spot. After lunch read *Carr* on seat above steps; didn't get very far as a poem began to fidget at the back of my mind. Gradually took shape as "The War Generation: Ave"; to go in front of first chapter to match "Vale" at the end. Lovely walk past Camber Castle to Winchelsea beach after tea (at which Miss Bellhouse & the cook provided a special cake decorated with seven candles in honour of wedding anniversary). Coming back lost our way on Marsh between Winchelsea &

Rye; recent floods had obliterated landmarks; got back rather late for dinner.

Monday June 27th

Seventh anniversary of wedding. So glad it is now & not then, when we were both unadjusted both psychologically & physically. Life can be very sweet, but for me all happiness for ever is a house built on shifting sands. Struggled away at poem in morning. Early lunch; spent afternoon sun-bathing at Camber. Hottest day of year; sand hills radiating heat; sun brilliant; sea very warm; had a semi-bathe.

Met Miss Bellhouse at the Loyal William at 5.15 & she took us in her car all over the Marsh to see various villages & isolated churches (built very large, centuries ago, to the glory of God & quite irrespective of the population). Usual brilliant green light lay all over the Marsh, giving sense of unreality, of having strayed into an enchanted country which is not quite England & not quite mortal life. Beans in flower; yellow flags in flower beside ditches; smell of new-mown hay everywhere, hot & sleepy. Back to dinner just in time; afterwards sat on seat above steps watching twilight come on, reading Carr & thinking about autobiography.

Tuesday June 28th London

Back to town by early morning train; finished poem on the way. Gordon out to lunch; Phyllis came in & we talked all afternoon. Felt tired & rather sleepy after much nocturnal intercourse during week-end, but went for a short visit to Dorothy who during my absence had to be removed to St Luke's Hospital for Women to have her appendix out. Operation to-morrow; the competent Winifred had already provided a temp. house-parlourmaid. Discussed books, frustrated women & plots for short stories with Phyllis; told her about Mrs & Miss Kershaw from Buxton who were staying at Rye; how they had read Not Without Honour before I came & were speculating with Miss Bellhouse over which characters were real Buxton people; but how Beatrice Kershaw's first remark to me was nevertheless: "You've got two children, haven't you?" P. says she is going to make this into a short story; I handed over the episode to her as she understands & can depict frustration in a way that I don't think I can yet. Gordon back to dinner. Wrote up letters till bedtime; all quite dull.

Wednesday June 29th

Dorothy had her operation; stood it well; Nurse saw her two or three hours after I had called & said she seemed quite fit already & not finding it too painful. Looked up Annual Registers in Chelsea Library & had my hair washed; gardened with John. Phyllis came in to dinner; went back with her to Crosby Hall & we talked about Carr, parents, families, the differences & likenesses between ourselves, and why I felt after reading Inheritance that though I had superficial scintillation & she hadn't, she was the kind of person I had always been looking for. Long talk with W. after coming home; apparently last week-end she had made to Phyllis the same suggestion as I did about putting money aside for the railway fare & coming down here whenever she felt intolerably bored or miserable in Halifax. Gordon dined with Clare & Brailsford.

Thursday June 30th
Small cheque for royalties for *Halcyon*; it still appears to go on mildly; 77 copies sold last year. Spent morning in British Museum reading *Annual Registers* & making notes for book. Took children in afternoon; hot but showery; we went for walk in Battersea Park. Phyllis came in for tea; looked tired. My copy of her book *The Partnership* arrived this afternoon; contains a typical description of what she obviously thinks herself; W. says she is a masochist—part of her fierce atheism is a fear of her own weakness, trying to get comfort from the fact that we don't know with absolute certainty that there is no survival & no hereafter. If she allowed herself to look outside this life for compensation she would depend too much on unproved possibilities; that, I feel sure, is what she feels. She left soon after tea to go to the theatre with an aunt. Rose Macaulay's 6d. collection of poems in the Benn series came this afternoon; I got it because it contains a poem called "Picnic, July 1917". Phyllis showed us her copy of Priestley's new book *Faraway*, out today. *Evening Standard* gave it only a painstaking & tentative review, & Roger Pippett's in the *Daily Herald*, entitled "Dull Mr Priestley", was quite devastating.

Friday July 1st
Sixteenth anniversary of the battle of the Somme. Worked all day at British Museum reading *Annual Registers*; had lunch at Romano's in Greek St with Phyllis, who had been to see Ellis Roberts at the *New Statesman*. Miss West & Miss Lewis at another table. Phyllis & I both got back home for a late tea; we argued about *Trio*, which she said she had intended for a study of human isolation from the point of view of the persons concerned & never to be present in her own character. Gordon then came in having tea'd at Oakwood Court & we all began a discussion of how far one could get out of one's private universe & how far it was possible to dramatise subjectiveness in a book. In the middle of the conversation he suddenly presented me with a charming yellow enamel cigarette-case as a seventh wedding anniversary present; Phyllis seeing our momentary absorption in each other suddenly got up with the hurt look that so often comes over her face, said she must go, & went.

Lady Rhondda came to dinner & Cicely Hamilton & Phyllis came in to coffee afterwards. Lady R. looked tired & was as stiff & constrained as usual; everything rather slow till after dinner when the appearance of the other two livened things up a little. But no specially good conversation;

Winifred v. tired & found the whole day rather too much. Gordon & I took Phyllis back to Crosby Hall & I gave her a copy of *Halcyon*.

Winifred had lunch with *T. & T.* Board—a brief but interesting conversation occurred with Rebecca, who suddenly said apropos of nothing: "Do you know I *did* feel embarrassed when I met Phyllis Bentley the other day—I was the only critic to give that book a bad review." W. said she herself had thought *Inheritance* a good book. Rebecca replied: "Did she mind?" & W. replied: "Well, one doesn't usually mind one bad review among so many good ones, only she does just happen to admire your work enormously & so it was rather bitter."

Saturday July 2nd
Exasperating day because no work owing to accounts & housekeeping in morning, & a boys' and girls' tea-party given on Gordon's behalf in afternoon—two young women (American) & two young men (English), one of the latter being Owen Parkinson of Hertford College, Oxford, who took the chair for me last year when I spoke to the Oxford Labour Club on Marriage. Phyllis came in after dinner; it was such a lovely bright evening that we went for a walk in Battersea Park & along the Embankment. When crossing the bridge saw the *Graf Zeppelin* which had flown over from Germany this morning coming up the Thames from Putney direction; against the clear evening sky it looked like a gigantic flying fish, very steady & powerful. We watched till it disappeared over Westminster.

Sunday July 3rd
Another rather exasperating day because again no work; children in morning; we turned out & tidied the shed amid clouds of dust & strong smell of tom cats. Oakwood Court in afternoon; Mother had bought some charming new clothes which she showed me. With great daring invited Rebecca in a note for lunch or tea & asked if she'd care—or rather could bear—to meet Phyllis. P. came in to supper & we discussed private universes again. She returned for a few moments to Crosby Hall & reappeared in evening dress looking really quite charming & behaving with a pleased assurance; I think it has given her real joy to feel that she isn't alarmed by Gordon & that he treats her as if she belonged to the household. Took her round to Swan Court for a party given by Ernest Milton & Naomi Royde-Smith.

Monday July 4th
Read Dreiser's *Tragic America* for review for *T. & T.* Phyllis called in for a few minutes in morning; said the Gollanczes were at Naomi Royde-Smith's & will also be at the Priestleys' dinner on the 8th. P. met Margaret Kennedy & neither of them said a word.

After lunch went to the Maternity & Child Welfare Conference at the Y.M.C.A. Hall in Gt Russell St, to make ten mins speech for Fed. of Babies

Clubs. All very badly arranged from my point of view; had to spend an hour in morning trying to get Miss Halford on the telephone to discover whether I was to speak or not; then at the Conference there was no one there to support me either from Chelsea or the Federation, so my brief speech had the effect of an irrelevant interruption in the real business of the Conference. Getting there, waiting to speak, speaking & getting back took at least 2 hours. I shall not speak for the Babies' Club or anything else any more unless they organise things better & avoid wasting so much of my time.

Dropped in at Oakwood Court on way home; Father told me he was giving me £500 saved over a long period to put on deposit at the Bank or buy Govt stock with, whichever I prefer. This [is] a very agreeable arrangement as it will enable my banking in general to be more elastic, so that I can overdraw (or withdraw from deposit) when I want to finish a book & not write articles, or if I should want to lecture in America. But Father's methods of saving are distinctly unorthodox; what my Bank Manager will think when I turn up with £500 in Treasury Notes in a suitcase I can't imagine!

Phyllis in to dinner; she obviously likes Gordon & is at ease with him. After dinner we all walked on the Embankment & indulged in much ribald conversation. The evening was delightfully warm & finished with a peculiarly lovely sunset. We stood with our backs to the parapet of the river & watched the lightly-massed flame and orange clouds behind Chelsea Old Church gradually deepen into fuchsia & purple. The Embankment was crowded with other people who were watching it too. I told Phyllis how good I thought *Carr*—and it makes me particularly happy to think that before she wrote *Inheritance* she had done another book almost as good, & more original in conception. One first-rate book may be an accident or an exception, not to be repeated, but something that has been done twice may be repeated indefinitely by the same person. I bet her 2/6 that she would have bought a small car by this time next year & 5/- that she wd have acquired a flat in town this time two years hence. We ended up by drinking lemonade & ginger beer at the little Lombard restaurant which has just gone in for pavement tables facing the river, like a continental café, and Phyllis said that she felt really happy; I remarked: "What an event." If we had sat there long enough all the writers & artists in Chelsea would probably have drifted past us; as it was we saw a good many strange-looking objects. Charles Morgan & Hilda Vaughan walked just past our table, almost brushing against us, but we did not recognise them until they were past.

Back home for tea at ten; Winifred remarked we *had* done a lot of pub-crawling to-night! But it was a charming evening—one of the nicest we have had this summer. At dinner I read aloud to Gordon (apropos of entertaining Halldor Hermannsson) my article in the *M.G.* entitled "Entertaining for Socrates". I think it took his breath away a little but he was quite a darling about being made fun of & entirely forgave me.

Tuesday July 5th
Wrote review of Dreiser's *Tragic America.*

Phyllis in to tea. After dinner went to "At Home" at the Harrods in Campden Hill Square. Deadly dull as usual; scarcely a soul there that we knew. Spoke for a few moments to Lady Forbes-Robertson. Escaped with great relief after an hour & went on to the party the Scott-James' were giving for Phyllis to meet Lancelot Spicer (brother of Eva) who has read & greatly admires her book. Sat next to a callow bob-haired young creature whom I was told was at Somerville with Anne; when I remarked that I had been at Somerville too she said: "I hope you're not going to talk about the dear old college!" (This to me! Do I look like that? Well, well!) Phyllis on the sofa in her red dress beside Lancelot Spicer was talking with great animation. He is big, fair, he-mannish & about 38; Phyllis liked him but Gordon thought he looked domineering & potentially cruel. The Davies' & two Scott-James girls—both now lovely—made up the party. Very pleasant. Sat next to the *Daily Telegraph* music critic, who obviously didn't like Rebecca's position on it & said that a "star" reviewer was a great burden to a paper. Lancelot Spicer left about 11.30 having to catch a late train for Scotland. We took Phyllis back in a taxi to Crosby Hall.

Wednesday July 6th
Took Elisabeth Ivimey's photographs of Phyllis over to Crosby Hall; one especially good. P. herself looked pale; said she had cried half the night at the thought of leaving this life in London & going back to family squabbles in Halifax. After coming to lunch she went on talking about them in the afternoon, especially about the everlasting conflict between her mother & second brother over the family car; she told me that if it weren't for her mother she would have nothing more to do with this brother & his family, especially as now she has made some money they are always criticising her for extravagance on account of what she spends.

Talking about it she began to cry again & couldn't stop. I told her how admirably she had fitted into this London life in spite of her dread of it & fear of me; she said I was the first really attractive & desired person to offer her friendship & that was why my friendship meant so much; she had got on well enough with the undesired but my kind of person had always snubbed her. I asked her if she thought the accidental possession of a pretty face impaired the values of an intelligent person & however she imagined that I rated the impermanent things more than the permanent; that having a pretty face gives almost as much satisfaction as possessing an agreeable new frock, but is in no way to be compared to the ability to write a great book. She said that the fact that I really seemed to want her had been a new revelation to her of her own possibilities & power to attract & life wouldn't be so intolerable so long as she kept in close touch with me & my world. She ended by fiercely asserting that if she repudiated her responsibilities & her hateful role of mediator for the sake of her own happiness she'd never be able to write another line. I expect this is true; sorrow & loss are such a spur to great ability, & happiness too often burns away in a flaming ecstasy.

Between lunch & tea she & Gordon discussed Winifred & how *Poor Caroline* showed a lack of co-ordination in her character between its romantic & efficient aspects which Lady Rhondda probably emphasises —thus hindering her development into an important writer.

Phyllis & I went to Queen's Theatre after dinner & saw Beverley Nichols' play *Evensong*, founded on his novel. Very good. Edith Evans magnificent in part of Irela. Came back to drink late tea & discuss families with Winifred.

Thursday July 7th
Winifred wrote a charming little poem called "House on Fire"; all about grief not happiness being the stabilising thing. We walked together in the Old English Garden in Battersea Park after lunch; a glory of campanulae, roses, delphiniums & stocks. Phyllis came in to tea; she had been seeing Gollancz & had told him of my Autobiography—persuaded thereto by Gordon's announcement yesterday that he had met Henrietta Leslie who had told him that Jarrold's were going to write to me & ask for it. When she said that Golly was going to write to me about it everything seemed to stand still & I felt too suddenly agitated to be very responsive. She says her own profits are not quite so much as she expected yet, but *Inheritance* is still selling steadily, about 200 a week. Gollancz very anxious to hear her plans for her next book but not anxious she should hurry it & very pleased that it was likely to be long. He gave her a cheque for £400 to be going on with.

After dinner Phyllis and I went to *Musical Chairs* at the Criterion. Very good & most unusual; John Gielgud as the consumptive piano-playing son who ultimately gets drowned rescuing the girl he didn't love was extremely attractive. Clare came to supper & Drummond Shiels dropped in to see Winifred after we'd gone.

Friday July 8th
A most satisfactory morning's post. First came the letter from Gollancz which Phyllis had mentioned but I didn't really believe in, asking to see my book; I replied saying he should see it before Curtis Brown sent it elsewhere. Then also there was a very charming letter from Rebecca, explaining how various catastrophes—including a serious operation on her sister Dr Fairfield—had prevented her from replying to mine. She concluded by saying that she would like to meet Phyllis if Phyllis would like it, & added (strangely & somewhat inconsistently) that she had always thought she would admire her if only she wouldn't follow what to her (Rebecca) are the falsest of false gods—Arnold Bennett & Priestley. (I do

wonder why she puts Bennett & Priestley in the same category; can't personally see that they have anything in common.) As there wasn't much time before Sunday I rang her up and after rejecting various suggestions of mine she asked me to bring Phyllis to tea at her flat at 4.30 to-morrow. P. was pleased if a little intimidated by this arrangement—said that two months ago she had thought it just conceivable that she & Rebecca might be in the same crowd somewhere & that R. would "spoil the party" for her—but the very last thing she had ever visualised had been going to tea at her flat. She was pleased & quite triumphant about the Gollancz letter—at least he'd got in first, which made things easier for me.

P. left about 3.0 to meet her second brother—the one who always upsets her—& see him off at King's Cross; I went on working most of the afternoon. Hilda dropped in about 6.0 to leave a book for W. & drove me round to Crosby Hall with a *Harper's* for Phyllis & her copy of the Arnold Bennett *Journal*; I made the return of these an excuse to go round as I thought her brother might have made her cry again, but I found her quite cheerful and looking really charming in the black & white dress with her face made up quite skilfully—she was just off to dine with the Priestleys.

Saturday July 9th
By first post a letter came from Jarrold's not only asking to see my book but definitely committing themselves to making an arrangement which would be financially satisfactory to me if only I would give them the offer of it. Funny that their letter & Gollancz's were written the same day—and lucky that as his was sent off more promptly I received & answered it first, thus giving him the prior claim. Jarrold's letter was most charmingly complimentary and I replied as agreeably as I could, saying that I had been already approached from other quarters but their very kind letter would of course have most careful consideration.

Phyllis came in about 3.30 & we took some snapshots in the garden of her with Winifred & me, & with the children. Then we set off for Orchard Court, she far more self-possessed & less nervous about it than I had expected. Indeed, I don't think I have ever known anyone whose confidence and sophistication has increased so much in so short a time; the gaucheness & provincialism of last May seem quite to have disappeared.

We found Rebecca out as usual—a prolonged luncheon & then a visit to the London Library—&, as usual, Henry entertained us with his slow, sententious, anecdotal conversation. This conversation, much to our amusement, betrayed considerable knowledge of Phyllis's work & even her local interests; Henry actually said he'd heard a great deal about her, & it was quite obvious that she had been very thoroughly discussed by them. Rebecca appeared in about half an hour—dressed, I think, in the same blue and beige frock as she wore at the *T. & T.* party, & looking very tired. Henry said they ought to have been away by now but for Dr Fairfield, &

her illness & the postponement of the holiday had obviously had a subduing effect.

It was a curious tea-party. The whole conversation remained entirely general; Rebecca was obviously determined (Phyllis said for my sake, but I don't know) to be as friendly & gracious to Phyllis as she could, but all the time there was a sense of sharp claws ready at any moment to pierce through the velvet. The whole thing was baffling, stultifying and politely alarming; Rebecca—partly because she was so tired—had evidently made up her mind to be impersonal & remote—to remain a safe distance away from all controversial topics. So (chiefly with Henry's help) we studiously avoided all mention of books, reviews, Phyllis's work, Rebecca's work &, above all, their opinion of each other—which for three writers was quite an achievement. Gordon was telephoned for (as Rebecca said she had meant him to come but I don't think she did at the time) but couldn't come. If he had, just possibly he might have absorbed Henry, & we could have had some more intimate conversation—but I don't think so; I'm sure R. didn't intend us to have it. The only dangerous moment came when Rebecca was talking about America & I—rashly but quite deliberately to see if it would draw anything—mentioned that Phyllis might be going over there in September; when R. asked why, Phyllis replied, with the only trace of embarrassment that she displayed, that her b-book was coming out there in September and she'd been asked to go over in connection with it. But Rebecca after one or two polite & slightly cold queries about it dropped the subject at once so of course I didn't pursue it. Phyllis behaved *admirably* all the time—was self-possessed without being dogmatic, & dignified without seeming distant or resentful. The conversation kept such an even & tepid tone that nothing special remains to report of it; I only remember Rebecca telling me (which I didn't know) that Ann Reid, the author of *We Are the Dead*, died soon after Gordon & I met her at Rebecca's New Year party and that Catherine Carswell's new book on D. H. Lawrence was inaccurate from beginning to end. When we left at 6.0 she came with us as far as the bus and told us a tale of how Eleanor Markel, the American who came to interview her for her lectures at the Plaza, remarked of Phyllis: "She seems to be doing some fine work in her little mining town." Rebecca suggested that Halifax might go up in flames if the remark were repeated there.

On the way home, & also earlier, Phyllis told me about the Priestley party, & how everyone carefully avoided the subject of *Faraway*. She sat next to Hugh Walpole both during & after dinner & found him very boring; wish I could have the same opportunity after his catty articles about me. Priestley told her he had liked me very much & seemed to be rather surprised about it.

We went along to the Savoy Grill after dinner & stayed there from 11.0 till about 12.30; P. & I were a little weary from late nights but it was great fun as we sat at a table by the window & saw all the beautiful creatures from the Eton & Harrow match coming in. The evening ended with an animated discussion on our methods of writing books. Phyllis came home with us in the taxi & Gordon saw her back to Crosby Hall.

She rather intelligently remarked this evening that Henry's conversation with Rebecca, her & myself was just like one bad player in an otherwise good tennis four; she made the characteristic gesture of three hard swift strokes followed by one high miserable lob just dropped over the net.

Sunday July 10th
Very hot & bright. Letters & diary in morning. Phyllis in to lunch. Afterwards gave her the blue-green enamel pencil which I got for her in Harrods' jewellery dept yesterday; wrote a card saying it was to remind her often of "the triumph of *Inheritance* & the summer of 1932". Winifred also gave her some woodcuts of old Chelsea, to look at when she felt homesick for London and this household. She said goodbye to the children & we all had tea at the Lombard; then we all saw her off in a taxi to Euston where she is meeting her Highgate friend & going off to a dull holiday in Ireland. She wouldn't let me go with her as she said she'd rather say goodbye to us in Chelsea where we belong.

Felt extraordinarily flat after she had gone; in some queer way she is one of the most stimulating people I have ever met, & her tendency to get easily depressed & feel shy and inferior doesn't prevent this. Tried to work after dinner but too depressed to do much—& of course in a typical way the girl at Cicely Hamilton's got involved in a motor smash & I had to go round & dress her head & then get Dr Higgs.

Monday July 11th
Very hot again; small thunderstorm with floods of rain after lunch. Messy morning; not much work done. Babies' Club Committee after tea; I took the chance to protest against the fiasco of the Maternity Conference & my unsupported speech. Consulted Miss Raynham-Smith about Miss Thomson's nursery school; she had no misgivings at all except very slight ones about diet, but brought up at the committee about the advisability of someone from the Club going to see it. I said I would & Mrs Stanley Robinson offered her car. Panted for air after supper; went for walk in Battersea Park; flower garden gorgeous.

Tuesday July 12th
Mrs Stanley Robinson's offer of the car materialised, though she can't go herself. Went over to see Miss Thomson & get all particulars; booked dates for the children; mentioned diet & she said it was being very carefully arranged by a dietician & a diet-sheet would be sent from the Club.

A p.c. from Phyllis written at Belfast station announcing her safe arrival in Ireland. Worked at notes in afternoon but morning broken up by dressing the head-wound of Cicely Hamilton's lodger, & visit to Oakwood

Court to fetch Father's £500. Gordon ultimately suggested that he put the cash in his bank & wrote me a cheque, owing to the assumptions that will certainly be made if I turn up before my unknown manager with an unexplained £500! I agreed to this. Kean Seymour very agreeable over whole transaction. Think I shall probably change my Bank; very bored with the dilatoriness & indifference at mine; also more convenient to have same bank as Gordon. Deposited the £500 in my Bank this afternoon (the cheque); also made a new will & deposited that at the same time.

Still feeling very flat; miss Phyllis immensely.

Wednesday July 13th
Went to Burford with Gordon in Mrs Stanley Robinson's car to see Miss Thomson's nursery school. Quite a delightful day; lovely run from Oxford to Burford in spite of mist & damp; can't think why I never went when I was up. Mrs Thomson, a very pleasing elderly woman, showed us over the school; I thought everything admirably adapted for children and felt I really could trust them with John & Shirley for three weeks. Had an agreeable lunch at the Cotswold Gateway; lovely vague view of the Cotswolds over towards Stow-on-the-Wold.

Came back just in time for dinner party; Balfours of Burleigh & Professor Hermannsson to dinner; Ernest & Natalie Davies in afterwards. Keen political argument most of the time; Lord Balfour a Tory who is spiritually Labour; Gordon a Socialist spiritually Tory. Lady Balfour rather silent but said she was glad that I was writing my kind of book as it hadn't yet been done. Ernest Davies delighted with Phyllis's *Clarion* article this week on "Novels as Peacemakers".

Letter from Jarrold's this morning regretted that other publishers have approached me about my novel but still very courteous in tone. Charming letter from Phyllis from Ireland beginning "My dear, my very dear, Vera" and says how very much—in spite of getting ideas for plots in quiet of Cushendall—she was missing us & Chelsea.

Thursday July 14th
Very fatigued all day after yesterday. John went with Nurse to David Weaver's party (son of Peggy Ward) so I put Shirley to bed. Wrote 11 letters in morning.

Friday July 15th
Collected the snapshots taken last Saturday; very good of everyone except Phyllis. But sent her a set in case they would do for Macmillan's who have asked her for some. After lunch went with Mother to Baird Lewis & bought at their sale a black coat & shirt, black evening dress & black hat with parchment-coloured ribbon. Got a parchment crêpe blouse at Marshall's & red and white spotted blouse at Peter Jones. At dinner had argument

with Gordon about educational expenses, which I'd rather find out of capital than reduce myself to a very narrow margin of income.

Saturday July 16th
Dull day. Finished taking notes on 1921. Children in afternoon. No letters.

Sunday July 17th
Took children all round Battersea Park in morning. Oakwood Court in afternoon; saw Margaret Jones' baby; ugly but not unpleasing. Gordon played very charmingly with John & Shirley. Started a deadly dull *M.G.* article on universities as a prelude to life as requested by the B.F.U.W. After supper discussed Dorothy Woodman & sex relations generally with G. & W.

Monday July 18th
Spent day at British Museum reading *Annual Registers* from 1900 onwards. I got in at S. Kensington Tube, & sat down to read Phyllis's novel *Carr* which I am just finishing, when a most strange coincidence happened. I noticed that the woman beside me—youngish middle-age, plain, rather red weather-beaten face, dressed in black leather coat & small black hat, was looking at my book in the rather inquisitive way that people in the Tube often do, when suddenly she said, in a rather harsh voice with a slight North country accent (but not at all the same as Phyllis's), "Forgive me for interrupting you, but I was at school with the girl who wrote that book you are reading."

Then occurred the following conversation (which I put down to retell to Phyllis as soon as I got to the B.M.):
Vera. Really! How interesting! I know her quite well myself; I'm a writer too & she's been staying with me in London. Were you at Cheltenham?
Stranger. Oh no; it was a little school in Halifax called Miss Rouse's. I lived in Halifax for 27 years & we knew all the Bentleys—Phyllis & her brothers. They were a very clever family, and they all wore glasses & had red hair.
V. All this interests me a good deal, because I only know P.B. as a famous writer who's just had a terrific success with her last book *Inheritance*. Have you read it?
Stranger. Yes, I read that; I thought it was awfully good. I didn't read her others because I go in for out-door things much more than reading, but I've noticed them coming out & been so interested because I was at the same school. Has she been in London lately?
V. Yes, she's only just left; she's had a perfectly splendid time here going to literary parties & making speeches at dinners & so on. Do tell me what she was like when you knew her—I don't know her from the point of

view of her early life at all. How old was she when you knew her at school
& what was she like?

Stranger. She was a good deal younger than I was—quite little, about 12 I
should say. She was a plain little girl & wore glasses, but had beautiful
auburn hair, very curly. But the chief thing about her was that she was
terribly high-strung & excitable—used to take it out of herself like
anything by rushing up & down all over the place. Of course she was *very*
clever, really brilliant at lessons & things; everybody thought her clever.
Is she just as excitable now?

V. Well—probably she is, but it doesn't appear much on the surface. She
seems self-possessed as a rule now, & rather reserved, but I suspect a
good deal of excitableness inside ("How different, different, different we
all are in our maturity," I thought to myself, "and yet how singularly the
same—our essential characteristics not altered but merely thrust in-
ward by the onslaughts of life"). Was she popular at school?

Stranger. Yes—quite; well, no, perhaps not exactly. You see, she was so
highly strung & absolutely absorbed in lessons & work; she didn't seem
to have much *outside* life, if you know what I mean.

V. Do tell me your name, so that I can mention it when I next write to her.

She told me that she was married now but her name was Irene Clarkson,
but that Phyllis would be more sympathetic to & more likely to remember
her sister Lydia who was lame; she said she lived in Wimbledon now, &
asked me my name, but it obviously didn't convey much when I gave it. By
this time it was Holborn & I had to get out; the general impression she left
on me as I departed was a kind of mingled pleasure & incredulity that the
excitable little auburn-haired girl had fulfilled what even then had seemed
her destiny & become so famous. By the time we'd finished talking the
other people near us in the train had become interested & we had quite a
little crowd listening to our conversation. As I walked to the B.M. it struck
me that the picture of the clever little red-haired girl running up & down in
sheer excitement was rather a pleasing one, but not in the least like the one
Phyllis gave me of herself; perhaps, after all, she didn't appear to her
childhood's contemporaries quite as unfavourably as she imagines.

B.M. was very hot & stuffy; felt quite dazed by tea-time when I dropped
in for a few minutes to Chrystal Macmillan's Chambers in Pump Court to
meet the foreign delegates to the Open Door International. Mrs Abbott
there but not Mrs Le Sueur. Talked to the Dane & the Belgian; Mme
Plaminkova there whom I met in Prague eight years ago but I didn't get
the chance to talk to her. Soon after I got back Evelyn Irons rang me up
from the *Daily Mail* & asked me to do an article on Careers for Daughters
for her Woman's Page. Letter from Phyllis this morning; also her really
excellent photograph. The letter was her real Yorkshire self; rather
withdrawn.

Tuesday July 19th

More *Annual Register*s at British Museum in morning. Children's party (for Shirley's birthday, eight days too soon) in afternoon; quite small as most of them have already gone away—we only had the Constable children, Davy children, Betty Lou Nidell & Lindsey Barry. Went off quite well in spite of only a hasty half-hour given to preparation; Mother & Katherine from Oakwood Court helped. Wrote long letter to Phyllis in evening telling her about the Tube encounter yesterday; then made some alterations in book. Getting now that I can hardly tear myself from it to do articles or anything else.

Wednesday July 20th

Wrote *Daily Mail* article, "Planning a Daughter's Future". Fitting at Baird Lewis after lunch. Went with children to Babies' Club; both passed very fit; Dr Waller thinks J.'s knock knees are really strengthening & his legs lengthening at last.

Thursday July 21st

Looked after children most of day as Nurse had to go off early to oculist & dentist, & Gordon was telegraphed for by his father to go to Oxford & solve some money complication. Very charming letter from Phyllis, discussing Arnold Bennett's *Journal*, & enclosing an inept reply from Benn's to her suggestion (prompted by me) that they should advertise her earlier books. My universities article in the *M. Guardian* to-day. Finished *Carr* in bed.

Friday July 22nd

All day in British Museum reading *Annual Register*s; very dark & stuffy; thunderstorm in late afternoon. W. & G. took John to Richmond by boat; storm broke just as they arrived there so they went into a tea-shop & didn't get wet, but J.'s afternoon was rather spoiled. Monica to supper; full of pep about her forthcoming visit to India with Ellen Wilkinson as the guest of the Congress Party. Got blue leather jewel case at Harrods for Shirley's birthday.

Saturday July 23rd

All day at B.M. again—verifying dates & events from small print till everything swam. Gordon went off to Digswell Park for to-night & Sheffield from Sunday to Monday. Winifred very worried bec. Evelyn Waugh, who has been to the Abyssinian coronation, is also producing a novel (like the one she has just finished about Mandoa) on a semi-mythical Central African state treated comically & politically. Lady Rhondda, who called in at tea-time, advised her to get Collins to race it out so as to run no risk of suspected plagiarism.

Very charming p.c. from Phyllis who appears pleased with my letters; wrote her another long one to-night all about the excellence of *Carr* which I think really does deserve Walpole's adjective "magnificent". I like parts of it—& especially the end—better than *Inheritance*; the spiritual insight which she showed in the York execution scene & the scene between Will & Mary at the Moorcock seems to run all through *Carr*.

Sunday July 24th
Packed in morning. Gave Shirley her blue jewel-case as birthday present for her birthday on Wednesday. After supper read Winifred extracts from the earlier chapters of "Testament of Youth"—she said she thought it moving & good, but I felt desperately dissatisfied—I had imagined it as so much better than it is.

Monday July 25th
Purely packing up. Saw Winifred off to Sidmouth at 3.0 to avoid fatigue of travelling with children; made her travel first. Read in Chelsea Library. Gordon came back from Sheffield; a scheme is afloat by which he may be offered a Chair in "Government" there in a year's time. At the Group Labour Conference at Digswell Park he met Laski, Cole, and Brailsford. G. went off after dinner to an I.L.P. meeting in Oxford Street.

Tuesday July 26th   5 York Terrace, Sidmouth
Came down to Sidmouth with Nurse & the children. John a perfect angel all day—the completely rational elder brother. No doubt, what with standing in the rain to identify our luggage, I did look somewhat dishevelled, for as I was standing with J. waiting for the rain to stop & allow the porter to bring our belongings from the train, the ticket-collector added final insult to injury by coming up to me and inquiring: "Have *you* any of the tickets, or has the lady got them all?"!! (The lady, presumably, was a lavishly-dressed but very vulgar-looking female who was standing a few yards away haranguing the porters!)

However, the rooms are delightful, the sitting-room balcony is so much on top of the sea that I feel as though I were in a boat, & the landlady Mrs Hazlewood loves children. J. has already made up his mind that he likes Sidmouth & wants to come again. A card from Phyllis from the Giant's Causeway was waiting for us.

Wednesday July 27th
Shirley's birthday; two years ago. She celebrated it by biting a piece out of a glass given her to drink from & making us all terrified that she had swallowed some, but no ill-effects are so far apparent. Spent day revising Chap. I & going two walks, one up Peak Hill & the other with Winifred along a flowery footpath beside the Sid. Day warm & showery; in the Sid valley we stood for some time watching the shadows of the clouds sweeping over a distant mown hayfield that looked exactly like green velvet. Went to local cinema after supper to see *Hindle Wakes* to see how far it was likely to

be a precedent for *Inheritance* if filmed; thought Phyllis's book might make a similarly excellent film. Found it was a Gaumont–Gainsborough picture produced by Victor Saville.

Thursday July 28th
Winifred heard to-day from Curtis Brown that Wishart's have accepted her *Virginia Woolf*. Rather miserable showery day; revised, worked, looked after children. John remarked on walk after tea that he wished his Christian name was "Pond's Cream"; while I was bathing him he told me a long, incoherent but passionate story about a lobster being presented with some beads. Shirley, after being put to bed, climbed right over the rails of her hired cot, which is an inch or two lower than the one at home, & fell with a terrific bump on the floor; I heard it in my room & dashed in to find her already at the door, roaring but apparently unhurt. She will now have to be strapped; where she gets all this adventurous rashness from I cannot imagine. As Gordon's mother is the only unknown element I suppose she must be responsible for S.'s terrifying traits.

Friday July 29th
Gordon's 36th birthday. Letter from him saying he isn't going to Russia because, like myself, he wants to get on with his book. Walked up to Mutter's Moor in afternoon; W. came half-way up the hill & sat on a seat while I wandered about among the woods & the heather. Finished revising Chapter I. Cutting from Durrant's showed the *Daily Mail* article (altered by Evelyn Irons out of all recognition!) to have appeared on July 26th.

Saturday July 30th
Went over by bus via Honiton & Kentisbeare to spend a day with E. M. Delafield & her husband & two children. Husband sandy-haired, agreeable but unexciting, rather like Clifton Roberts; boy, Lionel, aged 12, the image of Delafield; Rosamond aged 8 the image of her father. Pleasant house—spacious & informal; large garden full of flowers; view of Dartmoor from top windows. No special conversation all day owing to presence of children, their young male tutor, & a school-friend of Delafield's, Catholic, grey-haired & delicate-looking—as different as could be imagined from the graceful & elegant Delafield. (Family name really Dashwood.) Good deal of time spent in going over garden & playing paper games to amuse children. Delafield brought us back in her car in the evening & stayed to supper. While we were there Shirley fell & grazed one eye—on the pavement—about her fifth mishap since we came.

Sunday July 31st
Took children for a rambling walk round outskirts of Sidmouth while Nurse was at church. Tiresome showery day again—sudden downpours with intervals of extreme heat when mackintoshes felt atrocious. After

lunch Shirley was sick right in the entrance hall. Owing to the chaos involved by this I only got through revising about 15 pages of Chap. 2 instead of about 30 as I hoped.

Tuesday August 2nd
Long walk in morning up to Mutter's Moor & part way across; heavenly flowers, birds & butterflies. Gordon & his father came down in afternoon; we went to meet them. I hadn't thought of looking out & planning the journey for G. via Exeter & bus, so he had travelled for 8 hours & had four changes.

Wednesday August 3rd
Tried to bathe this morning but it wasn't very enjoyable; water too cold tho' the day was bright & sunny. Walked with G. to Mutter's Moor & across it after tea; weather gorgeous but wind too cold to see the place at its best. Revised from p. 121 to p. 142.

Thursday August 4th (18th anniv. of War)–Saturday August 13th
All very similar—revising (or rather re-writing, reduced to despair by notion of book being too long for any publisher to want), walking, bathing, sitting on beach or balcony, looking after children, reading Marjoribanks' *Life of Lord Carson*. E. M. Delafield, son & friend came over for day last Saturday—the loveliest day we have had though the weather has been good all along. All very pleasant. Delafield told us that when Arthur Watts, the artist who illustrated the *Provincial Lady*, was staying with her he wanted to visit the St John Ervines whom he had known well in the old days; she rang up Leonora who was very haughty, said she didn't think St John had much time etc., so Watts took the telephone from Delafield & called out: "What's that you say, Nora? Poor old St John—is that how it's taken him, too big for his boots, eh! Do commiserate him & say I'm sorry I've no time to come", etc. etc. Tableau! No communication since between the Dashwood and Ervine households!

Aunt Lillie, Uncle Arthur & Robin came up for tea last Sunday; long talk about Mr Jefferies & why he left Bryanston. She had seen my article "I Denounce Domesticity!" in the *Quiver*. My *Daily Mail* article on inventing your own career brought three persistent correspondents one of whom wanted to earn £3 a week without qualifications & *not* by domesticity! I turned them all on to the London Society for Women's Service.

Two or three letters from Phyllis—one brief note showed she was miserable & the next letter said she had been so though didn't say why. It also mentioned that the germ of a new book was growing—"very difficult if not impossible"—but it was making her happy.

Pa Catlin went back to Oxford yesterday, thank God. Gordon ran over to Farnham for the night last Thursday to lecture to the Fabian Summer

School. Have fixed up a lecture (only 3 gns though) for myself at Wanstead in Dec. on "The Problem Family" to a P.N.E.U. group.

Heard yesterday by *The Times* that Graham Wallas had died in Cornwall —75; a nice old man, always benevolent to Gordon & me; I'm very sorry. Also Ronald Mackenzie the author of *Musical Chairs* was killed yesterday in a motor accident in France; only 29. Life very precarious for the great.

Sunday August 14th
Children on beach in morning. Went over to the St John Ervines for tea. New house, Honey Ditches, at Seaton, most attractive—long view running downhill across to Seaton Bay; house white with bluish roof, looks south-east; St John's study a tiny place like a pagoda, joined to house but separate, & absolutely overflowing with books. Also there was a delicious terrace, & lower down the garden a small modern sun-house for working in warm weather, both looking over the view. Four-year-old garden going downwards in terraces; planned and largely made by Leonora; masses of colour in spite of the newness—gladioli in the usual scarlet but also deep shades of crimson; brilliant antirrhinums against a mauve mist of catmint; huge bushes of evening primrose both yellow & orange, rock plants everywhere & several unusual trees—maple, scarlet oak, & one or two varieties imported from America.

When we arrived St John was typing an article & Leonora finishing a letter; we made them both go on while the three of us looked at the garden. St John looked well & though vehement on the usual (& associated) topics of H. G. Wells & Maxton, was less bitter than usual in conversation, & Leonora, who took us back to the bus in her car after tea, was hardly catty at all—obviously much happier dominating her own house than always moving round to parties with St John's friends in London. But has let herself go stout & rather slovenly-looking. Tea—very pleasant—on dining-room table; two nice people, Dr & Mrs Cregan, there too—live in Sloane Square; he used to be St John's doctor in town. St John said that he & Leonora had speculated whether "Francis Iles" was Rebecca West or Winifred (we know of course it isn't W. & I privately suspect Delafield but didn't say so) but in the end concluded that "Francis Iles" was just Francis Iles, making a quick reputation by putting his name in inverted commas.

Altogether a very pleasant afternoon. Lovely sunset when we got back & bright moonlight streaming over sea. A good article likening Shaw to Socrates and called "That Gadfly" in this week's *Time & Tide* by Lady Rhondda.

Monday August 15th
Final bathe; final walk up to Mutter's Moor with Gordon. Picked a piece of white heather there; wish I could believe it is lucky.

Tuesday August 16th   London
Back to town with all our traps. Torrid day—hotter than any since we came. Train stifling & over ½ an hour late, but children very good; Shirley not sick & slept over an hour. Found waiting for me a very long and intimate letter from Phyllis which cheered my soul.

Wednesday August 17th
Very hot. Messed about all morning with interviewing temporaries, minor shopping, transferring Bank-account to Kean Seymour's branch of the Midland Bank, looking all over the place from the Town Hall to the Nat. His. Mus. for someone to tell me how to destroy the wasps' nest under our back steps, and finding no one. In afternoon Manager of Westminster Bank came round in great agitation about the transfer; I didn't want to get anyone into trouble by saying I couldn't endure the way his cashiers kept me waiting, so simply said I wanted to be at the same Bank as Gordon. Also a man came round from the Town Hall about the wasps' nest but as his suggestions only amounted to a treacle pit & syringing with disinfectant they weren't exactly inspired by genius. Then took children to see Dr Waller at Babies' Club—both very well; he thought nothing of S.'s habit of being sick & prescribed ointment for J.'s face. All this prevented me from doing much work so I wrote a long reply to Phyllis. At night a letter from David Higham asking after the Autobiog. so I told him about Gollancz's and Jarrold's inquiries. Winifred interviewed both Wishart's & Collins' today; her *Virginia Woolf* will appear on Oct. 7th & *Mandoa, Mandoa!* as an 8/6 book probably in November.

Thursday August 18th
Very hot—90° in afternoon shade. While I was putting children to bed Henrietta Leslie came in for a talk—said Sylvia Pankhurst had persuaded her to write round about *The Suffragette Movement* coming out in cheap edition. Also that Jarrold's are so keen to get hold of "Testament of Youth" that they keep on ringing her & Curtis Brown up about it. After dinner, Dr Schutze came in & extinguished the wasps' nest with some sort of powder. Posted long letter to Phyllis.

Friday August 19th
Still hotter—99° in shade at Greenwich this afternoon; hottest day for 21 years. Sat in garden all day sweltering & revising; managed to rewrite 30 pages. Children, espec. John, rather fractious from heat. Church invited us round after dinner but felt too done in after 30 pp. in such heat so let G. go alone. Mollison crossed Atlantic E. to W. Letter from David Higham satisfied with position re Autobiog.

W. had tea with Violet Scott-James who a) expressed great interest in "Testament" when W. told her about publishers' letters; b) said how much everyone had liked Phyllis when she was in town—so much more modest, human & objectively interested in other people than almost all successful writers; men apparently liked her as much as women.

Saturday August 20th

Very hot again. Actual temp. not quite so high as yesterday but atmosphere very close & tiring. Much delayed by loss of my reading glasses. Spent most of the day in Chelsea Library reading War-time *Annual Registers*. W. went off to Cottingham for 10 days after tea; Gordon saw her off at King's Cross.

Sunday August 21st

Thunderstorm last night so to-day somewhat cooler. Pursued references for "Testament" all day. Went to Oakwood Court with Gordon & John. Mother inclined to grumble about finding the basement untidy while the house was closed—evidently thinks I can't manage the maids. John rather trying all day; when I mentioned the possibility of a smack he merely replied: "Smack! Smack! If you want to smack anybody, smack yourself!"

Monday August 22nd

Rather wretched tiring day, buying things for children, renewing household equipment & getting hair washed. Absolutely in despair about "Testament of Youth"; just got to chapter I wrote last December after the election when W. was first ill & I was doing all her work & arrangements & having rows with Mrs Holtby & Lady R. at same time; should never have thought I could write anything so inchoate & *bad*. Shall I *ever* finish the damned thing—& will it be any good if I do? Had letter from W. to say she arrived all right at Cottingham.

Tuesday August 23rd

Further unavailing battles with wasps' nest. Henrietta Leslie & Dr Schutze to dinner; Gordon's friends the Gerrards from Longbland (Church's acquaintances) came in after; charming, rather over-conscious, agreeable woman of the super-barmaid type, with American accent picked up after 4 years' residence in U.S. Dinner not so badly done but general arrangements a little complicated by deafness of temporary parlourmaid.

Henrietta & I talked shop about books; she said she had heard *Inheritance* was the best novel so far this year. Mentioned her huge American correspondence over *Mrs Fischer's War* and I told her of Phyllis's English one while she was here. Henrietta said she wondered what it felt like to have such a success as Phyllis's, & how she must wonder whether she would be able to keep it up. As she seemed so impressed by Phyllis's performance I didn't mention that my greatest difficulty had been to get P. to realise that she had had a success at all or that anyone was in the least interested in her.

Wednesday August 24th
Very tired again—too much so for much work. Wrote review of the League *Year Book* for *Time & Tide*. Muddle with Miss West over a note supposed to be written by G. annoyed me. Short letter from Winifred.

Thursday August 25th
Phyllis sent me a copy of Ruth Holland's *The Lost Generation*, which she has been reviewing for the *Observer*, with a rather agitated letter fearing that R.H. had stolen my theme & covered the ground of "Testament of Youth". I wrote assuring her that she hadn't; there is no background of current events in *The L.G.* & no likenesses except those inevitable in writers who have lived through the same adventurous epoch—mere superficial similarities of incident. Nurse out—Mother came to tea—had children all day but got through fair amount of revision.

Friday August 26th
Worked all day, mostly in garden. Uphill work—part about Somme had entirely to be rewritten. *The Lost Generation* is a beautiful novel. Wish one could reserve a section of life—say three months—for one's own use as one reserves a railway compartment; no arrangements, children, maids or demands even on part of one's nearest & dearest. Feel Phyllis's society would be more tolerable than anyone's at the moment, simply because she has absolutely no claim on me except what I care to admit.

Saturday August 27th
In morning went to Library of Imperial War Museum to verify what posters actually were pub. in Feb. 1915. Saw a youngish man with bright, amused eyes who looked them up for me & seemed quite interested; told me that Radclyffe Hall went to him when writing *The Master of the House* as she wanted to get two white soldiers into Palestine at a time when there were really none there; he helped her to work out a way of doing it. Work rest of day—"T. of Y." gets on too, *too* slowly. Charming letter from Phyllis saying she was glad *The Lost G.* wasn't like it.

Sunday August 28th
Took J. & S. to Battersea Park in morning to see owls; Old English Garden full of gorgeous dahlias, & pond thick with water-lilies—pink & yellow. Phyllis's review of New Novels in Gerald Gould's place in the *Observer* this morning—*very* good; the change in her journalism since the Spring is nothing short of miraculous. Wrote to congratulate her—also to say that I felt rather more depressed [after] reading her review of *The Lost Gen.* than I did before—it seems to me she thinks it more typical than it is of the War Generation women, who certainly *did* as well as just suffered. Started revising the Malta chapter.

Monday August 29th

Took children to Dr Waller—he signed their health certificates. Was working in delightful garden at back of his home on the Babies' Club book. We discussed methods of publicity. Continued revision. 24 pp.

Tuesday August 30th

Winifred came back from Cottingham looking well—met her at King's Cross. Children had hair cut. *Very* charming letter from Phyllis, completely understanding my letter about her review; wants me to stay a week in November. Revised 22 pp.

Wednesday August 31st

Children, with Gordon & Nurse, left by 9.45 for Oxford to stay with Miss Thomson at Burford. Didn't go to Paddington for fear of upsetting them—but they didn't appear to mind leaving me at all! I'm glad they are less concerned than I am; whenever I see them drive off without me I always think of Isadora Duncan's two children being drowned in the taxi in the Seine. When they had gone, put up my new photographs of them & Phyllis. Nurse came back in the evening to say they had arrived at Cotter's Bow without mishap & were happy; Miss Thomson met them at Oxford with Jennifer & Mark; very understanding idea. Wrote all day; revised 50 pages. Finished Malta chapter.

Thursday September 1st

P.c. from Cotter's Bow this morning to say children happy—no tears. Started revising France chapter. Went to tea at Oakwood Court—brought back photo of self in 1917, copy of Chopin's "March Funèbre" (of which I want to copy a phrase into part about Sir H. Wilson's funeral) and Edward's setting of Roland's "L'Envoi", which I have decided to put into Ch. 2. Spent all evening copying it. Another reassuring p.c. about children by last post. G. came back from Oxford—ought to have dined with H. G. Randall who rang up v. indignant to say he'd been waiting in Greek St for over an hour & had 4 cocktails. Nurse went on holiday.

Friday September 2nd

Family went to Folkestone. More p.c.s to say all well with children. Feeling fed up about work (chiefly due to reviews suggesting the theme of the Holland book is not important—we shouldn't look back any more, says Naomi Mitchison in *T. & T.*; it's too long, says Pritchett in the *N. Statesman*—& it's only about ½ the length of mine). I went with W. to Peter Jones & bought a black and pink jumper and a green one. Very headachey; didn't get much done; went to bed early.

Saturday September 3rd

Still fed up; only revised 27 pp. G. took me to the Dorchester for tea & a vermouth; felt rather more cheered but W. had one of her headaches & had to stay in bed all day which was depressing. Another reassuring p.c. about children. Consulting Kean Seymour about investing my £500.

Sunday September 4th
Revised 30 pp. Lovely bright autumn day. G. & I walked round Battersea Park after lunch & tried to remember names & kinds of trees. Coffee all together at Lombard Rest. after supper.

Monday September 5th
Had a most extraordinary dream last night—probably due to rewriting yesterday part about seeing Edward off at Waterloo in Jan. 1918. I thought Mother and I were tidying up her flat (it was present day but the flat wasn't Oakwood Court) because both she & I were going away somewhere; amongst other things I had to do was to copy out some diary or other & get it up to date before we went. When we left the flat Mother came round to the door in a car, only it wasn't a proper car at all, but a bright orange suitcase, very large, made of a sort of spongy celluloid, quite transparent. It was on wheels but had no doors or windows; to get in she simply lifted up the lid as one would of a suitcase, & got inside. I said: "What a queer sort of car," and she replied: "Well, you can't expect much for 8/11."

I left her & went on to meet Edward, whom I knew that I was seeing off to India on some temporary engineering job which was to last for a year or two. I thought how queer it was that Edward of all people should go in for engineering. When I met him he looked the same as he always did, yet somehow different—more depressed, less vital, less tranquil, than he used to & in a queer way older without having changed at all. I said to him: "What do you want to go & do engineering for?" and he said: "Why not; it's as good as anything." I went on: "After all you haven't finished your education yet; why don't you go back to Oxford first?" He replied: "Well, they wouldn't take me as I am now, after all this time." I thought to myself, "Why shouldn't they? He's only eighteen—or is it twenty-two"—and then I remembered it was the present day and thought "But, good Heavens —he's thirty-six."

We got into an open taxi & drove on a dreary, colourless suburban road & I knew we were going to the station. In my dream I evidently hadn't seen him for a long time for I asked him: "Do you ever play the violin now, Edward?" He replied: "No, not now. You see, my arm still hurts at times and I can't get the finer tones." "Well, do you go to concerts?" I inquired. "No," he answered, "not at all." "Oh Edward!" I exclaimed, bitterly disappointed, "I've been going to them myself because I thought you'd be going to them and enjoying them." "In that case," he replied, very politely but quite without interest, "I must start going to them again."

We drove along a little further and I asked him again: "Do you really want to go to India & do this engineering job? It isn't quite in your line," &

he answered apathetically: "Oh, it's as good as anything else. You have to take what you can get nowadays. What's it matter, anyway?" And I thought in my dream: "Wouldn't it perhaps have been better if he'd been killed in the War, like the others?"

Then there was a sudden crash and I woke up to find Elizabeth bringing in my tea. It took me quite a moment to remember that Edward had been killed on the Asiago Plateau fourteen years ago. The dream reminds me a little of Hans Andersen's "Story of a Mother", where Death comes in & shows her the unhappy future of her son if he lives, & she tells him to take her baby away; "and then Death carried her child into the Unknown Land". Winifred said this dream would make a short story.

Got a p.c. from Phyllis this morning to say *Inheritance*, tho' not out till September 13th, is already in its 3rd edition in America & 16,000 have been printed. "I shall now go out & actually buy a new waste-paper basket," she adds. Revised a good deal but found myself obliged to turn aside & draft a short story called "Re-encounter", based on my dream.

Tuesday September 6th
Did more revising of "Loneliest Hour" chapter; also completed & typed "Re-encounter". W. showed it to Cicely Hamilton who came in to supper; they both liked it & said Lady R. should see it for *T. & T.*

Amy announced that her mother's baby—a boy—has at last arrived; 12 hours' labour, only a nurse for delivery; Mrs F. alone in house with small girl of 12 till almost the last moment. Whole thing sounds ghastly; am going to send Amy with eggs & fruit for her mother but never have been philanthropically-minded or felt that philanthropy is any good. What it *does* do is to make me more politically-minded than I can bear—seeing that I'm really a writer and it's no use trying to be otherwise—& I feel we all ought to put everything aside until a doctor and anaesthetics are available for *every* maternity case in the country. The moral for me, I suppose, is to go on urging it in books, articles & speeches until enough people care sufficiently to get something done.

Wednesday September 7th
Finished revision of Parts I & II—700 pp. reduced to 680. Gardened all afternoon. Wrote long letter to Phyllis in massacred handwriting.

Thursday September 8th
Started looking up letters etc. for Ch. X. Cicely Hamilton dropped in with some material from German paper *Das Bauerland* about German disarmt; W. arranged for her to do an article about it for *T. & T.* P.c. from Miss Thomson to say children well. Got Kean Seymour to invest my £500, ½ in Midland Bank shares, ½ in Conversion Loan. Very wet. W. reading "Testament". Magnificent article by Storm Jameson in *New Clarion* called "The Lost Generation"; wrote her long letter about it.

Friday September 9th

W. finished "Testament" last night; her opinion very consoling. Went through small errors pointed out; then continued letters etc. Gordon met John Middleton Murry in Cheyne Walk to talk over article for *Adelphi*; then on to town to meet Namier. Letter from Nurse, saying she has had tonsillitis. Fine & warm. Bought a grey & red inexpensive frock from Peter Jones.

Saturday September 10th

Uneventful day. Gordon went off in evening to Joad's "Progressive People's" week-end. Went through W. H.'s letters & took down extracts with help of wireless; oh! so much material for Ch. X; too, too much! Cecil Roberts mentioned "Testament" on his page in to-day's *Sphere*.

Sunday September 11th

Opened the *Observer* to find from Gollancz's advt that *Inheritance* has gone into yet another edition—the 8th. His notice says: "Phyllis Bentley's *Inheritance* has proved to be one of those rare books which, long after the first rush is over, continue to be bought day by day by bookshops throughout this country & the Colonies, & even on the Continent. We went to press yesterday with another impression—the 8th. We have always believed this superb novel to be one of the few which will outlast our generation."

She *will* be delighted. I wrote her a tiny note of congratulation, telling her that her epitaph ought to be some lines from *Adonais*:

> The splendours of the firmament of time
> May be eclipsed, but are extinguished not.
> Like stars to their appointed height they climb.

More revision, more letters, more paragraphs. Violet Scott-James came to tea; I told her something about my book & she was so thrilled about it that after tea when I'd gone back to work she & W. apparently talked about it all the time.

Monday September 12th

Long delightful letter from Storm Jameson; she's coming to town in Oct. to a tiny flat for University terms so that her son *and* her husband (both of whom she appears to be keeping) can attend the London School of Economics. G. says W.'s book on Virginia Woolf is *excellent*; congratulated her on it this morning; must read it as soon as I have a free moment from the "Testament". Storm Jameson seems thrilled about the "T. of Y." & says she wd do a large review of it for Orage's new weekly.

No letter from Phyllis in reply to mine of last Wednesday; hope she isn't having a misery. G. & I walked over Richmond Common this afternoon; rather a dull day but I felt better after it. Charming letter from Miss Thomson this evening about the children.

Tuesday September 13th
Long letter from Phyllis this morning; she's been in bed with a bad cold, hence the silence, but seems happy owing to the 8th edition and three large specimen posters sent her by Macmillan's in U.S.A. (her book is pub. there today). Went again over first two chapters of "Testament" so that Miss Lennox could take them away & type them; felt very queer seeing them go. New house-parlourmaid Maud Grey came to-day; pretty girl and seems agreeable. Mother & Father, owing to Father having an abdominal pain, returned to-night from Folkestone 2 days too soon—no maids in the flat of course.

Wednesday September 14th
Worked really hard at Chap. X & got chief subjects and their contents in order; sorted all the slips. Went over to Oakwood Court after lunch to see how Mother & Father were & to pick up my letter on going to Asiago the first time; Mother had also found one or two other missing ones including account of Queen's visit to Somerville. Nurse writes she will definitely have to be late coming back so have arranged with Amy to look after children for me & I to get in temporary cook for few days.

P.c. from Phyllis this afternoon to say she has had a 38-word cable from U.S. saying *Inheritance* reprinted 5 times before publication—feature front-page reviews in *N.Y. Times* & *Tribune*—"very hopeful for wide reading". W., G. & I sent a joint telegram to her—"Congratulations, all so delighted, allelujah!" Do hope she's a bit happy to-day.

Went on working at sorting chapter but at my present stage of "Testament" found the light of another person's extreme success rather painful to work by; still, I'd rather be jealous of Phyllis than of anyone—she has earned & paid hard for every scrap of success. I thought of her the other day when reading that letter of Winifred's written in 1921, in which she told me that her mother had been quoting Frances Ridley Havergal's lines to the child trying to write poetry:

> 'Tis not stringing rhymes together,
> With your heart's blood you must write it,
> Though your face grows pale, none knowing
> So the song will be worth singing.

Remembering Phyllis's drawn, tired face in the winter of 1930 & her pretty copper-coloured hair turning grey after writing *Inheritance*, I think she is one of the people whom F.R.H. would have held up as an example!

Thursday September 15th
Working really *hard* at Ch. X—awful mental exercise getting such diffused events on to one canvas without apparent strain, after the intense single-minded concentration on one issue of the War chapters. Did first 5 pages of actual writing this evening.

Ethelreda Lewis came to tea—not much changed since she was in England four years ago—a little older, a little more faded, since Dr Lewis died, but still the same plaintive voice, & enduring, resigned, disillusioned attitude to life; but there was rather less nervous strain, I fancied. Ethelreda had lately been in Tanganyika & Zanzibar; was almost ecstatic over the beauty of the latter. But the most interesting things she told us were that a) since publishing *Trader Horn* she had had no less than *83* old men coming to her house & wanting her to write their life story—only one or two (one died recently in a Johannesburg doss-house) any good; b) since *Trader Horn* Ethelreda Lewis is merely looked on as the "editor" of a brilliant old man's memories & cannot get stuff placed in her own name or impartial reviews if she writes in it, so she has actually started again under the name of Hernekin Baptist. In this name she wrote a novel recently recommended by the Book Society called *Four Handsome Negresses*; it was based on an old Portuguese legend wh. she had told W. when she was last here & said she wd make into a book. When *Four Handsome Negresses* came out W. was much upset as she thought someone else had got hold of the legend first & written it up; she tried not to see how good the book was & to refrain from recommending it. "You see, I thought *you* were going to write that story," she told Mrs Lewis, & Mrs L. answered "But I did." Then she described the difficulty of keeping her identity secret—even Cape who pubd the book tried to let it out—*so* she resolved she wouldn't tell any London journalist, not even Winifred. She did get magnificent reviews but didn't sell much; she was depressed about this as she said she *couldn't* write better than she had in that book—though as Hernekin Baptist she has had 3 stories in *Harper's* in six months tho' she could never get in as Ethelreda Lewis. But I said: "Try to think of yourself as the public & critics think of Hernekin Baptist—as a young man just publishing his first novel; for a *first* novel it had a magnificent reception," & she said she would endeavour to wipe out in her mind the long fatiguing past of Ethelreda Lewis & think of herself like this. She said that when she felt very tired it was a great relief to have another personality to escape into. The rest of the conversation was abt S. African Trade Unions & Ballinger.

G. took me to the new Piccadilly restaurant, Monseigneur, for dinner —very pleasant; sort of half-way stage between Trocadero & Quaglino's; we danced & didn't get back till nearly 2 a.m.

Friday September 16th
Feeling very-morning-after-the-night-beforeish all day. Tried hard to write Ch. X but couldn't get on very fast so read Gertrude Atherton's *Adventures of a Novelist*, sent me for review by the *Week-end Review*, most of the afternoon. Lively book but think G. A. sounds a perfectly *horrid* person. How the nasty side of people does unintentionally come out in autobiographies—I only feel the same thing will happen in the case of mine.

W. not at all well to-day; Dr Gray came twice to give her injections.

Lovely Beethoven concerto on the wireless in the evening; reminded me of Edward playing it. Letter from Miss Thomson to say she can keep the children till to-morrow week.

Saturday September *17th*
Long letter from Phyllis, telling me about v. pleasant correspondence with Hugh Walpole & an invitation to do a wireless debate with Prof. Pear of Manchester on Oct. 11. But she is v. indignant about my remarks on *The Partnership* & espec. my supposition that Lydia was herself! (though after all the portrait of L. is extremely similar to many impressions of herself that she gave me! even though it isn't my idea of her at all). But it was probably stupid of me to tell her that a likeness existed even if I thought so! But as I told her in a rather angry note that I wrote in reply, it's damned easy to be superior about other people's stupidities when you yourself are standing so serenely upon the pinnacle of the *fait accompli*. It's a little hard to be continuously in contact with so much success when one hasn't even finished one's own book.

Sunday September *18th*
Wrote for 6 hours on end, with lunch in middle; 18 pages. G. & I had supper at Oakwood Court.

Monday September *19th*
Such a charming note from Phyllis to Gordon; deploring Manchester Cotton Strike as showing how little apparent effect the artist has on the public; said one book shop in Manchester has sold an enormous number of *Inheritance* yet the very people who read its plea for understanding bet. capital & labour are now striking. She also told him that "never in all her life had she met with such warm-hearted & generous kindness" as she had from me. After this I had to write a letter apologising for Saturday's angry one. Went out with W. this afternoon & bought chest for lower bathroom; then walked alone in Battersea Park. Wrote all day but had too much to look up to get on as fast as yesterday; 11 pp. *Oxford Poetry* & Women's Degrees.

Tuesday September *20th*
Wrote 18 pp. again—i.e. 67 pp. in 4 days. Not too bad tho' might be better. W. & I went out & had tea at Candy Shop in Church St to get a break. Very forgiving little note (or rather asking to be forgiven!) from Phyllis saying that mine had made her tremble all over & quite incapable of food or work! I told Winifred about the dispute, and she merely remarked: "You've been the most important person in too many people's lives, you little bitch!" W. correcting proofs of *Mandoa*.

Wednesday September 21st
Yet another letter from Phyllis—very charitable, loving & forgiving; she
was jealous because I said Storm Jameson was coming to town, upset
because I had threatened not to go to Halifax, etc. etc. I seem to have set
out last May to go for a peaceful walk in companionable sunshine, & find
myself instead in company of a volcano, an earthquake & a thunderstorm
all rolled into one!

Did 12 pages to-day; didn't finish Ch. X as I hoped to do bec. 5 of them
were about my visit to the Asiago Plateau with Winifred to see Edward's
grave in 1921. Don't know why, for I never shed a tear over the parts about
the War, but as I wrote about Asiago I found myself blind with crying until
I had to take off my reading glasses & manage without. When the section
was finished I had such a splitting head & swollen eyes that I gave up
writing & walked over to Kensington to have dinner with the family. There
I read a strange, somewhat chaotic novel called *Parson's Nine* by Noel
Streatfeild, whom I hadn't heard of before; a section in it about the War
took me back to my own work of this afternoon, especially as there was a
twin brother and sister in it who felt towards each other much as Edward
and I, though not twins, felt long ago.

Thursday September 22nd
Finished Chap. X this morning—95 pp. written in a week, preceded by
quite five weeks of looking up. Almost like a book in itself. Felt as usual on
finishing a chapter very depressed—that it was bad stuff & all the work I
had put in thrown away. After it was done wrote to Phyllis—more
cheerfully than of late—& went for a walk with W.

At night went by myself to Embassy Theatre at Swiss Cottage to see
Chlumberg's play *Miracle at Verdun*. It had a colossal success in Leipzig in
1930 but the author never knew, as he died as the result of a stage
accident—falling into a deep orchestral pit—just before the performance.
Marvellous satire on hypocrisy; picture of the world celebrating the 25th
anniversary of the War in 1939 (!) when suddenly some of the much-
belauded War-dead come back to life in a world in which nobody wants
them & they ultimately return whence they came. It haunted me so much
afterwards with its savage bitterness & utter pessimism that I was glad
that for the moment I had no more to write.

Friday September 23rd
Wet, chilly day. Spent afternoon in Brit. Museum & finished *Annual
Register*s. W. had Dr Drummond Shiels to coffee after dinner. Card from
John this morning; he had written his own name.

Drummond Shiels had many amusing tales to tell of his time in the
Government—of Sidney Webb as his chief always calling Ministers &
others "tiresome people" because they picked holes in his perfectly logical
but somewhat inhuman White Papers; of MacDonald being isolated by his
Highland pride & J. H. Thomas acquiring influence over him because he

was the only person who cheerfully disregarded this pride and burst in on Ramsay without waiting to be invited; consequently was always offering to dispose of Ramsay's worries for him & interfering in all the departments. When Passfield pubd the White Paper about Palestine there was an outcry among the Jews; Passfield was sent off to Liphook out of the way by Ramsay, but Drummond Shiels, who wd now have to conduct the debate on it, couldn't get an interview with Ramsay or Henderson; finally he was told to see A. V. Alexander, who knew less than he did about Palestine so, instead of getting advice, he had to give it, & let A.V.A. have 2 of his best points for his speeches. Shiels didn't know, & wasn't told, whether he had to defend the White Paper or withdraw, so generally defended it; Alexander made a bad speech & left out the two salient points, so they were never made. Ramsay afterwards congratulated Shiels on the speech, but if it hadn't gone well wd doubtless have disclaimed responsibility & said Shiels had never consulted him! So we let down our junior Ministers!

He also told us an amusing tale of how when he went as a British Delegate to Geneva he had to make the British declaration re the Palestine Mandate, & Mrs Dugdale, who was being very pro-Jewish on account of the Balfour tradition, arranged with much persistence a secret meeting between Shiels & Dr Weizmann at the Beau Rivage. Shiels had already written his speech ten days before, but he courteously listened to Weizmann & then, the next day, delivered precisely the speech that he had written the previous Saturday week! He afterwards had a charming note from Mrs Dugdale thanking him for making it so conciliatory & remarking how providential it was that she had been able to arrange the meeting between them just in time!

Before I came in D.S. had been talking to W. about her high blood pressure; *his* theory is that it's due to endocrine glands & she ought to have a love affair!

Saturday September 24th
Went over to Burford with Ernest Davies' to fetch all the children. Ernest Davies somewhat subdued all the time; obviously much dominated by Natalie. Had lunch at Oxford, at St George's Café; food even worse than before (or perhaps my taste has improved) but nowhere better to go. Lovely day most of the time, tho' Thames Valley misty in places. At Cotter's Bow everything sunny and cheerful; Shirley & J. standing in passage inside door; J. of course knew me but S. stood looking vague, as much as to say: "I've seen you before somewhere—where was it?" Gradually a pleased look came over her face & she recognised me. Miss Thomson seemed sorry to let them go & they have obviously been very happy there; in the car on way home S. kept intoning disconsolately: "Miss Thomson—gone—ay-way!" and John said "I want to go to Miss Thomson's again for a long time—I want to go *seven* times!"

We stopped for tea at a rather nasty café at High Wycombe; very smelly lavatory to which both children of course demanded to be taken twice. As far as Wycombe S. sat on my knee & was quite good but from Wycombe home she crawled all over the back of the car. Peter & Bruce Davies quarrelled most of the time & for half of the way were in the back of the car with S. & me while John sat on Mrs Davies' knee. J. was a perfect angel all the time; he even let Shirley pull him about & never complained, but both were *very* tired when we got home &, although we had warned J. that Nurse would not be back yet, his private grief at leaving Miss Thomson's & then not finding Nurse here overcame him when he discovered Amy was putting him to bed; he burst out crying & begged me to do it, so I went down & we both undressed him. Darling little boy! He reminds me so much of myself as a child, with his way of feeling too proud to complain of his small sorrows & then being overcome by them. Both children fell asleep at once & hardly woke.

Sunday September 25th
Took children to Oakwood Court. W. had a succession of afternoon visitors—Clifton & Marjorie Roberts & Miss Todd who has become Woman's Editor of the *Sphere, Tatler*, etc. & wants W. to help her (wh. W. does not want at all!) in the task of introducing modern "make-up" into these papers.

Very tired all day; probably due to yesterday's "coping".

Monday September 26th
Took J. & S. to School to see Dr Nelson. Dr N. examined S. & said she was "a joy of a child". She went to school quite happily, without tears, though she asked for me at intervals all morning. I fetched her at 12.15 & she positively gurgled with joy at seeing me.

Don't seem to have done much work since I came back. Distracted by division of Ch. 4 for Miss Lennox. It must be cut & I don't know how. W. lunched with David Higham, who sensed the beginning of a reaction against long novels but didn't seem to think it mattered how long an autobiog. was. He told her his play at the Gate Theatre had been a failure owing to wrong casting. No special object apparently for the lunch.

Tuesday September 27th
Shirley stayed all day at school; seemed to stand it although she was a little fractious just before bedtime. Went to Baird Lewis in afternoon to have various garments altered or renovated. Mother there; we bought a new blue outdoor coat for Shirley; very nice but all rather a rush. Came back to find the copy of the *Herald-Tribune* for me wh. I ordered for Phyllis. Marvellous front-page feature review in the Book Supplement; double volume running on to next page, with a drawing of her in the middle done from the Ivimey photograph & making her look very interesting. Also found a big advt of *Inheritance* in *Harper's* which I cut out for her; sent the

H.T. & this off by the last post. Very worried by "T. of Y."—Chapter IV as usual; also where to keep anonymity & where to use names.

Wednesday September 28th

Finished revising Ch. 4 in morning; decided to put Victor & Geoffrey in book without their surnames. Walked with W. round Embankment in afternoon. Mother came in after tea & helped me play with children. W. had tea with Miss Body, the former headmistress of Queen Margaret's.

Thursday September 29th

Long letter from Phyllis saying *Inheritance* had printed 26,000 within 3 days of publication. W. Kean Seymour greeted me at the Bank this morning with: "Have you seen the American reviews of *Inheritance*—absolutely all out; washing in on the top of everything." Apparently Beatrice takes the American papers. Also got copy of *N.Y. Times* review; even better than *Tribune*. Walked with W. round Embankment again; had tea at Peter Jones as wanted to avoid G.'s guests the Hitchcocks from U.S.A. Nurse came back at tea-time. No work to-day at all.

Friday September 30th

Another *very* excited note from Phyllis to say that Peters had telephoned from London that his American agent had received an offer of $15,000 for the film rights of *Inheritance*. (£4,000 at present rate of exchange.) I wired at once asking if she'd like to come up for the week-end & discuss the offer with Peters, but she replied that details of the proposition weren't through yet from America and anyhow she has lectures over the week-end so can't come yet. Her earnings like her sales will soon be mounting into thousands. It's all very exciting & spectacular. I feel rather as if I were a spectator watching from the Dress Circle a play in which I wanted to play lead myself! However, it's better to watch someone you like very much playing lead rather than not to see the play at all, I suppose.

Gordon went off in afternoon to Labour Conf. at Leicester; had tea with W. & me first at Harvey Nichols. I felt so tired all day & also Phyllis's news excited me so much that I just *had* to do something other than work; so I bought a velvet afternoon suit at Harvey Nichols, 2 hats at Woollands & a powder-blue hat, jumper & shirt at Harrods to match the Baird Lewis tweed coat. Hardly any work all day.

Saturday October 1st

Worked most of the day but didn't seem to get through much; walk with W. round Battersea Park in afternoon in pouring rain. Another card from Phyllis explaining further that she couldn't come up because 8 books had suddenly arrived for review from the *New Statesman*; copy wanted Sunday. Obviously they have seen the *N.Y.T.* & *Tribune* & want her name while it is being discussed.

Sunday October 2nd

Ordinary day. Bad headache in morning so went for a walk round Battersea Park in windy sunshine. Work none too good. Children to Oakwood Court in afternoon; Shirley wore her new bright blue wool set that Mother knitted for her & looked adorable; she was very pleased with it too & kept looking at herself in the glass in all kinds of poses.

Winifred had lunch with Lady Rhondda & came back with numerous stories of E. M. Delafield, husband, children & relatives at Agay; Lady R. says Paul Dashwood is very selfish, & all the Dashwood relatives keep telling Delafield she's not a good housekeeper & pity Paul because *she* pays for everything (although he's been offered several good engineering jobs abroad & just won't take them because he prefers living like a gentleman in Devonshire!). None of the Dashwood relatives seem either to know or care that Delafield is a distinguished writer with a growing reputation.

I seem to be lucky over Gordon; most women writers seem either to have husbands who put upon them, like Delafield, or whom they have divorced, like Lady R., or else to be like Phyllis tormented with a sense of frustration because they haven't had sex experience at all. Companionate marriage is a partial solution but it doesn't meet the desire for children which physiologically-normal women like Phyllis do feel. Probably the only solution—and a slow one—is the education of men to the point where they really do give and take, really can be companions to women & feel as strong a sense of obligation to be unselfish and responsible as most women feel. I don't notice in John any *more* tendency to demand things for himself than I notice in Shirley, while he has a very strong feeling of responsibility for her as younger & more helpless. I don't *believe* irresponsibility is natural to men; it's simply bred [into] them by tradition, public schools and foolish female relatives.

Monday October 3rd

Worked all day at old *T. & T.* vols. Cut Babies' Club Committee. G. still away at Leicester Lab. Conf. After dinner tried without success to listen to Phyllis's broadcast talk from Leeds on Arnold Bennett's Industrial Novels. Late letter from her saying U.S.A. reviews are marvellous.

Tuesday October 4th

W. lunched with Editor of *Radio Times* & went on to *T. & T.* office. Radio man says you can't get the Northern Station from London except by a special "cutting-out" machine. Miss Lennox came in evening bringing back MS. of first two chapters & took away two more. Spent a lot of time having a persecution mania about the book & feeling that everyone will revile me for it.

G. came back late from the Leicester Conference with many amusing stories about the factions into which the Labour Party has split—the Cole party (Zip & the Socialist League) including Mitchison, E. F. Wise,

Brailsford, Horrabin & G. himself, Laski on the edge of it but deliberately left out of the main consultations & still sitting in the pocket of Arthur Henderson; the I.L.P.-ers now almost entirely Maxtonites; "official" Labour with Susan Lawrence & Morrison in the limelight; and finally the pure careerists—Kenworthy & Col. L'Estrange Malone. G. seemed to have a stirring time including a row with E. F. Wise bec. Wise as Chairman of the Socialist League wouldn't let him make a speech he wanted to make.

Copies of Winifred's book on *Virginia Woolf* came from Wishart's today—very nicely got up, blue-grey cover & jacket, good print, charming photograph of Virginia Woolf herself.

Wednesday October 5th
G., W. & I had lunch with H. G. Wells at Boulestin's. The *raison d'être* was that Wells wanted to know all about the new Socialist League (which is somewhat on the lines of his "Open Conspiracy") and when G. invited him to lunch indicated that he'd like to meet W. and myself as well. At first, when he appeared as we were all waiting for him in the cocktail-bar part of Boulestin's, I felt subdued & overwhelmed; because as long as I can remember Wells has been one of the two or three major stars on my literary horizon, and, far from having had an ambition to meet him, I have always regarded him as a person with whom acquaintance was quite outside my range. G. of course knew him from his *Realist* days, when both were on the Board of Directors. After a time I began to thaw—partly because of the effect of *crêpe de volailles* and some dry Moselle, but chiefly because of Wells himself, for he isn't terrifying at all but genial, forthcoming, magnetic and what Winifred calls "cosy". Though very "mellow" he doesn't somehow strike one as an elderly man at all; his manner is young & very vital & his eyes vividly blue. I can understand easily Rebecca "falling" for him but can't understand her being content with Henry afterwards; however, the Wells episode *was* exhausted and anyhow Wells' vitality may be tiring after a time—rather like living in a perpetual hurricane.

I didn't talk much nor did W., as most of the conversation was between G. & H.G.W. about the Socialist League, but a few remarks of Wells' are vigorous, memorable and too, too unrepeatable—i.e., that C. E. M. Joad is "squalidly over-sexed; he's got to be phallic or bust"; that the Bertrand Russells after so much sex-teaching are themselves on the verge of a divorce as B. wants to marry a "red-haired scalliwag" who wishes to be a Countess, & Dora feels she ought to marry the man who is father to her two younger children! H.G.W. had a great story of motoring over from Grasse to see the Mosleys at Antibes at the time of the crisis last autumn which led to the Gen. Election and the formation of the National Govt, & asking them what they were going to do about it. They seemed unable to think of anything except whether Mosley, who was going to England next day, ought to sit on the front Opposition Bench & what should be the colours of the Mosley party. So Wells, taking their mentality at the level it appeared incapable of surpassing, solemnly discussed with them the importance of "making a corner" in flame-colour before some other party appropriated it. He said that the day of the crisis, after Mosley had gone, Cynthia drove herself over to the Casino, danced deplorably in public, & then got drunk & smashed up her car driving it home. Wells gave this as an instance of the Mosleys' inability to exercise self-discipline even in a time of crisis, but it sounded to me much more as if Lady Cynthia had been driven to desperation & simply stopped caring what happened or what she did.

We sat talking over lunch till 3.30 & then Wells went off with a Russian woman, Baroness Budberg, whom he was taking out to tea & who happened to be in Boulestin's too; he was at great pains to explain that this coincidence was purely accidental. Walked part of the way home again via Adelphi, Charing Cross, Embankment & Victoria Street. Wore my Baird Lewis blue dress & hat with short fur coat & really didn't look so bad despite these ghastly weeks. But still got bad persecution mania about my book.

Thursday October 6th
Work on *T. & T.* volumes in morning. Letter from Phyllis who had been rehearsing her wireless debate in Manchester; she doesn't know about coming up on Oct. 18th yet.

At 4.0 went along to Reid-Lefevre Galleries at King St, St James's, to see the private view of Wyndham Lewis's "Thirty Personalities". Some—e.g. Rebecca—very good; others less so—e.g. Lady Rhondda & Chesterton. Round-faced people can't easily be reduced to cubes. I went with Gordon, Winifred & Edith Smeterlin; met there R. A. Scott-James & Roy Randall; saw Edith Evans, Kapp & several people who looked vaguely familiar. Wyndham Lewis wandering about in a hat as usual; was minus a front tooth which made him look definitely odd. We had tea at Fortnum & Mason's; a father and daughter (with a mother who was being "bright" with the waitresses & pretending to notice nothing) were quarrelling violently at the next table; the father—a King George-looking man —finally got up & went out leaving the daughter (aged about 20 & very fat) a large hump of huddled sulkiness.

Came in to put John to bed. Found in to-day's *M.G.* a long letter signed by the Archbishop of York, Headmaster of Eton, etc., protesting against Naomi's *Outline for Boys & Girls and their Parents*. 18 signatories altogether, & not one woman. I wrote to the *M.G.* to point this out, drawing the deduction that, as it was quite incredible that no woman should have been asked to sign a letter defending the institution of the family, whose preservation has been made her chief task, women now that they have power are evidently not prepared to defend its continuation at the usual sacrifice to themselves.

Friday October 7th
Work in morning; walk round Battersea Park with W. after lunch. Ernest
Rhys came to tea; gave John & Shirley his beautiful new nursery-rhyme
book with a long nonsense rhyme by himself as inscription; he also played
with them after tea, even to doing "bears" on the floor. He & W. discussed
"T. of Y."; he, like others, was interested & said the modern tendency was
all towards desiring greater frankness in autobiography. John behaved
beautifully to him—looked charming, like a little French boy, in a new
jumper-jersey mother bought for him.

Gordon had tea with Rebecca at Dorchester House; I had a brief
conversation with her on the telephone beforehand rearranging the time.
She says Anthony is now at Harvard; June Head told G. that he has
ploughed twice in Responsions; feels too grand for it, I suppose!—unlike us
humbler creatures who had to use it as a means towards getting the life we
wanted. That's the worst of belonging from birth to a circle which gives you
everything you could wish for. Rebecca told G. that on Thursday Wyndham Lewis had a cocktail party, after we had left, for the "personalities"
painted; she & Henry were there & saw Naomi Mitchison, who looked as
usual as if just about to produce twins. Henry said to Rebecca: "Good
heavens! She hasn't much further to go!" to which R. replied, "Oh, it's not
that at all; she *always* looks like it." To this Henry responded: "I see—she's
just the opposite of Vera Brittain; Naomi looks as if she is when she isn't,
whereas Vera always looks as if she isn't when she is!" Rebecca also
remarked that Naomi said to her, apropos of the Teachers' and Clerics'
letter in the *M.G.* and elsewhere, that "she wasn't going take the Bishops
lying down"!

Saturday October 8th
Phyllis sent me a large number of her American press-cuttings—all
excellent, of immense length & widely scattered over whole continent;
specially good notices in *Baltimore Sun*, *Saturday Review* & *Chicago Tribune*.
My letter criticising the Bishops appeared in to-day's *M. Guardian*.

Sunday October 9th
Took children round Battersea Park in morning, to Oakwood Court in
afternoon. Tried to explain point & purpose of my book to Mother &
Father but difficult to put anything over, especially to Father who was
absorbed by question of whether he should give Dr Gray a wedding-
present! Mother interested, & also interested to hear about the upset over
Naomi's book as she had just been to hear the Bishop of Birmingham at
Westminster Abbey; he had preached on the family & religion with
obvious reference to the attack on Naomi, & also was obviously on the
liberal side. Read proofs of Helena Wright's book for adolescents, *What is
Sex?* which she sent me to inspect; chapter on psychological aspects

particularly good. Own work practically nil. Very depressed because getting on so slowly.

Monday October 10th
Copy of the *Freethinker* sent me by unknown gentleman from Prestwick who deplores the fact that I "took cognisance" of the "silly letter" in the *M.G.*! (The fact that such things influence 70% of the population is, I suppose, ignored by this ardent agnostic.) Tiresome afternoon's shopping. S. after being quite all right all day does seem to be starting a cold to-night; has slight temperature tho' she seems quite cheerful. Unsatisfactory day's work; too many interruptions.

Tuesday October 11th
Thunderstorm in afternoon, during which I made my way to Harvey Nichols for a fitting. After dinner listened in with great difficulty on Winifred's wireless-set to Phyllis at the Northern Station debating with Professor Pear of Manchester University on "Is Northern Industrialism compatible with beauty?" She was taking the view that it was. From the disturbing midst of German music & scraps of French dialogue her voice sounded much more like Tallulah Bankhead's than her own, except that it was much warmer & less affected—vital, charming & gay. Only her laugh was occasionally familiar; it gave me a great desire to see her again. But W. & I shook with helpless laughter when she suddenly remarked: "The Northern woman has worked for her living for over a hundred years," & W. sent her a ribald postcard & I a letter teasing her about the working-powers of Yorkshire female centenarians. I hope she won't take this the wrong way, as really the whole debate was excellently done—natural, unaffected & just like a real conversation. But I shouldn't have known it was Phyllis talking if Professor P. hadn't frequently addressed her as "Miss Bentley".

When the ¾ hour conversation was over, I went across the road to Henrietta Leslie's party, & there—after a few words with David Higham, who was v. anxious for me to finish my book & kept on lamenting that it was three years since I'd published anything—I spent the evening talking with Mr Chance, the new Editor of the *Review of Reviews*, who wants me to do book reviews for him. I said I would after Christmas. He is partner to the new firm Lovat Dickson (Macmillan's London agent, the man who took Phyllis to see Charles Morgan & Hilda Vaughan in the summer, & who is going to publish Winifred's *rechauffé* of her "Astonishing Island" *Radio Times* articles in the spring). We talked about Italy, the new firm, Rose Macaulay's habit of writing her novels on very small loose-leaf notebooks which she can carry about, and the American sales of this year's "big three"—*The Fountain, Inheritance* and *Magnolia Street.*

Wednesday October 12th
Revising chaps 5 & 6 for Miss Lennox. Shirley's cold still in evidence. Fetched J. from school & took him for walk to Power Station; he disliked the noise and therefore said he hadn't wanted to go. P.c. from Naomi Mitchison this afternoon saying she'd liked my letter in the *M.G.* and was glad I had dealt with that particular point. Lovely bright warm day.

Thursday October 13th
Letter from Phyllis to say she is coming up to town from Monday till Wed., also from Storm Jameson inviting me to dinner in her small new flat in Abercorn Place. Children in afternoon; not much work.

Friday October 14th
Bought a dressing-gown & some underclothes, wh. took most of afternoon. Miss Lennox called at 6 to pick up 2 more chapters; confessed she wanted to go on quickly because so interested in the story. Letter from David Higham saying the Knopfs had also been inquiring about my book though they seemed to imagine it was about the feminist movement.

Saturday October 15th
Saw William Kean Seymour at the Bank; apparently he was responsible for Knopfs' inquiring about my book as he told Blanche Knopf about it at a dinner party tho' obviously in rather a garbled form. Long argument on & off most of the day with W. & G. (re her first chapter in *Virginia Woolf*) about whether it was best to be born the member of a cultural aristocracy (like Virginia and Naomi) or to be like W. & myself, forced to make one's way out of a wrong environment into a right one & become a little vulgar in the process. Personally I cannot think it anything but an incomparable advantage to have been absorbing platonic philosophy & acquiring a respect for scientific truth at an age at which I was wasting my time & ruining my taste by reading Longfellow & Mrs Henry Wood while W. endeavoured to find scope for the activity of her mind in lavatory copies of the *Ladies' Realm*.

Sunday October 16th
Shirley better. Children & W. with me to Oakwood Court. Hilda Reid came in after supper to read her new play on Byron to W. Gordon gave the afternoon sermon to a congregation of young men at Whitefield's Tabernacle.

Monday October 17th
Met Phyllis at King's Cross at 1.55. She was wearing a black dress & short black fur coat with a red hat & looked so smart I didn't know her at first. The change since this summer was quite remarkable; although her face has gone thinner she looked younger & *so* much happier & more confident. She

seemed so pleased to see me she could hardly speak & I felt rather the same. As we drove home in a taxi she told me I was the most charming letter-writer she had ever known & I explained how I really enjoyed writing letters—never found them a bore but much more of a temptation.

When we got in Winifred was talking to Naomi on the telephone about the Bishops, negroes etc., & subsequently I had 10 mins conversation with N. on similar themes. Shirley had meanwhile made her way up to my bedroom & sat on the floor there—where P. is sleeping—playing with a tea-set P. had given her. P. & W. & I had been going to have tea together but, just before, Wilfred Meynell's grand-daughter rang up to say the old man was in town for the day & so much wanted to see W., as he had appreciated her devastating review of Gertrude Atherton's book which was so rude to Alice Meynell. So W. went along to Palace Court & P. & I had tea alone—except for a brief interval when Gordon came in. We talked & talked about writing & *Inheritance* & "T. of Y." with slight interruptions from the children, both of whom seemed as devoted to P. as ever. John walked straight up to her & kissed her—most unusual for him, especially as she had not then given him the plasticine set she had brought him.

We all four dined at the Bolivar Restaurant next to the Langham Hotel so that Phyllis could walk across to the B.B.C. and broadcast & then come and finish. Amusing little place—old Victorian decorations kept and painted vivid colours. We got back in time to hear J. B. Priestley give his postponed talk "To a Highbrow" on the wireless; P. was angry with it because it derided highbrows. We all went to bed early—the maids below were having a riotous party for Amy's 21st birthday and I talked to Phyllis for about half an hour, sitting on her bed, before she went to sleep.

Tuesday October 18th
Did some work in morning while Phyllis went off to see Peters & Gollancz; Peters had heard nothing new about the Cinema contract. In afternoon we went to St Martin's Theatre to see *Strange Orchestra*; very amusing & moving play of a Chelsea boarding-house with Jean Forbes-Robertson as a girl who is deceived by her lover & goes blind. Moral: that nothing, however devastating, can deprive you of yourself. We got back just in time for our early dinner, to which Mother came in a new rust-coloured velvet; then she & P. & I went on to Mrs Piercy's house for a debate on "Motherhood should be a full-time job", with Rose Macaulay in the chair, Naomi Royde-Smith proposing & Mrs How-Martyn opposing. Rose Macaulay as fragmentary as usual & *very* amusing; Naomi R.S. was feeble & somewhat reactionary & Mrs H.M. violently communistic; Mrs Piercy & Natalie Davies, who spoke third & fourth, weren't at all good. One or two feeble speakers started when the debate was thrown open, & as nobody had spoken to the point I got up & talked about the improvement in national conditions for mothers & children, as such, since women, & espec. mothers, went into public life, & spoke of Mrs Pankhurst's discovery of the

fact that, as a Poor Law Guardian in Manchester, she was unable to improve matters for the mothers & babies in the Workhouse through being politically powerless though a mother herself, as responsible for her part in the Suffrage movement. I also spoke a little of the belief of modern psychologists that it was best for a child when the mother as well as the father completely fulfilled her own nature & intellectual development. Rose Macaulay, who had made me, tho' no one else, give my name, summarising the debate said that Naomi R.S. apparently wanted all women to be mothers, wh. would lead to overcrowding, & Mrs H.M. no one to be mothers, wh. wd mean extermination. R.M. said she wasn't quite clear whether men could have careers or were they only things that women went in for?

We dashed home so that Phyllis could go on to her 11 p.m. supper-party at Mary Leonard's for which she mainly came up; there she met Victor & Mrs Gollancz, Dr Cronin, & Naomi Royde-Smith once more; N.R.S. was greatly & justly annoyed bec. *The Times* had just reviewed "New Books by Vicki Baum, Margaret Kennedy & Rose Macaulay" in *that* order! N.R.S. spoke about the debate & was very generous about me considering how fiercely I had demolished her; said that I was brilliant, my speech was brilliant, I was the only person who spoke to the point, etc., & how much she would like to meet me. Phyllis also was talked to by a man representing Doubleday Doran, who told her how marvellously *Inheritance* was doing in the U.S.A.; how she'd *easily* sell the 26,000 they had printed & double that; how wonderful it was to have been on the front page of *both* the *N.Y. Times* & *Herald-Tribune*, a thing wh. had happened to one of their authors 3 weeks earlier & before that not at all for two years. She was brought home by some people whose identity I didn't grasp; was rather annoyed as Dr Cronin subsequently offered to take her.

Wednesday October 19th
Phyllis had breakfast in bed & played with Shirley. After she had got up & packed we went for a walk in Battersea Park (W. couldn't come as she was re-writing 2 notes for *T. & T.*). Battersea Park was *lovely*—trees gold & orange, & the sun making yellow lattice-work of the chestnuts. Bushes of Michaelmas daisies in the Old English Garden. I *must* put Battersea Park into a book—or write a story about it called "The Revolution Has Come".

Phyllis talked very intimately—about how my treatment of & attitude to her had completely altered life for her, because she had never been much wanted by anyone before, particularly by those whom others thought attractive. She said she had thought about it a lot after leaving here last summer—& had realised how in the old friendship with Barbara she had always wanted B. more than B. had wanted her & had been so often rebuffed that she came to think it was people's normal attitude to her. Apparently now that she is famous and desired for herself by me & others, B. wants her more than she wants B. She said she supposed it was possible for someone to be both a bane & a blessing at the same time, but I, thinking of W. who has never been anything but a blessing, said that I thought there was something fundamentally wrong with a relationship in which the person was a bane in the sense of being hurtful to one's deepest psychology, though surface rows didn't matter.

Strangely enough, just as we were hurrying back for an early lunch we met Naomi Royde-Smith at the gate of the park; P. introduced me formally, & we at once plunged into last night's debate argument. N.R.S. was *very* generous again & said how good my speech had been; she obviously was open to conversion & hadn't quite made up her own mind on the subject, as she was sympathetic to my remark that it wasn't only what mothers could get out of professions that mattered but what mothers could *give* to professions—[e.g.], the way in which a few married women doctors had changed the whole attitude of medicine & gynaecology & infant welfare. N.R.S. asked us to go in the park with her & continue the conversation but we explained that Phyllis was lecturing in Bradford this evening & just on the point of catching a train—so she asked me to go & see her sometime & said she wished P. had brought me along to her party last summer.

Then we had to take a taxi to get back to Glebe Place in time for lunch, after which P. & I dashed off in a taxi to King's Cross & had coffee there after she had taken her seat for Bradford. We talked a little of Winifred & both agreed mournfully that she didn't look or seem at all well. We went back to the train just before it went & said goodbye in the hope of meeting again six weeks hence; she looked less tired than yesterday & said the two days had cheered her immensely. I didn't quite watch the train go out, but got the Tube & walked from Hyde Park Corner to Sloane Square; the day was gloriously bright & all the shops looked very gay. I decided that King's Cross and Paddington were the only 2 terminuses I really liked— Paddington because it is associated with Gordon & with pleasant journeys to Oxford; King's Cross because it has meant so many pleasant meetings with Winifred & with Phyllis. Too many of the others—Victoria, Charing Cross, St Pancras—are associated with goodbyes during the War.

Thursday October 20th
Got through a good deal of work looking through letters to W. Children in afternoon; they were very good & seemed less of an interruption than usual; W. helped a good deal.

Friday October 21st
Winifred lunched at Quaglino's with Mr Collins (young), Rose Macaulay and Gerald Gould; said R.M. looked happier than she had ever seen her over the splendid reviews of *They Were Defeated*. R.M. said she had looked for me at the Piercys' after my speech the other night. She talked to W. about her *Virginia Woolf* & said she didn't see the necessity for the

biographical part (heaven preserve me if she ever gets "T. of Y." to review!). Gerald Gould was interesting about reviews—said most reviewers of novels were so overworked that the short, easy-to-read novel got an unfair chance of notice.

Dr Norman Leys called this afternoon to see Winifred & we talked a little before she appeared. G. lunched with Tawney. Lady R. is in bed with a painful shoulder which may be an abscess on the bone. Went through more of my letters to W. including the one about Lord Waring & the early ones about G.'s first letters. Charming little note from Phyllis saying how much she had enjoyed staying here—"You don't know what a terrific difference you have made to my life—I try to tell you but find it difficult to express the depth of my feeling." Had one or two inspirations about the Halifax lecture & got a good part of the first draft of it prepared.

Saturday October 22nd
Worked very hard all day at a final going-through of letters for Ch. XI so as to be able to take it away to Sidmouth on Monday. Felt very bad about my book as for this chapter I had to read the various letters and reviews I had for *The Dark Tide*, & *Not Without Honour*—all about immaturity, naivety, crudity, insufficient selectiveness etc., and they just made me feel that my work hadn't improved *one scrap* in ten years. W. had tea with Ethelreda Lewis—who is depressed about her daughter. W. & G. both very nice to-day.

Sunday October 23rd
Miserable soaking wet day. Thanks to W. & G. taking children between them in morning, got a good deal of planning of Ch. XI done. W. had tea with Lady R. who was ill in bed with two nurses waiting to see what would happen about her arm.

G. & I went to supper with H. G. Wells at Chilton Court. (Huge flat, about 10 rooms.) Party was 12 altogether—Brailsford, Ivor Montagu & wife, E. F. Wise, Lancelot Hogben & wife (very devitalised), David Low & wife, H.G.W.'s daughter-in-law, H.G.W., G. & me. Supper (at large dining-room table with chicken & ham, trifles etc.) was interrupted for the discussion of the new Socialist League & its projects, but never in my life did I hear so much "hot air" talked or see such an exhibition of egotism, incoherence, dogmatism & turgidity of ideas, coupled with an immovable conviction on the part of everyone who spoke that he had nothing to learn from anyone, let alone any one of the others. H.G.W., with his anxiety to discover forward-looking people & somehow organise them into an "Open Conspiracy", was the only person with a coherent plan & obviously none of the younger men really wanted to listen to him. I went there hoping to learn something but came away with nothing but a hopelessly depressed feeling that if all the "intellectuals" of the Labour Party were like this, each grinding their own little theoretical axe, each wanting to impress the other with his own ideas and no one formulating any practical plan or even evolving a set of lucid thoughts, it wasn't surprising that Labour in office did so little & that the National Govt got in so easily.

After supper we congregated in another room for whisky & soda, and the discussion turned on Naomi's *Outline*. Everyone, including H.G.W. (who obviously objected to his own patent notion of an Outline being used by anyone else), was very spiteful about it; H.G. said it wasn't an Outline at all but merely a collection of miscellaneous articles, and that Gollancz, being a clever shark who knew how to sell his books, had got hold of Naomi & diverted her very real talent for romantic novel-writing on to this kind of thing. (But I happen to know, through Naomi who told me so herself, & through Professor Cullis who told W. so, that it was Naomi who suggested the idea to Gollancz; N. is quite as keen on doing her own sex & family propaganda as she is on novel writing.) In course of general conversation I heard Gordon ask Low how he liked the "Ding" cartoons in *T. & T.* on Russia, & Low said he thought them awful & nothing but conservative propaganda (just bec. one picture happened to show an emaciated child). This made me more depressed than ever as I felt that, far from women being the spiteful sex, it seems to be men who are incapable of generosity towards the achievements of anyone working in their own field. The Hogbens took G. & me home in their car & although it was nearly 2 a.m. we argued for an hour (W. woke up & came & joined us in my room) about the futility of Socialist intellectuals.

Monday October 24th
Found Amy in tears this morning; reason being that now, owing to new tariffs, cheap meat, eggs & vegetables are unobtainable & her family have to live chiefly on bread & margarine. *Voici* one of the first results of Ottawa? I talked to Amy for some time about tariffs & how the only way to have the cheaper commodities accessible once more was to turn the Conservatives out at the next election.

W. & I went down to Sidmouth for a week; as we drove over Westminster Bridge & passed the County Hall (where the riot over the Means Test took place last week) we saw dozens of policemen assembling, for fear of another riot, for the weekly meeting of the L.C.C., when complaints from the local public assistance committees of course come up. On the train we met Mrs St John Ervine who has been in town for the week-end & was returning to Seaton; she gave us tea on the train and invited us to go over & see them on Sunday. At tea we talked about Shaw's play *Too True to Be Good*, the Wells supper-party, her new clothes and Lady Rhondda's illness. After Salisbury we ran towards a glorious fiery sunset, fleecy clouds with orange feathers of light in between, and the trees on either side of the line were like golden fleece, and burning bushes massed together with evergreens made a jade pattern in between. I can't remember when I was last in the English country in October.

Winifred told me that Lady R.'s article in *T. & T.* last week on Naomi & the Bishops has entirely patched up the quarrel between her & Gollancz. Several libraries—such as Hampstead, various exhibitions of children's books, & probably the B.B.C. (W. wired to Naomi to confirm this) are now banning the *Outline*; W. has to write a short leader about it, so got on to Gollancz on the 'phone yesterday. He sent her all the stuff about it—letters etc.—by special messenger quite early this morning; she said he was the first publisher she'd ever known to be in his office at 10.0 in the morning.

Sidmouth air soft & warm as usual; hotel not as comfortable as the Faulkner but food is good & my writing arrangements very tolerable —card table & gas fire.

Tuesday October 25th   Sidmouth
Lovely morning with sunrise reflected right over to the west; could see Mutter's Moor from my bed turning golden in the dawn light. Got up early & walked half-way there before breakfast; later W. & I walked across it; the lights & colours were most beautiful but I was a little afraid of it being too much for her. Worked rest of day, filling in references. Wire came from Naomi confirming B.B.C. ban on her *Outline*.

Wednesday October 26th
Not such a nice day—very showery—but we walked half way up Salcombe Hill, then down across the road to Lyme Regis & back by the path beside the Sid. Chestnuts vivid and orange-gold. W. got 3 telephones—one from Gollancz saying *he* had sent the information about the B.B.C. at Naomi's request & hoped *T. & T.* wd use it; one from Miss West asking W. to do Lady R.'s "Notes on the Way" next month as she is still too ill; and a third from Lady R. asking W. to book a room in this hotel for Miss Lewis who has been ill. We both reacted violently against this as Miss L. is a chatterbox who would disturb our work with gossip about the office & anyhow there wasn't a suitable room here, so W. found one outside & wired Lady R. to say so. Later Lady R. telephoned about it—hadn't realised we were down here to work, & as W. remained firm said she would try Delafield for Miss Lewis. Letter from G. to say children quite well. Got Ch. XI ready to write.

Thursday October 27th
Lovely bright morning though very wet later; walked along shore by sea. Letter from Phyllis about her mock trial at Leeds & the joy of her mounting bank account; 31,000 copies of *Inheritance* now printed in U.S.A., & Macmillan's have sent her $1,000 as a first instalment. Apropos of American royalties, W. told me a story about Charles Morgan which she had heard from V.S.J.; at one of the recent plays he was standing, looking very impressive in usual black flowing clothes in the foyer of the theatre and saying to an admiring group which appeared to be waiting for an

authoritative pronouncement on the play: "There's no security." V.S.J. approached nearer, expecting to be given a new theory of aesthetics, and heard him go on: "No security. Here's all this money pouring in from America and I'm damned if I know how to invest it!"

Got a letter—*2 sheets!*—from H. G. Wells apologising for having apparently several times addressed me as "Stella Benson" the other evening. Why two sheets, and anyhow what did it matter if he did; as I told him in my reply, if I had heard him doing it—which I didn't—I should have been only too flattered. I told him also how actually being at his party had made me quite speechless, and that when, in my Sixth Form at school, *A Modern Utopia* had opened for me a new world of experience, I should never have thought it possible that one day I should actually be his guest in his own house.

E. M. Delafield came over in her car & had tea with us in the lounge of the Riviera Hotel. She said she thought Lady R.'s autobiography very good, & asked me whether she would understand mine & whether it was personal at all! She talked about how gloomy it had been taking her family to Agay in the summer, & also seemed depressed because she uses her Bloomsbury flat so little that she'll have to give it up. It "didn't make for happy married life", she remarked ruefully, if she went up to town very much; apparently her selfish, incompetent and completely unattractive husband objects if she leaves him much, and she, being thoroughly immersed in the tradition of the submissive woman, gives way to him. It does seem a shame that the peace and happiness of so gifted a writer should be spoiled—as it is for Storm Jameson—by the possession of a child, or children, and a tiresome, dependent husband; it makes one feel that writing women oughtn't to marry, and yet when, like Phyllis, they don't, the results in tenseness and repression seem almost as tragic.

Poured with rain all evening; I started writing Ch. XI in my rather dark bedroom but felt that everything I did was rather below standard.

Friday October 28th

Very cold day but ecstatically bright; went quite long walk with W. round lower edge of Mutter's Moor & back through Sidford Village; went into small & very well-planned new church of St Francis of Assisi just erected there. Worked quite hard all afternoon & actually got about 10 pages of Ch. XI done. Letter from G. said Dr Waller thought Shirley looked pale after her cold; wrote urging Parrish's Food & codliver oil.

Saturday October 29th

Letter from Brittain's Ltd saying that my lost certificate for Preference shares can be reissued if I will sign letter of indemnity, which I have done.

Short walk round back of town; then went over in bus to Seaton to have lunch with the St John Ervines. Very nice lunch charmingly served; during the meal St John Ervine talked very amusingly about Orage & *The New Age* before the War & how though it never paid any of its contributors it was the one really courageous weekly, and all the Fabians & other left-wing people—Shaw, Wells, Bennett, St John himself, Katherine Mansfield —used to write for it. The War killed it by putting up the cost of paper; Orage went to America, divorced his wife, married a new American one & is now back in London running the *New English Weekly* with her money. But after lunch over coffee both St John & Leonora violently attacked *Time and Tide* & the way it is run—how it once wouldn't print something to the disadvantage of the *Daily Telegraph* in an article St John wrote about a hairdresser who was hounded to death by reporters over his mistress's suicide, because Lord Camrose is a friend of Lady R.; & again how Lady R. doesn't edit it properly because she goes off to the S. of France or Norway or Madeira, doesn't even come back when there's a political crisis, leaves the paper "marking time" just when it should be giving a lead to its readers, "follows the sun" & is away for about 4 months each year taking "schoolgirl holidays", ought to have flown back when the Govt crisis arose last Aug. year & instead ambled back after about 10 days. I told St John I thought that someone who hadn't had to work their way up from the bottom but came in on top without any tradition of work probably didn't really know what work was, & just because Lady R. is working harder than she did in her youth she thinks she is working as hard as anyone.

They brought us back to Sidmouth in the car; a wild gale & rainstorm had sprung up since the afternoon & red waves were breaking over the Esplanade. W. had quite a headache after St John's vehemence, so after tea we went for a walk in the storm & she told me that Lady R. had been told she'd wreck her health if she didn't work less & really *had* tried to find another Editor, had offered the job to W. herself at a good salary but W. doesn't want it as, health apart, she really doesn't like office organising & prefers writing books. And no one else suitable seems to turn up; either people are too Labour, like Ellen Wilkinson, or too highbrow like Theodora Bosanquet, or not feminist, or else want to write books rather than edit. I said I thought it wd be very difficult to get anyone to edit for Lady R. as she would never allow them any initiative & therefore wd never get anyone like Violet Scott-James—or myself—as we should quarrel with her in a week—and the only alternative was a cipher like Miss West, who became lazy through getting apathetic because never given initiative. The only other possibility is for Lady R. to work harder & be there more even if it *does* spoil her health, & be the real editor instead of the rich leisured woman who runs a paper as a hobby. I said the case of the Raverat woman—who has made a bad break over Elizabeth Bowen's new book almost as absurd as the one she made over Phyllis—was a proof of Lady R.'s obstinacy, as so many writers have impressed it on Lady R. that Gwendolen Raverat being a woodcut artist can no more do reviews than a novelist could criticise pictures, and yet Lady R. helps her on.

Sunday October 30th
Walked & worked; wrote about ten pages.

Monday October 31st   London
Returned from Sidmouth. Drafted article "While We Remember" for *M. Guardian* in town. Gordon met us at Waterloo. All seemed well; children stood on steps & shouted when we appeared. At tea-time manager of Embassy Theatre rang up & asked if I could do some publicity for *Miracle at Verdun* in its new run at the Comedy Theatre. Said I would do my best to introduce it into one or two articles. Tiresome evening—numerous cheques, etc., to write, but finished *M. G.* article before going to bed.

Tuesday November 1st
One of those interrupted days when one gets through next to nothing. Typed & sent off article for *M. G.* Had hair washed at Peter Jones.

Dined with Storm Jameson, husband & son at their new flat in St John's Wood, 139 New Abercorn Flats, in Abercorn Place quite near where W. & I used to live. All very new & varnished; three small rooms, central heating, everything done and found. I noticed at once how much S.J. had changed—grown to look tired, extinguished, almost middle-aged because of hair & complexion looking dull from overwork—obviously is leading a fierce & heroic life trying to keep everybody going. I thought her husband charming—shortish, grey hair, sense of humour, accepts his work at the London School [of Economics] & the fact that his tutor is 7 years younger than he with philosophical amusement. The boy Bill on the other hand was *very* tall—6 ft 2—seventeen, shy, rather nice-looking. We had dinner in the restaurant and afterwards S.J. sent Guy Chapman & the boy each into their separate rooms to do "homework" & we walked & talked; Guy Chapman dropped in again for a few minutes before the end & saw me off to my bus at 11.0. He has written a war book called *Passionate Prodigality* which is being published in January. S.J. and I talked about:

1) Her own semi-autobiog. war book—called, I think, *No Time Like the Present*. She doesn't much want to publish with Heinemann as she's quite fed up with them—they only care, she says, either for their very best sellers like Priestley, or people who have rich country houses and butlers like Lorna Rea. She said at the big "anti-depression" party they gave last March everyone was drunk except Beverley Nichols & herself; even Beatrice Kean Seymour was. Priestley half-seas over came to her & said "I've a bone to pick with you," and proceeded "to pick bones all over her" in a loud voice about her review (signed) of *Faraway* in the *New English Weekly*. I suggested Collins as a publisher.

2) Priestley and his family affairs. She obviously hates him—thinks he has let down the Yorks. character & is purely vulgar. Didn't know before that Mrs Priestley was formerly married to Wyndham Lewis & two of the

daughters are his. What a novel Priestley's story would make! Phyllis ought to write it since she knows his character from the inside.

3) Ethel Mannin, whom S.J. also hates—as E.M. stopped her publishing a novel about a successful & vulgar woman writer on the ground that this was an attack on herself. "Three months' work gone west," said S.J., and she'd never even thought of Ethel Mannin.

4) Phyllis Bentley. S.J. likes her enormously & thought *Inheritance* extraordinarily good; she wrote to tell Gollancz so, & thought the Book Society by not choosing it had done more harm to themselves than to Phyllis.

5) "Testament of Youth". I told S.J. fairly fully all about it; she was impressed espec. by the survival of the letters. She said I must not expect too much from its publication bec. a) war books were still ignored rather & it was pure chance whether they caught on; b) publishers were now so nervous owing to economic conditions that they caved in at once if someone took out an injunction against publication; hence a good many of these are taken out now (e.g. the Hammett book, Carswell book, Compton Mackenzie's *Gallipoli Memories*) & one or two firms of shady solicitors exist actually to persuade people into taking actions for things written in books. She said my best chance to get some notice & prestige for it was for a group of people who think the book worth-while to notice it instantly upon publication. She promised to do this herself.

Wednesday November 2nd
Reviews of Phyllis's book in the American *Nation* (critical, but very fair, valid criticism) and *New Republic* (bad & absurd; actually said that she obviously sympathised with the Oldroyds). Went to tea with Clare & took relevant parts of "T. of Y." to have facts about the Leightons vetted. Wouldn't let her see it as I want her to be able to disclaim all responsibility. She didn't think her parents either could or would do anything about it & undertook to give no assistance against it herself. She entirely saw & approved of the point & purpose of the book tho' she said she knew she'd find much of it harrowing. I said that my object partly *was* to harrow people, & make them realise exactly how events seemed at the time they happened. She was quite thin & didn't look very well; the toxic bug discovered by Obermer is still manifesting itself. She gave us one of her Christmas books of woodcuts for all of us & the children. W. came on to tea from Lady R.'s & looked at woodcuts while we did the book. She says Lady R. would like me to write a reply to a letter by Wyndham Lewis about Gollancz in this week's *T. & T.* Lady R. still has a nurse & her arm in a sling. Clare told me that Obermer said she "paralysed" him.

At 9.45 went over to Henrietta Leslie for party she was giving for Henri Barbusse, author of *Le Feu*. Barbusse wasn't a bit as I expected—tall, cadaverous, very pale, deep circles under dark penetrating eyes; rather like a 20-year junior of J. A. Hobson. He was very accessible; I had a word or two with him & he talked in French to a large circle of us about Communism in France. Met and talked to Amabel Williams-Ellis, Storm Jameson with husband & son, David Higham, Roger Chance, Dorothy Evans, Mrs George Strauss etc. Amabel W.E. anxious to get panel of authors ready to write letters to papers over the false news given about the London riots over the Means Test. Gordon, just back from Oxford, dropped in to the party a few minutes after me; met, talked to & liked Storm Jameson.

Thursday November 3rd
Revision for Miss Lennox. W. went to Yorkshire for four days as her mother thinks she's going to be made a County Alderman. Letter from Storm Jameson saying she'll come to tea on Nov. 11th. Nurse out, bathed both children; very good. John remarked at tea: "Bruce (Davies) treaded on Miss Bunner, and he did it again as we don't like her. I told him to do it." Great games of "cushions" and "pretending to be giants" in W.'s room.

Friday November 4th–Wednesday November 9th
Chiefly preoccupied with worries about "T. of Y."—have discovered letters written to me are the property of dead people's executors. This means I shall probably never get permission to publish Roland's letters or even his poems as the Leightons disapprove too much of all my present views and activities. All very worrying. Also Clare wants me to leave the Leighton name out of the book which I have promised to do. Probably it will be best to rewrite it all making everyone much more anonymous. Nov. 8th went to dinner with Randall at 22 Brunswick Square followed by quite dull but agreeable evening party at the David Highams. Long letter from Phyllis on Tuesday sympathising about the "T. of Y." difficulty. W. very helpful & sympathetic; is going to see the Society of Authors for me.

Thursday November 10th
W. found out from the S. of A. that all letters *are* the property of the writer—wh. means I can use my own & E.'s wh. Mother gave me, but not those of R., V. or G. Consulted Clare, who said I shouldn't get permission to quote the letters but just *might* for the poems if I write nicely & flatteringly to her parents. Spent most of Thursday composing the letter but don't really expect to get the permission. Anyhow shall have to rewrite large sections; the whole thing has made me feel like hell.
   Harry Pearson came to dinner—*very* good-looking after 7 years.

Friday November 11th
Armistice Day—my usual Armistice article in the *M. Guardian*. As usual went & stood on the Albert Bridge looking towards Westminster for the Two-Minutes Silence. My letter about Gollancz in *T. & T.* Storm

Jameson came to tea—saw the children; much taken with John who played "trains" & seemed to her very intelligent. W. talked business with her about Collins & she appeared much inclined to consider going to them.

At night made an Armistice Day speech at an *awful* meeting at St Paul's Hall, Paddington. Thought as it was in the Harrow Rd and my ex-V.A.D. acquaintance P. F. Storey was arranging it, it would be tolerable, so I made the same speech which went down so well at Chiswick Empire on Armistice Sunday last year. But the audience (mostly drab middle-aged Conservative women) disliked me, & the platform (nearly all smug clerics, with the Bishop of Kensington in the Chair) simply hated me! When the Bishop came into the small room where we were waiting he shook hands with the three men but completely ignored me, as though the "woman speaker" was of no account! Lord Rhayader made the chief speech (dry unillumined stuff about Manchuria & Disarmament). The final point came when Brendan Bracken, the M.P. for N. Paddington, in supposedly speaking to a vote of thanks, deliberately misrepresented what I had said (which was that we could elect M.P.s with a will to peace to Westminster, or turn them out; but *he* said that I had said the League of Nations could be governed from the House of Commons!). I had quite a scrap with him about it afterwards & we argued furiously on the platform. He said the H. of Commons was quite helpless—couldn't get peace questions discussed as the Government did everything overnight—so I asked who elected the Govt if not the people, & who gave our representatives, & Disarmt Confs etc., their mandates if not the H. of C. He was really quite angry—flaming red hair standing on end.

Saturday November 12th
Went with W. to see the Somerset Maugham play *For Services Rendered*. Felt angry with it because it seemed to take for granted that women in provincial towns whose men were killed in the War could do nothing but wait vainly & forlornly in the hope of marriage. No mention of jobs or going to a larger town to work though there were three of them. After it W. & I walked home from Shaftesbury Avenue to Sloane St & had an interesting conversation about sex-starved women in general & Phyllis in particular.

Sunday November 13th–Friday November 18th
Ordinary Sunday. On Monday quite unexpectedly cordial letter came from Mrs Leighton giving me permission to quote R.'s poems. She seemed glad I had remembered it all rather than envious about the poems. Later in week wrote to a) Aunt F. asking if she would like the name Bervon used or suppressed, b) Barbara Bervon asking if I might use one or two of Uncle Bill's letters. Aunt F. replied that she would prefer the name suppressed; Barbara telephoned & seemed agreeable but is coming to see the letters on Tuesday. Didn't get through as much work as I should have, owing to general feeling of agitation. On Thursday Miss Lennox brought back Chs.

VIII to X for re-examination. Friday, got the children to write cards for Phyllis's birthday & to send Mother small presents for hers—John a calendar, Shirley a small pink handkerchief. Had hair permanently waved on Friday.

Saturday November 19th
Mother's birthday and Phyllis's birthday. Went to Hay Wrightson's in morning in response to their invitation to have myself & the children photographed. Rather dull ponderous business; didn't much care for the man although his portraits are so fashionable. Worked hard all afternoon getting towards end of Ch. XI.

In evening went to dinner at Oakwood Court; took Mother's present—a rose quartz carved necklace that I got for her in Sidmouth, and Gordon gave her a peacock-blue pottery vase. Went on from Kensington to the Café de Paris; had small supper & danced a little. Enjoyed it much & should have done so more if I hadn't had on the wrong dress, the taffeta one which John calls the "tart" dress and which I put on because G. originally said we would go to the Café Royal. Got back about 1 a.m.

We sent Phyllis a large box of tawny chrysanthemums as a family & I sent her a green agate necklace, also from the Sidmouth shop. At lunchtime came a telegram from her thanking us all, which made me feel that she must have been surprised both by our knowing her birthday and taking any notice of it.

Sunday November 20th
Finished Chapter XI just at lunch-time; now only one more and the alterations. At 3.30 went to Victoria with Winifred, Gordon, members of the India League & distinguished individuals such as Bertrand Russell, to meet Monica & Ellen Wilkinson back from India. Talked to Mrs Whately and Miss Foot while we waited. The train came in only 10 minutes late; Monica & Ellen seemed about the only persons of importance on it. Several cameramen were there who took flash-light photographs of them. Winifred and I got just a second with Monica & gave her a few scarlet carnations we had bought. She looked rather pale, I thought, as if she wanted a good rest, but I never saw Ellen look better. She said they had sat up most of the previous night at a Paris café. Went on to Oakwood Court for a late tea while W. went to the Mannabergs. Helen Davies came to supper; measured me for a terra-cotta hat & put veils on two of my black ones.

Monday November 21st
Long letter from Phyllis (& others to the rest of us) apparently extremely pleased & touched by her birthday presents; said I had changed her life even more than her success [had]. Nurse had day off; looked after children; started to prepare Halifax lecture while they were at school this morning.

Tuesday November 22nd
Barbara Bervon came to tea; gave her Uncle Bill's letters to take away & read. I never know quite how to take her, but she said I could quote what I liked, so one more of "T. of Y." 's innumerable fences is surmounted. We talked a good deal about the way she has reorganised her life & found work of a kind since she was obliged to return home.

Dined with Storm Jameson & her husband at Abercorn Place; met Harrison Brown, who lives in and writes about Germany. G. turned up from House of Commons just before I did. He held forth about Labour Politics most of the evening; fortunately S.J. & the rest all seemed much interested & anxious to hear more. No talk other than political. We left very late.

Wednesday November 23rd
Winifred showed me Obermer's reports on her progress since he took her over; apparently her sclerosis of the kidneys can never be better as certain cells are destroyed, but she herself, though having to live partially as an invalid, need never be much worse if she follows his treatment & the routine he has suggested. She can write as much as she likes but not activise a great deal.

G. went to Oxford for the day & returned to say that Papa C. really does seem to be failing mentally & probably won't be able to come here for Christmas. Did rewriting of letters, etc., in Tawny Island Chapter. Tea at Oakwood Court.

Thursday November 24th
Mother rang up to call my attention to notice in *The Times* to say that Mrs Richardson—Maurice's step-mother—is dead. Later a letter came to Mother from Maurice to say she had died of pneumonia and was buried this afternoon. Strangely enough I was re-writing only last night in "Tawny Island" my brief conversation with her after Victor's death. Finished final revision of Chs. VII, VIII, IX.

Put children to bed; as usual told John tales about my nursing & he suddenly became quite upset by the thought that there might be another War. I told him as best I could about the League of Nations & good people working for peace & really think he took in a little.

Friday November 25th
Went to Millicent Fawcett Hall in evening to hear Amabel Williams-Ellis & Ellis Roberts debate on "That Modern Fiction is out of touch with everyday life". Storm Jameson in chair. Was asked to dinner first, & sat next to old Sir Squire Sprigge, the Editor of the *Lancet*, who told me all about the origin of the *Lancet* Commission on Nursing, & that St Thomas's Hospital represented all that was most immovable & archaic in professional conservatism. Donald Carswell opposite; said his wife's book was

coming out again in a fortnight. At the debate sat next to Catherine Carswell, whom I found I like; thought I shouldn't after her book on Lawrence. Debate very amusing; speakers good & S.J. very charming in chair. Thought of contributing to debate but felt too fatigued actually to do so. Someone in the hall mentioned *Inheritance* as evidence of the fact that modern fiction *is* in touch with modern life. After the debate talked with S.J. and Amabel W.E., and walked as far as Victoria Street with the Carswells.

Saturday November 26th
Getting up Halifax lecture. Rather a struggle. Tired.

Monday November 28th
Had hair done, face massage, manicure. Packed in evening; felt extraordinarily tired & rather ill; packing a nightmare; as in some dreams, I couldn't get it done. G. seemed to think me neurotic & fussy. Don't feel like giving a lecture.

Tuesday November 29th   Halifax
Finished packing. Couldn't eat lunch. Went up to Halifax by 2.0 train. Felt wretchedly ill in train; tried to eat tea without any enjoyment. Took two aspirins which pulled me together enough to finish the more "current" part of my lecture out of the day's *Manchester Guardian*. Journey 5 hours; seemed very long, espec. after it got dark. Phyllis met me at station; we drove up in car. House very typical—Victorian furniture, dark wallpapers, rather like our High Leigh, Buxton, house; opens out of gloomy ill-lit bye-road, probably pleasant in summer, but puddly & dank in winter. Mrs Bentley welcomed me warmly but is rather alarming; doesn't look anything like her 70-odd years, is stalwart, indomitable, potentially ruthless, keenly intelligent in a limited way; hair less grey than Phyllis's. Found I was expected to unpack *and* change before dinner, which had been postponed till 8.0; found this rather exhausting after so much fatigue & so little food. After dinner talked before fire.

Wednesday November 30th
Given my breakfast in bed, thank God. Felt very limp but managed to conclude getting up lecture with the morning's *Manchester Guardian*. Got up & dressed about 11.0 ready for luncheon at 12.30; wore black velvet suit. Just before we started a letter arrived from Mrs Leighton sent on by Winifred which made my heart jump into my mouth & nearly threw me completely out of gear for the lecture, as I thought it might be to withdraw the permission about Roland's poems; but it was merely amiable & discursive.

Went to luncheon hall in car; large room with gallery, crowded with women; members of the Covent Garden Opera Company visiting Halifax there as guests; all the women seemed immensely impressed with them. Most of the women much overdressed; several Americans among them. My chairman, Miss Scott, headmistress of local High School, & a Londoner, & plainly dressed, was in pleasant contrast to the others. Mrs Bentley sat next to me; I wouldn't have Phyllis, who had been put there. Couldn't eat any lunch, but Chairman made a pleasing speech which put me well in touch with the audience, & I got up on the little platform & talked for forty minutes on "Why Current Events Matter To Us". Started off with two comparative quotations, one from George Eliot's *Daniel Deronda*, & the other from an article by Phyllis in defence of the long novel. My quotation from Phyllis was clapped. The audience listened quite motionless all the way through, & gave me a tremendous ovation at end—went on clapping long after I sat down. I felt in command of the situation all the time & know it was one of the best lectures I have ever given (because it was done in front of Phyllis, of course). She said afterwards it was the best speech they had ever had and seemed tremendously pleased. Several people came up & congratulated me afterwards but I felt quite peculiarly done in & was glad to go back to an early tea.

It had been pouring all day but had now cleared, so Phyllis took me out for a walk along what she calls "the Rocks"—a road above a deep rocky valley filled with mill chimneys, tall, slender & tragically smokeless; indeed, the whole atmosphere seemed much cleaner & clearer than I had expected because so few mills are working. It was just before sunset; as we walked a thick mist rose from the valley enveloping the mills and chimneys & nothing more was visible but a long brilliant snake of lights moving away towards Lancashire. Phyllis told me that 31,000 of *Inheritance* have been sold in America & 43,000 printed, & Peters has just fixed her a new contract for her next novel with Macmillan's in which she gets £1,500 down when she signs the contract, which is any day now that she chooses. Walk was rather too long; a cold wind was blowing & my clothes seemed inadequate. Was taken after dinner by P. & her mother to see the Halifax Thespians performing *The World of Light* in a local hall; it was well done but I felt too tired & slightly sick to enjoy the short Shaw piece that followed it.

Thursday December 1st
Phyllis and I walked to Haworth; she had meant to do about ten miles over the moor but I told her definitely I couldn't manage it so the car took us half-way & we walked about five miles. It was a lovely clear day & the country outside Halifax was just like the country round Buxton—stone walls, bronze sun-flecked moors & running streams. But I couldn't really enjoy it because I felt dead tired & sick & had a pain, & even a fascinating conversation about sex and our own temperaments couldn't make me forget these things.

Lunched at the Black Bull at Haworth; fireless cold room, tried to eat eggs & bread & butter & tea without much success. Afterwards looked over the church & parsonage with all the Brontë relics; largest photograph that of the American gentleman who had given the money to the Brontë Society to found the museum; Charlotte's photograph relegated to side wall. Saw picture of Mrs Gaskell; Phyllis told me of the libel actions she had had over her *Life* of Charlotte & said that the book remained but who cared about the libel action now—a moral for me to apply to "T. of Y." Neither parsonage nor church as gloomy as I expected because of the bright day. We took the bus to Keighley instead of walking as Phyllis had intended. There she gave me tea in a restaurant between two buses; I sat beside the fire & felt warm for the first time that day. Nice tea & toast but couldn't eat much. We talked about the queer way that we'd "fallen in love" with each other.

In the bus on the way back to Halifax tiny sickle of new moon shone over the moor and I wished we had been walking there together beneath it if only the wind had been less cold & I less tired. Went to bed early & was sick. Too tired.

Friday December 2nd
Woke up still feeling sick; made myself get up but couldn't eat breakfast. Long conversation with Mrs Bentley about Phyllis; she actually seemed quite moved about how "good" we'd been to P. and said if she could ever do anything for me I must let her know.

Went in car with Phyllis to Huddersfield to hear her speak on "Yorkshire as a Novelist's County" to the Huddersfield Women's Luncheon Club there. Not nearly so good a room as the Halifax one; stuffy, noisy, crowded, odious with smell of food; couldn't touch lunch & don't know how I sat through it all without being sick. Phyllis, though not feeling very well herself, spoke excellently; very differently from her rather uninspired after-dinner speeches that I heard in the summer. The lecture was interesting & well constructed & she spoke in a charming deep voice & read Yorkshire dialect from the Brontës most attractively. She had an unexpectedly gracious and easy manner too. A very enthusiastic member of the Club next to me kept murmuring: "She's a *brilliant* woman! It's as good as a brain-wash."

Afterwards had to be sick in the gentlemen's cloak-room; then went with Phyllis to have tea with Miss Sykes, the local solicitor whom Winifred knows, & was sick again; finally had to stop car on way home (we went a long way round, over some high moors by a wireless station) for the same purpose. By this time concluded I must be going to have a baby again; told Phyllis so when we got in & she seemed almost as upset as I felt. Lay down for a bit; then dressed & went with her to the opera as she seemed bitterly disappointed at going alone, but it was sheer purgatory & I had to go out after the 1st act of *The Valkyrie*. She got me a taxi but stayed herself, so I went back alone in the taxi & had some difficulty in finding the house. Mrs

Bentley very kind; got me some hot milk & I went to bed but was pretty sick in the night.

Saturday December 3rd
Sick most of the day & didn't go out. Couldn't go to opera party in evening that P. had arranged. Both she & her mother thought it was a baby; I privately felt too ill to think it that alone, but didn't want to worry them.

Sunday December 4th
In morning made myself get up & go for short walk with P. but couldn't eat; was beginning to feel faint & light-headed; lay down again in evening while P. very nobly packed for me. Felt a fool & a nuisance & *furious* with myself for being so dependent on her. Too ill even to go down & see her brother so decided to go home next day.

Monday December 5th   London
After breakfast left with many apologies for being such a disappointment; felt miserably conscious all the time that P. was secretly exasperated with me for acting so much out of character & spoiling everything. But she kissed me very fondly when she put me on the quick Pullman train & seemed only sorry. Journey home a Purgatory; smells of food, meals laid round me & males—including the Bishop of Halifax—smoking heavy cigars in my non-smoking car just finished me off; was sick all second half of journey, couldn't even take Bovril, felt indescribable.

Gordon, to whom P. had telegraphed, met me at King's Cross; awful half-hour taxi ride home, trying not to be sick & held up at every turn. Was very sick when we got in; finally collapsed completely on bed shivering & sobbing, but so thankful to be home & able to stay in bed I didn't know what to do. Suspect whole thing started with all the awful legal bother over "T. of Y." & may be a sort of alternative to a nervous breakdown.

As Dr Gray is [getting] married we decided to call in Dr Joan Malleson (wife of Miles Malleson) who has been attending Lady Rhondda; she came—clever, calm, deep voice, fair fringe—& diagnosed acute gastritis plus colo-cystitis & prescribed various forms of treatment, not operative thank Heaven; I'd been so afraid I'd never finish "T. of Y." Sick again in night two or three times & very faint & thirsty because neither food nor water would stay down, but happy to be back & so sweetly looked after by G. & W.

Tuesday December 6th–Tuesday December 13th
Bed. Very queer at first; floating on a cloud, quite light-headed at times, the queerest dreams, nurse coming in to give me blanket baths & water-injections because I was so thirsty. Gradually stopped feeling sick & began to be able to take slops. Dr Malleson surprised that I neither drank nor

smoked much; said I didn't deserve to have gastritis. By week-end on solid food again & felt more normal. During week pulled myself together enough to write & have flowers sent to Mrs Bentley; wrote twice to Phyllis but apparently most deliriously & injudiciously. But did write her for S. K. Ratcliffe a testimonial about her lecturing for W. B. Perkins, the American lecture agent who inquired about her abilities.

Tuesday December 13th
Got up, wrote letters, slightly corrected an article for the *Quiver*. Very charming letter from Storm Jameson, who had been coming to tea but couldn't because her son had 'flu; sent me on proofs to read of a new little story she has written; also memorandum about Hunger Marches & inadequate news from Amabel Williams-Ellis. But chiefly a very stiff little note from Phyllis begging me not to write till I'm quite well again & saying my last two letters were too wild for her to understand. Apparently they *were* very rude & reckless as W. had a letter from her in great distress about them. Wrote & apologised & said I thought I must have got them mixed with some of my queer dreams last week.

Coming back from *T. & T.* Winifred met Henrietta Leslie who said she "had a hunch" (whatever that may mean) that the Book Society wants to choose it ["Testament of Youth"] but, quite apart from the fact that no one would suggest choosing a book that hadn't even found a publisher yet, let alone been read, no Club with Hugh Walpole & Clemence Dane on it would ever choose anything of mine. If only I could finish the damn thing I wouldn't worry about Book Societies or anything else.

Wednesday December 14th–Saturday December 17th
Feeling ill, tired & utterly miserable. Starting life & work again with wobbly feet & aching back. Phyllis insists on quarrelling with me for my silly letters—on Friday I got the coldest & cruellest of little notes from her saying she now regarded me quite differently & didn't feel she could resume our friendship again on the same terms. Of *course* I was in the wrong—but must this end everything? I can't think *how* she can let two foolish letters count more than all the things I tried to do for her in the spring & summer, all the other letters I've written her, & the conversations we've had about things so dear & sacred to us both. I wrote a long letter trying to explain this, and saying that I, at any rate, couldn't turn it all off like a tap. But I don't suppose it will be any good; she seems determined to be proud & haughty & offended & bitter. I can't alter suddenly towards people like that. I don't understand the unrelenting hardness of the Yorkshire temperament when angry. But I am too miserable to write about it any more.

Have tried to do my Christmas shopping & wrap up cards & parcels feeling ill & wretched & vainly remorseful. Half an hour's conversation would put all this misery & misunderstanding right at once. If only her house were hers & not her mother's I'd take the first train to Halifax and *make* her see me. But as it is, there seems to be nothing I can do but hope she'll relent in time. Yesterday as I walked along the King's Road I felt a familiar sense of heavy finality weighing me down and recognised it for the feeling I used to have in the War when somebody dear was dead—only this time not a person was dead, but a relationship that promised such lovely things. Having such a lonely past & such an inferiority complex, she is convinced that I meant every word I said—and of course it was really one of my idiotic flare-ups intensified by illness—half temper, half delirium. What a miserable *fool* I am!

Sunday December 18th
Oakwood Court—rather wretched; Father ill with breathless attacks, self feeling like nothing on earth. Took children short walk in Battersea Park in morning but felt very wobbly.

Monday December 19th
Winifred got a letter from Phyllis by first post apparently capitulating and saying she didn't resent my letters any more, but still rather cold & emotionally upset. No letter came for me—but felt better & went to a party at the Mitchisons' in the evening. Very pleasant—cheered me a good deal—usual crowd of young Socialists & Labour candidates—saw J.B.S. & Charlotte Haldane—talked to Louis Golding, Amabel Williams-Ellis & Naomi, & was picked up & danced with by a young don from University College, Leicester—very drunk on rum-punch but quite amusing, name Famacht, said he was at Oxford with me but I don't remember him. Introduced me to the eagle-faced D. A. Ross, whom I had often heard Gordon speak of but had never met before. Louis made bee-line for me & said at once: "Hallo! I hear you've been staying with Phyllis. How is she—and how's *Inheritance* going in America?" When I told him it had reached 43,000 in three months his face was a study; his jaw positively dropped & he exclaimed: "What! Do you mean to say she's got to that *without* the Book Club!" But obviously he feels very friendly towards her & seemed to think that she (and I've no doubt he added "himself") deserved both the James Tait Black Memorial & Hawthornden prizes much more than Kate O'Brien—about which I agree: *Without My Cloak* was a good & charming book but not great.

Got back to find a letter from Phyllis—cool & beginning "My dear Vera" but it said that she no longer felt any resentment & realised I had been more ill than she thought. But she seems emotionally quite exhausted and it's obviously going to take much tact and gentle treatment to get back to where we were.

Tuesday December 20th
Phyllis has started heaping coals of fire already—sent me a most charming blue "Flappach" powder case, & two most expensive-looking &
intelligently-chosen toys for the children—a toy piano for John & large
cuddly animal on wheels for Shirley. I retaliated with a black suede bag
with a white-edged flap & her initial in marquisite in a corner.

Went to farewell dinner to Dr Waller at Lady Jones's (Enid Bagnold's)
house; gorgeous & opulent dinner, followed by speeches. Dr Waller's very
interesting; he cut out sentiment & talked of the history of St Katherine's
College, Poplar, where he's going, and also spoke of maternal mortality &
how much of it probably would automatically disappear in twenty years'
time owing to the care now being taken at infant welfare centres over the
pelvises of girl babies. But after dinner Dr Gibbens said that in the present
state of our knowledge two of its chief causes—placenta praevia & the
formation of blood clots—cannot be foreseen. He also spoke of the heavy
damage rate due to lack of care in childbirth, & said that at one large East
End jam-making factory that he knows, it's quite usual for women (who
are paid at piece-work rates) to go off in the morning, produce a baby, &
return to their work in the afternoon. It was a shock to me to know that
such things still happen in a so-called civilised country. Dr Gibbens
interests me & I think I shall try to move to his clinic. Mrs Pickering
brought me home in her car—everyone, including Matron, very sympathetic over my jaded appearance.

Wednesday December 21st
John's fifth birthday—and the same day of the week. Had breakfast in
bed—they came up & I gave J. a motor-bus, with lights that turn on.
Shirley couldn't understand why J. should be receiving presents when she
wasn't; kept on taking possession of the bus and disconsolately reiterating:
"*My* bus!" whenever J. & I protested. Lovely morning, went for short walk
in Battersea Park, had Monica for lunch. She was as gay as ever, talked of
India, the end of Ellen Wilkinson's liaison with Frank Horrabin & her own
numerous homosexual relations, describing with gusto the mutual quar-
rels of her feminine lovers. She & Phyllis—sexual extremes—ought to be
violently shaken up together. M. admired Phyllis's photograph immensely
& was impressed beyond words by her sales.

Rest of day passed in Christmas letters & parcels—*no* work. John had
the three Davies children & Betty Lou to tea—pandemonium reigned,
crackers, Christmas tree, Christmas & birthday presents got mixed up
together & the ground floor looked like Bethnal Green Road on a Saturday
night. Shirley turned her back on the party & played in a corner with one
jig-saw puzzle all afternoon. Mrs Davies says that she has got through all
the Montessori apparatus in the school (i.e. up to six years old) & ought by
right to be moved up to an older group but is still too tiny—the youngest
but one. Feministically I am glad that in orthodox ways she seems likely to

be cleverer than John, but I have an instinctive fellow feeling for John & do hope the poor child hasn't inherited *only* my failings! Nice letter from Storm Jameson to-night.

Thursday December 22nd
A much nicer letter from Phyllis this morning—collapsed & in bed after another dental episode plus emotion. Says she was *bouleversée* by my letters, partly owing to financial demands on her by the family & partly to demands from the *Manchester Evening Chronicle* for more low-brow articles. But *Inheritance* has gone into a 9th edition in England & her two *Harper's* stories have been sold here to *John O'London's* & the *Woman's Journal*. Went to the entertainment at the Institut Français—standard of singing & dancing high & quite fair proportion of big boys.

Inundated by parcels (chiefly for the children) & consequent letters; no work possible owing to endeavour to keep my head above the flood.

Winifred lunched (alone) with Rebecca West, who was very benevolent & seemed most kindly disposed towards me—asked after "T. of Y.", said it was a great effort to bring up small children in their early years, that I often looked very tired & she wished I could have a real success. Later she took G. & me with her & Henry to see *Another Language* from a box which had been given her in the Lyric Theatre; good play by American Jewess adapted for English use, showing the isolation of two "high-brows" in a dreadful suburban family. Barbara Low also in the box; very fierce about D. H. Lawrence, whom she knew, when G. made a critical remark. After the theatre we dropped Barbara Low at her house & went back with Rebecca & Henry to their flat. Nothing special occurred in the way of conversation but R. remarked how much better Winifred was looking & how *chic* her clothes were. W. went up to Cottingham by afternoon train.

Friday & Saturday December 23rd & 24th
Inundated by parcels. No work. Visit to dentist on Christmas Eve; tooth satisfactorily dressed & aching checked. Loathsome tedious exacting Christmas. A p.c. from Phyllis saying she thought her last letter "graceless and egotistical" (it wasn't the former but perhaps a bit of the latter). Also a rather attractive specially-designed West Riding card with mills and a railway bridge.

Sunday December 25th
Usual sort of Christmas Day except for the evening & welcome freedom from Pa Catlin. Amy & Nurse out all day; took children & Maud to Oakwood Court; spent day there till children's bed-time. Not too bad; children very good on the whole. Put them to bed & then went out to dinner with G. to Kensington Palace Grill; very good dinner which I enjoyed though drunk & drowsy with fatigue. G. very sweet & charming to me all evening.

Monday December 26th
Feeling of terrific relief at being on hither side of Christmas. Blessed release from posts & telephones. Spent most of day finishing an experiment in *vers libre* called "Evening in Yorkshire" & written to Phyllis which was worrying me all last week. Fear it isn't a good poem but it does say what I want to say to Phyllis & can't in letters any more (it's on the text of "Out of this nettle, danger, we pluck this flower, safety") but its badness doesn't matter as she'll probably only think it emotional & hysterical anyway. Wish I could write more poems & better ones. Sent W. a copy but all her poems are so much better than mine that I'm sure she'll think nothing of it either.

Vile day, foggy & raw; have laryngitis & have completely lost my voice. Mother came in to see me this afternoon as G. went up to Oxford by early train to spend three days with Pa Catlin. At last have picked up again work for last chapter of "Testament of Youth".

Tuesday December 27th
Nurse woke with swollen face & rash; thought it looked like measles, her panel doctor away, got Dr Higgs to look at her; he said it was only an acute form of nettle-rash, but she was very sorry for herself & I had the children nearly all day. No work, of course.

Wednesday December 28th
Nurse still sorry for herself, finally went down to Bromley as her family wanted her to see her own doctor. She came back late at night to say it was no more than Dr Higgs had said, but of course I had the children all day again; also rows with both maids on account of the amount of off-time they still expected however much I was left in the lurch. Very miserable, laryngitis & tooth ache. No work again & feel vaguely worried all the time.

G. returned from Oxford to find me bathing both children, helped a little but dashed off almost at once to have dinner with Ethel Mannin—long arranged, of course, & it was only adverse chance that he seemed to be rushing off to enjoy himself & leaving me to cope unaided with domestic chaos, but if only it had been Rebecca or Naomi or Phyllis or someone whose mind I respect. Sat down to solitary supper (badly cooked by Maud because Amy as usual was out) & wept, feeling very sorry for myself. Letter came from W. this morning to say she liked the poem I wrote for Phyllis though she criticised one line which she mentioned.

Thursday December 29th
My thirty-ninth birthday & pretty miserable to start with. G.—in spite of having bought me a present—absent-mindedly forgot it until I reminded him; W. left me a present but of course wasn't here to give it me, & no letters came at all. There was one from Phyllis but it just turned out to be a rather snooty little note thanking me coldly for the poem & saying she

understood its main idea but couldn't feel adventurous—though she does seem to want to come here in January. Couldn't help contrasting this (unreasonably, perhaps, as I never told her when my birthday was) with my own efforts to find out the date of hers & make it agreeable. Wrote her a long letter about coming here & describing my birthday sensations—but I'm beginning to think it's all no good; she's too ill & neurotic & put off me to care any more about what happens to me. However, the day cheered up as it went on; I walked over to Oakwood Court for an early tea & Father gave me a box of fruit; came back for a late tea here to find Winifred just back. We all went on to dinner at Romano's in the Strand, & then W. went home & G. took me to see Noel Coward's revue *Words & Music* at the Adelphi—not as good as *This Year of Grace* but very amusing & typical Coward. Got back to find a copy of *T. & T.*—this week's issue—containing my story "Re-encounter", of the dream I had about Edward last September.

Friday December 30th
Worked on Chapter XII of "T. of Y."—old *Time & Tide*s for atmosphere. Went to dentist after lunch—not so bad as I expected—& then met G. in Knightsbridge to choose dining-room table, breakfast set, breakfast dish & coffee cups. Finished *T. & T.*s after supper. Letters from Amabel Williams-Ellis, Storm Jameson & myself in *T. & T.* & *New Statesman*.

Saturday December 31st
Quite a good day for the last of the year.
    Morning dissipated on housekeeping, but in spite of Nurse going off for day & a half after lunch, worked on a good many letters for Ch. XII. A really quite charming letter came from Phyllis this morning—so much warmer than all have been of late; she seemed really sorry not to have known my birthday, and also said: "I'm terribly sorry I was so stupidly obtuse about the poem; but you see I just wept the whole morning over it, and I just felt I couldn't bear any more. Now I am stronger & better, and understand what you meant."
    Also Gollancz's "Early Spring List" arrived to-day in the shape of his usual fat, intelligent and most exciting-looking mustard-coloured catalogue; it stated amongst other things that *Inheritance* & *Trio* go into cheap editions in March, and that Phyllis Bentley has a new novel in preparation provisionally entitled "As One". (News to me and I should think to everyone else.) W. & I tried to think what its rather intriguing vagueness could mean; I suggested "As one who on a lonely road doth walk in fear & dread . . ." Anyhow, the thought of her new book having at least this much of life seemed somehow to irradiate the future. Gollancz *is* intelligent; oh! if *only* he'd take "T. of Y."!
    G. went down to spend the day with Beatrice & Sidney Webb at Liphook; got back at 8.o. W. & I looked after the children & talked much

about Phyllis, & how I'm to get "Testament of Youth" finished and published. I only hope I shall feel myself a more worth-while person at the end of 1933 than I do to-day.

1933

Sunday, July 23rd   Hardelot-Plage
First advt of *Testament of Youth* by Gollancz in the *Observer*; in small
characters above the main advt (of Strachey's *Menace of Fascism*) he had put
"Ready August 28th, *Testament of Youth*". I conclude therefore that the
Observer note last week was the beginning of the campaign.

Came over to Hardelot-Plage. Smooth comfortable journey to Folkestone; Channel like a duck-pond; had tea on board boat & stood at prow
watching us go into Boulogne; had never felt well enough or free enough to
do this before. Car from Boulogne; went through St Étienne. As soon as I
saw Hôtel Aviation, felt convinced that—tho' renamed and repainted—it
was the hotel (mentioned in the France chapter of *T. of Y.*) at which Norah
Ashford & I stopped to have lunch in September 1917 but were ousted by
the Australian officer & his lady & returned to the Pré Catelan. Everything
much transformed now; a promenade has been built & many elegant villas
with brightly-painted windows and shutters. Process of "development"
has also produced many new roads through the pinewoods & along the
front. Hotel primitive but tolerably clean & meals are excellent. Lovely
views of wooded country from windows; agreeable short distance from sea.

Monday, July 24th
In morning Winifred & I walked in pinewoods to try to discover the road
by which I came here from Étaples, but new roads & erection of villas in
woods has confused everything. In hotel salon last night a young Frenchman asked me to dance; couldn't speak English but danced beautifully;
wondered if his father or elder brothers were in the War.

Sunbathed & slept on shore after lunch; after tea returned there & wrote
article "Sixteen Years After" for *M. G.* on my memory of Hardelot. We all
three walked by one of the new roads to the Pré Catelan & had coffee;
lovely garden but only vaguely as I remember it; thought it all much
smarter & more sophisticated. Perhaps with more tables & officers and
nurses about in uniform it actually was. Garden full of dahlias, roses &
gladioli. Scarlet pimpernel, blue and purple borage and white campions in
woods.

Tuesday July 25th
Quiet day. Cooler. Thick sea fog drifting in as far as pinewoods. Spent
morning making list of points to be emphasised in *T. of Y.* for Macmillan's.
In afternoon walked about misty sea-shore; after tea sat on sand dunes &
began specimen article for *Woman's Journal* on "Our Belated Children".
Walk in pinewoods with G. & W. after dinner; coffee at Grand Hotel
—pitch-pine, pretentious, non-national; might equally well have been at

Omaha. Card from Miss Thomson to say the children settled down all right.

V. interesting *Times* leader on Hitlerism suggested that one of the causes of rise of Fascism was the grotesque caricature of the War & disparagement of those who fought in it by War novelists in England & Germany. W. wrote Gollancz mentioning that Rebecca had thought my book a truthful picture & suggesting its quality of non-caricature as a line of publicity.

Wednesday July 26th
Very hot again. Nice letter from Miss Hutchinson of Macmillan's (publicity agent), saying how much she had liked my book & asking me for a statement of my activities this summer for publicity purposes. Sent this; spent much of morning composing it & replying to her letter. Enclosed a carbon of my *M. G.* article ("The Road from the Pinewoods"), which I also sent off to the *M. G.* Early tea, & sunbathed on shore afterwards till dinner time. Lovely evening; sun dipping into water, warm breeze; cannot remember having been on a western coast before. Walked to Pré Catelan after dinner with G. & W. for chocolate. Garden glorious; phlox in fading light showed a vivid magenta pink, like a deep sunset, against orange background of French marigolds. Sound of stream at foot of garden all the time running softly along edge of pinewoods. One little pond full of fish; another covered with exquisite water lilies. Electric light when turned on from outside of hotel showed clusters of trailing and orange nasturtium climbing wall, & a small furry mouse making its way upwards amid shadows towards the roof. Other flowers in garden were flame-coloured dahlias, white stocks, pink ramblers, scarlet gladioli, mauve sand-poppies. Wind scented with the smell of pines.

Thursday July 27th   Shirley's third birthday
Long letter from St J. Ervine, wh. started by confessing that he'd been unfairly put off me because I called myself Vera Brittain instead of Mrs Catlin. Said *T. of Y.* had entirely changed his opinion of me. Thought the first part "old stuff" and the last part too full of politics but most warmly commended the book as a whole; ended by saying that "many finely-written chapters of your story moved me to tears", and that he agreed with Stephen King-Hall that "here is a superb account of what the War did to our generation". Spent most of morning composing reply, chiefly dealing with his two points of criticism. Bathed just before tea; water gorgeously warm. Sunbathed again after tea, & walked to Pré Catelan for coffee after dinner. Hotter still.

Friday July 28th
Cooler. Strong wind. Finished article on "Our Belated Children" for *Woman's Journal*. Bathed before tea; too cold for sun-bathing after, so walked in pinewoods after that but couldn't find path to Étaples where

Norah Ashford and I walked in September, 1917. G. said my book was in
the Kiplingesque tradition—we had been talking about K.'s work; I didn't
agree, but said that what I had tried to do was not (like so many of the
war-book writers) to under-rate and disparage the heroism of those who
took part in the War, but to show that that heroism was wastefully
expended upon a futile cause.

Letter to Gordon from Curtis Brown saying Gollancz had turned down
"Preface to Action"—which he called "this brilliant book"—on the
ground that he didn't agree with it. Said that although he didn't think it
would sell he might have decided to publish on account of its quality but
could not do so since it ran contrary to his own opinions. G. not as
depressed as he might have been; decided to go to S. of France.

Saturday July 29th
Cold windy morning; got up late. W. got letter from Gollancz rejecting
Wickham Steed suggestion as "touching pitch"; was afraid he might
somehow turn my book into an apology for war.

After lunch walked through the pinewoods to the old château of
Hardelot; in 19c. belonged to Sir John Hare, now neglected & abandoned;
pseudo-Gothic tumbling to pieces, but lovely old trees & such contour of
the garden as is still distinguishable showed what it must have been in spite
of briars & weeds that now choke it. Country round a vast sweep of woods
& meadows with Hardelot, a village of red houses & a church spire, in the
distance, and several reed-crowded lakes, like mirrors, in the middle.
Woods contained trees of all kinds—pines, firs, hazels, holm oaks. In the
garden of the château, although the day was chilly & rather damp with
only periodic sun, butterflies sprang in dozens at the touch of a finger from
clumps of shrubs & flowers—red admirals, fritillaries, brown heaths,
white cabbage, powder-blue chalk butterflies. Wayside grass and
meadows very rich in flowers—rushes, ragwort, willow-herb, white campions, sea-purple, vetch both pink & purple, goldenrod, yellow toadflax,
tiny scarlet poppies, and blue and violet-shaded borage, with turquoise-
tipped magenta stamens, and tight pink buds sheathed in green cases.

Violet Scott-James arrived for five days or so just before dinner, very hot
after extreme heat—94°—in Paris.

Sunday July 30th
Day still too cool for bathing and sun-bathing. Changed room in morning.
Discovered by having tea at Golfer's Hotel that it has been built on the site
of the *old* Pré Catelan—which *was* at Hardelot, just beyond where the path
from Étaples turned into main road—so it is not surprising that the present
Pré Catelan was not familiar to me and that I couldn't understand how I
got to Hardelot-Plage from it in 1917. Golfer's Hotel, built in very modern
brick-red architecture, with terrace overlooking the lawn & the lake, &
many smart visitors, had so transformed everything that it was almost

impossible to remember what the garden looked like during the War. When we came back, read on sandhills. Coffee & conversation at Hôtel de Paris after dinner.

Monday July 31st
Full gale still on so decided to go to Le Touquet in afternoon. Spent morning writing a letter on the New Education for the *Week-end Review* in response to request. Bus to Le Touquet went through Neufchâtel (where the little war memorial is surrounded by exploded shells), Stella-Plage, Camiers, and Étaples. Very queer feeling of going back into a strangely distorted past, with so many of its characteristic features but not the chief. At Camiers passed blue Manor House where Faith Moulson & I so often had tea; the blueness of the paint and the mere are the same but it appears to be no longer a tea-place. Road from Camiers to Étaples, with sandhills and pinewoods, seemed unchanged, but the cemetery looks quite different with its immense stone monuments with their sculptured flags at each of the four corners. At marsh end of the cemetery Union Jack flies from a high pole, looking from the bus as though tied to the mast of a ship. The fields where the camps were spread—quite empty now and therefore making the whole camp area look curiously smaller—are much as I have described them in *T. of Y.* as seen from the windows of the Paris train, but I noticed nearer at hand that it is only on the side of the road to Camiers where the Sisters' Quarters were that vegetables & wheat are now growing. Except for very occasional patches of beet or potatoes, the huge part of the fields where the patients' huts were is rough, bumpy earth covered with coarse grass partly concealing, here and there, remnants of concrete foundations. Numerous boards on this side of the road between the cemetery and the railway bridge are marked "Danger. Défense d'admission." I wondered what the danger came from—tetanus, or the possibility of unexploded bombs?

The road from the railway-bridge to the harbour—once empty & very muddy—is now restored to smoothness, and transformed by new roadside villas, but the harbour looked just the same—same air of somnolence, same little ranked masts of fishing smacks. Bus went over same rather ornate bridge over the Canche that was the scene of the struggle in the 1917 mutiny. But road to Le Touquet also transformed with many rather ornate little villas in the woods. After looking at the front (which I don't remember having seen in the War—was it covered with Army huts, I wonder?) and at one or two shops, & changing our credit notes, we went back to the fashionable part & had tea at L'Hermitage where the Prince of Wales stays & Lord Beaverbrook mostly lives. This too I don't remember in the War; probably the whole area was covered by the Duchess of Westminster's Hospital. At any rate, although this is normally the middle of the season, the place was practically empty of its fashionable crowd; it was inhabited only by the French people who had come to see the society world that was not there. The newest & most expensive hotel, the Royal Picardy, failed (we were told by an English car driver in Hardelot) last year. In front of it three cars were parked & in front of the Hermitage four. The Casino was empty. In the lounge of the Hermitage we were the only people having tea. Our footsteps positively echoed along the marble corridors. In the Gentlemen's Cloakroom hung dozens of empty coat-hangers. The waiters explained that people came only at week-ends, or that the Channel was rough (though it had only been rough for three days!). No one ventured to suggest that it was all due to the Slump—and that the Revolution had in fact all but come—not through blood but through bankruptcy.

Tuesday August 1st
Walk on sands in morning. Letter from Mother enclosing press-cutting containing quite brilliant review by Phyllis of Beverley Nichols' *Cry Havoc!* Delightful tea at Pré Catelan; day less windy and growing warmer. Saw several red admirals, one tortoiseshell and two peacock butterflies among the zinnias & dahlias in the garden. V.S.J. told G. he was intellectually arrogant.

Drove after dinner to Golfer's Hotel for coffee; same devastating, echoing emptiness as in the Hermitage at Le Touquet, same pretence that the hotel was full at week-ends. Sycophantic waiters & porters touting for tips. Lovely walk home between scented pinewoods, with lights of fishing fleet out to sea & moon an immense Chinese lantern in the sky.

Wednesday August 2nd
Spent day in Boulogne; went in by car to see Gordon off to Paris for Monte Carlo by 1 o'clock train. Did not wait to see it leave but it started to go out as we were walking past the fish market before crossing the bridge; saw G. standing up looking out of the window in exactly opposite direction across the harbour. Boulogne very gay & noisy, full of markets & trams & cars & crowds. Had coffee & omelettes at Cavernis'. Then took tram to Wimereux to see Grand Hôtel des Anglais et des Bains wh. V.S.J. thought would do for me to bring the children in a year or two. Charming hotel, cheap, clean, lovely courtyard under trees; probably shall come one year. Wimereux urban & lively; pleasant shops; beach small but wonderful view over Channel from cliff running from Boulogne to Ambleteuse. Cliff edge mostly covered with wheat but saw indications of the large hospital (? 14th Stationary) that was there during the War, even to remains of outlines of Army huts.

Tea at hotel; back in Boulogne, W. went to rest in the church beside the market while V.S.J. & I walked up the hill to the Citadel de Boulogne—the old high part of the city where the Cathedral is & the old dignified houses. Here V.S.J. says is a life quite independent of the chattering proletarian life surrounding the harbour. Showed me the square inside the old walls where her father used to stay in a small very ancient pub with excellent food. We went into the Cathedral; lofty, light, beautifully proportioned, & hung with red and white flags ready, we imagined, for the anniversary ceremony on August 4th. Going back down hill walked through a "Fun Fair" beneath very walls of Cathedral; sea serpents, crocodiles, horses going round, cars knocking into each other, coconut shies etc.; all very gay & crowded. Rejoined Winifred at foot of hill; back in bus. Hardelot looking very lovely; country smiling again under warm sun. Sat with W. on shore till dinner. She went to bed early & V.S.J. & I walked over for coffee & conversation at Grand Hotel.

Thursday August 3rd
Letter from John this morning, illustrated by characteristic drawings, relieves my mind with regard to welfare of children. Meant to go to Amiens via Étaples but at last moment changed our minds & went to Boulogne owing to piece of stopping falling out of my tooth. Found an English dentist with a Paris degree who could not see me till the afternoon so we were unable to leave for Amiens till 4.3. Dentist, who refilled my tooth, queer contemptuous person suggesting some past history of crime or drugs. Winifred meanwhile made friends with a Mrs Carton of Sheffield who runs little 2/- tours of Boulogne & allowed us to leave our things there all day. Lunched at Hotel Meurice & sat in courtyard till dentist's app'ment. Then hurried to the Gare de Ville; tea at roadside café, took local train to Amiens, stopping at Étaples, Rang-du-Fliers (for Berck-Plage), Abbeville & various other places. At Abbeville consciously saw the Somme for the first time; dark sinister-looking river which during the War was said to fertilise surrounding country with blood. Read Beverley Nichols on way; decided to write to him from Amiens on 19th anniv. of War.

Reached Amiens at 6.8 & took rooms at Hotel Universe; then taxied to Cook's & made arrangements for drive round battlefields to-morrow. Amiens bright, gay & friendly—a charming, widely-spread town. After dinner at the hotel went alone (as W. was tired & sat in the flower-filled square of Park beside the hotel) to see the Cathedral; as I went in in the gathering twilight, the intense colour of its violet-blue rose window smote upon my eyes & reminded me that I had had precisely the same intense realisation of it in 1921. A service was going on in one of the chapels; I tiptoed towards it & noticed that the windows smashed in the 1918 German offensive were left still smashed and still boarded; apparently this is to be an everlasting memorial to the bitter hatred of those days. Noticed War Memorials put up (& in each case translated into French) to the British, Australian, Canadian, Newfoundland & American troops, who all helped to defend Amiens in 1918. Took down the British, Australian & American notices as interesting contrasts in post-war psychology. The British ran as follows:

A.M.D.G. In sacred memory of six hundred thousand men of the armies of GREAT BRITAIN & IRELAND who fell in France and Belgium during the Great War 1914–1918. In this diocese lie their dead of the Battles of the Somme 1916, the Defence of Amiens 1918, & the March to Victory 1918.

The Australians improved the occasion thus:

To the Glory of God and to the memory of the soldiers of the AUSTRALIAN IMPERIAL FORCE who valiantly participated in the victorious defence of Amiens from March to August 1918, and gave their lives for the cause of Justice, Liberty and Humanity, this tablet is consecrated by the Government of the Commonwealth of Australia.

But the Americans merely put:

In memory of the officers and men of the Sixth Regiment United States Engineers who gave their lives in defence of Amiens March 1918.

It is as though they had said: "We don't know much about the glory of God, & this liberty and justice business is all bunk, but we defended Amiens and here it is." Gave me idea for article entitled "Three Memorials". Had also idea for lectures on "War and its Aftermaths" (1921, 1924, 1933 travels) and "Stages of Post-War Psychology".

Friday August 4th
Nineteenth anniversary of the War. At 9.15, in the early morning sunshine of a perfect day, motored out from Amiens in direction of Louvencourt in private car hired yesterday. Chauffeur English, named Parsons, had been 29 years in France, married to French wife, served in War. Very full of information, much of it valuable. Talked French with a Cockney accent.

Road out towards battlefields rich with flowers—vivid blue flax, scabious, ragwort, meadowsweet, honeysuckle. First village Rainneville, still largely composed of old mud houses. Front line now ascertainable by presence of houses of new type; no mud huts in reconstructed area. Gas, light & water all brought to new villages. Passed through Pierregot and Rubempré. Lovely, mild agricultural country, productive & full of wheat; all over the Somme valley the French peasants were gathering the harvest. Made one understand France's hatred of Germany for ravishing her rich land. Impossible for anyone living in Somme area to forget the War. One vast open-air museum filled with memorials, but also exemplified the superb ability of nature to repair the ravages caused by man.

Came to *Louvencourt* by a different route from last time; remembered the two roads crossing, one uphill, and the thin line of elms beyond the cemetery. Had forgotten that Roland's grave is the first one comes upon when entering from the side path. Don't know why they put his age on the stone as 19 when he was really 20. Below his name & date of death is the motto of the Worcesters: "Firm"; and below that the crest of the Worcesters surrounded by the words "Honi soit qui mal y pense." Next to him Lt Jordan and next to Jordan Capt. Rolleston, who died of appendicitis in the summer of 1915. The cemetery is both English and French; the English are all in the middle and the French run round the inside of the encircling wall. The cemetery has both a memorial cross and a flat cenotaph with "Their name liveth for evermore." The path between the graves is paved and the grass very closely mown, giving an impression—as I said in *T. of Y.*—of suave velvet lawn.

On Roland's grave a pink rambler rose was growing, and a green plant with small yellow buds which I did not recognise. Picked a rambler rose for Mrs Leighton, and also a piece of rosemary from the grave of the French soldier which faces his, Pierre François Le Mer. Put on his grave, against the words "Never Goodbye" just under the edge of the grass, the two withered roses—pink from the Leightons' garden, red from mine—that I brought from London.

All around the cemetery the harvest was being gathered into sheaves, and the air was filled with the smell of mown grass and hay. Just over the wall of the cemetery, saffron and tortoiseshell butterflies flitted over a field of purple vetch. In the cemetery is also a Jewish grave, marked with the Jewish sign, to a soldier named Baum.

We left the cemetery & drove on; I did not see, this time, the château that was the Casualty Clearing Station where he died. We went on to *Hédauville*, which I remember as a bumpy, shattered road full of shell holes & ruined houses, as it was a place for stores & reinforcements and was heavily shelled. Then it was marked with a placard; now the name is painted in black on a wall & a barn. The road is now smooth & smiling; I remember going down the hill and turning the corner with a bump at the bottom; this time we went so smooth & swiftly that I was only just aware of "the long white road that ribboned down the hill".

Passed *Mailly-Maillet*—first Somme village wh. was in front line; all new houses. Was just behind front line all through War. The great part of the Church—built by the Spaniards after the Franco-Spanish War—was left standing in spite of various bombardments; the back was shelled to pieces and the joint between the old decorated front and the rebuilt back is very obvious. Some ruined houses, never rebuilt. Chauffeur told us that after War those whose houses were ruined were promised an equivalent sum of money by the State; did not get it immediately but were given an I.O.U. Went to dealers & moneylenders (who gambled on alteration of exchanges, value of franc, etc.) and changed the I.O.U. for cash down, with which they cleared off to towns & never rebuilt their houses at all—hence ruins still left standing. Children grew up in towns & refused to return to country to work on farms.

Devastated areas

These were not rebuilt by French—who would not go into these areas because of lack of gas & water & general discomfort & sentiment—but by Italian & Spanish labourers who were encouraged to come by the French. Millions of pounds were to be earned here and they could get more than in their own countries. The French (Parsons said) also encouraged the coming of hundreds of domestic servants from Russia, as French would not work as servants in these areas. French employers paid fare of Russians & kept back the amount out of their wages. Semi-official arrangement; agency in Amiens. Many Russians stayed on after year's contract, making much better terms for themselves than the first arrangement. Very hard-working at first. Many Italian & Spanish workers have settled on their own in these areas as builders etc. French welcomed them, as people who had drifted to towns during War through losing their homes refused to go back to country. Many Belgian farmers and Flemish workers also in these areas.

Beaumont-Hamel

Stopped here to visit "Newfoundland Park", the Newfoundland Memorial, crowned by a baying stag, in which the ground has deliberately been preserved as it was during the War—trenches, shelters, dug-outs, etc.; now all in a condition of self-conscious dilapidation. At highest point was a wall with arrows pointing in direction of various important points; one said "Newfoundland, 2600 miles". Ground was that over which Newfoundlanders marched on July 1st, 1916; bought by Newfd & Memorial was opened by Haig in 1925.

Struck by extent by which the Dominions had taken possession of Somme region, as though they had fought all the battles. No large British memorial except that to the Missing at Thiepval Ridge.

Valley of the Ancre

To reach Thiepval Ridge from Beaumont-Hamel we had to cross the Ancre Valley, where 35,000 men were killed, wounded and drowned in three months' fighting of 1916. The valley is verdant now with meadow-sweet and poppies and wheat, and the trees—almost alone in the Somme area—are the same as in 1913; the shells which passed between the ridges nearly all went over their heads. Each October when the beet-harvest is over, they still find 5 bodies a week in this valley, and the British War cemetery at Le Sars is being kept open for another two years to give them refuge.

Thiepval Ridge

On the left of the road as it reaches the top of the ridge is the Ulster Memorial to the 36th Ulster division. It looked rather too much of a pleasure park for souvenir hunters to suit my taste in memorials. The tower, which is a copy of Helen's tower near Belfast (where the Blarney Stone is—I suppose the whole thing representing the quintessence of the country for which they fought), has nothing about it to suggest War or death, but is more like an enormous water tower. The trees which line the path were planted by famous men & generals—one being Sir Henry Wilson. Close by are the Connaught and Mills Rd cemeteries—mostly Irish.

Thiepval is the only village in France not yet built up; there were 240 people there before the War. The new Church is just begun; after the foundations were dug and the building was in progress, eight German bodies were discovered beside it. They are still there but will later be moved into a cemetery.

Great Memorial to "The Missing of the Somme"
Unveiled on Aug. 2nd last year by the Prince of Wales. Thiepval Ridge during the Battle of the Somme was held by the Germans & dominated the whole of the British positions.

Upon the arch, inside and all around it, are inscribed the 73,367 names of those who fell on the Somme and whose bodies were never found or never identified. It made me realise what a comparatively few of the dead must have been found and buried beneath dignified tombstones inscribed with their names, for there appeared to be numbers of these memorials to the missing; I read in the *Daily Herald* that there are over 35,000 names on the one at Arras. I don't think this fact has ever been made public—or at any rate, ever emphasised.

Beside the names of the Thiepval Memorial the inscription runs as follows: "Here are recorded names of officers and men of the British armies who fell on the Somme battlefields July 1915 to February 1918 but to whom the fortune of war denied the known and honoured burial given to their comrades in death." I was interested especially in one name that I noticed under the heading Royal Naval Volunteer Reserve: "Doyle, W. Served as W. Higgins." Was Doyle, alias Higgins, a convict, I wonder, or just a boy who ran away from home?

Around the arch are also inscribed the names of the chief battle places on the Somme—Miraumont, Bapaume, Morval, Thiepval etc. In the middle below the arch is a flat cenotaph with the usual inscription: "Their name liveth for evermore." Below the memorial sloping downwards towards the Ancre is a cemetery where British and French are buried; hence Thiepval Ridge is the only British memorial in France with a French cemetery in front. The British graves are marked by the usual stones, the French by crosses. The cemetery was full of roses, pansies and lavender.

When we left the car I walked up the wide mown space of grass before the memorial, between flower-beds planted with violas and red roses, and stood below the immense arch of this brown & white stone memorial. Everywhere there was a scent of cut grass; and the larks were singing. In front of one lay the Somme country, miles upon misty miles of undulating verdant harvest land, rolling in its gentle curves towards the blue-grey horizon beyond which lay the spires of Amiens. And I thought what a cheating and a camouflage it all is, this combined effort of man and nature to give once more the impression that war is noble and glorious, just because its aftermath can be given an appearance of dignity and beauty after fifteen years. I never had before so clear an impression of the scene of Edward's Battle on July 1st.

The caretakers of these memorials must live a very strange, isolated life, in dug-outs, shelters and log-cabins.

Aveluy Wood

On the way from Thiepval to Albert we passed, in the near distance, Aveluy Wood, which was fought over in 1918 (mentioned in one of Edward's letters at that time). The original trees were all shattered but the undergrowth has now grown up sufficiently to create the distant impression of a wood. But between these new trees were sinister rust-red gaps of earth where trees grew only sparsely or not at all—and these seemed to me perhaps the most significant thing that I saw, for the chauffeur told us that their redness & their barrenness was due to the explosion here of gas shells, which chemically changed the quality of the ground. Comparatively few gas shells were used in the Great War, but where they fell mark the only places where the inexhaustible capacity of Nature to repair its ravages has failed to operate. It reminded me that after the next War there will be no one left to put up memorials to the missing, for we shall all be missing—a putrefying heap of pulped flesh and poisoned blood & disintegrating bones as soon as the raiding aeroplanes have passed over us.

Just before reaching Albert we passed the famous Crucifix Corner of the Somme battlefield. On July 1st it was a big German fortified position in a stone quarry; innumerable lives were lost here and it was one of the most terrible places of that day.

Aveluy is now rebuilt—new red-brick houses, white mortar, bright blue painted railings.

Albert

Just as clock was striking 12 we ran into Albert, which I remember in 1921 as a humped ruin of stones and dust, with a few huts of reconstruction workers dotted here and there. Now a clean, bright, new town, though considerably smaller than the original, which was, our chauffeur said, the Coventry of France, and made bicycles and machinery. Now makes aeroplanes at the factory of Potez—one of the best in Northern France, which employs workers from all parts. A civilian works under State control, where the men are known by numbers, not by names. A new machine works also employs all the working classes of Albert and many from Amiens.

On the site of the old shattered Basilica the new one has been built by the State; it is an exact copy of the old, which was only finished in 1900. In the midday sun it seemed to shine with its bright new paint, and the gold Virgin holding up her Child, as before, to look in the direction of the Albert–Bapaume road, gleamed in the sun. As we went past, the chimes were sounding for midday on the 19th anniversary of the War. Town has been adopted by Birmingham, and Birmingham presented a clock which was striking 12 from the tall tower of the new town hall surrounded by a French flag flying half-mast (the only flag we saw that day to suggest that anyone remembered it was a war anniversary). The chimes, we were told, are an exact replica of those of Big Ben.

As we ran into Albert the chauffeur told us the true story of the Virgin of the Basilica. One legend used to say that when she finally fell the War would end; another that as long as the statue remained on the steeple the French would never lose Albert and that it actually fell as the Germans entered the town (this latter repeated in *T. of Y.*). What actually happened was that after the Germans took the town in 1918 they used the Basilica as an observation post as it gave a marvellous view of the entire enemy forces. We ourselves therefore shot down the steeple (chauffeur says he was with the Captain who gave the order to fire at it), and the Virgin fell, was smashed to pieces on the pavement, and the fragments carried away by the Germans as souvenirs.

We lunched at the somewhat optimistically named Hôtel de la Paix, where the proprietor is an Italian who fought on the Italian front during the War, & afterwards worked as a waiter on the Riviera & at Vittel.

Road from Albert to Bapaume
Not far out of Albert we passed the craters of La Boiselle, which I remember seeing in 1921, in the midst of a completely devastated region. The craters (the biggest of which was used as German Headquarters in 1918) are now becoming grown-over with coarse grass & all gradually (though very slowly) filling up as the earth silts down into them in rainy seasons. Homely hens now peck peacefully around them and placid cows crop the rough grass at the edge. The chauffeur pointed out the hump of earth ¾ mile back where the shaft was let down for the tunnel to the mine; it was started three months before July 1st and made by coal-miners from Northumberland and Durham. This was the first time that mine craters (a method afterwards "perfected" at Messines Ridge) were used as an offensive measure in the War. The chief regiments at La Boiselle were the Irish and Scottish Tynesiders (Tyneside Scottish, 34th Division), mostly composed of employees of the Newcastle Docks. On the opposite side of the road to Bapaume is a memorial to these two regiments, on which the inscription concludes: "Think not that the struggle and the sacrifice were in vain." Here the old German front line ran through the village cemetery —now completely demolished.

Pozières
At Pozières is a huge cemetery, walled and colonnaded, where are 2,770

graves and, carved between the pillars, the names of 14,690 "missing".
(? What has become of all these bodily remnants? Are they collected
together in huge common graves, or have they been exploded, ploughed &
steam-rollered into the soil, & are we driving over them all the time? No
wonder the French do not care to live in this deceptively beautiful but
gruesome charnel house of a region.)

In front of the cemetery was an Australian memorial, marked with the
Rising Sun (the Australians captured Pozières, & the big cemetery was
started by them to hold the first Australian dead). The new red-roofed
mayor's house and school [were] built out of penny subscriptions from the
children of Melbourne.

The Canadians first came into action on Pozières Ridge. Here too is the
Tanks Corps memorial, on the first place where tanks were used; it
includes a model of the four different kinds of tanks used in the War & the
chains encircling it came also from tank wheels.

On the right of Pozières is Martinpuich, where is High Wood (also
containing a memorial to the 47th London Division, which lost 3,000 men
in 24 hours when first in action). They captured it on September 16th,
1916, with the aid of tanks. Here, between High Wood and Le Sars, the
first battle of the Somme ended. The 47th Division was chiefly composed of
employees of the General Omnibus Company.

Canadian Memorial at Courcelette
Massed with pink ramblers and surrounded by maples, grown from seeds
sent over from Canada. The only trees in France that change colour in
autumn.

Bapaume
Now all rebuilt with big station and large market. Like other towns rebuilt
since War is now complete with gas, water & electricity, which comes
mostly from Bethune—hence the pylons across the Somme country.
Chauffeur told us that everywhere the roads are being widened because huge 3-ton motor lorries hurtle down them 3 abreast during the
night. Thought Bapaume rather a messy mixture of old & new. Did not
stop.

Mont St Quentin
Hill captured by Australians who struggled through marshes below
dressed only in shorts and shirts, and took it with the bayonet. (River
Somme flows through plain beyond marshes.) Horrible memorial on road
up hill, showing statue of Australian pushing his bayonet into a recumbent
German eagle. Memorial is to the 2nd Australian Division.

Péronne
Big new town with modern hospital. Always very difficult to take because
so largely surrounded by water & marshland. Nevertheless, was taken in
both 1870 & 1914. Stopped in market square; went into chief Hôtel St

Claude (rebuilt in both 1870 & 1914) & bought postcards. Large place, much bigger than Bapaume, and has not a particularly new appearance as many of the old bricks were used in the rebuilding. One café marked as having been burnt by the Germans in both 1870 & 1917. Also a large shop (millinery and miscellaneous haberdashery) inscribed: "Built 1792. Destroyed 1870 & 1916. Rebuilt 1873 & 1924." Though the whole town was destroyed, it gives the impression of having been there for decades. After War adopted by Blackburn, which built the new Blackburn Bridge over the Somme Canal. (Some of these reconstructed towns don't have such a bad time &, if one can forget the dead, must be much more convenient to live in than the older ones.)

La Chapelette
On main road to Amiens, beyond Péronne. Indian soldiers first came into action here 1916. Indian cemetery similar to ours but no crosses on stone. Massed with pink roses.

We were now on "the great road from Amiens to St Quentin", along which the Germans both advanced & retreated in 1918. Was in French hands for greater part of the War. All flat rolling country like Yorkshire Wolds; harvest everywhere. French cemetery at Villers Carbonnel. French (and occasional Americans) spoil appearance of cemeteries by taking their dead out of them and removing them home. British not allowed to do this.

Proyart
Passed this village close to which is Big Bertha that shelled Amiens (in valley at Chuignes). Passed Heath cemetery and the so-called "Mysterious house", which though four times in the front line was never destroyed because no one was sure to whom it belonged (i.e. who was in occupation of the cellars), but after War all the apparatus there was found to be German.

Valley of Death
Passed through here beyond Proyart. So-called because full of British gun positions which were constantly shelled; also lorries of stores or reinforcements were forced to mount slowly road going up from valley on either side, & so were constantly shelled and hit.

Americans in action
Passed wood of Le Hamel where Americans were first in action on Somme, July 4th, 1918. Germans found here chained to guns. (First American attack in War made at St Michel in 1918.)

Villers-Bretonneux
Virtually a suburb of Amiens; last village Germans reached in 1918—got just beyond it to l'Abbé Wood. Australians held the line from here through Corbie and Bray. Adopted by Melbourne & Victoria. A *rosierie* here (rose garden) & old ruined château. French funeral taking place in local

cemetery. Passed also one of the 383 stones put up along 450 miles from the coast to the Vosges to commemorate the position of the front line. German front line (two black marks across road) just beside it. Stone marked: "Ici fut repoussé l'envahisseur 1918."

L'Abbé Wood
Germans reached here in the March–April offensive 1918, & were pushed back to where stone was. Here Adelaide cemetery—only one where all the dead were killed in 1918. No original trees—only undergrowth—in wood. Marvellous straight road—in front the gradually looming view of Amiens impressed me more than anything throughout the journey except the view from Thiepval Ridge, for it made me realise what the Germans must have felt as they came in sight of what must have been the largest town in France that they had the chance to take during the War. It must have seemed so near, so accessible, yet they never took it. The Cathedral, built in a hollow so that it recedes as you get near the town, yet so high that it dominates the whole countryside from a distance, must have been very easy to shell completely, yet they never destroyed it. Why? Did they mean to make the town their headquarters in final victorious campaign of War, & use Cathedral for observation? We ourselves used it in 1918 as observation post on German positions—advantage given us so great that this was a main reason why the Germans wanted to capture Amiens.

Back at hotel with half an hour to spare before train; wrote hasty letters to Mrs Leighton (enclosing rambler & rosemary) and Beverley Nichols whose *Cry Havoc!* I had carried with me all over the Somme battlefield. V. hot train back to Boulogne. Missed bus so drove back to Hardelot in car at sunset through roads scented with smell of mown hay.

Saturday August 5th
Started writing articles about battlefields. Very interesting letter in afternoon from Ernest Raymond about *T. of Y.*—he had got to p. 241, just after Roland's death, & couldn't stop thinking about it. Lost part of my *Clarion* article owing to wind on verandah; very much annoyed. Perfect night; orange moon.

Sunday August 6th
Finished & typed articles which I hope may be accepted by *Week-end Review* and *Clarion* & sent them off. Very hot—92° in London; must have been quite that here. Walked to tea at Pré Catelan over burning road. Entire population of Hardelot seemed to be talking & drinking round hotel so we walked after dinner to Golfer's Hotel for coffee, & back. Lovely scented walk through pinewoods under full moon.

Monday August 7th
Most perfect day since we came—hot but not tiring; constant gentle

breeze. Spent whole day on sea shore, bathing, sun-bathing, reading *Cry Havoc!* and walking. V.S.J. went off with her French count, so after tea W. & I walked across sands about 2½ miles to next village in direction of Boulogne. Real country fishing village, full of smells of drains & fish. Back over perfect sands in pearly light.

Tuesday August 8th
Cooler again. Tried sea but too cold, so returned & wrote up notes of battlefields. Tea at Pré Catelan; walk afterwards with W. through woods (dappled with clouds & sunshine) & sand dunes to old château. Wrote short review for *T. & T.* of Lady Stephen's book on Girton College.

Wednesday August 9th
Typed review & wrote letters. W. had one of her headaches & felt inactive, so V.S.J. & I had tea at Golfer's Hotel & walked on to the old château. Entrance now closed by wire as castle is supposed to be dangerous but we got under the fence & looked in. Inside ceilings all falling in, but outside seems likely to last for the present though topmost (red) turret looks very drunk. Huge cracks in walls & steps. "Gaudeam adfero" written over doorway a strange comment on situation. Garden which must once have been an exquisite dream now a wild tangle of grass, thistles & brambles below trees, which though dusty & dilapidated are still magnificent—ilex, alder, elms, walnut, poplars. Very much "they say the lion & the lizard keep . . .". Shouldn't like to be here at twilight—feel sure it is full of owls. A workman was inside the grounds mending his cart; V.S.J. asked him questions about the château & it turned out that his mother had been a servant there. Some years before the War it belonged to a Miss Guy or Gye—one of an English family all brought up there; then it became a restaurant, & during the War was commandeered for the Army & used as an instruction school ("Sports Shed" still written on one of the outhouses). Probably during War garden went to rack and ruin (one pink rose bush & a clump of goldenrod seem to be all that is left of it) and whole place was neglected, so that no one would take it on & spend money on it, & it is now rapidly becoming a ruin. Until a year or two ago Miss Guy wrote to the workman's mother regularly & always inquired after the castle. A year or two ago she came back to see it—and was evidently so much horrified at what she saw that ever since she has not written, or been heard of here.

Walked out along old carriage drive; ancient gates were firmly shut behind us by a lodge-keeper's wife. Walked back past mere (many fishers) and golf course; mere almost violently blue, & divine light on distant sandhills. Walked up old road to Étaples opposite Pré Catelan & came out on to big new white road to Le Touquet.

Thursday August 10th

Spent most of day drafting, on & off, 1,600 word article for *Daily Telegraph* on "What Shall I Do If My Son Wants to Join the O.T.C.?" By afternoon mail, gorgeous letter from Frank Swinnerton (to whom Odette sent a copy) about my book; says he has written the greater part of his literary letter to the *Chicago Tribune* about it, & Gollancz can quote from this if he likes. Also an engagement from Christy for lecture to Leeds Luncheon Club, Jan. 25th, on "Should Autobiographies Be Forbidden?" Dined at Pré Catelan as it was V.S.J.'s last evening; also had had enough of French families for the present.

Friday August 11th

Wet morning, windy, with thunder-storm, in spite of which V.S.J. departed by the 10.30 bus for the 11.30 boat. Very wet; worked most of day on *D. Telegraph* article. Tea at the Villa Les Roses—certainly *the* place to stay here. Discovered that Lady Cynthia Mosley actually stayed there with her children. Sat on sands after tea as sun actually came out. W. had letters about terrific quarrel between Wells and Odette Keun.

Saturday August 12th

Went over country by bus to see Étaples & Camiers. Lovely day; strong breeze, bright blue sky and clouds. Had long wait at Condette; ordered black coffee in roadside café where 3 French workmen (typical *poilus*) were drinking beer and *café au rhum*. All very gay and loquacious. Were shortly joined by a fourth from the wine-merchant's van. Among the bottles ordered were two empty ones, but this form of "try on" appeared to disturb and deceive no one. Man merely remarked philosophically "C'est la vie" (evidently the French equivalent to: "It came away in me 'and") and was invited by the vivacious young woman at the bar to sit down and have a drink with the other three, which he did.

We got off the bus at Camiers and walked towards Étaples along the once familiar road. We went into the churchyard at Camiers where we found the economical inhabitants had made the 1870 war memorial "Aux enfants de Camiers mort pour la patrie" do again by simply adding the words "1914–1918" under "1870". Of the old-fashioned, rather ornate and pointed type, it was in curious contrast to the bare, simple-formed memorials in most of the villages and cemeteries.

Then we walked along the path beside the mere just below the railway line to the "Manor House", which during the War was a restaurant where Faith & I had so many large & satisfying teas. It is still blue-painted, but is now a laundry, which looks somewhat dejected, & all the clamorous ducks and chickens have vanished. Then we walked between pinewoods and sandhills along the straight, switchback road to Étaples. In one place mounds of earth had grown over piles of old petrol tins; all along the left-hand side where camps had been was coarse grass and ragwort, toadflax, mustard and bugloss. I picked a piece of toadflax from the side of "the road to Camiers", and later a sprig of bugloss from where 24 General had been.

At Étaples cemetery we stopped for an hour. In contrast to the small cemeteries on the Somme it looked enormous, spreading like a huge open fan from the pinewoods on the top of the hill down the slope to the flat, marshy ground which surrounds the railway line. The graves must run into thousands and it is surely still the largest military cemetery in France. It was difficult in so enormous a place to tell just how the graves were arranged, but most of the officers appear to be together in the rows which start at the foot of the cenotaph and extend in lines of about twenty to the railway line. Among them was one V.A.D. and one or two Sisters—those killed in the Canadian hospital during the great air raid of May 19th, 1918. One—a certain Sister K. Macdonald who was evidently slain by a bomb while actually on duty—was described on the headstone as "killed in action". Above her name was the maple leaf, which is I suppose the emblem of the Canadian nursing service. The V.A.D.—named, I think, Hallam—was described as "Nursing Member, Voluntary Aid Detachment", and had above her name the combined emblem of the B.R.C.S. and Order of St John. I looked for the grave of my Corporal Smith—who died on Dec. 27th, 1917 in my ward and was apparently a vicar's son, which would account for his charming manners—but though I got the number from the register, I could not find it.

The German graves still have on them the original grey crosses (presumably the German Govt can't yet afford stones—I wonder where all the German cemeteries are) now very weather-beaten and many marked "Unknown German Soldier"—which seems curious; one wonders how men who died of wounds in hospital could be quite unknown. A few of these German graves (which just like the rest were richly decked with the magnificent summer flowers that filled the whole cemetery) were among the British, but most of them were away at the side nearest Camiers, together with the graves of Indians and other natives—"all the outcasts together", as Winifred described them, though the Indians of course had headstones. These were inscribed "Here is Honoured . . ." and then the name. The Portuguese were also buried among the British; they too have only the original wooden crosses but these have been painted white to resemble the headstones of those who are "honoured".

In one little corner on the right of the memorial stone (as one stood with one's back to the sea) was a tiny piece of cemetery surrounding a solitary Chinese grave, with the name inscribed in Chinese characters; it was that of a member of the Chinese Labour Corps and below the name were inscribed in English the words: "A good reputation endureth for ever." His number also in the Labour Corps was given in English characters, and the flowers and tiny hedge round the grave were arranged in a Chinese pattern. Beyond him, still further in a corner—were they perhaps unconse-

crated?—were about a dozen graves of other "natives"—West Indian and
S. African.

Before going round the graves we sat for some time on the steps leading
down to the cemetery and looked at the registers of graves from the two
closets in the ashlar wall. I recognised one or two that I remember of men
whom I had nursed or heard of. But still more interesting were some of the
inscriptions and the marks in the Visitors' Book for 1933 which was
enclosed with the registers. Winifred and I wrote our names with the date
in it thus: "Vera Brittain, 19 Glebe Place, London SW3. Nursed as a
V.A.D. at 24 General Hospital, Étaples, 1917–1918." "Winifred Holtby,
Q.M.A.A.C., Camiers, 1918." And below our names I wrote the words:
"No More War!"

Afterwards I copied down some of the mostly impressive remarks, which
were as follows: 1) Pierre Luick—no date & no address but simply the
words: "Et cela confirme mon opinion bas la guerre." 2) No signature, but
marked "Du Havre, 28.7.33." "Parmi nos amusements, nous n'oublions
pas ceux qui sont morts pour nous et souhaitons que leur exemple serve
aux vivants pour ne jamais revoir ces calamités." 3) Marked: "Lefevre,
Calais. Saisons, Calais." "'Le profit personnel est responsable de la
guerre. Seul le proletariat peut hitter contre la guerre. Proletaires de tous
les pays unissez-vous.' (Karl Marx)." 4) Marked only "Gaby." "Que ces
anglais reposent en paix pour l'éternité. Amen." 5) "G. P. Symonds, Hon.
C.F. Who buried many of those whose bodies lie here. Aug. 9th 1933. Well
done, gardeners!" 6) Anonymous: "Que tous les peuples prennent exemple. Les Anglais, Portugais, Canadiens, Indiens, Allemands, tous sont
unis dans une paix éternelle. Puissent-ils tous reposer en paix." And
finally, 7) "5 Réfugiés allemands, 10.8.33."

We left the cemetery at last and walked on to Étaples, down the road
where 24 General was, and the humped, ragwort-covered earth where the
huts were is marked everywhere "Danger. Défense d'entrer." I looked
across the wide tumbled field to the distant trees beneath which was once
the German ward. It was all very queer that it should be so quiet and still,
when I remembered it so full of hurry and anxiety, apprehension and pain.
To the right was a clear, beautiful view of Le Touquet, now unobstructed
by huts; above the woods appeared the roof of the Royal Picardy, whose
top windows must look straight on to Étaples cemetery. I wonder how
many of the wealthy people who stay there ever notice it, or remember.

Sunday August 13th
Finished & sent on *D. Telegraph* article on O.T.C. As usual Sunday
concourse was round hotel, W. & I took our lunch out and picnicked in the
pinewoods beyond the Pré Catelan. Sat in lovely dappled sunlight &
shadows on carpet of pine-needles; gorgeous scent of pine-needles everywhere. W. stung by wasp on way, but we got ammonia at once from grocer
& no apparent harm resulted. Stayed in wood till nearly 4.0; sounds of

distant thunder sent us back but no storm happened, only a few drops of rain. Walked up & down shore after tea, watching lovely children playing on beach. Gorgeous sunset. Drafted two more articles for *M. Guardian.* Press cutting from *Newsagent & Booksellers' Review* saying that *T. of Y.* looks like being another "winner".

Monday August 14th
Brief formal reply from Beverley Nichols to my letter sent from Amiens —typewritten, brief, insincere, obviously the "standard" letter sent off by his secretary. If I get any correspondence for *T. of Y.*, I won't have a "standard" letter.

Typed & sent off two *M. G.* articles, "Three Memorials" and "Ablutions in Picardy". This afternoon walked to Condette and back; had tea at so-called Hôtel Metropole. Kept by an English woman whom I didn't like; too voluble, a junior of Mrs Young, our ex-housekeeper. Walked back part of way through woods; scented & sweet as usual. Lovely clumps of purple loosestrife in meadows round golf-course; bullrushes in mere. Wild heliotrope, thistles, wild mignonette, growing at side of road by tram-lines.

Tuesday August 15th   London
Very windy morning, felt anxious about crossing. Had after-lunch coffee with Miss Davy of Transport House, who said she was being given *T. of Y.* as a present for correcting somebody's proofs. To Boulogne by crowded bus at tea-time; after various inquiries about crossing decided to go. Rough but not intolerable; never felt ill & even W. was not sick. Lovely lights going into Folkestone. G. met us at Victoria. Found letter awaiting me from Storm Jameson, enclosing one from Davey asking her to let the *Y. P.* have a review of my book first for the day of publication—so she has undertaken to do the *Sunday Times* one the following Sunday. Various cuttings announcing book as imminent.

Wednesday August 16th
Spent day straightening up correspondence, etc. W. went off to stay with Lady R. for 2 days. Telephoned Gollancz about Frank Swinnerton's letter (received my last day in Hardelot, giving permission to quote his first letter to me instead of the one in the *Chicago Tribune*, which will be too late) and V.G. said he had had one from F.S. too & also a very nice "quote" from Ernest Raymond. V.G. said he thought things were going well. Mother came in in early morning; still seems to feel perturbed because I haven't made her father sound important; thinks the aunts mayn't like it! Found that the *Week-end Review* had already put in my article on "Somme Battlefield, 1933," so it was worth while doing it in a hurry. My name on cover between Ernst Henri & Sir Norman Angell.

Thursday August 17th
Still clearing up. Went to Harrods after lunch & bought royal blue jumper, hat & blue & white shoes to complete check swaggercoat & skirt. Very becoming; ready for new Ivimey photograph next week. Letter for Winifred from Phyllis. Got Maurice Richardson a wedding present from Harrods for his wedding on Aug. 30th to Muriel Angus. Came back & gardened; creepers after 3 weeks like the Sleeping Beauty's garden. Cool & windy.

Friday August 18th
Delightful & very frank letter from Cecil Roberts (in Venice) about *T. of Y.*; says he "didn't think I had it in me". Tells me he has given it long review in *Sphere* of Aug. 26th—day before publication but more useful than a week late. W. back from Hampstead to do some packing; told me Ellis Roberts does not propose to review *T. of Y.* & has handed it over to Pamela Hinkson, who asked for it (Katherine Tynan's daughter). Lady R. pretended to know nothing about this (though she saw to it that Beverley Nichols was reviewed at length). Remembering that Cicely Hamilton had taken for granted that she was doing it if Roberts didn't, and that either Norman Angell or Stephen King-Hall would have done it gladly if asked, I felt that *T. & T.* had as usual let me down & said so with some force—with which W. actually seemed to agree. Went to Roberts (ex-Sutton) in Earl's Court Road at 4.30 & had hair permanently waved again.

Saturday August 19th
Met Cicely Hamilton in King's Road; she told me she had been expecting to review *T. of Y.* for *T. & T.* & is very disgusted about not being asked; has now written to ask if she can do it for *Morning Post* but fears it may be too late. Went to Oxford with Mrs Nedell to fetch children; everything very crowded but day tolerable. Lunched at Cadena & afterwards showed Mrs N. Tom Quad & the Cathedral. Miss Thomson came up quite punctually with children (whom she had driven down alone) all looking in radiant health. They have evidently enjoyed themselves as John remarked that another time he wanted to stay "a very long time, like Jennifer", but he seemed more reconciled to leaving than he was last year, & they both settled down quite happily. Press-cutting from *Yorkshire Post* saying great things are expected of *T. of Y.*—also Phyllis's weekly article (on books she would like to review) suggested—as I curiously enough did at Painswick —that W. ought to do a modern *Vanity Fair*.

G. & I discussed Phyllis after supper; he explained her reactions by saying that I treated her like a country cousin & she therefore compensated herself by treating *me* as a negligible writer. This cast a new & illuminating light on the situation. I decided too that as a writer she is rather like Dreiser—a literary architect, not a literary artist; does not produce a work of art but flings together an enormous fiction-cathedral (or as she is an agnostic perhaps "factory" or "county hall" would be more appropriate) which dominates without decorating the literary landscape. Her work has form and power, dignity and grandeur, but no beauty & no finish. But granite, though less pliable & adaptable, survives clay, & her work will probably endure. It is the product, partly subconscious & partly deliberate, of the student's intellect (a first-class and extremely forceful intellect) rather than the inspired expression of the artist's imagination; no sudden flame of delicate perfection lights its dark solidity with translucent glory. Behind it burns a restrained, sullen passion, that gives her work heat rather than light. It does not glow, it does not sparkle; it dominates, challenges & overwhelms.

Sunday August 20th
Wrote to W. in answer to a note left yesterday on my desk saying that Lady R. (to whom she apparently repeated my views about *T. & T.*) had instructed Ellis Roberts to feature my review & put it in early, and also says that if Gollancz likes he can quote her letter to me. A belated *amende?* I can't see much that is quotable in her letter but I sent it to V.G. on chance of usefulness.

Children very good. Played in garden all morning; John, following my instructions, pulled up & threw away all the old marigolds. Afternoon at Oakwood Court. Walk with G. round Embankment after supper.

Monday August 21st
Started to prepare lecture for Newcastle-on-Tyne on "The Changing Family". Face massage etc., Peter Jones.

Tuesday August 22nd
Hair shampooed again. Allan Young to lunch to discuss with G. what line of Labour policy to adopt. At 3.0 had another photograph taken by Elisabeth Ivimey in check coat & shirt & new jumper (dark blue, ties at neck) to try out on *Tatler*, *Sketch*, etc. Tea at Marshall's; bought new coral-coloured hat. Found I had just missed Mother when I got back; very much annoyed at her having long journey for nothing. *D. Telegraph* returned O.T.C. article; suspect too pacifist. Sent Miss Pearn a suggestion for *Daily Herald*.

Wednesday August 23rd
Note from Winifred. Odette has abandoned idea of publishing letters & memories about Wells; realises it will damage her Colonial scheme. Letter from Maurice Richardson thanking me for seal note-case sent as wedding present. Bought press-cutting book, looked after children, read *Changes in Family Life* (Beveridge etc.). G. went to Oxford for day. Held usual imaginary arguments with supposed critics of my book. Wrote to tell W.

about them & fear of numerous inaccuracies through queer tricks of memory.

Thursday August 24th
Letter from Nancy Pearn to say the *Woman's Journal* has agreed, like *Good Housekeeping*, to pay me 15 guineas for my articles. Restless wandering day; no work. Took collar to Baird Lewis to put on coat; called at Marshall's & bought blue evening dress to wear to-morrow at dinner to which Henry Andrews has invited us at Orchard Court. Acquired silver shoes & bag to go with it. Charming note from Harold Rubinstein this evening wishing luck to *T. of Y.* William Kean Seymour back at Bank this morning; said Beatrice somewhat rueful because Gollancz hadn't quoted her on cover of my book. Terrific hurricane in U.S.A. (Norfolk, Virginia, especially). No further developments about Mussolini & Dollfuss.

Friday August 25th
Two reviews out already; a lovely one by Cecil Roberts in the *Sphere*, & Beatrice Kean Seymour's in the *Woman's Journal*—which, though well-intentioned, reads rather stupidly beside his. Faults could of course be found with his—he confuses Roland and Edward completely, speaks of the book redeeming me from "obscurity" with a frankness that gives me rather a wry feeling (though it's better than the hypocritical "well-known novelist"). But the tone of the review is not as a whole patronising; it contains some magnificent commendations, & he gives me the entire page, with a photograph.

Dined at Orchard Court with Henry Andrews (Rebecca not home yet) to meet a youngish consular official who was interned with Henry at Ruhleben, & a Hungarian professor & his Russian wife—name so far as I could gather is Palyi—who have had to leave Berlin, where they were living, & come to England because P. is a Jew. Charming couple; wife dark, young & very pretty. Henry presented me with a copy of the *Week-end Review* with a review of *T. of Y.* in it by Naomi Mitchison; he seemed to think it favourable, but I thought it rather stupid. She too had intended to do me a good turn, but rides her own hobby-horses to such an extent that the general effect is disparaging, & she never says what the book is about.

Came home to find a charming letter from John Brophy (author of several novels) who tells me he is reviewing *T. of Y.* for the *Sunday Referee*, & uses that as an introduction to enlist my sympathy for oppressed shop-assistants (amongst whom he has been working as advertising manager in Lewis's, a provincial chain store). Ended up by talking about "your beautiful book; of course you know it is a masterpiece", etc. Told me that his wife, who was in the W.A.A.C.S., had been equally interested in it.

Saturday August 26th
Rang up John Brophy & asked if he & his wife would care to come round to

tea & discuss shop-assistants. Enthusiastic response; agreed to come on Thursday; delighted also at prospect of meeting Winifred. Spoke again about book; said review would be in to-morrow; rather disparaging about Cecil Roberts, who he seemed to think hadn't "understood" me. Very pleasant voice. After lunch John demanded to be taken to King's Cross to meet Winifred, so took him, forgetting holidays. Very hot, very crowded, Scarborough Flier very late & W. in second part, but J. was very good & did not fuss at all. Looked adorable in blue aertex shirt to match his blue linen knickers, & panama hat. Is a disturbingly beautiful child. W. looked very tired but cheered up on seeing us.

Just after supper a copy of the *Sunday Referee* was thrust through the front door—on it a note in John Brophy's writing to say he thought I'd like to see p. 11, & there was his *magnificent* review—1,000 words. He'd called it an exhortation over the telephone but *I* call it a eulogy; I've never had such a review or expected one. I wondered, too, if he had been specially to their office to get it & leave it round here. At twilight W. & I walked along the Embankment; warm, windless & very lovely.

Sunday August 27th
Huge advertisements of *T. of Y.* in both *Observer* & *Sunday Times*. About a third of the page and three-quarters of a column each, & he had collected "puffs" (which some of my reviewers will doubtless sneer at!) from no less than eleven sources—Sarah Gertrude Millin, Frank Swinnerton, Phyllis Bentley, Stephen King-Hall, Naomi Royde-Smith, Ernest Raymond, Beatrice Kean Seymour, Vernon Bartlett, *Sunday Times* (advance note), *Observer* (advance note) and Lady Rhondda—the extract from her letter which I doubtless sent after the rest of the advt was made up. I was rather disappointed that neither the *Observer* (which gave its main page criticism to Sisley Huddleston) nor the *Sunday Times* (which was doubtless fulfilling Storm Jameson's undertaking to the *Yorkshire Post*) carried a review, but consoled myself by thinking that after all more people will be coming back & will see it each week.

Sent copy of *Referee* to Clare & Aunt Florence, to whom I sent a copy of *T. of Y.* yesterday, together with May Wedderburn Cannan, Barbara Bervon, Mrs Holtby, Sir Owen Seaman, Walter de la Mare, Wilfred Meynell & Miss Thurlow. Went for walk to Old English Garden; a riot of rich, wild colours—dahlias chiefly, in scarlet & orange & bronze & flame. Very hot. Took children to Oakwood Court; W. came with me.

Monday August 28th–Sunday September 3rd
Oh, *what* a head-cracking week! Reviews, reviews, reviews, & reviews again. Never did I imagine that the *Testament* would inspire such great praise at such length, or provoke—in smaller doses—so much abuse.

Monday August 28th—day of publication. Excellent reviews in *Yorkshire Post* (by Storm Jameson and even better than I expected), *Star, Liverpool Post, Manchester Evening News* & quite good in *News Chronicle*, by E. E. Kellett, which provoked a controversy (begun by Winifred) about the attitude of the War generation towards the Younger generation's view of the War. Great interest provoked in Manchester by part in Chapter 1 which refers to my detestation of provincial towns but describes Manchester as free from provincialism. Leader in *Manchester Evening Chronicle* on the subject; called "The City of Progress". Later in the week was asked to contribute an article on this subject (to appear on Friday) to Allied Newspapers. Comment also in *Daily Dispatch*.

In morning charming telegram of good wishes arrived from Ernest Raymond, later another from Patrick Brand. A sweet letter from Storm Jameson and another from Miss Beatrice Hart, who had read Golly's advt. During morning a lovely bunch of pink roses arrived, a dozen and a half; later learnt they were from Phyllis. Gordon bought me some pink carnations too. Dreadful feeling of depression all day; cheered up somewhat when Winifred brought along the *Star, Liverpool Post* & Margaret's lovely review in the *Y. P.*

Tuesday August 29th Reviews in *Manchester Guardian* (by Evelyn Sharp, dull, as most of her writing is), *Birmingham Post* (very good), *Morning Post* (not too bad for it). Lunched Café Royal with David Higham, who told me sales already amounted to 3,300.

Wednesday August 30th First-rate review in the *Queen*, called "A Message to Humanity". Went to evening party at Miss Pearn's; met E. Arnot Robertson, Stella Gibbons, G. B. Stern, Yeats-Brown and wife, and Mr Lakin and wife (*Sunday Times*, which had previously rung me up asking for a photograph for Sunday's issue). Lakin made flattering remarks about both my book & the photograph & asked if I would do some reviewing for *Sunday Times*. Wore a new flame-coloured garment in thick crêpe, bought that afternoon at Peter Jones.

Thursday August 31st Spate of large reviews. *Times Literary Supplement* (splendid, a whole column), *Daily Mail* (by Compton Mackenzie, excellent), *Daily Herald* (by Roger Pippett, very favourable); both these two latter had splash headlines about my book, and my photograph. Also came the *Daily Express*; furious, insulting, vituperative attack by James Agate on both Gollancz and me—chiefly about way he is making a stunt of the book. No doubt, since I have now gone on record as pacifist, Socialist & pro-League of Nations, the *Express*, which is anti all these things, was glad enough to print the attack. Did not see this last until John Brophy and his wife (charming young man of 33, wife somewhat older, had been W.A.A.C. at G.H.Q. at Montreuil in War) came to tea bringing it. They seemed so perturbed that W. rang up Gollancz, who told me not to care a damn, said it was due to a personal row between Agate & himself bec. he didn't ask

Agate to his last party at the Ritz, thought the attack would probably help to sell the book, and said he'd ordered another edition (5,000 copies) on the strength of it. John Brophy said he was willing to answer the attack but Golly said this was useless as the *Express* wouldn't print it. We *loved* the Brophys—one of the most charming couples it has been my fortune to meet for long enough. They said they had been thrilled at the idea of meeting Winifred and me, as *Mandoa* and *T. of Y.* were the two books which had impressed them most this year.

Friday September 1st Fräulein Bleichenbach came at breakfast time to look after children; seems a very charming & attractive girl. Lovely review by Pamela Hinkson in *Time & Tide*; pleasant little review in *The Times* itself—a summary of the one in the *Lit. Supp.* Also an attack in a *Spectator* note on Gollancz for his method of putting *T. of Y.* across, though it spoke respectfully of the book itself.

Saturday September 2nd Saw family off for Brighton at Victoria; station crowded, family full of trepidation, Father started heart attack; nearly went down with them. Winifred had one of her bad headaches; got in Dr Boysen. Excellent review in *John O'London* by E. O. Lorimer. 3 displayed copies of *T. of Y.* on Victoria Station bookstall.

Sunday September 3rd Huge advts by Gollancz in both *Sunday Times* & *Observer*, stating "11th thousand printing" (which I suppose means about 5,000 sold!!) & quoting the lovely bit at the end of the *Times Lit. Supp.*, as well as the *Daily Mail* (Compton Mackenzie), *Man. Guardian, Birmingham Post, Liverpool Post, Yorkshire Post*, Brophy in the *Referee, John O'London, Queen, Lady*, & Cecil Roberts in the *Sphere*. Storm Jameson's beautiful & understanding review in today's *Sunday Times*, with a good photograph of me. Also a longish review in the *Observer*, unsigned; contained some lovely sentences but the writer never seemed to have quite made up his mind whether he approved of the book or not.

Children played with Fräulein all day. Margaret Green came to tea. This evening I was sitting here writing up this diary when the telephone rang; it was Eric Gillett, with whom I acted in *Raffles* at Buxton so long ago; he had just been reading my book for review in the *London Mercury* (having become a literary light about equivalent to myself—how far we have both travelled since 1914!), seemed to be much moved by it & couldn't resist ringing me up. We talked in great detail (since he too was in the War) about all the things that have happened to us both since 1914, and I asked him to tea.

Monday September 4th
Saturday reviews came in; nothing much that I hadn't seen. Got hair shampooed & was photographed by Swaine's; bad, irritating photographer & boiling hot room; very tired, shan't go there again. Saw piles of

T. of Y. in Truslove & Hanson & displayed copies in windows of various bookshops—e.g., Prince's bookshop in Piccadilly—so it must be selling somewhere besides Golly's advts.

Tuesday September 5th   Brighton
Letters congratulating me on book from Paul Bloomfield, Christine Brown, Aunt Belle, invitation from secretary of To-morrow Club to speak on *T. of Y.* in November. Went down with G. to Brighton; meant to go for day but stayed night as Father as usual ill & determined to go home before time; wanted me to stay & help them back. Lunched with family at Old Ship; dropped in for ten minutes to see T.U.C. Congress in the Dome; spent most of afternoon & evening walking up & down front with Mother & dropped in to see Father at intervals. Dined agreeably with Gordon at Grand Hotel; looked in at T.U.C. dinner afterwards & listened to speeches. Stevens of the *Clarion* came & talked to us & afterwards we sat till after midnight in the lounge, drinking beer & tea & talking to Allan Young, W. T. Thomson the solicitor (who had bought a copy of *T. of Y.*), & Mellor of the *Herald*. Was introduced to Stevenson, present editor of *Herald*. Very lovely day; hot on front; got very tired with so much coming & going.

Wednesday September 6th   London
Took family back to town; travelled in 1st class Pullman drawing room. Saw brief & rather unfair little review of *T. of Y.* in *Punch*. Answered voluminous correspondence.

Had Eric Gillett to tea; in face he hasn't changed much, but owing to thigh smashed at Passchendaele has gone about six inches shorter; very surprising when I remember him as a tall young man. Conversation long & interesting; he congratulated me on my prose & I told him that just because the book wasn't a novel most reviewers hadn't commented on its literary qualities at all. He said he had—asked me if I'd care to meet the *London Mercury* Group—said he may be going from Chapman & Hall to Heinemann's & wanted to see my early novels with a view to recommending them to make me an offer (though I said I didn't want to leave Golly, I wouldn't mind having the offer); suggested he might try to get me a job on the *Evening News*, and advised me to write to the B.B.C. proposing a series of talks.

Ellen Wilkinson came to supper; we discussed Fascism and talked chiefly about plans for entertaining the international commission on the Torgler Reichstag trial when it comes over next week.

Thursday September 7th
Answered letters. More voluminous press-cuttings—*lovely* review from the Glasgow Socialist *Forward*, putting over to Labour people just what I wanted; good reviews also in the *Listener* and the *Scotsman*. Took John to tea with Eric Gillett & his boy Tony, a thin fair-haired child who goes to Mrs

Spencer's & is about to have his tonsils out. E.G.'s wife left him—I gather when he was Prof. of English at Singapore—& his little girl died there of pneumonia. Talked to his old mother & a woman visitor who had seen most of my reviews. Afterwards he got me to sign his copy of *T. of Y.* & gave me a copy of his own *Men & Books*. Long & appreciative letter from Irene Rathbone, author of *We That Were Young*. Went with W. to cocktail party given by Margaret Goldsmith & Nora James to meet I.A.R. Wylie. Talked for some minutes to I. A. R. Wylie, who said she wanted to meet me. Otherwise met no one I knew except the Highams & found the party, though very noisy, rather dull.

Letter came in morning from Nancy Pearn containing offer from *Sunday Chronicle* to serialise *T. of Y.* for £200. Rang up Gollancz, who hesitated about it & said he wanted to consult his traveller on possible effect on sales. Told me book is going "extremely well"; is "thoroughly established", & he hopes it will sell on till Christmas. Rang up Nancy Pearn, who was obviously annoyed with me for ringing up Gollancz first; has usual antipathy of agent against publisher & apparently wanted me to disregard him, which I refuse to do. Ultimately convinced her we weren't against serialisation, got her into better temper & told her to put Higham on to Gollancz & leave me out of it. Later Gollancz phoned to say no objection to serialisation but hoped it could be postponed six weeks. Wrote to Nancy Pearn to this effect but she probably knows already. Feel in more of a hurricane than ever; too much going on all at once.

Friday September 8th
Spent most of morning & part of afternoon being drawn by the *Bookman* artist Ziegler (looks like a Russian Jewish Communist) for their October number. Drawing made me look very ugly but was quite interesting —certainly a different version of me from the photographs. G. had W. J. Brown (Civil Service Clerks T.U. organiser) to lunch; agreeable person with gingerish hair & pince-nez; has 3 children at Dartington Hall.

Looked after children in afternoon.

Saturday September 9th
Worked in morning; walk Battersea Park after lunch; had Miss Styer, Mrs Newbolt & Mme Nadaroff to tea. Critical reviews (though partly favourable) from *Church Times* & *Saturday Review*. Wrote private letter to *Church Times* reviewer. Telephoned Irene Rathbone, who has sent me a copy of her own book; invited her to lunch with me at Chelsea Grill on Wednesday. Has charming voice; Miss Styer told me she is very nice-looking, is Eleanor Rathbone's niece, & has acted in one or two London theatres.

Sunday September 10th
Wrote to Lionel Fielden of B.B.C. to suggest series of talks on "Women & the Passing World". Wrote Eric Gillett to say I had done it. Big advt (not

now alone but at head of others) of *T. of Y.* headed "Apology"; apparently 2nd impression of book ran out & it was unobtainable for two days; third impression will be ready to-morrow. Wrote for copies each of 2nd & 3rd edition. The remark in the advt "The 2nd Edition went out on Friday" seems to suggest that—owing to several days' demand which couldn't be met—I had the unusual experience of selling a whole edition of 5,000 copies in one day.

Took children & Fräulein to Oakwood Court.

Monday September 11th
Lovely letters about *T. of Y.* from Miss Street & Mrs Horrabin; the latter so moving that I had to stop reading it till after breakfast. Letter also from Storm Jameson saying Agate review was obviously due to personal grievance and doesn't matter. Got on during morning with "Changing Family" lecture in spite of Shirley falling down & cutting both knees. Mother rang up just after lunch; the other day she told me that the little Mudies in Ken. High Street sold 54 copies of *T. of Y.* in two days; to-day she had heard from Aunt Belle that everyone seems to be talking about it in Deal! (she hears them at her tea-shop). Told her how Sheila Lynd rang me up from Gollancz's this morning to report request for a review copy of *T. of Y.* from the *Macclesfield Times* & ask what connection with Macclesfield I had had. This morning also I carried Cicely Hamilton's case for her the distance between our house & hers, & she told me she had been staying at her caravan with Mrs Abbott, who had a copy of *T. of Y.*, & they had discussed it over the week-end. Letter from Rolfe Scott-James; said he'd sent on my letter to Nevinson, & that the snooty note last week about Gollancz & my book (though respectful enough to my book) was by Wilson Harris.

Went up Sloane Street & saw pile of seven or 8 copies of 2nd edition of *T. of Y.* in Truslove & Hanson; plain yellow cover this time, no "band", with Compton Mackenzie's review quoted on the front. Sight so unusual for me that I bought a charming hat at Eve Valère's on the strength of it; W. also ordered a grey hat & grey coat frock to be made there. F. L. Stevens this evening returned my *Clarion* article to be brought up to date but didn't—as I had suggested—give it back to me for use in another paper. Congratulated me on "great success" of *T. of Y.* & said their review was late. Henrietta Leslie also talked to me about it over the 'phone; she got back from Austria yesterday & I took her a little bunch of yellow roses this afternoon.

Wednesday September 13th
Life getting too hectic to keep diary in any detail. Lunched Irene Rathbone at Chelsea Grill; has been an actress. We talked war books.

Thursday September 14th
Tea with John Brophy & his wife at Ealing. Took the children—all ran round garden of bottom flat; Brophy v. nice with them. Afterwards W. took them back & I stayed to supper. We talked War books—success of *T. of Y.*—he mentioned his permanent attraction to Rebecca West & previous interest in Winifred & myself.

Friday September 15th
Lovely review of *T. of Y.* by Rebecca in *D. Telegraph.*

Sunday September 17th   Newcastle-on-Tyne
Went up to Newcastle-on-Tyne for lecture on Monday. Scotch express v. crowded, day warm. Wore black coat & skirt & scarlet white-spotted blouse. Stayed at station hotel; very comfortable. Secretary & her husband called on me after dinner & gave me coffee. Secretary professed anti-feminist & insisted on arguing with me, tho' I would rather have gone to bed.

Monday September 18th
Spoke to Newcastle Luncheon Club at Tilley's Restaurant on "The Changing Family". Very large attendance & talk seemed to go down well. Next door a book-shop with *T. of Y.* conspicuous in window. Back by late afternoon train.

Tuesday September 19th   London
Tea with Henrietta; she talked at length about *T. of Y.* and the 15,000 copies it is already supposed to have sold. Pleasant & quiet.

Wednesday September 20th
John started new school, Mrs Spencer's, 11 Brechin Place. I took him there & he ran all the way from excitement.
    Went to B.B.C. to discuss a talk on current affairs; saw Fielden & Miss Wace. Voice tested; O.K. Gordon decided to go to Leipzig by aeroplane for the trial to observe for the Zinkin Committee instead of Brailsford, who is suspect in Germany. Much complication over getting G. official letter to report for the *Y. P.* Eventually Major Church, who dropped in after supper, ran me over to Fleet Street in his car & I went to the *Y. P.* office myself & got the official letter out of Davey.

Thursday September 21st
Went down early to Croydon with G. to catch Dutch plane to Rotterdam; he was then going on by Czechoslovak plane to Leipzig. G. seemed unperturbed but I felt v. queer watching him disappear into the clouds in the tiny plane. Went back to tube by Charing X & there 'phoned David Higham to meet me at Hill's in the Strand about the *Sunday Chronicle*

serialisation of *T. of Y.*, about which he & Gollancz have been having a row all the week.

At 11.0 turned up at Bart's & was shown by Major Eccles all over the new nurses' quarters; he said our miserable quarters at Denmark Hill in the War & the death of the V.A.D. from pneumonia originally inspired him to raise the money. Remembered him well when I saw him. Quarters certainly are splendid compared to the old style; one bathroom to only six nurses, & the library has hot water pipes running under the window desks.

Had lunch at Hill's; David Higham turned up for coffee. We discussed the serial & I explained the importance of the cash owing to Leipzig; suddenly found myself, much to Higham's embarrassment, beginning to cry owing to strain & fatigue of past few days, & G.'s departure. Higham tried to be encouraging about both the serial & Germany without much success. Thankful soon after tea to get wire from G. saying he had arrived safely in Leipzig.

Friday September 22nd

Obliged to intervene in Gollancz–Higham dispute over serial by sending note to Gollancz (in answer to letter received 2 days ago) by Patrick Brand, explaining I hadn't replied before because of the Leipzig situation & saying that as I now needed the cash for G.'s work in Germany I desperately hoped the serial would now go through. In afternoon got note by hand from Gollancz saying he withdrew all objection to serialisation. Higham later rang up to this effect, but thought he could have got the better of Golly without my intervention but of course he couldn't. Agents generally useless in a crisis.

Tea with Guy Kendall at Authors' Club in Whitehall owing to his admiration for *T. of Y.* & especially the Malta chapter.

Huge crowded meeting at Kingsway Hall about the Reichstag trial; overflow so large that another meeting had to be held in Conway Hall. Had greatest difficulty in getting in through mob outside Kingsway Hall despite platform ticket. Ellen Wilkinson in chair; mentioned names of supporters on platform, including my own as author of "one of the best of the war books". Speakers included Laski, Pollitt, Dorothy Woodman, Kingsley Martin. Everyone asked after G., & Ellen Wilkinson & her sister both commented on his pluck in going off to Leipzig at a moment's notice. I was asked to go on a deputation to the German Ambassador but the request was afterwards withdrawn for fear it might prejudice G.'s work in Leipzig. Went home by Tube with H. J. Laski; we met crossing Kingsway after the meeting. He immediately remarked: "Doesn't Pollitt make you sick?" —typical, since he had talked in his own address about "the superb speech of Mr Pollitt"! Personally had never heard Pollitt before; never heard such roaring & ranting anywhere.

Monday September 25th
Went to coffee party at house of Mrs Dawson Scott, founder of the P.E.N. Club. The old snob is supposed to invite only those who have "arrived"; in her invitation she mentioned Rebecca's review, so I suppose she thinks I have! Wore flame-coloured crêpe dress. Met "John Lovegood", otherwise Grant Watson, a lean middle-aged man who said that whenever he looked in Golly's List for an advt of his novel *The Partners* he could only find one of *T. of Y*. Ernst Toller there; large dark eyes, grey-haired & solemn. He was in Switzerland when Hitler came into power & was warned not to return to Germany. The Nazis searched his flat & turned out his mother & sister, & he is now trying to make a living in England. Travelled home with Henrietta Leslie & Dr Schutze.

Tuesday September 26th
Went to *Sunday Chronicle* office in morning to interview Mr Simpson the Editor about the serialisation of *T. of Y*. I wore my royal blue & white check. He was pleasant, & flattering about book. Arranged for a *Sunday Chron.* photographer to go to Oakwood Court to photograph the portraits of Edward & myself. Promised many photographs of self, the War, etc.

Friday September 29th
Evening—went to B.B.C. to show Miss Wace the MS. of my current events & disarmament talk on which I had worked solidly for two days. She approved. Feeling completely exhausted & under the weather from over-work, over-excitement & too many consequences of *T. of Y*. all at once. Fan-mail letters beginning to come in.

Saturday September 30th
10.45 a.m., broadcast my talk on disarmament from the B.B.C. Didn't feel it was very successful or that the officials thought so. They seemed surprised that I thought 3 days a short time to prepare it but of course have no idea how beset my life is from all sides. In afternoon went up to Univ. College School, Hampstead, to have tea with Guy Kendall. Found a tea-party congregated to meet me; rather boring, & Hampstead is a terrible long way when one has too much to do. In evening Marjorie Roberts came to coffee to consult me about getting authors to lecture for the Red Cross Hospital Library; asked me to give one & I said I would. She urged me to employ a secretary & recommended Mrs Horter's school.

Sunday October 1st
Wrote 18 letters, mostly replies to fan-mails about *T. of Y*.

Monday October 2nd
Mrs Haden-Guest to lunch to discuss publicity for the Anti-war movement. John went to tea with Tony Gillett. Dined in evening with Mrs

Spencer; very agreeable; usual conversation about success of *T. of Y.*, but felt tired & ill, rather like gastritis.

Tuesday October 3rd
Another visit to *Sunday Chron.* office with photographs & things; trying bec. I still felt like gastritis & knew I looked ghastly. In evening went with Henrietta Leslie to the P.E.N. dinner at the Hotel Splendide, with H. G. Wells giving his Presidential address & a general meeting being held after. Sat at the high table between William Kean Seymour & Ellis Roberts; only person there not a member of the Committee. Much flattered; met Noel Streatfeild & Dr Dorothy Wrench, now married, Frank Hardie, the young Indian poet Chakravarty just over from Bengal, & many others. Philippa & W. G. Hole there, very anxious to claim relationship. Much flattery, felt better. Wore pale blue dress from Marshall's.

Wednesday October 4th   Hastings
Went down to Hastings to spend day with Storm Jameson attending the Labour Conference; Winifred meanwhile agreed to interview secretaries from Mrs Horter's and engaged one, Rosemarie Moore. At S.J.'s hotel met the Horrabins; Mrs H. had written me a charming letter about *T. of Y.* No v. interesting meetings—only one on Colonial affairs which I attended; in entrance of hall met Creech Jones & Miss Davy who was at Hardelot & introduced me to him; he wanted to talk about *T. of Y.* Met Monica there & we all had tea together; also Lilo Lihke, S.J.'s refugee. After tea S.J. and I had long delicious walk along the front for about 2 miles & talked. Later she came with me to the station; had dinner on train.

Thursday October 5th   London
Took chair at an evening meeting of Women's International League at which Miss Kate Courtney spoke on the Disarmament Conference, on the 4th floor of the Y.W.C.A. in Gt Russell Street. Meeting very full, though age & respectability of female audience (of members only) rather depressing. Miss Courtney made fine speech but later said to me: "They would not have come in such numbers as this if you hadn't been in the chair."

Friday October 6th
Went to interview Mr Cecil King at *Daily Mirror* office re doing them some articles; wore blue & white check & got on splendidly; talked to him most of the morning. Agreed to do series on upbringing of babies—about twelve, one a week; 800 words at 8d for each [word].

A "fan-mail", Mrs S. Maclagan from Kilburn, came to tea with small boy; had been a teacher but boy plain & badly-behaved, as children nearly always are when their mothers have given up their chosen work to try to look after them.

Saturday October 7th
W. & I spent delicious afternoon at Woking with Dame Ethel Smyth, whom W. had known before *Time & Tide*, but who had been enthralled by *T. of Y.* & wanted to meet me; had written several delightful letters about it both to W. & me. We sat in the garden & talked except when actually having tea (large loaf on table, slab of butter, pot of marmalade in grocer's pot; nothing else). Lady Betty Balfour, who had also liked *T. of Y.*, came to tea, & Dame Ethel said Virginia Woolf, who is her great friend, had been enthusiastic about it too. After tea walked round golf-links. Everyone excessively charming to me.

Monday October 9th
8.30 evening, called on Miss Raynham-Smith to get information about *Daily Mirror* articles. Very anxious to give it & get publicity for Babies' Club. Talked about *T. of Y.* Very pleasant.

Tuesday October 10th
John & Shirley to Babies' Club. Went to Wanstead P.N.E.U. branch to lecture on "Modern Ideals of Work & Play". Crowded drawing-room; pleasant tea afterwards. Usual talk about book & crowd of people trying to meet me.
   T. of Y. pub. in U.S.A.; cable from Latham saying 11,000 already sold.

Wednesday October 11th
Met Krishna Menon to discuss doing a book on "Marriage" for his series but mentally decided I hadn't time. At 6.15 called by invitation on Mrs C. S. Peel who had written to thank me for my review of her *Life's Enchanted Cup* & also to congratulate me on *T. of Y.* She gave me a glass of sherry & we talked agreeably for about an hour—also her husband & daughter for part of the time. Smart-looking oldish woman in black dress & hat, with kind manner & benevolent face.

Thursday October 12th
Visited Marie Scott-James at her nursing home at 30 Porchester Terrace —then went on to cocktail party at Curtis Brown's. *T. of Y.* much under discussion. Met Rose Macaulay, Dorothy Sayers, Doreen Wallace & Vernon Bartlett amongst others; V.B. looked very tired & heavy-eyed from effort to do in a hurry for Gollancz his book on Nazi Germany. Raymond Everitt of New York Curtis Brown there; arranged to see me later about doing articles & possibly a lecture tour in U.S.A.

Friday October 13th
Lunched Charlotte Haldane, who said *T. of Y.* made her feel she knew me very well. Everitt came to tea & we discussed my work in America.
   After supper made 10 mins speech at Kingsway Hall, on position of

literature under Fascism, for Relief for Victims of German Fascism Committee; other speakers Prof. Levy, Maxton, Lancelot Hogben, Isobel Brown. My own speech not v. successful; I can't accept the "hate Germany" anti-Fascism of the pure Communist. Last speaker, a young anti-Fascist, ended up with "Long live the fight against Fascism", which hardly seems a sensible invocation [for] someone who is presumably fighting Fascism because he wants to end it.

Saturday October 14th
Went (by invitation) to reunion meeting of 24 General at Overseas Club; sat with Coxon—now Mrs Jones, with three boys—and one or two others whose faces but not names I remembered; also Sister Wilson who seemed thrilled about *T. of Y*. At distance saw Norah Ashford & Dorothy Black-well (now Austin).

Tuesday October 17th
Young "fan-mail" girl to tea—daughter of Swiss minister, aged 16, who rang up & wanted to meet me. Spoke Six Pt Gp annual dinner, guest of honour; Helena Normanton there & suddenly very agreeable. Brought home in taxi by Geraldine Lennox.

Wednesday October 18th   Bolton
Went to Bolton; given hospitality in very comfortable house by Mrs Frank Taylor, J.P., who used to know Mr Catlin at Llandudno & showed me an old photograph of him when young. Studied German events all way up in train.

Thursday October 19th
Spoke Bolton Luncheon Club (Women Citizens' Association); not a great success; too political for them. On current events & the situation caused by Germany leaving the League.
    Went on to Huddersfield by tiresome cross-country journey; met there by Miss Mary Sykes, the solicitor whom I met before with Phyllis. So agreeable; felt so free after Mrs Frank Taylor! She & her nice mother put me up in their charming house above the town.

Friday October 20th   Huddersfield
Spoke Huddersfield Luncheon Club in same long-shaped café where I heard Phyllis speak a year ago. Room *crowded*, far more than then; they said it was a record attendance. Very good and friendly chairwoman. I gave same speech as at Bolton & it was a roaring success; the day was a delegates' day & several people from other towns, notably York, asked me to go & speak there. Taken to late afternoon train by Miss Sykes.

Saturday October 21st   London
Had tea with Mrs Ellinger & Maurice at their flat off the Edgware Rd, in consequence of her letter about *T. of Y*. She looked exactly the same, in carefully lighted drawing-room, as at Buxton in 1915; looked a young forty tho' she must be about 58. Maurice has grown very fat & middle-aged looking; earns a living of a sort by work at a wireless business, while Mrs E. teaches English to young foreign officials at Embassies & their friends. Evidently they have lost most of their money through the War. Both flattered me a good deal.

Sunday October 22nd
Supper at H. J. Laski's. Much talk about Germany & potential war situation, Laski favouring notion of General Strike.

Monday October 23rd
Dined Stanley Robinsons in Upper Phillimore Gardens. Thanked very warmly by Mrs S.R. in her bedroom after dinner for writing *T. of Y*. Her father Sir Victor Horsley & both her brothers died in War. Afterwards made speech about need for Babies' Club movement at annual meeting of Chelsea Babies' Club in large house opposite. Dr Eric Pritchard in chair. Room very crowded.

Tuesday October 24th
Sir Charles Trevelyan, who had written to say he had admired *T. of Y*. and would like to meet me, came to tea. We had it alone in my study and talked literature & politics.

Friday October 27th
Dr Fagan came to lunch & discussed Mosley movement with G.

Saturday October 28th
Tea with the Delisle Burns in Golders Green (D.B. had written praising *T. of Y*.). Agreeable house; largish party but no one interesting.

Sunday October 29th   Glasgow
Went up to Glasgow to give one of the celebrated Trinity Church lectures arranged by the theatrical minister the Rev. H. S. McClelland who read *T. of Y*. with great enthusiasm & wrote me melodramatic letter about it. Met and given hospitality by his friend & parish factotum Miss Winifred McLean who is an unoccupied wealthy spinster with large house left her by parents, magnificent car etc. She had a v. bad cold. Found supper waiting there when I got in (very late owing to train losing an hour or so). Greeted with enthusiasm by Mr McClelland who said he was "proud to know me" & altogether behaved more like an actor than a clergyman. Talked after supper about the various writers he had entertained (described by him as

"those great ones") including Rebecca West & Louis Golding, who demanded payment of his fee in guineas not pounds (wonder if he got 20 gns as I am or more? I suspect more, knowing Louis). Spent sumptuous night in magenta-coloured bedroom more like a large hotel sitting room, after going upstairs much later than I liked following the 8-hour journey.

Monday October 30th
In morning taken round in Miss McLean's car to see Glasgow; rehearsed brief portion of my speech first in Athenaeum Theatre, then saw main streets & slums, espec. one tall tenement house in the Brigate (? Bridge-gate) district near Clydeside docks. Steep spiral staircase coated with dirt; no glass in staircase windows; numerous children of Irish & Polish inhabitants might easily have slipped on worn steps & fallen out of any one of six or seven storeys. In afternoon drove along beside the Clyde to Loch Lomond, gorgeous in bright autumn day with brilliant burnt-sienna tints. Had tea at hotel beside Loch.

Got back in time for dinner, looked despairingly over lecture notes, felt v. tired after so much talking & travelling in trains & cars, tried to revive myself by cocktail but it proved a mistake, as half-way through the lecture its effect evaporated, I felt bored with myself & the lecture, & knew that for the last 20 mins. I was completely out of touch with the large audience. The Rev. Vera Findlay—youngish woman with fresh complexion, married to one Mr Kennard & going to have a baby—proposed vote of thanks; she had also been at dinner. In anteroom afterwards had coffee & sandwiches & changed hurriedly into train clothes. At door of theatre was stopped by several young men for my autograph; also asked by a representative of the Rationalist Press if I would lecture for them next year, which made me hope that that evening's lecture (on "Marriage & the Modern State") had perhaps not been quite such a ghastly fiasco as it seemed to me. Mr McClelland took me back to train & I tumbled thankfully into sleeper shared with three young women—one of whom, a teacher going back to Birmingham, recognised me from Press photographs & was full of curiosity & interest. Slept tolerably well for a train.

Tuesday October 31st   London
Lunched with Eric Gillett at 65 Earl's Court Square; met Clifford Bax & Ralph Straus; very agreeable. Later attended a meeting of the Anti-War Council at some office in Doughty Street where were also Beverley Nichols, Storm Jameson, Kingsley Martin. We were all somewhat anti-Council owing to the rigidity of Communist tenets. Dorothy Woodman spoke of the way S.J. and I had indirectly contributed to the cause of peace by *No Time Like the Present* and *Testament of Youth*. Beverley smiled at me agreeably despite my references to him in *T. of Y.*

Wednesday November 1st   Oxford

Went to Oxford to take part in O.U.W.D.S. full-dress debate at the Randolph. Invited (with effusiveness) to stay with Miss Darbishire, who said she had read *T. of Y.* with interest. (? Would this warm welcome have been offered if it hadn't been a success?) Felt that, despite its direct & indirect criticism of Somerville, I'd come full circle since days of *The Dark Tide* and been reinstated to favour. Met by President & Secretary of debating society at station; taken to Miss Darbishire's house, was welcomed & given visitor's room. She had wanted me to dine at Somerville & I had wished I could have—it would have been such a triumph to appear at the "High" as her guest—but I had promised the girls I would dine with them at the Randolph so had to do so. They were shy however & it was a bit dull. Marjorie Bowen (also invited to debate) joined us at coffee. She had dined with the Lindsays at Balliol. Found her taller, older, plainer, commoner but somehow much more good-natured & approachable than I had expected.

Room at Randolph packed with both men & women, including Miss Lorimer, though there were few Somervillians as I gather they still prefer their own debates to those of O.U.W.D.S. It would have been fuller still had not the "Free Speech" protest meeting at Ruskin been happening the same night. The girls spoke very dully—and I, seconding the motion that "This Age Has No Place For Romance", gained from the ineptitude of the proposer; think also my speech, which was loudly clapped, went down better than Marjorie Bowen's later. Finished evening with long talk in her room with Miss Darbishire & Miss Farnell, tho' now remember only that she said she didn't think ex-elementary school girls had the stamina for college life—and obviously disliked having them at Oxford. Also we contrasted my generation of students with the present one—though to whose advantage I cannot recall.

Thursday November 2nd

Hurried breakfast of orange juice & cereals with Miss Darbishire, who was going up to town; before leaving she bade me agreeable farewell & mentioned *T. of Y.* again. Then had long talk with Miss Lorimer, who seemed to have been genuinely moved by *T. of Y.* and said it expressed what a generation of women wanted to say. I explained what a pandemonium a best-seller caused in one's life; she thought however that it must be rather a pleasing pandemonium, & I should certainly be ungrateful not to agree. Finished up the morning by having coffee with the President (Honor Balfour) & Secretary of O.U.W.D.S. at the Pentagon Club (Women's Union) & saw over it; wished it had been there in our days of "cutting" dinner to work at the Camera. Then caught tea train home. It was a lovely day with a radiant afternoon sky, and as I watched the beginnings of the sunset I thought how queer it was that because of *T. of Y.* Oxford should thus have welcomed & reinstated me, and felt strangely thrilled to the verge of tears. Feeling further accentuated by long & very complimentary passages about myself and my "sensitiveness and charm" in the *Oxford Mail*.

1934

Friday September 14th   American Lecture Tour
Hair washed, face massaged, eyebrows plucked and hands manicured at
Marshall's in morning. Finished packing. Went to see Father at Collingham Gdns; he insisted he would never see me again and then presented
me with a silver book-mark & envelope-opener with magnifying-glass
attached (which he had actually been to Harrods during the afternoon to
buy), a charming bee brooch for Shirley & a bunch of Gloire de Dijon
roses. This effort on my behalf and the affectionate greeting on the
book-mark made me feel very mournful. Feeling continued all evening &
especially after dinner, when I went up at least four times to look at the
children asleep and wondered how I would endure being without them for
three months. Shirley as usual half woke up & put her arms round my neck.
Very hot evening. Went to bed late; had vague nightmares on & off for
most of the night and slept very little, espec. as G. was packing till 3 a.m.

Saturday September 15th   Berengaria
9 a.m., left Waterloo with G. for *Berengaria*. John, Shirley, Mother, John
Brophy, Miss Moore, Amy & Burnett at station to see us off; Winifred
(elegant lace blouse, hat with small veil) came with us to S'ampton. Wore
black coat with grey fox collar, black dress with grey & red spotted bar,
black Tyrolean hat with black & red feather. Mr Russell of Cunard Co.
spoke to me on platform; also two or three photographers snapped me
(carrying Father's Gloire de Dijon roses & some scarlet carnations given
me by G.) but most of them rushed forward right to front of train. Lord
Astor & Lord Lothian were going by boat, so they may have been after
them.
     Lovely warm morning; no wind. John & Shirley a little pale from
excitement, & Shirley burst out crying when startled by whistle from an
engine, but John Brophy put her on his shoulder to console her and neither
seemed extra perturbed by our departure. Shirley however kept urging me
to be back by John's birthday and demanded assurance from Winifred that
"Auntie isn't going to America too".
     Train went off at last; felt tearful, thought of leaving the children, &
Father struggling out of Collingham Gardens to buy me roses, Shirley's
brooch, & book-marker magnifying-glass, and wondered why in God's
name I had ever agreed to do the tour. Looked out of window of Pullman
coupé and felt wretched. Sun came out & country looked lovely. Soft
contours of Hampshire fields seemed so much more pleasing than anything
likely to be encountered in U.S.A.
     Seemed to reach S'ampton very quickly; embarkation pleasant and

easy; cabin C343 absolutely palatial—larger than W.'s room at home, two beds, two arm-chairs, dressing table, two wardrobes, bed-tables, trunk room, and superb bath-room with white tiles, washing-basin, toilet and shower. Two portholes in cabin, one in bathroom. It all seemed a very odd result of *Testament of Youth*. Dining-saloon next door to cabin; got pleasant table for two next to a pillar. Explored boat with W., visited lounge, library, palm court, sun & promenade decks. Irresistible comparison with my previous visit to U.S. as humble second-class passenger. Size & magnificence of everything seemed unbelievable. After gong had sounded for visitors to depart & W. had gone, we met Anthony West on stairs; he had been seeing off someone called Mrs Jardine White. Had turned into the typical American student complete with accent, and was (or pretended to be) entirely ignorant of whereabouts of Henry & Rebecca.

Boat did not start for ages after visitors had gone; finally left about 12.15. W. went to end of landing stage & stood against pillar; being taller than most of crowd she was very conspicuous in black, & beige-pink shadow-lace blouse; she used her bag-mirror as a glass to catch the sun which made her conspicuous until the boat turned to go down Southampton Water. Was reminded by the beautiful day & the many boats (*Doric, Balmoral Castle, Ascania* etc.) of going down the Solent in the September sunshine to join the *Britannic* eighteen years ago—then an obscure V.A.D., now a best-seller going to lecture in America but feeling very much as I did then. As we stood at end of promenade deck, G. waving his hat and I a red handkerchief, Harold Nicolson (whom we had seen joining the boat-train at Waterloo with Lord Rothermere's nephew to see him off) came and stood beside us to take a photograph. Don't know whether he knows us or not.

After W. was no longer visible we unpacked a little & then had lunch. Found letter from Storm Jameson in cabin. Superb & bewildering menu, containing all the things I adore but now dare not tackle; why is one always confronted with a chance of magnificent meals when one is not in a condition to partake? Lord Lothian seated himself not far from us but saw no sign of Lord Astor, who probably has a private suite. After lunch wrote postcards, got E. M. Delafield's *Provincial Lady in America* out of the Library (where the steward greeted my name with a start of recognition—I saw from his list that the library had a copy of *T. of Y.*) and attended a boat drill. Tea in the rather gloomy lounge which although the orchestra was playing gave a general impression of stuffiness and pink plush; saw Mrs Wintringham who is on board.

Soon after tea ran into Cherbourg; watched tugs in & then used interval of quiet to finish unpacking. Sea still smooth; air warm & misty. Had excellent but too large dinner, unwisely completed by a gin-and-ginger in the smoking room. Harold Nicolson (reading and obviously reviewing *Aristotle's Conception of Soul* by E. E. Spicer) again came & sat near us. Saw dancing on in ballroom, & in spite of fatigue G. & I did two dances before going to bed. Tolerable night though as usual on boats could not sleep soundly until daylight began.

Sunday September 16th
Fresh windy morning; rougher sea. Breakfasted on melon, haddock, honey & toast. Sat on deck in morning writing diary. Squall came on; it began to rain & got rougher. Lay on bed in afternoon & had tea down there. Struggled in to dinner, but felt mouldy & went to bed directly after. Took Sedibol & made up some arrears of sleep by sleeping soundly all night.

Monday September 17th
Woke up to find bright sun but high seas running. Day gradually became greyer & sea rougher. Sat on deck in morning but it was a mistake as boat was pitching so much that I felt almost too sea-sick to get through lunch & had a very brief one. Lay on bed again all afternoon. After tea weather appreciably improved; sea calmer, wind less fierce, fewer whitecaps. Got myself changed & went into Carnival dinner dance. Managed to eat caviare, sole, turkey & desert & danced a little afterwards. Ship's weather report for day: "Moderate gale; very rough sea"! Another good night.

Tuesday September 18th
Lovely fresh day; sea comparatively calm; hot sun; ship steady. Realised for first time why some people think voyages enjoyable. Victor Cazalet M.P. spoke to me when we were both handing in our passports at the Passengers' Office; said he was going over for 3 weeks to visit various towns but not to lecture. Spent morning walking round deck, exercising on various pieces of gymnastic apparatus & reading Sir John Marriott's *Modern England* on deck in sunshine. Harold Nicolson sat on chair next to me & passed me several times on deck but has never spoken. G. conversed with Lord Lothian for an hour last night after I had gone to bed. Our table waiter says Lord Astor is not on board but the curly-haired man we saw so much photographed at Waterloo is the Irish fisherman who played the chief part in *Man of Aran* film; he is travelling "tourist" but the producer is First Class & sits at next table to us in dining-room. Mrs Wintringham also exercising in gymnasium this morning. I really enjoyed superb meals for first time since going on board.

Later, lovely day turned to fog; fog-horn started sounding when we were at dinner & went on all night, for 16 hours altogether. Smooth sea, heavy humid air. Danced a little after dinner & went to bed v. late. Fog oppressive.

Wednesday September 19th
Fog-horn still sounding when we got up. At 11.0 Chief Steward at my request arranged for me to be taken over kitchen & hospital arrangements of the ship. G. came too, & two females & their husbands joined us.

Inspection reminded me more than anything of being taken over commissariat dept at Barts by the former Colonel of the 1st London General.

Lunched with Captain Cazalet & Harold Nicolson at their table in the lower dining-room. Liked Harold Nicolson very much & had not expected to; thought he would be "snooty" like V. Sackville-West, but he seemed straight-forward, kindly, without conceit, & very anxious to be helpful as soon as he heard about my tour & Colston Leigh—who was his & V.S.W.'s agent. I liked the way he always spoke about V.S.W., for whom he obviously has great affection; also of their two boys, both of whom have been to Eton, one is there now & one at Balliol. He seemed to think one couldn't do better than Eton unless one definitely went in for a "crank" school. At luncheon we talked of Mosley first (Nicolson knows him well & has done so from the time when Mosley was eighteen & had been thrashed at Sandhurst; later after he crashed in the War & was invalided H.N. found him work running round the Foreign Office). He said Lady Cynthia was "a stupid woman" intellectually but very loyal & charming, & that her death really did fill Mosley with grief & remorse. Said Mosley failure was due to various psychological weaknesses—impatience, instability etc.

We then spoke of lecture tours, tête à tête, while Cazalet, Gordon, & Lord Lothian, who had joined us, talked in a separate group. Nicolson said Colston Leigh was an awful man with an insufferable manner, but that he was honest & had an agreeable female assistant; H.N. also spoke very warmly & favourably of the Everitts of Curtis Brown's. Retailed various rows he & V.S.W. had with Colston Leigh—1) bec. V.S.W. lectured for 50 mins instead of an hour at Springfield, Mass., & the audience demanded part of the money back; 2) bec. H.N. put a lady in Toledo (who wd talk while he was trying to listen to Roosevelt broadcasting) into what he himself called a "cruel" article in *Vanity Fair* about Women's Clubs, & she was furious & said she would never have a Colston Leigh lecturer again; 3) bec. he wouldn't go and talk for money at a private dinner in Washington owing to his Embassy connections (though I gather that he subsequently attended the dinner & took the cheque without giving the talk!); 4) bec. he and V.S.W. wouldn't do anything so purely commercial as giving talks at bookshops (which E. M. Delafield did a good deal of, I gather from *The Provincial Lady in America*).

I rather got the impression a) that H.N. and V.S.W. hadn't done sufficient rough-&-tumble lecturing in England before going to America (he seemed genuinely surprised to hear about the Yorkshire Women's Luncheon Clubs, or that the experience I had of giving 9 lectures in one week last March was even possible); b) that they were too aristocratic and "society" for most of the company they had to keep (perhaps I being fundamentally provincial shall object to it less); c) that they hadn't —perhaps this applies only to her—taken quite enough trouble over preparing their stuff (I have heard this from other quarters). He appears to have realised this and urged me earnestly 1) to talk above rather than below their heads & generally give the impression that I have prepared the lecture with a great deal of trouble; 2) to assume knowledge on part of audience of any classic or modern novel one might quote—not to say "Some of you may have read . . ." but "You remember that in *The Waves*" (or whatever it is); 3) always to write very grateful bread-and-butter letter to hostesses.

After lunch we went up on deck & talked again chiefly about Eton and education, but also H.N. related the fiasco of Joad's lecture tour (he likes Joad very much). Apparently when Joad arrived in N.Y. he took such an acute dislike to it while driving from docks to his hotel that he 'phoned Colston Leigh he was returning at once by the boat on wh. he came. Colston Leigh took it quite calmly but came along at once to see Joad & kept him quietly in conversation on the situation until the hour for rejoining the boat had passed; then said that as he couldn't get another boat for 5 days he might just as well give the lectures booked for those days. Joad agreed, & gave them & a few more but did depart with most of the tour unfulfilled. It all sounded very temperamental.

Thursday September 20th
Another beautiful day. Packed & wrote letters. In evening was loveliest sunset I ever saw on Atlantic—smouldering sky with huge black mast of *Berengaria* quietly dipped against the flame as we sailed straight towards it. Sea like shot taffeta, flame and opalescent blue. In distance heavy bank of purple cloud so deep as to seem almost black looked like fast-approaching land. Sat up till nearly 3 a.m. in conversation first with Lord Lothian & then with the producer Flaherty who did the film *Man of Aran*. Woke up at 6.30 a.m. after short night to see light of small island and find boat running into Quarantine.

Friday September 21st   New York
Terrific day in N.Y.; did not get interviewed by reporters on way up river bec. I preferred to see wonderful outline of New York emerge through haze than to stay stuffily in cabin. Met by Bretts on dock; sweltering heat; took about two hours to find things owing to packed boat; went to Bretts' apartment next door to Macmillan office; dictated replies to about 12 letters, including one from "Scholastic" wanting my opinion in 100 words about how to prevent war; met Mr Latham & various members of Macmillan staff. Latish lunch, having had nothing since early breakfast; after lunch signed letters; felt terrifically hot & had sense of boat going up & down still but had no time to rest.

At 4.0 taken by Brett & Blanton the Sales Manager to see Colston Leigh—pale, rather oily-looking Jew, an astute variety of Leigh Groves, with splendid office on 37th floor & very pretty assistant named Theodosia Grey. Discussed tour; 34 lectures in 25 cities wh. Leigh proposes to raise to 40; it all sounded so appalling that I wondered not whether I should break down but when. Brett and Blanton wrangled with Leigh about me like dogs over a bone; Macmillan's and I naturally wanting to visit bookshops; Leigh maintaining that the organisations "which have purchased Miss Brittain" would object to my going to bookshops unless I allowed them to entertain me more than I might want. Eventually we compromised on bookshops in large cities only.

Left Leigh's office & tried to get thin frock in dept store just closing; could not find right frock so had to compromise on blouse; changed for dinner after resting on bed for brief ten minutes; taken to see the play *Dodsworth* based on Sinclair Lewis's novel; good play but I was hardly in state to appreciate it; finished up with iced orange juice at Hotel Brevoort. All this time had never been able to unpack; far too tired when we got home towards 1 a.m.; went to bed in midst of chaos & slept in sweltering heat.

Saturday September 22nd   Fairfield

Hurriedly repacked and opened banking account (which came to me in shape of girl clerk at Macmillan office; arranged like everything else with courtesy & efficiency) by 10.30. Macmillan's big front window on Fifth Avenue filled with my books yesterday to greet me; *T. of Y.* in red cover very impressive *en masse*.

At 10.30 left in car for Bretts' "shack" in country; very hot; Connecticut lanes rather like Gloucestershire; Long Island Sound 5 miles away; "shack" long low bungalow, very comfortable, carried out in green & yellow. Late luncheon; at 4.0 a man & girl who wanted to meet me dropped in; at 5.0 we went to a tea-party at the Richard Bretts' in my honour where everyone talked of *T. of Y.* Dinner party of eight here in my honour; one of the guests Stuart Chase; wore mauve frock; party lasted until about 12.30. About two hours before, I was ready to go to sleep & so was George Brett, who had bad cold.

Sunday September 23rd

Got up late; luncheon party arranged in my honour at the old Bretts' family mansion; having packed in so much hurry had nothing to wear but blouse & skirt. Various distinguished people there whom I had never heard of, including John Taylor Arms, an etcher, who sat beside me & was very agreeable. Sat on right of old Mr Brett, whom I like very much tho' I don't greatly care for his wife. After the luncheon, thank God, had a longish walk; then discussed Phyllis with George Brett, whom I find attractive. After supper went through all my contracts with him & we drafted out suggestions for Colston Leigh.

Monday September 24th

Bretts both went to N.Y. & I was left here in peace all day to write accumulation of letters & go for walks in the luscious lanes with their rich tangle of wild flowers & huge swallow-tail butterflies. Talked more lecture business with George after dinner. My poems were published here on Sept. 4th & have just gone into second edition. George said I ought to be able to serialise my next book, perhaps for $10,000. Conveyed to me that *A Modern Tragedy* did *not* succeed as they hoped; they advertised it heavily & lost money on it. Also Phyllis's lecture tour was a "flop" as Feakins never really believed in her; she only got about 14 lectures spread over vast distances in about 3 months, & was on the Bretts' hands about 6 weeks!

Tuesday September 25th
In morning went into Bridgeport with Isabel Brett; bought cotton frock, two pairs French knickers & 2 little cotton frocks for Shirley—much *chic*er than those obtainable at home. Hung about waiting to hear if I was to speak at the N.Y. Youth Convention, wh. was mooted; heard by 'phone from George Brett that I wasn't as person for whom I was to substitute had turned up after all. Article however arranged for me to do for Mrs Brown Meloney of *Herald-Tribune*; 100 dollars offered. Long walk in lovely but swampy woods with Isabel Brett after tea. George brought me copies of the 8th edition of *T. of Y.* & my poems, beautifully produced, from N.Y. Talked more lecture business; then motored out to Long Island Sound with intention of going out to Sound in Bretts' motor cutter under full moon; perfect night; lights visible from Long Island 18 miles away. Motor attachment on cutter wouldn't work so we had to stay in harbour; I saw over cutter & then we motored back to hear crickets in grass & trees, like chorus of miniature quacking ducks, crying "Katy did! Katy did! Katy *didn't*."

1935

Sunday May 5th   London
Jubilee Sunday. King's Road, Chelsea, one vast patriotic shriek like the rest of London; Cinema & Town Hall fronted with red geraniums & white daisies; red, white & blue bunting. All the flags sold out of Woolworth's.

Desire of John for flags of other countries & the vain search for them. "Does it matter if I put up a Greek flag?" "No—I don't think so—Princess Marina was Greek, wasn't she?" "I know, but p'raps I'd better not." Later, to Winifred: "Auntie, what are you wearing—a blue dress, & your lipstick's red & you're carrying a white book—Jubilee, I suppose!"

W. & I went to Hyde Park at 3.30 for the Labour May Day Demonstration. Platforms numbered only six; speakers included Herbert Morrison, Mrs Barton of the Co-op., & various near-celebrities of the movement; no real "lights". Park not at all full. No hostility & no enthusiasm; no sense of being keyed-up for a great purpose. Usual British crowd which is the despair of Continental countries—good-humoured, tolerant, long-suffering, nobody out at elbows yet nobody smart; air of patience & respectability rather than rebellion or daring. Usual facility for turning everything into a picnic (as for a long time it did the War) & refusing to be tragic about it. Probably many of the poorest people who actually would vote Labour if an election came preferred to putter amiably around looking at the decorations to supporting their own movement. In the Park itself many little family parties were seated on the dry ground (a hot lovely day) munching buns & apples & giving bottles to the baby. The police in their own compound were also eating buns without their helmets & sitting on the grass while one or two attended to all the horses. Showed no readiness to go if called & no expectation of being required. Such a sight would be impossible in N.Y., where the police would appear efficient but would actually be useless. No wonder we are the despair of active, energetic, violent America! What the crowd did reveal was exactly why we have had 25 years of an unshaken King & Queen during precisely the period when the monarchs of half the countries in the world have been flying for their lives. We are far too tolerant, agreeable, good-humoured, and accommodating to do anything so drastic & cruel as to overthrow a throne.

Later went on to Edwardes Square; had tea & supper with Mother & sat listening to the broadcast of the service "In Preparation for his Majesty the King's Silver Jubilee" & thinking over the events of 25 years.

Monday May 6th   Silver Jubilee Day
Took children to see procession, William Kean Seymour got us seats at 71A Queen Victoria Street Branch of the Midland Bank. Superb refreshments & loud speaker provided. Had to get there (in car hired for morning)

by 9 a.m.; actually arrived about 8.30. Had to keep children good till 12.30 as we could only see the return procession (after service at St Paul's) but both were angelic. Shirley sat by Winifred & drew. John wanted to watch everything & never leave the window; got so excited that each time I didn't see anything as quickly as he did he scratched my face, pulled my hair or pawed my white collar with his grubby little hands. He was just like an electric wire. Both children very sensible & good about refreshments; didn't eat much but mostly drank lemonade. Bank officials very charming & courteous. Could have had alcoholic drinks in profusion if I had wanted them.

Decorations in Queen V. Street looped right across from building to building. Excellent seats inside bank; ground-floor windows, stand inside raised just so that we could see over heads of crowd, which was only abt 4 deep in that narrow street, so we were almost on the top of the procession. Watched khaki troops—City of London Regt (? Rifle Brigade—Gordon's Regt) lining streets. Officers in new plus-fours.

John & I went through the programme. "And in that carriage," I said, "is the Earl of Athlone—he's the Governor of S. Africa." "Oh—is he *black*?" "No—you see the people who *govern* S. Africa are white." "Why are they? I thought the people were black." "Well, most of them are, but . . ." I endeavour to explain the Imperialist problem in S. Africa, not very successfully.

Day gets hot; luckily we are on shady side of street. Several people faint during morning—mostly men, including two soldiers—and one carried off by St John Ambulance men. Loud speakers broadcast service. Shirley wants to be "read to" while it is going on but is restrained. Procession comes at last—just King & Queen going at swift trot. Queen in silver cloak & pink turban—bowing & doing her duty as usual, conscientiously but not graciously. King looked tired & rather bored but not yet so much as 70. In rest of procession noticed only Countess of Athlone, "beautiful & gracious", Duchess of York, the York children, Prince of Wales almost eclipsed by large busby. Marina & Princess Royal eclipsed by hats, Elizabeth & Margaret Rose both waving with complete sang-froid. After they had passed, persons to get most cheers were Duke of Connaught & —of all people—Ramsay MacDonald. Looked rather isolated in carriage in court dress with two plain daughters (Ishbel & Sheila), one in blue & other in brown, but looked mildly pleased by cheers.

We got away quite early & were back by 2 p.m. London *lovely*, like an old etching, with all the flags in the brilliant sunshine. Rest of day as hot as July. Children played all afternoon at soldiers & Kings & Queens; demanded war stories & wanted to see my war medals. I'm afraid these official ceremonies with all their troops don't exactly help to educate the youngest generation in the way of peace!

Wednesday May 8th
John back to school. Bp of Bathurst to-day. Usual Australian face & voice, now so familiar. V. different from an English bishop; much more informed, very advanced in ideas; no pomp. Told me that at the Lambeth Conference, 1930, "the sacrament of love" was mentioned for the first time—i.e., recognition that the physical act had value in itself apart from its procreative significance. Talked about theme of "Hon. Estate"; much interested; gave me several ideas.

Thursday May 9th
Shirley back to school. Dr Nelson v. pleased with her. Afternoon—visits to Marshall's, Miss Mayo, American Consul to get my power of attorney witnessed to Stern & Reuben, N.Y., for income tax purposes.

Friday May 10th–Monday May 13th
Chiefly struggles with "Hon. Estate"—v. depressed over it with intermittent sense of its importance. Beginning of Chap. 2 very recalcitrant. Friday, nice letter from George.

Tuesday May 14th
Morning—went to City Temple to hear Angus Watson give address as new Chairman of Congregational Union. Place packed with dowdy but earnest men & women—some quite young. Gave idea that all religious vitality is to-day outside C. of E. Mr Watson read his address—at first difficult to hear but gradually became more audible—on stewardship, relations between business & morality; related remark of friend: "The devil took me up into a high mountain & showed me ten per cent"; commented on infrequency with which shareholders in a company inquire into conditions under wh. their money is made. Ended with reflection he made to me at Newcastle—moral progress of the universe; we are just on the threshold of revolution in morality; to-day ideals of men of fifty whom he knew in his boyhood are attained which then seemed impossible.
    Evening—Women's Freedom League Jubilee dinner at First Avenue Hotel; over 350 there. Did not have to speak; sat next to Kate Courtney. W. said a few words. Chief speakers Mrs Pethick-Lawrence (in chair), Mrs Corbett Ashby (reporting Istanbul Congress), Lady Astor, Nina Boyle. Lady Astor threw new light on evening in July 1922 (described on p. 596 of *T. of Y.*) when the Criminal Law Amendment Bill had passed its Third Reading & W. & I from the Gallery watched the debate which lasted till 2.30 a.m. Lady Astor was still the only woman in the House then, & said that several of the M.P. opponents of the Bill tried to get her to leave; said "You're making it impossible for us" (presumably to discuss the Bill in the "roars of laughter" spirit wh. wd have made it easier for them to oppose it). Lady Astor announced her determination to see the Bill through. "If you all take off your clothes & come into the House as God made you, I still

shan't budge," she said. She mentioned in her speech that though it seemed unfair that an American woman & not one of the English pioneers shd be the first woman M.P. to enter the House, she had certain "disagreeable qualities" wh. were very necessary in the first woman Member. Doubtless she was right—American women have a freedom from inferiority complex, & hence a quality of being unsnubbable, very seldom found in English women with their long tradition of repression & inferiority.

Nina Boyle made good racy speech; Winifred, Elizabeth Scott, Caroline Haslett, Betty Archdale and others also spoke on behalf of various interests in wh. women have made good. General feeling of satisfaction at progress made in 25 years. Telegram to this effect sent to King, who replied during evening. When meeting broke up talked to Lady Astor, Mr & Mrs Pethick Lawrence, Shukla Lal—also a few words with Mrs Littlejohn from Australia.

Wednesday May 15th
Wrote book all day. Cocktail party at Mrs Spencer's—met Mr Longman of Longmans, Green, again. Talked to Mrs Davies who brought me home.

Friday May 17th
Got up speech for Rationalist Press Dinner. Took John for walk to see Lot's Power Station. A few flags round World's End section of Chelsea counterbalanced by words scrolled on several walls: "FLAGS TO-DAY—GAS MASKS TO-MORROW."

Saturday May 18th
Book most of day—got on fast but badly.

Spoke in evening at Rationalist Press Dinner—first woman in its 30 years' history to propose toast of its prosperity. Wore mauve-and-blue patterned evening dress w' mauve coat. Lord Snell chairman—sat next him—rather dull & dry. Said he thought rumour of Oct. Gen. Election was correct; that Govt prestige had benefited from Silver Jubilee and they wd have forced the election earlier had it not been for the India Bill. Big & very sumptuous dinner—larger crowd than usual; perhaps 250 altogether. Prof. Levy, J. B. S. Haldane & Joad also there. Speech not one of my best efforts, though tolerable. Took Mother as guest & her conversation made concentration on speech rather difficult. Dancing afterwards—stayed till 11.45. Danced several dances—one with Eckersley who also spoke, but most with unknown young men who asked me to dance after stating that they were shy of approaching a "celebrity". Two of these had each bet the other that they wd ask me & one remarked: "The celebrities at these functions are mostly men so you can't get to know them but when it's a girl you can ask her to dance"!!

Got back to find letter from Gordon enclosing a purple poppy (faded from red?) picked on the Parthenon. Within past 48 hrs have had fan-mail letters about *T. of Y.* (nearly two years after publication) from 1) a married woman would-be writer from Belfast, 2) a Jewish girl from San Francisco, 3) a 24-year-old ex-Jesuit from Grahamstown, S. Africa, 4) an 18-year-old girl just about to take scholarship exam for L.M.H. from a village near Uttoxeter, 5) a Swedish married woman teacher of mathematics and chemistry with five children who writes most charmingly from Gøteborg.

Sunday May 19th
Lawrence of Arabia dead. What irony!—to go all through the War & liberate an enormous territory, and then be killed by an errand-boy on a bicycle!

Monday May 20th
Lunched Forum Club with Mrs Littlejohn (Australia) to meet Mrs Lyons (wife of P.M.). W.H. also there—& Mrs Pethick-Lawrence, Dame Rachel Crowdy, Maude Royden, Mrs Corbett Ashby, etc. I sat beside Mrs Lyons.

Tuesday May 21st
Julia Varley's farewell party (T.U.C.) at a doctor's house near Regent's Park. Met Ellen Wilkinson, who said, "Tell G. to look out for Sunderland."

Wednesday May 22nd
Dinner Storm Jameson.

Saturday May 25th
Gordon returned from Russia via Constantinople & Rome. Met him at Dover; went up in Pullman. He & I & W. dined at the Ivy.

Wednesday May 29th
Maude Royden had reception at Crosby Hall. Made short speech thanking Mrs Hamid Ali, the chief guest. Talked to Mr & Mrs Pethick-Lawrence; also Mrs Littlejohn again.

Friday May 31st
Have written 35,000 words of "Honourable Estate" since beginning of the month.

Saturday June 1st
Heard that Shakespeares & Gollanczes would come to Brett party.

Monday June 3rd
Lady Astor party—guests to Royal Institn Conference. Went with G.

Thursday June 6th
Sent basket of flame-coloured ramblers to Chesterfield Court. G., W. & I met the Bretts at Paddington, 8.30 p.m. (from Plymouth, S.S. *President Harding*).

Tuesday June 11th
Bretts dined here—saw John & Shirley. Took them to theatre—*1066 & All That*—had box. Went on to coffee etc. at the Savoy. George & I had violent altercation about my next book.

Wednesday June 12th
Called for Bretts at Chesterfield Court—took them to see presentation of *Femina–Vie Heureuse* prize to Elizabeth Jenkins by E. M. Forster. Talked to Charles Evans & Eliz. Sprigge there. Saw Phyllis there; & she & W. & Isabel & I went on to tea at Hyde Park Hotel. Then took Isabel to get books at Bumpus's while Phyllis told W. about her new book & Mr Latham.

Thursday June 13th
Luncheon at Savoy with Mr & Mrs Hugh Eayrs, Lovat Dickson, Mr Kyllmann of Constable, & W.H.—Mr Eayrs very keen on sound of my new book—congratulated me on doing a service by writing history of social change in this age.
　　George Brett picked me up after lunch & we talked business. "In my Father's house are many mansions."

Friday June 14th
Tried all day without much success to write article for *Woman's Journal* on "Is There a Second Chance in Marriage?"

Saturday June 15th
The seventeenth anniversary of Edward's death on the Asiago Plateau.
　　Lunched Beatrice Kean Seymour at the Ivy to discuss our joint article for *Good Housekeeping* on "What is the Main Business of Life?"—but we talked chiefly about a possible libel action being brought against B.K.S. by Sir Leo Chiozza Money, who thinks he recognises himself in *Interlude for Sally*.

Sunday June 16th
Winifred away. Tea Edwardes Square; Gordon came.

Monday June 17th
Finished *Woman's Journal* article.
　　Margaret Whitehead, her son & my cousin Hugh Brittain (Uncle William's son, who asked if he might) came to dinner. Intolerably boring. Whitehead stepson just gone to Cambridge; clever but insufferable.

Tuesday June 18th

Called for Bretts just before 12.30; took them to the Foyle Luncheon on
T. E. Lawrence (Chairman Lord Lloyd & afterwards Sir Herbert Samuel;
speakers Capt. Liddell Hart—a little dull—and Sir Ronald Storrs—good
& very moving in spite of "typical English gentleman" appearance).
George recognised & spoke to R. D. Blumenfeld. Wore my grey & coral
suit & Isabel & George both liked it. Isabel had to leave early, Gordon
stopped to talk to Mrs A. L. Lawrence, so George drove me back to Chelsea
in a taxi. Had only just got back when Gordon 'phoned me to come to
Piccadilly and help him choose yellow orchids for Isabel. Had tea with him
at Stewart's & then face done by Elizabeth Arden.

10 p.m. Our party at the Savoy, jointly with Archie & Mrs Macdonell.
A. rather tiresome about it; answered *no* letters, but all went well. Storm
Jameson came in to Glebe Place for coffee first & we went on to Savoy
together. My guests, with Gordon & Winifred & the Bretts, were Rebecca
& Henry, Storm Jameson, Mrs Shakespeare (Geoffrey could not come,
being kept at the House with a Bill), Victor & Mrs Gollancz, Dr Edgar
Obermer (with W.). Archie had Mr & Mrs Alec Waugh, Mr & Mrs Dan
Macmillan & several others I never grasped the names of, also A. D.
Peters.

Felt nervous before the whole thing started but it all went well and I
really enjoyed it. Victor Gollancz very agreeable & seemed pleased when I
said I had written 40,000 words; said in front of George that he didn't mind
if the book was 200,000 words. Another time George said to me: "I hardly
feel I can wait to read it. When will it be ready? How long have I to wait?"
At the Savoy I danced with him three times & he had one with practically
every other woman guest. Wore my blue and mauve chiffon with two
mauve orchids that George sent me beforehand. Party ended about 2 a.m.
& we took the Bretts home in our taxi. Archie somewhat drunk &
aggressive about arrangements discussed beforehand, but it didn't spoil
anything as I enjoyed it all too much to care.

Wednesday June 19th

3–3.30 p.m. "When that which is perfect is come, that which is in part shall
be done away."

Thursday June 20th

Tea-time—called for the Bretts at Chesterfield Court & took them on to
Time & Tide cocktail party. Very agreeable; wore black dress & cape &
George's orchids. *T. & T.* staff all fell for George; Lorna Lewis remarked:
"What a *young* man to be head of such a big firm!" Gordon talked to Odette
Keun, who wanted him to kiss her; & thought that it was because I was
there that he wouldn't & told him that I ought to have an affair! Talked to
Lady Rhondda, Lorna Lewis, Doris Stanhope, Mrs Stanley Unwin (who

seemed to click with George) & two American *T. of Y.* fans from Crosby Hall.

Friday June 21st
Wrote *Good Housekeeping* article nearly all day; after tea went with W. to get her birthday presents at Peter Jones.

Saturday June 22nd
Suddenly very hot after appalling weather. Did no work. Spent most of day shopping & in garden with children. Too full of grief to be of any use to anyone. Gordon at Digswell Park; W. went out to Hampton Court with James Anderson.

Sunday June 23rd
Winifred's 37th birthday. Very hot. G. all day at Labour Candidates' Conference. Tea at Edwardes Square. Began article for Stephen King-Hall's *Mine* on "Do You Want to Be a Writer?"

Monday June 24th
Gordon went up to Sunderland for Selection Conference. Saw him off at Paddington.
    Afternoon—called with W. at Chesterfield Court to take the Bretts to have tea at the House with the Shakespeares, & found only Isabel & Mr John Maxwell there—George couldn't come as he had to go into the country to see a film which H. G. Wells is making. Mr J. Maxwell took us to House & was hard to shake off. Tea on Terrace with Shakespeares, Cazalets, Robert Bernays M.P., Mary Shakespeare & a Chicago friend. Told them all about G. & Sunderland. Showed Isabel parts of the House & Westminster Bridge. Took her back to flat & found George there in dressing gown returned from seeing H. G. Wells.

Tuesday June 25th
Early morning—wire from Gordon to say he had been selected candidate at Sunderland. Terrific thunderstorm from lunch-time till tea-time— G.P.B. called here in midst of it to talk business; later took me up to Storm Jameson with whom I had dinner.
    "And the sun shall rise on these dangerous, these tide-torn waters."

Wednesday June 26th
G. back from Sunderland by night train; very happy at being chosen. Took Isabel Brett to lunch at Boulestin's (saw Harold Nicolson, Mrs Belloc Lowndes, Lovat Dickson, Mr Eayrs there), & then to Wyndham's Theatre to see Diana Wynyard in *Sweet Aloes*. Joined George & Winifred for tea at Ritz; Gordon came in later. George & Isabel went off to a cocktail party at

Lovat Dickson's & we three walked home. Wore red dress & black cape, as yesterday.

Thursday June 27th
Our 10th wedding anniversary; "tin wedding" as they call it in America. Got cable in morning from Ruth Gage Colby & Izetta Robb in Minneapolis. Gordon gave me a beautiful necklace of Egyptian scarabs and I gave him a gold glass cigarette box, and Winifred gave us both a superb blue-green and gold lustre bowl. Spent most of day getting ready for the party in the evening—a hundred guests & no "dead wood". Of course it was the one day in the week when it was too cold to use the garden, but I never saw the house look so nice. We decorated it with lilies & gladioli and at tea-time George Brett sent me some superb pink roses and yellow & blue irises—an absolute sheaf of both.

The party began at 9.0 (wore gold & blue dress), and the Bretts came very punctually—bringing an additional wedding gift of an enormous silver cigarette box inscribed in George's handwriting. The lavishness & the thought of the trouble it must have taken rather overwhelmed me and I felt I behaved tactlessly later in asking him to spare me yet another half-hour to talk about my book. Party very crowded—so many distinguished guests I hardly knew how to get the introductions accomplished, but managed to introduce George to Mr & Mrs Norman Collins, John Brophy, Ellen Wilkinson & Cicely Hamilton. The Bretts went early, being tired, and crowds more people came after they had gone, including the Gollanczes, Pritts, J. B. S. Haldanes & Eve Kirk with a group of friends. I began to get very tired myself and to feel the evening would never end—especially as Naomi Jacob & Odette Keun stayed till 2 a.m., and we had to clear up after that. Got to bed with dawn breaking and sun streaming into windows.

Friday June 28th
Felt very flat & tired all day. George rang up at tea-time to say their boat-train left Waterloo 8.30 a.m. Thursday. In evening went to reception of National Peace Conference—dull, everybody very elderly, but met Arthur Henderson—but ended up at a party in Bloomsbury which included Vyvyan & Mrs Adams, Norman & Mrs Bentwich, Joad & his daughter, & Gordon. Interesting conversation though I was too tired to take much part in it. Vyvyan Adams told me he was only 35—the only other member of my "generation" elected as a Vice-President of the National Peace Council. I said: "But I'm more than that; I was a nurse all through the War." He replied: "It would be rather difficult to conceal that *now*, wouldn't it?" Again did not get to bed till after 1.0. Very depressed all day; felt I had spoilt everything by behaving badly at my party. Everyone congratulating Gordon on Sunderland.

Saturday June 29th
Good for nothing all day; re-read novel to try to get back into atmosphere of writing it. Isabel telephoned in morning to say their boat left at midnight next Thursday, not midday. Hendon Air Pageant (to which they went); planes zooming over garden all afternoon. Gordon went to Oxford for day; walked with him on Embankment after supper.

Long talk over supper with Winifred, who told me for first time that when she was ill in 1932, Halls Dally only gave her two years to live unless the sclerosis could be arrested—as it has been, by Padutin. She told me how after she went back to Buckinghamshire, knowing this, she went for a walk on a very cold day there & was breaking the ice over the troughs with her stick for the new-born lambs to drink, when suddenly, as she was feeling she had lost everything, the words "having nothing yet possessing all things" came into her mind, and suddenly all desire to have things for herself fell away & had never really come back. She said it was the supreme experience of her life so far. I begged her to write her biography and make its crucial point this experience, as I feel it would give courage to many who have lost everything themselves. I told her then how I had always felt that she and Gordon (like T. E. Lawrence in a sense) had both laid hold of a world in which desire & worldly achievement counted for nothing because they had hold of the reality beyond life—philosophic truth or whatever one chooses to call it—whereas I am trivial, because I am so much in thrall to my strong earthly desires—for love, for fame, for beauty, for success & also position. I also tried to explain my experience with G.P.B. as an attempt to get at the larger morality by flouting the lesser—the larger morality which means the fuller understanding of humanity's needs and problems, and the end of all fear of being a prig, as my "fan-mails" have so often made me feel since *Testament of Youth*.

W. laid aside desire for love (since Harry had gone), children (since she was told she must never have any), fame (since she thought she would not live to achieve it). How trivial am I, who have these things yet never get from them all the happiness I should! If it is true that Winifred, having nothing (or at any rate so little) of what she wanted, possesses all things, it is sometimes equally true that I, possessing all things, so often seem really to possess nothing.

Monday July 1st
19th anniversary of Battle of the Somme. Still very many In Memoriam notices. Cocktail party at Doris Leslie's after tea (Talbot Square, W. 2). Wore grey & coral suit. Very hot. The Bretts there and Phyllis. George came up & shook hands in the usual cordial, impersonal manner; then got Eliz. Craig to move so that he could sit by me. He said nothing special; we talked of Kate O'Brien. Isabel on my other side said they were going on to Hurlingham. Doris Leslie, Phyllis and I seem likely to publish books at same time. I told G. this & teased him about next year's list. They went

early & I talked to Phyllis about her *T. & T.* letter over "Yellow Peril in Publishing" and the snub administered. We left together; she seemed ill at ease but actually walked with me as far as Paddington Underground.

Tuesday July 2nd

Bretts' cocktail party at Claridge's. Called there for them at 5.0; George & Lovat Dickson just leaving for Claridge's; Phyllis & a Mrs Thomas also with Isabel. Wore harebell blue with magenta tie & blue & magenta hat. Party very crowded; I seemed to know all the authors there—about one hundred, including Wells, N. Royde-Smith, Clare, Helen Ashton, Archie, & numerous publishers & agents. Worked hard introducing the less known. Decided I disliked Wells for his abominable manners; he refused one Martini because not dry enough, knocked the second all over Isabel & a waiter, & merely remarked before getting a third: "I suppose I'm going to get my cocktail sometime." Bretts very cordial with him but obviously being patient.

When nearly everyone had departed George came up to me & said he supposed I was going & he was sorry he couldn't manage another half-hour for tea but would 'phone me up in the morning. It may have meant a great deal or absolutely nothing but I felt snubbed & miserable. Talked to Winifred in flat after supper; such a queer feeling about it. Long talk with G. & W. about marriage, etc.; cried.

Wednesday July 3rd

Morning—long 'phone call with G.P.B. about business. I suggested someone else might "vet" the American Army Hospital chapter but he seemed surprised about this & said "Sure, I'll do it—of course I want to." Felt too tired to go to Heinemann Garden Party so had Faith Moulson to supper instead. Gordon in Sunderland.

Thursday July 4th

Lunched with Stanley Robinsons to meet Diana Wynyard. Did not "click" though she admired *T. of Y.*; thought her stiff and rather complacent.

After dinner the Bretts left Waterloo for the *Manhattan*, at 8.0; W. & I went to see them off. (Had previously sent Isabel a garden basket of pink carnations & lilies-of-the-valley to boat.) Wore my black dress, hat & cloak, & a button-hole of pink carnations & roses. Determined to seem gay & did. George reintroduced me to Henry Seidel Canby, editor of the American *Saturday Review*, who was also sailing; then G. & I talked together a little & I thanked him for what he had done over Curtis Brown. He said he was dead tired & would never come to England for a month again —either a shorter time or longer. Just as the train left he shook hands, said "I'll be writing you," and looked hard at me from the window as it began to move—but his expression really told me nothing, so I am left (as in the War) with a doubt which may never be resolved. Went home with W. &

had a cocktail & conversation at the Sloane Court Hotel. Then slowly to bed, wondering whether it was an end or not.

Friday July 5th
To dentist in morning; side-tooth out. Straight home to entertain Mrs Manning (G.'s co-candidate at Sunderland) to lunch; G. back in morning. Kept myself going by two liqueur brandies, but felt dizzy & miserable all day and went to bed early.

Saturday July 6th
Woke feeling rather better. Worked all day at final sections of Chapter 2 of "Hon. Estate".

Monday July 8th
North & Margaret Whitehead came to stay. Took them to *Noah* (John Gielgud) on Tuesday night. Left on Thursday. Very "Cambridge" but more tolerable than I expected.

Friday July 12th
Cocktail parties at Mitchisons & Glicksteins.

Monday July 15th
Lunched with David Higham at Café Royal. Discussed arrangements for "Hon. Estate" when written.

Wednesday July 17th
John's concert at school. He played quite well tho' I have heard him better at home.

Thursday July 18th
Went to Bethnal Green Rd in morning & acquired descriptive details for "Hon. Estate". Party in evening at the Raymonds (Chatto & Windus); lovely house in Hamilton Terrace but party dull because introductions inadequate.

Friday July 19th
Visited Putney Hill & Common & Putney Vale Cemetery to get details for book.

Monday July 22nd
Dined with David Lows at Golders Green. Party consisted of J. B. Priestley, A. J. Cummings, Robert & Sylvia Lynd & ourselves. Very pleasant.

Wednesday July 24th

G. & I lunched with Angus Watson (plus wife & daughter) at the Connaught Hotel. He seemed attracted by G. and disposed to advise the Sunderland Liberals to back him. After lunch went up to Staffordshire to stay at Ash Hall, Bucknall, Stoke-on-Trent (once the family residence of my Meigh ancestors & now a golf hotel) to get details for book.

Thursday July 25th   Staffordshire

Spent morning walking around Ash Hall & writing descriptive notes of it. Afternoon, hired car & went to look at Newcastle-under-Lyme, the Cloughs, & Keele churchyard where my great-grandparents, grand-parents, and two aunts are buried. Had seen Cloughs from road before but never Keele. Found Cloughs, where Father was brought up by his grandparents, in hands of housebreakers & already a ruin; garden a tangle of brambles & thistles. Keele churchyard peaceful & beautiful but the granite stone over the Brittain vault as laconic and unimaginative as the Brittains themselves. No flowers, or room for them to grow—just grey granite with bold laconic inscriptions, encircled by iron railing, giving impression that those dead are indeed forgotten. Great contrast to roman-tic inscriptions to Sneyd family inside the church. On way back to Ash Hall stopped at Bucknall church; went inside & around churchyard. In vestry found photograph of old church with inscription recording democratic victory of church authorities over Meighs and their claim to ownership of pew. Just outside church was ornate family vault of Meigh family, now falling into decay with growing moss & broken cobwebbed railings because the Meighs never attended Bucknall church again after the pew dispute. I thought: "What a veritable 'End of the House of Alard' "—the Meigh ancestral home turned into a golf hotel, the Brittain ancestral home falling into decay and being destroyed by the housebreakers; "ribbon development" causing small villas to invade what was once the country exclusiveness of both; the Brittains in Keele churchyard unvisited and uncared for; the Meigh vault covered with moss and cobweb. It all represents the death of a tradition and though I have probably done more than any member of the family to fight & destroy that tradition the evidence of its departure fills me with regret and sadness.

Friday July 26th

Went in to Hanley with G. and interviewed Mr Arthur Hollins (ex-M.P. for Hanley & Secretary of Potters' Union) on political & economic development of the Potteries since 1900. He gave me much valuable material. In the afternoon we took the bus to Leek and then to Buxton, and I saw for the first time since 1915 the moorland road over which Father used to drive daily before and at the beginning of the War; & the complacent little health resort which seemed to me to be less changed than any spot that I have revisited in recent years. Found the War Memorial in the midst of the Public Garden slope above the Pump Room—a cenotaph with bronze nameplates and a bronze angel with spread wings. Found Edward's name on it but without his M.C.—a fault I must rectify—and the names of many Buxton boys with whom I used to dance & play tennis.

Saturday July 27th   London
Shirley's fifth birthday. Returned from Staffordshire in time to give her her presents & for her party. Father & Mother gave her a tricycle. Just after I got in Father rang up & wanted to know all about Staffordshire; I suggested that he come round & hear about it & also see Shirley & her tricycle. I didn't think he would as he hasn't felt well enough to come to Chelsea for months; but in half an hour he & Mother came round, & we told him all about the changes in Staffordshire & Gordon gave him a stone he had brought from the demolition of the Cloughs. I thought he might be depressed by this but he didn't seem so. He saw Shirley and the tricycle & seemed much pleased by John's good marks, which I showed him, & his being top of his form at school; he said: "The lad's a credit to his father!" and I laughed & said "But what about his mother?"

In evening I wrote up Staffordshire notes & unpacked. W. away at Malvern Festival with Lady Rhondda, staying at same hotel as the Bernard Shaws.

Sunday July 28th
Wrote up notes in morning; afternoon, took children as usual to Edwardes Square. Father showed me photograph of the Cloughs as it was when he lived there; seemed rather better than usual but said he was in too much pain to go into the Square garden, and for once Mother did not insist, so we all sat comfortably in the morning-room and I mended stockings. Then the children came back and we left. There was nothing unusual in the way Father said goodbye to us, and certainly nothing to suggest that we should never see him again.

Monday July 29th
Spoke at Peckham Rye for Mrs Adamson, Chairman of Labour Party. Other speaker Sir Stafford Cripps. R. Minturn Sidgwick, who was on holiday in England, insisted on coming down with me. Cripps left early. Mrs Adamson warned me again [about] probable demands for cash on part of Sunderland. Was very sad because her daughter-in-law has just drowned herself off liner coming home from Canada or U.S.A.

Wednesday July 31st   Wimereux
Took children & Fräulein over for holiday to Grand Hôtel des Anglais et des Bains, Wimereux. Edith de Coundouroff & Margaret went with us. Good crossing. Shirley a little troublesome but John superb—thrilled with everything. Insisted all the way across on standing in wind on very front of

steamer. Stood there for nearly an hour. Clear day; both sides of Channel easily visible. Pointed out spire of Boulogne Cathedral as it gradually became clearer; he saw it almost as soon as I did. Didn't want to move even when we were ordered to landing deck; kept saying: "I want to see us arrive at France. I want to see us land." Long wait at Customs but car met us & we eventually got to hotel in time for late lunch. Given very pleasant room on top floor. After dinner walked on front with Edith & Mgt.

Thursday August 1st
Worked most of day at novel in pleasant garden of hotel with nasturtium-fringed ornamental pool. After dinner lovely walk with E. & M. to Wimille & back by road to Ambleteuse. Lovely mellow hay-scented countryside. From shore just after dark could see lighthouses of Calais & Boulogne & also three lights of lighthouses on English coast. A cool evening. At night a large moth flew into my room & I could not get to sleep. Felt very cold & restless all night.

Friday August 2nd
Worked at novel most of day. In evening walked with Edith & Margaret to the military cemetery just below the French municipal cemetery. In the military cemetery the grave-stones are laid flat—not standing up as in most others. Lovely peaceful place at sunset—not true of war, for it suggested as usual that war is glorious and death rest and serenity.

Saturday August 3rd
Worked at novel in morning. Had had letter previously saying Heinemann had turned down Gordon's "Face of Revolution" & knew he would be depressed, so arranged to go into Boulogne & meet him by the evening boat he had planned to come by. As we were sitting at lunch John suddenly called out, "Look, there's Auntie!" and I turned to see Winifred in her tweed coat in the lounge of the hotel. As she wasn't coming till next Saturday and it was Gordon I was expecting I knew at once something dreadful had occurred & that she had come to tell me. I went out to her at once & said "Something's wrong." She said "Yes"—I said "Is it Gordon?" thinking he had been depressed about his book, but she answered "No, it's your Father"—and told me that Father was missing, having disappeared from Edwardes Square sometime during the night of Aug. 1st–2nd—the night I felt so cold and couldn't sleep.

She said that Mother went to call him with his early tea at 7.30 a.m. yesterday and found his bed empty & then the cook found the front door open. Mother then remembered that she had heard a noise in the night & looked at her watch and it was 3 a.m. At the time she thought it just a loud creak on the stairs or something in the Square, but when Father was missing realised that it might have been the big iron bolt of the front door dropping against the side. Winifred said he had gone without overcoat or hat but had taken 30/- in notes & some loose silver. They didn't tell me yesterday as all day they expected him to come back having tried to frighten Mother, or that the police would find him wandering somewhere, but by Saturday morning there seemed little hope he could be still alive, as in his invalid condition he would soon be noticed & the family traced. I thought at once of the river at Hammersmith Bridge as he had talked of it so often & actually went down there once this year & came back saying there were too many people about to throw himself in. At the time we thought it just an attempt to alarm us. W. said that as soon as Mother realised he was missing she telephoned the Bentley-Carrs & they came over from Woking by 9 a.m. Then she rang Winifred up at Glebe Place & W. got hold of Gordon, who was at Cambridge seeing Lloyd George, & G. came straight back & was at Edwardes Square. He & Arthur Carr had been to the Kensington Police Station & to Scotland Yard, and a description of Father had been sent to London police stations & South Coast towns (as we thought he might somehow have got down to Brighton) & also to various taxi-shelters. She had come to fetch me home by the evening boat.

I packed & she lay on my bed while I did so; I took everything as I somehow knew I shouldn't come back; I felt sure Father was in the river because I had felt so cold that night. Edith de C. agreed to take charge of the children & I was obliged to leave them behind with her & Fräulein; Glebe Place was closed & anyhow I didn't want them to come into so much trouble. W. & I had an early tea-supper & she began to feel very sick over it owing to the strain of the journey & not having eaten enough, after being unwell at Malvern. She looked so ill that I thought she would never be able to go back with me, but she was anxious to return & get hold of her injections. She did look rather better after eating something, so we went off in the taxi together. Shirley was at the door with Fräulein & E. & M. to say goodbye, but John ran off before I left, to play with two little girls in the hotel garden! They were both told I had to go because Grandad was ill—& were so used to his being ill that it didn't impress them. By the time we got to Boulogne Winifred was much better; the boat was practically empty through everyone going the other way for the Bank Holiday week-end, and W. sat with me on deck for about half an hour & then went to lie down below. I stayed above; there was a most lovely sunset and the lights of Folkestone just appearing looked very beautiful as we came in just about 9 p.m.

We were supposed to arrive in town at 11.0 but owing to the crowd of morning trains to Ostend being sent back to Victoria we were an hour late. Gordon met us & W. went to Glebe Place & we to Edwardes Square; it was about 12.20 when we got there & Mother was sitting up with a tray of sandwiches. Everyone very tired, depressed & cross; neither of them seemed to expect *me* to be tired & were upset because I was late. No further news of Father had come in. I felt too tired to get to bed, though I only unpacked a little, & suddenly found myself weeping unrestrainedly at the

Wedding group, 1925, *l. to r*: Edith Brittain, the Rev. George Catlin, Gordon
Catlin, Vera Brittain, Thomas Brittain, Winifred Holtby

Thomas Brittain, Vera's father

Edith Brittain, Vera's mother,
with John *c*.1930

Left: Gordon Catlin and Vera Brittain soon after their marriage, summer 1925

Below: John Catlin, an unidentified friend, Gordon Catlin, Vera Brittain, and Winifred Holtby holding Shir Catlin, in the garden of 19 Gl Place, summer 1930

right: Winifred Holtby, *c.*1930

below: John Catlin, Phyllis Bentley, Winifred Holtby, Shirley Catlin, Vera Brittain, in the garden of 19 Glebe Place, 9 July 1932

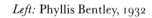
Left: Phyllis Bentley, 1932

Below: Gordon Catlin, Vera Brittain, Winifred Holtby, with E.M. Delafield, her son Lionel Dashwood and a friend, at Delafield's home near Cullompton, Devon, 30 July 1932

Vera and her two children, *c.*1934

Left: Vera Brittain, 1934

Below: Vera Brittain with John and Shirley Catlin on the beach at Sidmouth, August 1932

right: Winifred Holtby, from the painting by F. Howard Lewis commissioned by Vera Brittain and now Somerville College, Oxford

below: Vera Brittain in the United States, autumn 1937

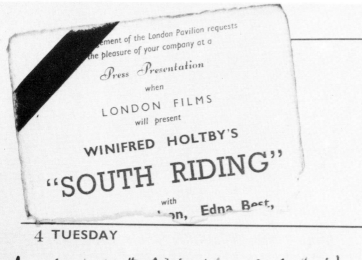

Left: Vera Brittain's torn admission-ticket the Press Presentatio of the film of *South Riding*, with her diary entry describing the occasion, 4 January 1938

Below: A P.P.U. Deputation to the Prime Minister, 1938 George Lansbury, Alfred Salter, Charles Raven, Laurence Housman, Vera Brittain, Stuart Morr

thought of Father in the river; realised how fond of him I still was in spite of all the neurasthenia & queerness of the past two years. Just couldn't bear to think of him going out into the chilly night without hat or overcoat, so feeble & frail, so much all alone when he was used to being accompanied everywhere. Couldn't think how any taxi-driver who picked him up could fail to realise he was ill, but suppose they often pick up people who are drunk in the middle of the night & only care to make what they can out of them.

Sunday August 4th
The 21st anniversary of the War. I had intended to spend part of it at the English church in Boulogne where I attended the service for the third anniversary on Aug. 4th, 1917. What an anniversary for us! No news of Father all day & we put in time somehow. Winifred had discovered from the river officials in Chelsea that the tide at Hammersmith was very full on the night of Aug. 1st–2nd—& if so he might have been carried out to sea & would never be found & we should never know what happened to him, but sometime in the day Mother suddenly said that she thought he might have gone not to Hammersmith but to Richmond, as he was so fond of Richmond & wanted to be buried there, & often used to take a bus & have tea there & walk along the towing path in the days that he was active. Towards evening I began to think we weren't doing enough, so we went to Kensington Police Station again but there was no news; and also got in touch with a private detective agency through Mr Cash the lawyer; but they advised us to use the police rather than themselves as they hadn't enough men to comb out the taxi-ranks. They also suggested that we get anyone of influence we knew to put pressure on Scotland Yard to get busier & I decided to do this in the morning.

Monday August 5th
Gordon left immediately after breakfast to put notice in "Missing" column of *Daily Mail*. Both Uncle Norman & Alfred Haigh, to whom letters had been sent, rang up early to know if there was any news of Father but I had to tell them there wasn't. Then I tried to get on the telephone everyone I could think of who might put pressure on Scotland Yard; tried Geoffrey Shakespeare, Percy Harris, Josiah Wedgwood, Lady Rhondda, Alfred Goodman, but as it was Bank Holiday everyone I tried was abroad or out of town or didn't answer. Just as I was sitting at Father's roll-top desk trying to think if there was anyone else I could find, the telephone rang again. It was the Kensington Police & they asked for "Mr Catlin". I said: "He's out; will you please tell me." The policeman at the other end seemed reluctant but I insisted & he then said: "I'm afraid I've got very disturbing news for you; a body corresponding to the description given of Mr Brittain was taken out of the river at Twickenham this morning." I knew then that Mother had been right & he had gone to Richmond, as Twickenham is on

the opposite bank. The man went on to tell me to go to the Twickenham Police Station & gave me the address.

I went upstairs to tell Mother, who was on the top floor, & just afterwards Gordon rang up to say he had put in the notice. I told him that Father had been found & asked him to come back as quickly as possible. Then I rang up the Twickenham police, & they told me that before going there we should go to Isleworth mortuary, where Father had been taken, to make formal identification. As soon as Gordon came back, we all went there in a taxi. We didn't want Mother to come, but she said she wouldn't stay in the house alone & insisted on coming; and talked & talked till we both felt nearly mad. We had some difficulty in finding the place, but at length we located it close to the West Middlesex hospital. We had to walk through Isleworth cemetery in terrific midday heat to get there, and the mortician took Gordon in to identify the body. Mother wanted to go too, but when G. came out again—looking greatly upset and saying that there was "no doubt whatever" that it was Father—he urged us emphatically not to do so. It came out afterwards at the inquest that owing to the heat and Father's age and ill-health, the body was very much decomposed; a police constable told me it might have been in the water a fortnight instead of three days. Gordon did describe it to me afterwards as "tremendously swollen, like an Epstein figure" and the face "black and red and swollen like the bruised face of a prize-fighter". The eyes were closed and no expression was perceptible, but there was no actual damage as from a fall or violence. The odour of corruption—one that I recall so clearly from tending the septic & dying bodies in the War—was of course intense.

Poor Father, I'm sure he never visualised this grim aftermath of suicide. He was always so fastidious about his clothes and had so strong a sense of propriety and of personal dignity, that these consequences of drowning himself seem not to fit him at all. I think he imagined that if he went as far as Richmond he would never be found, and that his body would remain at the bottom of the river. Mother said his mind had been running lately on one of his favourite songs, "The Diver", and how dreadful it must be at the bottom of the sea.

After the mortuary we drove on to Twickenham Police Station, where we were told that the Coroner's officer would call on us later in the day to give us instructions about the inquest. We went home, put the funeral arrangements in the hands of Harrods (who were there in spite of Bank Holiday), and I rang up Uncle Norman—who was terribly upset—and asked him to let the rest of the relatives know. In the afternoon, the Coroner's officer—a young policeman, but very considerately dressed in plain clothes—came to see us & gave G. instructions [on] what to say at the inquest. He was anxious at first to see if he couldn't establish the whole thing as an accident, but the weight of evidence—Father's state of health, his frequent threats of suicide, his actual attempt to gas himself in April 1934, & the [information] about his state of melancholia & neurasthenia given by Dr Yates to the police when he first disappeared—made a suicide verdict inevitable. The only thing, then, was to reduce the evidence to the necessary minimum.

The police seemed very indifferent and lethargic as long as Father was merely missing, but once he was found, their courtesy and consideration —and that of the cemetery officials at Richmond, Harrods assistants, and the people at the inquest—was beyond praise. The only people from whom we had neither kindness nor consideration were the older generation of Brittain relatives (except Uncle Norman, who was genuinely distressed but too ill to come up). Friends & acquaintances were splendid as usual. We got most kind & moving letters from Alfred Goodman & the Richard-sons. Edith de Coundouroff kept writing me reassuring letters about the children & Winifred went out to Wimereux to look after them a week after fetching me home.

Tuesday August 6th
Very hot again. Coroner's officer rang up in morning to say the inquest could be to-morrow morning, so we arranged for the funeral to happen immediately afterwards in the afternoon. Arranged with Harrods & went out to Richmond cemetery, where Father had wished to be buried and *not* by his relatives at Keele, to choose a plot for the grave. Some difficulties bec. the cemetery is supposed to be reserved for parishioners & a prohibi-tive fee is charged to those outside, but they allowed Gordon to purchase & charged only double fees since G. had been brought up in Kew. Lovely high cemetery; we chose a place just opposite a yew tree.

Afternoon—Aunt Florence & Ruby Williams came to tea, and Mr Dodd afterwards to explain family business. Later Coroner's officer came once more to make final arrangements for inquest.

Wednesday August 7th
Left Mother to go to Bank, and Gordon, Mr Dodd & I took a taxi to Isleworth to an Inn called "The London Apprentice" where the inquest was held. I thought it would be the back room of an ordinary public house and how Father would have hated the idea of it—but instead we turned off the main road at Isleworth and drove on until suddenly we stopped at a little cluster of country-looking houses and I found that we were on a most lovely reach of the river, which wound away into the distance with the willows on either side reflected in the dark green water. (I learnt later that it was only a short distance from the place where Father was found —Railshead Ferry—and that everything must have looked much as this did that early morning. It still puzzles me that he went so far upstream where the river is narrow; perhaps that seemed less frightening than where it is very wide & deep.) On one side of the river the houses with a grey-towered church above them looked exactly like a country village; on

the other were thick woods and meadows with the tall spire of Richmond Church standing out against the sky in the distance. "The London Apprentice" was a simple, pleasant-looking white building like a village inn and the inquest was held in its upper-floor billiard-room at the top of some twisting iron steps. The floor was covered with oars for the boats moored just below the inn against the river bank. (The Coroner's Officer told us that there are so few inquests in Isleworth that they just hire this room when required.)

When we arrived we found two reporters there and several policemen; later the police doctor appeared and a little under-sized boatman who turned out to be the ferryman at Railshead Ferry. The Coroner (Dr J. S. Crone, Deputy Coroner for Middlesex) was late, whereupon Mr Dodd waxed very indignant & said he represented the King & the King would never be late, so he ought to have been in time. But I didn't feel I really cared, about that or anything else, so I sat in the window & looked out at the river shining in the beautiful sun and the osiers dipping into the water, and thought & thought. I had been feeling that I should always hate the river henceforward, after loving it so much and liking to live near it, and hate having to see it; but its loveliness & peace that morning made me feel that instead I would try to think of it as a place that had brought Father the rest and release that he desired; not a place of horror but the solution of a problem that had grown intolerable; a place that at last enabled death to come to someone who had wanted to die and by a cruel fate, in spite of his age & his ailments, could not succeed in doing so naturally.

The Coroner at last arrived—an elderly man of benevolent appearance with a large grey moustache, looking like an estate agent or an undertaker —and we all stood up. Gordon was the first witness & replied briefly and well, giving evidence of identification, Father's state of health, his frequent threats to commit suicide and his one attempt to do so before. Then the boatman gave evidence of seeing the body floating in the river at 7.45 a.m. on Monday, and a police officer testified to helping him get it in and take it to the mortuary. The police doctor witnessed to having examined it—that it appeared to have been in the water several days; that there was the usual appearance of death by drowning & no mark of violence. (I kept thinking to myself "Drowned—drowned; whoever would have thought that Father would be drowned"; and the swift decomposition of the body seemed so dreadful until I realised that it was due to this that it had come to the surface so soon and we might well have had to wait a fortnight before hearing anything.)

When the doctor had done & there seemed to be no one else I said: "May I ask a question? Is there any evidence available as to how my Father got to the river?" But there was none at all; no taxi-driver had come forward, and as we know Father took about 37/- and only 17/- was found on him, I imagine that some man took a £1 to drive him to Richmond, which is only a 6/- fare, & either thought him drunk or disregarded his state of health

—and was afraid that he would either have the money taken from him or be blamed for not notifying somebody.

The Coroner then turned to us and said: "I suppose we all agree that this is a case of suicide?" and we nodded rather mournfully for we could do nothing else; and he then said: "I bring in a verdict of Suicide whilst temporarily of Unsound Mind, and I wish to tender my respectful sympathy to the relatives."

Curiously enough the inquest was held in G.'s old constituency and both the reporters obviously knew us both though my name was never mentioned throughout. He "squared" one reporter & on the way back called on the Editor of the *Chiswick Times*, whom he knew, & asked him to keep out the account—but one of the reporters though fulfilling their own promise must have passed it on to yet another paper which we didn't know about. The splurged headline with my name indicates what would probably have happened in the Press generally if we had not taken these precautions.

Just before lunch we looked at the flowers we had ordered from Hurley's—Ophelia roses for me, red for Gordon, red & white carnations for Mother, sweet-peas & scabious from the children, & a blue & mauve wreath from the Dodds. We put them all down in the maids' sitting room—Winifred had sent a lovely wreath from Harrogate, & there were flowers also from the Norman Brittains & from Barbara & Cicely. After lunch the funeral men with the hearse called for the flowers, & then the single carriage for Mother & Gordon & Mr Dodd & myself. We drove slowly, not wanting to be there too early for the three o'clock service, but we found the few people that were coming—Aunt Florence and Robin, Barbara & Hugh, Alfred Haigh—already there. Because of the intense heat & the sad condition of the drowned body the service had to be brief; we would have had him cremated but he often expressed himself strongly against the idea. I couldn't believe that the plain waxen oak coffin with its silver handles really contained the grim remains of Father who had been so elegant and fastidious in the days that I remember him best; and I was glad of the flowers covering the coffin; these at least were beautiful and seemed more like him.

The service was taken by a dark youngish priest with a beautiful voice; he stood before the coffin and said with intense and relevant earnestness the second part of the long Lesson: "Behold, I show you a mystery: We shall not all sleep but we shall all be changed, in a moment, in the twinkling of an eye, at the last trump, and the dead shall be raised, *incorruptible*, and we shall be changed. For this corruption must put on incorruption and this mortal must put on immortality."

Then the coffin was carried to the graveside & lowered after the first prayers and at the words "earth to earth, ashes to ashes, dust to dust", Mr Dodd picked up a handful of the dry red clay turned up by the grave-diggers and cast it upon the coffin as it descended. When the service was over I stood looking down at the coffin at the bottom of the deep grave with its silver plate just visible:

Thomas Arthur Brittain

Born April 6th, 1864

Died August 2nd, 1935

and thinking what a strange terrible end it was for that familiar figure [who] had always avoided enterprise and loved security. I had carried with me a tiny bunch of golden roses because he gave me a bunch of these when he said goodbye to me the day before I left for America, and I took them with me to my cabin on the boat. I threw the little posy down into the grave and it fell on the coffin just above where his head would be; and so I said goodbye.

Alfred Haigh & Mr Dodd came back with us to tea and after tea Mr Cash the lawyer came, and read the will in the morning room at Edwardes Square. I could hardly listen to the will with its chief bequest to Mother and its others to me (his jewellery & personal effects and a quarter of the estate) and to Gordon, Mr Dodd, Aunt Belle, etc., without reflecting how often he had visualised this moment, discussed it, prepared for it, talked about it to me so often and with such great interest all my life—how I and the children should be provided for, and so forth; and now at last the moment had come, on a summer's afternoon in the morning-room of a house he had lived in such a short time, looking out upon the beautiful paved garden with its bright antirrhinums and hollyhocks.

That evening I put away the only things I brought back from the inquest from the belongings found on Father—most of them had to be destroyed owing to water & decay—and I kept only his gold cuff-links and the Waterman fountain pen which still worked smoothly after four days in the river (what a grim advertisement for them, I thought, if they knew). I didn't tell Mother I had these things as they would only have given her what she calls "the horrors" and she gets these quite enough, and tells us about them, without any encouragement. I didn't want to take the 17/- found on him so told the police to give it to the local hospital.

August 8th–27th

Gordon became seriously ill with poisoning of the glands. Nursed him —first at Edwardes Square under great difficulties and disapproval—then sent for Amy & Burnett & brought him home where at least he had peace. Kept the children at Wimereux a week longer and Winifred and Hilda Reid went out to them.

Wednesday August 28th

Gordon getting better. Treatment all finished & himself up & sitting in the garden. Lunched with Bishop of Bathurst at St Francis Hotel. Met children & Winifred & Hilda at Victoria. All very brown & looking well.

Friday August 30th–Sunday September 1st

Lunched Edwardes Square & sorted out Father's clothes. Took away a good many for Gordon & the Bentley-Carrs had still more, including most of the suits. Winifred went to Yorkshire for week-end; apparently spent entire time discussing Peter's marriage with her mother; found it very tiring & came back exhausted.

Thursday September 5th

W. & I interviewed Society of Authors about agency business. Decided to leave Curtis Brown (except for myself in America) and go to Nancy Pearn's agency for articles, serials & films. W. very ill and tired; could hardly give her attention to interview & seemed scarcely able to walk back through Park. In evening heard Aunt Florence taken seriously ill & operated on for appendicitis at Chichester. Tried to ring up various people but could get no news.

Friday September 6th

10.30, took John to dentist to have two teeth out with gas for first time. Gordon went with me as I wanted to leave immediately afterwards to go to Chichester to see Aunt F. Helen Mayo took out the teeth very well but J. was very pathetic after the gas—eyes large & wild, hair ruffled; put out his hands to me for comfort. Strange effect of gas was to make him completely lose his "h"s; he kept saying "It 'urts! It's 'orrid! I 'ate it!"

As soon as he was properly round I left him with Gordon & caught train to Chichester; tedious journey but was able to travel most of the way on Pullman. Walked from station to hospital & was allowed to see Aunt Florence; she looked very old & ill but they said she was doing remarkably well for her age & the serious nature of the operation. She recognised me & was very pleased that I had gone to see her so promptly, but was still in a kind of painful dream after the anaesthetic. Sent her some red carnations from a flower-shop on my way back to town & went straight to Edwardes Square when I got back to tell Mother about her & to see John. Found that J. had gone to bed having felt very poorly after the gas & made the most of it! He had got Mother & Fräulein thoroughly alarmed but he had no temp. & I realised that a good deal of it was "playing up": left him sleeping peacefully after dinner & went home.

Saturday September 7th

Children came home again from their week's visit to Mother. W. not feeling at all well again—spent most of day in bed.

Monday September 9th

Lunched with Eric Gillett at the Ivy; he was very sympathetic & sorry about Father—said I'd obviously been much upset & ought to get away.

W. went to see Obermer this afternoon & he ordered her to bed for two or three days; thought some arsenical injection he had tried might have upset her circulatory balance.

Went with G. to a cocktail party at Jonathan Cape's to meet Sinclair Lewis & Dorothy Thompson—W. had been invited & asked if we could go too. Though she wasn't able to, we did—but found it chiefly a meeting for the Sinclair Lewises to give their views to reporters—in view of Lewis's novel *It Couldn't Happen in America* which Cape is about to publish. Didn't speak to Sinclair Lewis, who was surrounded the whole time with a solid phalanx of reporters, but had a brief talk with Dorothy Thompson. Impressive woman but very conscious of her own importance.

In evening Nancy Pearn came to supper to discuss the business I was transferring to her from Curtis Brown. W. had meant to see her too but was unable to get up. After Nancy had gone I found W. feeling much worse—very sick, which was most inconvenient for her in the top room, so about midnight I brought her down to mine & spent night—sleeping hardly at all—in Fräulein's un-made-up bed in Shirley's room so as to be near her.

Tuesday September 10th
In early morning found W. very sick & with violent headache—got down her hypodermic syringe etc. from the top room & helped her to give herself Impletol injection. Directly after breakfast got Dr Obermer on the 'phone & said I thought Winifred very ill & that someone more skilled & trained than myself should have charge of her. He promised to come round & see her in the afternoon & meanwhile to see G. & discuss her condition at 10.45.

G. agreed to come on & meet me at Helen Mayo's where I was taking John at 11.30 for his final small filling. Found him there when I arrived. J. was very good & much braver than last time—so while he looked at a magazine G. told me that Obermer had been very frank about W.'s condition—that owing to the process of renal sclerosis she must have been managing for the last 5 years or more with only about a quarter of each kidney; that when he saw her in the spring of 1932 he didn't think she could have more than two years; but as she had defeated his calculations she might go on doing so, & this new attack of illness might mean anything or nothing. Later when he came to Glebe Place in the afternoon he told us his policy had been to spare Winifred the sense of frustration—wh. wd depress her & be bad for her—& that was why he had said she could go to Liberia.

He went up to my room & saw W., & told her he wanted her to go into a special nursing home under his assistant Dr Bowde (a young German with Nazi views who is practising in England & is a specialist on kidney diseases) for a week of intensive treatment. She agreed; so I packed for her & helped her to get up, & took her to the home at 23 Devonshire Street (the Elizabeth Fulcher Home). She thought she would be sick in the taxi as she was when I took her to Courtfield Gardens in Nov. 1931, but she managed to avoid it & while I paid the taxi walked up to the nursing home door & rang the bell & walked in very bravely. She was wearing her black dress with blue pleated jabot, a black straw hat of the new "halo" style & her long black cloak. I was very worried about her but I never really thought that I should never see her dressed again or that she had left our home never to return.

They gave her a very nice room—large & quiet, looking out on to the new flats in Devonshire Place but with plenty of air & space—& she was pleased with it. I helped her to get into bed & unpacked for her—put her books near her on her bed table, did some red roses which I had given her in the morning to make my bedroom look cheerful for Obermer, & got her some muscat grapes from the grocer next door. Went home feeling very sad & depressed.

Wednesday September 11th
Had Victor Gollancz to lunch at the Ivy; found him remarkably co-operative since I had given up having an agent for my books; he made various suggestions by which I might serialise "Hon. Estate", & also gave up talking about May or June publication; suggested Aug. 28th as the date of pub. of *T. of Y.* and therefore lucky. I told him about Father; also about W.'s illness, my grief that such a valuable person should be thus handicapped & my fears that she might never get right again. Found him sympathetic & understanding. Said I'd like to read Mrs Swanwick's autobiography *I Have Been Young* & would try to review it for the *Sunday Times*. I also talked to him about Clare's early struggles & said I'd like to help her new book *Four Hedges* if I could.

Went on to see Winifred—she'd had a bad night & was still very sick & uncomfortable. Took her letters etc. and arranged for Miss Moore to come to the home & answer them for her to-morrow. Sat with her for an hour or so & had tea; then went on to dine with Storm Jameson; talked to her about Father's death & Gordon's illness & my fears for Winifred; and the general misery of this tragic summer. Said I wondered whether I [would] see every male friend die a violent death & take every female friend into a nursing home for *their* last days until in the end there'd be no one left to see me out of the world myself. She was kind & sympathetic as ever—one of the few people in my universe apart from Winifred who has a similar quality of understanding.

Thursday September 12th–Monday September 16th
G. & I gave up our project of going to Monte Carlo for our long-postponed holiday on Saturday because Winifred's condition made me feel too anxious. Each time I visited her she still had a bad headache—moved restlessly about the bed—screwed up her eyes—could keep nothing down, even fluids, & said that her beloved Impletol itself had failed her & she could get no sleep, though they tried one sort of injection after another till

there seemed to be bruises & sore places over the whole of her poor arms & body.

Discussed with Obermer sending for her Mother—to whom she had written cheerful letters saying she was only in for a week's treatment after a species of arsenical poisoning. Obermer was against Mrs Holtby coming —& even wanted us to go to Brighton—as he felt that the worst thing for W. wd be to have any idea that her state was really serious—felt that in such a complex and baffling case psychological factors were of the first importance.

On Sunday Dr Bowde still seemed optimistic but on Monday Dr Obermer really began to have misgivings—& reluctantly advised us to inform the Holtbys but not to tell Mrs H. of W.'s real condition for fear she would say anything to alarm her. We therefore rang up Cottingham—got Edith de Coundouroff as Mrs Holtby was away attending the funeral of their relative Dobson Peacock, & explained the true situation to her. Later in the evening she rang up to say she had told Mrs Holtby as much as Obermer had suggested & that both of them would arrive at King's X at 1.15 to-morrow.

Tuesday September 17th
Met Mrs Holtby & Edith at King's X after I'd been to see Winifred in the morning. I found her a little better, and managed to put over to her that Obermer wanted her to stay in the home another week. She seemed reconciled now to the idea of not going to Liberia—and said she had plenty of money for the home, as she could use George's advance of $500—which he had sent her from the Macmillan Co. in advance of her contract, to enable her to meet her Liberian expenses & on condition that she gave them her next two novels. I said I'd look after paying the home meanwhile.

Mrs Holtby & Edith had a cup of tea with us at King's X—situation very difficult—required much tact & management so I left it mostly to G., who manages her better than I do since she finds men on the whole more congenial than women. He finally persuaded her not to see W. or go to the home till she had seen Obermer that evening.

After dinner Edith de C. came in to tell us that they had both seen Obermer—that Mrs H. had liked him; that he had not gone into the serious details of W.'s illness but had told her he hoped to be able to pull her through—& finally agreed to let Mrs H. see W. to-morrow afternoon & said he would let her know about them coming beforehand.

Wednesday September 18th
Obermer rang up in the morning & asked me to take on the job of telling Winifred that her Mother was coming up, as he thought it would come more naturally from me than from him. So I went round to the home at once & after talking to her about other things for a little while said casually that her Mother had rung up & was coming to town to see her. I had to

make out that she was arriving that morning & probably was going back to
Yorkshire by the evening train. W. didn't seem alarmed about their
coming—though she was obviously tired & reluctant to make any effort, &
had told me previously that she didn't want to see Gordon or Mother again
till she felt better—but was only worried that the double journey might be
too tiring for her Mother.

They saw her that afternoon, & even before she went Mrs H. had
decided to go back to Cottingham by the evening train. Such optimism
seemed to me incredible—a combination of temperament & old age, I
suppose.

After they had seen Winifred we had tea with them at Stewart's in
Regent Street. Edith whom I met first said she thought W. looked very ill &
was greatly perturbed, but Mrs H. had been quite satisfied with her
appearance & general behaviour; I suppose poor W. made a great effort for
which she'll have to pay later. Mrs H. even remarked that "everything in
the garden was lovely"; said Edith & Margaret & Jessie would come to
town on Sat. & keep an eye on Winifred, & that as what W. was more
worried about than anything was our not having been away, we must
promise to go. We reluctantly consented to go to Brighton—the nearest
place within range—on Friday for a few days so as to give G. a change &
chance of recovery, but neither of us felt at all happy about going even so
far from W.

Thursday September 19th
Saw W. & told her that I would go to Brighton—but though she seemed
relieved I felt very miserable. She seemed to be suffering so much; said at
last that she was getting very tired of what she thought was the treatment &
its effects; hoped it wouldn't have to go on much longer & said the sleepless
nights seemed so long. She said "Of course if the treatment's making me
better I must put up with it. The one thing I want is to get better." I noticed
that her poor eyes were swollen—I feared with crying—& felt more
wretched & sad about having to go away so as not to alarm her, than I
could express even to myself. Sat with her about 2 hours & got her to have
some tea & a little bread & butter.

Friday September 20th
Went in to see Winifred and found that Lady Rhondda was back from the
Scillies and visiting her (she had sent a reply-paid telegram a day or two
ago asking for all symptoms etc. to be sent but a real explanation had not
been possible). I sent in a message to say I was there & would wait, but W.
sent back asking me to come, so I went in & sat on one arm of the arm-chair
& Lady R. on the other. Winifred was entirely herself—she looked &
seemed a little better but was probably making an effort for Lady R., as she
told me afterwards that the tea, etc., which I gave her so hopefully

yesterday had only made her sick in the end. She has really scarcely eaten or drunk anything since she came to the home 10 days ago. Lady R. & I sat there talking about nothing in particular for some time & I explained about G.'s illness & going to Brighton. Then she said she had to go, so I went with her along the passage to the lift & told her what the doctors really thought of Winifred, & Obermer saying she still had "a fifty-fifty chance", & our agreeing to go to Brighton so as not to alarm her & make her think she was too ill for us to go. At the lift Lady Rhondda, to my astonishment, suddenly turned & kissed me & said "Oh, Vera, I'm *so* sorry. It must be dreadful having to go away just now!" I didn't know how to prevent myself from crying or to prevent Winifred, to whom I went straight back, from seeing it, but evidently her eyes weren't very clear as she did not seem to notice much.

I stayed talking to her till lunch-time—amongst other things told her how the memory of George & last June had helped me to bear all the lugubrious conversations about sickness & death at Edwardes Square during the period of Father's suicide & Gordon's illness—and she said "Dear George, I'm sure he'd be glad." When her lunch came—barley water & some jelly—I gave it to her but she didn't like the jelly & could only take a spoonful or two. I did some red dahlias & pink roses wh. I had bought her with money given me by Aunt Florence, & I said I'd get her anything on earth she liked from Fortnum & Mason's—caviare, smoked salmon, turtle soup, or whatever it was—but she said regretfully that Bowde wouldn't allow her anything of the kind but she was to have a chicken sandwich for supper.

Left her very reluctantly indeed; wrote long letter about her to Edith who was coming to the Regent Palace in the morning, & went down to Brighton by the tea train. A vaguely familiar, common-looking, over-dressed, youngish woman in the 1st Pullman asked me if I was Vera Brittain & turned out to be Rita England of St Monica's days. We went to the Royal Albion as Eve Kirk's brother had commended it, also W. had sat next to Sir Harry Preston the proprietor at a recent Foyle luncheon & thought we might like it—but it was all red plush & sporting friends of Sir H. Preston (who came & spoke to us at dinner), & we were disappointed in the bedroom, the surroundings & the slow, reluctant service. Spent most of our spare time at the Metropole instead. Walked along the front just before dinner & saw a gorgeous sunset—violet clouds & golden palaces. Went to Metropole after dinner & watched dancing.

Saturday September 21st   Brighton
Long walk in morning as far as downs in front of Roedean; very warm & sunny & I felt cheered because the report about Winifred was that her condition was unchanged & she had had quite a good night. G. spent morning sitting on front. Afternoon, sat on shore reading *I Have Been Young*; tea at Metropole. Found encouraging telegram at lunch-time from Edith

saying she had had tea with Winifred & found her so much better. Much cheered, went to Metropole after dinner & had one dance with G.

Sunday September 22nd
Rather conflicting reports about Winifred; doctor's report said "Much the same", but nursing home pessimistic & said she had had a bad night. Decided to go over to Chichester & see Aunt F. for fear we should soon have to go back to W. but telegraphed Edith de C. to 'phone us at 7.30 p.m. as reports were so conflicting. Took early afternoon train to Chichester; went with some fruit to the Royal Sussex Hospital, & spent half an hour with Aunt F., who seemed much better—quite herself again & very sympathetic with our anxiety about Winifred. Had pleasant tea at A.A. hotel opposite Cathedral & got back just before dinner.

At 7.30 Edith rang up—her report was depressing & very alarming. She said she had been two hours with W.—that she had a cough & was very breathless, seemed very ill & kept saying she was so tired. I suggested I should come back at once but Edith said she was seeing Dr Bowde at 8.0 & if I'd wait she'd ring me up again at 8.30. Had a miserable scratch dinner between the two calls & then Edith rang up again to say that Bowde said there was no *real* change and that the coughing was due to the soreness of her throat after constant sickness & not to any defect in the lungs. We agreed that I would come back to town first thing in the morning. Felt desperately unhappy at having been away from her at all, even to reassure her by my absence; couldn't bring myself to go out or to the Metropole or anywhere; packed most of my things & went to bed with the heavy overwhelming sense of being back in the War again with doom at hand. Rainy, blustery day.

Monday September 23rd   London
Woke to see another lovely morning & was just getting up when I was wanted on the third-floor telephone. It was Mother, to say that a grave report had come from the nursing home to say that Winifred had had a very bad night & was "much weaker". A few minutes later Edith rang up to say Winifred had taken a sudden turn for the worse & she was telegraphing Mrs Holtby to come up at once; she said she was going to the nursing home immediately after breakfast & I said I'd catch the first train I could & go straight there. Just after this a waiter brought a message 'phoned through from the nursing home to say: "Miss Holtby is unconscious & her condition is critical." (We learnt later that some sudden change—such as Obermer & Bowde had said was *not* to be expected in this case—had occurred during the night, and that in the early morning she had relapsed into coma.)

I flung the remainder of my things into my cases, rushed downstairs & paid bills & things while G. finished dressing, & we caught the 9.25 & breakfasted on it—in so far as we could eat breakfast at all. I looked out of the window at the lovely morning with its bright autumn colours, thought perhaps I should find Winifred already dead or at rate unable to recognise me ever again, cursed myself for ever having been persuaded to go to Brighton—an ill-fated place where I got the worst of all news once before; and cursed the doctors for saying no sudden change could occur when it had. At Victoria I got G. to ring up the home from the Belgravia Hotel; and they told him that Winifred was still alive & still just able to recognise people. He took my luggage back to Glebe Place for me & promised to notify V.S.J., while I went straight to the home.

I was allowed to go up & found Edith sitting in Winifred's room, and Winifred herself lying semi-conscious, her face just slightly puffy & with the yellowish pallor I had seen in so many uremia & nephritis cases during the War. Edith & I went outside & talked for a few minutes; she said the doctors had realised that some "Factor X" had caused the unexpected change & now knew they must give her up. I told her Winifred had said last week that she wished Harry Pearson would come up & see her, & suggested that we telegraph him: "Winifred critically ill; still recognises people; has asked for you; come if you wish."

Later he telegraphed back that he was coming by a train that would arrive at 3.15 in the morning & come to Chelsea at 8.0; so I left a note at the King's Cross Hotel for him explaining where W. was & how she was.

Edith went out to send the telegram & I spoke to Winifred very gently: "Sweetie-heart—it's Vera." She smiled & put out her hand a little and said: "But I thought . . . Brighton . . ." I explained that Shirley had a cold (which was indeed the case) & that I had come back to see she had the doctor, & so on. Winifred murmured weakly: "She would."

Then two nurses came in to fix up a saline apparatus & I went down into the sitting-room. (It caused her to rally amazingly, as the Matron told me later she had thought she would not live until her mother came.) In the sitting-room I found Lady Rhondda talking to Edith, & a few minutes later V.S.J. came in; both were in tears. I took them up separately to see Winifred, who recognised them as she had me; I had to warn Violet that though W. couldn't see her (her dear eyes were all blank as she was no longer able to focus them) she might hear the tears in her voice. Later when they had gone I said to her "Sweetie-heart, I do love you," and she answered "I—love—you."

I stayed with her till just before Mrs Holtby was due to arrive and then went off to leave the coast clear. I came back later & Mrs Holtby was in the sitting-room of the nursing home. She had already taken possession of it and begun to hold court; having heard the report on W. from nurses & doctors, she was organising, executing, managing everything with what some of us called magnificent stoicism & the rest (including myself) colossal egoism. Already she was deciding where Winifred was to be buried (she thought London but I felt sure Rudston was where Winifred would want), sending for undertakers, dictating letters & sending telegrams to all

W.'s friends & her own relatives & acquaintances, sending for Winifred's
Will—which Miss Moore brought—and quite illegally opening it; giving
jobs to everyone. Lady Rhondda was in effect told: "Now you arrange the
Memorial Service"; under other circumstances it would have been quite
comic to see a great administrator being managed by a lesser, but Lady F
behaved magnificently all through and subordinated her private feelings in
a manner quite beyond praise. She was extremely generous to me too
—said she saw no reason why I should keep out of Mrs H.'s way, and that
she was ready to act as a "link between the generations". But I knew that
Mrs H. [had] better be left to Lady R. and Hilda Reid as much as possible
& that I was least able to endure her executiveness.

At tea-time went to Edwardes Square & saw Shirley—had told Mother
to get in Dr Yates. Only a throat cold but she can't go to school to-morrow.
Arranged for J. to go back to Glebe Place so as to separate him from the
cold—& S. to return there as soon as she is better.

Went back to home for one final visit to W. & then on to the King's X
Hotel with Harry's note. Mrs H. said she wanted the *Y.P.* and the Hull
Daily Mail & *The Times* notified of W.'s illness so we got this done at the
Hotel. Back home kept my door open all night & barely slept for fear of
being summoned by telephone. Mrs H. spent night in nursing home; had
taken rooms at Mandeville Hotel.

Tuesday September 24th
Notice about W. among the Invalids in *The Times*. Just after breakfast
Harry Pearson turned up looking for Pat Brand—in brown tweed suit,
blue-eyed, bronzed & handsome like an Army Major. Hilda drove us all to
the nursing home & I saw Winifred. She had rallied amazingly since the
saline injection & seemed now to have no pain or headache & very little
discomfort. She was in rapture because Harry had come (her mother had
told her he was coming the previous night) and also so pleased because
visitors, inquiries & flowers came all day, as the result of *The Times* notice.
She couldn't think who had put it in and asked "Does one have to pay for
that sort of thing?" Mrs Scott-James was much affected by the sight of
Winifred lying in bed & hand in hand with Harry at last, & furious with
Mrs Holtby for going up "to see that Harry did not tire Winifred".

I don't know quite how much Winifred suspected about herself through
the sudden concourse of visitors & flowers. I never quite knew all along. I
think she knew she was seriously ill, but thought that as she had defeated
medical prognostications once she could do so again, & had at any rate a
fighting chance which she was determined not to relinquish. She said
various memorable things to me during the day. "I've never had such a
lovely twenty-four hours as this . . . When I get better I shall have a terrible
character after all this flattery . . . I've never been so comfortable in my life
before" (this was to Dr Bowde). "It's worth having a headache because it's

so lovely when you don't—like the man who knocked his head against the wall because it was perfectly heavenly when the pain stopped."

She asked me in the morning to give Mrs Holtby the introductory dedication of "South Riding" to read and I did so—but of course, as I feared, Mrs H. never saw its intense pathos and beauty, but because the book is about a County Council only saw the possible effect of it on her own position on the East Riding C.C.! However Lady Rhondda & Gordon dealt with her over this—and I told Winifred that her Mother had loved the Introduction and (which was quite true) that I thought the last chapter one of the loveliest and most moving things she has written, and that the chapter about Sarah & Carne is not at all too brutal.

Later in the day Winifred said to me: "Are we by ourselves?" (she could not see anything now). "Vera, do you think . . . it's so strange—life seems to be rounding itself off in such a queer way . . . I used to want the things I did want so badly, but now I don't anymore . . . all impatience gone." I think she meant to say: "Do you think I'm not going to get better?" —feeling that I was the only person whom she could trust to tell her; and then perhaps she thought that it was not fair to ask me; or else that if she were really dying she would prefer not to know but to fight on as long as there was a fraction of a chance.

I think it was to-day that Mrs Holtby was talking about "too much having been said" about W. in the papers already, and that when Grace and Mr Holtby died they were "Winifred Holtby's sister" and "Winifred Holtby's father" instead of themselves. This tendency to resent the importance of Winifred made me realise that the one thing I must do for her was to make sure that the reputation for which she had worked so hard during her life must not be neglected or overlooked at the time of her death because of our private griefs. So I got on to Mrs Scott-James, who said that Davey had already written something for the *Y.P.* but I'd better send him all the details I knew that he mightn't; also that she'd do something about *The Times* & the *Manchester Guardian*. I got on to Lady Rhondda about the *Sunday Times*, and wrote to St J. Ervine about the *Observer*; I also rang up John Brophy who later undertook to see about the *Morning Post* and *Daily Herald*; & Gordon got on to Rebecca West about the *Daily Telegraph*.

I also think it was to-day that Mrs Holtby gave me to read the letter addressed to me found with Winifred's will; later I returned it to them. It was chiefly instructions about my being her Literary Executor (which I knew already she had left me, with a certain proportion of profits from her unpublished MSS. to go to me & another proportion to Somerville for scholarships) and where to find manuscripts, but it ended up: "I have been very happy. I have had a lovely life. I am not afraid of anything except of being a nusance" (characteristically spelt that way). I found myself thinking of her dear unseeing eyes with their kind, blank gaze and crying over & over again: "Oh, my poor sweet . . . !"

Wednesday September 25th

Winifred seemed worse again—quiet, tired & drowsy. She said to me in the morning: "So tired . . . life's too difficult"—but was still enjoining me to go back to Brighton & stay at the Metropole with Jan & Edith. I think it was to-day that Clare called, & was caught into the social court in the sitting-room; & that Edith Smeterlin—after seeing the notice in *The Times* about Winifred's illness—rang us up, & then sat for a short time with W. in her room; she was very slangy but obviously much upset and brought some superb lilies-of-the-valley. W.'s room was by now a bower of flowers —roses, carnations, lilies, violets, chrysanthemums. She kept saying "Thirsty" and thanking most courteously anyone who helped her to drink. When I offered her water or barley-water she chose the latter, though not liking it, "because it feeds you, and I mean to get better if I can."

I think it was this afternoon that V.S.J. told me she had been asked to write a 500-word Obituary for *The Times* & asked me to help her—so while Mrs Holtby, Hilda, Lady Rhondda & Gordon had tea in the café at the corner of Devonshire Street & Marylebone Street (which we all haunted during that dreadful week), Violet & I sat at another table & wrote the notice.

Harry had arranged to sit up all night with Winifred as she said she had so many people during the day (Obermer said she had too many & she asked him to cut down the number; "My room's like Piccadilly Circus," she told me later) but no one at night when she woke in sudden terror & felt lonely and couldn't see. I offered to sit up one night myself but Harry was obviously the person she wanted. ("He hasn't anything to do," she said. "It would worry me if you sat up—you're too busy.") At dinner-time he arranged for Mother just to go up & look at W. as she wanted to see her once again without disturbing her. Winifred was dozing & Mother stood in the doorway & looked at her lying against the pillows, so pale & quiet; she looked very young, she said afterwards.

I went back to dinner at Edwardes Square with Mother as she was feeling lonely, but returned almost immediately to the nursing home to see how W. was and give the final report to Lady R. & V.S.J. Found she was already asleep & Harry with her; no one else much was about except the Matron, who talked to me in her abrupt Irish way, & remarked that I'd got my home & children, and we all had to do the best we could with our lives by making use of what we had—or words to that effect. Found a message from Miss Isitt when I got home asking me to ring up in the morning to give her details about W.'s career. I knew Miss Isitt never appreciated Winifred & wouldn't be able to deal with her literary side at all, so over the 'phone I told V.S.J. that it looked as if I should be the only person who wasn't writing about Winifred; and after all the *M.G.* had been my stamping-ground for 8 years. She said she'd get on to Mr Bone of the London office & do what she could.

All day long inquiries had come & the Press Association rang up continually; they finally distinguished themselves with a call at 12.15 midnight, but promised to keep the rest of the Press from disturbing me during the night if I would undertake to let them know if there were any change.

Thursday September 26th
Usual 'phone calls, beginning at 8.30 a.m. Rang Miss Isitt up later & she told me that Mr Bone wanted me to write an appreciation of Winifred as well as her own notice.

I went to the home in the morning as usual and found Winifred more vigorous again—once more she had rallied & seemed anxious to talk. She was very decided on the subject of my visits—"They don't understand professional women here; don't ring up & ask when I want you, but say when you can come . . . I always want you whenever you like, but you must get on with your book—you've been interrupted far too much—it'll be 'Dishonourable Estate' before it's finished if you don't look out . . . You mustn't let them overwork you so; you're so small; you're looking much too thin and tired."

Later she said: "Whatever I may do, remember that I love you dearly . . . I'm intensely grateful to you—you're the person who's made me . . . You've got a mind like steel . . . It's the most honest mind I've ever known and the most lucid. Often when I've been all tangled up & haven't known how to get through you've said to me 'But this is the end . . . this is how to get out . . .' " I could say nothing but only, when she protested about my coming so often and the interruption of my work: "Sweetheart, you know I'd rather be with you than anyone in the world," and hold her hand & stroke her hair. She spoke of the happiness it had given her to have Harry with her during the night, & then said: "Don't think I mean I love him more than you . . . I love you quite differently."

One day she mentioned the debate at Oxford and I said: "But just think—if the debate hadn't happened I should never have come to you afterwards—and think what I should have missed." "And what *I* should have missed," she added.

After I had lunched with Hilda at the café I went into the hairdresser's next to the nursing home to have my much-neglected hair washed & set, and while sitting there began to make some notes for the article the *M. G.* had asked for. Then I walked down Wimpole St and finished it in, of all places, the rest-room at Marshall & Snelgrove's. It seemed so queer to be doing it as though she were dead, while she lay dying and I was still praying for her recovery. In fact while I was writing the notice Gordon was with her and she was telling him about a questionnaire she had seen recently in the *Daily Mail*, asking people to say what they wanted most if they had only two days to live. She told him that her own reply had been:

"A decided British foreign policy," and added "But I don't intend to clear out yet."

I went back later in the evening and found the usual cavalcade in the sitting room discussing funerals, memorial services (Canon Sheppard had already been approached by Professor Winifred Cullis) and various other arrangements. I then went up & saw Winifred again. She said: "I *am* better . . . Vera, have I been *very* ill—as ill as I was last time? I don't remember feeling quite as I have this?"

Again the dilemma. Was she entitled to the truth? Should I, under similar circumstances, want it? Obermer's view, & Lady Rhondda's (that she should be persuaded to take an optimistic view of herself on the chance that there still might be a faint vestige of hope which encouragement would aid) again prevailed and I said: "Well, you've probably been *as* ill as last time, but they understand your illness so much better now that they've done various things that have made you feel queer." This seemed to satisfy her & she began talking about what she wanted to do while she was recovering. (She had previously asked about the *Good Housekeeping* reviews & I had assured her that I had found someone else to do it temporarily for one month only.) I didn't stay long as Harry was again going to sit with her all night.

Friday September 27th
Owing to number of letters and inquiries I got to Winifred rather late (Edith & Gordon having already been with her), & found her quite rampageous on the subject of her visitors. She said: "When Obermer told me I could only have three visitors I asked for you and Mother and Harry, and I got Edith and Gordon." She had obviously wanted me badly for she started talking at once on what was in her mind—all the fundamental things which had lain hidden in her heart for years began to come out. She spoke of her relationship to Harry & how much she wondered whether he really loved her and had done so all through, and did I think, if she spent her convalescence in a cottage in the country, that he'd come & look after her. "I feel as if I'd like someone to look after me for a bit." She wondered, too, if he would be willing to marry her. I said: "Does that matter? Couldn't you be happy together in a cottage without bothering about an actual ceremony?" She replied: "I feel I *want* to be married somehow—I want some sort of security now." (Previously she had said to V.S.J.: "There can't be many people who have been in love with the same man for thirty years and not married him in the end.") She added imploringly: "But would it be fair to marry someone when I can't have children? Vera, you wouldn't let me do anything ignoble, would you . . . ?" I assured her that Harry didn't strike me as at all the sort of person to want children & that if he had done so he'd probably have taken steps to get them before now, and anyhow I could lend them John & Shirley; but mentally I decided that the one thing she still wanted to make her life complete she

must have, & that Harry must be persuaded to play his part before it was too late.

After she'd finished saying all she wanted to about Harry—and half-apologising for it, but making the inner preoccupation very clear—we went on to other things, and I read her a letter Phyllis had sent. She told me with a kind of mischievous smile to answer it on a postcard if that would amuse me . . . I noticed how her dear face in repose was entirely benevolent & sweet—and hardly any suffering now. She asked me for several drinks —lime-juice, which she told me she had sent out for—and I gave them to her, raising her head against her pillows in my arms.

Finally I went down to find Mrs Holtby and Chakravarty (who had sent Winifred numerous flowers & had haunted the home for two days) & several others, much elated because Obermer had been and said that Winifred's increased vigour of interest in things *might* be a good sign; that he'd never before seen so much vitality displayed by anyone he'd given up; and that if by any chance her blindness was due to a slight haemorrhage behind the eyes, it was an excellent symptom. He said he would at once take another blood test, and send a specialist to-night to look at her eyes.

We all felt enormously elated, as though we had been granted a sudden reprieve, and Mrs Holtby (as though something final had been discovered) began making arrangements for Edith & Harry to leave town on Sunday and herself the following Wednesday! Edith and Hilda & I had lunch together & then went for a walk in Regents Park, where the sun was shining brilliantly and the dahlias all aflame. Edith said she didn't see *how* Winifred could recover bec. the doctors had said her kidneys were almost solid, & even with the catheter she was hardly passing anything; but Hilda & I both felt that (as Obermer had suggested) Winifred was so many times more than an ordinary person that if anyone could fool the doctors & defeat death, she could; & that even if she could be kept alive another six months, some way of making dead tissue grow might be discovered. On the way to the Park I telephoned Lady Rhondda, who was almost tearfully grateful, that there might be a chance of better news.

Between tea & dinner I got hold of Gordon, who came to the home, & told him that I thought Harry ought to tell Winifred he loved her & always had; that he'd like to marry her when she was better; and that only another man could put this over to him in such a way that he wouldn't be offended & frightened; and that it should be done at once because, for all our renewed hopes, time might be short. He agreed to try & see Harry that night.

I went up to see Winifred again for a few minutes before the eye specialist was due; she was lying in clean white embroidered night-gown with a little red rose in her hand. More of them were standing in a vase beside her, and she said: "Who *do* you think sent me these? Helen Waddell!" and I found a little card "With love & gratitude from Helen Waddell" with the roses. She said the front of her night-gown, which lacked ribbons, was "indecent", so

I fastened it together for her with the rose. When I'd done this she began to talk about John & Shirley, and said: "They've taken my flowers out now, but I've got so many; choose two of the nicest roses and take them to my two darlings—you know, when I was in France with them I *prayed* that I might bring them back to you safely—perhaps it was silly but I wasn't taking any chances . . ."

I wanted to cry but said instead: "May I take a rose for myself too?" and she said: "Oh, darling, haven't you got one? Why, of course take one." Just then Dr Bowde came in with the eye-specialist to see her eyes, so I went away; and later Edith went up & brought two tea-roses for the children and a red one for me.

Mrs Holtby and Harry & Gordon went off, and Edith and I stayed, with thumping hearts, to hear the specialist's verdict & the result of the blood-test. They came, & threw us into the depths, for the eye-specialist said that Winifred's blindness *was* caused by the disease, and that all he could do was to correct a certain amount of double vision by drops and an eye-shade; while the blood-test showed that the amount of urea in her blood had increased by three times since the last test and that there was literally no hope. Obermer said later that with such a blood-test she ought to have been dead already & that it was only her astonishing vigour of personality which was keeping her alive & so comparatively lucid.

We went back to the Mandeville Hotel hardly able to walk for the bitterness of grief & disappointment after our raised hopes. Mrs Holtby insisted that I stay there for dinner, and afterwards I stayed talking for some time with her & Edith (Chakravarty was there for a little while too, but left quite soon, evidently finding the "executive" nature of the conversation too much for him). Meanwhile I heard that Gordon had taken Harry off to dine, & hoped & prayed he would achieve something before it was too late. I went home & carefully pressed my flowers; tears were falling on them by now & I was thinking again: "Oh, my poor sweet . . ."

Gordon came in a good deal later, to say that he had had a long talk with Harry (who, as I learnt later, never suspected Gordon of "putting anything over" but thought he was a charming individual who was letting him unburden himself—which says a great deal for G.'s tact). He told G. that, without ever having been violently attracted to Winifred sexually (he prefers temporary diversions with the venal, apparently) he had always thought he would marry her in the end—when perhaps he would mind the contrast between their positions less. Gordon said how important it was for W.'s happiness that Harry should speak to her now. He said he would, but feared only to cause her a shock or too much excitement. Gordon said he would take the responsibility for this as what mattered most now was Winifred's happiness. Harry agreed; he was going to bed to-night after two nights with Winifred, but said he would seize the first opportunity to-morrow.

Saturday September 28th

Obermer got us on the telephone in the morning, on the subject of keeping Winifred under morphia for her last hours, in order to let her final consciousness be that of her present happiness & not of some cruel shock of sudden realisation. Apparently this is a moral rather than a medical question, about which relatives & friends have to be consulted. On grounds of humanity we agreed, though somehow I imagined that it couldn't be done till she went to sleep to-night. It seemed a sin deliberately to put out that lovely, kind, radiant personality—but what else could be done to spare her pain when death anyhow was to take her so soon?

Went early to the nursing home & found she was asking for me. I went up at once; she didn't seem quite so clear in her head as yesterday and said to me: "I don't want you to bother to come back again during the day, but will you come last thing at night, after everyone else has gone, to straighten out the tangles in my mind?" I promised I would, and then she said: "I never saw Harry all yesterday, & he wasn't here last night," and I promised that as soon as I went down I'd find him & see that he went to her without delay—and she seemed satisfied. Her eyes were darkened with drops & beside her was a black eyeshade which she asked me to put on for her. When it was on, she could see a little—she could see me, for instance, and said: "What's happened to your eyebrows—surely they're lighter than usual." I said that probably too much had been plucked off them at the hairdresser's when I was last there, and she said: "You mustn't let them do that—you've got so much character in your face—don't let them spoil it . . . Your eyes are different from everybody else's eyes." She looked past me & said "I see some lovely gladioli"—they were tall mauve ones, sent by Mr Kyllmann of Constable's. She asked me then to get the nurse to bring her a cup of tea made with milk; and I said "I'll go down now & get Harry"—wanting him to come & see her as soon as possible. She said: "Yes, I think we've discussed everything important for the moment . . . of course I can always say that I love you . . . but you'll come back to-night, won't you?" I promised faithfully that I would, & kissed her, & left her with the nurse giving her the tea—never thinking that I had had the last conscious words that I should ever hear from her in life.

In the passage I found Lady Rhondda coming up for a few minutes & told her W. was not quite as clear as yesterday. Shortly afterwards she came down & said W. seemed to her quite clear—the tea had roused her—but she (Lady R.) wanted to see Harry as soon as he arrived. (It turned out later that Winifred had been dwelling, as she did with me, the day before, on whether he loved her & would want to marry her.) I told Lady R. that I knew Harry wanted to say something private to Winifred, & begged her to keep Mrs Holtby out of the way, and she said she would. In the meantime I had sent the message to Harry that Winifred wanted him—though both Mrs Holtby & Edith seemed to feel he oughtn't to be hurried or have pressure put on him when he was so tired. I felt fiercely that at this juncture it was Winifred who mattered, not Harry. Gordon said he knew Harry was going to speak to her that morning, & that we'd better disappear & not seem to be enjoining anything; so I went into the little café while Gordon stayed to make sure that Harry had got the message & did come. Eventually I saw Harry crossing the road to the nursing home with a big bunch of scabious & knew that it was all right; and Gordon joined me & took me to the basement floor of the café while Lady Rhondda brought Mrs Holtby to the upper one & kept her talking there for about an hour.

Gordon & I walked down Marylebone High Street on our way home, for as W. didn't want me till the evening I thought I might as well go back to Glebe Place. When we reached Spanish Place we saw that St James's, Spanish Place, where we were married, was open, and the organ playing most beautifully. So we went in & knelt down for a while beneath the dim light from the high windows as I used to do when I was grieving for Roland during the War. It seemed strange to look at that altar where Gordon & I had stood only ten years before with Father Bede Jarrett in front of us and Winifred & Father standing beside me, & Lord Stamford beside Gordon; and to think that Bede Jarrett was gone, & Father was gone, & soon Winifred would be gone; and only Gordon and I (and Stamford, whom we never see) be left. As the organ rolled over my head so beautifully, I knelt and prayed that the one thing Winifred had most desired throughout the sixteen years I have known her might be coming to her at that moment — "Oh, my darling, may God give you happiness at the last."

And suddenly, as I looked at the altar, I saw five figures in deep mourning go up to it — a man and a woman, the woman's father, her friend as maid-of-honour, and the man's friend as best-man — and realised I was watching a marriage take place, but an unusual marriage, for the little scattering of their friends in front were all in deep mourning too. It was the strangest coincidence — they seemed like ghosts of ourselves ten years ago — and yet I felt it a happy augury too.

We went home & to lunch, and while there the nursing home rang up to give me a message from Winifred: it was just: "Yes, all through." At first my brain was dull & I didn't quite understand & sent back a message asking if she'd like me to come round earlier; but the reply came "It's all right — I'll explain when you come to-night." Meanwhile it had flashed upon me that the message referred to Harry and that it meant he had loved her all through & she wanted me to know at once — so I sent back another message that I understood, and would she like me to come round at once? I was told later that this message *was* delivered to her, but I have never known for certain, as I got no reply. Harry meanwhile rang up to say that everything had gone that morning just as we all wished — that he'd said what he wanted & she seemed very happy . . .

Then, about three o'clock, I got the worst shock of the whole week, for Hilda Reid rang up to say that Obermer had been round to the home & had already put Winifred under morphia; she was now unconscious &

would never be permitted to come back to consciousness again. Later I learnt that Obermer did this because after Harry had been with Winifred she was so happy & excited that he feared a violent convulsion for her, with physical pain & mental anguish; and that he thought it best to let her go out on that moment of happiness, without the cruel realisation that what she was hoping could never be fulfilled. No one saw her after Harry but Mrs Holtby; Winifred was quite ecstatic, told her Harry wanted to marry her, and said: "You don't mind, do you, Mummy?" and Mrs H. said "I'm delighted; I've just lost one son-in-law" (meaning Peter, who has married again) "and now I've got another instead." Winifred said: "It's just an understanding between us—no engagement." She had already had the morphia when Mrs Holtby came, and she drifted into sleep & faded from consciousness with those words and in that state of happiness.

But when I heard she'd been given the morphia already, something died in me. I realised then how deeply I'd been counting on seeing her conscious and herself once more & hearing about Harry from her own lips. It was pure selfishness, of course; but I just wanted to feel that I'd been the instrument of bringing her the one happiness she had wanted all her life and never had; and to see that happiness for myself. I raced to the nursing home in the hope that a flicker of consciousness might be left; but Edith who was in the sitting-room told me that it was all gone, and I began to cry then; knowing that I should never see Winifred, as Winifred, again; and wishing bitterly that I'd stayed in the home and got just a word with her as soon as Harry had gone, instead of trying to make things go more smoothly for her by keeping out of the way. Edith said "Cry, darling," but I felt that what I wanted then was not to cry but to see whatever was still left of Winifred, so I checked myself, and went up.

Mrs Holtby was there, & Winifred was lying quite unconscious, breathing heavily as those under morphia do. Mrs Holtby told me that Obermer had said that the morphia by subduing the symptoms might prolong her life for a few days—but I privately thought that it was Winifred's will that had kept her alive in spite of her body, & that as soon as her personality was put out she would probably go. Mrs Holtby said she had arranged that if Winifred died in the night, no one was to be called till 7 a.m.—"We can't do anything, and we should only be in the nurses' way ... You do agree about not being called." I didn't say anything, for I didn't agree at all that Winifred, so dear & beloved, treasured by so many who would do anything for her, should be left to die alone amongst strangers. I just said good-night to Mrs Holtby and kissed Winifred and left, feeling unable to discuss any more "arrangements" within a few yards of her as she lay dying. Downstairs I telephoned Lady R. about the situation and also about her own message "Yes, all through", which the home had telephoned by mistake to V.S.J. Fortunately she let me know of the mistake, or Lady R. would never have known that W. sent her a message at all.

As I came out of the home leaving Winifred dying & unconscious, a newspaper placard confronted me: "Abyssinia Mobilises". Everything that Winifred and I had lived & worked for—peace, justice, decency —seemed to be gone.

Later Gordon and I went back to the home, after Mrs H. had gone, & told the night nurse that if any change came in Winifred during the night, *we* wanted to be told at once. Gordon took three of the violets from a vase beside her, & the sprig of lily-of-the-valley that she had had from the bunch the children gave her. She was still breathing heavily but as we stood just above her pillow she looked like her ordinary self asleep and we kissed her good-night.

Sunday September 29th

We slept with the door open as usual, and at 4.30 a.m. the telephone bell rang. We both sprang out of bed, knowing what it meant, & Gordon, being nearer, got to it first. It was from the night sister, to say that Winifred's breathing & pulse had changed, and she had gone suddenly much weaker. We were dressed in ten minutes, & I called Amy & sent her up to the top to be with the children. I sent for a taxi from South Parade but when the man came he was quite drunk, so we took another from Sloane Square. It was a very dark night & had been raining heavily.

At the nursing home we were let in at once and crept upstairs. The clock outside struck five just after we arrived. The room was dim, with a shaded lamp, but I saw at once that Winifred had changed, and though her pulse was still tolerably strong, she was breathing very shallowly, and wore the look that I had so often seen on the faces of dying men in the War. Her lips were only slightly parted; her eyes were serenely closed & her hair brushed back from her forehead. She looked utterly at peace—"like a tired child", as Gordon said afterwards, "who has at last had a good night after many bad ones".

The night nurse, standing above her—a kind, understanding girl—said that Winifred had rallied a little since she telephoned, but that the end would probably come quite suddenly. Gordon sat down in the arm-chair under the lamp and I sat beside Winifred, sometimes holding her hand, sometimes with my fingers on her wrist. As I watched beside her an hour slipped almost imperceptibly away. All the time the words kept running through my head: "When thou passest through the waters I will be with thee: I will not fail thee nor forsake thee." The lovely benevolence of her face remained unchanged; no glimmer of pain or sorrow challenged its calm, but shortly after six o'clock I realised that *she* had changed again, & was breathing more shallowly, while her pulse was slower & weaker. After almost a quarter of an hour her pulse, which I was holding, had almost stopped, and her breathing seemed to come from her throat only. I nodded to Gordon and he came and stood beside her. It was strange, incredible, after all the years of our friendship & all that we had shared together, to feel her life flickering out under my hand.

Suddenly her pulse stopped; she had given two or three deeper breaths and then these ceased and I thought she had stopped breathing too; but after a moment came one final, lingering sigh, and then everything was at an end. I whispered to the night nurse: "Gone?" and she nodded. I looked at the clock—Dot McCalman's carriage clock which Winifred had been so fond of and asked me to bring to the home two days before. It was 6.25.

The night nurse cut off a strand of her hair for me and I put it in an envelope in my bag, and then Gordon and I stood beside her to say our last goodbye. She looked very peaceful and utterly happy, as if she had just fallen asleep, with her fair eyelashes lying lightly upon her cheeks & her lips slightly parted. We both of us kissed her high, generous forehead and the place where her hair grew from it—first I, and then Gordon, and then I again—and said: "Goodbye, Winifred dear."

Then we went straight out of the room—looking back for a moment at her lying so quietly against the pillows—and then out of the nursing home and into Marylebone High Street. It was night when we began to walk down one end of it, and dawn when we reached the other. We found St James's, Spanish Place, already open for 7 o'clock Mass, and we went in again and knelt there for a few minutes, and as we left I lit a votive candle for her soul, wherever it might have gone or whatever become.

Almost next to the church we found Durrant's Hotel open—the entrance full of upturned carpets & vacuum cleaners, & decided to stay there until it was time to go to the Mandeville Hotel on the assumption that we hadn't heard about Winifred till 7.0. (We decided not to tell Mrs Holtby that we had been with Winifred when she died unless she asked us direct; and in fact she never did. Edith & Harry also later both agreed that we shouldn't tell Mrs H.—Harry even urged us to lie if asked—as, though Mrs H. didn't want herself to be with Winifred, she wouldn't like anyone else to be—and would want to feel she was the last person to see her. I didn't care; I didn't mind lying if necessary; all I cared was that my darling Winifred should not die alone. I believe that there may well be means of communication between one spirit and another even after one person's consciousness is gone; there was always so strong a telepathy between Winifred & myself that I feel my presence did make a difference to her, and that the quietness with which she died, the lovely tranquillity of her face just after death, may well have been due to the fact that the person who loved her best and with most understanding was beside her at the last.)

At Durrant's, in order to stay, we ordered tea & toast that we didn't want (the night-sister had already given us some at the nursing home as soon as we arrived) and telephoned to the Press Association, Mother, Lady Rhondda & Storm Jameson. Gordon telephoned to them all except Storm Jameson; when I rang up Guy answered first, & I knew by his voice when I said who I was that he understood what I had to say—I had scarcely

realised when we did all the calls that it was still only between 7.0 &
8.0 a.m.; we seemed to have been up such a long time.

At 8.0 we went along to the Mandeville & Mrs Holtby insisted on our
having breakfast with them. She was quite extraordinary—started to tease
Harry & then said: "But we mustn't be uproarious to-day"—and described how they had all been awake & what they were all doing (Harry &
Edith having tea & biscuits & looking down the wet length of the High
Street) when Winifred died. None of them attempted to go near the nursing
home the whole morning, as Mrs H. was terrifically making arrangements
& requiring everyone's co-operation. I had to write notices for *The Times*,
Daily Telegraph etc. at least five times—Mrs H. continually thinking of
different things she wanted to put in—until when I had written the words
"Winifred Holtby, aged 37" for the fifth time the whole thing came over me
& I started to cry—so moved away from the group, which had now been
joined by the undertaker & by Lady Rhondda, who was forced to stay and
discuss, discuss, discuss the funeral arrangements & the Memorial Service. Finally, when the group broke up, I flew out at Lady R., of all people
(though she understood it wasn't directed at her & never resented it), and
said that apparently the only thing that mattered about Winifred was that
she should be buried—and departed home in a storm of irrepressible tears.

I can't quite remember what I did with the rest of the morning—but
found when I got home that Mother had already been & taken the children
again, & that Miss Moore had come to do various odd jobs—typing out
notices & so forth. Margaret Storm Jameson came to lunch—she was very
comforting, & as G. said that in spite of everything he *must* go down to the
Labour Conference at Brighton & make a speech, I was to go home with
her for the night—I was more than grateful, not wanting to be left all alone
just yet.

In the afternoon after consulting her I decided to send back the $500
advance for "South Riding" to George—Winifred hadn't endorsed the
cheque so it remained technically the Macmillan property—as it had been
sent before the contract especially for Liberia, & she could never now fulfil
the stated conditions (her next two novels). I didn't see why I, who as her
literary executor am the chief beneficiary from unpublished manuscripts,
or Somerville College either for that matter, should profit in a slightly
questionable manner at Macmillan's expense from Winifred's death. So I
sent the cheque back with a brief note asking George to use it to promote
her book & help to crystallise her reputation.

Then Margaret went home & I took the *Times* notice & the Memorial
notice for the Social column (how short a time it seemed since I had been
there with Father's notice!), saw Gordon go on by the Tube to Victoria &
to Brighton, & went up to St John's Wood to rejoin Margaret.

In the Tube to Maida Vale I was looking gloomily out of the window
(dressed rather conspicuously in mourning, I suppose, & with my eyes full
of tears) when a woman who had been sitting opposite and got up to go out

suddenly put a hand on my shoulder & said: "Take heart" (or rather "Taike 'eart"). I said to Margaret afterwards: "What a lot of undirected benevolence there is in the world!" They welcomed me most kindly —listened to all I wanted to say—in fact Guy gave me a very strong vermouth so that I became quite drunk & talked & talked; and then Margaret made me take a hot bath early & go to bed. She brought me some hot milk & I took two Alasils & did sleep a good deal because for the first time for a week I had not the telephone to listen for (though how I wished & wished that I had).

Monday September 30th
Came home early from Margaret's flat—in a taxi in heavy pouring rain—and bought all the chief papers. They were full of notices of Winifred—the ¾-column notice by Violet & myself in *The Times*, the combined notices and appreciation by Miss Isitt & myself making a column in the *Manchester Guardian*, as well as a London note by Edward Garnett & an announcement on the main page; Rebecca's article in the *Telegraph*, John Brophy's in the *Morning Post*, & the Obituary by Charles Davey and a whole column by Phyllis in the *Yorkshire Post*. I knelt by the fire looking over them, quite unable to read them properly or take in the fact that it was Winifred about whom they were written. It still seemed quite impossible that she should be dead. I had known of her danger, had feared this calamity for so long, and yet I had never really believed in it; she seemed too vital & radiant a creature for death to touch.

Hilda came to lunch with me, & then Edith came to pack Winifred's clothes (what an intolerable task, & how noble of her to spare me from it—Amy & Burnett helped her). She said she had just taken Mrs Holtby to see Winifred in her coffin at the mortuary chapel at the undertaker's—and how lovely & content she looked. I was going out to order our flowers for the funeral, & suddenly felt impelled to go there first and see her face for the last time.

The undertaker took me into the little chapel, and there was her long coffin—closed—of light unpolished oak with silver handles, and her flowers from the nursing home—Chakravarty's roses and Helen Waddell's roses and Mr Kyllman's gladioli—standing on a narrow mantelshelf above it. I asked if I could see her face, so he drew the coffin lid back a little & pulled back the lace handkerchief that covered her. I looked at her for the last time, but now with incredulity, for though she was still lovely and tranquil, it was a different loveliness & a different tranquillity from my last glimpse of her face at dawn on Sunday, when the warmth and colour of life still remained in it. Her features, now, had the stillness and colour of a beautiful wax-work—the wax-work of a nun or a bride; her lips were just parted in a tiny fixed smile; she looked altogether happy & serene as a statue is serene, but the life & the light of her had gone clean away—more completely gone & extinguished than those who died in the War, except perhaps Victor, whom I saw dead, whereas the others merely ceased to write.

Clearly, definitely, with an annihilating thoroughness, the Winifred I had known for sixteen years had vanished; that generosity, that eagerness, that lovely kindness, had utterly departed and its place knew it no more. Whether it had become nothing I did not know. I felt it had, despairingly. If it still existed, it had gone, very far away, and was nowhere near me; the only trace of it, and that now to pass from my eyes for ever, lay in the sweetness that her character had given to her face. Her closed eyes, & her eyebrows, alone seemed the same; but they were those of the Winifred I knew at college, rather than the Winifred of recent years, who used lip-stick, & eyebrow pencil. Until I saw her in death, looking so young, with her fair eyebrows which had grown a little in the nursing home, & the purplish tinge beneath her eyes (as I had so often seen it in sleep when she was tired) just where her fair eyelashes rested, I hadn't realised that make-up, by adding sophistication, causes people to look older, not younger.

With her in the coffin was the tiny sprig of white heather attached to Lady Rhondda's card which she had with her all the time at the home since Lady Rhondda's return, and one of the sprigs of lily-of-the-valley from the children. I had stopped at a flower-shop in Marylebone High Street to buy four Ophelia roses—one from me, one from Gordon, one from each of the children, & I asked the man if I could put one in the coffin. He said I could, so I laid it there with the other flowers, & he put the other three roses in a vase beside her. I asked him to leave me alone with her, and I knelt down beside the coffin, but I didn't really feel alone with people coming & going in the office in front, and anyhow I was quite unable to pray to an unknown and—it seemed—unmerciful God, or to have any feeling in my heart but overwhelming grief & loss. So I looked at her—the effigy of her—one last time, & then went out into the heavy rain in Marylebone High Street.

I took a taxi to Sylvester's in Sloane Street, and ordered a cross of Ophelia roses & lilies-of-the-valley & rosemary for myself; a laurel wreath with purple gladioli for Gordon; a chaplet of pink lilies & purple carnations for Mother, & a tiny Victorian posy of yellow roses & forget-me-nots for the children. I came home to find that Edith had just finished the clothes, & had left for me the turquoise ring I gave Winifred after my American tour, and Odette's scarab & Ballinger's brooch to return to them; and a cigarette lighter for Gordon; also the cigarette case which Lady Rhondda gave her. I undertook to return these to the people who had sent them.

I went over to Edwardes Square to dinner & said goodnight to the children. Mother told me that she had heard Winifred's death announced in the News on the wireless yesterday evening as so many people did. I went home & began to answer some of the numerous letters that were already coming in. I was alone but I had pulled myself together enough now not to fear being alone. I even felt nearer to Winifred, somehow, by myself at the top of the house which we had shared for so long, than I felt kneeling beside her coffin or looking at her dear dead face in its waxen peace.

The cheaper papers to-day all carried a sob-story about "Miss Winifred Holtby, told that she had only a few years to live, set out to finish two works", etc., suggesting that she had set herself, & won, a deliberate race against time. I don't think this is quite the case, even though the facts approximate to the truth. Winifred was certainly told that, if her disease continued, she might only live for two years, and through that strange spiritual experience in Buckinghamshire of which she told me, she had brought herself to a philosophic acceptance of the possibility—had taught herself not to want anything very much; but when the two years were up & she felt better, not worse, & her blood tests seemed encouraging, & Obermer was pursuing his consistent policy of optimism, she began to believe that she was a "freak" who had defeated medical prognostications and would continue to do so. As Bowde said, she was one of those people who dissimulate their symptoms, whereas the more neurotic types (e.g., Father) aggravate them. I think she felt too vital, too eager, too much in love with life, really to believe in the possibility of her own death even though she accepted the threat as an academic fact. She did feel—as when she said once to me "Look at me—I'm damned & doomed," and again in the back garden of the Blue Cockatoo where we were having tea together last spring and she told me that Obermer had said she couldn't expect to live to be very old—that her time was probably shorter than most people's and therefore she made the very most of it (though never at other people's expense). But I don't think she ever carried on that conscious race that the papers suggest and I believe she fought, gaily and optimistically, for life up to the very last. Even the remark she made to me on the Tuesday when she had so many visitors—that it was so lovely to be free from pain, because she was beginning to be afraid of it, and St John Ervine would understand this because he knew what pain was—was made, I think, on the assumption that the pain was due to "treatment" & was the penalty of her recovery. Had she not been given morphia, I am sure that—unless she had had the convulsion that Obermer feared—her hope and faith would have kept her alive a few days longer. It was by her will that she continued to live when by all the symptoms she should have been dead, and this seems to be proved by the swiftness with which she died when the flame of her personality had been put out.

Tuesday October 1st
Storm Jameson, Hilda Reid and Mother came to fetch me & we went to Winifred's Memorial Service at St Martin-in-the-Fields, taken by Canon Sheppard with whom she had had a friendly correspondence owing to the likeness of his recent novel to her story "Judgment Voice".

At the request of the Holtbys we were there early, & sat in the front on the right. Gradually the church filled up behind me till I had the sense that it was quite full; I realised afterwards that it was crowded—crowded not only with writers but with the representatives of the innumerable interests which Winifred had served. When the Holtbys came—later than ourselves —Harry sat just opposite me at the end of the pew on the left. It was not a cold day but I couldn't help shivering & my service paper wouldn't keep still in my hand. I was conscious that Lady Rhondda came & sat just behind the Holtbys & behind her W. A. R. Collins & Rose Macaulay, but I saw no one else.

The service began with the prayers & when the coffin was brought in covered with a long cross of hundreds of violets (her favourite flower, one of the papers said, but if so I didn't know it) I found myself shivering so violently that Storm Jameson held on to me till I recovered. I couldn't think of her dead and inside it. She lay there, appropriately enough, between Harry and me—the two people whom I think she loved best. It was better when the quiet ended with the prayers, & the music began with a psalm they used to sing every morning at Queen Margaret's School —"My heart is inditing of a good matter." Then the hymn which I chose—Bunyan's Pilgrim Song that we used to sing at Oxford—came next, and then the lesson—"The souls of the righteous are in the hands of God"—and after it "The Sower went forth sowing"—the words of which were written by the author at Rudston shortly before Winifred was born. Then her cousin, Daisy Pickering, sang "Crossing the Bar", & some prayers followed; nearly everyone was crying by now, which felt better than shivering. Finally Canon Sheppard said that because those who were left must carry on the struggle, we would end the service by singing "Jerusalem"—again my choice for her. I felt able to look at her coffin, then, and to sing the last four lines as a final vow to her gallant body and her unquenchable spirit:

> I shall not cease from mental fight,
> Nor shall my sword rest in my hand,
> Till we have built Jerusalem
> In England's green & pleasant land.

We stood, finally, when Chopin's Funeral March was played through —Winifred and I both loved it & I shall always associate it, incongruously enough, with the day that we stood in Fleet Street in 1922 and watched the coffin of Sir Harry Wilson carried up to St Paul's. When it ceased after its triumphant burst of chords, the Holtby family left and I thought that all the congregation would follow and I could creep out at the end, but instead everybody waited for me to go—a tribute to my friendship with Winifred which moved & touched me when I recalled it afterwards. By this time I couldn't see or recognise anyone, but I learnt afterwards from the *Times* list that the people there included Henry Nevinson (now 79) and Evelyn Sharp, Mrs Swanwick, Cicely Hamilton, Elizabeth Delafield, Mrs Abbott,

Mr & Mrs Innes, Monica Whately, Miss Underwood, Chakravarty, nearly the entire staff of *Time & Tide*, and many representatives of organisations.

Mrs Holtby was already holding court outside the church & I introduced Storm Jameson to her, & then John Brophy—who had been crying himself—came up to me, & suddenly I saw Phyllis Bentley coming down the church; she went up to me in the porch & kissed me, and said: "Oh, my poor Vera!" After that Margaret & Guy got a taxi & detached me from the crowd & we drove home, with Hilda Reid; Mother had apparently gone off with Clare, who was there with Brailsford. Margaret & Guy took me home & then had to drive off, but Hilda stayed for lunch.

At tea-time Harry joined us, & Gordon just back from the Brighton Conference (where he made a speech on the Colonial question—Winifred would have wanted him to do that, he rightly said, instead of going to her Memorial Service), and we all caught the 5.45 to Hull, for Cottingham. G. & I travelled up with Lady Rhondda & I gave her Winifred's cigarette case from her. At Hull Henry Burt met us & we were driven out to Cottingham. Most efficient preparations; everything ready, everyone comfortable; Lady R., G. & I, & Hilda, all put up without fuss. Lady R. gave me some Medinol to help me sleep and I did get quite a good night.

Wednesday October 2nd   Cottingham
Lovely sunny morning. Got up early & went out into the garden & looked at the little paved square in the middle of the lawn which was being made when Winifred & I were last here—in March 1934, when I came up to speak to the Hull Luncheon Club & make 3 other speeches after a week's lecturing in the north, & she came over from Withernsea to join me. It seemed so strange & pointless to be at Bainesse without her; I looked at the tennis court & thought of all the games we had there during college vacations; how we heard the results of Schools there and congregated there for Grace's wedding after the Corfu dispute at Geneva in 1923.

About 10 o'clock the cars came & we drove the 35 miles to Rudston —Lady Rhondda & Hilda with Mrs Holtby in the first car, & Gordon & I with Edith in the second. We drove through the flat land of Holderness first, and then through Beverley with its beautiful Minster—to which Winifred & I walked one day from Cottingham, over the fields—till finally the flat land began to rise, & we passed through Driffield & were among the Wolds of which Winifred had so often spoken to me—those undulating curves of land that she told me, almost when I first met her, had become part of her being. And suddenly we were in Rudston, where the sheds covered the recently unearthed tessellated pavements of the Romans, and we were passing Rudston House—ivied, solid & spacious, with its lawns & dells—where Winifred was born, and opposite, folded into a curve of the hill, stood the small church with its triangular roofed tower flanked by the ancient pagan monolith about which her story was broadcast only last August, and the village churchyard where she was to lie.

We drove up to the back of the church & got out; Alec Lightwood was there waiting & Winifred's cousin Robin, & other members of the family. We went into the small church, crowded out with the farm people and villagers, and friends and acquaintances from the districts round. The bell was tolling gently, & it was all such a contrast to the service in St Martin's that I realised that my instinct about where she should be buried was right, and that you couldn't commemorate the two aspects of Winifred in one service.

The coffin was there when we arrived—it had lain in the church all night with its cross of violets, a little faded now but still filling the air with their scent. As I went into the church I caught a glimpse of a distant bank of flowers at the lower end of the churchyard—beside the family burial ground of the Macdonald of the Isles, I learnt later, and in full view of the windows of Rudston House.

Immediately we entered the church the organ began to play—Blake's "Jerusalem" amongst other things; it was the Vicar of Rudston himself who was playing but he stopped when the Vicar of Cottingham came and began to read "I am the Resurrection and the Life . . .". The service was simpler than yesterday's but otherwise much the same; we had "The souls of the righteous are in the hand of God" for the lesson, & "The Sower", but no solo, and the service ended, instead of "Jerusalem", with the "Nunc Dimittis", played as we followed the coffin out of the church. This time it was not carried shoulder-high, but swung between the bearers, led by the shepherd with whom Winifred used to play when she was a little girl. It all seemed so right—all the people who came from London with Gordon and me, Lady Rhondda & Hilda & Mrs Scott-James, said how fitting it was that she should be brought back here, "bringing her laurels with her", as one of the onlookers said. It was right, too, that the service in London, where the people with whom she worked were continuing the fight, should end with "Jerusalem", but the service in Rudston with the "Nunc Dimittis", where her body, which had finished the fight, was to be committed to the ground.

We followed the coffin down the gently sloping path to the grave, which had been lined with ivy from Rudston, and clematis and chrysanthemums, by the village people. It didn't look harsh and raw as poor Father's had looked, but a gentle bower of leaves and flowers. Violet Scott-James & one or two others moved aside for Gordon & me to stand near the grave, & there I saw the immense bank of flowers that I had glimpsed from a distance—wreath upon wreath and cross upon cross of roses, carnations, lilies, chrysanthemums, gladioli, dahlias, forget-me-nots. A woman reporter who was there, & who had attended many famous funerals, wrote afterwards in a Yorkshire paper that never, except in the case of Ellen Terry, who was twice Winifred's age, had she seen so many flowers sent in honour of a distinguished woman. It was a lovely autumn day, not sunny but bright, with a fresh, leaping wind which carried the exquisite perfume of the flowers across to us as we stood near the grave. We [moved] aside a little as they lowered the coffin gently into it, and then went close again as the committal service was read and I heard the words that always touch me so poignantly: "O God most Holy, O Lord most mighty, O blessed and merciful Saviour, suffer us not at our last hour, for any pains of death, to fall from Thee!" Whatever may have been true of poor Father, no pain or fear of death had separated Winifred from any God or any Good that rules—or —it may be, more truly—strives to permeate a sad and cruel world.

When the service was over we took a last look at the coffin lying beneath us with its cross of violets; again I whispered, "Goodbye, Winifred dear," and then Gordon and I walked together up the path to the gate. On the way there we were joined by Mr & Mrs H. D. Rowntree of Scarborough, who put me up last year when I spoke there for the L. of N. Union & so many Queen Margaret's girls came to the meeting; they said they would give anything to help us in some way, & that they would like to work for Gordon at Sunderland during the election.

We went back to Cottingham for lunch—back there I told Lady Rhondda how deeply I admired her for the way she had subordinated her own feelings & supported Mrs Holtby, and then we all left for the afternoon train, leaving Edith & Mrs Holtby alone in the house looking forlorn & sad. What an annihilation of a family & a lifetime—Grace, Mr Holtby & Winifred all gone within little more than seven years, & the oldest of them all surviving her entire household.

We travelled back once again with Lady Rhondda & spent the time talking about Winifred & how best to enshrine & crystallise her literary reputation.

Thursday October 3rd–Friday October 11th
Spent in a whirl of answering letters—I must have had over 200—, sending in press notices, packing up Winifred's books, which she left to Queen Margaret's School, & seeing Harold Rubinstein about the legal side of being Winifred's literary executor. He also prevailed on me to remake my will—which this time I did properly—since the deaths of Father & Winifred made the old one out of date.

Father's will was in the papers on Saturday Oct. 5th & Sunday Oct. 6th—approx. £62,000 without the death duties. *The Times* put nothing about the manner of his death, the *Evening Standard* & the *Observer* put "Found drowned in the River Thames on Aug. 5th", but the *Sunday Express* made a story of it—a reporter visited Mother on the Friday & she treated him with injudicious roughness. She was very much upset about the publicity but I was past caring. Oddly enough, none of the papers seemed to realise Father's connection with myself, or at any rate they didn't emphasise it & quite inaccurately described me as "Vera Mary Catlin";

possibly it was done out of decency, to spare me over recent events, but this is hard to believe of the popular press.

We discussed innumerable holiday plans—at first Margaret Storm Jameson (whom I have now made my literary executor instead of Winifred) thought of coming with us, but then she had to go to Watford to a nursing home—where I took her in a car—and we finally decided that we would go on a cruise on an American boat to Palestine & the Eastern Mediterranean & look at the international situation at first hand. Packed & got all ready to go on October 12th.

Saturday October 12th
Cancelled the Palestine cruise at Friday's breakfast, six hours before we were due to start, owing to news that General Election would probably be about November 19th. Ellen Wilkinson emphatically, & F. Pethick-Lawrence more gently, advised G. not to leave the country, so to-day we came down instead for a week or ten days at Fowey, in Cornwall. Neither had been there before. Took Cornish Riviera train & got in to Fowey on a local line just after dark. Had lovely bedroom looking on harbour; got beautiful impression of dark, smooth water & lights of ships, & brilliant moonlight illuminating the hills. Very comfortable hotel, the Fowey Hotel.

Sunday October 13th–Sunday October 20th   Fowey
Darling little place, delightful walks not spoilt by prevailing atmosphere of warm, grey mistiness. This was restful, but two sunny days of walking along the rocky coast put more life into us. But the more lovely the world was, the greater became my overwhelming sense of loss—not just mine but Winifred's; as George Brett wrote to me in the most significant sentence that came in all my hundreds of letters: "It hurts to think of the years she has missed."

Our peace here was somewhat broken, not only by the vast correspondence which followed us down here in spite of a notice in *The Times* that we had gone abroad, & Miss Moore's endeavours to spare us, but by intimation of the General Election which put political pressure upon G., & the endeavours of various publishers (Mr Kyllmann of Constable's rang me up here twice) to get me to do an immediate biography of Winifred. Finally wrote in desperation to Gollancz, who also wanted it, & also immediately, but who at least will—I hope—help me to do it in connection with the rest of my work instead of in conflict with it. We are to discuss the whole matter when I get back to London. I no more feel equal now to doing an immediate biography of Winifred than I felt equal to writing *T. of Y.* immediately after the War, but I feel even less like continuing my novel at present, and perhaps with the need the power will come.

Sunday October 20th
Gordon left early to look over Hunger Strike area of S. Wales miners.

Lovely morning after heavy rain. Wandered around headland & coves & felt more at peace than all the time here. In afternoon corrected typescript of "South Riding". Evening, talked over fire with young man who lives at Ditchling and is writing life of Frank Brangwyn. He had read *T. of Y.* & knew about Winifred.

Monday October 21st   London
Another lovely morning; superb orange sunrise over the harbour. Walked round woods & headland again before catching midday train back to London. Found beautiful flowers from Storm Jameson & from Mother; also masses of letters, including a charming one of real sympathy from Mr Latham & one from George acknowledging the return of the $500 advance wh. I sent back to him on the day Winifred died. Lady Rhondda rang up—was kind—wanted me to take more than 3 months over doing a book on W.; said she would try to persuade Mrs H. that I was the person to do it. Also rang up S.J. but she had a party of Norwegians there to dinner & couldn't talk much.

Corrected W.'s typescript all the way back in the train—such a lovely, gracious book, full of human benevolence & understanding. Oh, what a loss—what cruel stupidity of fate to take her away! Decided to ask George & Latham to call it "South Riding", not "Take What You Want". This suggests a snappy, trivial book; and Winifred's is great & ought to be a classic.

Tuesday October 22nd
Wrote & dictated about 25 letters. Walked to Edwardes Square for tea; started before the children came in; welcomed by dear John (who has been so sweet to me since Winifred died); hardly noticed by Shirley, who was staring at the cakes on the table. Read *The Garden of Time* to them after tea & then went home.

Listened to Gordon's election address after dinner & composed last sentence. Most of the evening corrected the typescript of Winifred's beautiful book. Oh, the publishers *must* make "South Riding" into a classic. So full of wisdom, compassion and understanding, so rich with pity for human frailty and admiration of human courage. She has never written anything finer than these lovely country scenes of birth and death, seed-time and harvest—as though she went back to the beginning because she knew, subconsciously, that the end was near. Looked up at her photograph just above me and thought: "Oh, my dear love, I shall never do anything to equal this! I shall never produce work worthy of you, of your kindness and wisdom and pity! Oh, my poor dear love, my poor sweet!" The first-rate are taken and only the unworthy are left.

Wednesday October 23rd
Afternoon—saw Harold Rubinstein about literary executorship business; says Holtby family are satisfied, & grateful for what I am doing; got on well with family solicitor. Gordon went to Cambridge to make speech. Heard from Sir Charles Trevelyan that he will speak for him; also Mrs Corbett Ashby may. After seeing Rubinstein went to London office of *Sunderland Echo* & got a copy that Gordon wanted; then dined with Storm Jameson. We discussed Winifred's book, the Holtby family, marriage, finance, etc. Found snappy letter from Mrs H. when I came back about packing of Winifred's books; Harrods' charge much larger than their estimate; also takes for granted that I never sorted them out before sending them, after the awful day Hilda & I spent in doing so! Gordon came back from Cambridge very late. Both of us tired & cross, he worried about the election & I about the book on Winifred & my eyes. Sat up arguing till nearly 3 a.m.

Thursday October 24th
Lunched with Gollancz & found comfort, help & support where I least expected it. He didn't seem in a hurry, he cared, sympathised, & understood about Winifred; thought it indecent of other publishers to harry me as they did directly after the funeral & when I was trying to take a brief holiday; said he got Daphne du Maurier's book because others did the same to her but he waited for 2 months. Eventually found myself telling him of Winifred's last hour; of our drive to her through the night, of our walk from Marylebone High Street as night opened into day. Was on the verge of crying till he gave me a second brandy, & there were tears in his eyes too. He said he thought Mrs Holtby very extraordinary to want not to be called, & that he agreed with me that some kind of communication is possible even after consciousness is gone. We discussed the book about her & he gradually revised his opinion about doing a hurried book to catch topical interest; said it always seemed to him a little indecent, as though one wanted to make capital out of the dead & that this would certainly bring criticism even if undeserved. Eventually on the strength of his "flair" he decided that the book should *not* be a formal biography nor be published now, but should be a biographical novel of the type of *T. of Y.* I said I wanted to write not just the portrait of Winifred but of a woman in her time & he caught me up & said: "That's the title! We'll call it 'A Woman In Her Time' & add in a subtitle that it's the story of Winifred Holtby."

I walked all the way home feeling strengthened & comforted as I had not been since Winifred died. Gordon came in at dinner-time; had been making contact with Angus Watson & seemed fairly satisfied with it. Went to King's Cross & saw him off to Sunderland by the night train; Duke of Northumberland also in it, & several men who looked like M.P.s or candidates going north after the Dissolution of Parliament.

Friday October 25th

Lady Rhondda rang up just after breakfast saying that Mrs Holtby agreed (history doesn't relate how reluctantly) to my doing the biography of Winifred, & a note from Edith de C. said the same thing—so that is a great weight off my mind.

At noon went to the Memorial Service for Arthur Henderson at Westminster Abbey. By saying I was representing Gordon & using name of Sunderland, I got a seat among the party organisers & M.P.s close to the choir stalls where the Members of the Government were sitting. Just opposite me were Ramsay MacDonald & J. H. Thomas (whose thoughts must have been strange, to say the least of it), Major Attlee & Mr Clynes. It was an impressive service, with the hymns & prayers suggesting work for international peace; it wasn't as poignant as Winifred's, because there was not the sense of premature death but of one who had stayed his time & fulfilled his course even though at the end nearly everything he had worked for seemed at its lowest ebb. If only both he & Winifred (who worked so hard for Gordon's advancement, & he just *might* get elected) could have lived to see the results of the coming campaign, which though they won't mean victory are at least not likely to be as bad as 1931. As I looked at the glowing topaz & ruby & sapphire of the rose window above me, & the sunlight flecking the tall grey arches where they join the vaulted roof, I thought of Winifred & Henderson together—the young writer and the old statesman—and how in their different ways they had both worked for peace.

Paid the £350 for the election over to Gordon & transferred the sum from my deposit to my current account. If only these *Testament of Youth* royalties can help him to win his seat!

Saw Mr Williamson Noble the oculist in evening—nothing much wrong—reading glasses need changing. He said trouble accentuated by shock.

Monday October 28th

Took Winifred's novel to W. A. R. Collins; said he was going to do a special limited edition as well as the ordinary & asked me to write introduction. Much upset because I was doing her life for Gollancz; had wanted me to do it for him.

Drops put in eyes & further test.

Tuesday October 29th–Friday November 1st

Mostly election business for Gordon. Got Sir Charles Trevelyan, Betty Morgan & Dr Albert Belden to promise to speak for him. Inundated by wireless, letters & telephone calls. Found time to write an Introduction to W.'s book on Thursday—splitting head, thought it due to new glasses.

Friday November 1st
Spent day in bed with slight chill—evidently origin of headache. Charming letter from George urging me not to hurry "Hon. Estate", to postpone lecture tour if I wished; he also enclosed my royalties' cheque (£566.11.0) which I had asked if I might have as soon as it was due at the end of November. Enclosed also a letter to Everitt sending their commission and saying that he had been "glad to accommodate me". Sent some news of Sunderland for Hannen Swaffer's page in the *D. Herald.*
Dictating & working most of day; not much rest.

Saturday November 2nd
Sunderland one of the two towns won for Labour by municipal election; Labour after aldermanic elections will be in control. 6 Socialist Councillors unopposed; increase of Socialist vote in Tory wards.
G. telegraphed asking me to go up to-morrow; said I would. Sketched out two speeches. Mother came to help look after children.

Sunday November 3rd   Sunderland
Went up to Sunderland—still feeling a little groggy from chill. Harry Pearson met me with car at Newcastle. Arrived at Grand Hotel to find party meeting of Councillors Hoy, Cohen, Ford & Hied. G. obviously over-tired & not entirely at ease. They asked me to make short speech at Miners' Hall that night—said I would. G. said somewhat contemptuously "Don't be too ladylike," but I take no notice of such remarks nowadays.
Went to meeting; crammed full. Somerbell, prospective mayor, in chair. Made my speech at end; got such a rousing reception when I first appeared & again at the end of it that I had to stand up to take the applause. Harry told me later that Jos. Hoy, the Chairman of the Labour Party & a checkweighman, said to him later that G.'s speech was a great improvement on his past efforts, but *"she* got them". Staying at Grand Hotel; very comfortable.

Monday November 4th
Went to Labour office (9 Murton Street) in morning & started getting to know the workers & managing G.'s correspondence. Spoke in afternoon at Co-op. Hall. Nomination meeting in evening. Sir Charles Trevelyan came over from Wallington to speak at it & dined with us first. His interest in me (due to *Testament of Youth*) seemed in no wise diminished & I was as conscious as before of his stimulus & fascination. The Victoria Hall was crammed, chiefly with enthusiasts. Dr Betty Morgan arrived with Leah Manning (G.'s fellow candidate) soon after the meeting had begun. Sir Charles spoke first (very interesting speech—largely on Russia—wh. G. however thought dangerous), then Betty Morgan—good & attractive —then G. (not very good, too nervy, too much movement, not enough constructive ideas), then Leah Manning (good & solid), & I wound up in a

brief 10 mins. Jos. Hoy made a first-rate Chairman. Very successful meeting.

Tuesday November 5th
Correspondence, writing up material for Press. Several meetings in wards in evening.

Wednesday November 6th
Spoke at Gaiety Theatre meeting in afternoon; crowded with our supporters. Councillor Jenkins took me afterwards to see some slums that had just been cleared—one a terrible underground basement, no light or heat, holes in boards of floor with unspeakable rubbish beneath. Ward meetings in evening.

Thursday November 7th
Went round Monk Wearmouth housing with Mrs Cohen; more terrible slums, & crowded rooms with indescribably filthy bedding. In one house saw family of man & woman with nine children all living in two rooms —man an ex-serviceman who had never had a job since the War; woman looked very ill, shapeless & entirely overwhelmed by life. Children only semi-clothed. The couple had been there 20 years & obviously had not turned out the rooms all that time as there was nowhere but the street to put the furniture. Realised as so often what an expensive luxury cleanliness is. Have never seen such terrible housing before—not even in Glasgow. No meetings this evening; cried off & did stuff for the Press instead.

Friday November 8th
Met Mrs Silva-White at Carnick's for coffee. Large aggressive overdressed woman (Canadian); suspect she joined Labour Party in order to meet me. Walked round Central Ward with her & made short speech at a street corner.

At 3.0 met Ellen Wilkinson at Committee rooms, coming to speak for us at Gaiety Theatre & Roker Baths; she listened & followed carefully, in true statesmanlike fashion, all I told her about the constituency. She had a sore throat & was obviously much tired. I told her just what I thought abt George Ford as an agent & she understood.

Was picked up at Gaiety Theatre by Councillor Hied; went round Thornhill Ward with him & did a little canvassing; had tea with him & his wife. He "coached" me as to how best to speak there, & later that evening I talked in one of the Thornhill schools on why I became a Socialist. V. successful; Hied an intelligent man. Spoke at 2 other meetings, one even more Conservative, & another very crowded & full of supporters—the Bede Hall. Margaret Bondfield had spoken there before I arrived, & left; Chuter-Ede (standing for South Shields) was speaking, very amusingly, when I arrived. Mrs Silva-White in chair. G. had spoken before I came &

said he had stopped an uproar in the meeting. Went to Mrs Silva-White's
house when it was over, had glass of wine & cake, & met the Canon (dry &
desiccated but preferable to Mrs S.W.).

Saturday November 9th
10.45, meeting with Sunderland teachers at a room in the Y.M.C.A. (G.
talked to a gym instructor there who told him that a large proportion of the
Y.M.C.A. members were too under-nourished to profit by gymnastics.) At
12.0 went to Town Hall for institution of the new (and first Labour) mayor,
Somerbell. Speeches by various councillors & aldermen—Ritson, Taylor,
Nicholson etc. Furness & Storey on platform but not near us.

2.30, went to watch Football Match at Stadium; sat next to Furness, who
rushed to Leah Manning & me as though we were going to protect him
from Storey, who sat at other end of row next to Gordon. F. & S. never
spoke to each other at the whisky-drinking in the interval, G. said. After
match, had tea with Miss Moul, headmistress of the Bede School; mixture
of domineering teacher & enthusiastic undergraduate; reminded me of
Sarah Burton, the heroine of Winifred's "South Riding".

Evening, open-air meeting in damp street near hotel; large crowd.

Sunday November 10th
Morning, went over to Seaham Harbour & G. sat on Shinwell's platform at
one of his meetings against MacDonald.

Afternoon, spoke for Jos. Ritson & Tom Sexton at Usher Moor, beyond
Durham. Noisy miners' meeting but was favourably received. At the end
the owner of the cinema theatre where we spoke addressed the meeting on
the iniquities of the Means Test and its ill-effect on the entertainment
business.

Evening, Peace Council meeting at the Miners' Hall. Mrs Zangwill
spoke before me, less drearily than usual, on the absurdity of the official
defence against gas regulations.

Monday November 11th
Armistice Day. Morning, parade & service at the War Memorial.
Marched down Fawcett Street with huge crowds lining road. Wore War
ribbons, also G. Storey in silk hat & frock coat, looking very inappropriate.
In afternoon Dr Belden turned up to speak at evening Armistice meeting at
Victoria Hall. In actual speech became too political—contrary to under-
standing with Tories—& annoyed the British Legion, which walked out.
They stayed however for my speech which came first & which G. said was
one of the best I had made—on memories of Aug. 4th, 1914; on tour of
Central Europe 1924; & Thiepval Ridge 1933. Furness & Storey in front
row of dress-circle; some of our supporters hissed when they came in so G.

at once got up & shook hands with them. Furness congratulated G. on my speech.

Tuesday November 12th
Canvassed in Bishop's Wearmouth with Mrs Humphreys; lunched with her; later we both visited the Infirmary (of which Storey is chairman) & encountered Mrs Manning there with Mrs Silva-White. Our visit considerably embarrassed the Matron, who showed us round, as Furness & Storey were having a meeting at the same time & she feared they would run into us.

Evening, spoke for Ellen Wilkinson at two meetings in schools at Jarrow; returned to address enormous open-air meeting in West Park (through microphone, standing in bitter wind on top of a lorry with footlights below; crowd looked black & indefinite against vivid glare). Walked through Park to Victoria Hall & tried to get admitted to Furness & Storey's big meeting but policeman wd not admit me although a supporter of ours in the crowd gave me a ticket. No one came out from the hall to address the overflow meeting in the street & every entrance was guarded by the policemen, so I shepherded the crowd to West Park & went to make a final speech at the Herrington Street Mission Hall.

Wednesday November 13th
Eve of poll. Afternoon, spoke at Co-op. Hall where Jack Lawson was the chief speaker (the Miners' chief M.P.); he remained there during my speech and said he was glad to meet someone he knew so well by repute. Also heard G.'s speech, which was good & wh. he obviously approved. Packed meeting.

Evening, went all round wards with G. & made 5-minute speeches after his to crowded meetings in schools; to three read first letter ever written me by Shirley, received a day or two ago and beginning: "Dear Mummie & Daddy, I hope you will get into Parliament." Always went down very well. Ended up at big demonstration in Miners' Hall, crowded with our own supporters, who had waited patiently there for nearly three hours while we spoke at the other 6 meetings. Big final ovation to G. & Leah Manning.

Thursday November 14th
Polling day. In morning drove round with Leah Manning (who had a frightful cold) and visited polling-booths and committee-rooms. After-noon, spent most of time in damp & dark East End, canvassing in houses with pitch-dark stairs worn & broken in many places; tin baths & buckets on landing; walls felt shiny & damp to touch. Habitations more fit for monkeys than human beings; wondered how many bugs I was picking up. Taken round by very intelligent little boy of 13. Got impression that most of East End population were voting for Storey. Ended up with late dinner & then went on to Leah Manning's hotel at Roker to hear results on

wireless. All of us somewhat depressed, as return of polling cards didn't indicate a very favourable prospect for us, and first results on wireless showed that, though a few old Labour strongholds were won back, the great towns in the North, such as Newcastle, were still voting National Govt with large majorities. Heard that D. N. Pritt (former candidate for Sunderland) was returned for North Hammersmith. Got back to Grand Hotel long after midnight. G. very tired & eyes inflamed after being out with the [loud] speaker all day.

Tuesday December 31st: New Year's Eve   London
After dinner G. & I went to St Paul's, where a watch-night service was being held both inside & out, to see the New Year in. So thankful to get rid of 1935 that we wanted to do something to mark its passing. Got out of bus at Aldwych & walked to Ludgate Hill. Got there about 11.30; mob there so thick that we couldn't get nearer than about 200 yds from the steps. Couldn't hear a word of the Service, or the community singing of war songs and "Abide With Me", for the shouting & yelling of the mob & their constant performance on squeakers. Frightful struggling & pushing mob, many of them drunk. But for G., who put his arms in a circle round me & made a barricade, I couldn't have kept on my feet; as it was I got bruised all over & could hardly breathe. In distance saw Canon Sheppard announcing & gesticulating before microphone in front of the statue of Queen Anne. Dome floodlit but rest of Cathedral, in front of which stood Christmas trees, lighted up with brightly-coloured electric bulbs—green, orange, blue & red. Trees from the King's garden.

Finally the striking of twelve did prevail over the noise of the mob; an occasional flash illumined the clock face; & then everyone, even down to us on Ludgate Hill, started singing Auld Lang Syne—1935 had really gone; what of 1936? Winifred in dying took with her that second life that she initiated for me just after the War; can I make a third? Can I, once more, begin again? Are children and books enough incentive for living? Have I any hope of repeating the success of *Testament of Youth*? Does one make new friends when the thirties are over? Does love, orthodox and unorthodox, still abide? Time only can answer.

We walked back from Ludgate Hill to Piccadilly, after going into the emptied Cathedral and looking at the little effigies showing Christ in the stable. Various forms of semi-drunken mirth going on—suggest that the wearing of false noses is a peculiarly English method of demonstrating gaiety. Men everywhere carrying enormous bunches of coloured balloons. People dancing animatedly in the street or talking to partners on the pavement. Strangers taking off hats with excessive flourish & wishing me a happy New Year. Most restaurants open; cheaper ones crowded; got some coffee & sandwiches at Honey Dew in the Strand; Savoy emptying as we passed. Damp, mild night; ground wet and muddy but no rain. In Strand, outside Strand Palace, a few ladies somewhat drunk parading street in evening dress. Wondered why the passing of anything and the coming of anything new causes humanity to celebrate and rejoice. Is transition a good in itself? After all, we have it all the time.

Picked up a taxi in Piccadilly; got home about 1.30 & to bed about 2.30. Goodbye to 1935; the worst, cruellest and saddest year since the War.

1936

Wednesday January 1st   Sidmouth
Went down to Sidmouth with Mother. Not so tired as I expected after last night's battering by New Year celebrators outside St Paul's. Another batch of Winifred's letters from Creech Jones; also a request by the *Teacher's World* for a "message" to children to go in their "Messages from Famous People" series. Wrote it going down on train. Another letter was from Mrs Ethelreda Lewis from Dar-es-Salaam; she had been travelling and only heard belatedly and casually of Winifred's death.

Pleasant rooms at Sidmouth—7 York Terrace—not been to them before. Mother quite pleased. Lovely sun when we arrived & a gold and red sunset. Sea apparently calmer than it had been for days though the waves are quite high. Walked up cliff walk towards Mutter's Moor & then (alone) up path through woods on side of Salcombe Cliff; went as far as Miss Chattell's where Winifred stayed exactly four years ago this month, & seemed to see her everywhere.

Thursday January 2nd
Lovely morning sun. Walked along Esplanade and up Salcombe Cliff. Rooms seem quite comfortable to me though Mother complains a good deal (about the cold, the bathroom, the lavatory, the cold, the way the grate doesn't fit, the fact that the early morning tea isn't brought up promptly at 7.30, the cold, her bedroom window, which lets in a draught, the size of the lumps of coal, which burn up too quickly, etc. etc.). Alone I should notice none of these things; I don't feel cold after London. The peace seems exquisite and would be perfect if I were by myself. Oh Winifred darling, why aren't you here to share the peace with me and with me to appreciate it, and the sun, and the sea, and all the simple everyday things we both loved!

Spent most of yesterday correcting the proofs of *South Riding* and admiring it more than ever. I wish "Honourable Estate" could be even half as good. Walked up to Mutter's Moor after lunch—and along the Sid with Mother before tea.

What a strange experience of communion with her spirit this proof-correcting is! In her book, all the time, she says the things that we both thought and said to one another.

Friday January 3rd
Pleasant letter from Harold Latham, repeating that he wants to use my Introduction to *South Riding* as an afterword. Letter from G. describing luncheon with Ellen Wilkinson at the Gargoyle (which pleased him) and saying that the children were all right. Corrected W.'s proofs all day but

kept getting ideas for "Hon. Estate" instead. Advance review (good) by John Brophy in *T. & T.* of Phyllis Bentley's new novel *Freedom, Farewell.* Very cold. Walked a good deal in morning & afternoon but too chilly to be pleasant.

Saturday January 4th

Winifred's probate papers came from Rubinstein—attested & signed them before Mr Mossop, a Sidmouth solicitor. So odd to be reading papers about "Winifred Holtby Deceased" while looking at this prospect of red cliffs and tossing sea which we so often watched together from a similar balcony. Astonished to see that her estate amounted to £24,000 odd till I realised that this included capital coming to her under her father's will of which she never enjoyed the income. She never mentioned this £19,000 in her will and I'm sure never realised it was hers to leave; as she would not have simply let it go back to her nieces, who have enough already. Lawyers are very culpable in not explaining to heirs of estates just what they are entitled to do. I should never have known I could will away the £5,000 coming to me absolutely from Father if Harold Rubinstein had not told me. To think what W. could have done with this money—and the Tolmie relatives have no social sense.

Letter from Tyrone Guthrie giving me his impression of W. at their luncheon. I wrote back saying I did hope he would produce "Hope of Thousands". Corrected proofs of *South Riding.* Lovely morning, chiefly spent in probate business. Long walk round Sidford in afternoon; gorgeous sunset over sea when we returned.

Sunday January 5th

Long review by Gerald Gould in *Observer* of *Freedom, Farewell*; interesting but not altogether flattering; questioned Phyllis's motive in writing it and the worth-whileness of the whole performance.

Very wet all day; terrific storm, waves dashing over esplanade. Went out for two short, wet, gusty walks; otherwise worked all day at proofs except for long letter to Gordon. Proofs seem interminable; nearly 600 pages.

Very worried about next section of "Honourable Estate"—how to do it. Wish I could get on to it.

Monday January 6th

Finished & sent off proofs. Avalanche of letters. Weather slightly better but ground very wet.

Tuesday January 7th

Began on Book II of "Hon. Estate". Got section 2 (Wife) sorted out. Wrote to Mr Latham, Margaret S. J., Gordon, & sent M.S.J. parcel of honey, cream etc.

Wednesday January 8th
Went on with "Hon. Estate"; sorted out Book II, section 1 (Husband).
Wet and stormy day again. Completed typescript of Part I came from Miss
Moore.

Thursday January 9th
Another storm in night; part of the cliff, fenced off as dangerous a week ago,
gone down beyond Jacob's Ladder. Got out very little all day. Refused
speaking invitation from Nat. Peace Council (a youth group at Hampstead). Worked on Staffordshire history & politics for "Hon. Estate".

Friday January 10th   London
Returned from Sidmouth. Blustery there but sunny day away from coast.
Gordon met me at Paddington. All seemed well at home. Usual boring
avalanche of letters & papers to sort. *Times Lit. Supp.* had a none-too-
enthusiastic review of Phyllis's book, but a leading article on the present
popularity of Greece and Rome as scenes for novelists.

Saturday January 11th
Afternoon, went to Somerville Annual S.S.A. meeting at Bedford College,
with Hilda Reid who drove me there. Was glad I had had hair, eyebrows,
nails done, as gathering was even more ghastly exhibition than usual of
sartorial monstrosities—dating from the days when intellect in a woman
was supposed to annihilate any pretensions to personal attractiveness and
any obligations to improve one's appearance. Chief exception Dorothy
Sayers who while grown enormous & deliberately eccentric is at least not
dowdy. Has been recently elected Chairman of S.S.A. & as Chairman was
trying to get alteration in the Constitution passed which automatically
gave the Chairman a seat on the Somerville Council. She obviously
enjoyed being Chairman & took three times as long as was necessary in
putting all the points, especially considering intelligence of the audience,
who were largely headmistresses, writers etc. Not many of my years at
S.S.A. meeting but met Marjorie Barber, Muriel Byrne, D. Lord, Joyce &
Kit Simpson, & Jane Harvey, whose husband is now a master at Eton.
Hilda came to supper & helped put the children to bed.

Monday January 13th
Read History of T.U. organisation in Potteries for "Hon. Estate". Afternoon, made myself go to West End & do a little shopping for myself and the
house.
    After dinner met Harold Latham at Euston (boat-train from S.S.
Georgic, which landed at Liverpool) with Gordon; Lovat Dickson there
also. All three of us went along with him to Brown's Hotel & had coffee etc.
& talked about nature of the novel. Lovat Dickson maintained that in a
political novel the politics were simply an accident & that what mattered
were the human relationships—I that the novel if capable of further

development must include large social & political movements & show their effect on the individual; that political & social movements are themselves the product of human emotions (i.e. the desire for power, the impulse towards mercy, etc.). Later G. showed me his account in "Face of Revolution" of his talk in Russia with the Russian writer Pilnyak (Chairman of Revolutionary Writers' Committee), who commented that no one can exist outside history.

Asked Latham to dine with us here on Friday & wrote asking Margaret Storm Jameson if she would come too & stay night.

Tuesday January 14th
Morning—read History of Potters' T.U. organisation. Afternoon—took John & Shirley to be overhauled by Dr Hamilton—one or two small things wrong with John; Shirley commended for good health, perfect teeth & general fearlessness. Went on to Collins & discussed W.'s book— apparently some chance of the Book Society taking it. Agreed that my Introduction should be an Epilogue as in America. Another letter from Mrs Holtby to Collins generally grousing at Winifred's prefatory letter because it refers to her, and her public work that is apparently sacrosanct —which he hadn't answered. We looked over photographs but they still preferred the old one for the frontispiece to the Special Edition. Was not offered any tea, so at 5.30, feeling tealess and depressed, went along to Maison Prunier and ate oysters.

Wednesday January 15th
Lunched with Mrs Littlejohn at her flat (very attractive modern one at top of Prince's House in Kensington Park Rd) to meet Sybil Thorndike. Had met her before at a luncheon with Sarah Gertrude Millin, in pre-*Testament of Youth* days, but as she didn't recall this I pretended not to either. Must be in the fifties now—dressed in vivid green, gay, vital, strong, charming, *very* energetic. Somewhat difficult to hold much of a conversation as she talks a good deal & in her stage voice in an ordinary-sized room. The room was charmingly furnished & the lunch excellent (tomato soup, poached eggs on stewed corn, jellied chicken surrounded by salad, sweet made of pink meringue with passion-fruit juice & cream. Wish I could manage anything of the sort here!).

Mrs Littlejohn had just been in Germany & lunched with Goering—as, though she had written articles adverse to the regime, they thought her worth taking trouble over owing to her influence in Australia. They showed her everything they thought would impress her favourably & she came away feeling as adverse to the regime as ever & that the younger generation don't know the difference between truth and falsehood. They are consistently taught, she says, that they are the finest nation in the world but that other nations are jealous and work against them, so they must fight for their rights.

Thursday January 16th
Very cold snowy day. Worked at Book II Part 1 of "Hon. Estate" till tea-time; then went to tea with Dr Jane Walker at 122 Harley Street—it had been suggested to her by Bp Crotty (Bathurst), who returns to England at end Feb., to take a living in St Pancras (largely through Dr Walker & Dr Mansbridge having approached Matthews, the new Dean of St Paul's). Borrowed *Life of Mandell Creighton*—from which I am quoting something in my book. Harold Latham sent me the contract for *South Riding* wh. I sent on to H. F. Rubinstein.

Friday January 17th
Book in morning; then got flowers etc. for dinner & did them. Had Harold Latham & Margaret Storm Jameson to dinner. Margaret stayed the night in Winifred's room. We talked of *South Riding*, of Margaret's new book published now with New York Macmillan, of Gordon's "Face of Revolution", of Charles Morgan's new novel. Latham said George had been quite perturbed when he got my letter saying he needn't publish my book on Winifred if he didn't want to; went down into Latham's office wondering whatever he'd done. Pleasant dinner. Daffodils & mimosa about the house. Latham seemed to think there was a chance that the American Book of the Month Club might choose *South Riding*.
   Very cold. Kipling critically ill at Middlesex Hospital. Rumours that the King is seriously ill again. Gave Harold Latham the corrected proofs of *South Riding*.

Saturday January 18th
Kipling's death announced this morning—took place in early hours. Papers full of obituary notices & remarks containing contradictory estimates according to whether writer was Imperialist or Socialist. King's illness demanding several doctors. Kipling was at Brown's Hotel—where Mrs Kipling is now.
   Went to watch a class at Macpherson's Gymnasium before deciding to send John & Shirley; thought it would do for them. Took them into Battersea Park this afternoon where they snowballed. Very cold but some sun. Among my afternoon press-cuttings (mostly about Winifred) was a curious one stating that she was a friend of Cynthia Stockley's & that it was partly out of grief for Winifred's death that C.S. committed suicide the other day. As I feel pretty certain that Winifred never knew or had even corresponded with Cynthia Stockley this puzzled me somewhat—especially as the cutting (from the *Daily Mail*) further said that W. had prophesied C.S.'s death in a short story not long ago. Sent it on to Lady Rhondda to see if she could elucidate the mystery.
   Did a little book but not much. Margaret S.J. had to go back to Reading immediately after breakfast. John went to dentist, & Amy to Rubinstein's

office again to testify once more to her witness of Winifred's will. G. went to
Maidstone for a political conference.

Sunday January 19th
Bitterly cold but turning warmer & wetter towards evening. Aunt Belle at
Edwardes Square; took the children as usual. G. returned unexpectedly
from Maidstone; I wasn't as welcoming as I might have been as my book
was in my head and I wanted to get on with it. He then began to scold me &
I broke down completely & violently from griefs of past few months. Went
to bed about 3 a.m. with swollen face & splitting head.

Further disquieting news of the King's health. All the Royal family gone
to Sandringham.

Monday January 20th
Announcement that Kipling is to be buried in the Poets' Corner at noon on
Thursday; only the third person this century to be buried in this part of the
Abbey (the others being Sir Henry Irving in 1905 & Thomas Hardy in
1928). Wrote to Canon Barry asking if there was any chance that I could be
admitted.

G. nice to-day. Some sun, with showers; walked round Battersea Park.
Evening papers contained no fresh news of the King, but at 9.30 this
announcement was made on the wireless & signed by three doctors: "The
King's life is moving peacefully towards its close." At 10.0 this bulletin was
repeated and a service followed, giving the psalm "The Lord is My
Shepherd", prayers for the King, and the words: "In quietness and
confidence shall be your strength." Weather turning colder again & wind
howling as I sat on the kitchen stairs listening to Burnett's wireless. The
same bulletin was repeated at 10.30. G. was going to a theatrical party so I
went along with him and got out at Buckingham Palace and watched the
crowds waiting for news from 11 p.m. till after midnight. Very cold;
snow-laden wind blowing again; ground wet & muddy. Crowds not only
pressing against railings but were mounted on Queen Victoria's statue &
fountain, together with press-photographers & cinematograph workers
with flashlights. Above the Palace—closed with drawn blinds but one or
two lights in the top windows—the clouds occasionally parted revealing a
solitary star. Conversations in the crowd: "It's very sudden." "Yes, it is
sudden, isn't it." One little man remarked to two females: "They said he
really died this afternoon." "Oh, but the 9.30 bulletin didn't say so." "No,
they never does. Look at Queen Victoria; she was dead a fortnight before
the people was ever told." "Oh . . . but what about buryin' her?"

Took taxi home; taxi-man told me 12.15 a.m. wireless had said that the
King died at midnight. Later this was confirmed by G. who heard it at a
theatrical party. The actual time of his death was 11.55 p.m.; so he missed
dying on the same day as Queen Victoria only by 24 hours & 5 minutes.

Tuesday January 21st
All papers full of enormous obituary notices of the King and biographies of
"Edward VIII". After a life-long association of kingship with elderliness
and Nestorian wisdom, it seems odd to have a contemporary as king.
Walked about London this afternoon getting impressions in case I want
them for sequel to *T. of Y.* Half-mast flags from all chief buildings, against
wintry orange & grey of a sky that looked snow-laden. Bitterly cold with
East wind. Drapers' and milliners' shops all decorated in black with
occasional white or purple. Groups of people still walking round Buckingham Palace, & a crowd round St James's Palace entrance waiting to see the
new King attend a Privy Council. Fact that he flew to London, & that
everyone heard of King George's death by wireless, marks vast changes
since death of Edward VII.
   Saw a school (90 Queen's Gate—Rowland's) to-day, for John, but too
conventional.

Wednesday January 22nd
Went down to St James's Palace to hear the Proclamation of the new King
at 10 a.m. Too much of a crowd to see much, especially as we could only get
to the back, not the front, of Friar's Court, but I heard the words of the
Proclamation through the loud speakers, and saw the Herald's carriages,
the green-uniformed trumpeters on horseback, and the Life Guards with
draped colours.
   A typical London winter's day, with subdued sun and a slight mist. G.
and I walked back through St James's Park as far as Hyde Park Corner.
Worked all rest of day on "Hon. Estate" and finished Chapter 4, which
means half of it done.
   Letter from Phyllis, asking me to tea to-morrow; also from Miss
Hutchinson thanking me for Winifred's poems, and one from George's
secretary, Miss Stone, acknowledging my last to him & saying that he has
gone on a trip to the Pacific coast till the beginning of February.

Thursday January 23rd
Went to Kipling's funeral in the Poets' Corner in Westminster Abbey.
Clear bright day, very cold. Sat in North Transept; music lovely; moment
especially impressive when choir and clergy with their uplifted crosses
moved in front of the coffin to the Poets' Corner at the far end of the South
Transept, and the Dean uttered the Committal Prayer standing beside
Addison's statue with its outstretched hand. As they returned the "Reces-
sional" was sung—softly instead of with the usual pompous violence.
When the service was over I moved up to the front with the rest—and saw
the purple-covered grave between the graves (incongruous companions) of
Hardy & Dickens, and the beautiful wreaths of spring flowers.
   In afternoon looked over a school (Gibbs' in Sloane Square) which Lady
Balfour of Burleigh recommended; a P.N.E.U. school, fairly progressive,

which will probably do for John. Then went on to tea with Phyllis Bentley at the Halcyon Club; very pleasant and peaceful, and we talked chiefly books—*Freedom, Farewell, South Riding* and "Honourable Estate". I told her I'd recognised the extent to which Elaine in her *Modern Tragedy* was due to me but that I realised that with a good novelist no one was ever a photograph but merely the inspiration for a portrait which developed quite otherwise.

Mother got a window in Oxford & Cambridge Terrace for us to see the King's Funeral. The body came back from Sandringham this afternoon to lie in state in Westminster Hall but I didn't attempt to see the procession, having had more than enough of crowds in the past few days. Reflected afterwards that in the crowd at Kipling's funeral I didn't see a soul I knew, whereas at Galsworthy's Memorial Service I seemed to know every second person. Concluded that the crowd at the Abbey this morning was not a literary crowd at all but chiefly soldiers & civil servants.

Friday January 24th
Lunched Violet Scott-James at the Ivy; we talked of Winifred & *South Riding* and her John. Gollancz was there with the Lynd girl; came over and shook hands with us. V.S.J. & I talked till after 3.0; then I dropped in to the News Theatre for half an hour & saw the film of yesterday's procession, etc. Agreed on telephone to do next week's Book of the Week for Thomas Moult (*Sunday Referee*). Rubinstein rang up to say that the re-drawing of one clause of W.'s contract with Macmillan would be necessary owing to the separation of the ordinary & literary estates by her Will.

Gordon at Oxford for night (staying with H. H. Price).

Saturday January 25th
Worked all day at "Hon. Estate"; wrote 11 pp. of Part II. Took children out with tricycle after lunch. At 5.0 Burnett took John to see Bertram Mills Circus. Put Shirley to bed. G. returned from Oxford. Rubinstein returned reworded contract wh. I sent on to Latham. After supper read book on China for *Sunday Referee*.

Sunday January 26th
G. & I lunched with Dr Jane Walker at 122 Harley St; met her nephew (Foreign Editor of B.B.C.) and another male & female whom I didn't identify. General pleasant conversation; good deal of it about the Royal family & the funeral. Lovely morning; walked partly there through the Park; everyone dressed in smart mourning after church. Blackness but no desolation.

Edwardes Square later. Jessie & Alfred Haigh there to tea. Worked at "Hon. Estate" after supper but back ached badly & I went to bed comparatively early.

Monday January 27th
Felt so tired that I cancelled my lunch with Find Graucob & stayed in bed
till the evening. Lectured at 8.o at Central Y.M.C.A. on *Testament of Youth*.
Short speech first by official who said the hall was called after King George.
Everyone solemn, in black, and easily moved to tears. Large audience,
some in gallery. Went to Regent's Park afterwards to have coffee &
sandwiches with Mrs Grace MacDougall of Rhodesia (in England for a
year) who founded the F.A.N.Y.s. Wore black dress with lattice-work
silver top & black mortar-board hat.

Tuesday January 28th
Got up very early to take John to 3 Oxford Terrace to see the King's funeral
procession but it wasn't early enough; taxi came late. Got involved in
terrific scrum of crowd round Oxford Terrace; had to negotiate five
crossings of barriers; was afraid J. would get crushed to death, & we should
never have got through without Gordon. Mother battered & much upset.
Aunt Belle also battered but remained brisk & cheerful. J. behaved
splendidly; was never frightened, seemed to have complete confidence in
us & was only anxious to get to his window. We did get there at last & saw
excellently from third floor—corner of Edgware Rd & long perspective
down Oxford Terrace. Crowd very obstreperous; inquiry was held later on
general breakdown of police arrangements. Crowds of people fainted &
were attended to below our window. Never saw such a concourse of
people—result of mass hysteria worked up by wireless. Procession itself
not very well drilled or organised but somehow pathetic—especially the
smallness of the coffin on the gun-carriage—and the massed bands were
beautiful. Saw Edward VIII—who looked very tired & walked haltingly
—quite clearly; also the backs of York & Gloucester—but the foreign
royalties were too higgledy-piggledy to be identifiable except for the yellow
cockade of the tall Crown Prince of Sweden.

Walked most of the way home through the Park; J. keeping up manfully
& saying he wasn't tired. Got back in time to listen to the service at
Windsor; everything behind schedule—the two minutes' silence when the
coffin was lowered into the vault was ¾ hour late—but the service was very
moving.

Gave tea for P. Nehru, president of the Indian Congress—people we got
here to meet him included Ivor Thomas, Leonard Barnes, Creech Jones,
Mrs Abbott & Monica Whately—who usually dresses all in black but was
wearing conspicuous red-striped collars & cuffs to show her contempt for
royalty. I was impressed by the composed intelligence of Nehru, who
answered questions for over an hour & stayed till everyone had gone. He
told me that *Testament of Youth* had been one of the last books sent him while
he was in prison & that he had been released before he had time to read it.
Monica stayed after everyone else & talked to G. about constituencies.
Wrote review for *Sunday Referee*; very late to bed, & tired.

Thursday January 30th

Doris Leslie's luncheon at the Sesame Club. Other guests were Sheila Kaye-Smith (whom I met for the first time), May Edginton, Trevor Blakemore, Watt the agent, Dr Hannay (who must be George Birmingham's son, I think), a female and male whom I didn't identify, and of course Mr Latham. He sat between Doris Leslie & myself & we talked books all the time. She had finished her novel. Sheila Kaye-Smith looked older than I expected—must be well into the fifties. I liked her. She said she'd admired *Testament of Youth* & I told her that *Challenge to Sirius* had helped me through part of the War. Walked home afterwards to Chelsea.

Clare (back from America) & Miss Wilson (one of John's schoolteachers; works for Labour Party & League of Nations Union) came to supper. Clare suffering from post-American reaction. Conversation lively but too general to be particularly significant. Clare stayed three weeks with the Bretts; disliked Isabel, liked George but thought he'd never grown up! She had "clicked" with three men but made it clear that George wasn't one of them. Said Isabel had tried to find out what she thought of him and told her that he was "potent"! I asked: "For what?"

Friday January 31st

Saw some pussy willows in the flower-shop windows this morning & remembered how Winifred hated them—she said they were frightening when they came out in brilliant yellow bloom.

Took John (with Gordon) to Miss Mayo this afternoon to have two small stumps out. Was overhauled myself by Dr Sharp but nothing wrong except over-fatigue. Blood pressure 120, heart & lungs all right. Had bromide & tonics prescribed. Brought John home in taxi while G. went to Brown's Hotel to see Mr Latham. J. felt sorry for himself & slightly sick but soon recovered on his bed. I took Shirley out & we bought him a peach & several small animals.

After tea Collins rang up to say that *South Riding* had been chosen as Book of the Month for March, and will be published on March 2nd. Why, why couldn't this have happened before? Why couldn't she have lived to know it? Oh, my poor sweet! And in her life she always felt that no book of hers really came off.

Wrote to Mrs Holtby, Lady Rhondda, Phyllis, Storm Jameson, St J. Ervine, etc., to tell them. Rang up Violet who like myself was more conscious of the bitter irony of life than of any feeling of satisfaction.

Saturday February 1st

Wrote most of day. Children in afternoon. Miss Wilson took John out & I took Shirley to cinema to see pictures of King's funeral procession & two Mickey Mouse films—preceded by lurid Tallulah Bankhead picture called *Between The Devil and the Deep Sea*—lady in beautiful evening dress on ˙submarine, husband drowned, lover rescued, etc. etc.!

Note on Winifred's Will (of which probate has just been granted—*and* to me in my name) in *Evening Standard*. Of course comments on the supposed £24,000-odd—which is quite absurd as it is half the income on which Mrs Holtby is now living. I am sure Winifred didn't know she could will this away.

Sunday February 2nd
Worked at "Hon. Estate". Edwardes Square. My review of the Lin Yutang book *My Country and My People* in the *Sunday Referee*.

Notes on Winifred's Will in *Observer*, *Sunday Express* etc. All pick out for comment the section relating to myself & the literary executorship. Press kept ringing me up about it—Press Association, *Manchester Evening News*, *Yorkshire Post*, etc.

Monday February 3rd
Mosley case begins to-day but was told I need not attend. Later learnt that only those who had seen weapons at Olympia or elsewhere were required as witnesses. More paragraphs on Winifred's Will in *Times* & many other daily papers—all picking out the same sentences.

Tuesday February 4th
Lunched with May Edginton at Ladies' Carlton Club. She made me drunk with a double "White Lady" and told me there was a ghost in Edwardes Square. Said all sorts of ill-luck happened to her while she lived there.

After lunch got head clear again by walking to Brown's Hotel and leaving note for Mr Latham. Had him to dinner at the Ivy, where we talked mild business (in which his usual antagonism to George came out), & then took him to see *Mary Tudor*. Very pleasant unexacting evening. Flora Robson excellent as Mary Tudor—also Joyce Bland as Princess Elizabeth. Mr L. brought me here in taxi.

Wednesday February 5th
G. away. Worked at "Hon. Estate". Felt under the weather with usual duodenitis but went in spite of bitter cold to hear John Spivak—the American journalist now writing in the *Herald* parts of a book which he is ultimately publishing with Gollancz—speak at Gollancz's house to a large crowd. The party as usual loud, over-crowded & blatant; Gollancz's parties always make me wish I published with Macmillan. Talked to Dr Stella Churchill, Evelyn Sharp, Mrs Harold Munro; also a few words with D. N. Pritt, J. L. Hodson, H. W. Nevinson, Norman Collins.

Spivak very interesting but most of the audience got a little restive—wd obviously rather have drunk and gossiped. Told tales of expedients wh. he adopted in meeting anti-Nazis (notably a Munich cabaret where his man was disguised as a Nazi leader in full uniform) & said that from what he saw he was convinced War was coming in a year or two but the longer it could be postponed the shorter it would be (I suppose because Russia is gradually getting better armed). Left after speech & went home alone in atrocious cold.

Thursday February 6th
Call from Lady Rhondda anxious to refute false impression of affluence created by Winifred's Will; said I thought appeal for African memorial fund wd be best place for public statement. Rang up Lewin & asked him to let me have draft at once.

Letter from Mrs Holtby urging me to use W.'s legacy from her books for myself or the children—*not* to create or further other memorials to her! I replied that I would not be obstinate—but shall lie low & see. A portrait of her for some institution where it will be seen is what I have in mind. Collins sent proofs of my Introduction—now Epitaph at end—for correction.

A *lovely* morning—so lovely that I abandoned my lecture & walked on the Embankment. The river looked beautiful this morning—I am getting over the feeling about it which Father's death gave me. Wish we could get a house on the Embankment.

Started getting up Sheffield lecture "The World To-day".

Friday February 7th
Worked at lecture "The World To-day" and at book. Mosley case ended. Mosley got ¼d damages & no costs!

Saturday February 8th
Worked most of day in getting half of "Hon. Estate" ready for Mr Latham. At night saw & wept over film of *I Was a Spy*. Going very cold.

Monday February 10th
Lunched Brown's Hotel—Mr Latham's Macmillan party. G. came with me but had to leave early for train to North. In much fear and trembling took MS. of half "Honourable Estate" and left it there with him. To my surprise Margaret Storm Jameson & Guy were there but hardly saw Margaret, who looked charming in a new brown coat. Phyllis also came —greeted me stiffly; apparently still offended over my purely amused identification of myself with Elaine in *A Modern Tragedy*. Talked also to Charles Morgan, H. E. Bates, Willie Collins, etc. Hotel warm but day colder than anything I have felt since the War; bitter N.E. gale; hat would have been off in Piccadilly if I had not pinned it on. At lunch talked to Harold Macmillan M.P. & Mary Ellen Chase about the Gen. Election & lecturing in America.

Went straight from lunch to dentist but had practically nothing done. Came back & changed into warmer dress for Kingston lecture. Took train to Surbiton, bus to Kingston & lectured in Memorial Hall behind Congregational Church on *T. of Y.* Audience quite good but chairman said bitter weather had kept many away. Taken back to station by a Malden minister who was an enthusiastic *T. of Y.* fan.

Tuesday February 11th   Cottingham
Went to Cottingham by 1.30 to Hull; day so cold that train never got warm. Mrs Holtby met me in Hull. Crouched thankfully over fire & sat there talking (except for supper) till bed-time. Granny not critical or aggressive and seems to have resigned herself to *South Riding.*

Wednesday February 12th
Breakfast in bed. Walked with Harry, who came over in morning, for about an hour, in sunshine which made the cold more endurable. Got back at tea-time. Granny & Edith motored me over to Bridlington for lecture on "Youth Morals" at Alexandra Hotel. Pleasant room; talk seemed to go down quite well though owing to intense cold I did not feel inspired. Granny very agreeable. She showed and gave me to keep a photograph of Winifred's grave with the stone newly on—an opened book beautifully carved with just the words "In loving memory of Winifred daughter of David & Alice Holtby. Died in London Sept 29th 1935 aged 37 years" and on the opposite page the quotation Granny likes from Annie Swan:
> God give me work till my life shall end
> And life till my work is done.
The grave is outlined by a long plain surround of white marble and in the middle is a white marble vase, sunk in the ground, for flowers. (But *was* her work done? No, oh *no!*)

Thursday February 13th   Sheffield
Still ferociously cold. Granny presented me for my breakfast-in-bed with first lot of typescript copies of W.'s letters to Jean McWilliam. They were so lovely, fresh and full of spring and youth (1920–1922) that I couldn't put them down till I had read them all. Went to village (sun out but air fierce) to get Valentine for Gordon. Left Cottingham for Sheffield by 2.50 (I suppose I have seen Bainesse with all its memories for the last time as Granny goes so soon to Harrogate).

Bad train, no tea; arrived 4.30; met by Mr Lamb & shown over City Library; then taken to the Misses Gillott (my hostesses, small house but comfortable, know the Pethick-Lawrences & are typical Rationalists) & at last got tea & felt warm over big fire. Told that there was greater demand for tickets for my lecture than any that season; all seats sold long ago, people fighting for tickets & complaining to the Press when they couldn't get them. Wore gold shirt blouse & long black skirt for lecture; very effective against velvet curtain shaded gold & red by stage lights. Mrs Jonathan Barber in chair (vigorous & very pleasant Quaker lady aged 70 with enormous contralto voice; prominent social worker in Sheffield). Felt in good form though not well; lectured for 1¼ hours & was told at end I had had more applause than any other lecturer who had been there.

Friday February 14th   London
Lectured Sheffield City Hall on "The World To-day" to 1,000 children (boys & girls between 16 & 18) from all the Sheffield secondary schools. Seemed to go down well. Good questions afterwards (an innovation for them). Caught the 11.5 back to London. Good train, sun came out, less cold. Found children well. Mother arrived to do flowers & I went for walk along Embankment with her after dictating letters. At 6.30 went to Henrietta Leslie's Valentine Party & talked to Beatrice Kean Seymour (afire with projects after recent Chiozza Money libel case), David Higham, Nancy Pearn, Dorothy Evans, Evelyn Sharp.

Saturday February 15th
Wish I could know whether Mr Latham likes "Honourable Estate"; fear he can't or he'd have let me know at once.

Less cold—damp & rainy. Thick fog in afternoon so only took the children out a short time. Worked at Sect. 5, Chapter 5, of novel, though should feel more inclined for it if I could hear from Mr Latham. Expected Gordon back; as he wasn't here by 8 p.m. rang up Edith at Cottingham, who said he was going to Oxford or Birmingham to-day & wouldn't be back till to-morrow evening. Letter from G. by late post confirmed this.

Sunday February 16th
Worked on another section of Ch. V of "Hon. Estate" this morning. Major article by Ellen Wilkinson (who flew to Germany on Friday) in *Sunday Referee* describing Hitler's plans for marching to the Rhine. (Like a pre-war Blatchford article.) Took children to Edwardes Square & found Gordon there, back from various visits & speeches & with slight cold. Mother came to supper.

Very late Burnett came in & reported that Latham had rung up while I was out. Burnetts had not left the message & when they told me it was too late to ring up so I still don't know what he thinks. Damn & damn.

Monday February 17th
Latham telephoned early this morning to say that he is more than pleased, he is thrilled & delighted with "Hon. Estate", and that it has made him so disgusted with the other fiction manuscripts he has been given to read that he has turned down the lot wholesale! Felt enormously relieved. Went jubilantly to hairdresser & had shampoo etc.; then lunched with Eric Gillett at Ivy. Happened to mention, in discussing *South Riding*, that I'd rather have a book chosen by the *Evening Standard* than Book of the Month Club. Eric thereupon said he knew Howard Spring & wd send him a proof of "Hon. Estate" if I let him have it in time.

Evening, Mr Latham called for me & took me to dinner at Scott's (where I hadn't been before), then to the Little Theatre to see *Lady Precious Stream* (Chinese play beautifully done; a genre that doesn't attract me much but excellent of its kind). He talked again a good deal about "Hon. Estate"; said he thought its success in fiction should be as great as that of *Testament* in biography; that it wd be very interesting to promote & he looked forward to telling George about it. I promised to see him off Friday morning early at Waterloo—boat-train for S.S. *President Harding*.

Tuesday February 18th
Started on final three sections of "Hon. Estate" Chapter 5, much cheered by Mr Latham's opinion.

Wednesday February 19th
Book in morning; evening, went down to Dartford, Kent, to dine with Sir Stephen Tallents at his house St John's Jerusalem, Sutton-at-Hone, & to lecture to Dartford Co-op. on *T. of Y.* Sir Stephen joined me at St Paul's station & we went down together; told me something of his new work at the B.B.C.

Saturday February 22nd
Still felt a good deal under the weather but got up as Margaret Storm Jameson was coming to lunch and I had the children to cope with. Scolded Margaret (I afterwards thought perhaps unkindly) about the attitude of resignation shown by *In the Second Year*. I also said that—good as it is—I didn't really think it could have happened in England. She said she had really meant it to be after another Great War (when it would have been credible) but couldn't face drawing the aftermath of such a catastrophe. We discussed our Libel letter for *The Times*, and also Margaret's contract with Colston Leigh, which we are trying to combine with mine for 1937 as regards dates, and about which I gave her a good deal of advice based on my own tour. We didn't have much time & after lunch I took her to her Labour Conference in Markham Square Church of which she was Chairman.

Mother came & looked after the children for me & then the Burnetts took them over so I got on a bit with "Hon. Estate". Just as I was putting them into bed a long searchlight appeared in the sky—a sinister reminder of the last War & the approaching horror of another about wh. we have all been talking. Shirley said: "I can't go to sleep with that thing in the sky" but I told her there was no danger to her. Not yet.

Sunday February 23rd
Still feeling pretty mouldy. Stayed in bed for breakfast, told Mother I wouldn't go to Edwardes Square with children to-day. Long notices about *South Riding* in both *Observer* (Books & Authors) and *Sunday Times*. After

lunch when they had all gone I settled down to the final section of "Hon. Estate", steadily wrote 10 pages in 3 hours and was just writing the last words of Chap. 5 when they all came back for supper just before 7.0.

Mother showed me the sketch for Father's gravestone in Richmond Cemetery. We are having a sundial because he was always so much interested in clocks, and in time, and on it the words: "So teach us to number our days, that we may apply our hearts unto wisdom." At the other end of the grave is a square tilted block with his name and dates and beneath them the words: "Comfort us again now after the time that thou hast plagued us and for the years wherein we have suffered adversity." We thought that those verses from the Psalm "Lord, Thou hast been our refuge" seemed singularly appropriate to both his life and death.

Monday February 24th   Farnworth
Took midday train to Manchester, for Farnworth. Small industrial town undistinguishable from rest of Manchester–Bolton area. How often now I seem to have been on railway journeys through industrial Lancashire & Yorkshire. Lectured to a parish church Mutual Improvement Society (12 guineas). Good audience in long schoolroom but two front rows of quite juvenile children rather putting off, especially as the subject was "Youth Morals To-day & Yesterday" and I had to leave out one or two of my best stories.

Stayed with some very pleasant people, Mr & Mrs Johnston, who had also put up Phyllis Bentley, Rosita Forbes, etc. They liked Phyllis but weren't convinced that Rosita Forbes's journeys were genuine. One or two people came in to supper who had been at my Bolton Luncheon Club address two years ago. Very comfortable; really hot bath & fire in bedroom.

Tuesday February 25th   Liverpool
Breakfast in bed; got up late; journeyed via Bolton to Liverpool, where Mr James Macdonald met me. He was unwell from overwork & later retired to bed at home but managed to take me to the docks & the river (too foggy to see across) & show me the entrance to the Mersey Tunnel. We lunched in town—and talked a great deal about Winifred, & Father, & his son who was killed in the War a fortnight after Edward was wounded. The eldest Miss Macdonald drove me out to my lecture at St Helens (origin of Beecham's Pills & Vita Glass) & back. A large Congregational Church, reasonably well-filled. St Helens much as I expected—dark, dirty, foggy, indeterminate; only saw it after dark. New Liverpool–Lancashire highway very wide & modern—almost as good as an American main road.

Wednesday February 26th   Manchester
Left the Macdonalds & Liverpool for Manchester (dark, dirty, raining, as it always seems to be, whenever I visit it). Stayed at Queen's Hotel &

lunched there. After lunch went to office of *Manchester Guardian* & *Manchester Evening News* & got them to scrap the appalling photograph of me they always publish. Instead they took another (five positions) in the *M.G.* library.

At 7.30 lectured in Memorial Hall, Albert Square, for Nat. Union of Women Teachers, on *Testament of Youth*. Enjoyed lecture, felt completely at ease. Hall was packed to overflowing, gallery full & people standing in doorway. About 50 copies of *T. of Y.* were on sale on a stand in the hall; I promised to autograph any sold after the lecture. They all went & there was a demand for more. After the lecture scene of crowd pressing round me rather like U.S.A. Went to *M.G.* office afterwards & called on Madeleine Linford but didn't much like her; she wasn't "warm" at all. Said she had been reviewing *S. Riding* for the *M.G.* Went back to Queen's Hotel, had some milk & retired to bed. I believe it is the Manchester hotel W. put into *S. Riding* where Sarah & Carne were "temporarily insane".

Saturday March 14th   London
Situation seems slightly calmer internationally. Miss Lennox called & I gave her Part I of "Hon. Estate" to type. Went on revising Part 2 to post to her. Mother took children for walk in afternoon & I did some looking up in Chelsea Library before tea & putting them to bed. Letter from Somerville trying to get me to agree to Winifred's bequest being transferred in certain contingencies to general scholarship fund. Drafted reply objecting as before. Talked late with G. about European situation.

Sunday March 15th
No answer yet from Hitler as to whether Germany will send a delegate to the League Council here this week. Decided unless explosion blows up that G. & I will go to Germany for the election—and thence to Rhineland & Verdun. Showed G. some of the National War Aims Committee pamphlets which I have quoted in "Honourable Estate"—suggesting that a "German peace" (1917) would breed future war!

Edwardes Square as usual. Mother to supper. Garvin's article in the *Observer* actually roughly represents our own views of the European situation. Can't get on with my novel in this atmosphere.

Monday March 16th
Hitler replies he is willing for Germany to be represented at Council discussions on condition of 1) equality, 2) discussion of his peace proposals in due course. (This last word "alsbald" was at first translated "forthwith" & caused alarm; but mistake was later corrected through German Embassy.) Council later replied (at 7.30 to-night after its afternoon sitting) accepting 1) but saying that 2) was not for the Council to decide (i.e., Locarno Powers?).

G. & I went to American Consulate after lunch to find out how the children and I could go to America with him on a non-quota immigrant visa in case of a War which we could not endorse. Procedure far more complicated than it used to be but can be done. Then we drifted down to St James's Palace; got in by asking for members of the Press; and we found ourselves in midst of the world's press, jostling & pushing in a long narrow lobby while locked out of secret Council meeting. Greeted Miss Ward, of the Geneva Press Dept, who used to give me Press tickets. Saw Knicker-bocker, John Gunther, Zilliacus, W. N. Ewer of the *Herald*, Gordon-Lennox of the *D. Telegraph*, von Kreiss of the *Berliner Tageblatt*. In the Press room were rows of long tables covered with blue crash—obviously hasty improvisations—telephone booths beside them; electric candles of sconces between tall light windows; low ceiling supported by white pillars. One or two women—? Press—dressed in black moved among the crowds of men. Conference room where Council was sitting was up the stairs beyond a lobby (used as a cable room) where the wall was appropriately decorated with specimens of antique guns. Had to go—work couldn't be put off—after about an hour, but G. waited & finally heard the Council declare in public session that Germany had violated the Treaty of Locarno.

Colossal correspondence this morning; answered it but still can't get on with novel. I fear War more than Fascism; anyhow I am sure that you can't use Satan to cast out Satan; that Fascism which sprang from colossal injustice will only grow stronger if the injustice is rammed home; that the only way to kill it is to ostracise it as we have the Mosley movement. The Press and all the people I meet seem to be divided into 1) those who hate murder in Germany but don't mind it in Russia; 2) those who hate murder in Russia but don't mind it in Germany; 3) a few minoritarians like myself who hate it anyway. Well, I seem to have lost everything; not only is Winifred gone, and Father, but all that we have worked for in the last 15 years seems to have failed—all that she wore herself out for and literally gave her life in support of. As she wrote in *South Riding*, I feel "the deep fatigue of those whose impersonal ideals do not march with history". What a generation! "What shadows we are & what shadows we pursue!"

Tuesday March 17th
More & more about the crisis. Very difficult to write in this tense atmosphere. G. & I lunched at the H. of Commons with Col. Josiah Wedgwood—nominally to meet Bromfield, the Member for Leek, but he couldn't come. Col. Wedgwood seemed v. anxious to press our claims on Staffordshire owing to my being native there—G. as candidate for a Staffordshire constituency; myself as (in Staffs) "the successor to Arnold Bennett"! Invited us to Moddershall Hall for the week-end to see various people.

Lovely day. Walked back to Chelsea from Westminster. Gave party at Gargoyle in the evening; John Gunther, now London & formally Moscow correspondent of the *Chicago Daily News*, & his wife, dined with us; Walker of the B.B.C. & Herr von Kreiss, London correspondent of the *Berliner Tageblatt* (not a Nazi; still more to the right) joined us after dinner. Violent arguments all evening, as was to be expected; Gunthers not only vehemently anti-German but anti-negotiation with Hitler; we on the contrary tried to discover what was still left that might make for peace. When von Kreiss came various stories of the Fascist regime were told & then arguments became hotter. Gunther in effect attacked von Kreiss for the monstrosities of Fascism & especially of the 30th June shootings, which von Kreiss tried to defend on grounds of "counter-revolution". Neither quite lost their tempers which says a good deal for newspaper correspondents. Got home after 1 a.m. with a crashing headache.

Wednesday March 18th
Germans agree to come to London. Warm day; tried to get on with book but crisis, headache & complete flatness owing to lateness & fatigue of previous controversial evening made it a day when I did nothing much but deal with my usual enormous correspondence.

In evening went to speak to the Youth Fellowship at St Martin-in-the-Fields; had supper first with the Pat McCormicks. McCormick himself not there as he had gone off to France with a party going round the battlefields, but Mrs McCormick entertained me (formal & very charming; looked much younger than she actually must be) & her lovely Gainsborough-like daughter Kiki. Mrs McC.'s old mother was also there, & the young curate who was conducting the proceedings & who succeeded Mr Appleton (who helped Dick Sheppard with Winifred's funeral service & originally invited me). Intelligent & very pacifist group of young people—as many men as women. Spoke for about ¾ hour, nominally on *T. of Y.*, actually on present crisis. Then answered questions for nearly another hour. One or two of the audience came with me to 11 bus & another got into it & earnestly questioned me all the way home. Got back very tired & with sore throat from so much talking when so fatigued.

Thursday March 19th
G. went down to St James's Palace; insinuated himself among journalists, got into Council and heard von Ribbentrop make his statement. Knew that (as female & as myself) should be too conspicuous to have any success, so worked all day in garden on Chap. 6, Section 3. Very hard for the moment to throw one's mind back to Gallipoli.

At 4.30 attended meeting of National Peace Council at Baptist Church House, Southampton Row. Don't usually bother to go but felt I should to-day as they were discussing the crisis. Opinion absolutely divided between those who wanted to stand on white sheet & forgive Germany owing to our past iniquities, & those who want to take firm stand with France & Russia against her aggression owing to the militaristic basis of the Fascist philosophy. Division shown by voting on N.P.C. letter to Press on sentence deploring Germany's breach of Locarno—20 for keeping it, 19 for having no sentence condemning Germany at all. I voted for keeping it as I am all for resistance against aggression provided it is *collective*, but I am much more nervous than most anti-fascists seem to be of our being dragged in the name of the League into a purely military alliance with France of the old nationalistic type—*called* the collective system but actually the Balance of Power all over again. And I think that resistance to what Norman Angell calls the "guilty nation" theory is also of first importance.

Friday March 20th
Time & Tide & *New Statesman* both have comments on our Libel letter in last Friday's *Times*.

Itinerary came from Wayfarers about German & French tour next week; discussion of this took up a lot of time & I only got a page or two of "Hon. Estate" written in consequence. Warm day but showery. Tension in press somewhat less. Carlisle organiser angry because of my cancelling my luncheon club engagement to go abroad. Wrote her a firm letter; sorry for their inconvenience but don't see the fun of being dictated to by a body which was anyhow under-paying me for taking so long & expensive a journey. G. says I am too easily exploited.

Went to Bedford at 4.30 to lecture on autobiographies to a girls' teachers' training college. Seem to spend half my time in trains owing to the enormous demand on me from all quarters to do things. Had a delightful old chairman, aged 85, & a most enthusiastic & responsive audience of girls. Had supper afterwards with Miss Spence, the Principal, & a member of her staff who heard me give the same lecture at Bumpus's two years ago. Felt that they really had all enjoyed the lecture & that the evening was a success. Got back at 10.45 but owing to correspondence etc. was not in bed till 1.0 as usual.

Saturday March 21st   Staffordshire
Took 10.40 train to Stafford to stay for night with Col. Josiah Wedgwood. (G. went up to Stoke last night to see Rev. Mr Horwood of Etruria about the Leek constituency.) Col. Wedgwood & Mrs met me with the car at Stafford & motored me up to Moddershall Oaks for lunch. (Long bungalow house with verandah front like S. African stoep, on top of oak-covered hill looking over Moddershall Mill & Mere across Staffordshire towards the Wrekin. Beautiful woods, semi-cultivated round house; oaks interspersed with rhododendrons & azaleas. Bungalow & woods all reminded me of the Bretts' "shack" at Fairfield, Connecticut—an Anglicised version.)

After lunch discovered by telephoning from Moddershall village that G. was waiting to be picked up at N. Stafford Hotel; Col. Wedgwood placed car at our disposal, so I drove down to Stoke to fetch G. Noticed in driving the cobbled main streets, & pot-banks all interspersed with private houses.

Went in car to Trentham Rd to call on John Thomas the W.E.A. man to see if he would "vet" "Hon. Estate" for accuracy regarding Staffordshire; but he was out. Drove back through Trentham, which I barely remember except for vague recollection of Trentham Hall (now a public gardens; Duke of Sutherland gave it up owing to dirtiness of Trent wh. received all industrial refuse of Potteries). Stream over road where I used to fish for minnows is gone. Back via Barlaston; got a glimpse of Park Fields & the Tittensor country. A Wedgwood nephew came to dinner, after Col. Wedgwood & G. & I had had a long evening walk round the woods.

Sunday March 22nd
Breakfast in bed & up late; wandered round woods for half an hour in lovely mild morning sunshine; then went off to Stoke in car to find John Thomas again but he was still out. Drove back by Park Fields & this time stopped; inside of house much modernised but got impression of it as it must have been when extensive Brittain family lived there. Very attractive white-fronted low house looking over view of sloping green fields interspersed with little clumps of trees. Whole district called Park Fields; Brittain house really Park Fields cottage; bigger Park Fields house across the way. Called on way home on Col. Wedgwood's brother Ralph's family; met his sister-in-law & three nieces; Mrs Wedgwood remembered the Brittain family going to church from Park Fields to Barlaston. Back to Moddershall for lunch; conversation intermittently continued about desirability of G. getting adopted as candidate for Leek. Caught 2.13 from Stoke in order to get back to town in time for Mosley meeting; G. obliged to come later as he had to see a certain Mr Price, chairman of County Labour Party, at Stone.

GERMANY AND FRANCE
March–April 1936

Wednesday March 25th
Left London at 8.30 for Harwich & Hook of Holland. Quiet crossing. Slept in snatches. Very few English on train going down.

Thursday March 26th
Got up 5.30; in train for Berlin at 6.19. G. says that when I showed my passport at Harwich, the customs official nudged his colleague & said "Famous authoress there."

Never been in Holland before. Flat, tranquil, prosperous, green; everything looked clean & unhurried. Breakfast in a pleasant restaurant-car of chromium & green leather; cost 2 florins each which totalled 13/6! Went through clean agreeable cities which had been names to me before —Rotterdam, Utrecht, Deventer. Contrast immediately frontier passed at Bentheim; Germany more desolate, less prosperous. Politics of which

Holland seemed unaware confronted me immediately with a railway poster: "Der Führer has increased railway wagons. We thank the Führer with you." Passed through more flat country to Osnabrück, but wider stretches; no more dykes as in Holland intersecting meadows into little fields. Wooded country of Westphalia beyond Osnabrück; no flowers yet except for a few white anemones in a Dutch wood. In train met Dr Bowde, Winifred's doctor at the nursing home, going to Berlin to do some work for the German Ministry of Education. He lunched with us; we talked chiefly of medicine not politics.

At Hanover Station confronted by two more black & red posters: "Der Führer hat Wort gehalten. Deutschland dankt ihm am 29 März." Another had a red ball lying in a black cross & above it in huge red letters the word "So!" At Bentheim luggage was not examined, & passport only cursorily, but we had to give full account & show all foreign money brought in in cheques or cash, & have paper filled in giving amount, to be shown to customs on leaving.

Railway line & all stations very vocal indeed about elections. Just outside Stendal, an hour from Berlin, passed a railway train with the engine carrying a huge white Swastika & scrawled across its length with the white-painted letters: "Wir stehen zum Führer!" Germany suffering at the moment from the one-track mind.

Berlin

Walked over from station to Coburger Hof. Pleasant hotel, everyone very polite; obviously no dislike of the English as individuals. Dropped bags & went off to see American United Press & make sure if *Sunday Chronicle* arrangements were O.K. Americans very helpful indeed; told me Hitler was speaking at Essen Friday afternoon, Goering in Berlin Friday evening, Hitler in Cologne Saturday evening. Decided to go on to Cologne Sat. morning, hear Goering Friday evening, & hand in my *Sunday Chron.* article to be wired by Amer. U.P. after hearing Goering.

Berlin a city of flags flying from innumerable windows (long crimson flags with black Swastika on white circle in middle). Also countless posters in various varieties of black, white & red—black letters on white banners; red capitals and black letters on white banners; etc. etc. This vast, insistent, universal propaganda is terrifying in its skill and efficiency due to unstinted expenditure of public money. Made me feel that we have everything to learn about propaganda at home.

Examples of some of the posters were: "Arbeit—Ehre—Frieden." "Deine Ehre—Treue dem Führer!" "Wir schützen die Welt von dem Bolshevismus." "Der Geist des neuen Deutschlands ist der Geist des Friedens." "Danke dem Führer mit deiner Stimme." "Ein Volk—ein Reich—ein Führer!"

Went out to find the Taverna in the West End where the journalists congregate. Walked down the Hermann Goering Strasse (formerly the

Friedrich Ebert Strasse just as the former Stresemann Strasse is now the Saarland Strasse) when G. pointed out a large ornate building with a big "To Let" notice & heaps of débris & scattered papers in front. He said: "I lunched there with Treviranus (one of Brüning's ministers) in November 1933." It was the Herrenklub, the fashionable meeting place of the Right, approximately like our Carlton Club. Treviranus is now in exile in Scotland and the Klub deserted, abandoned, "to let". Protests from the Right against this most absolute of all tyrannies have been silenced as completely as those from the Left. Not unity, but unanimity, achieved by whatever methods the Government finds convenient.

Took bus; spent a short time in a picture-house hoping to hear news but it was just a terrible translated American picture with Sylvia Sydney & Herbert Marshall. Went on to Taverna; at first found at the usual reserved table only a young German journalist representing some foreign Press agency, but later we were joined by Miss Schultz of the *Chicago Tribune* & an older German Nazi journalist. Talk frank & general, all about the crisis; gathering seemed a gathering of conspirators who all tacitly agreed to spy on each other. By this time was getting too tired to take in much but remembered the following.

I remarked on politeness of Germans to us. Miss Schultz: "Oh yes —they're expecting your country to do something for them next week." The older Nazi journalist remarked: "There will be a new Locarno; then Hitler will get his 25-year Peace Pact and all will be well." But Miss S. kept on dropping hints about the unreliability of peace promises. "Go to Aix (Aachen). It is said they are fortifying there and have armies of workmen." "They are saying in diplomatic circles that Hitler's foreign policy is modelled on the way he acquired power. When he raised his Storm-troops they were illegal but the Government needed their help. His Putsch was illegal but he got away with it. Now he is presenting the Powers with illegal *faits accomplis* and getting away with those too!"

We taxied back & got to bed about 2.0. Recalled that American Press Agency had shared view of Miss Schultz. A large fair young man (Oestner's assistant & reminiscent of John Gunther), when telling me that part of the Essen programme was one minute's silence for "inner contemplation", said: "I can't imagine a Nazi having anything to go into inner contemplation about." He also said about this election campaign: "Hitler's getting damned dramatic. He always does, but his voice is holding out. He hasn't got this cancer of the throat people try to give him. But if he does not stop speaking soon we shall all be in strait waistcoats."

Friday March 27th
Breakfast in bed late. Came down in time for interview with Herr Dänkwerts (a journalist; editor of a monthly paper) & a lady who came with him to interpret—middle-aged woman whose mother had been English.

Substance of interview (on colonial question)

Jugo-Slavia: French control not now so strong as formerly.

Turkey: French control absolute over finance.

Czechoslovakia: French control not strong financially but very strong politically.

Romania: French influence strong both commercially & politically.

Greece: French influence practically destroyed by recent death of Venizelos.

Germany strong in import & export in all these countries.

Russia: Trying to get influence on Balkan countries by means of trade & to destroy German trade—but not wealthy enough to have much influence yet.

G. asked: "By what diplomatic method could German economic control be restored in Danubian countries?"

Answer: Not much can be done diplomatically but only by establishing the superiority of German goods. Germany maintains a "compensatory" exchange—i.e. of goods but not of cash. Neither Germany nor any of these countries has money. Increase of exchange arrangements will improve German influence but this is not easily re-established unless internat. situation is tranquil. New materials are not obtainable from Danubian countries. Increase of influence in border states is not an alternative to regaining of colonies. If raw materials are obtained from colonies, this is useless unless they can be exported as finished goods. Raw materials not obtainable because loans not obtainable—Germany would be ruined trying to buy them.

Debts

Private debts wd be greater if value of German mark was again reduced. Devaluation of mark would be disadvantageous to German middle classes & wd also increase size of German private debts to other countries. City of London would probably extend credits if tranquillity cld be restored in political world—i.e. acceptance of Hitler's proposals! No withdrawal of British credits since recent crisis—but French & Russians have. Russia had given credit in goods but this has been withdrawn since crisis. (N.B., this suggests that the City's policy is pro-German, which also probably explains pro-German policy of Baldwin.)

As a result of crisis Dänkwerts thought there were *two alternative polices*: 1) German isolation, with demand for return of colonies; 2) commercial arrangements with England, France & Russia if tranquillity restored.

Political question

We said that England was not so much disturbed by the present breach but by possible future threats to Austria, Czechoslovakia, colonies, Channel ports. Dänkwerts replied: "Hitler will not have a war with anybody—and a war with Italy wd follow the absorption of Austria."

Italian–Abyssinian War
Germany cannot forget that Italy left them in Great War. German people in favour of sanctions until time came that sanctions might be applied to Germany!

Attitude toward L. of Nations
German people do not quite understand why Hitler wants to return to L. of N. Actually it was a gesture to show that he did not mean War by occupying Rhine. L. of N. has hitherto been unpopular because identified with inequality. That is why Hitler demands guarantee of equality before returning to L. of N.

Austria
If an insurrection occurred there Germany wd not do anything. Hitler wd take risk of unpopularity rather than invite a war with France & Italy. Austrian young men now largely in concentration camps—and in Tyrol are put into Italian army & sent to Abyssinia.

Went out to United Press & found they had got me two tickets for Goering's meeting to-night. Very courteous & co-operative. Went to small café on way back to hotel & drafted out to-night's article for *Sunday Chronicle* over a cup of chocolate. Then lunched & went out by bus & taxi to Charlottenburg to hear the broadcast of Hitler's Essen speech from Frau Osler's house over a cup of tea.

Essen arrangements as given me by United Press were:
Essen Speech (No. 11 or 12 in Election stunt)
3.45. All German radio stations transmit order to hoist flags.
4.0. Siren of Krupp foundry in Essen sounds—signal for everything that whistles in Germany to join in for one minute. (Presumably this was the "silence" for inner contemplation as no other time for it was given.)
4.1. Silence. All traffic to stop except aeroplanes in flight.
Flags to remain up till Sunday night.

Found Frau Osler's house—pleasant flat; tea laid out with bread & butter & jam on bread. Her two children there—young son of 16 & daughter rather younger; all very keen Nazis, especially the boy. He explained to me that Hitler wrote *Mein Kampf* (which I gave as reason for much English anxiety) when he was out of power, but that now he had power & responsibility he knew that many of his projects could not be carried out! Frau Osler asked me about myself and my work. I told her & gave her a card—probably rashly.

Essen Broadcast
Locomotive Hall in Krupps works. Broadcast to entire factory. 120,000 people.
3.45. Goebbels gave order to raise flags—spoke for 10 minutes. Sound of music & marching feet approached at 3.55. Badenweiler March—

favourite march of Hitler, always played when he approaches (Baden-weiler scene of small struggle between French & Germans in Great War). Cries of "Führer! Führer! Der Führer Hitler!" swelling to great crescendo of shouting.

4.0. Sound of siren—repeated by all whistles in Germany. Dies away —March repeated—more shouting.

4.5. Leader of the workmen welcomes Hitler.

4.8. An officer speaks for soldiers in all garrisons. Speech punctuated with loud shouts. Officer concluded: "Nun sprecht der Führer."

Hitler spoke. Began in deep, sonorous voice, slow & clear.

"I come to speak not only to these workmen but to all workmen in all parts of Germany." The Essen works are only a symbol. There is one class in Germany—the workmen are neither better nor worse than other people. "What would this great work be if no nation was behind it?" "All that has been done could be done only as one man did it, not many parties." He did not take to his work with 47 parties and half a dozen faiths. "It must be that I succeed in my work and I shall succeed." (Young man says Hitler is an artist in giving new content to familiar speeches.)

Voice goes shrill and cracks in moments of emotion. "There will be no peace until all nations are equally armed." "There must be no victory & no defeat, but reason by which we shake hands."

"I can work only if the people sustains me." He belongs to no one party or faith but to the whole people. "We do not want people to mix in our affairs. We do not mix in theirs." "I have done nothing secretly but everything in public."

Speech punctuated with roars from huge audience of 120,000.

"We must do things ourselves and not leave them to our children. The people will never be so strong if the parents have not been united." "No peace if people are forced to sign—it must be free will." "Treaties have never been so often broken as in recent years."

Said he had put on the elections bec. he wanted to show the other countries that this was not just one man but the whole people. Towards end of speech began to shout; voice rose. "On the 29th the world will see that not only one man speaks but the whole nation."

Meeting ended with singing of "Deutschland über Alles" and the Horst Wessel Lied.

Took taxi on to Deutschlands Halle, Charlottenburg—huge building of grey concrete, modern in construction but reminiscent of Olympia in size & construction. Got there about 6.0—detachments of Brown-shirts and men in black-shirted uniform & black steel helmets already drawn up there. Good restaurant attached—nearly empty—so large that waiters had to walk miles & were very slow—everything very much polished & modern-looking.

Got good Press seats though rather cramped & hard. Quite near platform as relative distances went—hall held about 20,000. Platform draped with red—in front of it two long tables with red-draped sides & white tops. Behind chairs on platform, row of four shallow steps stretched almost entire width of dais, with background of small firs; these steps were later occupied by standard-bearers. Front of platform decorated with laurels & pink hydrangeas. Black swastika on white circle in centre. Stewards all Brown-shirts.

Above back of platform over gallery enormous black flag with silver German eagle above black swastika on silver ground. Ceiling lighted with big square inset lights. Red flags with black swastika on white circle hung all round top gangway above gallery.

Round end of gallery ran slogans in huge black letters on white sheets: "Zwietracht und Verrat machen uns rechtlos—Einigkeit und Treue sichern uns Freiheit und Recht." "Die Garnisonen Deutschlands sind Garnisonen des Friedens."

The meeting began. Goering came in in brown-shirt uniform with red swastika armlet. (We were told later that he is very vain about his uniforms and changes them about five times a day.) A few minutes earlier Frau Goering had come in—tallish woman dressed in grey with big grey hat; sat near the front; everyone stood up. When Goering entered everyone stood with arms raised in Hitler salute—G. & I stood but did not salute. Goering very much like von Kreiss. Went to platform—sat down—audience sat down. Then came in procession of Fascist flags & pennons—the most highly organised pageantry in the world, to which Mosley's Wagnerian displays are childish toy demonstrations.

Goering's face & figure
Even bulkier than photographs suggest; heavy masculine type, nothing feminine about him as there is in Hitler. Wide flat forehead with dark brushed-back hair & one deep furrow across it. Eyes small, slit-like and narrow; well above centre level of ears. Mouth hard, flat & ruthless. Prominent chin spoiled by rolls of fat underneath. Very deep, raucous voice, soon rises to shouting. Like a sledge-hammer, rasping, exhausting, overwhelming. Mechanical & un-human; gave impression of highly organised mechanical instrument for all the technique of demagogic gestures which accompanied it.

Fascist legions, black & brown, stood behind him with pennons & standards while he spoke. (Standards of workers have cogwheel on top.) Background of troops occupied entire steps.

Speech terrifying, like the letting loose of some enormous impersonal force—undirected, amoral, overwhelming, irresistible as a flood or an earthquake is irresistible. G. remarked: "A political meeting reduced to the level of a football crowd." No possibility of thought, reason, consideration here—only mass emotion on the largest possible scale. Thought of all the books I have ever read on herd-instinct & mob psychology. Pageantry is raised to the nth degree of decorative hysteria. Applause wh. punctuates speech like the roar of a titanic waterfall.

Notes from speech

"Germany, once powerless, now can say No." "So long as a nation is to have peace the others must be peaceful on their side—the people ask it for their family & people." "Germany is determined to remain through & through National Socialist." Constant talk of "Germany's honour". "Our watchword is peace & reconciliation."

Attack on Bolshevism. "Hetzen, Hetzen, Hetzen." "No peace with weakness, no peace without honour." "A new life, a new outlook." "A weaponless folk is everyone's victim." "Pacifism is a phrase—what matters is honour & freedom." "The international Jews are talking about morals—this is the most grotesque of all their grotesqueries."

"We only demand to be lords in our own house—we demand neither gifts nor pity." "Do not confuse our demand for peace with weakness; no peace without honour, the most lordly idea & the most powerful force. Honour is the greatest, the highest."

"Germany is going to re-arm. Peace can only be maintained if we have a sword at our side." "We will not move our troops from the Rhineland whether we are promised Paradise or threatened with Hell!"

Drove back in taxi through Tiergarten to hotel after meeting. Huge radio station flashing through night just outside hall. No difficulty in getting away. Typed out first article for *Sunday Chron.* wh. I had written at intervals during the evening. Took it to Internat. Press in Unter den Linden; everything locked & shut but luckily in a moment or two someone came out & I walked up pitch dark stairs & found a German Press-man, to whom I gave it in the office. Had two sandwiches at the Automat & got back v. tired. G. typed his article for the *Y.P.* till nearly 1 a.m.

Saturday March 28th   Cologne

Took early morning train from Berlin to Cologne to hear Hitler's speech there to-night.

Have noticed that German women nowadays are scarcely made up—all gone pure—skin often greasy & unpowdered; hair not waved & dressed unbecomingly, showing the ears. Strange that when all that matters about a woman is her sexual aspect, the accepted methods of emphasising that aspect disappear.

When crossing the Lüneburger Heide (immense stretch of moor & woodland between Berlin and Hanover), got into conversation with agreeable German doctor—a women's doctor from Essen; said (as everyone says) that the last thing Germany wants is war & that as foreigners always come here when something special is happening they invariably see more troops about than usual!

Got to Cologne at 3 p.m.; but could not get through the mere hundred yards between the Station & the Dom Hotel across the Domplatz because Hitler was due to arrive in half an hour and the whole place was packed with people. Had no choice but to stand in the crowd & wait too. Not only the Domplatz and the Cathedral steps were thronged but the main thoroughfares through which he was to drive.

I was struck immediately with the contrast between Cologne to-day and Cologne under British occupation in the bleak, cheerless autumn of 1924 (as I tried to describe it in the last chapter of *T. of Y.*). Then it was poor, sad, oppressed; the people moved like silent ghosts up and down the Höhe Strasse; the very lights were dim and the Cathedral looked a black sinister shadow looming up into the night.

To-day the spring sunshine was warm & bright; an air of cheerful excitement prevailed everywhere; the hawthorn sprang freshly green, the forsythia vividly yellow against the grey walls of the superb Cathedral. Everywhere music was sounding and the red swastika flags were flying; they draped the station building & fluttered from the huge bridges over the Rhine. The Hohenzollern Bridge is now painted a dull green but still looks like the skeleton of a prehistoric monster at night; the suspension bridge beyond is a brighter, fresher green. Aeroplanes doing stunts near Cathedral.

The contrast between the two Colognes is the whole story of German Fascism.

Saw nothing of Hitler as the crowd was too great but learnt he was dining later at the Dom Hotel which accounted for the crowds around it & the impossibility of getting there. Heard cheering as his car drove through; everyone gave Nazi salute as usual. Decided to go to Propaganda Ministry's office to get our tickets for Hitler's meeting at the Merse Halle but had to walk miles before we could find a taxi. When we finally got to the Propaganda Ministry on the outskirts the whole office was closed. Got the address of the Press Office in the Gibizenich House (where Hitler that afternoon received the delegates from Rhenish districts) & went on the way back again. There by means of much questioning & telephoning we discovered someone at the Propaganda Ministry who knew where the tickets were & promised to leave them with the guard below. So we went all the way back to the Ministry, got the tickets at last, & then, as it was now nearly 6.0 & the Press Office had advised us to be there 2 hours beforehand, decided to drive straight to the Merse Halle (Exhibition Hall). As the Hohenzollern Bridge was closed to traffic we had to drive all the way along the Embankment (Kaiser Wilhelms Ufer) and cross at Köln–Mülheim. Some distance from the hall motor traffic was stopped so got out for another long tramp; crowds already assembled. After various officials had looked at our permits we got into the hall at last. Had hoped a restaurant wd be attached as at the Deutschlands Halle, as by this time we were in need of a meal but there was nothing but a beer-tavern with a kitchen attached where the staff were frantically trying to make ham sandwiches in response to a large demand from Blackshirts & Brownshirts; G. had to stand in a queue for about 20 minutes to get one. Left his coat first on two seats in the "Press Gallery". Very bad & crowded accommodation; two straight benches & the rest hard chairs. Saw Mrs Anne O'Hare McCormick there from the *N.Y. Times.*

Merse Halle a long dull red building but actual hall smaller than Deutschlands Halle; holds perhaps 10,000 people. Inside draped with red; at back of platform a large red satin curtain with colossal wooden silver painted swastika fixed on it. Just before Hitler came, one of the Nazi officials went carefully beating behind it to see if anyone was hidden there; they also scrutinised from the wings all the movements of the Press. We were told later that Hitler was much afraid of attack in Cologne as the wives of several Communists, etc., who had been "bumped off" were still living here. Galleries here draped with green—imitation laurel wreaths above them.

Gen. Blömberg, head of the Army, came in first; blue uniform. Also staying at Dom Hotel. Then Hitler entered to sound of Badenweiler March. Could not see him from Press Gallery till he was just below the platform. He then stood still, smiled & saluted. Exactly like all his photographs—must be the most photographed man in the world—features in all shop windows, hotels etc.; also busts. A man in the prime of life apparently unimpaired by stream of internat. negotiations combined with election campaign. Voice anything but falsetto—as English rumour sometimes hopefully asserts; it begins by being clear, sonorous & impressive, though it begins to crack and shrill when he gets emotional. At the same time he clenches his fist & beats his breast like a penitent in an agony of religious fervour. Did not strike me as wily diplomatist but religious maniac. Was accompanied by complete Nazi ballet—Frick, Goebbels, Ley, Darré, Blömberg. Soldiers' March from *Faust* played.

Gauleiter Groke introduced Hitler. Said that Germany from being a land of impotence was now one of the proudest on earth. The old garrison towns had again been given soldiers—the whole nation & the newly-risen honour of Germany behind Hitler.

Points from Hitler's Speech

"A new movement of inner knowledge grew." "I am the best democrat in the world." "A new community to build . . . I must go this way. I could go no other." ". . . to forget all & learn to be German . . ." "Geistlich, organised, constructed movement, impossible to solve the problems of unemployment etc. by the old methods."

"We are an island in an evil world." "Not possible to continue with 47 parties." "What we have suffered in this Rhineland." "An army stark und gefertigt—we now have become a People." "Who first crosses these borders will be turned back."

"This senseless war must be ended—we have waited sixteen years . . . A people of sixty million stretches out its hand and is asked in return for some symbolical gesture." "No man has worked more for peace than I have." "A war is not a useful event . . . Peace by God's help."

End of Meeting
When Hitler finished audience sang, & all German radio stations relayed the "Alt-Niederländisches Dankgebet". Everyone in Germany expected to stand at attention & join in. At last line of last verse every church bell in Germany had to peal for 15 minutes. They were still pealing when we got outside the hall.

Found our way up wooden steps to Hohenzollern Bridge; walked across with about 10,000 other people, mostly in uniform. Flag-draped Nazi lorries thundered past. From centre of bridge saw all the beautiful buildings on left bank of Rhine fully flood-lit, and the twin pinnacles of the Cathedral, no longer a sinister black shadow, scintillating against the dark sky of the lovely warm night.

Reached hotel about 10.0 at last; Hitler just leaving as we arrived, saw the car run through the crowd. Little black, white & red sentry boxes on either side of the hotel. Had late but excellent dinner; felt ready to drop off.

Sunday March 29th
Day of the elections; woke to see flying flags and to hear sounds of jubilant bands & marching feet. Lovely spring morning. At 9.15, while we were having breakfast in bed, saw the two Zeppelins—the *Graf Zeppelin* and the *Hindenberg*—circling Cologne dropping pamphlets. People standing on their roofs & cheering them. The two Colognes again—as last night.

Got up & walked across to Cathedral; congregation crowding aisles & even entrances; every seat full. Again as in 1924 singing echoed back from vaulted roof but spirit of congregation very different. Looked at tall beautiful East window with its main tints of dull green & bright orange, & wished Winifred were here to observe the contrast with me instead of being in her grave.

Dom Predikant preached with passion but several members of congregation assured us there was nothing political in his sermon. Went out at close of High Mass and walked about in sunshine; saw poster near the Cathedral: "Studenten! Seid Propagandisten des Führers!"

Lunched at café in Höhe Strasse; couldn't find the Hotel Disch where W. & I stayed in 1924. On way back to Embankment visited polling station at Bahnhof; very quiet; G. got voting paper & gold button specimen worn by people who have voted.

After lunch walked to Rhine Embankment & sat at outdoor café looking over Rhine; drank coffee & cognac & wrote up diary. Old insanitary buildings opposite Rhine being replaced by new ones on same structure to keep design. Saw another poster, evidently designed for women, of cheerful-looking boy & girl & Mother with very sentimental smile kissing a laughing baby. Inscription was: "Unser Kindern die Zukunft durch Adolf Hitler."

When it was too cold to sit, walked along to see the Reuter agent whom the American United Press had telephoned to on my behalf from Berlin —Captain Charles Bennett, 4B Kasino Strasse. Found middle-aged ex-Army man, red-faced, obviously somewhat given to toping but very friendly & well-informed. Had German wife or mistress who looked Jewish. He gave us potent cocktails & talked.

Told us that the rumour about the Germans fortifying the Eifelbrige (mountainous district between Aachen & Mosel) that we heard from Miss Schultz in Berlin was untrue as far as his information went. Knew a maid-servant who came from that district & wd certainly have told him if anything had gone on. Said it was very difficult to be sure of information here—e.g. he was informed that Hitler wd come to Cologne in evening & visit barracks, so told Press; but Hitler didn't visit barracks or come till the afternoon. Told us Hitler was spending week-end at his favourite Rhineland hotel—the Hotel Dreeson at Bad Godesberg; used to go there before he came to power; other visitors departed bec. of Hitler but hotel proprietor continued to have faith in him. Now repaid bec. hotel is always full of Nazis.

Was a very fair-minded man about regime; didn't like it but didn't like French either, espec. their attitude now. Said the Jews *do* get the dole here the same as Germans. Many English ex-service men still here from Occupation, married to German women; were employed until Hitler regime but now sacked as foreigners; living on German dole & their wives' families.

Advised us when in Frankfurt to see Reuter's agent there—Paul Freye. Wife advised us to read German book giving true picture of French occupation: *Der Jüngling im Feuerofen* by Steguweit. They said Goering & Goebbels seldom seen on platform together; Goering here last Tuesday going round in a car looking like a carnival figure.

Described entrance of troops into Cologne. A surprise to population —notice given to town about 5 a.m. Trains went to Rhineland full of troops—many made to march very long way—half-dead when they arrived about 2 p.m. Great welcome by town. Pandemonium at Capt. Bennett's house—he was the only person on the spot—telephone from newspapers went all day—towards end of day correspondents began to arrive by air & all came to his house for information. Said Cologne was quite flat to-day in comp. with yesterday—always like that—no real excitement over elections—many people with French blood in Rhineland.

We asked him to come to our hotel and have a drink with us another day but he said: "No, you come back here; at the hotel we shall be seen & we can't talk."

Advised us to go to Saar whenever we wanted real news of regime; many people dissatisfied there & will talk. Told us—important this—that before

Hitler's meeting the Gauleiter Groke went to see the Cardinal-Archbp Schultz of Cologne & implored him to come to Hitler's meeting but the Archbp refused—said his appearance would create wrong impression that he countenanced the wrongs done to Catholicism by the regime.

Went back to hotel & had dinner late. At ten results began to come in by radio—all tending to final 99% backing for Hitler—listening-in in hotel, had impression of entire city cheering results. Looked out of hotel door; street strangely empty. Too tired to walk further but G. went along to Neumarkt, centre of city, where results were being given. Found six loud-speakers blaring results & cheers into night but square deserted. Whether enthusiastic reception of Rhineland "Liberation" came from Berlin or the radio studio or the highly efficient Propaganda Ministry we didn't know, but they certainly did not come from Cologne.

Monday March 30th
Spent all morning & afternoon writing & typing second *Sunday Chron.* article, sent off two copies, by air-mail & ordinary. After tea went for walk with G. along Rhine Embankment towards Köln–Mülheim; pleasant evening; cobbled quai; big flat-bottomed barges along Rhine carrying coal; various nationalities. Trees across Rhine near Mülheim a bright burnt-sienna colour as if it were autumn. In public gardens magnolia trees in full bloom & yellow forsythia. Lovely view of Cologne in evening light; one of the most beautiful cities in Europe.

Dined at hotel; went along afterwards to Capt. Bennett's; heard many stories of French occupation of Rhineland. French hated because they left houses in filthy condition; English welcomed; petition from Wiesbaden that they might go there instead of French. Favourite cartoon of time showed French Colonel & wife leaving a German house with broken egg-shells, cobwebs etc. behind them; English Colonel & wife entering, holding noses & followed by army of charwomen. One French family simply covered a drawing-room carpet with heap of sand; left baby of house to play there & do its business when it liked; whole place simply a manure-heap when family left.

Capt. Bennett billeted on old couple at Bonn; both over 80, spotlessly clean; very kind; treated him like a son, left sandwiches etc. for him at night. When he left, French officer came in; imported whole of his family; banished old couple to attic; forbade them to use their own kitchen so that they had to build a separate one & only allowed them to use back door. Old man went mad under treatment & died; old woman endured it for a time & then left to live with her son-in-law.

Heard some stories of Jews. Mrs Bennett has friend living in Cologne married to youngest railway inspector; inhabited block of flats on floor below a Jewish family. Did not really know people but used their telephone etc. One night wife went up to use telephone—had bridge party down-stairs—found Jews very depressed owing to threat to their financial position etc. Said: "Won't you come down & join our party." Jews came; shortly afterwards young man was sent for by railway authorities and told he was relieved of his job; sent to another place, where no work for him. Evidently someone at party who wanted his job had reported him as friendly with Jews.

Bennetts said a good deal of discontent with regime exists [among] those whom it does not favour—e.g. workman he knew got chance of job after 5 years unemployt; went along to local labour exchange to get permission to take it & register; was told, "Oh, no, there are many people who have been in the movement longer than you who need the job"; therefore he is still unemployed. Bennett says the place is full of spies & everyone watches you. We noticed on leaving our hotel that the manager asked us where we were going—"To a café?" We said "No" only—but had sense that he knew & had noted where we were going owing to our telephone call to Bennett earlier in the evening to ask if we could come along.

At midday we read results of election in *Mittag*—99% for regime, as engineered. Only substantial votes against were in Frankfurt-am-Main (10,000 odd) and Hamburg (37,000 odd). About 5,000 voted against at Cologne—but no. of those entitled to vote at Cologne & Frankfurt was not given. We tried to find this out (in order to get number of abstentions); G. went to Propaganda Min. in Cologne to ask & they made great pretence of telephoning but in the end said they didn't know! Tried again later at Frankfurt in office of *Frankfurter Zeitung* but could only get 1933 figures —not accurate for now as so many Jews have to be counted out. Election by which Hitler came into power (March 1933) the last time Jews were on the register.

In the end we never did find out. Were told that at beginning of election results wireless announcers began by giving number of those entitled to vote—and then suddenly ceased—evidently by instructions from headquarters.

Thursday March 31st   Aachen

Took train to Aachen to spend day—really because of Miss Schultz's remark about fortifications & Bennett's denial. Think he is probably right as we saw no workmen all day. Typical German provincial town; no good hotels; odd to think it was once capital of the Holy Roman Empire. Now just a frontier town to which few visitors come. Walked about town; went up to Cathedral—old round Basilica style with piece of poor Gothic & an unimpressive spire added on. In square in front, flower-sellers seated round clusters of spring flowers; gorgeous colours.

Went into Treasury which was full of relics, crowns, robes etc. One large gold erection rather like a glorified kennel is said to be Charlemagne's tomb, and his forearm is supposed to be enclosed in a large gilt hand & arm. Walked from Cathedral to Rathaus behind—green copper roof, modern copy of an older building. Getting round to the front of it, we saw another propaganda stunt—two huge futurist soldiers in uniform painted on gigantic sheets for nearly whole height of tower and high between them the lettered notice: "Unsere Garnisonen sind Garnisonen des Friedens." And between the soldiers, just below the notice, was a little seated statue of Christ with a sceptre in one hand & the other held up in blessing! Again, as we walked through the town towards the road leading to the Dutch & Belgian frontiers, we passed a big glass frame containing anti-Jewish propaganda, including pages from *Die Stürme*, and just behind it above a fountain was erected a large statue of Christ on the cross. German propagandists evidently have no sense of incongruity. Nor did they evidently mind eclipsing the comic-opera figure of Charlemagne on the fountain in the centre of the square—as he was pro-French!

We found quite a good Vaterland café for lunch & then walked out to the Belgo-German frontier with a little help from the tram. Frontier lies beyond a wooded hill about 3 miles out of the town; woods evidently a favourite place for pictures etc. in summer & have many paths running through them—and a lovely view of Aachen & its numerous churches from the top. Similar half-wooded, half-meadow country running right up to the frontier village, in which we had to walk under a triumphant arch of firs with the usual flags and election notices. Frontier itself marked by a white painted, black and red striped, barrier across the road & a small Customs house. Nothing could be more innocent than the village & its surroundings of pleasant woods with anemones beginning to come out. I picked & pressed three. Looked over barrier to church spires & tranquil sloping fields of Belgium in distance. Walked back part of way & then took tram to the town. Had tea in a dullish hotel café & returned to Cologne in time for dinner. Packed afterwards & went to bed early.

Wednesday April 1st   Frankfurt
Early train from Cologne down Rhine to Mainz for Frankfurt; breakfasted on it. Lovely run beside river; passed Bad Godesberg where Hitler stays and many famous castles and mountains—Drachenfels, Lorelei, Silben Gebirge at outset. Blossoms out everywhere & trees vividly green; hillsides near Bad Godesberg white and mauve with cherry & plum blossom. Got to Frankfurt about 11.30; pleasant spacious residential town, now much hit financially by exit of Jews. Made straight for British Consulate; saw Vice-Consul first; typical Civil-Service Army Englishman. While waiting for the Consul (who was with the Reuter man, Paul Freye, whom we had been told of) we asked the Vice-Consul for number of *contra régime* voters in Frankfurt. He said many people here sympathised with Jews; also several thousand maid-servants (Germans) had lost their jobs because girls not now allowed to work in a house where the man is a Jew. Meant exit of many maids because Jewish women are not domesticated like Germans (& why German women should be in a country so full of cafés beats me). Jews must now employ Jewish maids or German men.

Eventually went down to Vice-Consul, who was still talking to Paul Freye & evidently welcomed the interruption. Then ensued a 4-party conversation, Freye & the Consul both being Die-hards (Freye not a Nazi but a nationalist). Consul said there was a good deal to be said for the Nazi regime. When we mentioned the suppression of opinion he said that the Press hadn't much influence anyway (instancing the Northcliffe Press in England, tho' we pointed out the influence of *The Times* in creating the British opposition to the Hoare–Laval negotiations) and that most people everywhere wanted to be told what to think! He said it was a pity that the Nazis had faked their election results (which he agreed they had—he couldn't supply the Cologne or Frankfurt voting figures) as they would have got 87% support without any hanky-panky. I asked why the Govt had spent so much on propaganda when their victory was certain & he said they hadn't—most of the work was voluntary; printers produced voluntary posters & other Nazi supporters stuck them up & took them down again. Painting on engines, etc., quite voluntary.

We asked why the regime got so much support from Social Democrats & other obvious opponents, & he & Paul Freye both agreed that it was due to German fear of Bolshevism—they fear Bolshevism more than they hate Hitler—country of small capitalists, delicate mechanism, not agricultural [like] Russia, could only be turned over to Communism by violent readjustments.

Paul Freye so eloquent—urging that as foreign journalists we learn the truth about the elections & tell the world—that I deliberately winked at the Consul—who responded, and ended by asking us to come back for cocktails at 6.30.

We went off with Paul Freye whom we asked to lunch to get more information, though we didn't quite reckon on being run round to the extent that we were! He had been a Professor of German in Siam —interned in India during War but seems to bear us no malice for it— now lectures on Far East to help impoverished middle classes—very fond of imparting information. Took us to see Goethe's house & the church (Katharina Kirche) where the Goethe family used to worship; showed us plate in aisle where Goethe as a child got permission to sit on little chair bec. church so crowded. Church Baroque; gave me the impression of crowding & restlessness that Baroque always does.

Walked on to old town (it was now beginning to rain) and into streets still as they were in the Middle Ages—saw the Romerhof, the Coronation hall of the Emperors of the Holy Roman Empire—pictures of them all round the walls of the chief hall; also inner room where the T. of Frankfurt was signed in 1871. By now hoped for lunch but were made to go into a completely medieval corner, buy 2 Frankfurter sausages and a piece of bread & sit on a bench and eat them; were told the King of Spain had done the same. At last got lunch, about 3 p.m., in large underground restaurant in one of the main streets; Paul Freye talked a mixture of German history, the Far East & modern politics.

Points in conversation

1) *Austria*   Germany could not afford to incorporate it—Austria was financed by L. of N. & this wd stop if Germany occupied it. If invited might make friendly gestures & economic agreements, but that would be all.

2) *Rhineland occupation*   Hitler could have had this by *agreement*—also raw materials from colonies on same terms as England—but would not have this as wanted to denounce Versailles Treaty by military gesture. Patriotic mania. Four interviews between Hitler & Sir Eric Phipps before Christmas. Sir E.P. failed to persuade him to do things diplomatically. (Presumably mere paper agreement would not have diverted national attention from international conditions.)

3) *The Jews*   In 1932 Frankfurt had popln of 34,000 Jews but now 20,000. Whole popln of Frankfurt 550,000. Many Jews trying to go to Palestine —Consul's office flooded with them (espec. those with children who cannot bear humiliations of their education; many whose parents never particularly thought of themselves as Jews now obliged to leave German schools & mix with children from ghetto). British demand (in addition to quota system) a deposit of £1,000 or a year's training as agricultural labourer (through Jewish agencies). Those who leave Germany are not obstructed by German govt but are only allowed to realise total of 27% of their capital paid to them over period of six years.

Between Spring 1933 & Spring 1935, approx. 40 liquidations a month took place among Jewish firms. (Many Nazis themselves saying Jewish policy a mistake, owing to its bad effect on German finance, espec. in such towns as Frankfurt.) Figures slightly diminished in Summer 1935 but now have increased again to about 25 liquidations a month. Number now entitled to vote in Frankfurt about 384,000 (after deducting Jews, who have not been able to vote since the Hitler regime).

4) *Frankfurter Zeitung*   The Reich's Angabe of the *F.Z.*—signed "Berlin, R.K." (Rudolf Kircher)—represents the Govt's point of view, given daily. R.K. represented *F.Z.* in London—wrote *Englishmen Among Themselves*. Now edits paper from Berlin. The *F.Z.* was formerly democratic—had a comment of Editor's—to-day regime has insisted that it must have a Chief Editor—this is R.K., who is intimate confidant of Hitler & Neurath, tho' not a member of the Party. *F.Z.* now financed by chief shareholders of the I.G. Chemical Trust and of other industries including Krupps. Represents German finance & industry—fully Aryan paper, though still has several Jewish editors on its commercial staff bec. they are experts and high industrialists protested against their dismissal. (Aryan = 75% German capital & staff. *F. Zeitung* has no Jewish capital now.)

When we had finished talking Freye took us for coffee and *Schlagsahne* to the Café Rothschild—a Jewish café and one of the only two in Frankfurt where Jews are allowed. Hardly a German in F. wd venture to go there because he would be thought friendly with Jews & might lose his job—but Freye can go bec. it is known that for his newspaper job he must have converse with everyone. This café was closed not long ago bec. it had 250 lbs of butter in store and authorities said the Jews were "hoarding" butter—but they submitted the amount to catering experts, who said it was not only reasonable but below normal for a café of that size—so though stormtroops had closed it, it was reopened after two or three days. Staff is not Jewish—shop was not closed down bec. Germans wd have lost jobs. Paul Freye was urged to "cut down" his intercourse with Jews to lowest minimum. Editors of newspapers not allowed to respond to-day if Jews accost them in streets.

Café gave one a queer feeling—the collective sense of humiliation was oppressive; marked admixture of classes who would normally not talk to each other driven together by common misfortune. Both upper & lower rooms were crowded. I felt as if I were among a gathering of Girondins under the Terror—or prisoners of War—or exiles in a foreign country.

Went from there to have cocktails with Vice-Consul—strong cocktails, pleasant room (in which I noticed a copy of *South Riding*—they belong to the Book Society), beautiful Norwegian wife, very fair & charming. Did not talk much politics but she spoke a little of the suffering of the better-class Jews, & also of Hitler—how much more "gentlemanly" he had become in the last three years—did not bang & thump so much when speaking or look round furtively for possible assassins.

Caught train to Heidelberg 7.30—journey about 1½ hours; swinging local train; felt sleepy & rather sick from strong cocktails. Went to Hotel Damstadterhof—pleasant, with very courtly proprietor. Took walk in dark before going to bed—looked at outline of castle on hill & old bridge over the Neckar.

Thursday April 2nd   Heidelberg
Woke up to sunny morning—small detachment of troops marching through, also little bands of hiking girls, singing. Got up & went for walk; lovely place, perfect for work; hillside on other side of the Neckar covered with white blossom. Shops everywhere selling wild daffodils & clusters of primroses. Yellow pansies in square in front of a University building (purple in a square in Cologne). Went up to old Schloss on top of hill (castle of Electors Palatine; red sandstone, statue of Electors on front wall). From terrace outside had gorgeous view of Heidelberg on both sides of the Neckar.

Looked at the map given us by hotel for directions; noticed two slips of paper pasted over names. Held them up to light; one was an advt by a Jewish shop, Löwenthal; the other (among the list of interesting places to visit in Heidelberg) covered the suggestion that the house where Friedrich Ebert was born was such a place. Decided to go & look at the Pfaffengasse near the river, where it was, & see if anything had happened to it. In Pfaffengasse found the house—a small workman's cottage with plants in the window; over it had been a notice on a plaque, which was now thickly plastered out! The regime is nothing if not thorough. In a little cake shop & café in a side street the notice was conspicuously displayed: "Juden sind hier unerwünscht."

Bad day—misty & dull, began to rain. Went in & wrote some letters; lunched, then walked to other side of Neckar. Had tea at a café & wrote up diary. At 7.30 took train to Karlsruhe; changed there & went on to Strasbourg, over big Rhine bridge.

Friday April 3rd   Strasbourg
Sense of relief at being in France—conscious of being watched & supervised in Germany; letters opened, conversations listened to, telephone calls noted. Still don't know if my *Sunday Chronicle* article got through, though I sent one copy by air mail & one by ordinary. Germany a bitter country for progressives; what a task for England to mediate between one country with a detestable domestic policy and another with a deplorable foreign policy!

Went out after breakfast—looked into Cathedral. Built of red sandstone; one enormous spire like a huge finger pointing heavenward. Superb stained glass inside; section below spire in basilica style; tiny west window like little gleaming jewel, looks as if it was cut in wall later. Superb rose window—black in shape of spokes of wheel, with circular patterns of green & deep blue.

Walked on towards office of American Consul whom Bennett had advised us to see; new buildings on Quai Koch. Strasbourg a very pleasant town; stream or canal running through midst of it, though surrounded by shopping streets & commercial buildings, looks like a country stream; green banks with magnolias & forsythia in bloom; men peacefully fishing in it. Beautiful twin-spired church near University Place reflected in it. Population seems to converse in German. All streets have new French names but old German names left below. In hotel the older sanitary fittings had "Warm", "Kalt" on them, [with] the new French additions "Chaud" & "Froid". Statue of Goethe still retained near University, but statues outside post office (did not find out of whom) were decapitated when Alsace went back to France after War.

Called on American Consul, Mr Green (agreeable, unimpressive, kindly little man), who said:

1) Very little change here since Rhine occupation. Census taken (a habitual proceeding) on day of March 7th–8th—the day of the occupation —among soldiers in garrisons gave 8,000, the usual number.

2) Very little excitement among population when occupation

announced but soldiers thought it meant immediate War; left barracks & occupied forts along line; much weeping among relatives.

3) No one really expects War but for sake of precaution no one is buying very much; trade very quiet. (Cf. Nancy Pearn's remark to me that none of the magazines are taking articles very far ahead.) Population here more tolerant than in most parts of France—cf. street names.

4) Newspaper correspondents writing up situation here made a great deal of events that happen as a matter of course—e.g. mentioned soldiers at Cathedral services, but soldiers are always at services as this is a garrison town. On Occupation Sunday probably fewer than usual were there as all were in barracks & forts. Barracks were heavily guarded that day & no one was allowed near.

Mr Green told us where to go if we wanted to see the new Rhine fortifications—so we took No. 15 tram to its terminus by the old Laval Tor (part of the older fortifications which are now being taken down). Sunny day, very warm. Walked along straight path by Rhine Canal for about ½ mile to place where it joined the Rhine; got at once into area of enormous cranes & innumerable barges flying the French flag & carrying chiefly slag & coal. Roar of huge cranes dropping slag into barges. Came to the Rhine & the frontier; wide river here, flowing quietly between green banks. The village of Kehl on the opposite bank looked very innocent & peaceful; no German flags flying; perhaps people there have been ordered to avoid provocation.

Walked along the Rhine to the left, looking as casual as possible & appearing to notice nothing; eventually came to an area of petrol dumps & the first modern fort—a low round fort of stone surmounted with small steel turrets, the roof covered with earth & grass. A notice said that photographs were forbidden. On the other side of the military road were barbed-wire entanglements & petrol dumps; the ground was bare except for half-dead scrub as though it had been dug up for the burial of stores beneath. Amid all these sinister military symbols fluttered a single white butterfly. Woods beyond road turning freshly green; looked as if they might conceal further fortifications. About three hundred yards further along the bank was another low fort.

Saturday April 4th

Took morning train to Metz; excellent Pullman train called the Edelweiss, running from Zürich to Amsterdam. Two Dutch ladies (both very plain & rather unpleasant-looking) very much interested in us.

Dull, damp day. Got out at Metz—a spacious but incredibly desolate-looking city; very wet; typical French-German commercial town; heavy buildings; no show places of any kind. Walked from station past large military barracks and parade ground to Cathedral; felt we must be the only two English people in Metz. Looked at outside of Cathedral, which was closed; early Gothic, built of yellowish stone which had grown discoloured;

copper roofs of a tarnished green; whole place looked as if it wanted restoring. Pigeons flapped about the buttresses; roof & entrances soiled with pigeon-droppings which seemed to have accumulated for a long period.

It started to rain & we hastened to the Grand Hotel—large & shabby —Gordon said exactly like most Russian hotels, but we got quite a good meal. Rain poured down in torrents while we lunched; it stopped about 2.30 & we hastened under dripping roofs to a cinema half-way to the station which advertised that it gave the news. Sat through a Mickey Mouse film & an incredibly long & dreary informative picture of the French Sudan—*Le Pays de Soif*—which went on for about 45 minutes, showing endless pictures of laden camels tramping across deserts, acres of sand, oases & natives who inhabited them, more sand, more natives, some geographical information about products & distances, more sand, a lonely camel left by the cavalcade, more natives, a most gruesome series of pictures showing the camel dead in the sand & going through various processes of decay until all that was left was a few clean-picked bones, camels being intractable in whirlwinds of sand, more natives, more customs, more sand with human skulls lying about, more cavalcades with evening coming on, pictures of tropical towns all looking the same. Thought the thing would never end but at last it did. Then came the news—the *Queen Mary*, American floods, the Grand National; finally & most interesting, the German elections (Hitler at Cologne, Goebbels voting, etc.), preceded by a notice imploring the audience to "prenez le grand calme" as if there were any disturbances the film could not be shown. Went out, to great disturbance of Zouave at entrance, before the chief film—a Jewish production.

Raced to station with rain still dripping all round. Got no tea. Found train for Verdun & discovered as last straw that it was an "omnibus". It poured with rain so that we could hardly see the high wooded hills which once formed the natural frontier between France & Germany. Passed through Amanvillers which obviously used to be frontier station. Reached Verdun at last; stopped at the Coque Hardi—very pleasant little modern country-style hotel, rebuilt after War, stone-floored lounge, little tables with bright cloths, parquet-floored dining room, good dinner, pleasant bedroom with comfortable beds & bath; good sanitation. Pictures in lounge showed Coque Hardi smashed by bombardment & Coque Hardi rebuilt. Placard in lounge giving full instructions of what to do in case of gas raids.

Letter from Miss Moore saying Albatross Library may reproduce *South Riding*; also Sir Charles Trevelyan wanted me to speak on May 3rd but I decided I *must* refuse in interests of "Hon. Estate".

Sunday April 5th   Verdun
Cold wet day; east wind; rain gradually diminished as day went on. Went

out of hotel into Verdun, where the twin towers of the grey Cathedral stand high above the olive-green waters of the Meuse. Coque Hardi in Avenue la Victoire, built after War; Verdun "adopted" by London, so enlarged Embankment along Meuse (houses used to be right up to river) is called "Quai de Londres". Walked up hill through rain to Cathedral—Verdun stands high above country around; promontory obvious reason for its being a fortress.

Cathedral built of grey stone; frontage damaged slightly by shells & still not repaired. Roof was smashed & is completely renewed. Many new houses or parts of houses among older buildings. Huge brand-new water tower just beyond Cathedral given by City & County of London. Pale grey stone. Pre-war fortifications very large & conspicuous, commanding open country to South-east; shell-scarred walls but not seriously damaged. Country almost invisible owing to rain & damp.

Went into Cathedral—Passion Sunday—High Mass very long—crowded congregation below new roof—stained glass new; Bishop of Verdun in red skullcap seated in chair. Singing much less musical than in Cologne. Came out & walked past covered market-place; noticed that hundreds of places were set with a bottle of wine each; on outside wall of market-place a poster advertised actually a peace pilgrimage.

Had early lunch; came back to market at 1.30; saw pilgrims assembled there. Given a medal & several copies of the oath by a woman pilgrim at table in doorway. Tried to find committee; pursued them to Hotel de Ville in rain, saw pilgrims visiting various Verdun War Memorials; finally encountered some of the officials as the whole lot were getting into motor-buses to visit battlefields near Fort de Vana. Spoke to a plump dark man whom we afterwards learned was Jacques du Clos, a well-known Paris Communist. With him was a local organiser who spoke English; told us that there were 1,600 pilgrims, mostly from Paris, among them not only du Clos but Perrin, Socialist Deputy for 18th Arrondissement of Paris; that the Anciens Combattants had brought together various left-wing organis-ations of the Front Populaire (Socialists, Radicals, Communists). He said to us: "Tell the English people about our pilgrimage for the French Press will be silent." We said we would; G. wrote a letter about it to the *News Chronicle* & I to the *Manchester Guardian*.

Going back to market, was reading poster again when a woman in black posted small green leaflet on wall beside me:

> Les profiteurs de la guerre sont les marchands de canons et de muni-tions, les gros industriels et les banquiers. Les victimes sont vos Enfants! Mères! Défendez vos fils de vingt ans. Comité Régional de Femmes contre la Guerre et le Fascisme.

Went back to hotel; spent rest of day writing up diary in café & hotel. Arranged to drive in morning to Romagne-sous-Montfauçon to see the American cemetery about which George told me.

Monday April 6th
Drive round French & American battlefields—French chauffeur Joseph
—spoke some English. Started from Verdun at 10.0. Hills opposite V. the
Belleville Hills—low along horizon; Germans used to shell Verdun from
other side; Fort of Belleville never lost. Vauban fortifications round
town—now being taken down. Fort St Michel on extreme right of Belleville Hills in small wood. We passed long line of blue-clad soldiers with dark
blue steel helmets. Officers in khaki which will ult. be uniform of all French
army.

Long country road to Montfauçon. Military barracks on left. Open
green country all round—rolling, wide & spacious; must have been v.
difficult to fight in as everything so conspicuous from great distances.
White houses with red roofs & green shutters. Little woods with green
feathery trees against darker background—chequered with narrow strips
of brown ploughed fields—cherry & blackthorn in bloom everywhere like
trees white with snow. Black & white cows feeding in meadows full of
daisies & cowslips. Fortifications on hills. As we approached Mont
Homme saw pits made by shell holes, still bare.

Turned off by village of Charny for Mont Homme—in distance white
monument of Douaumont finished in 1931. Acres of ploughed fields;
numerous magpies darting among them. Blue-grey asphalt road winding
through open meadows—new villages, white red-roofed new houses in
place of ruins half-covered with grass. Delicate mauve mayflowers in fields.

Past Chattancourt to Dead Man's Hill—meadows still tumbled &
rough with trenches & dug-outs; cowslips growing among them. Blackthorn bushes standing up against pale blue sky. Hills pock-marked with
shell-holes. Grass on them still coarse & brambly—many dead still hidden
beneath them.

Immense view from Dead Man's Hill of wide rolling country—
brambles & thistles growing over old trenches—ground silting in—above
blue sky with feathery tufts & strips of white cloud. Larks singing in spring
sunshine. Monument—Dead Man with hand upraised—back turned
towards German troops & addressing France: "Ils n'ont pas passé."
Inscribed: "Aux Morts de la 69th Division." Pock-marked & tumbled hills
all round—clumps of dandelions & rusted tin cans lying about old
trenches—heaps of greyish-white stones here & there—a desolation.
Little red-roofed villages in valleys & young woods beginning to grow up.
Remnants of rusted stake & wire. German front line along top of Dead
Man's Hill. Ground tunnelled. Little palm-bushes ("sole") growing
among old trenches.

Misty blue-grey lines of hills on horizon. Dead still lying under humps
on hills. Barbed wire; clumps of cowslips & violets growing among
shell-holes. Cowslips everywhere. White blossom everywhere against pale
clear sky. Grass rough & coarse over trenches & shell-holes. Nature
struggling to repair ravages. Woods show thin white trunks of birches

—bright tufty green heads against darker part of woods. New houses growing up among villages literally razed to the ground. Hill 304— fighting all in shell-holes—terrible, worst [of] battlefields—bayonets; constantly re-taken.

Bois Camère Disappeared in one night from German artillery; now little bushes.

Malancourt Village taken by 79th American Division (New York Divn). Dead Man's Hill held by 80th American Division. Sept 27th—took Malancourt at 9.0 and Montfauçon later on same day. Picked palm from Mont Homme & cowslips from Hancourt (now non-existent) near Malancourt. Yellow butterflies flitting over trenches. Remnants of "pill-boxes" visible on hills. Birds—finches, magpies, larks, hawks with slow hovering flight.

Montfauçon Great American monument (huge column surmounted by statue of Liberty; dominating country for miles around as far as the Argonne), made of Italian granite & erected just beside ruins of formᴄ: 12th-century church in Montfauçon on top of highest hill for miles around. New village now further into valley; church not a copy of old one wh. was very large of grey stone. Column vivid white against blue sky.

Main inscription [on Monument]: "Erected by the United States of America to commemorate the brilliant victory of her First Army in the Meuse–Argonne offensive Sept. 26th–Nov. 11th, 1918, and to honor the heroic services of the Armies of France on this important battle front during the World War."

Lunched at Montfauçon—good & ample meal in simple village restaurant—ham & pork, large mutton chops with stew of potatoes, carrots & lentils; cheese, bananas, jam & biscuits. Place has been rebuilt since War but still runs to earth closets.

Drove on past Nantillois—80th Div. Monument erected by State of Pennsylvania—two houses—arms of Penn. Village occupied by Americans for 4 years. Inscription on arms: "Virtue, Liberty & Independence."

American cemetery at Romagne

Car drives through great marble gateway—two gates crowned with American eagles—all very simple in spite of feeling of great ornamental museum—big sweeping lines—vast area of 128 acres on two sides of a valley—graves on one side—Superintendent's house, visitors' hostelry, stores etc. on the other. (Hostess-house just like a sitting-room in N. Carolina—American even to sanitation.)

Cemetery fronted by ornamental lake full of goldfish—long beautifully-mown lawns on either side—straight gravelled road runs all round—all very tidy & ornamental—a bit of America in the midst of France. Four short yews round the lake, like a great national park.

Sense of tremendous green space and in the midst of it acres & acres of the dead. From distance owing to vividness of both green sward & white crosses the white turns blue & gives impression of an enormous field of bluebells planted in rows.

Sun dipping towards low hills to right as one faces chapel. (Flag in 1924; also marble crosses were not put up till 1927. In 1924 were rather taller wooden crosses, more slender, painted white & stencilled in black.)

Cemetery reached by wide flight of marble steps with huge square columns on either side (columns not there in 1924). Shrubs & small firs grow around columns on side away from steps. Sense of oppression given by vastness (over 14,000 graves). Paths lead up to chapel on either side of wide central grass path closely mown.

Crosses Each grave now marked by white marble cross—now (& probably formerly) marked as follows:

Eugene C. Meury

Capt. 271st Inf. 59th Division

New York. Oct. 7th, 1918

D.S.C.

D.C.M.

Air filled with lovely smell of mown grass. Swallows darting over it. Graves have no gardens round them as in English military cemetery. Stand straight up out of immense green sward cut short but not mown; in the midst of it, growing about graves, patches of daisies and violets & cowslips. Bare, ungardened bases of graves add to sense of vastness and regimentation. One vast open field of the dead. Graves 160 in number walking across cemetery.

Eugene's grave should be at far north-western corner of cemetery —close to a thin copse of trees in blossom—cherry trees; others just beginning to bud. Feathery leaves. Groups of young firs. Trees lining path cast their shadows like larger & darker cross over the end graves—shadow falls in front of shadow cast by Eugene's cross from western sun. Graves face east. Sun sets behind & at side of them.

Warm sun—birds singing loudly in trees—newly-awakened bees humming—bronze beetles with a burnishing of iridescent green creep through grass—air mild & gentle, with sense of coming summer added to by gentle throb of distant lawn-mower. Only village in sight Romagne, among trees; only country sounds—birds, mower, tap as of a wood-cutter, lowing of cows.

Clumps of daisies in grass at foot of cross & longer grass in copse thick with daisies and cowslips. Trees close to graves are chestnuts. Acres upon acres of the dead. Crosses ranked in long straight lines like soldiers marching.

In distance gentle outlines of wooded hills and ploughed fields. Enormous pale blue vault of the sky—cloudless except for tiny tufts of feathery white. Church of Romagne in valley, visible among small houses & fruit trees in blossom, from top of hill. Graves slope down immense hillside into valley with white road running along bottom of it, and huge white marble gateposts surmounted by American eagles at either end. Graves divided down centre by wide slope of mown grass running down hill towards lake in centre at bottom of valley. No horror or agony of death here but a beautifying & concealing of it. An attempt to make tolerable the rawness of memory. Sun slowly dipping down towards wooded hills at north-west of cemetery.

The Argonne Forest

Heard cuckoo for first time this year. Saw remains of old observation post in tall tree. Deep ravines full of trees. Dug-outs covered with shrubs & brambles—remnants of occupation. Chimney pots, broken trees; undergrowth here mostly broom. Patches of violets. Muddy paths through brambles. Pussy willows. Impossible-looking tangle; enemy wd be quite invisible. Pigeons cooing, blackbirds chirping, ivy on ground; afternoon sun filtering through thick trees.

Passing through section fought over in 1915 by French and in 1918 by Americans—road runs between La Harazée and the ravine Four de Paris; the 77th Division of Americans—George's division—were here. Broken trees and dead brown bushes lying in heaps among silver birches; thick broom, much of it dead. Old dark boards along rough muddy path; old communication trenches. Violets, cowslips. Open spaces in many parts where trees have been completely cleared. Palms, catkins, pussy willows out. Forest full of lilies-of-the-valley in May. Ground all bumpy with trenches—many American dead probably lying under here. Broken trees with sharp dead ends lying amongst the others; broken moss-grown trunks; dead leaves everywhere. Little thin birch trees & cherry trees, in blossom, growing up. Catkins & pussy willows everywhere.

In middle of Forest, near Harazée, French monument & shelters—put up also to American division which fought in Argonne—names them: "Aux Morts de l'Argonne."

"Eugene at Romagne"

"And all that remained of the beautiful young body with which hers had once been united was the sorry fleshless structure of a man, decently hidden beneath the bright green sward, its horror and pathos covered by the external dignity of spring flowers & Christian symbols. Disillusion swept down upon her."

Tuesday April 7th

Left Verdun 8.56—passed along edge of Argonne again by railway seen yesterday; went through Ste Menehould & Valmy. Changed at Châlons-sur-Marne; passed Épernay, Château-Thierry. Spent 3 hours in Paris; 4.30 train back to London. Cold windy day with intervals of bright sunshine.

Monday April 13th   London
Worked at "Hon. Estate" most of day. Children came over in morning.
Went to tea with Mother & to say goodbye to them in afternoon.

Tuesday April 14th
Saw children off to Guildford with Fräulein. Trains running late & station
crowded. Sent off first five chapters of "Hon. Estate" to Macmillan &
Curtis Brown.
   Baird Lewis in afternoon—hair done at Marshall's.
   Mother rang me up to say that Alfred Goodman died suddenly on
Friday morning. Spoke to his maid when she called him & seemed quite
normal but when she went back he was dead. Must have been sudden heart
attack due to his recent bronchitis. He was 79. The older generation is
going fast. John Williams, Father, Uncle Norman & Alfred in less than two
years. It reminds me of Winifred's story "The Casualty List"—but who
would have believed that she would be one of the first casualties herself.

Wednesday April 15th
Large correspondence. Dentist in afternoon. Finished Section 3 of Chap. 6
of "Hon. Estate".

Thursday April 16th
Went to Alfred Goodman's cremation at Golders Green. Garden of
Remembrance full of daffodils.
   Visited Miss Mayo—Elizabeth Arden. Tea with Maurice Richardson
& his wife at Stewart's—talked about Germany & the Carlisle Luncheon
Club.
   Prepared speech for luncheon lecture to-morrow.

Friday April 17th
Spoke at American Women's Club Annual Federation Luncheon on "The
Public & a Peace Policy". Wore new black rose-patterned dress & black
hat with long veil; pleased with both. Experience much like similar
women's clubs to which I spoke in America. Mrs Curtis Brown in chair;
very good lunch; about 50 present. Spoke of my recent experiences in
Germany & France. Somewhat hampered by cough but got through all
right. Lovely afternoon; walked home.
   Worked at Sect. 4, Ch. 6, of "Hon. Estate".

Saturday April 18th
Finished Section 4, Chap. 6, of "Hon. Estate". Worked hard & painfully
among ceaseless interruptions.

Sunday April 19th
Started off for Dutch lecture tour. Packed all morning. Ructions with Amy

before I started; temperamental & uppish; told her off for once & of course produced tears. Tea with Mother. Left Liverpool Street 8.30; beautiful day but rather windy. G. saw me off; gave me bunch of mauve tulips. Dined on train. Decent cabin but it was slightly rough & port-hole could not be opened; slept badly in consequence. Harwich to Hook. Went as guest of the English Association in Holland.

Monday April 20th   Holland

Arrived Hook at about 7.30; stayed on boat till 8.0; took train for Hague, changed at Schiedam. Cold & rather dull. Holland all water, windmills & flat green meadows. Took taxi at Hague to Roelofsstraat 52; met at door by Mrs Te Winkel-Tadema; tall, voluble young woman, going to have a baby; very energetic; instructions all very detailed & efficient. She gave me breakfast—fried egg, strips of ham & cheese on slices of bread as usual in Holland. Spent morning unpacking things & writing to G. Poured with rain in afternoon; got quite damp walking only to end of road to get stamps. Dutch houses in this part of the Hague very modern, well-planned, good balconies; area of gardens at back. Gardens bright with bulbs—daffodils, tulips, grape hyacinth. Was regaled with tales of previous English lecturers —S. P. B. Mais, my predecessor, forgot slides, lecture superficial, trailed round wife with bad cold; Randolph Churchill, bumptious, insufferable, ran down Americans, said women only useful as instruments of procreation; Rosita Forbes, good lecture but had had cocktail party at Amsterdam Hotel & put down cost, 100 guilders, to English Association; Phyllis Bentley, good lecture, but was always tired, & went to bed with hot water bottle in each place!

Early dinner—first solid meal of the day; drove to lecture at Hotel des Indes. Audience about 100; fairly distinguished; wife of British Minister there, Rosalind Wade & her father & sister in audience; was introduced by a very tall Dutch Admiral. Somewhat hampered by bronchial cough but got through lecture all right; ¾ hr, then interval for tea, etc., then another half hour. Talked to Wades & Lady Montgomery in interval; promised to come back on 30th & speak to Dutch L. of N. Union.

Tuesday April 21st

Stayed at Hague till afternoon; taken round to Peace Palace by Colonel Wade, who turns out to be the interpreter whom W. & I often met at Geneva & who made the slip (mentioned in *T. of Y.*) about "le vilayet de Parmoor" instead of "le vilayet de Mosul". Peace Palace a vast museum of precious things—porcelain fountains, tiled floors, Japanese tapestries & Chinese ornaments; statue of Christ of Indes looking over staircase. Queer to think of all that strange collection being inspired by last Czar of Russia.

Lunched at British Legation with Sir Hubert Montgomery, wife & son. Pleasant people; house in middle of town with long narrow garden at back full of spring flowers. Taken by Mr Te Winkel to train & went on to

Amsterdam. Met by Mrs Kalff de Vries-Robbe & taken to house of her mother & father. Old Mrs de Vries-Robbe a Scotch woman who came to Holland 44 years ago as a bride. Tall house with pleasant balcony & back garden—found big tea party in progress to meet me—Dutch, German, English. Dr Bonten, the acting Chairman, & his wife also came. Early dinner; lectured in lecture room at a club on "Youth Morals". No break. Back very tired; felt I lectured badly but the audience seemed quite pleased. The Bontens & one or two others came back to van Englenstraat after the lecture; & we sat up late having tea & talking.

Wednesday April 22nd
Came down late to pleasant breakfast. Then taken by Mrs Kalff to see the Rembrandts in the Rijks-Museum; saw especially "The Night Watch" and "The Jewish Bride". Cough still troublesome.

After lunch Dr Bonten (who entertained Rebecca when she was here & says all the women lecturers from England are nicer than the men) called for Mrs Kalff & me & took me over Amsterdam. We saw the canals circling round the city & intersecting the streets; the churches, halls & numerous bridges; the workmen's quarters full of new modern planned buildings, fringed by the sand dunes. Then he picked up his wife & we drove out to the bulb-fields near Haarlem—lovely patch-work quilts of colour laid over the green land. Day very bright but cold with a terrific wind. Had tea at fashionable restaurant by a river; old farm house with ancient sleighs filled with growing pansies in the garden. Large & excellent tea. Then the Bontens took me to the house of Mr & Mrs Tadema, where I was to stay. She formerly English, gymnastic instructress from Lancashire; he the brother of Mrs Te Winkel. Two little boys, eldest very beautiful, Kees, 4½; the other Roger in England with his grandmother. Lecture in a Haarlem hotel; very pleasant; excellent chairwoman who spoke charming English. In interval was presented with a yellow orchid by Mr Perrebot, editor of the chief Haarlem newspaper.

Thursday April 23rd
Morning breakfasted in bed (too much of this very demoralising & I don't really like it), walked in lovely Haarlem woods with Mrs Tadema & fetched Kees from school. Directly after lunch took train for Apeldoorn via Amsterdam—amid sand dunes & low hills with firs; small park-like town where Queen of Holland has her summer palace. Hotel quite comfortable & spotlessly clean; but bedroom very bare & rather cold; no hot water but only cold laid on, as so often here. Most of Apeldoorn still has earth closets; these gradually being changed for ordinary sanitation. Met at station by Mrs Polma, a translator of English; taken to tea at her house. She was very kind but her English was at first poor & conversation rather tiring. Dined alone at Hotel; lecture there afterwards to small but agreeable audience though rather of the elderly spinster type; branch has only 35 members.

Got to bed early for once. Demand for bath caused some activity; finally a tepid one achieved with help of a geyser.

Friday April 24th
Poured with rain in morning. Could not get out so stayed in & wrote long letter to G. & sent cards to children. Lunched with Mrs Polma & her son; pleasant lunch; her English had improved with practice. We talked of books, translation, etc.; the sins of Mr Mais, who had complained bitterly of the hotel; & of Phyllis Bentley, whose lecture they liked but who was *so* tired & spent all her time in bed with a hot water bottle. After lunch as it had stopped raining we wandered about Apeldoorn country roads. Son took me in train for Amersfoort; there met by a teacher of English who took me to his home for tea & dinner. Small red-haired daughter in bed in dining-room. Rather a depressed couple; conversation a bit difficult. Lecture in a kind of class-room at top of a hotel; Mrs Te Winkel & her husband there. Small audience as again small branch but lecture seemed successful. Afterwards taken to station by chairman & had to take 20 mins journey to Hilversum to spend night at house of a Mr Bakker, wealthy Dutchman who had spent many years in England. Mr Bakker met me; I nearly got carried on as train stopped only 2 minutes & I was left with porter. Nice house but I felt my presence somewhat embarrassing to him. Tall spare elderly man with tragic face due to loss of son 3 years ago; wife already gone to Rotterdam for exhibition of son's pictures.

Saturday April 25th
Comfortable night; breakfast in bed again; Mr Bakker already departed to Rotterdam when I got up. Had asked elderly Dutch lady who spoke English to show me over Hilversum. Saw very modern & extremely lovely town hall of yellow & ochre brick with blue clocks & tiles; saw all over it; interior all straight modern lines & colours in exquisite taste. Especially struck by coffee-room with black & white tiled floor & chromium chairs with yellow leather seats & orange-painted cupboards. Then walked round Hilversum (really a pleasant suburb of Amsterdam), saw shops, modern cinema, etc. Lunched at Mr Bakker's house; elderly lady then saw me into train & I went back to the Tademas' for week-end. Arrived in time for tea; thought I might get time for some letter writing during week-end but was never alone long enough except when in bed. After tea young English-speaking secretary called for Mrs Tadema & me & took us ride in her car through lovely country of beautiful houses, gardens & dunes to Zaandvoort by the sea where the Kaiser sometimes comes, but sudden thick mist obscured all views & even the sea itself. No lecture; talked after dinner till bedtime.

Sunday April 26th
Lazy day, breakfast in bed, but tiring bec. never alone afterwards. Went for

walk with Tademas in morning. Quite decent standard of hospitality though she had only one industrious little Dutch maid & a part-time nurse for the child. After lunch the Editor Mr Perrebot called for us with his car; took us again to Zaandvoort, which we could this time see—a sandy health resort of the Margate variety; then to the bulb-fields again; then on to see Dr Roorda of Haarlem, who initiated the joint letter addressed to the *Statesman* by about 300 psychiatrists from many countries emphasising war as a disease of the mind which should be tackled in a medical way. Promised to make this propaganda known. Back to Tademas for supper & talked again idly; wrote letters in bed.

Monday April 27th
Repacked; again walked in woods with Mrs Tadema & Kees; then took train via Amsterdam for Enschedé, on German border. Longest of all these short journeys, 3 hours; wrote long letter to G. Went through Amersfoort & Apeldoorn again; also Deventer, where last lecture is. Met at Enschedé by Mrs Rozendaal, English Jewess from Norfolk, married to a Dutchman & strangely enough the sister of Daphne Haldin, who used to work on *Time & Tide*. A dark, pleasant woman, easy to talk to, but apparently has no children & not enough to do & is far from contented with life as a rich Dutchman's wife. Enschedé a little Dutch Manchester—textiles, chiefly cotton. Rozendaal home at Lonneker, suburb of Enschedé, very luxurious & beautifully decorated; heaps of flowers. Had tea as soon as I arrived —then changed & had dinner to which came her plump agreeable Dutch husband & 3 other members of the English Assoc. Committee. Drove to lecture—in a kind of club; very tiny audience as everyone had been put off by Mais on previous occasion. Followed Mrs R.'s instructions not to be "high brow"; talked about Englishwoman's life in England & during War; Mrs R. very pleased; said it was by far the best lecture of the season & my English clear & easy to follow.

Tuesday April 28th
Taken by Mrs R. over Enschedé—shopped with her in market & had cup of chocolate; sent Kees Tadema some chocolates & bought Mrs R. some flowers, & she presented me with 2 Dutch bowls for ashtrays & chocolates for the children. Got to station rather late, only just caught train; felt too tired to write, so read Delafield's *Humbug*, wh. Mrs R. had given me. Weather turned quite warm but still dull. Nearly missed connection at Zwolle through having tremendous distance to go & only 5 minutes to do it; also couldn't understand anyone's explanations & as usual couldn't get a porter for ages.

Met at Groningen (big University town in north—like Edinburgh or Aberdeen) by agreeable secretary; took me out to house of Professor & Mrs Leo Polak—Jewish-Dutch Professor of Philosophy; wife a feminist; tall & dark; 3 daughters; old mother of 80 who spoke only German. Perfectly charming family—far the best yet; hospitality perfect; nice bedroom; bathroom to myself. Big audience for lecture, very intelligent & most appreciative; admired my English & subject; Professor Polak delighted. Committee came back & talked afterwards including former Prof. of Dutch at Univ. College, London.

Wednesday April 29th

After breakfast looked over Prof. Polak's wonderful library—first editions of Luther, Hobbes, Locke, Rousseau & most famous philosophers. Promised to send him a book by G. Walked in sunshine with Mrs Polak; lovely warm day; family delightful; same way of thinking as myself about war, politics, feminism etc. Inspired by reading Prof. Polak's books to new enthusiasm for my Mary Wollstonecraft book "Behold, This Dawn!"

After lunch took train for Deventer; Mrs Polak saw me off at station; this time managed change at Zwolle quite easily.

Met at Deventer & stayed with an elderly teacher of English, Miss M. Elshout. She had a nice little house & was most kind to me; it was all very simple & peaceful. After tea she took me over Deventer—saw Cathedral (big, bare & Protestant), church with twin spires & great river LJssel with bridge of boats; high & flooded. Two typically Dutch women in to dinner, which was very good; standard of hospitality with small resources here is amazingly high. Lecture at a hotel; good audience including many students, but the committee sat on the platform with me, the room was very hot, & I was so tired & bored with the lecture that I had to grind every word out of myself with immense effort; no vitality.

Thursday April 30th

Left Deventer 10.5; breakfasted alone as Miss Elshout had to leave early for her teaching. Changed at Amersfoort. Arrived at Hague just in time to speak to a League of Nations Union meeting at cheap hotel. Presented with immense purple orchid. After the luncheon went to see the Mauritzhaus and gazed for a long time at Rembrandt's "The Anatomy Lesson". Spent rest of day with Mrs Te Winkel-Tadema; bought quantities of flowers to take home. Got night boat from Hook; good crossing.

Wednesday June 10th   London

George arrived at 3 a.m. with Isabel from S.S. *Washington*; stayed at Lansdowne House. He rang me up about 6.30 & came straight round to fetch the MS. of Chap. 6 of "Hon. Estate". Stayed & talked to me for an hour, till Gordon came back from Oxford.

Went to *Femina–Vie Heureuse* Prize Giving in afternoon; presented by Max Beerbohm to L. H. Myers for *The Root & The Flower*. Margaret Kennedy in the chair.

Thursday June 11th
Got up late; was still in my bath when George rang up to say he thought Ch. 6 superb; offered to come round & go through American dialogue with me in the afternoon. Said he had sat up till 1 a.m. last night reading it. Of course I said "Come," so he was here all afternoon. He sent for & presented me with (by special messenger from Bumpus's) a copy of *Company K* & a gorgeous edition of *Drums* to help me with the dialogue. Isabel picked him up here about 5 o'clock. He said I was a superb novelist and that the seduction passage was such first-class literature that he would go to court about it if necessary.

Friday June 12th
Taken out by the Bretts; picked them up at Lansdowne House. We dined with them at the Eiffel Tower; then went to Noel Coward's *To-night at 8.30* & afterwards on to the Savoy where George & I danced & talked. Gorgeous evening.

Monday June 15th
Faith Moulson gave me dinner at Artillery Mansions Hotel & took me to the Russian ballet at the Alhambra.

Tuesday June 16th
Attended Council of Civil Liberties sub-committee on law of libel at Leonard Woolf's flat, 52 Tavistock Square.

Took the Bretts out to dinner & the cabaret show at the London Casino. Got Sarah Gertrude Millin & her husband & John Brophy to come as well; Storm Jameson wouldn't. We had cocktails at the Gargoyle first. Adorable evening. We were a woman short & Sarah didn't dance, so George danced with me all the time.

Saturday June 20th
Great Dorchester Peace Rally.

Monday June 22nd
George Brett came here and spent the afternoon with me. We talked about the publication of "Honourable Estate", my American lecture tour—and ourselves. I read him the poem written last year. I promised to see him off on Thursday. It will again be a year, I suppose, before I see him—but I recollect Olive Schreiner's words "Sometimes such a sudden gladness seizes me when I remember that somewhere you are living and working."

Thursday June 25th
Saw George & Isabel off at Waterloo by the boat train for S.S. *Roosevelt*. Phyllis Bentley & Archie Macdonell there too.

Sunday June 28th
Writing Chapter 7, Section 4 of "Hon. Estate" (the sleigh ride to Shimorka). Tea at Edwardes Square. Mother came to supper. Walked along the Embankment afterwards as far as 2 Cheyne Walk.

Monday July 20th
Finished first draft of "Honourable Estate" about 7 p.m. Dined with Sarah & Philip Millin; had them to the Gargoyle. Felt tired, flat and depressed. Book seemed no good.

Monday July 27th
Shirley's sixth birthday. Children's party. I gave her a cargo boat. (She started by asking for a battleship, but finally it became "any boat that goes".)

Wednesday July 29th
Gordon's 40th birthday. Asked me to ignore it so I did.

Saturday August 1st
A year ago Father died—the night of August 1st–2nd. "Comfort us again now after the time that thou hast plagued us: and for the years wherein we have suffered adversity."

Sunday August 2nd
Finished "Honourable Estate", 11.45 p.m.

Monday August 10th   Sandown
Came to Sandown. G. brought children in morning; I followed by evening train because of appointment with dentist. Revised "Hon. Estate" alone in garden all day.

Thursday August 27th
Sent G.P.B. a night-letter telegram saying I would send off typescript of "Hon. Estate" by *Bremen* on Saturday.

Friday August 28th
Full-rate cable from George saying "Cheers will look for arrival *Bremen*". (He addressed it merely to "Vera Brittain, Sandown" and it reached me without any delay!) Finished the revision of Macmillan's copy of "Hon. Estate" and sent it off in two registered parcels to catch the *Bremen*. V. nice letter from George by afternoon post. Wrote to both him & Harold Latham by *Bremen*.

Thursday September 3rd
Midnight. Finished revising Gollancz's copy of "Honourable Estate".

Gordon went to International Conf. at Brussels to discuss Spanish affairs.

Friday September 4th
Handed in typescript of "Hon. Estate" to Gollancz at 11.0. He sent it straight off to printer by passenger train. Publication date Nov. 2nd or 9th. Cabled George to this effect.

Wednesday September 9th   Italy
Left London for Rome, Naples & Capri. Took train at 2 p.m. from Victoria for Rome Express.

Friday September 25th
Before leaving, copied some of the inscriptions on the walls of houses in Anacapri—usually black notices on white ground.
   " 'Ad atti di guerra risponderemo con atti di guerra.' Mussolini." " 'Il grido d'Italia è un grido di giustizia ed un grido di vittoria.' Mussolini." " 'L'Italia non farà più una politica di rinuncia et di viltà.' Mussolini." Another on the wall of Capri harbour: " 'Molti nemici, molto onore.' Mussolini."
   Crossed from Capri to Naples. Tea with Vera Mikol at café near station. Went on by late evening train to Rome. Spent the night there (Lago Maggiore Hotel).

Saturday September 26th
Left Rome by Rome Express, 11 a.m. G. came as far as Pisa; then got off to stay at Lavorno with il Duca di Cesaro. Began proofs of *Hon. Estate* on train.

Monday September 28th   London
Corrected proofs all day.

Tuesday September 29th
Winifred died at 6.29 a.m. a year ago to-day. Corrected proofs. V.S.J. put an In Mem. Notice in *The Times* too. Sent her a bunch of carnations in memory.

Wednesday September 30th
Finished proofs of *Hon. Estate*. Called in to see Granny Holtby at Rembrandt Hotel for ten minutes with Shirley. Took S. to meet Gordon at Victoria. Train late, so gave her a strawberry ice-cream at Stewart's while we waited.

Thursday October 1st
Started replying to accumulation of letters. Phone call from Miss Horsman

of Gollancz thanking me for speed in correcting proofs. At 3.0 saw W. A. R. Collins; we decided to publish Winifred's McWilliam letters next.

Engaged a "help" till I can get a governess. Tea with children; put them to bed.

Tuesday October 13th
Lunched at the Ivy with Gollancz and Norman Collins to discuss preliminary preparations for "Hon. Estate". Gollancz said I must expect a bad press as *T. of Y.* had aroused so much jealousy, and the minor writers get their own back in reviews. He said I should probably recapture it with the biography of Winifred. They are getting out subscription cards for first edition, accompanied by my photograph, to all the bookshops. Yeats-Brown, whose new book on India is being also published on Nov. 2nd, & I, are to have a big double advt, and double displays in the shop windows.

Went on to tea with Clare—we discussed V.G. & how he was the first person to help & "stiffen" me after Winifred's death. I told her I was always uncertain whether he liked me or not. Brailsford came in to tea and we talked about Spain.

Went later to the Savoy, to the P.E.N. Club dinner to celebrate H. G. Wells's 70th birthday. Brilliant if naughty speech by Shaw; good solid speech in response to the others by Wells. The other speakers, Maurois, Julian Huxley & G. B. Stern—were all dull & somewhat inadequate. Had to leave immediately after the dinner as G. didn't feel well.

Thursday December 3rd
Crisis about King's marriage began. Read leaders in *Times* & other papers on way back from Leicester.

Monday December 7th   Manchester and Wigan
Left Euston at 10.30 for Manchester & Wigan. In reading about King's marriage crisis in *News Chronicle* on way up, found it had at last reviewed *Hon. Estate*, with several other novels—a typically scathing review by my (& Winifred's) old enemy Ellis Roberts who in calling me "old-fashioned" displayed his ignorance of the cultural difference between London & the provinces. Crisis still unresolved, but public opinion, which seemed to be swinging towards the King at the end of the week, now seems to be turning against him.

In Manchester visited two shops—Sherratt & Hughes, & Cornish & Barber. Just before my arrival a black fog came down & emptied the streets so I hadn't many books to sign. Mr Hughes however ordered 50 more copies of *Hon. Estate* on the strength of my visit & said he thought *H.E.* a much better book than *T. of Y.* He presented me with a copy of Hone's biography of George Moore. Went on to Wigan in cold & fog; met by Miss Sachett, the headmistress of the local girls' school, who put me up at her flat for the night. She had gone to endless trouble over fire, meal, my room (wh. she had obviously turned out of). Lecture at a municipal college to the Wigan Education Society was well-attended—about 500—& I had many books to sign afterwards.

Tuesday December 8th
Very comfortable night with two hot bottles; got up late; peaceful breakfast alone after Miss S. had departed to her school. Few things move me more or testify better to kindliness of human nature than the immense trouble taken by those who give me hospitality to make me comfortable. It makes me feel worthless & wonder why they want to do it.

Went to Starr's bookshop in Wallgate at 11.0; many customers there; I signed their whole stock & we took down the window display also as in B'm. Afterwards I was taken by the Sec. of the Educn Society & the Librarian over the public library; saw books, coins, local documents relating to Civil War etc. Interesting but rather fatiguing; left time for only hasty lunch before I departed to Bolton. At Bolton went to Swan Hotel; then to Read's bookshop in Newport Street; entertained for 2 hours by Mr Read, plus local librarian & a local doctor. Given tea & presented with gorgeous bunch of pink roses & freezias. Similar experience to Wigan; signed entire stock including window display.

Large audience in evening at George St Cong. Church, on "Why I wrote *T. of Y.*". A fifteen-guinea engagement and my 36th lecture or speech since Oct. 19th. It began at 8.0 but ended by 9.15 so I was able for once to get to bed early.

Wednesday December 9th   Dumfermline
Thick fog at Bolton. My train to Edinburgh for Dunfermline left an hour late. Clear day by time we got to Preston. Country beautiful outside Carlisle—olive-green fields & brown woods lightly powdered with snow; sun shining from clear pale-blue sky.

Crisis still continues. Difficult to see reason for King's delay since he must have faced situation for weeks—*unless* at some earlier stage Ministers gave him some reason to think morganatic proposal wd be sympathetically considered. This may be part of the facts withheld from Parliament. Difficult to understand Parliament's acquiescence in being kept in ignorance. Surely from point of view of Commons, dictatorship by Cabinet is almost as dangerous as dictatorship by Crown?

Met by Rev. Mr Cairns at Dunfermline. He told me rumour all over D. said King had abdicated but Duke of York wd not take Crown. We hurried over high tea to listen-in to 6 o'clock news, but it only said that Baldwin wd make statement to-morrow. Opinion here very hard on King—purely in view of Mrs S.'s "morals". Women—Mrs Cairns & Miss Lepage, Sec. of the lecture soc.—espec. intolerant; Minister himself much less harsh. My suggestion, that if Mrs S. had been a foreign princess with whose country we had desired an alliance her past wd not have been so adversely scrutinised, received in silence. Lecture only moderately attended owing to news but audience keen & asked many questions.

Thursday December 10th   Middlesbrough

Left Dunfermline 9.24; seen off by Sec. of local Carnegie Institute who took chair for me last night. Headlines & news in all newspapers suggested impending abdication to be announced this afternoon. Changed at Edinburgh; over an hour to wait so walked up & down Prince's Street. Keen consciousness of tension & suspense in Scottish capital; street full of newspaper vendors selling special late editions; people going in & out of cafés or standing on station with bundles of papers under their arms. At 11.20 caught Pullman train to Darlington. Read various newspapers —*Scotsman, Bulletin, D. Express, News Review*—a very different selection from my customary *Times, Herald, News Chronicle*.

Changed at Darlington & arrived Middlesboro' 3.27. Met by Mabel Bigland, who was with me at Millbank. Drove to a main-store café in the town where the "reception" that I had promised to give to help the Cleveland Lit. and Phil. Society was being held. Met by Miss McCrombie the President (headmistress of a local secondary school and Labour in politics) and the Secretary, Mr Morris. As we heard that one of the most dramatic announcements of our history was to be made at 4 o'clock, I asked if the proceedings could be delayed for ¼ hour so that everyone could listen-in. The café was crowded, the wireless-set a poor one, but in spite of this the words announcing the King's abdication came clearly through in all their momentous simplicity:

"After long and anxious consideration I have determined to renounce the throne to which I succeeded on the death of my father, and I am now communicating this, my final and irrevocable decision.

"Realising as I do the gravity of this step, I can only hope that I shall have the understanding of my peoples in the decision I have taken, and the reasons which have led me to take it.

"I will not enter now into my private feelings, but I would beg that it should be remembered that the burden which constantly rests on the shoulders of a sovereign is so heavy that it can only be borne in circumstances different from those in which I now find myself.

"I conceive that I am not overlooking the duty that rests on me to place in the forefront the public interest when I declare that I am conscious that I can no longer discharge this heavy task with efficiency or with satisfaction to myself.

"I have accordingly this morning executed an instrument of abdication . . ."

No sound accompanied these words except that of the store lift going up and down and the opening and shutting of the gates. The announcement had been expected by everyone, & after it was over the people in the store—mostly women—drifted quietly to the tea-tables and sat down. I had tea with Bigland, Miss McCrombie & one of her "old girls", now a reporter on the local paper.

Miss McCrombie agreed with me that:

1) The facts about the King & Mrs Simpson should have been made public long ago—i.e., when the story first appeared in the American Press—so that public opinion would have had time to crystallise and the King to know more clearly what it was. Also, so many coronation orders would not have been placed nor so many firms—especially those in the Potteries—suffer heavy losses. For this the Government is entirely to blame.

2) The morality of the older generation—as represented by Baldwin & the Archb. of Canterbury—is no longer endorsed by the younger generations (the War generation to which the King belongs and its successor).

3) The case of Mrs Simpson has shown a) that the semi-mystical significance attaching to royalty is out of date; b) that the public life of this country is permeated with the worst (because most self-interested) type of moral hypocrisy—i.e., if Mrs S. had been a foreign princess belonging to a country with wh. we desired an alliance, her past would not have been scrutinised in the same way & Press propaganda would have made her acceptable to public opinion.

4) We are both unutterably ashamed of what America must be saying and thinking (and with justice) of us and our self-deceptive national morality.

Before this I had "received" the guests, who all had tickets & came in crowds despite the crisis. After tea I gave my little speech for the society, saying that despite national crises life must go on, & pointing out what it would have meant to me had such a society existed in Buxton. I suggested various methods of publicity they might use.

After this I signed numerous books brought to the hall by the local W. H. Smith, & Bigland drove me to the Highfield Hotel. Had only just time to change, glance through my letters, look at the evening paper & have some dinner, when another car appeared to take me to the lecture. I was the "star" speaker of their season & everyone commented on the extraordinary appropriateness to the day of my topic—"The Changes in Manners & Morals in the last Thirty Years". I wore my black & white and gold-lacquered silk tunic dress, with three of the pink roses given me in Bolton at my neck. The platform was charmingly decorated with plants but the room rather cold & draughty.

I began with an introduction based on the aphorism "Happy is the country which has no history", in which I said that I, like King Edward VIII, belonged to a generation which had seen almost more history than any generation could bear & was still only on the early side of middle age—the greatest War in history; the greatest Strike in history; the greatest experiment in international co-operation, which had given promise of success but now was suffering what I hoped was only a temporary eclipse; the rise of the strangest & the most formidable dictatorships in history; and to-day one of the greatest & most tragic crises in the story of England's monarchy. I pointed out that at least one factor in this crisis was the profound and unbridgeable gulf between the attitude of the older generation towards morals & that of the war generation. And I quoted later the words of "Ruth Alleyndene" in *Honourable Estate*: "To love the wrong person too well, without calculation—that's the only 'moral offence' our society calls by that name."

I made the speech a plea—based on the growth of mercy & toleration, linked with the development of the science of psychology in the past 30 years—that in all cases, whether national or private, of which the morality seemed to us questionable, we should suspend judgment & condemnation, & try to understand.

To bed late—too much tension both public & personal for sleep to come easily, despite being given best state bedroom with huge bow window & private bathroom at the hotel.

Friday December 11th
Left Middlesboro' at 10.0 & caught the *Silver Jubilee* at Darlington. Large mail with masses of American press-cuttings forwarded from London; papers to read; diary to write up. We have indeed had too much history! The trouble with all momentous periods of my life—whether due to public or private events or to a mixture of the two—is that I never have time while they are going on either to take things in properly, or adequately record them. I realised only the other day in going over 3-year-old press-cuttings that I hardly took in any of the reviews of *T. of Y.* and the same thing is now happening over *Hon. Estate*. I don't have time to read them properly, or consider them in such a way as to make myself a better writer. Popular success is blinding and deafening, and when combined with momentous national events it annihilates meditation.

Found *Silver Jubilee* astonishingly smooth in its running—more like an American train. It did not seem to be going as fast as many much slower "expresses", & I could write in it quite easily. All country we went through grey, foggy, and frosty; bitterly cold day, somehow appropriate to the sad & regretful national temper. Bought *Times*, *D. Herald*, *News Chronicle*, & *D. Express*, & tried to read and take in their various points of view. All emphasised regret but some had more implicit condemnation of the King than others. In my view none expressed sufficient condemnation of Baldwin & the Govt for its ineptitude, its long postponement of information to the public, and its consequent rushing through of the crisis when the facts did emerge. Papers expressed general sympathy with D. of York for the awkward circumstances of his accession. I cannot believe that that stiff, shy, slow-brained man & his snobbish, limited little Duchess will do anything to increase the prestige of the monarchy, but Baldwin & the

Archbps will doubtless be delighted at replacing the high-spirited & determined Edward with a wooden figurehead exuding all the domestic & family virtues so dear to the older generation.

Tuesday December 15th   London
Went with Mother to Foyle's Grosvenor House Luncheon for the "descendants" of classical writers. About 20 descendants & relatives present, of George Eliot, Sheridan, Milton, Charles Reade, Lucas Malet, Wordsworth, Herrick, Macaulay, etc. Luncheon memorable for 3 bon mots.

1) Rose Macaulay, proposing toast to Lady Oxford, the chief guest: "Lady Oxford was married to the only great Prime Minister we have had in the past 30 years. Well—perhaps I ought to modify that; I've always thought Mr Ramsay MacDonald had a good deal of ability!"

2) John Drinkwater, replying for "The Classics": "My ancestors came from Canterbury, but thank God they were only publicans." (This was too subtle for most of the audience, even though the Archb. of Canterbury's bitter & uncharitable broadcast on the ex-King last night was summarised in this morning's *Times*, together with 29 other sermons, nearly all equally un-Christian.)

3) Ian Hay—on "The Future Classics" (we simply don't know, he said, who they are): "When a man wakes up to find himself famous, you can bet your life he hasn't slept."

Went on to Caxton Hall bazaar in aid of Ethiopians & signed copies of my books presented by Gollancz & myself. After dinner indignation over sermons caused me to send a short letter to *Time & Tide*.

Friday December 18th
John's end-of-term play at Remembrance Hall, Flood Street. J., in the Hiawatha scene, looked very pretty in his Indian suit and spoke his little piece well & clearly. Took Shirley, brought her home after, then joined G. for tea at the school, 134 Sloane Street.

Crowds of other Gibbs parents there—including Mrs Marsden Smedley, woman's editor of *Sunday Express*, whom I met at Hilda Reid's some time ago. Mr Taylor introduced me to Flora Robson, who had been helping them get up the plays. Got home to find we had just missed the Bentley-Carrs who called to bring the children's presents; telephoned them later at Woking.

At 7.30 G. left for Paris, via Newhaven & Dieppe, to attend the Spanish Aid Committee there to-morrow.

1937

Friday January 1st   London
Started in on year's work after three days' holiday at Bexhill. No celebrating or "seeing the New Year in". Doing this in 1935 and 1936 brought no luck.

Tuesday January 5th
Took children to be overhauled by Dr Yates. Both quite fit. John ordered calcium to help in eruption of his teeth.
    Captain Philip Mumford came to tea to talk to me about pacifism & the Peace Pledge Union. What really made me join & promise to speak, however, was not his conversation (though he is a decent, agreeable & clear-headed person), but Bertrand Russell's *Which Way to Peace?*
    Felt too fatigued to go to Mrs Littlejohn's At Home for Miss W. Mayo, so got G. to ring up & say I had a headache.

Wednesday January 20th
Worked all day at letters, telephone etc. to help G. to get off to Spain. At 8.30 lectured for Red Cross hospital library at W. H. Smith's headquarters lecture room in Portugal Street. Marjorie Roberts took chair as Pethick-Lawrence unable to come. Room quite full in spite of 'flu, bad night, etc. Spoke on "Manners & Morals"; explained to audience why I had to leave early & therefore could not answer questions, sign books etc. Got away on time to see G. off at Victoria by Dunkerque–Paris sleeping car train. Had ten minutes before train went.

Tuesday February 2nd
Very wet day. Drafted article for *British Legion Journal*. At 6.0 went to cocktail party at the Geoffrey Manders', 4 Barton Street, Westminster. Small house, very crowded, good cocktails. At doorway greeted quite enthusiastically by Rose Macaulay because I had joined Peace Pledge Union; told me they had elected me as a Sponsor at their meeting yesterday. Talked to the Pritts, a certain Cartland, M.P. for King's Norton & brother of Barbara Cartland, a young man who had written an autobiography to be published by Hamish Hamilton called *Growing Pains*, Archie Macdonell, who seemed to have it on his conscience that he did not answer my letter from Birmingham. I said I had forgotten writing it. Had a "White Lady" & a "Martini" & felt more cheerful. Nice party.

Wednesday February 3rd
Lunched at Waldorf Hotel with a "fan"—young solicitor called Hignett from Knutsford, Cheshire. Usual desire to talk to me about nothing in

particular, usual political & literary aspirations—but seemed to have made his own way & to have some experiences worth recounting.

Evening, was guest and only woman speaker at Centenary Dinner of Booksellers' Provident Institution at Hotel Victoria, Northumberland Avenue. Chairman was William Longman (whose grandfather or great-grandfather helped to found institution) and most publishers had representatives there, including Norman Collins from Victor Gollancz. Other speakers were Prof. G. M. Trevelyan (v. like Sir Charles but looked older instead of younger & much more glum), Sir James Jeans, William Longman himself, Mr Taylor of Dent's, & Harold Macmillan. There were also many comic musical items. My own speech came so late that it could only be short & not very telling. Chief interest of evening was sitting between William Longman & Harold Macmillan—who said he had read *Hon. Estate* while in bed with 'flu & much admired it—espec. the objective reconstruction of War part. He said it was quite ridiculous of George to say it hadn't done well enough in America when it had been in the best-seller list for so many weeks—but that George was never satisfied with the way any book did because he always pictured to himself how much better it might do. H.M. said he was going over to U.S.A. in 3 weeks & therefore George might not come this year. Told me how Latham discovered *Gone With the Wind* at Atlanta by being constantly told about it at parties—that the author kept wiring him that she didn't want it read or published as it was about her family & she couldn't bear to run risk of having it refused. He said E. M. Delafield had gone to America again—that she wrote too many books for financial reasons & they were helping her to make the intervals longer; that A. G. Macdonell had it in him to write much greater book (of the Thackeray type) than he had yet done. In making speech thanking me for coming, H.M. remarked he was half my publisher—i.e. in the United States—& judging by my sales there, the better half!—at which Norman Collins, who met me when I arrived, looked somewhat rueful. Copy of *Herald-Tribune* for Jan. 24th showed *Hon. Estate* again in list—9th week running.

Thursday February 4th
Cable from Gordon from Barcelona to say he expects to return on Sunday. Letter from Rubinstein saying Somerville agrees to his interpretation of W.'s Will. Amy in bed with 'flu.

Bought two hats at Baird Lewis, & had tea with Nancy Lord—the Australian girl who is trying to get on to *T. & T.*—at Marshall & Snelgrove's. Walked home.

Friday February 5th
Spent most of day doing Amy's work, tidying up, preparing for evening. Harold Latham came to dinner. We talked about Winifred's Letters—he agreed that if I had sole control & no other publisher could get them, he

would rather do them after her more mature work & my biography. We discussed my lecture tour; he asked me to spend two or three days with him in his country house first. In talking about Winifred he told me—which I hadn't known before—that when Macmillan of N.Y. were simultaneously publishing *Mandoa* & *Testament of Youth*, she wrote & asked him to concentrate their advertising on *T. of Y.* She must have already known that she had not long to live. He said he had been greatly touched by her generosity—and of course wrote to say that Macmillan's had money enough to advertise us both. He told me Phyllis's recent tour was much more successful than her last & that she was mostly away from N.Y.—also that she didn't stay with the Bretts when she first arrived because George's father died just then. It was the first I had heard of old Mr Brett dying; I felt terribly guilty for not having written to George when he wrote me such a nice letter after Father's death.

I showed Harold the letters about *Hon. Estate* from the Newark bookseller & George himself. He told me—as I suspected—that the Newark bookseller evidently had some grievance against the Macmillan Company and was trying to cause trouble between them & their authors—for the price-cutting on *Gone With the Wind* & other books was done not by publishers but by a booksellers' ring against whom 4 of the chief American publishers, including Macmillan, had brought an action for this & lost it. Harold said that apart from *Gone With the Wind* (of which he described the discovery, calling Margaret Mitchell by her married name "Peggy Marsh"), *Honourable Estate* had done the best of their autumn novels, and that George's letter didn't mean he was disappointed, but only that he wished he could tell me it had sold 100,000. Harold said—oddly enough, "Oh, George just wrote to you off-hand like that because he knows you so well. It's the kind of way he would write to his wife"!!

Saturday February 6th

Wrote to George about his father—explained that I hadn't known. Brilliant sunny morning with cold wind. Amy still in bed but better. Met Philip Sargant Florence for tea at Cumberland Hotel to tell him what I knew about nursing conditions & sources of information, preparatory to an inquiry they are having in Birmingham through difficulty of getting nurses for new hospital.

Sunday February 7th

G. 'phoned from Paris to say he returns to-morrow. Very wet day; could not go out in morning. Drew up questionnaire for Ballinger about W.'s African interests. Tea 37 Edwardes Square. Read review novels after supper.

Monday February 8th

Met G. with children at Victoria (night train from Dunkerque; arrived

9.40, half an hour late). He said he had seen three ministers & went to front line at Madrid; spent two nights there; town being bombarded all the time. He seemed to have done everything he wanted & to be pleased with his experiences. Looked quite well.

Tuesday February 9th
Clothworkers' Hall dinner in aid of Newnham College building fund. G. & I very well placed; sat quite close to Duke of Kent & Dick Sheppard. Other speakers were Hon. Rupert Beckett, Prof. Winifred Cullis, Master of Clothworkers' Guild and Dr Alan Garrett Anderson, son of Dr Elizabeth. Went on afterwards with G. to Gargoyle & we danced.

Wednesday February 10th
G. & I lunched with Dick Sheppard at 1 Amen Court to discuss Peace Pledge Union. Luncheon began late & was somewhat brief. Sheppard was racy—told stories of Bishop of London & his animadversions against pacifists. G. said he reminded him of Charlie Chaplin.

Wrote a hurried article for the *Star* on the population debate in the H. of Commons this afternoon; got it all drafted between 5.30 & 7.30 & helped to put children to bed as well.

Dined quietly with Lady Balfour of Burleigh & Barbara Miller, née Buckmaster.

Thursday February 11th
Took chair for Eric Gillett at the To-morrow Club, in British Industries House. Small gathering of would-be authors. He talked on "What We Are Reading Now"—& told me he is lecturing in Holland in April, in accordance with my recommendation to Christy. After the meeting we escaped, & ate oysters & talked at the Maison Prunier.

Friday February 12th
Letter from Harold Macmillan asking whether I was by any chance thinking of changing my English publisher; if so they would regard it as great honour if I would entrust my books to them. Wonder what is in the wind. I have a feeling that—Gollancz quite apart—George & Harold Latham would rather I didn't.

Saturday February 13th
Replied cautiously & non-committally to Harold Macmillan—tentatively inquiring what terms they would give me if I ever *did* publish with them. Also said all the flattering things I could think of about Harold Latham & George.

Sunday February 14th
G. decided to go to America to organise fund-raising for Spain. He went up

to Newcastle-under-Lyme to speak for the Labour Party—I to Edwardes Square with children as usual.

Monday February 15th
Large Macmillan luncheon given by Harold Latham at Brown's Hotel. Sat between Wilkins, formerly of the *Daily Express*, whose historical novel *And So—Victoria* is the book Harold Latham was on tenterhooks about the night he dined with me, and Laurence Whistler, who is apparently a poet and critic. Talked briefly to Phyllis Bentley, John Brophy, A. G. Macdonell, Cecil Roberts, W. A. R. Collins. Others there were Rose Macaulay, Hilda Vaughan, Harold & Dan Macmillan, Helen Ashton & husband, Doris Leslie & new husband (Dr Hannay), G. B. Stern, Arnot Robertson. About 30 there altogether. Very enjoyable. Walked home.

Tuesday February 16th   Manchester
Went to Manchester for day to give book talk at Kendal Milne's (now Harrods). Cadness Page, Harrods' manager, met me at station. Was photographed first at Schmidt studio in St Ann's Square. Room crowded for speech ("My Books and the Ideas Behind Them"). Extra chairs had to be brought. They had expected 60 as that was the number they had yesterday—but actually got about 150. People crowded round afterwards & I signed copies of my books.

Wednesday February 17th   London
Going through W.'s files for biography, came across two letters from St J. Ervine full of extremely unflattering references to myself. Just like him to have no respect for friendship between women. If he had written the letters to me direct I wouldn't have cared—and I daresay Winifred took no notice since she knew his prejudices so well—but it was mean to write like that all the same. I wrote him an unposted reply, which I clipped to his letter—as it oughtn't to be destroyed, yet I don't want that account of myself to go down unchallenged to posterity.

Mrs Abbott had dinner with us. We discussed abdication crisis, P.P.U., and the Open Door Council annual meeting at which I am speaking in March.

Thursday February 18th
Depressed all day over Ervine letters. Don't know how far such vehement prejudices as his go to undermine my whole reputation and even prevent my getting work—such as articles etc.—which wd otherwise be offered me as a matter of course.

G. attended N.P.C. meeting on Spain.

Friday February 19th
Met Leslie Birly of the B.B.C. at the Ivy at 12.50 to discuss my part in

"Scrapbook 1912". Lunched with Nancy Pearn there; for two hours we hedged round the subject of my exclusive rights, which she wants, and never actually discussed them.

At 6.0 went to Mr & Mrs Longman's sherry party at 23 Glebe Place; there met Mrs Ernest Heathcote, formerly of Buxton, who remembered seeing me there as a child. We discussed Buxton & its limitations & she told me a story of 1915 there—how they were playing bridge one evening when the evening paper arrived. Mrs Heathcote, who was dummy, opened it and at once exclaimed: "Good Heavens! Kitchener & all his staff have been drowned in the North Sea!" Whereupon her partner, old Mrs Hubbersty of Burbage (who never called on Mother!), remarked reprovingly: "Be quiet Gladys; I said 'One No Trump'!"

Called for G. at Cyril Connolly's at 312 King's Rd; found them all, with the Sykes artist brother of Mrs Elwes, in studio room at the top. After we had had supper at home I drove with G. to Waterloo to catch his boat train for the *President Harding*. Also said goodbye to Harold Latham, who was not only going by same boat but was in same first-class carriage. The Divines & Lovat Dickson also there to see him off. Boat train left at 9.0, very empty; G. & Harold glad of each other's society.

Saturday February 20th

Oddments of work. Finished "unposted letter" to St J. E. Walked over to Edwardes Square & had tea with Mother. Cold bright day, strong east wind; fear G. has a rough sea.

Monday February 22nd

Saw H. F. Rubinstein about contract for "Letters to a Friend". Walked to Gower St from Chelsea. He said he had greatly enjoyed the Letters.

Tuesday February 23rd

Dr Lockhart—medical officer to Boot's, who wrote me a v. interesting letter about *Honourable Estate* & *T. of Y.* came to tea. We talked for two hours—chiefly about effect of modern conditions on human psychology, especially in industry. He is a feminist, & agrees with O.D.C. that women & young persons should be separated, not lumped together, in factory regulations. Told me that both palpitations & duodenitis are almost pure "anxiety" troubles, not originating in physical causes at all. They were due to imaginary "lions" and my own "lion" (Doctor Hughes' wrong diagnosis of incipient gallstones) was quite sufficient to increase the symptoms. He said hard work often dissipated them by diverting the mind & it was natural that my last American tour should have worked a cure.

(*Note*. Doctor Lockhart subsequently killed his wife in fit of amnesia at outbreak of Second War & I went to his murder trial at Nottingham as possible witness for defence. He was sent to Broadmoor, let out after 2

years, married again & had two children. After a short period of country
practice in Cornwall, he & his family emigrated to Australia.)

Thursday February 25th
Afternoon—hair done & face massage. Was guest (for dinner, at Connaught Rooms) of the Women's Soroptimists' Annual Dinner. Sat next to
R. C. Sherriff with whom it was agreeable to talk "shop". He seemed well
pleased with V.G. as a publisher. We both made speeches—he on the
drama, I in response to toast of "Optimism" (which I tried to make funny)
after it had been proposed by Humbert Wolfe in an excellent speech. Very
good dinner.

Friday February 26th
Very nice letter from G.P.B. about the misunderstanding over *Hon. Estate*;
saying he had meant to be nice, and was always discontented with the sales
of a book, whatever it was! Explained what a disadvantage the three
thousand miles of Atlantic was, between friends.
     Lunched with Leslie Birly at Trocadero to discuss the revised version of
the B.B.C. "Scrapbook for 1912". He told me his father was a Conscientious Objector in the War. He himself was just too young for it.
     Children did a "play" for me after tea. Spent evening reading about
rearmament.

Saturday February 27th
Another nice letter from George, thanking me for the one I wrote about his
father's death, & saying what a blow to him it had been.
     Read up newspaper etc. on the rearmament programme all afternoon in
preparation for the Hyde Park protest to-morrow & various other lectures
for the P.P.U. Had supper with Mother & wrote out my lecture by the
morning-room fire afterwards. Getting very cold.

Sunday February 28th
Bitter day, colder than any this winter; strong east or north wind with
flurries of hail & snow. After lunch went off to Hyde Park to speak in Dick
Sheppard's Peace Protest against the Govt rearmament programme as
outlined in the White Paper of Feb. 16th. I hardly expected to find any
speakers or audience but quite a number of the speakers were there & we
got quite a good audience, who circulated round the two "platforms" (i.e.
carts). Dick Sheppard, Laurence Housman & one or two younger men
were on one cart, & Philip Mumford, Canon Morris, Allen Skinner &
myself on another. Rose Macaulay, in long brown leather coat, was
wandering round in support, saying at intervals "Is it really worth-while
our all getting pneumonia?"
     As I stood on the cart—though I was warm enough while speaking—the
wind literally thumped my back & the sleet lashed my face, but I couldn't

complain, when so many "crocks" had bravely turned up. Dick Sheppard began "I'm afraid you won't be able to hear me in this gale, I'm an asthmatic." Laurence Housman said: "I hope you won't mind if I keep my hat on, but I'm over seventy." Canon Morris said "I'm keeping *my* hat on too, as I've only just recovered from scarlet fever"! How the audience —200 or 300 at least—endured as they did for over an hour is beyond my comprehension, but the English are incredible. They mostly seemed to be with us too.

Had tea at Marble Arch Stewart's with Peggy Smith and a man from the audience whose name I never learnt tho' he paid for our tea. He said he had read *T. of Y.* & come 15 miles to hear me speak, as he wanted to be a pacifist but couldn't feel convinced. We talked over the whole subject and he seemed more—though still not entirely—convinced when he left. A nice man, & really honest.

G. should have arrived in N.Y. to-day.

Monday April 19th
Four invitations to speak at peace meetings, two to send messages to "Peace Weeks", one to take the chair at a District Nursing Association Conference—all this morning or last night! My life is not my own—and everyone all over the country is doing their best to prevent me being the writer which alone makes me of value to their cause! What a world!

Wednesday April 28th
Had 5.30 cocktails at the Savoy with Mr & Mrs Casey (Australian Minister over to attend Sugar Conference). Mrs Littlejohn introduced me & was there—as Casey had said Dorothy Sayers & I were the two English writers he most wanted to meet. However D.L.S. wasn't there & Casey, who arrived late, talked most of the time to W. N. Ewer. Monica Ewer was there too; also Helen Simpson & husband. Helen Simpson just off to Australia & then to America for a lecture tour. She will be there when I am. I gave her several tips. Mrs Casey very charming—small, slim, short skirt, very young-looking in spite of grey hair.

Thursday April 29th   Edinburgh
Took *Flying Scotsman* to Edinburgh; met by the Rev. Oliver Dryer & taken out to The Manse at Lasswade (small industrial town making paper & carpets six miles from Edinburgh). Day started coldish but became radiantly warm & was like summer when I arrived so Mr Dryer & two daughters took me for a walk near golf-links. Wore no hat or coat. After supper went down to Usher Hall, Edinburgh, to speak with the Rev. Mitchell of Glasgow & Donald Soper at the annual meeting of the Scottish Church Christian Pacifists (last year they had Sheppard & Lansbury—it is the biggest peace meeting in Scotland). Car hired to be "grand" for my benefit broke down half way & had to be mended, so we only just arrived in

time. Hall full except top galleries—about 2,000. Rev. Macpherson a prosy chairman; Mitchell sound but a little dull as he read his speech. Mine—wh. was not so good as I intended bec. our lateness in some subtle way seemed to put me off—went down well & was lengthily applauded. Soper not as good as at Dorchester. Meeting ended about 10.30 but I sat up till nearly 1.0 talking to Dryer family.

Friday April 30th
Between 10.30 & 11.30 Mr Dryer took me for car ride followed by short walk up nearest of the Pentland Hills. At 12.0 went down to Prince's St & was taken by Mr Small, Gollancz's Scottish traveller, to some of the main booksellers—mostly a conservative & rather formidable crowd. At 1.0 they gave a complimentary luncheon for me at the Loxburgh Hotel, Charlotte Sq.; Miss Muriel Ritson, Secretary to Scottish Board of Health, took the chair. Made short speech afterwards on women's place in literature. After luncheon (at wh. I autographed several books), I went home with Margaret Robertson till train time. Had tea & then she motored me to Queen's Ferry to see the Forth Bridge from below; also a glimpse of Holyrood. Early supper; then she motored me to the station to catch the 7.50 night train back to London.

Saturday September 18th   American Lecture Tour
Left Waterloo in *Georgic* boat train 9.29 a.m. G. came to South'ton with me; Mother, John, Shirley & Burnett at Waterloo. In the Booking Hall, as I was following the porter with my luggage, Shirley, running after me, crashed down on her face. I thought she had broken her nose but it was only bruised; the poor little love was very white & shaken, but brave as usual & tried to smile. It upset me a good deal, reminding me of all the possibilities of accident to the children. John too was pathetic; someone said "You don't mind Mummy going to America, do you?" and he answered "No-o, I don't mind; it's babyish to mind things." Felt like weeping as I kissed them goodbye, but didn't.

Two American women in our carriage saying English shops were full of "junk"—& various other things of the type usually said by English people in U.S.A. Lovely morning; Hampshire country vivid with sunlight & yellow mustard-fields. Great hustle on board the *Georgic*; G. rushed on shore after only about ten minutes; stood at end of quay & waved to me in sunshine. On the other side of the C.W.S. lock I saw the *Empress of Britain* sailing exactly the same moment as ourselves. Boat very full; 1,400 passengers. Got table to myself in dining-room & decent outside cabin. Talked on deck & again in evening to Morgan Jones M.P. & Rhys Davies M.P. who were also going to U.S.A. to lecture.

Sunday September 19th
Docked in Queenstown (Cobh) harbour early in morning; warm sunshine;

coast of Ireland velvety & green. Gave up resolution to stay in bed & got up after breakfast to sit on deck in sunshine. By evening however weather turned muggy & oppressive & I was glad to go to bed before dinner.

Passenger list published; no one of any special interest. Long talk over tea with Morgan Jones & Rhys Davies about future of Labour Party. They emphasised prosperity of working classes owing to various forms of social insurance etc. & said that in one sense a successful Socialist movement killed itself.

Boat half-full of Americans, including the staff.

Monday September 20th
Morning sea smooth & grey; turned rough & rainy towards evening. Talked to Morgan Jones & young Purser whose father is next Lord Mayor of Liverpool. Got note from four women saying that as I chose to travel "under such a distinguished name" they hoped I would pardon their request to me to come & talk to them. Ultimately agreed to do this on Wednesday.

Every tenth person on deck seems to be reading *The Citadel*. Other books being read include *And So—Victoria, Northwest Passage, American Dream*. One woman reading *South Riding*, another *Letters to a Friend*.

Talked in evening to a Mrs Mason, occupying next cabin to mine, an American who was enthusiastic about *Testament of Youth*; likewise her daughter, a teacher.

Miserable evening; only just managed to get down to dinner. Went to bed directly afterwards.

Tuesday September 21st
Very rough in morning; gradually got smoother towards evening but I stayed in bed all day. Couldn't read so made up arrears of sleep.

Wednesday September 22nd
Weather calm, grey & muggy. Got up late to write to Gordon on deck. At lunch time met Morgan Jones & Rhys Davies, who took me down to see their palatial cabins & bathroom—given them *after* they got on board in exchange for inferior inside accommodation, because they are M.P.s.

Over tea met the group of American ladies who invited me to talk to them; they had developed into about 20, three being English. As I couldn't lecture to them owing to my contract, they sat around a table in the card-room & asked me questions which I tried to answer, about peace, European situation, position of women etc. This went on for two solid hours. They were agreeable enough, but I found it trying, as there was a considerable swell on, & the card-room appeared to be hermetically sealed. Got a splitting headache which persisted all evening. I gathered from their conversation that they had been "thrilled" at seeing my name in the list & had tried to spot me, asked the stewards to identify me, etc.

Sat up after dinner to see a sound picture, *A Star is Born*, in lounge in the hope of diverting attention from headache but it still persisted. I must be the world's worst sailor—not from acuteness of sea-sickness but bec. of its chronic persistency so long as the boat moves.

Thursday September 23rd
Very depressed this morning. Woke up with headache still there; lay in bed & howled for sheer home-sickness. Wished I had asked Mother to telegraph to Queenstown whether Shirley's nose was broken or not. Keep seeing her with her poor little tear-stained face, trying to smile. The news also was depressing; little "Ocean Times" concentrated on fact that we are approaching U.S. about their attitude if we withdraw our Ambassador from Japan. Spoke to Morgan Jones about this when I got up; asked, does it mean war? He said, No, America would never agree to making war on anybody with Cordell Hull as Foreign Secretary; we may withdraw our Ambassador & they theirs, but there it will end, especially as Japan owing to her position is quite unconquerable. He thought that such War as there was would remain confined to the Far East. I only hope it is so, but it is an anxious moment to have to leave home. Cannot help remembering that in 1914, when our eyes were fixed on Ireland, war came from Serbia. To-day, when our eyes are fixed on Germany, might it not come from the Far East?

On deck, an English woman I met yesterday, a trained nurse, suggested that I should feel less sick if I played a game of deck-shuffle with her. I did so & certainly felt better. Afterwards she talked about Winifred's books & mine, all of which she had read (the more recent ones).

Friday September 24th
More cheerful day. Invited to cocktails with the Captain in his private room on the Bridge just before lunch. Autographed his private album containing names of various celebrities who had sailed on *Georgic*. Played game of deck-shuffle with Rhys Davies after tea; then went all over ship's Diesel engines with one of the junior officers. Very hot & rather alarming experience.

Nasty night; ship suddenly started to roll violently. Got very little good sleep.

Saturday September 25th
Lovely day & gorgeous sunshine; sea looked agreeable enough but tremendous deep swell caused boat to roll terrifically. While I was having tea with Rhys Davies, it almost seemed as if it would roll over & he looked quite alarmed. Afterwards learnt that we were in the tail of a Florida hurricane, which though over affected the depths of the sea from far away. Walking difficult but no longer felt seasick. Grand sunset. Terrific noise at dinner; everyone wearing masks & blowing whistles. Afterwards a ship's concert, at which Rhys Davies took the chair & I sat with Morgan Jones.

We reached Quarantine about 9 p.m. & docked. Strange sudden quiet & warmth; air on deck like midsummer; all around the lights of Staten Island & the Jersey shore. A soloist at the concert sang "Ich liebe dich . . .". I vividly remembered leaving dear, dear New York nearly three years ago, & wondered what I was coming back to. Later a mist fell & the fog-horns of the ships waiting to go through Quarantine seemed to blow all night. Couldn't sleep anyhow for anticipation.

Sunday September 26th   New York
Docked about 9 a.m. Very hot. Statue of Liberty & outline of buildings shrouded in mist. Felt rather heartsick as I saw everyone's friends waving to them & imagined no one would be there; but to my delight A. J. Putnam was on the dock to meet me. We got through the Customs in about an hour. *N.Y. Times* reporter interviewed me on the dock, & then Putnam took me to the Fifth Avenue Hotel. Found my bedroom a bower of flowers—dahlias, lilies, gladioli—from George, as well as four of Macmillan's latest books. Also lovely box of dahlias from Harold Latham. Almost immediately I was in my room George rang up from Connecticut to greet me & ask if I wanted to go out there. I told him I had to see Colston Leigh in the morning, so he asked me to breakfast with him & go out to Fairfield later. Putnam took me to a second breakfast at the Brevoort, & I spent the rest of an incredibly hot day in my dressing-gown, re-packing. Room seemed to go round so much that I had to lie down at intervals. Felt rather better when packing finished & I'd had some tea, so went out with Lois Cole of Macmillan & her husband to a cocktail party & supper.

Monday September 27th
George called at my room at 9.15 to take me to breakfast. Felt shy after not seeing him for over a year & I think he did too though he never shows it. I thought he looked, not older, but thinner, from strain of greater responsibilities & family troubles since his father's death. We had a most agreeable breakfast together; then I greeted people at Macmillan office, opened bank account after borrowing $500 from Macmillan through George to save supertax by not taking royalties, & went up to see Colston Leigh. Leigh most agreeable; has a grand tour for me including a trip to the South; talked to me for about an hour. Palatial quality of his offices greatly increased; also efficiency. Later went through schedule with his assistant Miss Hollingsworth; hasty sandwich lunch & back to Macmillan office to be interviewed by a newspaper editor from Portland, Oregon.

About 4.0 George called for me at hotel. We had highballs first & then drove off to Connecticut, past George Washington Bridge, wh. I hadn't seen, & along new Hudson Parkway. Glorious evening, with lovely sunset before us. Talk intimate & absorbing; stopped somewhere for tea. Reached Fairfield & Isabel about 8.0. She greeted me affectionately. I had same room as 3 years ago.

Tuesday September 28th   Fairfield, Connecticut
Wet miserable day. Very different weather from 1934; no crickets or butterflies. Isabel took me up to Easton to see beginnings of the large new house they are building for $85,000! Then went out to lunch at a smart country restaurant which was half-empty because of the wet; with old Mrs Brett & Mrs McKerney, George's sister, who seems to have been monopolised by her mother since Mr Brett's death.

A dinner party at old Mrs Brett's house in the evening in my honour —mostly a family affair, but one or two others there including Thompson, a dramatist, to whom I talked. George came back late & seemed vexed with life & overpowered by his family, which is certainly too numerous & very trying.

Wednesday September 29th
Motored by Isabel to have lunch at a little country farm-house about an hour nearer N.Y., with her mother & two sisters. Hot lovely day again. Drove back with Isabel & after tea we went off for a walk together round the Brett estate. Returned to find that George had come home early & gone for a walk by himself. Small dinner-party given by them to which came John Taylor Arms, the black-&-white artist whom I met in 1934. Hardly spoke to George at dinner when I sat next him. Party broke up early & we went to bed at a reasonable hour—or rather we should have, but Isabel & I sat up late talking about the Brett family problems, & how Winifred—who died two years ago to-day—had told Isabel that last summer that she couldn't live more than six months. It seems as though she *had* to tell someone & deliberately chose people who lived abroad, & wouldn't meet anyone [in England], like Isabel & Ballinger.

Thursday September 30th
Woke up when George left for N.Y. & waved to me from the porch. Had had a night disturbed with dreams since our conversation, so got up at 7.30 & went for a walk alone through the lovely Connecticut country in the early morning. Just off the main road came across the entrance to a field almost carpeted with windfalls of ripe apples smelling delightfully in the morning sun. Ate one; it was warm & sweet. Back to breakfast on the porch in shorts & shirt, & wrote letters. Isabel had two school-friends to lunch & we motored again to Easton & walked around the new estate. Another dinner-party; amongst the guests Herschel Brickell of the N.Y. *Evening Post* who said he would give me Introductions in the South. Talked to George a little after dinner; at dinner sat beside Richard Brett. Went to bed as soon as party broke up, quite tired after long day. Had to finish packing before I could sleep.

Friday October 1st   Onteora
Got up early & drove 2½ hours with Isabel into New York. Warm lovely

morning. Got there about 11.30; washed & brushed in still-unopened Brett house; reported to Harold Latham at office about midday. Lunched at Longchamps with Harold, Lois Cole, Mr & Mrs Putnam—who together with Lois's husband were all going to Onteora for week-end. A. J. Putnam & his wife took me. It turned out to be a drive of 125 miles into the Catskills; took about 5 hours as we stopped for tea & they didn't know the last part of the way. First part lovely, along the banks of the Hudson & across several bridges; "burning bushes" everywhere. But I got very tired before we arrived, after the previous drive as well. Last section meant mounting 3,000 feet; my head swam as we got to the top. Found Harold, his mother & rest of the party there. "Content" a somewhat elaborate baronial residence looking over superb mountain view which was shrouded in mist. Rich furniture, rugs & food. Had a very fine guest room to myself with magnificent bathroom attached. Glad to go to bed early but head swam all night & I kept feeling I was still on the boat.

Saturday October 2nd
Went for walk first round Harold's most spacious flower & vegetable garden; then through damp forest on mountain side. Mist gradually cleared & we had amazing view of changing trees, mountain lakes, & higher mountains of about 5,000 ft in distance. Still felt dizzy & rather sick but walk did me good although I felt tired. Walked first with Lois Cole & then Mrs Putnam. Passed Mark Twain's shack.

In afternoon sun came out & the others told me to sleep on lounge chair in verandah as guest of honour at tea party while they prepared it. I did fall asleep in the lovely sun with the mountain view in front of me, and it about saved my life, for 85 people from Onteora who had stayed a week longer than usual to come, appeared at the party. Not typical Americans at all—a highbrow community, more like inhabitants of a Cathedral city at home. Harold & his mother delighted with the way the party went off. Got to bed at reasonable hour & slept really well.

Sunday October 3rd
Another walk in morning; got stranded far from home & had to telephone Harold to fetch me in car. Lunch of exceptional weight & richness; lasted till 3 p.m. At 3.30 we started back for N.Y., I this time with Lois Cole & Alan Taylor. We deviated somewhat in order to go through Poughkeepsie & drive round campus at Vassar; also stopped for tea in Vassar village. Darkness came long before we got to N.Y.

Monday October 4th   New York
Day spent mostly catching up on mail & re-packing. George dropped in to the Board Room for a few moments while I was working there. Made engagement for us to have tea together on Wednesday.

Interviewed in afternoon by Mary Cameron of the N.Y. *Evening Post* for her Saturday column.

Found a cheap café on 8th Street called the University Restaurant where I can get lunch & supper for 50 cents.

Tuesday October 5th   Bryn Mawr

Luncheon engagement at Hotel Warwick with a professional women's group called "The Woman Pays", got together by Miss Schuler of the *Christian Science Monitor*. Was a guest of honour though not allowed to do more than just announce myself. Ralph Bates, over from Spain, another guest of honour, but saw him only for few minutes as I had to leave early to catch train to Bryn Mawr, Pa. Met there & taken to tea by my organiser, Mrs Chadwick. Incredibly hot, stuffy afternoon; terrific thunder, & rainstorm broke just after I got to the College. My bedroom there, which was *heated*, registered over 80° all night! Changed & went down to cocktails & dinner-party given in my honour; sat beside the Principal, Mrs (Dr) Park. Formidable, but more genial than head of an English women's college would be. Lectured on "Literature & World Peace" to audience of almost 1,000 students & faculty; spoke badly owing to thundery air & terrific heat of auditorium, in bath of perspiration all the time; also need a lecture or two to get acclimatised to U.S.A. Another meeting for questions with students afterwards, then taken by a member of the Faculty to her house for a highball. To bed late but couldn't sleep for headache & heat.

Wednesday October 6th   New York

Taken over Bryn Mawr Campus by member of Faculty; still very warm & damp though rain had ceased. In one of the dining halls met Margaret Ayer Barnes (author of *Years of Grace* whom I met in Chicago at Harold's luncheon in 1934), a former student of the college who was staying there.

Back to N.Y.; wrote letters etc. in afternoon. About 4.0 George called for me in the Board Room & took me to his office, where we discussed chiefly Gordon's books; George wouldn't let me pay my debt, but said he'd persuade G. to write him a book to fulfil his second contract. We also discussed briefly *Letters to a Friend* & my biography of Winifred, which George seems really keen on now. We then went to Fifth Avenue Hotel; had tea in my sitting-room & he was perfectly charming to me. He left about 7.0 for a dinner date & I had supper at the little café in the state of keen exhilaration to which his society always lifts me.

Sunday October 24th   Chicago and St Louis

Left Chicago for Tulsa, Oklahoma, via St Louis. Passed across great bridge over Mississippi & saw famous view of St Louis in the distance across the river which I missed last time through arriving at night. At Union Stn Chicago a keen-faced young porter said of my large suitcases: "Don't you want to check these through?" I said: "I can't, I'm on a lecture tour & I've got to have my stage clothes with me." He said eagerly: "Say, can you give me any hints about public speaking; I'm taking classes in it at the University." I said: "Then you don't mean to do this always?" He: "Sure not; I'm going to be a —." I didn't catch the name of his intended career, but enlightened him as best I could on the results of 15 years' speaking experience.

On train read par. in *Chicago Tribune* that Dick Sheppard had *won* the Rectorial Election at Glasgow University by a big majority, beating Winston Churchill & J. B. S. Haldane. A pacifist Rector where once Lord Birkenhead, as Rector, made his speech about glittering swords! It shows that there *are* times when the powers of self-interest & materialism can be conquered by the spiritual forces of the world. Wrote Sheppard on the train, enclosing a striking cartoon from the *Chicago Tribune*, & cabled him from St Louis. Took 15 mins walk round Negro quarter outside St Louis station & then got on Texas Express for Tulsa.

Sunday November 7th   Atlanta
Arrived 7.30 from Nashville with Norman Berg, who took me to the Biltmore—then called for me about 10.0 & ran me round Atlanta. Grand view from hotel window of rich red-brown trees softened with mist. City like a garden—homes all hidden by trees. Margaret Mitchell not at her house & didn't come, but found traces of her everywhere. In historical book & print shop in basement of Biltmore saw exhibited the cover of her Danish translation—literally "Blown by the Blast". Norman Berg drove me out to his house & we passed Mgt Mitchell's—a very modest second floor apartment in a grimy-looking apartment house known as the Russell on West Peachtree Street. House of yellowish-cream stucco brick; the bay window of her apartment looks out on rather a dreary back yard. I suspect this refusal to spend any of ½ million dollars on more comfortable living to be a kind of inverted swollen-headedness—espec. as her father lives in quite an ornate column-fronted white house further down the same street. Taken to the Bergs' home—2 charming little boys, one 4½, one 4 months. Signed their copies of my books; they said Mgt Mitchell had never offered to do this though she had signed hundreds at his office. They took me to see the cyclorama (grim realistic picture & relief work of New Orleans battle), gave me excellent lunch at Athletic Club, ran me round environs again & took me to station.

1938

Tuesday January 4th   London
Press show of *South Riding* film. G. & I attended preliminary luncheon
given by John Mayer at Trocadero. He asked me to take the chair & make
a short speech about Winifred. Edna Best, Marie Lohr & Ann Todd all
there. Sat next to *Evening News* film critic. Saw film afterwards at London
Pavilion—beautiful & impressive. Winifred's name & *South Riding* on red
sky signs dominate Piccadilly Circus.

Cable from George Brett that Victor Gollancz wants "Thrice a
Stranger".

Saturday March 12th
Germany marched into Austria.

Sunday March 13th
Germany annexed Austria. Hitler appeared in Linz & Vienna. Communist demonstrations in West End.

Monday March 14th
The oppression of the beautiful bright days of this amazing March when
the international situation is so precarious.

L.N.U., Labour Party & all the so-called peace-lovers (except the
P.P.U.) are shouting war! For 20 years they have been propaganding in
favour of negotiation rather than war. But in this, the acid test, they are
back again preferring war to negotiation.

1939

Sunday January 1st   London
Had Christmas dinner [to-day] instead of Christmas day. Edith & Margaret came; brought me lilac & daffodils. Tea Edwardes Square. Walked home in dark with children.

After supper worked on biography of Winifred—went through notebooks & poems.

Tuesday January 3rd
Very cold. More work on notebooks. Took children to see Bertram Mills' circus at Olympia.

Wednesday January 4th
Worked on W.'s notebooks for *Land of Green Ginger* & *South Riding*. Gertrude Arends, daughter of the Dutch Consul in Boulogne, came to tea; she is writing a thesis on Winifred & her work for her Doctorate at the Sorbonne and wanted information. I showed her photographs of Winifred, copies of her books, "The Runners", *New Voter's Guide*, translations etc. She was especially interested in the Dutch translation. A small vivid person with black hair & very red lips. I should think she will do an intelligent thesis. She hopes ultimately to publish it in France & that it will help the translation of W.'s books. She saw Lady R. & Hilda Reid when she was over last year & I was in America.

After she had gone, listened to broadcast of President Roosevelt's message to Congress—a vehement fighting speech, anti-dictator, pro-rearmament & continued expenditure. Hardly likely to improve relations bet. U.S.A. & Germany, but these are already so strained that anything short of war can hardly make them worse. Congress more or less unmoved by references to internat. situation; cheered only when he referred to Opposition desire for retrenchment. Ended by saying they [were] determined to be an eighty, not a sixty, million dollar nation.

Thursday January 5th
Went with John to see Helen Mayo. Nothing wrong with his teeth or mine.

Two speaking invitations by first post—Soroptomist Annual Conference at Southport & a London pacifist group. Refusing both. Plum cake arrived made for me as Christmas gift by Ruth Gage Colby.

Evening, spoke to City of London branch of the British Legion Women's Section, on "Constructive Peacemaking"—not propaganda, but the account of war experiences which made me a pacifist, and what I thought peace-lovers shd do now. About 50 women present. Chair taken first by Lady Maurice, who had to go early, & then by Miss Sprott of the B.B.C.

Meeting at the Langbourn Club in Upper James Street. Had supper there with Miss Sprott & a few others after the speech. Pleasant evening. Speech seemed to go down well. Got back to find huge evening mail.

Friday January 6th
Worked most of day on Winifred's files—S. Africa & literary. Walk with John in afternoon. Very cold. Victor Gollancz Ltd sent me a copy of Archibald Baxter's *We Will Not Cease*—the autobiography of a conscientious objector. Is this a gesture of sympathy towards pacifism? To-night I read V.G.'s "After Munich" editorial in the November *Peace News* with a greater sense of agreement with him than I have felt since he published *Testament of Youth*. He seems to admit that extremists in the Left Book Club have run away with it into paths of propaganda rather than thought.

Saturday January 7th
Worked all day on biography. G. took John to see *Sixty Glorious Years* at Clapham Junction Cinema; Shirley went to party at Mrs Guinness's. Much milder but dull & damp after rain storm last night. Long walk with Shirley after lunch before party.

Sunday January 8th
Going through W.'s letter files—H.P., Rhondda, Odette, Sarah Millin, Stella Benson, etc. Had looked over them all once but this a more intensive search for biography. Confronted with literary executor's usual difficulty of whether to destroy, return to writers, or put away & keep. In view of fame & importance of most of correspondence, decided to keep for posterity. Left the intimate letters unread—their writers won't have the same objection to posterity as they would to me. But what I saw in sorting & filing was quite enough to indicate their interest in time to come.

Tea Edwardes Square. Mother had pretty new dress—black with mauve bead embroidery, & the gold chain I gave her for her birthday looked charming on it. Wore own new black cloth coat with Persian lamb collar. Mild pleasant day.

Monday January 9th
Irritating day as secretary didn't turn up owing to fact that her children's nurse was given a week-end holiday & simply did not come back last night. Gave no notice or anything. Married women's work in this country is difficult owing to no lack of ability or organising power in themselves, but to deplorable domestic system of individual household management. Strongest possible argument for state-supplied creches, nursery schools, communal kitchens etc., as in Russia. Half the population's intellectual power running to waste from avoidable thraldom to domesticity. Absolutely no real reason why a woman shouldn't have best of both worlds as a man has always had.

Tuesday January 10th
Invited to address Conference of Northern Branches of Nat. Union of Women Teachers at Newcastle-on-Tyne on Feb. 25th. Refused owing to book.
    Shirley went back to L.C.C. school.

Wednesday January 11th
Wrote Gollancz re *We Will Not Cease*; also mentioned possibility of French Revn novel. Spent most of day on a 1,000-word article—"A Square Deal for Nurses"—for *Local Govt Service*. John & Oliver Evans-Palmer running about together all day bargaining over stamps. Had face massage at Barker's & tea with Mother.

Thursday January 12th
Tiresome day because so much interrupted. Letter from Colston Leigh in morning which involved making out new lecture synopses, signing contract & seeing after photographs. Large other mail in addition.
    Went to Sarah Millin's cocktail party at 42 Upper Brook Street. Philip there; being a judge has made him thinner than he was two or three years ago. (How odd it is that one never sees so many of one's friends "in action" professionally & they never see one at work either—thereby mutually missing the most essential part of ourselves.) G. & I talked to Henry Andrews, the Weizmanns, Dame May Whitty, Victor Cazalet.

Friday January 13th
Another interrupted day owing to large correspondence & necessity of reviewing a book for *Peace News*—*Franklin Roosevelt* by Basil Maine. Pleasant & easy account of Roosevelt's career; rather "external" & not intimate, but revealing as regards the early lack of sympathy between Franklin & Eleanor.
    Invitations to speak from Cheltenham Ladies' College & Glasgow Fed. of University Women; refusing both on account of book. Letter from Gollancz saying that my description of the possible Mary Wollstonecraft novel is "extraordinarily interesting" & he would like to talk it over with me sometime. Sent signed contracts & lecture synopses to Colston Leigh.
    This evening finished working on W.'s letters to Phyllis. By last post came the gift of Chakravarty's book— *"The Dynasts" and the Post-War Age in Poetry*, by Amiya Chakravarty.
    Short-handed to-day; Amy in bed with 'flu.

Saturday January 14th
Foggy; then very wet. Correspondence minus secretary again took most of the morning. Children went to a party at the James Lavers; Mrs Laver (Veronica Turleigh) said "They were so nice" when I fetched them & remarked how helpful to her John had been.

Began on Winifred's letters to me. Gives me the "Nessun maggior dolore" feeling so habitual now.

Sunday January 15th

Wet wild night last night; this morning mild & lovely so that I could work (reading W.'s letters to me) at the open window, but wetness & wildness came on again after tea. Amy still in bed. Children uproarious all day long—banging doors & generally throwing their weight about. V. tiresome when I took them to tea at Mother's—being generally tactless, pushing glass crooked on dressing tables etc. Finally on way home dashed out of bus at Chelsea Town Hall & escaped from me across King's Rd, then down Flood Street & lost themselves in wild roaring wet, so that when I got in they were not there & I had to wait for them. When they came in I was really angry & packed them off to bed without supper. Went up later & found Shirley quite uncrushed, bobbing about in her bed, but poor John very subdued.

Did Winifred's 1925 letters to-day.

Monday January 16th

Worked all day at 1926 letters (S. African tour). V. slow work because so much material—each letter full of fascinating descriptions. Must publish many of these.

Discussed question w' G. of country cottage for self to write in & children to spend holidays in event of war, & he suddenly remembered his property in Leamington & that present tenants are due to leave the better of the two houses in Sept. Decided to investigate situation.

Read parts of Hone's biography of George Moore. Margaret R. & other busy "executives" should have had *his* procrastinations to deal with! Every great artist takes his own time, refusing to be hurried by other people, & Moore took longer than any of them. He was writing *Esther Waters* for about six years & then completely re-wrote the second half on the proof.

Tuesday January 17th

Secretary back again. Huge mass of accumulated letters to dictate, including a v. difficult one to the *M. Guardian* about the case of the imprisoned French pacifist Eugène Lagot, wh. the War Resisters' Internat. wanted me to take up. K.N.E. says I shouldn't bother with any of this but spend all my time writing books. Oh, if only I could! If only people would let me *alone*!

Didn't get to work on my biography till 6 p.m. owing to letters & odd jobs, mostly occasioned by J.'s return to school to-morrow. Sent Colston Leigh collection of photographs wh. I have at last succeeded in getting together.

Wednesday January 18th

John went back to school to-day, 1.45 from Paddington. Sat writing quietly all morning at table & I thought he was doing stamps; afterwards found he had left a notebook for me with 3 pages of most pathetic reactions about going back to school & his tears outlined on the cover! But he was very good at the station; much cheered by the sight of Roger Morgan & Adrian Marston; also because Mother, who was at the Station to see him off, gave him 2/- & Shirley gave him sixpence. He got into a carriage with Roger Morgan & about 6 others—one small boy sobbing bitterly. Charles & Hilda Morgan on station, also Hester Marsden-Smedley & Jeffrey & Doreen Marston, seeing off offspring.

Later went to cocktail party at the Kean Seymours & met the Marstons again; Doreen finally took us home as far as the King's Rd. Good party—besides Marstons, Henrietta Leslie, Trevor Blakemore, Maisie Greig & husband, Spencer Curtis Brown, etc. Margaret S.J. not there, & couldn't come to supper with us later, because of 'flu. Rosalind looked pretty in long purple dress with silver collar, & my godson Philip was flourishing though very solemn. Had 4 cocktails to try to drown desolation of saying goodbye to John. Shirley full of ebullience at lunch; not at all subdued by his going back to school.

Thursday January 19th
Still on the 1926 letters—a very long job bec. so full, so detailed (& so new to me) about S. Africa.

To-day accounts came in for the half-yearly distribution of W.'s estate —money seems now to be mostly swallowed by income tax & legacy duty—to say nothing of lawyers' charges. By letters to-day was invited to: 1) speak at a No-Conscription meeting on Sunday; 2) speak at a P.N.E.U. luncheon on Feb. 16th; 3) be a guest at Bart's Appeal dinner; 4) attend Labour Book Service Luncheon in March; 5) be guest of honour at the N.C.E.C. "21st Anniversary of Suffrage" luncheon at the Criterion. Refused first three; accepted last two.

Saw Sarah Gertrude Millin off (& Philip) at 11.15 at Waterloo by *Winchester Castle* boat train. Sarah in her element with photographers, gifts & indeterminate group of friends; wore a pretty new blue tweed coat & skirt, & charming blue hat.

P.P.U. telegraphed for the £200 wh. I put on deposit for them; sent it. In Tube this morning saw a poster with pictures of Stalin, Hitler & other dictators above a Madame Tussaud's advt. "The only place in the world where they all live together at peace."

Miss John. Wished all day that we never sent him to boarding-school —tho' threats of war & approach of Eton did seem to make it inevitable.

Friday January 20th
A bad day—constant relays of correspondence and "jobs". No work—yet nothing else to show for it. Telephoned Mother at night & found she had an

attack of 'flu—started Wed. night, temp. 102 but now normal. Wrote Mrs Hoyland to warn her that John might have it.

Usual tedious set of requests by post to: a) attend opening of Workers' Empire Exhibition; b) write a 2,000-word essay (for nothing) in honour of Gandhi; c) read proofs of a book by a stranger called *The Madhouse of Civilisation* & give him a puff for publicity (publisher Jarrold's, so it can't be much good!); d) attend a reception of the N.P.C. Refused all but the last. In evening a further request to attend, & distribute synopses of, a pacifist Economic Conf. at King's Weigh House next week-end. Shall be in Wales.

Bad headache, so went to bed early myself. Ann Watkins wrote that Mabel Search of the N.Y. *Pictorial Review* will pay $500 for my article but wants it re-written and made "more intimate". Another 3 days of interruption to my book!

Saturday January 21st
Mother better; telephoned. Shirley went to Gym after usual wrestle. Wept all morning over W.'s 1926 letters with their reminder of just what we lost—*I* lost.

Took S. in the Park after lunch. G. spent morning talking to political group at the Duchess of Atholl's house. American woman teacher, Helen Fogg, introduced by Lois Cole of Macmillan, came to tea. *Very* tall, pleasant, & easy to talk to.

Sunday January 22nd   Bournemouth
Went down to Bournemouth for day; stayed at Highcliffe Hotel. Long walk by sea in afternoon—somewhat spoilt by high wind, rain, & an incipient cold. Hotel comfortable except that bath-water was tepid at night. Mostly full of old ladies.

Monday January 23rd   Swanage
Took late morning train from Bournemouth to Swanage & looked over Oldfeld School as a possibility for Shirley. Favourably impressed—Mr & Mrs Hickson sane & intelligent, building & farm attractive, but best of all gorgeous views all round of sea & downs. Couldn't spend much time in the little town as the gale had become a hurricane—which we afterwards heard had capsized the St Ives lifeboat in the early hours & drowned 7 of its 8 crew. We could hardly stand going up the hill to Oldfeld. Lunched at pleasant inn in the town called The Ship. Back to London by the 5.40; pleasant journey & found Shirley well. Secretary had done correspondence, which for once was not extensive. Letter to G. from George Brett somewhat grieved because he hadn't heard from us for so long—but I think I wrote last from the *Queen Mary*!

Tuesday January 24th   London
Felt ill & miserable all day with on-coming cold.

Harold & Mrs Latham to dinner. Discussed G.'s book, mine, & suppression of Mrs White's.

Wednesday January 25th
In bed with 'flu & bronchitis—no temp.—but vile cough, streaming cold & headache. Dr Yates came & advised me to cancel Welsh engagement. Bitter day, with strong wind & heavy falling snow. Large correspondence; struggled to dictate answers & send telegrams to Wales. P.P.U. got Ethel Mannin to go instead of me to the Dolgelly meeting.

Thursday January 26th
Still in bed. Another avalanche of letters. Read *The Crowded Street*.

Friday January 27th
Sat up before fire in bedroom. Aberystwyth telegraphed fixing next Friday for lecture. Finished *The Crowded Street*.

Saturday January 28th
Came down & went out for few minutes in sunshine but wind was cold & it didn't do much good. Struggling all day trying to write letter to *Peace News* disagreeing with "anti" campaigns for pacifists & urging more constructive work & philosophy. Brain wouldn't work, but letter was quite lucid when finally achieved. Fear it will infuriate a good many of the would-be persecuted.

Mother came to see me in morning & brought a lovely bunch of pale orange tulips. We discussed Oldfeld & decided to send Shirley there next term owing to: a) war risks; b) desire to give her three or four years in the country before she goes to St Paul's at 12 or 13—D.V.

G. got 400 pp. of proof of *The Story of the Political Philosophers* to correct before sailing.

Listened in to Chamberlain's 9.30 p.m. speech at the Birmingham Jewellers' dinner—résumé of armaments progress, warning to Hitler before H.'s speech on Monday plus gestures of friendship. Went *very* slowly—obviously with intention of enabling foreign listeners-in to understand.

Sunday January 29th
Still 'fluish. Bitter N.E. wind so dared not go out. Worked most of day on *Land of Green Ginger* & W.'s 1927–1929 letters. Went to Edwardes Square & back in a taxi to have tea with Mother.

Monday January 30th
Invitations to speak from Swansea Soroptomists, Hampstead Women's Freedom League, Fellowship of Reconciliation (big meeting Kingsway Hall, Feb. 27th). Refused first two; tentatively accepted last, as it is on day

I come back from Malvern so I shan't be working anyhow.

Violent head cold & headache still persists; also bitter wind, so that I can't get out for more than a breath of air.

Letter from Ethel Mannin, raising conscription question; wrote a long reply not really for her sake but to clear my own head about what I feel.

Wrote to Mr & Mrs Hickson of Oldfeld & asked if Shirley could go next term; also to St Paul's inquiring age of entry, scholarships etc.

At 7.45 listened in to Hitler's speech to Reichstag—usual aggressive, intermittently sarcastic voice but *much* faster than usual—listened till nearly nine, when he was still slating Jews, Catholics, England, France, America etc. Couldn't understand much & finally decided I couldn't bear the forceful, provocative tones any more—so shut him off before he had finished. Later translation showed that it was a more pacific speech than everyone had expected, & stocks & trade generally improved at once in consequence.

Tuesday January 31st
Went to the Macmillan lunch at Brown's Hotel; usual pleasant function & met the usual pleasant people—Margaret & Guy, the Lovat Dicksons, Cecil Roberts, the Charles Morgans, Harold Macmillan, etc. Successfully avoided W. A. R. Collins—who equally avoided me!

Margaret S. J. came back to tea & supper. We discussed a) my immediate resort with Shirley to her flat in event of war while we make plans—agreed I would send a telegram & just come w' all the documents for the biography of W. to get them out of London; b) possibility of our jointly resigning as Sponsors from the P.P.U. (not as members) so as to concentrate on writing & avoid so much pressure to speak, do organising, etc. Also because we agree that their no-conscription campaign & other "*anti*" campaigns are a putting of the cart before the horse and what should be concentrated on is finding alternatives to *war*—not resisting just one or two of its consequences. We also agreed that in event of war our policy wld be to urge an early & just peace by writing & speaking so long as we were allowed to do it—& then some form of non-military relief work—but that the biog. of W. should be done before all else. She says Ellis Roberts still hasn't finished his book on Stella Benson, who died in 1933.

Wednesday February 1st
No secretary; K.N.E. got a touch of my 'flu I am afraid. Worked all day on my correspondence & re-writing article "American Mothers Are Lucky". Had hair & eyebrows done in afternoon; looked much better and consequently felt much better.

Thursday February 2nd
Worked all day on re-written article & correspondence. Tea with Mother; walked slowly all the way to Edwardes Square but regretted it later as legs

ached from after-effects of 'flu. We discussed & agreed about taking possession of & furnishing G.'s house in Leamington owing to a) war risks, b) value of having some place away from London in which to write.

Friday February 3rd   Aberystwyth
Took 11.5 train to Aberystwyth; latter half of journey (from Shrewsbury) slow & tedious. Very cold; Welsh hills grey & snow-covered but had a desolate beauty, especially round the Borth estuary. Met by President of Union & another member; they put me up at the Queen's Hotel (very comfortable) where we had a ceremonial dinner first. Sat between the student President & Dr Campbell Jones the Vice-Principal of the University.

After dinner gave my official lecture as Hon. President for the year of the Univ. debates union (and the first woman to be elected to this office—some of my predecessors have been Sir Austen Chamberlain, Walter de la Mare & Dean Inge!). Huge mausoleum of hall; students kept up clamour for first ¼ hr, mostly in Welsh, but listened attentively to the rest; I was told later that they always do this & if they don't like the lecture keep it up till the end! I was more than ever glad I didn't attempt it when "under the weather" & cancelled last week. Got good reception at end after a woman student & the Prof. of History had proposed vote of thanks. Proceedings ended by singing of official Aberystwyth song. Taken back to hotel by Vice-Principal & 3 students; talked with them there till bedtime. Good night though bedroom right on sea which was rough.

Saturday February 4th
At breakfast conversed across tables with a lady from Liverpool, who having wanted to hear me speak for some time, had attended lecture last night. Went up to my room & put on outdoor things & found a complete stranger (a small middle-aged woman in outdoor things) waiting there with a large album & a *Testament of Youth* for me to autograph. President of Union called at 9.45; took me in taxi round the front & University buildings. Saw big church, St Michael's, where my grandfather was organist & Mother was christened. At 10 o'clock break spoke to the assembled students in the Quadrangle, standing on the iron grid where only distinguished men visitors had spoken before. Talked for 3 minutes & was well-received; then had to rush off & catch 10.15 train.

Sunday February 5th   London
In bed for breakfast. Got up to find Shirley with slight temp. and a 'flu cold, & inclined to weep. Put her to bed for the day & dosed her. She brightened at once; temp. was down by this evening. Tea with Mother; only stayed till 5.30; then came back & got S. bathed and tidied for evening with help of Burnett. Too interrupted all day to get much done but wrestled with Jan.

accounts & revised typescript of "American Mothers" article. Cheque from Gollancz for £71.19.4 came by last post last night.

Monday February 6th
Shirley better. Lots of letters. Started work on lecture "America To-day & To-morrow" for Trinity Church, Glasgow. Lovely day, brilliant sun; the best this year. Long walk in afternoon round Chelsea & Battersea Park.

Tuesday February 7th
Another lovely day, but more wind & high tide in river. Worked on Glasgow lecture & walked in park again. Mgt Storm Jameson arrived just after tea, & she & G. & I went on to the P.E.N. refugee party where I was acting as a host (M. of course President). Other hosts were Henrietta Leslie, Ernest Raymond, Richard Church (Margaret Kennedy didn't turn up), Berta Ruck & about ten others. Forty refugee writers were guests; many could only speak German. When they arrived most of the hosts appeared to be talking to each other & bulk of introducing fell on Hermon Ould, Margaret, Henrietta, & me. Dr Alfred Neumann the Viennese author, & Dr Steinberg who lunched with us recently, were there & helpful; also Henry Nevinson as ex-President. What with standing for two hours, talking German & only getting a few mouldy sandwiches etc. very late for supper, it was all somewhat exhausting, but refugees obviously enjoyed themselves & were more manageable than I expected & fore-gathered without difficulty. Margaret made a charming little speech telling them that this was old Europe as well as future Europe & they were to be at home. Henrietta translated.

Wednesday February 8th
Letter from St J. Ervine enclosing copies of W.'s letters to him, w' covering note to me full of usual bombastic accusations about egotism, "causeness", aggressiveness, inferiority to W. & exploitation of her etc. Decided time had come for worm to turn, so wrote him long letter, v. frank, & enclosing still franker one wh. I wrote & did not post after reading one of his attacking letters to W. about me two years ago.

Went to All Soul's, Langham Place, at 3.30 for Christening of Lovat Dickson baby, now 8 months old. Lovely child but looks as if it didn't get enough fresh air. Marguerite looked very beautiful. Dan Macmillan one of the godfathers. Foregathered afterwards for tea in their charming little house at 79 Brown Street; Cecil Roberts & various other guests turned up & we drank tea & champagne.

Thursday February 9th
Finished American lecture. Walked over to tea with Mother. After supper read *Eutychus*. Mlle Piaget sent a book *The Good Master* for the children.

Friday February 10th
Worked on letters, *Eutychus* & began *New Voter's Guide.* Creech Jones to lunch to tell me about more recent history of I.C.U. Took away Ballinger's account of his meeting w' W. & going out to S. Africa & said he would amend & add to it for me; also promised to read the three chapters on S. Africa.

Gordon's host in Hungary, Dr Balogh, who is arranging his lectures with the British Consul, to tea. Amiable strange-looking man—mixture of Babylonish priest & Mussolini. Asked me to go to Hungary with G. but G. isn't keen on sharing publicity etc., so I don't suppose anything will come of it.

News reports the Pope dead at 81 and the end of the Spanish war likely to come next week.

Saturday February 11th
Mother, Aunt Muriel, G. & I went to St Anselm's Church, Hatch End, to see Hugh Brittain married.

Came back to find Shirley with a temp. of 103°; got in Doctor Yates who diagnosed tonsillitis & said at last he was sure of the reason of the sudden high temps. & that she should have her tonsils out in the spring. By the time he left, her temp. was down to 99° & after I had washed her & sprayed her throat & nose she seemed her normal self again. He said she would be all right in a few days if she was kept in bed till I come back from the North & her nose & throat sprayed three times daily.

Sunday February 12th   Newcastle
Went up to Newcastle by 1 p.m. train to speak for P.P.U. Shirley better before I left; temp. down to below 100°. Met with Maurice Browne (producer of *Journey's End*, a decorative figure in a fur coat) at the barrier by the organisers. Given tea. Huge meeting, nearly 3,000 (almost as many as for Dick Sheppard) in the City Hall. A local barrister, Mr Robson, took the Chair. Maurice Browne spoke excellently, & I followed; it seemed to go quite well. Very well organised meeting; short effective speech from Chair, no interrupting appeals, no tedious questions to spoil the final effect; whole thing only took 1½ hours & audience left while still interested. Wrote later to Roy Walker to commend organisers. The secretary, Thomas Large, even put some daffodils in my room at the hotel. Maurice Browne went back to London by the night train & the organisers left with him saying they were "much encouraged", so I got to bed reasonably early. Rang up G. to find out how Shirley was; her temp. was 101 but G. said Yates had seen her just after I left & was quite satisfied.

Monday February 13th   Glasgow
Went on in morning to Glasgow after short walk round city. Tedious journey which took 5 hrs as an overturned coach on the line ½-an-hour

from Glasgow delayed the train for nearly an hour. Everybody was very nervous in Newcastle about the Irish bomb outrages as the King is going there next week to launch a battleship. Gunpowder was found on Saturday on the line between Durham & Newcastle over which I passed on Sunday.

Rev. H. S. McClelland of Trinity Church picked me up at the Hotel (Central) for my lecture to his Forum just before 8.o. No wire from G. about S. so I assumed she was going on all right. Lecture was on "America To-day & To-morrow"; audience v. interested in the international relations aspect of it. Felt confident & indifferent as so often, so gave a lecture wh. obviously pleased the audience, Mr McClelland & the Jewish-American mover of the vote of thanks, Rabbi Barsune of Texas. After lecture went on for tea at McClelland's Manse & met again the American Consul General & his wife, Mr & Mrs Davies, who came to my autobiographies lecture.

Tuesday February 14th
Returned to London by the 10 o'clock train. Journey comfortable & seemed to go quickly bec. I was reading Winifred's admirable study of Virginia Woolf; finished *Poor Caroline* on my way up. Kept on wondering, as so often, why the very measure of my indifference to lecturing seems to make me so successful as a lecturer, whereas I care so much more about books & succeed so much more hardly. Lecturing is of course a trivial art compared with writing, but I get quite irritated with myself when I find my college-trained brain selecting the right facts & presenting them lucidly, my well-developed voice rendering them audibly, & my possibly instinctive clothes sense enabling me to make a pleasant appearance. Mr McClelland said that the Duchess of Atholl, who lectured the time before me, appeared in tweeds & spats, & gave a dull address in wh. no one could see the wood for the trees. Yet she surely ought, as a politician, to lecture well. It is a trifling & unsatisfying thing to be good at, somehow.

Got back to find S. with normal temp. & not too many letters.

Wednesday February 15th   London
Lovely day. S. got up after breakfast & played in nursery all day. Card from Mrs Hoyland to say John was in their sick-room for two days with feverish cold but is now better. Went longish walk in sunshine & did some shopping. Working on Winifred's 1932 letters. Letter from R. Ellis Roberts to say that the letters to Stella Benson cannot be traced unless they are in China with James Anderson's possessions. His second wife (who wrote a p.c. to this effect) now evidently has two children.

Thursday February 16th
Large American mail in—several "fan-mails" to add to the number I found after Glasgow. One from George Brett, at last in favour of Roosevelt for bluffing Hitler & angry with politicians who have tried to make him eat

his words. Long & charming letter from Phyllis in Chicago; she had spent about a month with the Bretts & also saw Clare in N.Y.

Went to P.N.E.U. luncheon in honour of the new Chairman, Sir Fabian Ware (of the Imperial Graves Commission); made speech proposing toast "The Children's Future" & heard the Hon. Mrs Franklin describe it as "magnificent" when she didn't know I was just behind her, so it must have gone well enough. Mr & Mrs Hickson of Oldfeld were there & said they now knew what I wanted done for Shirley! Met also Antoinette Devonshire who wrote the pacifist book for children to which I wrote an introduction. She said that the P.N.E.U. board, which is "Collective Security", wouldn't adopt it. Bought some shoes & then went on to a reception given by the Nat. Peace Council to its new President, the Bishop of Chelmsford. Bishop Barnes there, & told story of himself & the Bp of London presenting contrasting sermons in Temple Church during War. Mrs Hoyland was there to my surprise; she is daughter of Dame Elizabeth Cadbury & was there representing her. She said that John is now quite fit again.

Friday February 17th
Trying to work on Winifred's letters, but somehow impeded by G.'s preparations for departure. Went to Euston after lunch & saw Harold & Mrs Latham off to Liverpool for the *Samaria*. Gave Mrs L. a box of sweets from Page & Shaw. No one else there seeing them off but Lovat Dickson, the Deverils & a man I didn't know. Harold said it was the hardest trip he remembered but I didn't gather it had produced much in the way of MSS.

Mother called just after tea-time to say goodbye to G. He somehow got cleared up & we dined out together at the Café Royal Grill. Cold day, turned wet at night.

Saturday February 18th
Went with G. to Southampton by the 8.54 a.m. boat train for the *Queen Mary*. Bright morning & less cold. At S'ampton it seemed no time at all since we last saw the docks & the boat. We go to U.S.A. in much the same way as other people go to Brighton! This is G.'s 33rd crossing. He was travelling economically so as to make all possible profit on his lectures, & had a Tourist cabin on D Deck, but with a porthole & to himself. Small & a little Spartan-looking but quite good for work. Boat sailed at noon; went to the upstairs level of the farther shed & watched the ropes loosened, the tugs attached & the flag raised to the top of the mast. G. walked round the boat keeping me in sight as she turned to go out of the dock. I walked to the end of the shed & waved to him so long as I could see him; then watched the boat till she slid smoothly round the corner of the shed & was almost out of sight.

Some v. nice proofs of G.'s new photograph by Elliott & Fry came just before we left; am ordering some. Also a letter to me from the Duchess of Atholl asking if I would speak at her first public meeting of the "Hundred

Thousand" group; she evidently thinks my internat. politics similar to G.'s. Refused explaining that as a member of the Dick Sheppard group my appearance on her platform would be of no value to her.

Sunday February 19th

S. got up for breakfast; took her out. Worked on 1933 letters.

Report published in *Sunday Express* that Roosevelt is returning from a fishing holiday owing to "ominous reports" about situation in Europe, but no indication what these are.

Edith & Margaret came to lunch; Edith gave me various pieces of information for the biography. Tea with Mother; found her rather miserable owing to servant troubles & feeling under the weather since 'flu—but she cheered up before we left. Showed me a nice blue two-piece & hat bought from Baird Lewis.

Edith agreed with me that Lady R. was really W.'s evil genius—used her time, health & energy, & gave little worth having in return for all that she took. The idea seems to have been dawning on Edith for some time—as it has on me since that lunch with Lady R. & since reading in W.'s letters how even in the appalling days of work & correspondence after her father's death she was apparently still expected to do Notes for *T. & T.* E. said Jean McW. had always felt strongly abt Lady R.'s selfishness & possessiveness.

Monday February 20th

Work. Actually no engagements or important letters. Doing 1933–1934 correspondence. Lovely day. Walked round Battersea Park after lunch. Happy letter from John; had been for an 8-mile "hike". Also seems to be getting popular & enjoying it. Dear love—neither excessively "intellectual", nor disgustingly ambitious, what a comfort he will be in a family which has hitched all its waggons to inaccessible stars!

Wrote Jean McWilliam, as Edith thought she wd like to see me.

Tuesday February 21st

Again able to concentrate on work—did 1934–35 letters all day. Bright day, though cold & windy. Went to Harrods for two new jumpers & a few "accessories" & walked back.

Wednesday February 22nd

Finished reading Winifred's letters. The Great War series *I Was There*, edited by Sir John Hammerton, Nos. 21 & 22, came tonight, with the long extract from the Somme part of *Testament of Youth*.

Had hair set, nails done, face massaged etc. Tea with Mother—she was overhauled by her doctor after tea for after-effects of 'flu but he says she could manage Malvern all right if she takes things quietly. Invited to be hostess at W.I.L. reception on March 22nd; refused.

Thursday February 23rd
Doing W.'s letters to St John Ervine; also wrote first draft of the Epilogue, being inspired to do so by all the evidences of exploitation (particularly by Lady R., her mother & me) in W.'s letters.

Lunched at the Univ. Women's Club with Mrs Corbett Ashby to meet two Arab women—wives of Arab delegates to the present Palestinian Conference. Freda White & Miss Albertini (of one of the Women's organisations but I can't remember which) were there too. The two Arabs were lovely creatures, like smart Parisians. One—the more beautiful —spoke only French; but the other, older one, talked fluent, vehement English rather like Odette Keun's. Of the four English women, I was the only one who painted my lips, varnished my nails & wore clothes that didn't look as if they'd been put on after hanging in a cupboard for 5 years. Why, why, must social reform & political intelligence in the women of this country be associated with shiny noses & unwaved hair? Is it hubris—the feeling that you're so important that it doesn't matter *how* distasteful your appearance may be—or simply that most English women have no taste & don't even know it. Oh! that University Women's Club—full of grim-looking desiccated spinsters in appalling tweeds. Heaven preserve Shirley from an academic career! A youngish woman visitor was there with two small girls & the University women looked astonished & quite affronted at their presence.

It was refreshing to hear the Arab view of the Jews, who apparently behave to the Arabs in Palestine exactly as people in other countries behave to *them*!

Cable to-night from Gordon, just saying "Benedictions", so he has arrived in New York. Rapidity of transport by *Queen Mary* seems quite incredible.

Friday February 24th   Colwall
Mother & I came by the 1.45 to Malvern & took a car from Gt Malvern to the Park Hotel, Colwall, for John's half-term week-end. John not available till to-morrow. Perfectly lovely day, getting warmer as the train went further west. Worcester looked like a heavenly city in the light of the sinking sun. Reached Colwall just at sunset; sky aflame & the Malvern hills shone with a luminous roseate glow. Went for a short walk directly we arrived to show Mother the school before dark; heard cheerful voices & sounds of piano-practising coming from it. Walked on up the hill through the wood beyond; rich country scents everywhere, & clucking of chickens from the school farm. Radiant sky & hills growing darker against it as we went home. Hotel *very* comfortable; excellent food. Started to re-read *Mandoa, Mandoa!*.

Saturday February 25th
Weather changed during night; bitter wind sprang up; very cold; had

nearly to close window. Raining at breakfast time. Went to fetch John at 10.30; found him standing hatless in rain waiting for me. Brought him to hotel & dried his hair as he still had rather a stuffy cold. He had lunch with us & then as the rain had stopped the three of us walked over the hill to Malvern; it started raining just before we arrived. We had tea at the Abbey Hotel; met Hilda Morgan & Roger there, & all went together to the cinema to see *Adventures of Tom Sawyer*, etc., as it was still raining. Got a taxi back at 7.0; dropped John & Roger at school & came back to hotel ourselves. Went along to the Hoylands' evening At Home at the School; spoke to both Mr & Mrs Hoyland & told them G. was in America. I asked Mr Hoyland if he wanted to see me about J. as otherwise I wouldn't bother him, & he said No, he seemed to enjoy everything tremendously & had no problems except the ordinary problems of growing up. Put through trunk call to London when I got back at 9.30 to see how Shirley was—had previously tried to get on without success. She was quite all right but still awake & said goodnight to me herself.

Sunday February 26th
Lovely day again, though bitter wind. Had unusual experience this morning of lying in bed in my east-facing bedroom & watching the early morning sun creep over the edge of the hill opposite till it flooded the room with light. Went for a long walk with John over that hill this morning; got nearly as far as the British Camp on the top of the highest hill; then descended through woods & fields to Colwall. Wonderful views every-where—brilliant yet misty, with the blue-grey bareness of February.

After lunch went for another short walk round Colwall; then Hilda Morgan & Roger came to tea; discussed lecturing, writing books, schools, etc. This morning John & I saw a finch with a green head & pink breast; & this afternoon we passed a farm-orchard filled with baby pigs with bright pink ears. At 6.45 we went to the evening service. It was even more moving than last time—nothing is quite so poignant as boys' voices. Mr Hoyland told a little parable about people who lost their railway tickets & the Christian being someone who had taken a ticket to the City of God.

Monday February 27th   London
J. came to breakfast—afterwards returned to school for the expedition. For the first time he left me without tears, waving his hand & running cheerfully in to the side door, & at last I feel satisfied that he is happy there. Took rooms at the hotel for G. & myself for next half-term. Mother & I came back to town by slow & rather tedious trains; got back 3 p.m. & found Burnett in bed with an "influenza throat" but Shirley quite well. Had her down to sleep in my room to keep her off the top floor. No special letters.

Early supper—went along to Kingsway Hall to be the only lay speaker at the "Christian Pacifist Message" meeting to launch the renunciation of war by the joint pacifist group from the Christian churches. The Hall was packed, with people standing in the Gallery, & I found the meeting —which was as much a service as a meeting—really most moving. We sang "God moves in a mysterious way", which I hadn't heard since it made me weep during the War, the Oxford version of Luther's "Ein Feste Burg", and "Jesus shall reign where'er the sun". Canon Raven & Donald Soper were the other speakers beside myself. I felt a little strange among so many clerics, but spoke as a lay person representing the other lay people there who were looking to the pacifist message from the Christian churches to give us a lead & become more widespread. I *do* like Canon Raven—a natural dry academic who forces himself to give people the emotional inspiration they need. After the meeting two eager & earnest young men took me off for coffee to a restaurant in S'ampton Row. Went home to find that Storm Jameson had sent me her collected essays and papers in a volume called *Civil Journey*.

Tuesday February 28th
Worked all day on book & correspondence. Doing more letters now (mine to W.). How naïve & long-winded I was in my post-war twenties!

Wednesday March 1st
More work on own letters. In evening went to Old Vic with Hilda Reid to see Tyrone Guthrie's production of Ibsen's *An Enemy of the People*—the modern rendering being by Norman Ginsbury, who gave me the tickets. Excellent version & production—espec. the public meeting scene wh. is always so difficult to convey on the stage. I had forgotten the theme, which in so far as it is a study of municipal graft is extraordinarily like that of *South Riding*. Would the highbrow young critics who say that W. was "not an artist" because her books dealt with social & political themes be prepared to maintain the same thesis about Ibsen, I wonder?

Hilda & I discussed W.'s biography on the way home; she completely agreed with me that such a book must have time to mature & ripen, & be written with the detachment that only a long interval can give. I told her about Lady R.'s attempts to hurry me owing to the exigencies of a supposed "topical market"—& H. agreed that this was purely due to the unliterary values of a journalist, & that no one cared a damn now that Mrs Gaskell's *Life of Charlotte Brontë* was published in 1857 & not in 1855.

Friday March 3rd
Working on own letters.

P.P.U. Sponsors' meeting in afternoon, at new premises in 6 Endsleigh Street, opposite Friends' House. A good centre. Useful discussion on gen. policy of the P.P.U. & its tendency to get away from its simple main object on to side-issues. Donald Soper especially made this point. Some discussion also as to the resignations of Aldous Huxley, Margaret S.J., Eliz. Thorneycroft & myself as Sponsors in so far as this involves executive work. Nothing could be decided before the Ann. Gen. Meeting next month, but I did explain briefly, on behalf of myself & Margaret, what I thought the function of writers in the movement should be—& when I said that what we needed most was not to be always activising but to go away quietly & do a little thinking, Canon Morris heartily agreed. Walked most of way home afterwards; lovely day, light till 6.0.

Saw in *Evening Standard* that Canon Raven is the new Master of Christ's at Cambridge. Wrote to him; also mentioned G.'s application for Barker's job. Letter from G. by *Queen Mary* mail this morning.

Saturday March 4th
Lovely day of uninterrupted work—own letters.

Sunday March 5th
More work. Have now reached 1933 with own letters. Took S. to tea at Edwardes Square. Pleasant mild day—lovely sun this morning—but strong wind.

Sunday Express full of optimism about the internat. situation & even the *Observer* less gloomy than usual.

Monday March 6th
Interrupted day—also felt mouldy from something or other which had upset my inside. Too stupid for work this morning so turned out clothing for the Women's Service Bargain Sale. Went to first meeting of Labour Book Service at a luncheon in the Connaught Rooms; sat next to Lloyd and the Secretary to the Service, & made various suggestions through lunch. I was told—I don't know how truly—that the Left Book Club is losing money & V.G.'s other business suffering through his exclusive attention to the Club—but that may be merely malice. Francis Williams as Chairman & Hugh Dalton, Tawney & Mrs Hamilton spoke as Selectors; then various advisers made suggestions, Hannen Swaffer talked about the importance of stressing the ethereal side & G. D. H. Cole wound up—as a heretic who had written for the Left Book Club, & was now a supporter of Sir Stafford Cripps. Cole said he was just going to be 50 but he now looks as though he were 10 years older. The Service, like anything that promotes books, is a good idea & there is plenty of room for it in addition to V.G.'s group, but I didn't feel that anyone who spoke to-day was exactly going to bring in the New Jerusalem. I was sorry G. couldn't be there as the whole thing was originally his idea, & as usual he was given no credit for it. Talked to Williams, Mrs Hamilton, Gaitskell & Dr Eileen Power.

Got away about 3.30. Had hair washed at Peters & went to bed early having done nothing for my book.

Dr Yates rang up to-night about Shirley's tonsils—advises having it done on April 5 & by Mr Denis Browne, Helen Simpson's husband. William Hillman's secretary rang up to say he is still in Rome but has cabled his friends in the Hearst Press in Washington to call on G. at his hotel.

Tuesday March 7th
Work; face done at Barker's; got back just in time for Margaret S.J., who came at tea-time to stay the night. Just before tea Yates telephoned to say arrangements made about S.'s tonsils operation; also Christy to say Stoke Luncheon Club was a mistake & I wasn't to go. Margaret & I had a leisurely tea; talked about her new book *Civil Journey*, about the P.P.U., Winifred's biography, & Lady R., whom Margaret thinks has v. little influence now & certainly no standing as an author.

We went along together to the P.E.N. dinner—I to meet Compton Mackenzie, next whom I sat (he was guest of honour). *Very* full of animation & easy to get on with. We talked of St Paul's, *Sinister Street, Guy & Pauline*, and I said that during the War the "lighted door" in the verse at the end always symbolised Oxford for me. He told me that though the door isn't in Oxford in the book it actually *was* an Oxford door—in Worcester College, as it was the Provost of Worcester's daughter to whom he was engaged & who was "Pauline". Talked also to the Nevinsons; Horace Shipp; Pamela Frankau. Philippa Hole was at a table just opposite. Margaret made an amusing little Presidential speech, then Compton Mackenzie, then Mr Stanley Cursiter of the Scottish Nat. Gallery—quite good but too long after C.M.'s brilliance. It was a "Scottish dinner" to celebrate the opening of the Scottish Exhibition. After dinner Margaret, C.M., Pamela Frankau, another female & I went along with Humbert Wolfe to his flat in Euston St. Pamela was doing the honours but I couldn't make out whether she lived there with him or only visited. He showed me a photograph of Viola Garvin & told me her lameness resulted from the removal of her knee-cap muscles as a child. Showed us all his review books with autographed letters in them. Mgt & I didn't get back till 1 a.m.

Wednesday March 8th
Margaret & I had breakfast together; then went out & looked at flats in the neighbourhood as she wants to come back to town in Sept. & to be near me. She liked Dolphin Square & put in for a two-room top floor flat with a balcony. She then left for various engagements & I spent most of day on the 1934 letters, with a break to go to Lady Reith's cocktail party at 6.0. Talked to Hilda's brother-in-law (very "Left") about Palestine where he had worked, & to Hester Marsden-Smedley amongst others.

Thursday March 9th
Finished doing W.'s letters to me—now ready for the remainder of her books.

Took Shirley to tea with William & Rosalind Seymour for Philip's first birthday. Shirley played with him—very fascinated. Later became very boisterous. Philip is a magnificent healthy baby—not pretty but very strong, animated & vivacious. Henrietta also there, also Trevor Blakemore & one or two of Rosalind's relatives. I took P. a blue & white striped Buster suit & Shirley a coloured woollen ball with a cowbell inside.

Friday March 10th

Large correspondence. Read *The Astonishing Island*. Went with Mother in afternoon to see film of *The Citadel*—better as a film than the book is as a book. First half—the Welsh section—excellently produced; latter half somewhat confused & crowded. Whole thing a fine sermon on integrity.

Invited to speak by Oldham P.P.U.; refused. Also to write two free articles! One refused; sending an old one to another.

News in afternoon of another crisis in Czechoslovakia—Slovakia asking for separation & autonomy. And only to-day *The Times* said that the whole European outlook was better!

Saturday March 11th   Swanage

4 speaking invitations this morning; 3 P.P.U., one an educational body. All declined.

Went down to Swanage at 4.30 with Mother & Shirley, to show her Oldfeld. Pouring with rain. Stayed at Ship Hotel; comfortable & very reasonable; only 12/6 a day all found for us, & 7/6 for Shirley.

Sunday March 12th

Bitter cold day, east wind lashing the waves but no rain. Took Shirley to Oldfeld, where she was shown round everything, including the farm, by two children slightly older, one a girl much taller than she, the other the smaller Hickson boy. I looked out of the window to see the three children wandering with complete sang-froid among the cart-horses & ponies. The Hicksons much less stiff than last time—in fact really charming & cordial; I think they were somewhat on the defensive before, & did not want to appear to cadge for a useful pupil. They showed me the really delightful dormitory where S. is to sleep; it has only three other beds & looks away from the town to the lovely hills. Shirley was so pleased with everything that she didn't want to go back to London, & threatened to escape from us & find her way to Oldfeld.

Monday March 13th   London

Weather changed; lovely sunny morning; at last saw Swanage as it must usually be. Took S. for a short run on the beach before breakfast; she tripped happily along the sand in the sunshine, loving everything. We returned home directly after breakfast; got back in time for lunch. S. very good; I thought with thankfulness how little I have ever had to punish or think of punishing either of the children.

Finished *Mandoa*; made various notes on it; straightened up at home.

Now, I hope, no more nights out of London till most of my book is done.

Tuesday March 14th
Reading *Truth Is Not Sober*.

Took Shirley in afternoon to see Mr Denis Browne abt her tonsils operation. Said the need not "catastrophic" but she was too pale, & dark under the eyes; her general condition was consistent with constant slight poisoning. Arranged for her to be done at Tite Street, not Great Ormond Street, on April 5. She was v. good & lively—not at all nervous. Bought her a little leather horse from Abbott's which she fingered lovingly; promised her she could have it the day she went into hospital & she at once began to look forward to that.

Czech reports looking grave. Premiers of both Czechoslovakia & Slovakia itself gone to see Hitler.

Wednesday March 15th
Grave news; Hitler proclaimed "protectorate" over Bohemia, Moravia & Slovakia, & destroyed the country & the Munich settlement. Hacha, the premier, compelled to give in under threat of bombardment of Prague. All Europe boiling again. No knowing where it will end. Called G. to know his immediate movements.

Spent most of day telephoning to Home Office, Miss Ashberry, etc., to see whether anything could still be done for Dr Schreiber.

Tea with Edith to get various facts for biography—but concentration again very difficult.

Thursday March 16th
Hitler's troops marched into Prague yesterday & took possession; he himself followed to-day. Moravia occupied & protectorate declared over Slovakia. Chaos in Central Europe. Same old method of taking over by force & of striking suddenly just when internat. sky appeared to be clearing. Rang up again about Dr Schreiber; learnt that 6,000 refugees, all with their papers in order to come here, are unable to get out of Czechoslovakia; all air-ports in hands of Nazis. Brit. Consulate in Prague has had to close owing to pressure of people wanting to escape. Margaret S.J. rang up from P.E.N. & confirmed this.

In evening went to Brighton for a P.P.U. meeting to speak with Lord Ponsonby at the Dome. Both dined beforehand with the charming chairman, Dr Crow. Felt rather scared all day in the internat. circumstances. I expected a rough house—but Dome was full of apparently sympathetic people & questions afterwards were very sensible. Ponsonby made a *magnificent* speech—the best intellectual exposition of the pacifist case I have ever heard, & I listened as intently as the audience. Both of us got a grand reception. Got back to London at 11.25; v. tired. Cable from G. saying Washington till 23rd; then returning on *Bremen*.

Friday March 17th

Morning papers all raging about Hitler; rumours of further "swoops" in Eastern Europe; Tory M.P.s said to be discontented with Chamberlain; everyone restless.

Went as guest of honour to 21st anniversary of women's suffrage luncheon given at the Criterion by the Nat. Council of Equal Citizenship. Miss Picton-Turbervill in Chair; Eleanor Rathbone chief speaker; short "messages" given by Philippa Fawcett, Mrs Hubback, Edith Summer-skill, Dr Maude Royden. This part broadcast. I spoke after the broadcast; also Mrs Corbett Ashby & Mrs Pethick-Lawrence. Mrs Corbett Ashby told me that one of the 5,000 arrested by the Gestapo in Prague is almost certainly Senator Plaminkova, the Czech woman political leader who showed me round Prague in 1924 & whom G. met last summer. What a bloody world.

Heard Chamberlain's speech at the Town Hall, Birmingham, broadcast to-night. First part an explanation of Munich policy & extenuation; second part a condemnation of Hitler for his latest coup; third part a definite warning to him that if he tries to dominate the world by force England will defend her freedom by arms. Seems odd that anyone supposed she would have any freedom if war came again.

Saturday March 18th

Another day of intense anxiety. Rumours printed headline size in papers about Hitler's march eastwards & alleged ultimatum to Romania about her economic resources. Meditated cabling G. not to return on *Bremen*.

In evening meeting at Queen's Hall to celebrate the obtaining of 1,062,000 signatures to the Nat. petition for a new Peace Conf. Alas, both the celebration & the deputation to present the Petition to Chamberlain on Monday have been spoiled of what would have been their overwhelming effect by Hitler's latest coup, but meeting was packed & we all took view that situation rendered immediate calling of a conference not less but more urgent as a last-minute possibility of saving Europe. The Bishop of Chichester in the chair read a friendly message to the German *people* wh. the B.B.C. promised to try to broadcast on the foreign wave-length. Speakers were, in this order, C. E. M. Joad, myself, H. G. Elvin, Miss Tanner the Headmistress of Roedean, & George Lansbury. Was congratu-lated on my speech (made on behalf of the writers supporting petition) by the Chairman, Lansbury (who sat next me) & Nevinson, who was on the platform. The Fleet Street choir sang exquisitely between the speeches, & we finished up with "Jerusalem", the more moving bec. of the situation.

Sunday March 19th
News still much the same. Papers full of repercussions after Chamberlain's speech—approval in democracies, fury in Berlin. Denial in both Berlin & Bucharest that any ultimatum, or anything more than trade negotiations, was presented to Romania. Exceedingly gloomy article in *Observer* by Garvin entitled "The Truth"—all the old 1914 stuff about German militarism run rampant & it being our duty to withstand it. All the Press tumbling over itself with self-righteousness, as though no power but Germany had ever broken its word before, & we ourselves had never invaded anybody. *Sunday Express*—enjoying a complete switch-over from its peace-at-any-price policy of the past three months—publishes a picture of a steaming battleship & announces a series of forthcoming articles on Britain's Glory. *Plus ça change plus que c'est la même chose*—alas, alas! If only G. was here or Winifred was alive to join in with the wry faces I am making alone.

Managed to make myself do final preparations for biography by allocating notes to diff. files. Took Shirley to tea Edwardes Square; discussed the possibilities of Lesser House at Woking as refuge for children these holidays if war came again.

Monday March 20th
Began to do the actual writing of Winifred's biography. Did the Introduction and started Chapter 1. Very cold & windy day.

After supper Hilda Reid & I went to Chelsea Town Hall for a Left Book Club meeting at which Victor Gollancz was to speak & Sir Stafford Cripps to explain his policy. Cripps was late, & after the Chairman—a young man called Lester Hutchison—had spoken, Gollancz had about ¾ hour. He used it to make the most terrible, emotional, irrational attack on Germany & Fascism which reminded me of recruiting meetings in 1914. It was full of all the old illusion about a War to end War, smashing German militarism & making the world safe for democracy, & he used hysterical atrocity arguments (as if Soviet Russia, Republican Spain & ourselves in Palestine committed no atrocities) quite unworthy of an intelligent person. There is an excellent case against Fascism but this hate-mongering does not strengthen it. I was horrified by the rapidity with which the audience was roused to passion. Cripps' sane, rational speech with its exposition of an economic peace policy sounded, after Gollancz, like a statement from a P.P.U. platform & the audience was quite bored! Asked a question which caused him to state categorically that he *was* prepared to negotiate with Germany.

Tuesday March 21st
Miserable interrupted day. Felt very troubled about V.G.—wondered if I should go on publishing with him. Rang up the P.P.U. (John Barclay) & suggested some ways in wh. local groups could counter this terrible

propaganda by careful questions which I drafted out & sent.

Lunched with the Geoffrey Manders. Very pleasant tho' I ran into a regular den of lions, as the other guests (all men) were Claud Cockburn of *The Week*, Frank Pakenham from Oxford, & a National Labour man whose name I didn't catch—all different politics but all equally determined to catch me up on pacifism. Though so weary of arguing I stood up to them—even Cockburn. Cockburn talked about Romania & the temp. lull in Eastern Europe & thought it just possible that war might not come for four or five months—the "real" as distinct from the "apparent" war, he said. Had to walk home via Embankment bec. of President Lebrun's arrival at Victoria.

Hilda came to tea & we talked over the Gollancz matter; she was against penalising him for his political views & I decided I was too deeply committed over the biog. & his kindness abt it to do anything at present. Proofs of *Take Back Your Freedom* arrived from Cape.

Wednesday March 22nd

Cable from G. to say that he cannot catch the *Queen Mary* without breaking his contract & that if the *Bremen* seems inadvisable he will wait for the *Aquitania*. Cabled back to ask whether in this case he wants me to go ahead with Shirley's operation in his absence.

News quietening down somewhat despite announcement of Hitler's long-expected occupation of Memel. Goering has gone back to Italy for his holiday & general idea seems to be that for at any rate this month Hitler will consolidate his gains. No more news of Romania except that trade discussions w' Germany are discontinued. But how long to wait for more developments? Nothing can settle as things are—yet even twelve hours seems a breathing-space after such continual crisis.

Aunt Lillie & Uncle Arthur came to tea to discuss arrangements if situation gets acute again & I have to take Shirley to Woking—but Heaven preserve me from being obliged to do it.

Went on writing to-day. Finished Chap. 1 of biography & made out scheme for Chapter 2.

Thursday March 23rd

Letter from Cambridge Vice-Chancellor announcing that Brogan of Corpus Christi—alas!—has been elected to Barker's chair, so G. does not get it. Bang goes £1,200 a year & the financial burden continues to rest on me. Still—no matter, if only he can get into Parliament. Cabled him, thinking he ought to know at once.

Began writing Chap. 2 of biography & did 9½ pages (about 2,000 words).

No fresh news. Hitler at Memel saying as usual that he hasn't any fresh demands to make. Read *The Week* to-night remembering that Claud Cockburn had said on Tuesday that he thought War four or five months away. But all the press talking war. A terrible article in *Evening Standard* by Viscount Castlerosse saying it doesn't matter if 1 million men are killed in war as they have to die someday anyhow. Then why should they or any of us be born? As terrible as Duff Cooper's letter in yesterday's *Times*, saying that if we hadn't crushed Germany to the earth in 1919, she would have made the present demands on Europe all the sooner—as though the 1919 German Govt were not a decent non-military democracy wh. we ought to have supported at all costs.

Miss Ashberry rang up—all Dr Schreiber's permits now through—she had a letter from her.

Friday March 24th
Letter from G.; has various lectures at Columbia, Syracuse, Duke Univ. N.C., which please him. Spent most of morning answering mail, writing to M.S.J. and drafting a letter against "hate-mongering" for the *New Statesman*. Mentions Duff Cooper, Castlerosse, & Gollancz's Chelsea speech, though without using his name.

Took Shirley to Barker's this afternoon & got all her equipment for Oldfeld for £15/8/11, which was less than I expected. She talked unceasingly about every object bought.

Got back for late tea, when William Hillman rang up; said he returned from Rome about 4 days ago. We discussed the international situation; he said he gave it about 3 months before War if things went on looking as they do now; that Hitler would probably keep quiet for a while if the trade agreement with Romania gave him all the oil he wanted—but if not Germans & Hungarians would foment discontent as in Czechoslovakia & Hitler would then march in. This would probably start the trouble; if not, he might suddenly strike west at Denmark & then it would begin. H. said Hitler had made his first fatal mistake by annexing Czechoslovakia & now knew it—& that Goering had been violently opposed to doing it.

Saturday March 25th
Wasted sort of day. Spent morning running round—quarter day, housekeeping day, so had to visit Bank; then to find shop where I could get some decent fruit for Margaret de C., who has chicken-pox, & Hilda, who has 'flu! Wrote a bit in the afternoon, but can never get on in afternoons. Then had to go to a late tea (5.0) with the travelling section of the Hockaday School under Miss Jameson at Athenaeum Court. Charming *chic* girls —eight of them, & as different from English college girls of that age as anyone could imagine. Two young men (met at St Moritz) with them, & a gramophone playing. Nothing *gauche*, hoydenish or unsophisticated. If only the world lasts, I feel all the more determined to send Shirley there before Oxford. They were all pleased with themselves at having engineered a European tour between two crises, but as they are not due to start back

for a month, wonder a little if they will return without impediment or alarm.

It is now after midnight & all day I have only written 2½ pp. Somehow I can't go to bed in these days of crisis—hate my lonely room & dread waking up to the shock of the present world, as in the War.

Sunday March 26th

Sunday papers full of depressing news; talk of conscription, of Poland mobilising one million men, of possibility that Mussolini's speech might intensify the crisis. Garvin, having executed a complete *volte-face* on Germany & Russia, now quoting *Mein Kampf* & fulminating about the necessity of "counterforce". Lunched with the Lovat Dicksons; met there Von Rintelen, the German—now an anti-Nazi living in England & a lecturer to schools & others—who was a spy during the War & put on board the *Lusitania* the time-exploding cigar boxes wh. wrecked the ship. L.D. said that if Mussolini's speech was aggressive he would send his wife & baby to her mother in Montreal.

Arrived late for tea at Edwardes Square. Went from there to Mr Howard Lewis's picture show at his studio; saw Mother's portrait & thought it excellent. Asked him to do me one of Winifred from various photographs wh. I gave him—to be reproduced in my biography. Met Angela Thirkell there; also Mrs Jarman & the Hockaday girls again. At 6.30 & again at 8.45 listened to the broadcast reports of Mussolini's speech; it sounded aggressive enough to me, but the announcer said it was regarded as very moderate in Germany & in France as not materially changing the position.

Monday March 27th

According to this morning's papers, Mussolini's speech seems to be regarded as "moderate" and liable, if anything, to relieve tension a little, but the N.Y. *Herald-Tribune* is quoted as reminding its readers that Hitler made a "moderate" speech shortly before marching into Czechoslovakia.

Worked nearly all day at Chapter 2 of biography, wrote 14 pp. and finished it. Have done 45 pp. in a week.

At 6 o'clock went to a Committee of Friends of Africa at the H. of Commons; Creech Jones in the Chair, Julius Lewin, Carol Johnson and a Jamaican negro called Lewis there besides myself. Before the meeting, Creech Jones promised to send me the Ballinger material, which he is revising very soon. Julius Lewin is leaving in 10 days for a three years' University job in S. Africa and will definitely see about the founding of a Memorial Library to Winifred in Johannesburg.

Letter from G. this morning. Though written on March 15th, he took the international situation very calmly and couldn't think why I asked him to cable his immediate plans!

Tuesday March 28th
Worked all day at Chap. 3 of the biography (Winifred's schooldays, for which I had immense masses of material to handle). By working steadily from 11 a.m. till midnight & only leaving my desk for an hour or two, I got it into shape by the end of the day and wrote five pages.

News of the crisis still indeterminate except for much talk of "compulsion", so I suppose G. will sail by the *Bremen* to-night. K.N.E. took Shirley to see Miss Mayo, who says her teeth are perfect & the new ones coming well. K.N.E. gave her a large ice-cream & a cake on the way home, & they amused themselves going down Piccadilly by counting horses. Shirley got seventeen & apparently won.

Wednesday March 29th
Last night about 1 a.m. I was lying half-asleep in my bath when suddenly I heard a dull roar so reminiscent of air-raid bombs that I was wide awake in a second thinking confusedly: "Heavens, can Hitler be bombing us already—I'd better get some clothes on." Then, more rationally, I listened for the fire-engines, etc., which would immediately follow a raid, & heard nothing. No other noise occurred & I concluded that a car in the street must have back-fired, though it hadn't sounded like that. This morning I read that, through a new I.R.A. outrage, part of Hammersmith Bridge had been blown up by a bomb, & learnt later that only the presence of mind of a man crossing the bridge—who saw a second bomb in a suitcase & threw it into the river where it exploded—prevented it from being blown up. It happened at 1 a.m. & this must have been the sound I heard, travelling down, in the silence of the night.

Worked at Chap. 3 all day at intervals. Had Dr Schreiber & Miss Ashberry to tea. Dr S. a charming woman; glad I helped to rescue her. She goes soon to work as a maternity nurse at Woolwich Hospital under the National Midwives scheme with which Ruth Fry is associated. As yet she knows little English, but I mustered all the German I could. She seemed in very good spirits considering her experiences in Prague—which I gathered were potentially rather than actually terrible. I found her more grateful to me than I really deserved for what I did & was constantly addressed as "Gnädige Frau".

After supper went along to the P.P.U. "consultation" meeting at Kingsway Hall—expected a small group meeting in a side room, but found instead the big Hall filled with all the group leaders who could get there, anxious for guidance—Lansbury, Morris, Donald Soper, Plowman, Mumford and I, all tried to give it—& in doing so I became more conscious than ever of my job to stay here & help to maintain & organise all the sanity that remains.

Thursday March 30th
Morning news of Daladier's speech answering, with new defiance, Musso-

lini's speech, so disturbed me that I could think of nothing but war prospects all day, and by way of reply to the reflection provoked by a letter from G. this morning, spent the time till lunch drafting a kind of moral "credo" & my reasons for remaining here to face the music. Did a little shopping at Harrods & struggled w' Chapter 3.

Friday March 31st

Chamberlain announced in the H. of Commons this afternoon a British guarantee of Polish "independence" (whatever precisely that is) which seems as liable to cause the loss of millions of lives as the similar guarantee of Belgian neutrality which brought us to the War of 1914.

Met John at Paddington this morning. The train was about ¼ hour late & I talked to Doreen & Jeffrey Marston & their six-year-old boy while waiting. John & Adrian Marston arrived together. J. looked rather taller & much broader; he said he had put on abt 6 lbs this term. He was very tired this evening from the early start & heavier air.

Took Shirley to be overhauled by Dr Yates—she was in very good condition except for the gland trouble from her tonsils. He reaffirmed that she would be better without them, tho' he said the operation could be postponed if the situation was looking very grim after G. returned. She was very lively & to-day brought back from school her *excellent* report—only 6 marks lost on a total of 250, & full marks for many subjects. Even Arithmetic was good.

Finished Chap. 3 to-night. Went to bed very late & for abt 20 mins watched 5 people standing on the Embankment, very still, & wondered if I should ring police but decided they were drunks.

Saturday April 1st

Took John & Shirley to the Franklins' house to see the Boat Race—we watched from their drawing-room balcony. On lower Mall, they are only some four or five houses from the Bridge, & showed us a picture of their smashed windows on Wednesday morning. They said they thought they were killed when the explosion came. The Bridge was boarded up where the explosion was, & closed to traffic; pedestrians were only allowed across in large groups accompanied by policemen. Half a dozen policemen remained on it during the race. Cambridge won easily & were obviously the better crew; they were well in front of Oxford when they passed us less than half-way through the course. It was a very calm, misty day, with smooth water & little wind. Got the children home again quite early. Cicely Hamilton was with us on the Franklins' balcony.

After lunch took children round to Hilda & got gas-masks for them, as she was so insistent they should have them *before* the crisis got worse. I took one too as Shirley seemed so alarmed at the idea of my being without. A.R.P. Wardens came this morning in my absence & measured the basement. To-night Hitler's Wilhelmshaven speech (launching of *Von*

Tirpitz battleship) was reported on the wireless but there was nothing sensational in it & he did not mention Poland.

Sunday April 2nd

Worked all day organising Chapter 4 (the War); wrote about three pages of it. Took Shirley & John to tea with Mother.

Cavalcade has a headline "Cris-isteria". Another Sunday paper had a poster "That Bore Hitler". Garvin in the *Observer* had a huge recruiting article entitled "The Great Call" & side by side with it a leader maintaining in the *same* column: 1) that "encirclement" was the miracle which defeated Germany in the Great War since no less than six nations were actively responsible for defeating her; 2) that the German fear of encirclement is hysterical, senseless and unfounded! How truly wonderful some of our editors are! But the *Sunday Chronicle* did print last week my denial that the inflamed paragraphs attributed to me in their "We Have Been Warned" extracts were in fact mine!

Monday April 3rd

John & I went down to Southampton to meet Gordon from the *Bremen*. Arrived at 12.0 & found that the tender would not arrive at the new docks till about 3.30—so had a mouldy lunch at a café & put in time at a cinema. It was a miserable, wet day not fit to walk about in. We got to the new docks at 3.15 & saw the tender already coming up the river—though someone told us it wasn't the *Bremen* tender as the red & green flag hadn't gone up on the jetty, & we weren't taking any particular interest in it till John suddenly saw Gordon standing on it & shouted "There's Daddy!" I was profoundly thankful to see him again, & that war hadn't come with the Atlantic still between us.

Only 35 people were on the tender, of varying nationalities—German, Japanese, etc. Very few English. G. said the *Bremen* was practically empty, with only 48 First Class passengers (among them Jean Monnet, the French financier & L. of N. man). *But* all the Germans on board had expressed an anxious concern for peace. Some Czechs with German passports bitterly resented this, but were dancing with the Germans before the end of the voyage. When we got the boat-train (with "Norddeutscher Lloyd" outside the carriages), people in the stations we passed through stared hostilely at us as though we (practically all English) were a collection of German spies, but a very nice porter at Waterloo, when G. remarked how peaceful the Germans had been in the boat, said: "I'm thankful to hear it, sir! What do we want to fight each other for? There's been no business in this station since the crisis—nobody travelling."

G. & I finished up the evening by dining at Athenaeum Court, & going on for a drink to the Berkeley Buttery—where Gordon-Lennox told us Chamberlain was now really roused.

Tuesday April 4th

Rang up Dr Yates & Mr Denis Browne to confirm Shirley's operation to-morrow. Worked on largish correspondence in morning. In response to two pamphlets, sent Percy Bartlett 3 gns for Embassies of Reconciliation, & offered to go on one if they ever wanted it written up.

Between heavy April showers G. & I took dear Baba to the children's nursing home attached to Victoria Hospital, Tite Street. She was very brave & good; marched in cheerfully, armed with Gordon's "Ferdinand" & the little horse I gave her. She had been excited all day & seemed quite unafraid, but asked Amy if *she* was nervous about her operation. The pleasant Sister whom I saw the other day received us, & Shirley was given the bed next to Adam Currie, who goes out to-morrow. She was taken off to the bathroom to be weighed & was almost too interested in the pleasant ward & the newness of everything to kiss us good night. We arranged to wait at home in the morning & let Dr Yates telephone us about the operation, as we are so near.

After dinner wrote about Winifred & Harry in Chapter 4.

Wednesday April 5th

Poppy had her tonsils [operation], at 9.0 this morning. We seemed to wait ages to hear, and finally just before 10.0 G. rang up the hospital to find that it had been successfully over twenty minutes earlier. Dr Yates rang up immediately after; he had tried before but couldn't get on because Edith & Mother were telephoning me. He said that her tonsils were much bigger than Mr Browne expected—also she had adenoids as well, & should be much better now they are all gone. They asked us not to go round till 6.0 as she would be under the anaesthetic, and when we did go she was still fast asleep—a little flushed & frowning a bit but otherwise quite placid. The Sister said she had been astonishingly good—she had woken up once or twice and talked, but made no fuss at all and wasn't sick. Adam, next door, said she had been asleep practically all day.

The peace & convenience of having all done in hospital is quite unbelievable after the fuss I remember over John.

Mother dropped in to tea; she had been to take flowers to Aunt Florence's grave. Wrote 8½ more pp. of Chapter 4 in spite of gloom of international situation. A fuss in the evening papers about a speech by Lord Stanley.

Thursday April 6th

Went in at 10 a.m. to see Poppy & found her reading. She looked reproachful, wouldn't smile at us & was able to talk very little, but Denis Browne—who came in when we were there—said she was doing very well—& she herself said it didn't hurt much. She looked very large-eyed & pretty, & not too pale.

International rumours still filling the air. Lord Stanley in his speech said to have remarked that, just before he began, it "became necessary to man the anti-aircraft guns of the Fleet" (presumably in response to a threat to bomb it by Germany). Hence all the fuss. German papers sarcastically wondering whether Lord Stanley was expecting the Martians to descend on the earth.

Ultimatum said to have been sent to Albania by Italy; evening papers announced that Italians were leaving Albania.

Interrupted day owing to visits to Poppy & reading to her; also getting her the various things she wanted. Took her ice-cream, grapes, book & papers. She played the invalid grandly & took it all as her due!

Friday April 7th
Very cold. A little sunshine early, but it soon went. Found Shirley paler but more lively. Dr Hamilton came to see her this morning; also Mr Browne. Then Mother came, with her Easter chicken & a little bunch of primulas from the garden; then Amy later. Dr Hamilton seemed surprised when I said she was going to boarding school & remarked: "What—so soon?" But when I said that London just now was no place for a child he agreed —especially, he said, in the case of a child like Shirley, who knew & noticed too much. This afternoon I saw her again & she really could talk quite well, but did not because a little tired. John played almost all day with Oliver Evans-Palmer, who came to lunch.

The day seemed very calm & peaceful with its lack of letters, newspapers, and rumours—until we learnt from the six o'clock news that Italy had invaded Albania & was meeting with resistance—one day after the birth of a son to the Albanian Queen. Is this the alternative to pressure on France over Tunis & Djibouti?

Saturday April 8th
Albania occupied, ports & capital bombed, young Queen & 3-day-old son hurried for 14 hours over mountain roads into Greek territory. King later yielded to force & joined her the following day. What a *grand* victory for Mussolini! Rumours flying round about further trouble in Balkans, Ministers back in London, Premier returning from Scotland to-morrow—so we go on! Denis Browne, whom I met outside the hospital when I was coming back from seeing Shirley, remarked that it reminded him of the nursery saying "The better the day, the [worse] the deed."

Lovely morning. Remained sunny all day. Shirley recovering so quickly that she was allowed to dress & go out in the hospital garden into the sun for a while. Reading at an enormous rate & was presented to-day with no less than 15 comics.

Did another small section of Chapter 4. If only this tension would cease I could get the whole book done so quickly.

Sunday April 9th

Lovely day, but international tension appalling & papers full of alarmist reports. Gordon rang up Hillman, who said the Albanian invasion is probably a "blind" to distract attention; that Germany will probably walk into Holland, Denmark or Poland before the end of the week, that in a few days we shall be in the pre-ultimatum period, & probably have a crisis similar to the Sept. one in ten days or so. So G. & I decided to take the children to Bournemouth & keep them there for the rest of the holidays, directly Shirley comes out of the hospital. Rang up & booked rooms at the Crag Head Hotel recommended by William Kean Seymour. Whether war comes or not, London is not a fit place for J. & S. just now. Discussed matter over tea with Mother & agreed to go to her for week-end when I attend the P.P.U. Ann. Gen. Conf. unless war is actually upon us. Wrote Storm Jameson about Hillman's information as she intended to go to Paris on Tuesday. Urged Mother to go straight to Woking & then on to Bournemouth if tension increases.

Monday April 10th

Morning papers contained further news about the Albanian occupation & talk of a guarantee pact to be given by us to Greece and the possible fortification of Corfu by ourselves. Posters announced "Parliament Recalled". Later news said this was to be on Thursday, for one day, to discuss the proposed Greek pact.

London deserted. Loveliest Easter for about 12 years. Long hours of sunshine; temp. nearly 70. Spent most of the day packing my most important diaries & papers, to get them out of London & if necessary keep them there; also a largish selection of clothes for various weathers. If necessary could store them all somewhere in the country & run up & down to London myself. The beauty of the day made all the war rumours so incongruous. Rumours as usual flew round—Germany going to attack Poland, or Holland (both are mobilised), or in the long run Romania; Italy going to move from Albania to Jugo-slavia, to Greece, to French Africa, to the French frontier of the Pyrenees; Franco said to be contemplating ultimatum to us about Gibraltar—so it goes on.

Definitely heard to-day from Denis Browne via Sister that S. can leave hospital to-morrow. Mother came to tea. After supper we went over to Kean Seymours for port & conversation. Philip v. flourishing.

Tuesday April 11th   Bournemouth

V. busy morning with packing, letters, going through 1935 *T. & T.*s, etc. Work much impeded as K.N.E. didn't come through her nurse being ill—so had to do all secretarial work for myself. Lovely day again—temp. over 70°. Picked up Shirley from the hospital at 2.0 & presented nurses with chocolates. Took the family to Bournemouth by the 3.30 train. Stayed at the Crag Head Hotel recommended by the Kean Seymours. It was everything they said—a perfectly lovely garden belonging to an old manor house running right to the edge of the East Cliff edge. Good food & lovely flowers everywhere. We had the best bedroom in the hotel, with private bath, as it was the only one vacant—but fortunately the cost was offset by that of tiny rooms given to the children. Shirley was *very* good on the train, but was tired when she got here & cried a little (pretending it was because I "treated her soft"). She soon recovered & I put her to bed immediately we got our rooms.

Internat. situation still tense. I looked at the Embankment in the sunshine and wondered if War would break out while I was away & it would still look as lovely & peaceful when I returned. Train full of soldiers & very crowded.

Wednesday April 12th

Another beautiful day; woke up to see the sun streaming on the sea & the lovely garden. Shirley had her breakfast in bed but got up in great spirits; the last deterrent to perfect health having been removed, she seems more irrepressible than ever. Unpacked for the children & took her out later, while G. visited house-agents; she tore strenuously round the garden & up & down the cliff roads outside & was not to be deterred. In the afternoon one of the house-agents motored us round to see various small houses for sale in the Parkestone–Lilliput–Poole neighbourhood; two close to Poole Harbour with woodland gardens were very attractive, espec. one with views of the sea.

Rumours of new German demands on Poland in the newspapers but the wireless denied them & said that the German propaganda against Poland has been called off.

Sent Denis Browne cheque for 20 guineas for Shirley's operation. She & John went with us to the houses—she climbed a gate & tore her skirt, raced round the gardens of all the houses we saw & kept G. amused in the car by telling Cockney stories in excellent imitation of both tone & accent.

Thursday April 13th

G. left by morning train & went up to town. Day turned very wet; children played for most of it in downstairs playroom with draughts & dominoes that I bought for them. Faith Moulson came to tea; approved cottage idea; gave various hints about districts. Got through no work, as usual when quite alone with children.

Evening papers contained Chamberlain's speech to Parlt to-day. Mussolini's invasion of Albania condemned but Anglo-Italian agreement not broken. Pacts to be given to Romania & Greece. More encirclement.

Friday April 14th

S. had nightmare in middle of last night about an air-raid on Cheyne Walk & a "headless body" falling into the nursery when she was sleeping. She was sweating & shivering with fear, poor little soul. Took her into my room for rest of night.

Day started wet but cleared up—shopped a little in morning with children & wrote letters. At lunch-time K.N.E. rang up with message from John Barclay that Gollancz "categorically denied" my *New Statesman* account of the Left Book Club meeting—& was there anyone to corroborate it? Told her to get in touch w' Hilda Reid. After tea took children for long seashore walk as far as The Square, where I bought a *New Statesman* at Smith's. Found as I expected that V.G. had summarised his speech in a manner quite different from the effect it made on the audience, but—what I didn't expect—that his letter ended with a sneer about our American trip of last September (justifiable comment, if true facts unknown, but caddish & quite irrelevant). Raises whole question of future publications. Spent evening drafting a reply.

Saturday April 15th
G. returned at lunch-time. Went up to London by afternoon train for P.P.U. Annual General Meeting. Had tea at home, discussed letter to *New Statesman* with Hilda who came along, & dictated it to K.N.E. Hilda drove me to Friends' House & I attended the 6.30 P.P.U. session (chiefly discussion of constitution) till nearly 11.0, when Stuart Morris got hold of an evening paper & announced from the chair that Roosevelt had called an international conference, & invited the Dictators to refrain from aggression & get economic benefits in return. Hopes ran high & I took the bus to Kensington to spend the night with Mother in a state of elation, feeling that our troubles were over.

Sunday April 16th
Morning papers announced Roosevelt invitation unlikely to be accepted by Dictators. Evening, exhilaration departed.

Attended P.P.U. Annual General meetings all day. Much talk, little said. Back to Bournemouth by late evening train; G. met me at Central Station.

Monday April 17th
Taken round by Ormiston's Mr Link to see more country properties. Saw cottages at Highcliffe-on-Sea & Midford; neither suitable. Finally he ran us over to Lyndhurst to see one further property though it was outside the area—Allum Green Cottage, on the edge of a large estate, Allum Green House, & probably once its game-keeper's cottage. Owned by owner of large house, Mrs Drury-Lowe, cousin of the Admiral with whom I used to work at the L.N.U. We loved it at once; glorious position, right on edge of forest, 200 yards from main road up private path, with 20 miles of unspoiled country at its front door & a tiny but sufficient cottage garden at the back. Rather primitive, would need doing up, but quite spacious;

7 little rooms, kitchen, scullery, bathroom, lavatory, & lounge hall. We asked at once for the first refusal.

Wednesday April 19th

Walked along the sea-shore with the children to Bournemouth Square. Visited Ormiston & Knight's office to say we definitely preferred Allum Green Cottage to anything else, & learnt that other people were after it—but that Mrs Drury-Lowe very much preferred us & hoped we should take it. Ormiston got hold of Hopkins the surveyor and decorator, & went over his report. Found nothing wrong, but various things such as pumps & kitchen ranges would need modernising, involving the expenditure of about £75 apart from furnishing & the decorations. So I made an offer of £1,125 instead of the £1,200 she asked. He rang her up & she accepted immediately—so I made an appointment with the decorator to go over on Friday afternoon.

Spent afternoon on the beach with the children & after tea in the garden, starting my article for the Fellowship of Reconciliation. Lovely day.

Nice letter from Harold Macmillan this morning, saying that he had read the author–publisher controversy in the *New Statesman* with some surprise & asked me to meet him & talk things over when I am next in town.

Thursday April 20th

One of the most marvellous spring days I have ever known, as hot as summer. Spent whole day on the beach with children; except for lunch we were there from 10.30 to 6.30. We took our tea down there & I wrote an article on "From War to Pacifism" for the Fellowship of Reconciliation while they played. Misty blue sea, cloudless sky & brilliant sun, as hot as the Riviera. Great activity of bombing & fighting aeroplanes overhead; the children were excited, wondering if they were looking for the German fleet which is on its way to Spain.

G. telegraphed in the evening that he was seeing Harold Macmillan to-morrow morning, & would be here in the afternoon. Telephoned him to go to Brockenhurst & meet us there.

Pleasant letter from Eric Gillett this morning, saying his firm was on good terms with Macmillan & arrangements might be possible.

Thursday April 27th

Mother arrived by midday train for week-end to see cottage & help me furnish it.

Shirley went to school; looked a darling in her navy & white uniform. She joined the carriage of London girls at Bournemouth. Complete sang-froid and no tears. She was immediately captivated by a white wire-haired terrier belonging to the mistress in charge of the party and hardly turned to say goodbye to us. It was we who walked home feeling forlorn!

Friday April 28th
P.c. from Poppy who already has found a girl she likes.

Went to Bournemouth in afternoon & ordered part of furniture for cottage.

Saturday April 29th
Took Mother over to see Allum Green Cottage. Cold day, bitter wind; not best type for it, but it still looked charming. Measured windows & floors for curtains & carpets. Travelled by coach; had lunch & tea in Lyndhurst. G., John & I walked the distance 3 times; Mother spent the afternoon resting in the hotel.

Monday May 1st
Spent day buying furniture for Allum Green Cottage, at Bealson's & Woolworth's.

Still no reply from V.G.

Wet & chilly.

Tuesday May 2nd   London
Returned home from Bournemouth.

Packed all morning, unpacked in evening. V. tired.

Wednesday May 3rd
John returned to school.

Walked back from Paddington with Hilda Morgan through Park as far as Kensington.

Interviewed W. Kean Seymour; got promise of Bank loan with limit of £2,000 but probably use only £1,500.

Thursday May 4th
Sorted file of 3 weeks' letters. Wrote 9 pp. of "King & Country" chapter of biography.

Friday May 5th
Biography. W.A.A.C. chapter. Was going for walk with Hilda but it rained in afternoon so went to Bank & talked with W.K.S. over insurance etc.

Long telephone call in evening from Hester Marsden-Smedley about my luncheon with Mrs Roosevelt as she is doing a write-up of her.

Phoned Lovat Dickson about the Gollancz situation & his failure to answer my letter; also asked him to inquire whether Macmillan would ever consider acquiring the English rights of *T. of Y.* Asked him & Marguerite to dinner on 19th. Sent off letter to Harold Macmillan saying that I would like to see him before doing anything further.

Saturday May 6th
More W.A.A.C. chapter. Hilda forgot about the walk postponed till to-day & came in just before dinner to say so. Read my letter to V.G. & thought it entirely courteous & deserving of a reply.

Telegram from Margaret Storm Jameson asking me to tea on Monday. Wired I could go.

Sunday May 7th
Wrote last 10 pp. of W.A.A.C. Chapter. Tea with Mother; went over the furniture, curtains, etc., that she is giving me for Allum Green Cottage.

Monday May 8th
Went to Reading to see Storm Jameson. Talked about her finances, Bill's impending marriage, weariness of writing anonymous "humour documents" in addition to her own novels; promised to help her get literary criticism.

Told her about the Gollancz affair; she agreed that my criticism was purely political & entirely justified as political comment. She thought his personal attack in reply quite monstrous. Offered to write to him & get him to break my novel contract if Harold Macmillan agrees.

We walked in the park opposite her flat after tea; lovely spring day; all the May flowers out in the meadows. Discussed as usual whether war was coming; she said that she like myself couldn't feel that it was, but this might simply be that our minds could not visualise a catastrophe of such magnitude.

Guy came in to supper; when he realised that I seriously intended leaving V.G. he congratulated me on so doing & showed signs of wanting me to go to Cape, but I told him I was committed to Macmillan. Felt the same kind of confidence in Margaret as I used to in Winifred. Is it a Yorkshire quality?

Tuesday May 9th
Worked revising five chapters of biography so that K.N.E. can do a typed copy. Walked with Hilda Reid in Kensington Gardens—lovely in first spring freshness, with feathery young leaves on all the trees.

Wednesday May 10th
Finished revising first five chapters of biography & went through two *Time & Tides* for W.'s articles. Called in at Cecil Howard Lewis's studio to see his portraits of Winifred & of Mother. Mother's is good but has caught her more apprehensive look—Winifred's seems to me really remarkable for a portrait done from photographs by an artist who has never seen the

original. It has inevitable minor faults—eyes slightly too dark, shades in hair too chestnut—but he says he can easily alter these & he gives a remarkable impression of her personality; her vitality, eagerness, intellectual alertness, & even has right the lines of her face & the crookedness of her nose. Had tea with Mother. Lovely warm day.

International news very quiet. Nowadays I suspect it when nothing special seems to be happening. Much doubt about real result of negotiations with Russia.

Thursday May 11th
Spent morning at Bank wrestling with details of loan on cottage and with solicitors who apparently imagined they were going to have a leisurely correspondence lasting several weeks & that I was going to wait all that time to start the repairs. Startled Mr Young & gingered him up by announcing that I had already begun them.

Señor Madariaga came to lunch—brilliant talk about international affairs. Said that Sir Eric Drummond (Lord Perth) was put at head of League by Brit. Govt in order to see that it never became of any importance in European affairs.

Dentist at 4.30; one front tooth stopped. Bought a cheap navy coat & hat at C. & A. of all places. No work today.

Friday May 12th
Went down to Lyndhurst for day. Country beautiful tho' not sunny & rather chilly—blossom coming out, beeches bright green. Gerald Hopkins met me at Lyndhurst Rd & we lunched together at the local hotel. Decorations going on quite well; garden in a wild tangle but white broom & purple lilac were out & white lilac coming out. It will be a joy.

Saw the local Forestry Commissioner—a charming Civil Servant, who shook hands & said he had been putting no difficulties in the way about the provision of water, etc. I also saw Mrs Drury-Lowe, who said that her title to the estate had been thoroughly investigated & was perfectly good. So I wrote my solicitors pointing out the unnecessary delay of her solicitors & urging them to go ahead.

Sent Hopkins cheque for £50 towards decorations.

P.M. announced a Pact with Turkey.

Saturday May 13th
Mr Cash rang up & said he would try to expedite the house business. Worked all day at arranging Ch. 6 of biography—but handicapped by bad headache.

Nice letter from Max Plowman who cannot come to the party next Saturday but thanks me for having it; also for remaining as a P.P.U. Sponsor in time of stress.

Dictated publicity material (replies to questions) for Colston Leigh; also wrote him about my income tax in U.S. Advance copies came of Winifred's play *Take Back Your Freedom* from Cape.

Sunday May 14th
Got Chap. 6 of biography finally arranged. Worked all morning at it. Sunny then—sat in drawing-room window—but it rained later.

Beatrice Hasburgh (the English–American music teacher who was so kind to me in Georgia & is over here on holiday) came to lunch. Tea Edwardes Square—Muriel Nicolson later. After tea we all went (G. also) to see Howard Lewis's portraits—G. agreed in thinking both good—espec. the one of Winifred, which he has improved. Muriel Nicolson came back for a few moments to look over our house—I always forget how lovely it is & the treasures it contains till I show them to someone.

Monday May 15th
Started Chap. 6 of Biography. Trying to analyse Oxford in 1919 yet make it different from "Survivors Not Wanted" in *T. of Y.* Slow difficult work.

Went with G. to a cocktail party at the Butterworths (American Embassy people). Noel Coward there but didn't speak to him. Went on to Lovat Dickson's house & had a very satisfactory talk with him about giving Macmillan my future work in England. L.D. drove me home. Pouring wet afternoon.

Wrote various letters about *Take Back Your Freedom* to dramatic critics, etc.

Wednesday May 17th
Work, but a tea-party here (Mrs Maurice Guinness, Marsden-Smedleys, Mrs Polson—met at Butterworths—& all arranged by G. for a certain Mrs Stromenger who wired to say she couldn't come after we'd started) a great interruption. Kept me from book from 3.30 till 7.0, though in itself pleasant enough.

Thursday May 18th
Work. Chapter 6 moving forward a little at last. Sent publicity material (replies to questions) to Colston Leigh. News in *Herald* that Ronald Gurner (headmaster of Whitgift, author of *The Day Boy* & once an admirer of Winifred's) has committed suicide. *Evening Standard* reported it as due to money troubles. Pathetic end to distinguished career.

About 100 so far coming to P.P.U. party.

Friday May 19th
Work. Gave small dinner-party just before Fred Howard Lewis brought Winifred's picture—quite perfect, I thought, except that hair needed to be very slightly warmer in tone. It had all her personality—vitality, intentness, humour.

Lovat Dickson came early to talk business & was charming. Greatly admired Winifred's portrait & suggested that Macmillan should reproduce it in colour. Other guests were Susan Lawrence, Mr & Mrs Hutchinson of the Home Office, & the Vyvyan Adams' (he in a bad temper & quarrelsome; she charming).

Saturday May 20th

P.P.U. Council in afternoon on ground-floor room of Dick Sheppard House. Large contingent from provinces added to many of original Sponsors. Sat beside Sybil Morrison.

Gave second large P.P.U. party here in evening—even bigger than first. Must have had nearly 200 guests—Canon Morris received them with me. Members of the Council who came included Dr Alfred Salter, John Barclay, Andrew Stewart, Maurice Rowntree, Sybil Morrison, Mary Gamble. The Howard Lewises came—also Mother, Edith de C. & Mary Dimishky, & Hilda Reid. Winifred's portrait was greatly admired.

House looked lovely—we had drawing-room windows open & many of the guests stood on the verandahs & looked at view over river. Guests this time mostly Group Leaders from North of Thames. Put Thomas Large of Newcastle up for the night.

Sunday May 21st

Recovering from party. Thomas Large left after breakfast. Work. Tea Edwardes Square.

Monday May 22nd

Work. Lovely hot day. Draft contract arrived for Allum Green Cottage; signed & sent it back.

Tuesday May 23rd

Another lovely day. Went for first time to Macmillan's magnificent office in St Martin's Street. Received with great courtesy—talked business for an hour with Harold Macmillan—who didn't keep me waiting at all!—& signed contract for the biography before I left. Saw Lovat Dickson for a few minutes afterwards & went into Dan Macmillan's office for a second to shake hands. Harold Macmillan said he would approach Gollancz himself about announcement to trade. Wrote to George Brett, Harold Latham & Hugh Eayrs in afternoon announcing move to Macmillan.

Wednesday May 24th

Work. Finished Chapter 7 & started revising.

Lunched at Café Royal to help G. talk to Mr Ragg of Routledge.

Got back just in time to discuss W.'s portrait with Macmillan's art director, who came to see it. He agreed it was good & should be reproduced in colour.

Friday May 26th
Work. Finishing revising last two chapters.

Saturday May 27th
Work. Arranging Chap. 8. Lovely day.

Sunday May 28th
Finishing arranging Chapter 8. Lovely Whit-weekend; never saw London more beautiful. Odette Keun came to lunch. Ecstatic about her new lover & our house!

Monday May 29th
Packing up all day for Allum Green. Another perfect day. Finished up note-taking, etc., for work to go down to cottage. Mother came over for a few minutes after tea.

Tuesday May 30th   Allum Green Cottage, Lyndhurst
Macmillan's photographer came at 10.0 & took W.'s portrait away. Directly after breakfast G. left to go to Southport for the Labour Confer-ence, & Amy & Burnett started off for Lyndhurst in a hired car with provisions & their own belongings. I left myself by the 12.30 train & found to my annoyance that I had to change at Southampton, where there were no porters & everything still chaos from the Whitsun holiday. Burnett met me at Brockenhurst & I found the cottage looking *lovely* even though the garden was a jungle. The surrounding beeches were fully out, & in the garden, blooming all together, white & yellow broom, white lilac, magenta & crimson rhododendrons, lupins & cabbage roses. Everything came as ordered from Bealson's & Woolworth's, & by evening we were as straight as we could get without the things from London. Forest just heavenly; *why* have I put up with every summer in town just bec. G. doesn't like the country? Mrs Drury-Lowe gave me a cup of tea; told me the cottage was down for quite a time with a Lyndhurst agent before she gave it to Ormiston's, but such awful people came after it that she always found an excuse for not selling & was thankful when we came after it to let us have it for less than the full amount.

Heavenly cottage, heavenly spot! At least *Testament of Youth* has given me this!

Monday July 31st
Telegram came about midday from Edith to say that Mrs Holtby had died in her sleep early that morning.

Worked all day and finished revising "Testament of Friendship", re-writing much of the last chapter and a little of the Epilogue. Very strange that Winifred's mother should die on the actual day that I completed my biography of her when I had been working on it for three years.

Wired G. in town. Later rang Edith up & found that the funeral was on Wednesday. Then telephoned G. & we decided that we could just manage to go to it after he had met John & brought him here.

Wednesday August 2nd
Mrs Holtby's funeral at the Priory Church, Bridlington.

Wednesday August 9th
Took completed typescript of "Testament of Friendship" up to Harold Macmillan in London. Long talk with him. We discussed the possibility of war & both felt it might still be avoided.

NOTES

NOTES

(The numbers refer to text pages; "VB" and "WH" refer to Vera Brittain and Winifred Holtby. Quotations are from VB's *Testament of Youth, Honourable Estate, Thrice a Stranger, Testament of Friendship*, or *Testament of Experience*. In general, personal honours have not been noted.)

1932

Although not a complete daily record, the diary-entries for this year give a detailed picture of VB's very busy literary and social life. It was a crucial year for her: the year of frantic effort to complete *Testament of Youth*, in the midst of an intense but doomed friendship with her fellow writer from the North, Phyllis Bentley.

29   **19 Glebe Place:** In April 1930 this "tall ugly house" in Chelsea, with its "small sunny back garden, which proved to be an ideal place for writing", had become home for WH, VB, her husband G. E. G. Catlin (when he was back from his teaching-duties at Cornell University) and their two small children. The Catlins moved from there to another Chelsea address, 2 Cheyne Walk, in May 1937.

29   **Buxton:** The Derbyshire health-resort where VB grew up; she had found it claustrophobic.

29   **Phyllis Bentley:** A well-known and prolific novelist and critic (1894–1977) whose regional historical novels, especially *Inheritance* (1932), earned her international popularity and critical respect. She lived most of her life in Halifax, Yorkshire, and never married.

29   **John Edward; Shirley:** VB's son, John Brittain-Catlin, was born on 21 December 1927, and her daughter Shirley (Shirley Williams, the prominent political leader) on 27 July 1930.

29   **Rebecca and Henry; Anthony:** Rebecca West (b. Cicely Fairfield), the admired and provocative journalist, novelist, critic, feminist and political writer (1892–1983), married Henry Andrews, a banker (d. 1968), in 1930. (They first met at the Catlins': Andrews and Catlin had been contemporaries at New College, Oxford.) Anthony West (b. 1914), Rebecca West's son by H. G. Wells, became a novelist and critic, and published a biographical study of his father in 1984.

29   **G. B. Stern; Pamela Frankau:** Two prolific writers: Gladys B. Stern (1890–1973) wrote *Pantomime* (1914) at the age of twenty, and by 1932 had

published several other novels; Pamela Frankau (1908–67) published the first of her many novels, *Marriage of Harlequin*, in 1927.

29 **Winifred, blood-pressure:** In 1931, aged thirty-three, WH began to suffer seriously (with high blood-pressure, recurrent headaches and bouts of lassitude) from Bright's Disease (sclerosis of the kidneys); in November that year she had entered a London nursing home for rest, treatment and (inconclusive) medical tests.

29 **Sidmouth:** A Devon seaside resort near Exeter where VB and WH spent several holidays.

29 **St John Ervine:** An influential playwright, novelist, critic, biographer and academic, of Irish birth (1883–1971); *God's Soldier*, his biography of General Booth, founder of the Salvation Army, appeared in 1934. WH dedicated *The Astonishing Island* (1933) to him.

29 **Gordon:** In 1925 VB married (Sir) George Edward Gordon Catlin (1896 –1979), called "Gordon" in the family and usually "G." in VB's books and diary. A prominent socialist, political scientist and academic, he tried three times to become a Labour M.P. He was a Professor of Political Science at Cornell (1924–35) and McGill (1956–60) Universities, published several books including *A Study of the Principles of Politics* (1929), and was a fervent proponent of Anglo-American Union.

29 **the Mitchisons:** Naomi Mitchison (b. 1897), prominent as writer, socialist and political activist, was married to (Gilbert) Richard (Lord) Mitchison (1890–1970), barrister and Labour M.P. 1945–64.

29 **Brailsford:** (Henry) Noel Brailsford (1873–1958), an influential socialist, writer, editor and journalist; he crusaded for women's suffrage, pacifism and colonial emancipation.

29 **Clare:** Clare Leighton (b. 1900), the well-known woodcut artist and writer. Younger sister of Roland Leighton (VB's fiancé killed on the Western Front in 1915), she was a close friend of both WH and VB, and for several years lived with Noel Brailsford, before moving permanently to the United States in 1939.

30 **Vernon Bartlett:** A distinguished journalist (1894–1983), he was London director of the League of Nations Union 1922–32 and an Independent M.P. 1938–50.

30 **Joan Temple:** A playwright and actress (d. 1965), she collaborated with Henrietta Leslie in dramatising the latter's best-known novel, *Mrs Fischer's War* (1931).

30 **Henrietta Leslie; Dr Schutze:** A novelist, playwright, travel-writer and devoted internationalist, Henrietta Leslie (1881–1946) was married to Dr Harrie L. Schutze (b. 1882), an Australian-born bacteriologist.

30 **Randall:** Roy Randall, an "extremely cultured young acquaintance" of VB who had literary ambitions and died young; his tactless remark annoyed and stimulated her.

30 **Lord Cecil:** Robert Gascoyne, Viscount Cecil of Chelwood (1864–1958), worked for women's suffrage and the establishment of the League of Nations;

President of the League of Nations 1923–45, he was awarded the Nobel Peace Prize in 1937.

30 **W.I.L.:** The Women's International League for Peace and Freedom, founded during the International Women's Conference at The Hague, April 1915.

30 **L.N.U.:** Established in November 1918, the League of Nations Union evolved into the most influential anti-war organisation in Britain by the late twenties; but in the mid-thirties its leadership espoused rearmament and the policy of collective security, alienating VB and many left-wing and pacifist members.

30 **Ellen Wilkinson:** A cotton-worker's daughter (1891–1947), she was a prominent Labour M.P. (from 1924), union-organiser and feminist. In 1935 she led the Jarrow march of the unemployed, and was appointed Minister of Education by Clement Attlee in 1945.

30 **Duff Cooper:** (Alfred) Duff Cooper (1st Viscount Norwich), the eminent statesman and historian (1890–1954); he was Secretary of State for War 1935–37, First Lord of the Admiralty 1937–38, and Minister of Information 1940–41. His wife was the beautiful Lady Diana Cooper.

30 **C. E. M. Joad; Shaw:** Joad, a well-known moral philosopher, writer and broadcaster (1891–1953), and George Bernard Shaw, the famous playwright, critic and controversialist (1856–1950), both vociferously supported liberal social reform.

30 **reception for G.:** Catlin stood unsuccessfully as Labour candidate for Brentford and Chiswick, London, in the 1931 General Election; in January 1932 he was returning to Cornell to resume his teaching duties.

31 **Basil Blackwell:** The Oxford publisher and bookseller (1889–1984). As a keen undergraduate journalist at Oxford in 1920, VB had got to know him quite well, and co-edited *Oxford Poetry* that year on his invitation.

31 **Horrabin:** Frank Horrabin (1884–1962) was an artist, cartoonist and lecturer; a Labour M.P. 1929–31, he helped to set up the Fabian Colonial Bureau.

31 **Marie Stopes:** The famous pioneering advocate of birth-control and sexual reform (1881–1958); her Mothers' Clinic for Constructive Birth Control (C.B.C.) in London (founded in 1918) was the first in the world.

31 **Paul Bloomfield:** A writer, lecturer and critic (b. 1898), he published studies of Disraeli, William Morris and the Bloomsbury Group.

31 **Monks Risborough:** A village in the Chilterns where Clare Leighton and Noel Brailsford were living; they invited WH to convalesce in a cottage near them.

32 **Monica Whately:** A socialist and feminist, she was an unsuccessful Labour candidate in the 1929 General Election (helped by VB and WH), and worked for Indian Independence in the thirties.

32 **Patrick Thompson:** He was a Director of *Time and Tide*.

32 **Aunt Florence:** Eldest sister of VB's mother, Florence Bervon ("Aunt F.")

was VB's godmother and Co-Principal (1904–31) of St Monica's, Kingswood, the school VB attended as a boarder from the age of thirteen. She died in 1936.

33 **C. K. Webster; Morgan Jones:** Charles Webster (1886–1961) was Professor of International Relations at Aberystwyth University College 1922–32, then Professor of International History at the London School of Economics; Morgan Jones (1885–1939), Labour M.P. for Caerphilly from 1921, was Chairman of the House of Commons Public Accounts Committee 1931–38.

33 **postscript to** *Goodbye to All That*: The account by Robert Graves (b. 1895), the eminent poet, novelist and critic, of antagonistic responses to his famous memoir (1929) was entitled "Postscript to *Goodbye to All That*" and printed as the first piece in his collection *But It Still Goes On* (1930).

33 *Kameradschaft*; **Pabst:** The film *Kameradschaft* ("Comradeship"), directed by Georg W. Pabst, a German film-director (1885–1967), was an anti-war work showing an upsurge of comradely feeling between French and Germans at a time of crisis.

33 **Gollancz:** Victor Gollancz, the prominent publisher, writer, socialist and humanitarian (1893–1967).

33 **Babies' Club:** The Chelsea Babies' Club, a welfare centre for subscribers, was founded in 1926, and before it closed in 1965 dispensed "scientific advice" to benefit some 3,600 children. VB strongly supported the Babies' Club and Nursery Schools Movements of the twenties and thirties, recognising that they were important contributions to the further emancipation of women and the improved health of children.

33 **Hilda Reid:** A novelist and journalist (1898–1982), she had been a contemporary of VB and WH at Somerville College, Oxford, and remained a friend; she co-edited, with VB, the posthumous collection of WH short stories, *Pavements of Anderby* (1937).

33 **Amy:** Employed as housekeeper, Amy Francis later married Charles Burnett, and they remained in the Catlin household, as servants and family friends, for most of their lives.

34 **Lady Rhondda:** Margaret Thomas, 2nd Viscountess Rhondda of Llanwern (1883–1958); she founded the feminist-oriented weekly *Time and Tide* in 1920 and the feminist Six Point Group in 1921.

34 **Helen Mayo:** She was Secretary of the feminist Six Point Group, as well as a dentist.

34 **J. B. Priestley:** The eminent and prolific man of letters (1894–1984); his novel *The Good Companions* (1929) and play *Dangerous Corner* (1932) were popular and critical successes.

34 **Obermer:** Edgar Obermer was a "German-Austrian specialist in arterial diseases" who alleviated WH's pain with drugs and so "enabled her to write *South Riding*"; in 1935 he published *Health and a Changing Civilisation*.

34 **Halls Dally:** Dr John Halls Dally (d. 1944), author of *Blood Pressure* (1931) and other books, was a leading London physician and consultant.

35 **Edward Marjoribanks:** A politician and biographer (1900–32), he published the first volume of his *Life of Lord Carson* (1932) as well as the *Life of Sir Edward Marshall-Hall* (1929).

35 *Ending in Earnest*: This was a collection of Rebecca West's critical pieces (1931).

35 *M.G.*: The *Manchester Guardian*.

35 *Clayhanger, The Mill on the Floss*: Admired regional novels by Arnold Bennett (1867–1931) and George Eliot (1819–80) respectively.

36 **Edith Street**: She was a teacher (and colleague of Florence Bervon) at St Monica's, the school VB had attended.

36 *T. & T.*: *Time and Tide*, the "independent non-party weekly", feminist in orientation. WH was one of its Directors and, like VB and many of their friends, wrote regularly for it. (The dispute with Gollancz, mentioned again later, arose from an apparent editorial reluctance to advertise his publications.)

36 **Ernest Davies:** A journalist (b. 1902), he was Editor of the *Clarion* and *New Clarion* (in which VB published several articles) 1929–32, and was a Labour M.P. 1945–59. His wife Natalie ran a nursery-school in Chelsea.

36 **Sir W. Beveridge; Family Life Questionnaires:** Sir William (Baron) Beveridge (1879–1963), the eminent social worker, economist and economic historian, Director of the London School of Economics 1919–37, is best remembered for the Beveridge Report of 1942 which was the blueprint for social welfare legislation 1945–50, including the National Health Service.

36 **Roger Pippett:** A critic (1895–1962), he wrote for the *Daily Herald* and later the *New York Times*.

37 **Geoffrey Thurlow:** Killed in 1917, he had been a close friend of VB's brother Edward.

37 **Dr Waller:** Dr Harold K. Waller, the chief consultant of the Chelsea Babies' Club, was a "pioneer paediatrician".

37 **Lady Jones:** Enid Bagnold, the novelist and playwright (1889–1981) best remembered for her bestseller *National Velvet* (1935); like VB, she nursed as a VAD during the First World War and published a fine memoir, *Diary Without Dates* (1918); she married Sir Roderick (later Lord) Jones in 1920 and with VB was a member of the Chelsea Babies' Club Committee.

37 **Asiago**: The battle in Northern Italy during which Edward Brittain was killed.

37 **Viola Garvin:** A journalist (1898–1969), she was Literary Editor of the *Observer* 1926–34.

37 *Femina–Vie Heureuse* **Prize:** Founded in 1904 by the reviews *Femina* and *Vie Heureuse* "to encourage literature and strengthen the bonds between women of letters", it was awarded annually for a novel.

37 **Stella Benson:** A novelist and travel-writer (1892–1933), she lived many years in China; *Tobit Transplanted* (1931) was her last novel.

37 **Northcliffe Prize:** Alfred Harmsworth, 1st Viscount Northcliffe (1865
-1922), the very successful newspaper publisher, financed many literary
awards.

37 **Jean Schlumberger:** A French novelist and critic (1877–1968).

37 **Harold Nicolson:** A diplomat and writer (1886–1962), married to the poet
and novelist Victoria (Vita) Sackville-West; he resigned from the Diplomatic Service in 1929, in 1932 was on the staff of the *Daily Express*, and became a
National Labour M.P. 1935–45. He published several literary and historical
works, two novels, and diaries.

37 **Amabel Williams-Ellis:** A writer and journalist (1894–1984); one of her
books was a study of *Women in War Factories*.

37 **Noel Coward; Richard Hughes:** The famous man of the theatre (1899
-1973); and the novelist and poet (1900–76) best known for *A High Wind in
Jamaica* (1929).

38 **Robert Nichols,** *Wings Over Europe*: A writer and academic (1893–1944),
Nichols is remembered for his war-poetry; *Wings Over Europe* (1929) was
co-written with Maurice Browne, later one of VB's pacifist friends.

38 **"daimon":** An overwhelming, mysterious impulse or influence; an "inner
command".

38 *The Miracle*, **Diana Cooper, Tilly Losch:** Revived in 1932, Max
Reinhardt's play *The Miracle* (first performed in 1911) was a transatlantic
"rage"; Lady Diana Cooper (b. 1892), beautiful wife of Duff Cooper, played
the Madonna, and Tilly Losch (1907–1975), the famous Viennese-born
dancer, was the Nun.

38 **Oakwood Court:** VB's parents, Thomas and Edith Brittain, lived in a block
of flats in Kensington; later they moved to two addresses nearby (Collingham Gardens and Edwardes Square), all within two miles of VB's house in
Glebe Place.

39 **Margaret Kornitzer:** A journalist and writer (b. 1905); VB attacked her
book for "Libelling the Modern Woman" (10 May 1932).

39 **Aunt Lillie:** A sister of Edith Brittain, she lived in Woking with her husband
Arthur Bentley-Carr and son Robin.

39 **Cecil Roberts:** A novelist, poet, journalist and socialist (1892–1976), he
went on six North American lecture-tours between 1920 and 1939.

39 **David Higham:** A well-known literary agent, and later writer (b. 1895); he
served in both world wars.

39 **Evelyn Isitt**: A feminist, she was on the *Manchester Guardian* staff.

39 **Miss Davison:** Women's Editor of the *Week-end Review*.

39 **Miss West:** She was Lady Rhondda's editorial assistant.

39 **the Scott-Jameses:** Violet Scott-James (V.S.J.), a journalist from Yorkshire
(d. 1942) "whose 'London Letter' was a regular feature of the *Yorkshire
Post* for many years", was a close friend of WH. Her husband, Rolfe
A. Scott-James (1878–1959), a journalist and critic, was Assistant Editor of

the *Spectator* 1933–35 and 1939–45, and Editor of the *London Mercury* 1934–39.

41 *Vile Bodies*: A play adapted from the satirical novel about the twenties (1930) by Evelyn Waugh (1903–66).

41 **Canon Percy Dearmer:** An influential writer on religious and social questions (1867–1936); he was appointed Professor of Ecclesiastical Art at the University of London in 1919 and Canon of Westminster in 1931.

41 **Percy Harris:** VB and WH had worked for the election of (Sir) Percy Harris (1876–1952), a Liberal and a member of the League of Nations Union, in 1922 and 1923; through that work they "came into intimate contact with the homes of the poor" and in 1924 became socialists. He was Liberal Chief Whip 1935–45.

41 **Mrs Hobman:** D. L. (Daisy) Hobman (b. 1891) later published a biography of Olive Schreiner (1955) and a lively feminist study *Go Spin, You Jade!* (1957).

41 **L. A. G. Strong:** A well-known journalist and man of letters (1896–1958), he published over seventy volumes of criticism, poetry, novels and short stories.

41 **Rose Macaulay:** The eminent novelist, essayist and travel-writer (1881–1958), best remembered for *The Pleasure of Ruins* (1953) and *The Towers of Trebizond* (1956). She had been VB's admired predecessor at Somerville, and, a keen pacifist, welcomed VB to the Peace Pledge Union in 1937 as a fellow Sponsor.

41 **Norman Collins:** A novelist, critic and journalist (1907–82) who in 1932 published *The Facts of Fiction*. He was a member of the Gollancz staff.

41 **Louis Golding:** A prolific novelist, essayist, poet, critic and travel-writer (1895–1958); his best-selling novel *Magnolia Street* (1932), about life in a Manchester Jewish Community, came out a few months before Phyllis Bentley's *Inheritance*.

42 **Ellis Roberts:** A journalist and writer, (Richard) Ellis Roberts (1879–1953) was Literary Editor of the *New Statesman* 1930–32, on the staff of *Time and Tide* 1933–34 and published biographies of Stella Benson (1939) and Dick Sheppard (1942).

42 **Viola Meynell:** She was a writer (d. 1956) and daughter of the writers Alice and Wilfred Meynell.

42 **Pa Catlin:** VB's father-in-law, George Catlin (1858–1936), was an "explosive little clergyman" with "conventional judgements"; previously priest at St Luke, Richmond, 1912–16, he lived in retirement at Summertown, Oxford.

43 **Mrs Ensor, New Education Fellowship:** Mrs Beatrice Ensor, a Theosophist and Editor of the magazine *Education for the New Era*, founded the New Education Fellowship in 1920. Like other organisations in the "New Education" movement of the twenties and thirties—much influenced by the work of Froebel, Montessori and other educationalists—its members believed in co-education, respect for each child's individuality, free self-

expression, avoidance of punishment, and emphasis on co-operation rather than competition.

43   **the Pethick-Lawrences:** Frederick (1871–1961) and Emmeline (1867 –1943) Pethick-Lawrence were prominent socialists, pacifists, and leaders (with the Pankhursts) of the campaign for women's suffrage. He was also a Labour M.P. 1923–31 and 1935–45, and Secretary of State for India and Burma 1945–47; VB wrote his biography (1963).

43   **Maude Royden:** A well-known feminist, socialist and Christian activist (1876–1956), she was a pioneering woman preacher.

43   **Romieu book:** By the French critics Émilie and Georges Romieu, *The Life of George Eliot* was published in English translation in 1932.

44   **Norman Leys:** A socialist and physician who worked for sixteen years in Africa, he was a prominent critic of colonialist oppression and is reflected in the uncompromising humanitarian Arthur Rollett of WH's novel *Mandoa, Mandoa!*

44   **Cicely Hamilton:** A journalist, feminist and actress (1872–1952), she published political studies of several European countries in the thirties and *Lament for Democracy* in 1940.

44   **Charles Morgan, Hilda Vaughan:** These prominent writers married in 1923. Morgan (1894–1958) was admired in the thirties for the novels *Portrait in a Mirror* (1929) and *The Fountain* (1933), which was a best-seller. Vaughan (b. 1892) published many novels set in Wales.

44   **Macmillan's London agent:** i.e. Lovat Dickson.

45   **"The Superfluous Woman":** VB's poem appears as the epigraph to Chapter XI of *Testament of Youth*.

46   **Richard Sickert:** Walter Richard Sickert (1860–1942), the painter best remembered for his picture of "Ennui" (1913).

46   **Dr Stella Churchill:** An authority on maternity and child welfare (d. 1954), she was a member of the London County Council 1925–32, a Labour candidate in two elections, and author of such books as *Nursing in the Home* (1924) and *On Being a Mother* (1936).

46   **Barbara Drake:** A feminist and socialist (later Barbara Mienertzhagen); a niece of Beatrice Webb, she wrote the influential *Women in the Trade Unions* (1920), and was a London Alderman.

46   **Mrs Rubinstein:** Wife of the solicitor-playwright Harold Rubinstein.

46   **"From him that hath not . . .":** St Matthew 25, 29.

47   **Agnes Grozier Herbertson:** A Swedish-born novelist, poet, journalist and children's writer.

47   **Dr Cronin:** A. J. Cronin, physician turned popular novelist (1896–1981); *Hatter's Castle* (1931) and *The Citadel* (1937) were among his best-sellers.

48   **Hardy and Arnold Bennett:** Thomas Hardy (1840–1928) and Arnold Bennett (1867–1931), recently dead; both major writers wrote admired regional novels.

48 **Dorothy Whipple:** A novelist and short-story writer (1893–1966) who was a friend of WH; several of her novels were Book Society choices and two were filmed.

48 **P.E.N. Club:** An international association of Poets, Playwrights, Editors, Essayists and Novelists, it was founded in 1921 to promote co-operation, freedom of expression, and international goodwill. It helped many European writers and intellectuals to flee Nazi and Fascist persecution.

48 **Ernest Raymond:** A novelist (1888–1974) who served as Chaplain in the First World War and published over fifty books (including *Tell England* and *We, the Accused*); he greatly admired *Testament of Youth* and became a friend of VB.

48 **Mrs Dawson Scott:** Catherine A. Dawson Scott (d. 1934), a feminist and poet, founded the P.E.N. Club in 1921.

48 **Nora Heald:** A journalist (d. 1961), she became Editor of *The Queen* and *The Lady*.

48 **Bradda Field:** A Canadian-born novelist (1904–57) who won the *Femina –Vie Heureuse* Prize for *Small Town* in 1931.

48 **Lady Rhondda; row over Winifred:** During WH's first collapse and confinement in November 1931, VB, on medical advice, "kept Winifred's friends, both eminent and humble, away from the nursing home", took over many of WH's tasks, and turned back requests for material.

48 **E. M. Delafield:** Elizabeth M. Delafield, a prolific novelist, playwright and critic (1890–1943); she was a VAD nurse during the First World War, contributed frequently to *Time and Tide* (of which she was a Director), and achieved great popularity with her witty *Diary of a Provincial Lady* (1931). She lived with her husband, Paul Dashwood, and two children at Cullompton, Devon, near Dartmoor.

48 **Professor Cullis:** Winifred Cullis (1875–1956), Professor of Physiology at the University of London, a Director of *Time and Tide*, and President of the International Federation of University Women 1929–32.

48 **Miss Head:** June Head was on the staff of *Good Housekeeping*.

48 **Jean Lyon:** A journalist at *Punch*, she was a Director of *Time and Tide*.

48 **Miss Pearn:** Nancy Pearn, a literary agent; initially with Curtis Brown, VB's agent, she, David Higham and Laurence Pollinger established their own agency in 1935.

49 **Agay:** A resort in the South of France where Lady Rhondda and her friends went on holiday.

50 **"Yo-yo":** This toy had just reached England, setting off a "craze".

50 **Lee Keedick:** One of the foremost American lecture-tour managers (1879 –1959).

50 **Sir Alfred Fripp:** An eminent physician (1865–1930), he was Royal Surgeon to Edward VII.

50 **Galsworthy:** John Galsworthy, the well-known novelist (1865–1930), author of *The Forsyte Saga*.

50 **Sir Philip Gibbs:** A popular journalist, war-correspondent, novelist and editor (1877–1962); among his many works is *The Golden Years* (1931).

51 **Helen Ashton:** A novelist (1891–1958); married to a barrister, Arthur Jordan.

51 **Miss Thurlow:** Sister of Edward Brittain's friend Geoffrey, who was killed in 1917.

52 **Ernest Rhys:** An eminent man of letters (1859–1946), but best remembered as the founding editor of the popular *Everyman's Library* of reprints.

52 **Eleanor Farjeon:** She published over eighty volumes, including novels, plays, poetry and children's books (1881–1965), as well as a fine memoir of the poet Edward Thomas (1958).

52 **Laski:** Harold Laski (1893–1950), a prominent socialist, political scientist and writer; he was Professor of Political Science at the University of London from 1926, and a member of the Executive Council of the Labour Party 1936–49.

52 **Stephen Gwynn:** An Irish-born critic, biographer, essayist and journalist (1864–1950); his many books include a *History of Ireland* (1923).

52 **Wyndham Lewis:** The controversial modernist writer and painter (1884–1957), he led the Vorticist movement; his satirical *Apes of God* and admiring *Hitler* appeared in 1930 and 1931 respectively.

52 **Norman Angell:** Pseudonym of Ralph Lane, writer and economist (1872–1967); his anti-war book *The Great Illusion* (1910) was translated into twenty languages, he was a Labour M.P. 1929–31, and in 1933 he was awarded the Nobel Peace Prize.

52 *Farthing Hall*: VB reviewed this collaborative novel, with other "New Fiction", in *Time and Tide*, 22 March 1929, incurring the annoyance of both authors.

52 **Walpole:** (Sir) Hugh Walpole, a prominent and prolific novelist and critic (1884–1941) whose popular family-saga *The Herries Chronicle* was emerging in the early thirties.

53 **Keynes:** John Maynard (Baron) Keynes (1883–1946), the highly influential economist (and member of the Bloomsbury Group); his *Treatise on Money* appeared 1930.

53 *The Dynasts*: Thomas Hardy's epic verse-drama (1903–08) based on the Napoleonic Wars.

53 **Philippa Fawcett:** An eminent educationalist (1868–1948) and daughter of the suffragist leader Dame Millicent Fawcett.

53 **"Miss Beale and Miss Buss":** Victorian headmistresses who pioneered high academic standards in girls' schools; they were traduced in the anonymous verse "Miss Buss and Miss Beale / Cupid's darts do not feel. / How different from us, / Miss Beale and Miss Buss." Walpole's comment was much resented by VB.

54 **Conference on the Family:** It was organised by several groups, including the New Education Fellowship and the Nursery School Association.

54 **Mrs Sidonie Gruenberg:** A writer and educationalist (1881–1974), she was Director of the Child Study Association of America.

55 **Dora Russell:** Bertrand Russell's second wife (b. 1894) founded with him the progressive school Beacon Hill and published a lively feminist polemic, *Hypatia* (1925), as well as *The Right to be Happy* (1927).

55 **Susan Lawrence:** A socialist politician (1871–1937), she was organiser of the National Federation of Women Workers 1912–21, Labour M.P. from 1923, and Parliamentary Secretary to the Minister of Health 1929–31.

56 **Peters:** A. D. Peters (1892–1973), the journalist and well-known literary agent.

57 **H. V. Roe:** Marie Stopes married H. Verdon Roe, an aviation pioneer and brother of A. V. Roe, in 1918, and with him established in 1921 the London Mothers' Clinic for Birth Control (C.B.C.).

57 **National Birth Control Association:** Evolving in 1930 from the Malthusian League, it was later re-named the Family Planning Association and by 1960 had over 300 clinics.

57 **Mrs How-Martyn:** A prominent suffragette (1875–1954), she founded the Women's Freedom League in 1907, was the first woman member of the Middlesex Council, and wrote *The Birth Control Movement in England* (1930).

58 **Harold Rubinstein:** A London solicitor with literary interests (1891–1975), he wrote several plays and handled legal affairs for VB, who noted that "his benevolent skill has brought help and comfort to many writers of my generation".

58 **Ernest Milton:** An actor and writer (1890–1974), he was married to Naomi Royde-Smith.

58 **the Rector of Stiffkey:** A focus of popular scandal, the Rev. Harold Davidson, previously an actor, was in 1932 found guilty of immoral sexual conduct after a long and sensational trial.

58 **Sylvia Lynd:** A novelist and poet (1888–1962), she was married to the writer and journalist Robert Lynd.

58 **Alan Thomas:** A barrister and detective-novelist (1896–1969), he was on the staff of the League of Nations Union 1921–36 and later became Editor of the *Listener*.

59 **Sinclair Lewis:** The famous American novelist (1885–1951), who won the Nobel Prize for Literature in 1931.

59 **James Laver:** A novelist, dramatist, poet, biographer and author of many books on the fine arts (1899–1975).

59 **Lady Warrender:** She published several autobiographical books (1870–1945).

60 *Not Without Honour*: VB's second novel (1924), largely based on her youthful experiences in Buxton.

60 *Annual Register*s: VB was consulting these to gather and check facts for *Testament of Youth*. Founded in 1758 and first edited by Edmund Burke (1729–97), the *Annual Register* is a review of the year's important events.

61 *Halcyon*: VB's feminist "squib" wittily attacking conventional views of marriage (1929).

61 **"Picnic, July 1917":** VB quoted Rose Macaulay's poem in Chapter VIII of *Testament of Youth*.

62 **Naomi Royde-Smith:** A novelist, playwright and biographer (d. 1964); *The Delicate Situation* (1931) is one of about forty novels she published.

62 **Dreiser:** Theodore Dreiser (1871–1935), the American naturalistic novelist best known for *An American Tragedy* (1925). *Tragic America* (1932) was a "social commentary".

62 **Margaret Kennedy:** A novelist and playwright (1896–1967) who had been VB's contemporary at Somerville, she is best remembered for *The Constant Nymph* (1924), popular as a novel and a play.

63 **Halldor Hermannsson:** An Icelandic-born historian (1878–1958), he was a colleague of G. E. G. Catlin at Cornell and author of many works about Iceland. (VB's article in the *Manchester Guardian* (17 May 1932) humorously excoriated husbands for expecting wives to give automatic precedence to the role of hostess.)

64 **Lady Forbes-Robertson:** Gertrude Elliott, an American actress (1874–1950), wife of Sir Johnston Forbes-Robertson.

64 **Eva Spicer:** A missionary and teacher (b. 1898), she was a contemporary of VB's at Somerville College. Her brother Lancelot (1893–1979) won the M.C. in the First World War.

65 *Poor Caroline*: WH's fourth novel (1931) satirised the "do-gooding" impulse.

65 **Beverley Nichols:** A popular journalist, writer and broadcaster (1898–1983), he was a contemporary of VB's at Oxford. His *Cry Havoc!* (1933) was an influential anti-war book, but in the late thirties he fell under the influence of Mosley's Fascists.

65 **Edith Evans; John Gielgud:** The internationally famous actress (1888–1976) and actor (b. 1904).

65 *Musical Chairs*: This play was by Ronald Mackenzie, who died young in 1932.

65 **Drummond Shiels:** A Scottish physician and politician (1881–1953) who served in the First World War, was a Labour M.P. 1924–31, and devoted much of his life to colonial advancement and emancipation (in 1946 he helped to found the Colonial Economic and Development Council).

65 **Curtis Brown:** Spencer Curtis Brown (1906–1980), the well-known literary agent.

67 **Ann Reid:** Pseudonym of Mrs Louis Marlow (b. 1889); she wrote *Love Lies Bleeding* (1930).

67 **Catherine Carswell:** A writer and critic (1870–1946); *The Savage Pilgrimage* (1932) is one of the most detailed and sympathetic accounts of D. H. Lawrence by a friend.

68 **Miss Raynham-Smith:** Ethel Raynham-Smith was Matron of the Chelsea Babies' Club.

69 **Kean Seymour:** William Kean Seymour (1887–1975), a poet, novelist and journalist, was also a bank-manager. His first wife, Beatrice (d. 1955), was a novelist, journalist and critic.

69 **Burford:** A town on the edge of the Cotswolds about twenty miles west of Oxford.

69 **Balfour of Burleigh:** George Bruce, 11th Baron Burleigh (1883–1967), was an active bureaucrat and board member, and Chairman of the Kensington Housing Trust 1926–49.

70 **B.F.U.W.:** The British Federation of University Women.

70 **Dorothy Woodman:** A close friend of Kingsley Martin (Editor of the *New Statesman*), she was a Communist and a member of the National Peace Council (d. 1970).

71 **Chrystal Macmillan, Mrs Abbott, Mrs Le Sueur, the Open Door International:** This organisation was founded in 1926, with representation from all the main feminist groups, to seek "complete equality in the economic and industrial spheres" for women. Chrystal Macmillan, Elizabeth Abbott and Winifred Le Sueur were joint leaders of the British Open Door Council.

71 **Mme Plaminkova:** Franciska Plaminkova (1875–1942), a "large, fair, kindly woman", was a Czech feminist, educationalist and politician; the first Chairwoman of the International Council of Women, she was a Czech Senator from 1929 and "one of the first to be arrested by the Gestapo when Hitler marched into Prague".

71 **Evelyn Irons:** A distinguished journalist (b. 1900), she was a contemporary of VB at Somerville College, contributed to *Time and Tide*, and as a war correspondent 1939–45 was awarded the Croix de Guerre.

72 **visit to India; Congress Party:** Ellen Wilkinson (who lost her parliamentary seat in 1932) and Monica Whately were keen supporters of Gandhi and his Congress Party, like many of VB's friends.

72 **Winifred worried:** Although Evelyn Waugh's satirical *Black Mischief* came out about a year before WH's *Mandoa, Mandoa!* (1933), both novels were highly-praised and best-sellers.

73 **Cole:** G. D. H. Cole (1889–1959), an economist, political journalist, and Professor of Social and Political Theory; a prolific contributor to the *New Statesman*, he was seen as one of the most influential socialist thinkers of his time.

73 **I.L.P.:** The Independent Labour Party, the individual members' section of the Labour Party, became increasingly radical in the twenties under James Maxton, disaffiliating from the Party in 1932; but some of its members, under E. F. Wise, joined the S.S.I.P. ("ZIP") to form the Socialist League.

73 *Hindle Wakes*: A popular comedy (1912) by Stanley Houghton (1881–1913), it was set in the cotton-mill districts of Lancashire.

74 **Victor Saville:** A film producer and director (1897–1979), he made the film of WH's *South Riding* in 1938.

74 *Virginia Woolf*: WH's book, a pioneering critical study of the eminent novelist (1882–1941), was published in October 1932.

74 **Gordon's mother:** Edith Kate Orton, "a turbulent, thwarted, politically-conscious woman" sixteen years younger than her clergyman husband, "had joined the suffrage movement in spite of his disapproval", so "their marriage had faltered" and she "had died prematurely in 1917". VB fictionalised Catlin's mother, and her story, in the novel *Honourable Estate* (1936).

75 **Arthur Watts:** He was well-known for his posters and humorous illustrations (1883–1935).

76 **P.N.E.U.:** The Parents' National Educational Union advocated (and founded) schools which would not create an artificial "child-environment" but, along Montessori lines, allow children to live and learn in a "natural home atmosphere".

76 **Graham Wallas:** A political scientist (1858–1932), he was Professor of Political Science at the London School of Economics 1914–23. Catlin dedicated his *Principles of Politics* (1929) to Wallas.

76 **H. G. Wells:** The famous and prolific writer (1866–1946), extremely influential in the thirties.

76 **Maxton:** James Maxton (1885–1946), a journalist and politician; he was a pacifist during the First World War, became Chairman of the Independent Labour Party and in 1932 led it to disaffiliation from the Labour Party.

76 **"Francis Iles":** They were all wrong! This was the pseudonym of Anthony Cox (1893–1970), a mystery writer and journalist.

77 **Sylvia Pankhurst:** The second of Emmeline Pankhurst's three daughters, she remained a pacifist through the First World War and worked in the London slums; her long account of *The Suffragette Movement* was published (and reviewed by VB) in 1931.

77 **Major Church:** Archibald G. Church (1886–1954), a politician, public servant and journalist; he co-founded the *Realist* with Catlin and was a Labour M.P. 1923–24 and 1929–31.

77 **Mollison:** The aviator James Mollison (1905–59) married Amy Johnson in 1932; his flight in August 1932 was the first solo westward crossing of the Atlantic.

78 **Cottingham:** A village (now a suburb) near Hull, Yorkshire, where WH's mother lived in a house called Bainesse.

79 **Ruth Holland:** This novelist (b. 1898) published several books; VB praised *The Lost Generation* for its honest representation of war.

79 **Radclyffe Hall:** A novelist and poet (1880–1943) who became notorious for her "lesbian" novel *The Well of Loneliness* (1928), which was suppressed after a trial for obscenity. VB defended it, both at the time and in her last book, *Radclyffe Hall: A Case of Obscenity?* (1968).

79 **Gerald Gould:** A prominent journalist, critic and lecturer (1885–1936).

80 **Isadora Duncan:** The famous American dancer (1878–1927); her children were drowned in 1913.

80 **Cotter's Bow:** Miss Thomson's house and school at Burford.

80 **Sir H. Wilson:** Sir Henry Wilson (1864–1922). Chief of the Imperial General Staff from 1918, he was murdered after making anti-Sinn Fein statements; VB and WH watched his funeral procession near St Paul's Cathedral and were deeply moved.

80 **Pritchett:** V. S. Pritchett, the respected short-story writer, novelist and critic (b. 1900).

82 **Storm Jameson:** A prolific Yorkshire novelist, critic and social activist, Margaret Storm Jameson (b. 1897) became a close friend of VB in the mid-thirties; she was a pacifist in the thirties, and worked indefatigably through P.E.N., of which she was Chairman from 1938, to help refugee European intellectuals.

83 **John Middleton Murry:** Critic and journalist, socialist and pacifist (1889–1957), he edited the *Adelphi* magazine 1923–38 and *Peace News* (then the organ of the Peace Pledge Union) 1940–46; in 1932 he published *The Necessity of Communism*.

83 **Namier:** Sir Lewis B. Namier (1888–1960), an eminent historian best known for his *Structure of Politics at the Accession of George III* (1929).

83 *Adonais*: The long "Elegy on the Death of John Keats" by Percy Bysshe Shelley (1792–1822).

83 **Orage's new weekly:** Alfred Orage (1873–1934), a well-known editor, established the *New English Weekly* in 1932.

84 **Miss Lennox:** VB's typist.

84 **Queen's visit to Somerville:** See *Testament of Youth*, Chapter X, Section 10.

84 **Frances Ridley Havergal:** Author of several popular hymns (1836–79); her collected *Poetical Works* appeared in 1884.

85 **Ethelreda Lewis:** A South African novelist (1890–1946), she achieved world-wide fame with *Trader Horn* (1927), the edited reminiscences of an English adventurer, Alfred Aloysius Horn (1861–1931); a friend of WH, whom she had strongly influenced, she was an active worker against *apartheid*.

85 **Ballinger:** William G. Ballinger (1894–1974), a labour organiser in Scotland, went to South Africa in 1928 to help the only black trade union, the Industrial and Commercial Workers' Union; Ethelreda Lewis supported his efforts.

85 **Gertrude Atherton:** An American writer (1857–1948) who published many novels.

86 **Prof. Pear:** Tom Heatherley Pear (1886–1972), Professor of Psychology at Manchester University and author of many books, such as *The Art of Study* (1930).

87 **Noel Streatfeild:** A novelist and children's writer (b. 1895).

87   *Miracle at Verdun*: An anti-war play by Hans Chlumberg (d. 1930).

87   **Sidney Webb:** With his wife Beatrice (1858–1943), Sidney Webb, Baron Passfield (1859–1947), was a very influential social reformer, historian and member of the Fabian Party. He was Secretary of State for the Dominions and Colonies 1929–31, with Drummond Shiels as his Under-Secretary.

87   **MacDonald:** James Ramsay MacDonald (1866–1937), a Labour politician of Scottish origin who was Prime Minister 1924 and 1929–31, and (of a coalition National Government) 1931–35. In 1931 he divided the Labour Party in dealing with the serious financial crisis which brought his Labour Government down.

87   **J. H. Thomas:** James H. Thomas (1874–1949), a trade-union leader and politician; he joined MacDonald's National Government in 1931 and lost union support.

88   **Palestine:** Under the terms of the Balfour Declaration (1917), British policy favoured the establishment in Palestine of a national home for the Jewish people, but protests and rioting by Arabs led to the White Paper of 1930 which virtually prohibited further Jewish immigration.

88   **Henderson:** Arthur Henderson (1863–1935); a trade-unionist and Labour M.P., he was Foreign Secretary 1929–31. With Catlin he co-edited *New Trends in Socialism* (1935).

88   **A. V. Alexander:** Albert Alexander, later Earl Alexander of Hillsborough (1863–1935); a trade-unionist and Labour M.P., he was First Lord of the Admiralty 1929–31.

88   **Mrs Dugdale:** Blanche Dugdale (d. 1948), a niece of Balfour and an ardent Zionist supporter, was a member of the British Delegation to the 1932 League of Nations Assembly.

88   **Balfour:** Arthur, 1st Earl Balfour (1848–1930), statesman and writer; he was Conservative Prime Minister 1902–05, and as Foreign Secretary under Lloyd George was responsible for the declaration on Palestine.

88   **Dr Weizmann:** Chaim Weizmann (1874–1952), Israeli leader; he helped to secure the Balfour Declaration, and in 1948 became the first President of Israel.

90   **Queen Margaret's:** The girls' school in Scarborough which WH attended 1909–15; Agnes Body was its first Headmistress.

91   **Zip:** A popular variation of S.S.I.P., the Society for Socialist Inquiry and Propaganda, founded June 1931 by G. D. H. Cole and others as a "ginger-group" in the Labour Party.

91   **the Socialist League:** It was founded on 2 October 1932, just before the Labour Party Conference at Leicester, by E. F. Wise and other former I.L.P. members, in conjunction with S.S.I.P.; an "intellectualist group", whose original Council also included Pethick-Lawrence, Dr A. Salter, Sir Charles Trevelyan and Stafford Cripps, it disaffiliated from the Labour Party in 1937.

91   **E. F. Wise:** Edward Wise (1885–1933), a barrister and Labour M.P.

92 **Morrison:** Herbert Morrison, later Baron Morrison of Lambeth (1888
–1965), Labour statesman; he was Minister of Transport 1929–31.

92 **Kenworthy:** Commander Hon. Joseph Kenworthy, later Baron Strabolgi
(1886–1953), Liberal M.P. 1919–26, Labour M.P. 1926–31.

92 **L'Estrange Malone:** Lt. Col. Cecil L'Estrange Malone (1890–1965), suc-
cessively Liberal, Communist, Independent and Labour M.P.; he and other
S.S.I.P. dissidents formed the "1932 Club", opposing the Socialist League
and favouring alliance with the Liberal Party.

92 **"Open Conspiracy":** H. G. Wells' book of this title (1928) advocated
extra-parliamentary radicalism by the intelligent minority to control world
affairs. VB reviewed it in *Time and Tide*, criticising its totalitarian tendencies
and exclusion of women.

92 *Realist*: In 1929 Catlin co-founded with Major Archibald Church this
socialist "intellectual monthly . . . dedicated to 'Scientific Humanism' '"; its
board included many illustrious socialists, including Arnold Bennett, H. G.
Wells and Rebecca West; but it fell victim to the 1929 Crash and ceased
publication in 1930.

92 **Bertrand Russell, divorce:** The famous philosopher and social activist,
3rd Earl Russell (1872–1970), and his second wife Dora annulled their
marriage in 1935. His third marriage, to the red-haired Patricia Spence, was
annulled in 1952. Dora had two children by Barry Griffin, an American-
born journalist.

92 **Mosley:** Sir Oswald Mosley (1896–1980); after serving in the First World
War, he became Conservative M.P. (1918–22) and Labour M.P. (1926–31),
then, in 1931, founded a progressive socialist movement, but dissolved it in
April 1932 and six months later established the British Union of Fascists.
Catlin, who had supported Mosley in his efforts to deal effectively with
unemployment, had "ended his brief connection with Mosley immediately
Sir Oswald left the Labour Party".

93 **Cynthia Mosley:** Half-Jewish first wife of Oswald Mosley, Lady Cynthia
Mosley (1898–1933) was a Labour M.P. 1921–31 and joined her husband's
British Union of Fascists reluctantly.

93 **Baroness Budberg:** Maura Zakrevskaya (Countess Beckendorff, Baroness
Budberg), a vivacious Russian spy, became H. G. Wells' mistress in Russia
during his 1920 visit, and when she arrived in London in 1931 the affair was
renewed.

93 **Chesterton:** G. K. Chesterton (1874–1936), the prominent essayist, novelist and poet.

93 **Edith Smeterlin:** A schoolfriend of WH, Edith Mannaberg was a naturalised Austrian who in 1925 married a Polish-born concert pianist, Jan
Smeterlin (1892–1967). VB and WH heard him perform several times when
they visited Vienna in 1924.

93 **Kapp:** Edmond X. Kapp (1890–1978), an artist who fought in the First
World War.

93 *Outline for Boys and Girls and their Parents*: This big book, edited by Naomi Mitchison and published by Gollancz in 1932, aimed to provide "the foundations of knowledge"; it contained about thirty essays, under the broad topics of Science, Civilisation and Values, most of them by eminent socialist experts. The essay that aroused most antagonism was "Physiology, or What Am I?", an account of human reproduction, with diagrams of the sexual organs, by Professor Winifred Cullis and Dr Evelyn E. Hewer.

94 **Teachers' and Clerics' letter:** i.e., the open letter (in the *Manchester Guardian*) attacking the *Outline for Boys and Girls*, which had now become the focus of a battle between conservative and liberal thinkers.

94 **Bishop of Birmingham:** Rt Rev. Ernest Barnes (1874–1953); see also later note "Bishop Barnes".

94 **Helena Wright:** A gynaecologist, she was an Executive member of the Family Planning Association's Executive Committee, and published several books on sexuality and birth control.

95 **Tallulah Bankhead:** The husky-voiced American actress (1902–1968).

95 **Mr Chance:** (Sir) Roger Chance (b. 1893), a writer and journalist; he was press attaché at the British Embassy, Berlin, from 1938.

95 **Lovat Dickson:** A writer, publisher and editor (b. 1902); born in Australia, he moved to Canada in 1917 and then to England in 1928; while London agent for Macmillan's of New York, he established his own publishing firm, but in 1938 joined Macmillan's of London, becoming a Director in 1940. He came to know VB well.

95 **"Astonishing Island":** A series of satirical sketches of English life, as experienced by the amazed "Robinson Lippingtree Mackintosh from Tristan da Cunha", *The Astonishing Island* (1933) has lost its sparkle to time.

96 **the Knopfs:** Well-known American publishers, Alfred and Blanche Knopf.

96 **Longfellow; Mrs Henry Wood:** The popular moralistic American poet (1807–82) of *Hiawatha* fame; and the highly conservative writer of moralisingly melodramatic novels (1814–87), such as *East Lynne* (1861).

96 **Whitefield's Tabernacle:** George Whitefield (1714–70) was a nonconformist evangelist whose supporters built him a chapel in Tottenham Court Road.

97 **Wilfred Meynell:** A respected writer (1852–1948), he edited the collected works of his wife, the poet and essayist Alice Meynell (1847–1922).

97 **Jean Forbes-Robertson:** A popular actress (1905–62), daughter of Sir Johnston Forbes-Robertson, the actor. She was especially notable for having played the part of Peter Pan for eight consecutive seasons, 1927–34, and was to play a ninth in 1938.

97 **Mrs Piercy:** Mary Piercy was Chairman of the Chelsea Babies' Club.

98 **Vicki Baum:** A popular novelist and playwright, born in Vienna (1896–1960); her best-selling *Grand Hotel* appeared in 1930.

98 **"The Revolution Has Come":** VB put Battersea Park into her *article* of that title (*Manchester Guardian*, 7 July 1933).

98   **Barbara:** Barbara Clark (d. 1948), a close friend of Phyllis Bentley from their schooldays.

100   **Tawney:** The eminent historian, socialist and pioneer of adult education, Richard H. Tawney (1880–1962), author of *Religion and the Rise of Capitalism* (1926).

100   *The Dark Tide*: VB's first novel (1923), largely based on her memories of Somerville College and much resented there at the time.

100   **Ivor Montagu:** A writer, journalist and film critic (b. 1904), he wrote for the *Daily Worker* 1932–33 and 1937–47, and was awarded the Lenin Peace Prize in 1959.

100   **Lancelot Hogben:** A zoologist, physiologist and expert in linguistics (1895–1975), he was Professor of Social Biology at London University 1930–36 and published the popular *Mathematics for the Million* (1936).

100   **David Low:** A well-known political cartoonist, born in New Zealand (1891–1963), he was a member of the *Evening Standard* staff 1927–50 and became famous for his "Colonel Blimp" cartoons.

101   **his Outline:** Wells' encyclopaedic *Outline of World History* (1919) was enormously popular and influential.

101   **Ottawa:** The Imperial economic conference held at Ottawa in July–August 1932 agreed on Dominion Preferences which led to a decrease in British foreign trade.

101   **Means Test riot:** Introduced by the National Government under Mac-Donald after its overwhelming victory in 1931, the Means Test was an extremely unpopular measure to achieve economies by withdrawing the unemployment benefit from people with savings or wealthy relatives. There were many demonstrations against it.

103   *A Modern Utopia*: An early blueprint for the future (1904) by Wells.

103   **Brittain's Ltd:** The family paper-mill near Stoke-on-Trent of which Thomas Brittain had been a director until his premature retirement in 1915.

103   *The New Age*: Orage and Bernard Shaw bought this weekly review in 1907, and under Orage's editorship it became widely influential, promoting socialism and publishing many new as well as many famous writers.

104   **Katherine Mansfield:** The brilliant short-story writer (1888–1923), born in New Zealand and married to John Middleton Murry.

104   **Lord Camrose:** William Berry, Baron Camrose (1879–1954), Editor-in-Chief of the *Daily Telegraph* from 1928.

104   **Government crisis:** In August 1931 a financial crisis forced the resignation of the Labour Government and the formation of a coalition under Mac-Donald.

104   **Theodora Bosanquet:** A journalist (1880–1961), she was Literary Editor of *Time and Tide* 1935–43.

104   **Raverat; Elizabeth Bowen:** Gwendolen Raverat, a wood-engraver and

book-illustrator (1885–1957); she reviewed *Friends and Relations* (1931) by the admired Irish-born novelist (1899–1973).

105 **"While We Remember":** One of a series of Armistice Day meditations VB wrote for the *Manchester Guardian*.

105 **Guy Chapman:** Storm Jameson's second husband, Guy Chapman (1889 –1972), who served in both world wars, was a writer, publisher and historian; his *Passionate Prodigality* (1933) is one of the finest memoirs of the First World War.

105 *No Time Like the Present*: Storm Jameson's memoir of the "war generation", it was reviewed admiringly by VB in April 1933.

105 **Lorna Rea:** A Scottish-born writer of popular novels (1897–1978).

106 **Ethel Mannin:** An extremely prolific novelist, essayist, editor and journalist (1900–84), she was of London working-class origin and in 1932 a member of the Independent Labour Party; her *Confessions and Impressions* (1929) were thought scandalous.

106 **Hammett book:** *The Thin Man* (1931) by Dashiell Hammett (1894–1961) was banned in Britain for obscenity.

106 **Compton Mackenzie,** *Gallipoli Memories:* (Sir) E. M. Compton Mackenzie (1883–1972), a prolific novelist best remembered for *Sinister Street* (1913) and *Whisky Galore* (1947); *Gallipoli Memories*, a volume of his *Memories*, was suppressed in 1932 under the Official Secrets Act.

106 **Henri Barbusse:** A French novelist and journalist (1874–1935), he became internationally famous on the publication of *Le Feu* (*Under Fire*), a harshly-realistic war novel, in 1916.

107 **Dorothy Evans:** A pioneer feminist, she worked for an international Equal Rights Treaty at the League of Nations.

107 **Mrs George Strauss:** Patricia Strauss (b. 1909), wife of a Labour states-man, (Baron) George Strauss, Minister of Aircraft Production 1942–44.

107 **W.'s mother, Alderman:** Alice Holtby had been elected first woman member of the Yorkshire East Riding County Council in March 1923.

107 **the Leightons:** Robert Leighton (d. 1934), a critic, journalist and author of many boys' stories, helped VB and WH considerably in their early journal-ism; Marie Connor Leighton (d. 1941) published over forty popular novels and an anonymous memoir of her son Roland, *Boy of My Heart* (1917).

107 **R., V., G.:** Roland Leighton, Victor Richardson, Geoffrey Thurlow: VB's fiancé, and two friends, all killed in the First World War.

107 **Harry Pearson:** WH's perpetual boyfriend. In *Testament of Friendship*, VB called him "Bill": "tall and very slim", his "long brown lashes, a little deeper in colour than his bronzed cheeks, curled lazily over his amused blue eyes, and his vivid, humorous smile creased his thin face into characteristic lines of cynical benevolence." His experiences in the War, she believed, had changed him "from an ardent idealist into a soul still benevolent but without purpose or integration". Son of a Driffield bank manager, he became a friend

of T. E. Lawrence (Lawrence of Arabia) when they were both aircraftsmen on the north-west frontier of India in the late twenties.

108   **Bishop of Kensington:** Rt Rev. John P. Maud (1860–1932).

108   **Lord Rhayader:** A well-known politician (1862–1939), he was a Liberal M.P. 1905–18, 1923–24 and 1929–31.

108   **Brendan Bracken:** A Conservative politician, (Viscount) Bracken (1901 –58); he was Churchill's Private Secretary 1940–41 and Minister of Information 1941–45.

108   **Somerset Maugham,** *For Services Rendered:* One of several popular plays by the well-known novelist, short-story writer and playwright (1874–1965).

108   **Barbara Bervon, Uncle Bill:** W. H. K. Bervon (also "Uncle Willie"), Edith Brittain's brother, who died in 1925 (VB had a close and affectionate relationship with him, especially during the First World War); Barbara, his daughter.

109   **Mannabergs:** Relations of Edith Smeterlin, WH's close friend.

110   **Mrs Richardson, Maurice:** Maurice Richardson (b. 1899), a retired teacher, and younger brother of Victor, the friend of Edward Brittain and Roland Leighton killed in the War. In *Testament of Youth*, Mrs Richardson is Victor's "aunt" (she married his father later) who, at the end of Chapter VII, consoles VB "with an affectionate warmth of intimacy which had not been possible before and would never, we both knew, be possible again".

110   **Sir Squire Sprigge:** A physician and writer (1860–1937), he was Chairman of the Society of Authors; among his books is *Physics and Fiction* (1921).

110   **Donald Carswell:** Catherine Carswell's husband (1882–1940) was a public official.

112   *Daniel Deronda:* VB's quotation from George Eliot's last novel (1876) was no doubt her favourite "There comes a terrible moment to many souls when the great moments of the world . . . enter like an earthquake into their own lives . . .".

112   **Haworth:** Phyllis Bentley was an expert on the lives and work of the Brontës (she edited their works and published two critical studies); she had clearly looked forward to showing VB around the parsonage and walking with her over the moors.

113   **Mrs Gaskell:** The great biography of Charlotte Brontë by her friend and fellow-writer Elizabeth Gaskell (1810–65) appeared in 1857, after considerable opposition from Charlotte's father and husband.

114   **Dr Joan Malleson:** (1888–1969), she was the second wife of the actor and playwright Miles Malleson.

115   **S. K. Ratcliffe:** A journalist and editor, Samuel Ratcliffe (1868–1958) was a prominent lecturer in England and the United States.

115   **Clemence Dane:** A well-known novelist, essayist, and playwright (1888 –1965); her novel *Broome Stages* (1931) was very popular.

116   **J. B. S. and Charlotte Haldane:** Naomi Mitchison's brother, he was a

leading genetic scientist, writer and socialist (1892–1964), author of *The Inequality of Man* (1932); on retirement he lived permanently in India. His wife was a journalist, novelist and essayist (1894–1969).

116　**Kate O'Brien:** An Irish novelist and playwright (1897–1974); the novel *Without My Cloak* was published in 1931.

119　**"Evening in Yorkshire":** VB's poem refers to Bentley's "solitude" and "incommunicable anguish", urging the warmth of friendship—"the summer days will return".

119　**"Out of this nettle . . .":** The quotation is from Shakespeare's *King Henry IV, Part I.*

119　**Panel doctor:** Before the advent of the National Health Service only those in certain occupations (among them domestic service) qualified for free medical attention from a registered panel of doctors, their "health cards" being obligatorily stamped at their employers' expense.

120　**"As One":** Phyllis Bentley's projected novel was probably the one she referred to as "very difficult if not impossible" (see August 4th), and in her autobiography *"O Dreams, O Destinations"* as "a large (perhaps too grandiose) brother-of-man novel" that "perished".

120　**"As one who on a lonely road . . .":** Misquoted from Coleridge's *Rime of the Ancient Mariner.* (Perhaps Bentley's title quoted from the Book of Judges: "The people arose as one man.")

1933

VB made no entries in her diary until 23 July, when she was on holiday in France with WH and Catlin. In January 1933 *Testament of Youth* had been accepted, before completion, by Macmillan's of New York; she finished it on 16 February and it was immediately accepted by Victor Gollancz, who "enjoined the utmost speed in revision". Then began a series of wearing problems as VB submitted the text to family and friends for approval, and sought permission to publish various quotations: "To my growing dismay nobody seemed willing to 'pass' anything and, while my publisher daily demanded corrected proofs, constant requests to add, alter or eliminate material recreated the strain which I had hoped was over." By July all problems were resolved: *Testament of Youth* would be published on 28 August.

125　**Hardelot-Plage:** A resort "some eight miles from Étaples, the scene of my war service in France".

125　**Strachey,** *The Menace of Fascism*: (Evelyn) John Strachey (1901–63), writer and statesman, was a Labour M.P. 1929–32 and 1945–63, and Minister of Food 1946–50; his book (1933) was one of several political studies.

125　**Norah Ashford; hotel incident:** She was a "senior VAD" (b. 1891) whose "humorous common sense made her a pleasant companion for the sixteen-mile walk to Hardelot and back". See *Testament of Youth*, Chapter VIII, Section 6, for VB's account of the hotel incident.

125 **Pré Catelan:** An "old chateau with a beautiful garden which had been converted into an expensive restaurant".

125 **"Sixteen Years After":** Retitled "The Road from the Pinewoods", this meditation appeared in the *Manchester Guardian* 4 August 1933.

126 **Stephen King-Hall:** A writer and Independent politician (1893–1966), he served in the Navy during the First World War.

127 **Kiplingesque tradition:** Catlin may have been remembering the importance of courage and duty in works by Rudyard Kipling (1865–1936), who attacked British indifference towards "Tommies".

127 **"Preface to Action":** Catlin's book appeared in 1934.

127 **Wickham Steed:** A journalist, editor and lecturer (1871–1956), he was a well-known broadcaster on world affairs during the Second World War.

127 **Sir John Hare:** A celebrated actor and manager (1844–1921).

128 **Faith Moulson:** Called "Hope Milroy" in *Testament of Youth*, she was Sister-in-Charge of the German Ward in 24 General Hospital at Étaples in 1917 (see Chapter VIII). After the War, she and VB continued their friendship, visiting each other and exchanging letters for many years.

128 **1917 mutiny:** This serious disturbance among Allied soldiers at Étaples lasted for several weeks in September and October 1917; known locally as the "Battle of Eetapps", it was caused by "the repressive conditions in the Étaples camps and was provoked by the military police".

128 **Prince of Wales:** He acceded as Edward VIII in 1936, but abdicated the same year and was created Duke of Windsor (1894–1972).

128 **Lord Beaverbrook:** The Canadian-born newspaper-magnate and Conservative politician (1879–1964) was Minister for Aircraft Production 1940 –41 and of Supply 1941–2.

129 *Cry Havoc!*: Published in July 1933, Beverley Nichols' emotional anti-war tract ("not so much a book as a scream", according to one reviewer) was controversial and influential as fear of another world war increased.

131 **"Three Memorials":** Published in *Bart's Annual* for 1934.

131 **1921, 1924, 1933 travels:** During the summer of each of those years VB and WH travelled extensively in Europe, in 1924 as accredited journalists reporting on the League of Nations Assemblies at Geneva and on the state of Europe, in 1921 as in 1933 touring the trenches and cemeteries of the Western Front.

132 **"Never Goodbye":** The concluding line of a favourite poem of Roland Leighton and VB, "Echoes: XLII" by W. E. Henley (1849–1903).

132 **"the long white road . . .":** From Roland Leighton's "Hédauville, November 1915", which is quoted in *Testament of Youth* (Chapter VI, Section 4).

133 **Haig:** Sir Douglas Haig (1861–1928) was British Commander-in-Chief in France 1915–19.

135   **Edward's Battle:** Edward Brittain was badly injured on the first day of the Battle of the Somme, 1 July 1916; he was awarded the M.C. for conspicuous bravery.

139   **"Ici fut repoussé . . .":** "Here the invasion was repelled in 1918."

139   **articles about battlefields:** Similar anguished pieces, "Somme Battlefield, 1933" (*Week-end Review*, 12 August 1933) and "Illusion on the Somme" (*New Clarion*, 30 September 1933).

140   **"Gaudeam adfero":** "I bring rejoicing".

140   **"they say the lion . . .":** From *Omar Khayyam* by Edward Fitzgerald (1809–83): "They say the Lion and Lizard keep / The Courts where Jamshyd gloried and drank deep . . ."

141   **O.T.C.:** Officers' Training Corps, common at British public schools.

141   **Frank Swinnerton:** A prolific novelist, critic and journalist (1884–1982).

141   **Odette:** Odette Keun (b. 1890), a journalist and writer, whose tumultuous ten-year affair with H. G. Wells ended bitterly in 1933.

142   **B.R.C.S.:** British Red Cross Society.

143   **Q.M.A.A.C.:** Queen Mary's Army Auxiliary Corps.

144   **"standard" letter:** VB always answered fan-letters individually.

144   **"Ablutions in Picardy":** A humorous article; *Manchester Guardian* 24 August 1933.

144   **Davey:** Charles Davey, a friend of Catlin; he was a journalist on the *Yorkshire Post* and later the *Observer*.

145   **Pamela Hinkson; Katherine Tynan:** Pamela Hinkson, a novelist and journalist; her mother (1861–1931) was a prolific poet and novelist of Irish birth.

145   *Vanity Fair*: The great panoramic, satirical and sentimental novel (1847–48) by William Makepeace Thackeray; WH may well have taken this advice seriously, for *South Riding* has some similarities.

146   **Allan Young:** A political commentator, he had joined Mosley's New Party in 1931.

147   **Mussolini; Dollfuss:** In August 1933 the Italian dictator guaranteed Austrian independence on condition that Engelbert Dollfuss, the Austrian Chancellor, implemented Fascist principles; in September Dollfuss forced the Austrian parliament into dissolution to form a "Corporate State", but was assassinated by an Austrian Nazi in 1934.

147   **John Brophy:** A prolific novelist and journalist (1899–1965), he had enlisted at the age of fifteen to fight in the First World War.

147   **W.A.A.C.s:** Women's Army Auxiliary Corps.

148   **Sarah Gertrude Millin:** A prominent South African novelist and biographer (1889–1968), she published *The South Africans* in 1934; she and her husband Philip, a Judge in the Supreme Court of South Africa, were friends of WH and VB from the late twenties.

148 **Sisley Huddleston:** A writer and journalist (1883–1952), he became a naturalised Frenchman and wrote on French topics; in 1933 he published *War Unless—*.

148 **May Wedderburn Cannan, Sir Owen Seaman, Walter de la Mare, Wilfred Meynell:** VB sent them copies of *Testament of Youth* in gratitude for permission to quote from poems by them and by Alice Meynell.

149 **E. E. Kellett:** A writer and critic (1864–1950).

149 **Patrick Brand:** A member of Victor Gollancz's staff.

149 **Evelyn Sharp:** A prominent writer, lecturer, journalist and relief worker (1869–1955), she was a militant suffragette when young.

149 **E. Arnot Robertson:** A writer, broadcaster and lecturer (Lady Turner) (1903–61); she published *Ordinary Families* in 1933.

149 **Stella Gibbons:** A novelist and poet (b. 1902), best known for *Cold Comfort Farm* (1932), which was awarded the *Femina–Vie Heureuse* Prize.

149 **Yeats-Brown:** The writer Francis Yeats-Brown (1886–1944); he served in the First World War and in 1930 published his popular *Bengal Lancer*.

149 **Mr Lakin:** Cyril H. Lakin (1893–1948), a barrister, journalist and broadcaster; he fought in the First World War, and was Literary Editor of the *Sunday Times* 1933–37.

149 **James Agate:** A well-known writer and critic (1877–1947) who published many books on the theatre.

150 **Fräulein Bleichenbach:** The children's governess for three years. She later married an Englishman named Clarke.

150 **E. O. Lorimer:** Emily Lorimer (1881–1949), writer, translator and scholar.

150 **Eric Gillett:** A writer, journalist, academic and critic (1893–1978); he and VB acted together in *Raffles*, the popular play by E. W. Hornung, in June 1914, before he was wounded at Ypres in 1917; he became well-known as a drama and film critic.

151 **Aunt Belle:** Isabel Bervon, sister of Mrs Brittain.

151 **Stevens:** Frank L. Stevens (b. 1898) was Editor of the *New Clarion* 1932–34.

151 **Mellor:** William Mellor (1888–1942), a writer, journalist and socialist, was Editor of the *Daily Herald* 1926–31.

151 **the Torgler Reichstag trial:** The Reichstag fire of 27 February 1933, shortly after Hitler assumed office as Chancellor of Germany, was blamed on five men, one of them Ernst Torgler, Chairman of the German Communist Parliamentary Party, and their trial was scheduled for September in Leipzig. Torgler was imprisoned and survived the War, but one of his fellow-accused, the retarded Dutchman Marinus van der Lubbe, was executed.

152 **Irene Rathbone:** A writer, whose *We That Were Young* was published in 1932 with a Preface by E. M. Delafield.

152 **Nora James:** A novelist (1901–1979); in 1933 she published *Jealousy*.

152   **I. A. R. Wylie:** A prolific novelist and short-story writer (1885–1959), she published *The Things That We Do* in 1932.

152   **W. J. Brown:** William Brown (1894–1960), Labour M.P. 1929–31, Independent M.P. 1942–50.

152   **Eleanor Rathbone:** The influential Labour politician, feminist and pacifist (1872–1946); she was President of the National Council for Equal Citizenship 1919–29.

152   **Lionel Fielden:** A journalist and broadcaster (1896–1974), he was head of the BBC's General Talks Department 1930–35.

153   **Sheila Lynd:** A daughter of Robert and Sylvia Lynd, the writers, and a member of Gollancz's staff.

153   **Nevinson:** The well-known writer, journalist and philanthropist Henry Nevinson (1856–1941); he was a distinguished war-correspondent, and published his autobiography, *Fire of Life*, in 1935. He was married to Evelyn Sharp.

153   **Wilson Harris:** (Henry) Wilson Harris (1883–1955) was Editor of the *Spectator* 1932–35.

154   **Zinkin Committee:** "At Ellen Wilkinson's flat, British anti-Fascists from all parties formed a body ... to 'defend' the Reichstag prisoners at a 'counter-process' in London and to send an international delegation to the trial itself." One of the Committee's leading members was Pincus Zinkin, a well-known Communist.

155   **Bart's, Major Eccles:** St Bartholomew's Hospital (the oldest London hospital), at which VB nursed in 1918, was excoriated as "St Jude's" in *Testament of Youth* (Chapter IX) for its "unillumined routine" and "rigid sectarian orthodoxy". William M. Eccles (d. 1946), a noted surgeon, was Governor of St Bartholomew's in 1933.

155   **Guy Kendall:** A schoolmaster and writer (1876–1960), he was Headmaster of University College School, Hampstead, 1916–36, and in 1933 published *A Headmaster Remembers*.

155   **Pollitt:** Harry Pollitt (1890–1960); he was a founding member of the British Communist Party (1920), its General Secretary from 1929, and its Chairman from 1956.

155   **Kingsley Martin:** An influential journalist and lecturer in Political Science (1897–1969), he was Editor of the *New Statesman* 1930–60.

156   **"John Lovegood", Grant Watson:** Herbert Grant Watson (1881–1971), a novelist and diplomat.

156   **Ernst Toller:** A "German refugee writer" of expressionist plays (1893–1939), a pacifist and socialist: "Grey-haired and sad, with large dark eyes", he tried to make a living in London, then went to New York and committed suicide there.

157   **Frank Hardie:** A writer and socialist (b. 1911), he published many historical or political studies, including *Young Oxford and War* (1934).

157 **Chakravarty:** Amiya Chakravarty (b. 1901), a Bengali poet, once secretary to Rabindranath Tagore; he became very friendly with WH, published a critical study of Hardy's *The Dynasts*, and taught at New York State University College.

157 **Philippa and W. G. Hole:** Related to VB by marriage, he was a poet and playwright; his daughter Philippa wrote poetry, and edited a poetry magazine.

157 **Creech Jones:** Arthur Creech Jones (1891–1964), trade-unionist and politician, socialist and pacifist, Labour M.P. 1935–50 and 1954–64; his main interest was in colonial affairs, and he was Colonial Secretary 1945–46.

157 **Kate Courtney:** Kathleen Courtney (1879–1974), a feminist and social worker, was a prominent member of the League of Nations Union.

157 **Cecil King:** Later Lord Harmsworth (b. 1901), he was Director of the *Daily Mirror* from 1929 and has published a study of *The Future of the Press*.

158 **Dame Ethel Smyth:** The well-known composer and feminist (1858–1944), who was a Director of *Time and Tide*. At seventy-five, "she appeared no older than an energetic sixty, and her lively blue eyes seemed to snap with gaiety as she talked."

158 **Latham:** Harold Latham (1887–1969), a writer and editor, was head of the trade department of Macmillan's of New York 1919–52, as well as a Director and Vice-President: a "huge smiling man, whose benevolent countenance so effectually concealed the shrewd skill of his critical intelligence". In January 1933, he accepted *Testament of Youth* for publication before VB had completed it.

158 **Krishna Menon:** V. K. Krishna Menon (1896–1974), an Indian statesman; he worked in England for Indian independence, writing (with Ellen Wilkinson) *The Condition of India*, then became High Commissioner for India 1947–52 and a member of the Indian cabinet 1956–62.

158 **Mrs C. S. Peel:** Constance Peel, a writer and journalist, was Editor of *Hearth and Home*.

158 **Dorothy Sayers:** Dorothy L. Sayers, the famous writer of Lord Peter Wimsey detective stories, translator of Dante and Christian apologist (1893–1957); she was VB's contemporary at Somerville College.

158 **Doreen Wallace:** A prolific novelist and journalist (b. 1897); she was an undergraduate at Somerville College during the First World War.

158 **Vernon Bartlett's book on Germany:** *Nazi Germany Explained* (1933).

159 **Prof. Levy:** Hermann Levy (1881–1949), a German-born Professor of Economics who came to England in 1933.

159 **Isobel Brown:** A prominent Communist, member of the Committee for Spanish Medical Aid 1936.

159 **24 General:** The military hospital in Étaples where VB had nursed in 1917.

159 **Six Point Group:** The feminist pressure-group founded by Lady Rhondda in 1921.

159 **Helena Normanton:** A lawyer (1883–1957), she was the second woman called to the Bar in England and was a pioneer worker for equal pay.

160 **Mrs Ellinger and Maurice:** Mother and son, once neighbours of the Brittains in Buxton; Edward Brittain and Maurice Ellinger were boyhood friends and often played music together.

160 **Stanley Robinson, Sir Victor Horsley:** (Sir Edward) Stanley Robinson (1905–74), a scholar and numismatist, married Pamela Horsley, daughter of Sir Victor Horsley (1857–1916), an eminent surgeon and medical pioneer who strongly supported women's suffrage.

160 **Dr Eric Pritchard:** A noted paediatrician and consulting physician (1866 –1943), he published *The New-born Baby* in 1934.

160 **Sir Charles Trevelyan:** A well-known politician (1870–1958) who, as a Liberal M.P. 1899–1918, resigned from the Board of Trade in 1914 in opposition to Britain's entering the war; he was a Labour M.P. 1922–31 and President of the Board of Education 1929–31.

160 **Delisle Burns:** Cecil Delisle Burns (1879–1942), a lecturer and writer, Editor of *Ethics* and active in the League of Nations Union; he published *Challenge to Democracy* in 1934.

160 **Rev. H. S. McClelland:** The Rev. Henry McClelland (1882–1961), Belfast-born minister of Trinity Church, Glasgow, 1915–56. An emphatic personality, he attracted many "big names" as speakers in his very popular lecture series.

161 **Rationalist Press:** This association was formed in 1899 to promote "free thought" in religious matters by promoting reason as the ultimate arbiter. All her life, VB was influenced by the "free thinking" of writers like Olive Schreiner who had impressed her in her youth.

161 **Clifford Bax:** A playwright and writer on art (1886–1962).

161 **Ralph Straus:** A novelist and biographer (1882–1950).

161 **Anti-War Council:** The Anti-War Movement, a Communist-controlled organisation founded in 1932, was renamed the British Movement against War and Fascism in 1934, but soon afterwards dissolved.

162 **O.U.W.D.S.:** The Oxford University Women's Debating Society, which met at the Randolph Hotel.

162 **Miss Darbishire:** Helen Darbishire (1881–1961); Tutor in English Literature, author of major editions and studies of the poetry of Milton and Wordsworth, she was Principal of Somerville College 1931–45.

162 **days of** *The Dark Tide*: VB's first novel, "a lurid but guileless caricature of life at the Oxford women's colleges", had been resented at Somerville.

162 **Marjorie Bowen:** Pseudonym of Margaret Long (1888–1952); she wrote many novels, plays, biographies and historical studies, her best-remembered novel being *The Viper of Milan* (1917).

162 **Miss Lorimer:** (Elizabeth) Hilda Lorimer (1873–1954), Tutor in Classics 1896–1934, University Lecturer in Homeric Archaeology 1929–37, and

author of *Homer and the Monuments* (1950). VB, whom she tutored in 1914, remembered her with great affection and respect.

162 **Miss Farnell:** Vera Farnell (b. 1889), Librarian 1915–28 and Tutor in Modern Languages 1934–47 at Somerville College.

1934

The only entries in VB's diary are for the brief period 14–26 September, covering her and Catlin's journey to the United States, and the four days in and near New York preceding her three-month fifty-lecture tour. The tour itself—a "brilliant interlude" in VB's life—is described in *Thrice a Stranger* and summarised in *Testament of Experience*. The calm of the preceding nine months of 1934 had been punctured by an Italian holiday, a visit to Sidney and Beatrice Webb, the death of Roland Leighton's father, and, in June, a violent Mosleyite demonstration at Olympia which VB and Catlin witnessed.

167 **Miss Moore:** Ada Moore, a prominent member of the Six Point Group.

167 **Lord Astor; Lord Lothian:** Waldorf, Lord Astor (1879–1952), politician husband of Nancy Astor, was Chairman of the League of Nations Committee on Nutrition 1936–37; Philip Kerr, Lord Lothian (1882–1940), was Director of United Newspapers and in the India Office 1931–32.

168 **my previous visit:** Soon after her marriage, VB spent a year in the United States (September 1925 to August 1926)—in Ithaca, where Catlin taught at Cornell University, and in New York.

168 *Britannic*: On that ship VB had journeyed to Malta on 19 September 1916 as a VAD nurse.

168 **Mrs Wintringham**: Margaret Wintringham (1879–1955), the second woman elected to the House of Commons.

169 **Victor Cazalet:** Lt. Col. Victor Cazalet (1896–1943); after service in the First World War, he became Conservative M.P. for Chippenham from 1924.

169 **Sir John Marriott:** An eminent historian, academic and Conservative M.P. (1859–1945); he encouraged VB's ambition to study at Oxford, and published several historical studies.

170 **V. Sackville-West:** Victoria (Vita) Sackville-West (1892–1962), wife of Harold Nicolson and friend of Virginia Woolf, was a novelist, poet, critic and biographer best known for *The Edwardians* (1930).

170 **Colston Leigh:** (William) Colston Leigh (b. 1901); he set up his very successful lecture and entertainment agency in 1929. VB thought him a "human dynamo"—"shrewd as a ferret and tough as a Brooklyn boy".

171 **Flaherty,** *Man of Aran*: An American film-maker (1884–1951), he was a pioneer of the "contrived documentary" and best known for *Nanook of the North* (1922); *Man of Aran* (1934) was filmed off the west coast of Ireland.

171   **Bretts:** George P. Brett Jnr ("G.P.B.") (1893–1984); son of "one of the greatest publishers of his generation, who founded the Macmillan Company of New York in 1896", he was gassed while serving in the U.S. Army in France, and became the "youthful-looking President of the Macmillan Company" 1931–58. VB had first met him and his "friendly, hospitable" wife Isabel in London, during June 1933.

172   **Stuart Chase:** An American writer and social scientist (b. 1885) who believed that "we must put men first and money second"; in 1934 he published *The Economy of Abundance*.

172   **John Taylor Arms:** An American etcher (1887–1953) who worked extensively in Europe.

173   *A Modern Tragedy*: Phyllis Bentley's long Yorkshire novel was published in 1934.

173   **Mrs Brown Meloney:** A leading woman journalist (d. 1943), she edited the New York *Herald-Tribune*'s Sunday Magazine.

1935

Diary-entries begin on 5 May and are frequent, but not daily, until the end of July; after that, they are long, detailed and almost daily until they break off abruptly at the end of November. For several months after returning from her exhausting American lecture tour, VB was immersed in "domestic disturbance", but early in 1935 began to write *Honourable Estate*, the long novel which preoccupied her for over two years. She worked hard on it through spring, and enjoyed discussing it with George Brett, her debonair American publisher, with whom she had fallen in love. But summer brought a double disaster: her father's suicide, and the painful death of Winifred Holtby. This "cruellest and saddest year since the War" ended with energetic support for Catlin's bid to become a Labour M.P.

177   **Jubilee:** On 6 May 1935, George V (1865–1936) celebrated his Silver Jubilee: 25 years on the British throne.

177   **Princess Marina:** The wedding of Prince George (Duke of Kent) to Princess Marina of Greece in December 1934 was a very popular event.

177   **Edwardes Square:** VB's parents moved into a "small period house with a paved garden", in this "historic square off the Kensington High Street", early in 1935.

178   **Gordon's Regiment:** Catlin, as a rifleman in the London Rifle Brigade, was sent to France in 1918 "just in time for the Armistice".

178   **Earl of Athlone:** He (1874–1957) was Governor of South Africa 1923–31, Governor General of Canada 1940–46, and Personal A.D.C. to George VI.

178   **Queen:** George V's consort was Mary (May) of Teck (1867–1953).

178   **Duchess of York; York children:** Later Queen Elizabeth (b. 1900) when her husband, second son of George V, became George VI on the abdication

of his elder brother, Edward VIII, in 1936; his daughter Elizabeth (b. 1926) succeeded him in 1952.

179 **Bishop of Bathurst:** Horace Crotty (1886–1952) was the Anglican Bishop of Bathurst, New South Wales, 1928–36.

179 **theme of "Hon. Estate":** VB's "novel of transition" focused on the changing nature of the institution of marriage.

179 **George:** George Brett, President of the Macmillan Company of New York.

179 **Angus Watson:** He was the owner of the *Observer*.

179 **Women's Freedom League:** A feminist group formed in 1907 by suffragists, led by Mrs Despard, who did not accept Mrs Pankhurst's policies.

179 **Mrs Corbett Ashby:** Margery Corbett Ashby (1882–1981), an activist for women's rights, twice President of the Women's Liberal Federation, and Editor of *International Women's News*.

179 **Lady Astor:** American-born, Nancy Viscountess Astor (1879–1964) became in 1919 the first woman M.P., and was the only woman M.P. in the House of Commons 1919–21.

179 **Nina Boyle:** A writer, lecturer and feminist (1866–1943), she was three times arrested for suffragette activities.

180 **Elizabeth Scott:** An architect (1898–1972) who achieved prominence for designing the Shakespeare Memorial Theatre at Stratford-upon-Avon.

180 **Caroline Haslett:** An engineer (1895–1957), she was instrumental in opening that profession to women.

180 **Betty Archdale:** Honorary Secretary of the Equal Rights Committee 1933–35, she was the sole woman (and top) candidate in International Law 1934.

180 **Mrs Littlejohn:** She was the wife of a prominent Australian headmaster.

180 **Mr Longman:** William Longman (1882–1967), founder of the publishing firm, was President of the Publishers' Association 1929–30.

180 **Lot's Power Station:** "The great electrical plant at the unfashionable end of Chelsea", in Lot's Road.

180 **Lord Snell:** A Labour politician, Henry Snell (1865–1944) was committed to "Socialism and Rationalism"; he was Chairman of the London County Council 1934–38 and led the Labour Party in the House of Lords 1935–40.

181 **L.M.H.:** Lady Margaret Hall, an Oxford College.

181 **Mrs Lyons:** Enid Lyons, a gifted speaker, wife of Joseph Lyons (1879–1939), Prime Minister of Australia 1931–39.

181 **Dame Rachel Crowdy:** A prominent public servant (1884–1964), she was the VAD Commandant in the First World War, and worked for the League of Nations until 1931.

181 **Julia Varley:** A suffragette, trade-union organiser and social reformer (1871–1952), she campaigned for better working conditions for women and was a member of the T.U.C. General Council 1921–35.

181 **Sunderland:** This Northern constituency encompassed a heavily-industrialised region east of Newcastle-on-Tyne.

181 **Gordon, return from Russia:** Catlin accompanied the delegation of Anthony Eden, appointed Foreign Secretary later in 1935, to see Stalin in Moscow. While there, Catlin decided to resign his professorship at Cornell so as to enter active politics in England.

181 **Shakespeare:** Sir Geoffrey Shakespeare (1893–1980), Liberal M.P. 1922 –23 and 1929–45, was Parliamentary Secretary to the Minister of Health 1932–36. He was distantly related to VB.

182 **Elizabeth Jenkins:** A novelist, critic and biographer (b. 1907).

182 **E. M. Forster:** The admired novelist (1879–1970) best known for *A Passage to India*.

182 **Charles Evans:** A publisher and critic and text-book writer (1883–1944), he was Managing Director of Heinemann's from 1932.

182 **Elizabeth Sprigge:** A writer, lecturer, translator and play-producer (1900 –74).

182 **Hugh Eayrs:** An English-born Canadian publisher (1894–1940), he was President of Macmillan's of Canada from 1921.

182 **"In my Father's house . . .":** St John 14, 2.

182 **Sir Leo Chiozza Money:** A flamboyant writer, journalist and Liberal politician (1870–1944), he switched to the Labour Party in 1918 but was not re-elected.

182 **Margaret Whitehead:** A friend made in the United States during VB's 1934 lecture tour, she was married to Professor T. North Whitehead of Harvard.

183 **Lord Lloyd:** Lord George Ambrose Lloyd (1879–1941); a politician, public servant, traveller and writer, he served in the First World War.

183 **Sir Herbert Samuel:** A writer, academic, and public servant in Israel (1898–1978), he became 2nd Viscount Samuel in 1963.

183 **Capt. Liddell Hart:** The eminent writer on military tactics and military history, (Sir) Basil Liddell Hart (1895–1970).

183 **Sir Ronald Storrs:** A public servant and specialist in Middle Eastern affairs (1881–1955), he was Governor of Jerusalem 1917–26 and Governor of Cyprus 1926–32.

183 **R. D. Blumenfeld:** Ralph Blumenfeld (1868–1941), an American-born journalist who was Editor of the *Daily Express* 1902–32.

183 **Archie Macdonell:** A writer and journalist (1895–1941), he served in the First World War and worked for the League of Nations Union 1922–27; his books include the popular *England, Their England* (1933). Like VB he had made an American lecture tour in 1934, and they had met at the Bretts' country house in Connecticut. She was distressed when, in 1937, he eloped with Dick Sheppard's wife Alison.

183 **Alec Waugh:** Brother of Evelyn Waugh; a novelist (1898–1981) best remembered for *The Loom of Youth* (1917) and *Island in the Sun* (1956).

183   **Dan Macmillan:** Elder brother of Harold Macmillan (1886–1965), he was Chairman and Managing Director of Macmillan's in London 1936–63.

183   **"When that which is perfect . . .":** I Corinthians 13, 10.

183   **Mrs Stanley Unwin:** Wife of the publisher (1884–1968), who was Chairman of George Allen and Unwin Ltd.

184   **James Anderson:** Stella Benson's widower, he worked in the Chinese Customs service.

184   **Robert Bernays:** A politician and journalist (1902–45), he was Liberal M.P. for Bristol from 1931.

184   **"And the sun shall rise . . .":** Possibly by Vera Brittain.

184   **Mrs Belloc Lowndes:** A prolific popular writer (1868–1947).

184   **Diana Wynyard:** A well-known stage and screen actress (1906–64), she was nominated for an Oscar for *Cavalcade* in 1933.

185   **Ruth Gage Colby, Izetta Robb:** Two close American friends made by VB during her 1934 lecture tour: Ruth Colby (1899–1985), wife of a child specialist, Dr Woodard Colby, was "a poet, an artist, and the Minneapolis Chairman of the Women's International League for Peace and Freedom"; Izetta Winter Robb (b. 1904), "a brilliant young woman trained at the University of Minnesota", became "an administrator of education in the Duluth area" and later an editor.

185   **Pritt:** Denis N. Pritt K.C. (1887–1972), a socialist, pacifist and writer, was a Labour M.P. 1935–50 who pressed for closer relations with the U.S.S.R.

185   **Naomi Jacob:** A writer, actress and feminist (1884–1964).

185   **National Peace Conference:** The National Peace Council was established in 1904 to organise annual Congresses and co-ordinate the peace movement.

185   **Vyvyan Adams:** A politician (1900–51); M.P. 1931 and 1935–45, he was the leading Conservative advocate of disarmament in the House of Commons.

185   **Norman Bentwich:** A writer, public servant and academic (1883–1971), he was Professor of International Relations at the Hebrew University of Jerusalem 1932–51; cousin, by marriage, to Victor Gollancz.

186   **Buckinghamshire, walk:** WH's "supreme spiritual experience" occurred at Monks Risborough, when she was living in a cottage near Clare Leighton.

186   **"having nothing . . .":** II Corinthians 6, 8.

186   **Doris Leslie:** Lady Fergusson Hannay, novelist, biographer and historian.

187   **Henry Seidel Canby:** A writer and journalist (1878–1961), he was co-founder and Editor of the *Saturday Review of Literature* 1924–36.

188   **Mrs Manning:** Leah Manning (1886–1977), a teacher, writer and politician; she was a Labour M.P. 1931 and 1945–50, and on the Party's National Executive 1931–32. She became the first woman to be Chairman of a Trade Union when she was elected to the position in the N.U.T. 1929.

188   **North Whitehead:** (Thomas) North Whitehead (1891–1969), Professor of Business Studies and Economics at Harvard University 1931–39 and

1943–58, Adviser to the Foreign Office on American Affairs 1940–43; son of the eminent philosopher A. N. Whitehead, he was "one of the most charming, gentle and perceptive people I ever met".

188   **A. J. Cummings:** Arthur J. Cummings (d. 1957), a journalist and political commentator, was the Political Editor of the *News Chronicle* 1932–55.

189   **Meigh ancestors:** The family of VB's paternal grandmother.

189   **"End of the House of Alard":** A reference to the title and theme of a novel (1923) by Sheila Kaye-Smith.

189   **Arthur Hollins:** A trade-unionist and politician (1876–1962), he was General Secretary of the National Society of Pottery Workers 1910–47 and a Labour M.P. 1928–31 and 1935–45.

190   **Winifred at Malvern:** On that visit, WH and Lady Rhondda were photographed with G.B.S. on his seventy-ninth birthday.

190   **Mrs Adamson:** Janet L. Adamson (1882–1962) was a member of the National Executive Committee of the Labour Party 1927–47 and a Labour M.P. 1938–46.

190   **Sir Stafford Cripps:** A prominent statesman (1889–1952), he was a Labour M.P. 1930–50, Solicitor-General 1930–31 and Chancellor of the Exchequer 1947–50.

190   **R. Minturn Sidgwick:** An "immensely tall and disarming young man" when VB met him in Chicago in 1934, he was a nephew of Ellery Sidgwick, Editor of the *Atlantic Monthly*.

190   **holiday; Edith and Margaret de Coundouroff:** In 1915 Edith married George de Coundouroff, a Russian orphan who came to England as a boy and spent summers at Rudston with the Holtby family before fighting in the First World War and then going to Russia during the Revolution. Edith went to live with the Holtbys in 1916 and, after her husband's disappearance and presumed death in 1919, continued to live with them, as WH's "sister", for twenty years. Her daughter Margaret was sixteen at the time of the holiday. WH remained in London, working desperately to finish *South Riding*, which she had written while living alone at Withernsea and Hornsea on the Yorkshire coast for periods in 1934 and 1935.

191   **"Face of Revolution":** Catlin's book was never published.

192   **Bentley-Carrs:** VB's Aunt Lillie and Uncle Arthur.

193   **Alfred Haigh; Alfred Goodman:** The first was a business associate, a Director of Brittain's Ltd, the family paper-mill; the second a family friend from Buxton.

193   **Josiah Wedgwood:** Col. the Rt Hon. Josiah (Baron) Wedgwood (1872 –1943) was an M.P. (Liberal, Labour, finally Independent) 1906–42, and Mayor of Newcastle-under-Lyme 1930–32.

194   **"The Diver":** "Der Taucher": a setting (1891) by Schubert of a poem by Schiller.

195   **Mr Dodd:** Arthur Dodd was the family solicitor and an old Buxton friend.

197 **G.'s old constituency:** Isleworth was in the Brentford and Chiswick constituency, for which Catlin was the unsuccessful Labour candidate in 1931.

197 **splurged headline:** The 300-word article in the *County of Middlesex Independent* was titled "Vera Brittain Bereaved / Writer's Father Commits Suicide / Dr Catlin's Evidence at Inquest / A Sufferer from Melancholia".

199 **Peter's marriage:** Seven years after WH's sister Grace died (in 1928), her husband, a Scottish doctor, remarried.

200 **Dorothy Thompson:** A well-known journalist and writer (1894–1961) who married Sinclair Lewis in 1928; his book was of course entitled *It Couldn't Happen Here* in the United States.

200 **go to Liberia:** In April WH "accepted an invitation from Liberia, issued on the strength of *Mandoa, Mandoa!*, to be the guest of its Government that winter and write them a confidential report. . . . She longed to see the country because it was a portent, a symbol of African independence . . .".

201 **Mrs Swanwick, autobiography:** Helena M. Swanwick (1864–1939) was a prominent feminist, socialist, internationalist and journalist; she was a British delegate to the League of Nations Assemblies 1924 and 1929, and Editor of *Foreign Affairs*, published for the Union of Democratic Control; *I Have Been Young* was published by Gollancz in 1935.

201 *Four Hedges*: Written and illustrated by Clare Leighton, this book (1935) is a joyous "gardener's chronicle" of her life at Monks Risborough.

204 **Sir Harry Preston:** Journalist, *bon viveur* and hotel proprietor (1860–1936), he published many articles on boxing and other sports.

204 **Roedean:** A famous public-school for girls near Brighton.

206 **ill-fated place:** At Brighton, in December 1915, VB was informed that Roland Leighton had been killed.

206 **Rudston:** WH grew up in Rudston House, built by her father David on his large farm near the village of Rudston, on the Yorkshire wolds near Bridlington.

208 **Mrs Holtby; the introductory dedication:** WH's "Prefatory Letter to Alderman Mrs Holtby", printed in *South Riding*, is an affectionate "explanation and apology" for the novel's biographical indebtedness, and records "the proud delight which it has meant to be the daughter of Alice Holtby".

208 **brutal chapter about Sarah and Carne:** In Book VII, Chapter 5 of *South Riding*, Sarah Burton and Robert Carne, though deeply in love, quarrel violently—and Carne, who has *angina pectoris*, dies abruptly in the next chapter. (Or perhaps the reference is to Book VI, Chapter 6, in which Sarah, "temporarily insane", spends a night with Carne—who is drunk, and has a heart-attack! Both chapters qualify as "brutal".)

209 **Mr Bone:** James Bone (1872–1962), London Editor of the *Manchester Guardian* 1912–45.

210 **the debate at Oxford:** This is described fully in *Testament of Youth*, Chapter

X, Section 5. VB had felt humiliated by WH and other speakers after aggressively endorsing "those who suffered deeply from the War".

211 **Canon Sheppard:** Dick (H.R.L.) Sheppard (1880–1937), Vicar of St Martin-in-the-Fields, Trafalgar Square, from 1914, and Canon of St Paul's Cathedral from 1934; a pioneer of religious broadcasting, deeply admired for his humanitarian work and his pacifism, he founded the very influential Peace Pledge Union in 1936.

212 **Helen Waddell:** A respected Irish historian (1889–1965), she was a member of Somerville College 1921–22, and widely known for *The Wandering Scholars* (1927), *Medieval Latin Lyrics* (1929) and *Peter Abelard* (1933).

215 **Father Bede Jarrett:** Provincial of the Dominican Order in England, and a respected scholar and historian (1881–1934), he married VB and Catlin (who was a Catholic).

215 **Stamford:** Roger Grey, Lord Stamford (1896–1976), Deputy Lieutenant of Cheshire 1937–74; a contemporary at New College, Oxford, he was Catlin's Best Man.

217 **"Abyssinia Mobilises":** War between Mussolini's Italy and Abyssinia (Ethiopia) began in October 1935; following ineffectual League of Nations sanctions, Italy invaded and occupied Abyssinia in May 1936.

217 **"When thou passest . . .":** Isaiah 43, 2; Joshua 1, 5.

218 **Dot McCalman:** Educated with Edith de Coundouroff in a Belgian convent, Dorothy McCalman (1888–1930) taught in elementary schools in England; helped by WH to fulfil her educational ambitions, she entered Somerville College in 1922. WH endowed a Somerville Scholarship in her name.

220 **Edward Garnett:** A writer, critic and editor (1868–1937).

221 **Victor:** Victor Richardson died of his wounds in London two months after being blinded at Vimy Ridge, April 1917.

221 **its place knew it no more:** Psalm 103, 15.

222 **St John Ervine knew pain:** He was badly wounded in the First World War, losing a leg.

222 **"Judgment Voice":** WH's first play, never performed or published; she turned it into a short story, "The Voice of God" (in *Truth is not Sober*).

223 **W. A. R. Collins:** (Sir) William A. R. Collins (1900–76), Chairman and Managing Director of William Collins, WH's publisher.

223 **"My heart is inditing . . .":** Psalm 45.

223 **Bunyan's Pilgrim Song:** The poem ("He who would valiant be . . .") by John Bunyan (1628–88) set to a traditional melody.

223 **"The souls of the righteous . . .":** Wisdom of Solomon 3, 1.

223 **"The Sower . . .":** The words of this hymn are by the Rev. William Bourne (1846–1929); they are set to a melody by Sir Frederick Bridge (1844–1924).

223 **"Crossing the Bar":** A setting of Tennyson's popular lyric by (Sir) Joseph Barnby (1838–96).

223 **"Jerusalem":** The poem by William Blake (1757–1827) set by Sir Charles Parry (1848–1918).

224 **Bainesse:** The name of Mrs Holtby's house at Cottingham. (Renamed Holtby House, it is now a student hostel of Hull University.)

224 **Corfu dispute:** Conflict between Italy and Greece during which Mussolini attacked and occupied Corfu, August 1923; the League of Nations negotiated Italian withdrawal after Greece paid Italy a substantial indemnity.

225 **story about the monolith:** WH's "The Legend of Rudston", reprinted in *Pavements at Anderby* (1937).

225 **"I am the Resurrection . . .":** St John 11, 25.

225 **"Nunc Dimittis":** "Lord, now lettest thou thy servant depart in peace . . .": St Luke 2, 29–32.

225 **Ellen Terry:** The extremely popular and respected actress (1848–1928).

226 **"O God most Holy . . .":** Burial service, prayer at the graveside.

227 **Hunger Strike, S. Wales miners:** Monmouthshire miners remained underground until management agreed to discontinue employing non-union men.

228 **young man, life of Frank Brangwyn:** Presumably William de Belleroche (b. 1912) who published a biography of Sir Frank Brangwyn (1867–1956), the artist.

228 **"Take What You Want":** The epigraph to *South Riding* is an "old Spanish proverb": " 'Take what you want,' said God. 'Take it—and pay for it.' " VB was surely right to reject this title, which is also only partially appropriate to the novel's theme.

228 *The Garden of Time*: By Mrs (Gwendoline) Davidson, this "tale for children" (1896) had been read to VB when a child.

229 **Daphne du Maurier's book:** The best-selling novel, *Jamaica Inn*, was published in 1936.

230 **J. H. Thomas, strange thoughts:** Arthur Henderson had been appalled by the "betrayal" of 1931, leading the Labour Party into opposition to Ramsay MacDonald's coalition, but Thomas had joined the National Government and so lost union support.

230 **Major Attlee:** The statesman Clement (1st Earl) Attlee (1883–1967); he was a Labour M.P. from 1922, Leader of the Opposition 1935–40, and Prime Minister 1945–51.

230 **Mr Clynes:** John R. Clynes (1869–1949), a trade-unionist and politician; he was a Labour M.P. 1906–31 and 1935–45.

230 **as bad as 1931:** The Labour Party was very badly defeated in the General Election of 1931, winning only 52 seats to the National Government's 554.

230 **Williamson Noble:** (Frederick) Williamson Noble (1889–1969), an ophthalmic surgeon.

230 **Betty Morgan:** A journalist, broadcaster and scholar.

230 **Dr Albert Belden:** Superintendent Minister of Whitefield's Tabernacle in London 1927–39, he published many religious books (1883–1964).

231 **Hannen Swaffer:** A flamboyant and influential journalist and drama critic (1879–1962).

232 **Margaret Bondfield:** The Rt Hon. Margaret Bondfield (1873–1953), an eminent trade-unionist, public servant and politician; she was a Labour M.P. 1923–24 and 1926–31, worked with the League of Nations at Geneva through the twenties, and was Chairman of the T.U.C.'s General Council 1923.

232 **Chuter-Ede:** James (Baron) Chuter-Ede (1882–1964), Labour M.P. for South Shields 1929–31 and 1935–64, was Home Secretary 1945–51.

233 **Furness and Storey:** Catlin's and Manning's opponents: Stephen Furness (1902–74), Liberal M.P. for Sunderland 1935–45; (Sir) Samuel Storey (Baron Buckton) (1896–1978), Conservative M.P. for Sunderland 1931–45.

233 **Shinwell:** The statesman Emmanuel (Lord) Shinwell (b. 1884); he was Labur M.P. 1922–24, 1928–31, and 1935–70; Minister of Fuel and Power 1945–47 and Minister of Defence 1950–51. He stood against Ramsay MacDonald and defeated him.

233 **Joshua Ritson; Tom Sexton:** Ritson (1874–1955) was a Labour M.P. 1922–31 and 1935–45; Thomas M. Sexton (1879–1946) was a Labour M.P. 1935–45.

233 **Mrs Zangwill:** A writer and pacifist (d. 1945), she was married to Israel Zangwill (1864–1926), a well-known novelist.

234 **Jack Lawson:** Lawson (1881–1965) was a Labour M.P. 1919–49 and Parliamentary Secretary to the Minister of Labour 1929–31.

1936

This year began for VB with intense literary effort as she prepared WH's *South Riding* for its publication in February, and her own *Honourable Estate* for publication in November. In the spring she travelled with Catlin to Germany and France, keeping a detailed record of her observations. Then, after a short lecture tour in Holland, came "a turning point in my life" when, under the influence of Dick Sheppard, she became a pacifist and (early in 1937) a Sponsor of his Peace Pledge Union. The diary has many gaps (especially in the latter part), but gives a fairly full impression of an important year in VB's life.

239 **Introduction to** *South Riding*: It was printed as "Ave Atque Vale: An Epitaph", an afterword, in the American edition, and gives helpful background information for WH's "story of universal values mirrored in local experience".

240 *Freedom, Farewell*: An historical novel about Julius Caesar, *Freedom, Farewell* (1936) was a striking departure by Phyllis Bentley from her regional base.

240 **Tyrone Guthrie:** (William) Tyrone Guthrie (1900–71) was an admired theatrical director, Administrator of the Old Vic and Sadler's Wells 1939 –45.

240 **"Hope of Thousands":** Earlier title of WH's play *Take Back Your Freedom*.

241 **S.S.A.:** The Somerville Students' Association.

241 **Marjorie Barber; Muriel Byrne:** They had been acquaintances of VB in 1914: Barber (b. 1894) was a Chaucer scholar and lecturer; Muriel St Clair Byrne (1895–1983), a lecturer in English Literature, published several editions and critical studies, including *The Lisle Letters* (1981).

241 **Brown's Hotel:** Quiet, select and expensive, it was Rudyard Kipling's favourite hotel and a prominent literary meeting-place.

242 **Pilnyak:** Boris Pilnyak was the pseudonym of Boris A. Vogau (1894–1937), author of *The Tale of the Unextinguished Man* (1927), who was expelled from the Soviet Writers' Union in 1929 and "disappeared" in 1937.

242 **Sybil Thorndike:** The famous stage actress and firm pacifist (1882–1976).

242 **Goering:** Hermann Goering (1893–1946); Minister for Air Forces from 1933 and founder of the Gestapo, he was Hitler's First Deputy until late in the War.

243 **Dr Jane Walker:** An expert on consumption (1859–1938), she was very concerned with social problems and published several medical books for women.

243 **Matthews:** The Very Rev. Walter Matthews (1881–1973), Dean of St Paul's 1934–67, was the author of several books on Christian belief.

243 *Life of Mandell Creighton:* WB's quotation is an epigraph to Chapter VIII of *Honourable Estate*; the biography (1906) of this eminent ecclesiastic and scholar (1843–1901) was by Luisa Creighton, his wife.

243 **Charles Morgan's new novel:** *Sparkenbroke* (1936).

243 **Cynthia Stockley:** A South African novelist and journalist.

244 **Sir Henry Irving:** The eminent Shakespearian actor (1838–1905).

244 **Canon Barry:** (Frank) Russell Barry (1890–1976), later Bishop of Southwell, author of several religious books.

245 **Addison:** The famous poet, essayist and journalist Joseph Addison (1672–1719), co-founder of the *Spectator*.

245 **"Recessional":** Kipling's popular patriotic and moralistic poem.

246 **Lynd girl:** Sheila Lynd, who worked at Gollancz Ltd.

246 **Thomas Moult:** A journalist, writer and critic (d. 1974).

246 **H. H. Price:** Henry H. Price (b. 1899), an eminent professor of metaphysics whose *Perception* (1932) was admired.

247 **Find Graucob:** A businessman of Scandinavian origin.

247 **F.A.N.Y.s:** The First Aid Nursing Yeomanry.

247 **P. Nehru:** Pandit Jawaharlal Nehru (1889–1964), the Indian national

leader and statesman; for many years a leading member of the Congress Party, he was the first Prime Minister of India after independence was gained in 1947.

247 **Ivor Thomas; Leonard Barnes:** Thomas (1861–1942) was in the Indian Service until 1916; Barnes was an adviser on African affairs to the Labour Party in the thirties.

248 **Sheila Kaye-Smith; May Edginton:** The first was a well-known novelist (1888–1956), the second a prolific popular writer (d. 1957) one of whose novels was adapted as the musical *No! No! Nanette.*

248 **Trevor Blakemore; George Birmingham:** Blakemore was best known as a poet. George Birmingham was the pseudonym of the Rev. James Hannay (1865–1960), a prolific novelist, humorist and religious writer; his son Dr Hannay later married Doris Leslie.

249 **Lin Yutang:** A writer and academic (1895–1976) who wrote many books about China and was Professor of English at Peking University 1923–26.

249 **Mosley case:** Sir Oswald Mosley brought a slander action against John Marchbank, General Secretary of the National Union of Railwaymen, who had claimed that Mosley urged his followers to carry and use weapons.

249 **Flora Robson; Joyce Bland:** Robson was a greatly admired stage and screen actress (1902–1984); Bland (1906–1963) also starred in films, including *The Citadel* (1938).

249 **John Spivak:** An American journalist and writer (b. 1897), he published *Europe Under the Terror* in 1936.

249 **Mrs Harold Munro:** Widow of the poet (1879–1932) who founded the Poetry Bookshop.

249 **J. L. Hodson:** James L. Hodson (1891–1956), writer and journalist; he investigated European unemployment 1932–33 and was a war correspondent 1939–42.

250 **Julius Lewin:** His work for social justice in South Africa includes such books as *Africans and the Police* (1941) and *An Outline of Native Law* (1944). Lewin was Professor of African Law at Witwatersrand University.

250 **H. E. Bates:** A popular novelist and short-story writer (1905–1974).

250 **Harold Macmillan:** The famous statesman (Earl of Stockton, 1984) (b. 1894); Conservative M.P. 1924–29, 1931–45 and 1945–64, Prime Minister 1957–63, he was also a Director of the family publishing firm (Chairman 1963–74).

250 **Mary Ellen Chase:** An American academic and novelist (1887–1973).

251 **Granny:** i.e., Mrs Holtby (affectionately called "Granny" after the birth of her daughter Grace's first child).

251 **Annie Swan:** A popular writer, especially for children; her autobiography, *My Life*, appeared in 1934.

251 **Jean McWilliam:** A predecessor of WH and VB at Somerville, Jean McWilliam (1881–1963) was a teacher in South Africa; she and WH became

close friends in France during 1918 when they met while serving in the Women's Army Auxiliary Corps, and their subsequent lively correspondence was published as *Letters to a Friend* in 1937.

252 **pre-war Blatchford article:** The influential journalist Robert Blatchford (1851–1943), founder and editor of the *Clarion*; he published *My Eighty Years* in 1931.

252 **Howard Spring:** A novelist, critic and journalist of Welsh birth (1889–1965).

253 **Sir Stephen Tallents:** A public servant (1884–1958), he was Controller of Public Relations at the BBC 1935–40.

253 *In the Second Year*: Storm Jameson's novel (1936) imagined Britain falling under fascist dictatorship.

253 **Libel letter for** *The Times*: Signed by thirty-four eminent writers, it pleaded for "reforms in the law relating to libel" since "at present the law is so heavily weighted against authors" that it severely diminished their freedom of speech and so threatened the quality of English literature.

254 **"So teach us . . .":** Psalm 90, 12.

254 **"Comfort us again . . .":** Psalm 90, 15.

254 **Rosita Forbes:** (Joan) Rosita Forbes (d. 1967) was a well-known travel-writer.

255 **Madeleine Linford:** A writer and journalist, she edited the *Manchester Guardian*'s Women's Page and published a *Life of Mary Wollstonecraft* (1924).

255 **Sarah and Carne "temporarily insane":** In Book VI, Chapter 6, of *South Riding*.

255 **Situation calmer internationally:** After denouncing the Locarno Pact and remilitarising the Rhineland on 7 March 1936, Hitler agreed to attend a Council Meeting of the League of Nations in London.

255 **"German peace":** i.e., one that (unlike the Treaty of Versailles) treated Germany generously; in 1917 such a peace was advocated by pacifists and others.

255 **Garvin:** James Garvin (d. 1974), author of a biography of Joseph Chamberlain, was Editor of the *Observer* 1908–42. Father of Viola Garvin.

255 **Locarno Powers:** The Locarno Pact of December 1925 comprised a series of agreements whereby Germany, France, Belgium, Great Britain and Italy mutually guaranteed peace in Western Europe; it was an attempt at rapprochement after the First World War.

256 **Knickerbocker; John Gunther:** Prominent American journalists: Hubert Knickerbocker (1898–1949) won the Pulitzer Prize in 1930 and 1933; John Gunther (1901–70) became prominent with a series of travel books such as *Inside Europe* (1936).

256 **Zilliacus:** Konni Zilliacus (1894–1967), a journalist, writer and Labour M.P.; he worked in the Information section of the League of Nations Secretariat 1919–39, and in the Ministry of Information 1939–45.

256   **W. N. Ewer; Gordon-Lennox:** William N. Ewer (b. 1885) and Victor Gordon-Lennox (b. 1897), journalists who specialised in foreign affairs.

256   **"the deep fatigue . . .":** *South Riding*, Book V, Chapter 3.

256   **"What shadows we are . . .":** Edmund Burke (1729–97), speech at Bristol 1780.

256   **Bromfield:** William Bromfield (1868–1950), a trade-union organiser 1919 –42 and Labour M.P. 1918–31 and 1935–45.

256   **"successor to Arnold Bennett":** Presumably as an important writer from Staffordshire who, in *Honourable Estate*, was to use the Potteries as a setting.

257   **30th June shootings:** The Röhmputsch or "Night of the Long Knives": in 1934 Ernst Röhm and his Stormtroopers were "purged".

257   **Pat McCormick:** The Rev. (William) Patrick McCormick (1877–1940) succeeded Dick Sheppard as Vicar of St Martin-in-the-Fields in 1927 and was appointed Chaplain to the King in 1928.

257   **von Ribbentrop:** Joachim von Ribbentrop (1893–1946) was German Ambassador in London 1936–38 and Foreign Minister of the Nazi Government from 1938.

259   **Duke of Sutherland:** George Grenville, 5th Duke (1888–1963), held many public appointments.

260   **"Der Führer . . .":** "The Fuhrer has kept his word. Germany thanks him on 29 March."

260   **"Wir stehen . . .":** "We stand with the Fuhrer!"

260   **the posters:** "Work—Honour—Peace." "Your honour—have faith in the Fuhrer!" "We are defending the world from Bolshevism." "The spirit of the new Germany is the spirit of peace." "Thank the Fuhrer with your vote." "One People—one Reich—one Fuhrer!"

261   **Friedrich Ebert; Stresemann:** Ebert, a socialist politician (1871–1925), was the first President of the Weimar Republic 1919; Gustav Stresemann (1878–1929), as Chancellor and Foreign Minister 1923–29 of the Weimar Republic, achieved Germany's entry to the League of Nations in 1926.

261   **Treviranus; Brüning:** Gottfried Treviranus (1891–1971)—Minister of Transport from 1931, under Heinrich Brüning (1885–1970), Chancellor of the Weimar Republic 1930–32—fled to England in 1934.

261   **American picture:** *Accent on Youth*, starring the English-born actor Herbert Marshall (1890–1966) and the very popular American actress Sylvia Sydney (b. 1910).

262   **colonial question:** Hitler took Germany out of the League of Nations in 1933, and refused to accept the Treaty of Versailles (1919) as valid; he demanded the return of all Germany's colonies and ceded territories.

262   **Venizelos:** As Greek Premier 1928–63 Eleutherios Venizelos (1864–1936) pursued pro-French policies, and fled to France in 1935.

262   **Baldwin:** Stanley (1st Earl) Baldwin (1867–1947) was Conservative Prime Minister 1923–24, 1924–29 and 1935–37.

263   **Essen, Krupp foundry:** The huge steel and armaments factory owned by the Krupp family; it was of major importance to German military might.

263   *Mein Kampf:* Hitler's two-volume work ("My Struggle", 1925–27) set out his political ideas and objectives.

264   **"Nun sprecht . . .":** "Now the Fuhrer speaks."

264   **"Deutschland über Alles"; Horst Wessel Lied:** The German National Anthem; and the song by a young German "martyr" (1907–30) which in Nazi Germany became a second anthem.

265   **slogans:** "Discord and treachery make us lawless—unity and faith assure us of freedom and justice." "The German garrisons are garrisons of peace."

266   **"Hetzen . . .":** "Agitate!"

268   **Mrs Anne O'Hare McCormick:** A journalist (1882–1954), foreign correspondent for the *New York Times* from 1920, she was the first woman to win the Pulitzer Prize for Journalism (1937).

268   **Gen. Blömberg:** Werner von Blömberg (1878–1946); Field Marshal and War Minister of the Nazi Government 1935–38, he resigned over a scandal involving his wife.

268   **Frick, Goebbels, Ley, Darré:** Senior members of the Nazi administration: Wilhelm Frick (1877–1946) was "Protector" of Czechoslovakia; Josef Goebbels (1897–1945) was Minister of Propaganda; Robert Ley (1890–1945) organised the German Labour Front through which workers were controlled; and Richard Darré (1895–1953) was Minister of Agriculture, but in 1942 was stripped of office for criticising Hitler's war policies.

268   **Gauleiter:** Area Commander.

268   **Geistlich:** Vigorous.

268   **stark und gefertigt:** Strong and prepared.

269   **"Alt-Niederländisches Dankgebet":** "Old Low-Country Prayer of Thanks".

269   **"Studenten! . . .":** "Students! Be propagandists for the Fuhrer!"

270   **"Unser Kindern . . .":** "Our children's future through Adolf Hitler."

270   *Der Jüngling im Feurofen:* A novel ("Youth in Torment") by Heinz Steguweit (1897–1964) published in 1932.

270   **the Saar:** This industrial area was under resented League of Nations and French control 1919–35.

272   **Charlemagne:** King of the Franks, he became Holy Roman Emperor (742–814).

274   **the Northcliffe Press; Hoare–Laval negotiations:** The Hoare–Laval Plan (September 1935), devised by the British and French Foreign Secretaries, hoped to solve the Abyssinian problem by ceding half of Abyssinia to Italy; made public and vociferously opposed in the popular press in December, the plan was repudiated and Sir Samuel Hoare (1880–1959) forced to resign.

274   **Goethe:** The great German writer and polymath (1749–1832).

275   **Sir Eric Phipps:** A diplomat (1875–1945), he was Ambassador Extraordinary and Plenipotentiary in Berlin 1933–37.

275   **Angabe:** Statement, declaration.

275   **Rudolf Kircher:** A prominent journalist (b. 1885); several of his books about England were translated into English, *Engländer* (1925) being the most widely read.

275   **Neurath:** Konstantin von Neurath (1873–1956), Hitler's Foreign Minister 1932–38 and then Protector of Bohemia–Moravia until replaced (because considered too lenient) by Heydrich in 1941.

276   **Schlagsahne:** Whipped cream.

277   **"Juden sind . . .":** "Jews unwelcome here."

279   *Queen Mary:* Recently launched, this liner set a new record for a transatlantic voyage in 1936.

279   **Zouave:** Soldier (in the colonial Algerian infantry).

281   **"Ils n'ont pas passé":** "They were stopped here."

282   **Penn:** The founder of Pennsylvania State was an English Quaker and Admiral's son (1644–1718).

283   **Eugene C. Meury:** The inscription is imaginary. Eugene Meury is a major character of *Honourable Estate*. Ruth Alleyndene, its heroine, while nursing in France towards the end of the First World War, meets a handsome, "very tall, black-haired" young American soldier with "brilliant smiling eyes" and a "questing vivacity of countenance". They fall deeply in love. But he is killed, and after the War Ruth visits his grave. VB "lived" Ruth's experience in the American Cemetery at Romagne, collecting impressions which appear in Part III, Chapter VI, Sections 11 and 12, of *Honourable Estate*.

284   **"Eugene at Romagne":** This passage was incorporated, almost word for word, in *Honourable Estate* (p. 499).

285   **"The Casualty List":** WH's short story appears in her collection *Truth is not Sober* (1934).

286   **S. P. B. Mais:** Stuart P. Mais (1885–1976), a prolific novelist, journalist, broadcaster and academic.

286   **Randolph Churchill:** Son of Sir Winston Churchill, Randolph Churchill (1911–68) was a lecturer, journalist and writer.

286   **Wade:** Col Henry Wade (1869–1941), served in the First World War. His daughter Rosalind, a novelist, became William Kean-Seymour's second wife.

286   *"le vilayet de Parmoor":* VB's account of this slip—relating to a dispute over the boundaries of the Iraqi province Mosul ("vilayet" being a Turkish word for "province")—is in *Testament of Youth*, Chapter XII, Section 5.

286   **inspired by last Czar:** Nicholas II (1868–1918), killed during the Russian Revolution, called an international Peace Conference in 1899 at The Hague;

the delegates met in the Peace Palace and signed the Hague Convention, which attempted to discourage and control warfare.

286 **Sir Hubert Montgomery:** A diplomat (1876–1942), he was British Minister at The Hague 1933–38.

287 **Rembrandt:** VB's deep admiration for the great Dutch artist (1606–69) was expressed in visits to the Rijksmuseum and Mauritzhaus to see his paintings.

288 **the Kaiser comes:** Wilhelm II (1859–1941) fled into exile in Holland just before the First World War ended.

289 **Professor Leo Polak:** When VB visited Holland again, in September 1945, she was told that Leo Polak had died during the War.

290 **Mary Wollstonecraft book:** VB's projected biography of the pioneer feminist (1759–97), which she also called her "French Revolution book"; it was to have placed Wollstonecraft's life in the historical context of the French Revolution, which she observed in 1792.

290 **Max Beerbohm; L. H. Myers:** The celebrated caricaturist and humorist (1872–1956); and Leo H. Myers (1881–1944), whose *The Root and the Flower* (1935) was part of his Indian tetralogy of novels, *The Near and the Far*.

291 *Company K*; *Drums*: Two American war novels, the first (1933) by William Campbell (William March) (1893–1954), the second (1925) by James Boyd (1888–1944).

291 **Leonard Woolf:** A historian, autobiographer, critic, publisher and socialist (1880–1969), he was married to the novelist Virginia Woolf.

291 **Great Dorchester Peace Rally:** This "turning point of my life" is described at the beginning of Chapter V in *Testament of Experience*; when VB participated as a speaker at this large outdoor peace rally in Dorset, she was thrown into contact with some of the foremost advocates of Christian pacifism —Laurence Housman, George Lansbury, Donald Soper and, particularly, the charismatic Dick Sheppard. Within six months she had joined Sheppard's Peace Pledge Union.

291 **"Sometimes such a sudden gladness . . .":** *The Story of an African Farm*, Part II, Chapter 11.

292 **2 Cheyne Walk:** The Chelsea house VB and Catlin were to buy in May 1937. A "typical eighteenth-century dwelling" with "perfectly-proportioned rooms", it "stood at the east end of the long terrace facing the river where some of Britain's best-known artists and writers had lived."

292 **Sandown:** A resort on the Isle of Wight.

.293 **conference, Spanish affairs:** The Spanish Civil War had just broken out, in July 1936. After attending this international conference, Catlin supported Labour Party criticism of the British Government's non-intervention, "served on a Spanish Aid Committee which met in Paris", and visited Spain in January 1937.

293 **Anacapri inscriptions:** "To acts of war we will respond with acts of war." "The cry of Italy is a cry of justice and a cry of victory." "Italy will no longer

pursue a policy of renunciation and humiliation." "Many enemies, much honour."

293 **Vera Mikol:** An American writer (b. 1899), she worked in the U.S. Foreign Office at Naples 1931–36.

294 **Yeats-Brown book on India:** One of the sequels to *Bengal Lancer* (1930).

294 **Maurois; Julian Huxley:** André Maurois (1885–1967), the French novelist and biographer; (Sir) Julian Huxley (b. 1887), the eminent biologist and first Director-General of UNESCO 1946–48.

294 **Crisis, King's marriage:** Edward VIII (1894–1972), who acceded to the throne on 20 January 1936, had known the American divorcée Wallis Simpson since 1931; he insisted on marriage to her, against political and ecclesiastical objection, and their affair became public knowledge on 3 December 1936.

294 **Hone's biography of George Moore:** This biography of the Irish novelist, essayist and autobiographer (1852–1933), by Joseph Hone (1882–1959), was published in 1935.

297 **Archbishop of Canterbury:** At that time, Cosmo Gordon Lang (1864–1942).

297 **the greatest Strike; the greatest experiment in international co-operation:** The British General Strike of 1926; and the League of Nations, established in 1919 to promote peace and settle international disputes by arbitration, but seriously weakened by 1936.

298 **Duke of York, his Duchess:** VB fully recognised that she had been wrong about George VI and Elizabeth (now the Queen Mother), and when he died at the beginning of 1952 queued for five hours in the cold to pay tribute at his lying-in-state. (See her article "Memorial Queue" in *Testament of a Generation*.)

299 **Lady Oxford:** Widow of Herbert Asquith, 1st Earl of Oxford and Asquith (1852–1928), the Liberal statesman who was Prime Minister 1908–16.

299 **John Drinkwater:** The eminent poet and playwright (1882–1937).

299 **Ian Hay:** Pseudonym of Major-General John Hay Beith (1876–1952), best known for his account of the early volunteers to fight in the First World War, *The First Hundred Thousand* (1915).

299 **Mrs Marsden-Smedley:** Hester Marsden-Smedley (d. 1982), Woman's Editor of the *Sunday Express* and sometime Chairman of the Poetry Society.

1937

Diary-entries are frequent but not daily during three months (January, February and April); then daily from 18 September to 6 October, recording VB's voyage and her first few days in the United States; ending with two entries made during her travels. In January, VB began "to work systematically on the biography of Winifred" which was to occupy her for over two years (with a break to write *Thrice a Stranger* in 1938). After moving to 2 Cheyne Walk in May, she and Catlin went on a walking holiday in Cornwall before she prepared for her second American lecture tour.

303 **Captain Philip Mumford:** He served in the First World War and (with the RAF) in Iraq 1927–32, then became an internationalist and pacifist, joining the PPU in the summer of 1936 as a Sponsor and member of the Executive Committee; but he resigned in May 1940, at the same time as his two fellow Sponsors, Bertrand Russell and Storm Jameson.

303 **Peace Pledge Union:** Formed in May 1936 from the Sheppard Peace Movement, it incorporated the No More War Movement in February 1937 and became the British Section of the War Resisters' International; in 1940 it had some 136,000 members and was extremely influential as the major British anti-war organisation.

303 **Bertrand Russell's** *Which Way to Peace?*: This very powerful tract was published in 1936. It began: "The governments of Europe disagree on many subjects, but on one point they are in perfect harmony: they all believe that a new Great War is imminent." His argument led to the conclusion that "the duty of every friend of mankind" was "TO ABSTAIN FROM FIGHTING, AND FROM ALL VOLUNTARY PARTICIPATION IN WAR BETWEEN CIVILISED STATES; TO USE EVERY EFFORT TO PERSUADE OTHERS TO DO LIKEWISE . . ."

303 **the Manders:** (Sir) Geoffrey Mander (1882–1962), a barrister, was a Liberal M.P. 1929–45 and joined the Labour Party in 1948.

303 **Sponsor:** PPU Sponsors, of whom there were about thirty, composed its "collective leadership" until May 1939, when a National Council took over; the Sponsors represented many variations of pacifist opinion.

303 **Cartland:** John R. Cartland (1907–1940), a Conservative M.P. from 1935, was later killed in action during the War. His sister Barbara is the well-known romantic novelist.

303 *Growing Pains*: This autobiography, by Basil Harvey (b. 1909), was published in 1937.

304 **Prof. G. M. Trevelyan:** The eminent social historian (1876–1962) who published many volumes of popular historical studies in English history; he was Professor of Modern History at Cambridge 1927–40.

304 **Sir James Jeans:** A physicist and astronomer (1877–1946); his popular scientific books include *The Mysterious Universe* (1930).

304 *Gone With the Wind*: This best-selling novel by Margaret Mitchell (1900–49), a journalist on the *Atlanta Journal*, was published in 1936 and won the Pulitzer Prize.

305 **Philip Sargant Florence:** A noted economist and educator (1898–1982), he was interested in labour efficiency and urban and regional planning; in 1933 he published *The Logic of Industrial Organisation*.

306 **Newnham College:** The Cambridge women's college founded in 1871.

306 **Hon. Rupert Beckett; Dr Alan and Dr Elizabeth Garrett Anderson:**
The first was a J.P. and bank-director (1870–1955); (Sir) Alan Garrett
Anderson (1877–1952), a Conservative M.P. 1935–40, was the son of a
pioneer woman doctor (1836–1917) who was also the first woman elected as
a mayor in England (at Aldeburgh in 1908).

307 **Wilkins:** (William) Vaughan Wilkins (1890–1959), a journalist and writer,
was Assistant Managing Editor of the *Daily Express* 1929–33; *And So
—Victoria* was published in 1937.

307 **Laurence Whistler:** A poet, art critic and glass engraver (b. 1912).

307 **St John Ervine letters; unposted reply:** None of these (VB's reply *was*
posted, two years later!) is among VB's papers.

308 **Kitchener:** Secretary of State for War 1914–16, Lord Kitchener (1850
–1916) was drowned on his way to Russia.

308 **Cyril Connolly:** The prominent writer and critic (1903–74); he co-founded
the literary magazine *Horizon* in 1939 and is best known for his partly-
autobiographical *Enemies of Promise* (1938).

308 *Letters to a Friend:* This selection of WH's letters (1920–1935) to her friend
Jean McWilliam was published in 1937.

308 **Dr Lockhart:** As the note VB added later (probably about 1945) indicates,
Leonard Lockhart, who had been badly shell-shocked in the First World
War, was found "guilty but insane" of the murder of his wife in 1939; VB's
interest in the case led her to fictionalise it in her *Account Rendered* (1944).

308 **O.D.C.:** The Open Door Council.

308 **"lions":** Tyrannical or hurtful things.

309 **R. C. Sherriff:** Robert C. Sherriff, the playwright and novelist (1896–1975)
best known for *Journey's End* (1929), his play about the First World War.

309 **Humbert Wolfe:** A poet and essayist (1885–1940).

309 **Laurence Housman:** A prolific playwright, poet and artist (1865–1959), he
supported women's suffrage, and became a leading socialist and pacifist
after the First World War.

309 **Canon Morris:** Stuart Morris (1890–1967), a Chaplain during the First
World War, became Travelling Secretary 1936 then General Secretary 1939
of the P.P.U.

309 **Allen Skinner:** Imprisoned as a conscientious objector during the First
World War, Allen Skinner (1890–1972) joined the P.P.U. in 1937 when it
absorbed the No More War Movement.

310 **Mr Casey:** Richard Casey (1890–1976), later Baron Casey, an eminent
Australian politician and diplomat; he was Federal Treasurer 1935–39.

310 **Helen Simpson:** A novelist (1897–1940) whose works include *Boomerang*
(1932); she was married to Denis Browne, a surgeon.

310 **Donald Soper:** A Methodist minister (b. 1903) and fervent pacifist (Baron
Soper 1965).

310   **Lansbury:** George Lansbury, politician, social activist and journalist (1859 –1940), was a Labour M.P. 1922–40 and Leader of the Labour Party 1931–35, founder of the *Daily Herald*, and a leading pacifist.

311   **Miss Muriel Ritson:** A public servant (1885–1980), she served on many commissions and was Controller of Health and Pensions Insurance in the Scottish Department of Health 1929–45.

311   **C.W.S.:** Co-operative Wholesale Society.

311   **Rhys Davies:** A trade-unionist and politician (1877–1954), he was a Labour M.P. 1921–51.

312   *Northwest Passage; American Dream*: A vivid historical novel (1937) by Kenneth Roberts (1885–1957); and a novel (also 1937) by Michael Foster (b. 1904).

313   *A Star is Born*: This version starred Janet Gaynor and Frederic March.

313   **withdraw Ambassador from Japan:** After occupying Manchuria in 1931, the Japanese invaded China in July 1937, causing diplomatic uncertainty in Britain when the British Ambassador in Peking was attacked and injured.

313   **Cordell Hull:** An eminent diplomat, statesman and judge (1871–1955), he was Secretary of State 1933–45 and was awarded the Nobel Peace Prize 1945 for helping to create the U.N.

314   **"Ich liebe dich":** A very popular setting (1863) by Edvard Grieg of a poem by Hans Andersen.

314   **A. J. Putnam:** Macmillan executive connected with the NY branch of P.E.N.

314   **Lois Cole:** A writer and editor (b. 1902), she published many novels under various pseudonyms.

315   **Herschel Brickell:** (Henry) Herschel Brickell (1889–1952); an editor, writer and reviewer, he was a book-columnist and then Literary Editor of the *Evening Post* 1928–35.

316   **Vassar:** The famous women's college founded in 1861.

317   **Ralph Bates:** A writer and academic (b. 1899), he lived in Spain 1930–37 where he was active in anti-Franco politics, and was Professor of Literature at New York University 1948–68.

317   **Bryn Mawr, Dr Park:** Marion Edwards Park (1875–1960) was (from 1922) President of Bryn Mawr, the women's college founded in 1880.

317   **Margaret Ayer Barnes:** A novelist (1886–1967), she won the Pulitzer Prize for her *Years of Grace* (1930).

318   **Dick Sheppard, Rectorial Election:** He had polled 538 votes to Churchill's 281, but a few days later was "found dead in his study chair with a half-finished letter before him".

318   **Lord Birkenhead:** F. E. Smith, 1st Lord Birkenhead (1872–1930); a Conservative statesman, he was Attorney General 1915–19, Chancellor 1919–22, and Secretary for India 1924–28.

318   **New Orleans battle:** During the American Civil War, New Orleans was bombarded and subsequent martial law imposed by the Unionist victors was very harsh (1862).

1938

"From the beginning of 1938, political events made a too-convulsive background for literary composition." Nevertheless, VB completed a book about her three visits to the United States, *Thrice a Stranger* (published in September 1938), and continued her work on *Testament of Friendship*. The year opened with the joy of seeing the successful film of *South Riding*, but the international situation darkened steadily before, on 29 September, came the temporary relief of Chamberlain's Munich Agreement, which VB strongly supported as a necessary attempt to avert the worse darkness of world war. Earlier in September, VB and Catlin travelled to the United States; on this brief visit they took both children, intending to "leave them in American schools" if war began in Europe.

321 **Edna Best, Marie Lohr, Ann Todd:** Three well-known film-stars: Edna Best (1900–74) played Sarah Burton, the heroine; Marie Lohr (1890–1975) Alderman Mrs Beddows; and Ann Todd (b. 1909) Muriel Carne. (Ralph Richardson played Robert Carne.) VB thought it a "memorable" but "over-romantic" treatment of WH's "moving but astringent story".

321 **Communist demonstrations:** Among several demonstrations in London on the eve of Hitler's invasion of Austria was a march by Communists through Whitehall; they shouted "Chamberlain must go!"

1939

From the beginning of this year VB again kept a daily "reflective record", with very few gaps. Hard work on *Testament of Friendship*, the desperately worrying international situation—these are qualified by domestic events such as school-arrangements for her children, an operation to remove Shirley's tonsils, and the acquisition of a country cottage where, in the first ten days, "I wrote 100 pages of *Testament of Friendship* . . . and had done nearly 500 at the end of another month", finishing it just before the storm finally broke.

325 *Land of Green Ginger*: WH's third novel (1927). "For the light that it throws on her personality and the continual conflict in her thoughts, this novel is among the most illuminating of Winifred's works."

325 **"The Runners",** *New Voter's Guide*: The first was a long novel, never published, about the religious reformer John Wyclif; WH finished it in November 1925, but it was refused by John Lane on the advice of J. B. Priestley. In the second, a booklet published just before the General Election of 1929 (the first in which all women over twenty-one could vote), WH discussed the questions a "young woman voter might put to the canvassers of all three political parties".

325 **President Roosevelt:** Franklin D. Roosevelt (1882–1945) was President from 1933 to his death.

326 **Archibald Baxter's** *We Will Not Cease*: "The autobiography of a New Zealand pacifist."

326 **Left Book Club:** Founded by Victor Gollancz in May 1936 to resist the rise of Fascism and Nazism, it was immediately successful: by the end of 1937, in addition to its widely-distributed Left Books of the Month, there were over seven hundred local discussion groups.

326 *Sixty Glorious Years*: Starring Anna Neagle, this 1938 film featured scenes from the life of Queen Victoria.

326 **H.P.:** Harry Pearson.

327 **French Revolution novel:** VB's projected study of Mary Wollstonecraft's life and work, against the background of the French Revolution, was never written. It was to have been entitled "Behold, This Dawn!"

327 **Dame May Whitty:** Professional name of Dame May Webster (1865–1948), an actress and social activist.

327 **Basil Maine:** The Rev. Basil Maine (1894–1972), a prolific biographer and musical journalist, published *Franklin Roosevelt* in 1938.

327 **Veronica Turleigh:** A well-known actress (1903–71).

328 **"Nessun maggior dolore":** From Dante's *Inferno*, this is the beginning of a favourite quotation: "There is no greater pain than to recall the happy time in misery".

328 *Esther Waters*: George Moore's most popular novel, it was published in 1894.

328 **War Resisters' International:** This organisation was founded at The Hague in 1921 to "co-ordinate socialist pacifism".

328 **K.N.E.:** Katherine Nixon-Eckersall became VB's secretary towards the end of 1938.

328 **John to school:** He was now at the Downs School, near Malvern—a boys' preparatory boarding-school.

329 **my godson:** Philip Kean Seymour, b. March 1938.

329 **No-Conscription meeting:** The No-Conscription Fellowship (1914–19) was revived in 1938 as the No-Conscription League, but was not influential.

329 **Bart's:** St Bartholomew's Hospital, where VB had nursed at the end of the War.

329 **Labour Book Service:** An attempt to promote socialist literature, apparently in competition with the more radical Left Book Club.

329 **N.C.E.C.:** The National Council for Equal Citizenship. Originally the National Union of Women's Suffrage, its primary object was to "ensure that women's rights were constantly brought to the attention of Parliament"; it opposed "protective legislation" for women workers since this limited their earning capacity.

330 **Hoyland:** Geoffrey and Dorothy Hoyland, Quakers, ran the Downs School.

330 **Gandhi:** VB deeply admired the Indian nationalist leader and social reformer (1869–1948).

330 **N.P.C.:** National Peace Council.

330 **Duchess of Atholl:** Katharine, ("Red") Duchess of Atholl (1874–1960); a Conservative M.P. 1923–38, she was a League of Nations delegate 1925 but opposed women's suffrage and appeasement; her *Searchlight on Spain* appeared in 1938.

330 **Oldfeld School:** In September Shirley Catlin was sent to this "P.N.E.U. school at Swanage in Dorset where she had cheerfully agreed to go after seeing it with me in March".

330 **from the** *Queen Mary:* i.e., on the voyage back from the United States a few weeks earlier.

331 **Mrs White's book suppressed:** The book was *War in Spain* by Freda White.

331 **Welsh engagement:** This was postponed to early February; VB had been elected Honorary President of the Debating Society of Aberystwyth University and was to deliver a lecture to the student body. Like the election of Dick Sheppard as Rector of Glasgow University, this was an indication of pacifist sympathy among British students.

331 *The Crowded Street:* WH's second novel (1924), set in rural Yorkshire; its title is a quotation from a poem by VB.

331 *Peace News:* Then the organ of the P.P.U.

331 **"anti" campaigns:** VB felt strongly that campaigns such as that against conscription diverted effort and attention from central pacifist issues, and were damagingly negative.

331 *The Story of the Political Philosophers:* Catlin's most popular and successful book, published in 1939 and several times reprinted.

331 **Chamberlain's speech:** Neville Chamberlain (1869–1940), British Prime Minister 1937–40, was trying to persuade Hitler to respect the Munich Agreement of 1938.

331 **Fellowship of Reconciliation:** Founded in 1914, this Christian pacifist organisation developed into an international movement with particular strength in the United States.

332 **avoided Collins:** Because she was to publish *Testament of Friendship* with Gollancz although Collins were WH's publishers. (It was eventually published by Macmillan.)

333 **Sir Austen Chamberlain, Walter de la Mare, Dean Inge:** Respectively eminent as Conservative statesman (1863–1937), poet and novelist (1873–1956) and influential Christian apologist, Dean of St Paul's Cathedral (1860–1954).

333 **my grandfather, organist:** VB's maternal grandfather, John Bervon, was an organist and composer of Welsh origin.

334 **P.E.N. refugee party:** Under the Chairmanship of Storm Jameson, P.E.N. was very active in the late thirties, and through the War, helping European intellectuals to flee Nazi and Fascist repression.

334 **Richard Church:** A respected poet, novelist, autobiographer and critic (1893–1972).

334   **Berta Ruck:** A popular novelist (1878–1978), she was married to the writer Oliver Onions and published over 150 books.

334   **Hermon Ould:** A playwright, poet and critic (1885–1951), he became General Secretary of P.E.N.

334   **"causeness":** Too devoted to various social and political causes.

334   *Eutychus: Eutychus or the Future of the Pulpit* (1928) was WH's "short treatise in the form of a Plain Dialogue" wittily proving that "the authority of the pulpit is passing to the public platform" (the original Eutychus was an early Christian who fell asleep, and out of a window, while St Paul was preaching!).

334   **Mlle Piaget;** *The Good Master:* The book sent by one of the famous educationalist's daughters was by Kate Seredy (1935).

335   **I.C.U.:** The International and Commercial Workers' Union. Founded in 1919, this was the only Black trade union in South Africa; supported by WH, William Ballinger helped to reorganise it.

335   **Dr Balogh:** Thomas (Lord) Balogh (1905–1985), a Budapest-born economics expert, worked for the League of Nations and the U.N., and was Minister of Energy 1974–75.

335   **Pope dead:** Pius XI, who sought good relations with Mussolini and Hitler but attacked totalitarianism when his strategy failed.

335   **Roy Walker:** From 1937 he worked full-time for the P.P.U. and was the driving force behind many of its campaigns, notably the campaign for Food Relief during the Second World War in which VB worked closely with him; he resigned from the P.P.U. later after a serious conflict over policy and became a dramatic critic and lecturer.

337   **Sir Fabian Ware:** An educationalist (1869–1949), he was also founder of the Imperial War Graves Commission.

337   **Hon. Mrs Franklin:** An educationalist and lecturer (1866–1964), Hon. Mrs Henrietta Franklin was Secretary of P.N.E.U. and founded a girls' school.

337   **Antoinette Devonshire:** Her pacifist book was *New Valour* (1938).

337   **"Collective Security":** The policy of rearmament to dissuade aggression.

337   **Bishop Barnes:** Ernest W. Barnes (1874–1953), Anglican Bishop of Birmingham 1924–53, and a well-known writer and theologian, was the only Bishop advocating pacifism at the time.

337   **Dame Elizabeth Cadbury:** A prominent philanthropist (1858–1951); mother of Mrs Hoyland of the Downs School.

337   **"Hundred Thousand" group:** A movement, seen as right-wing, to "convince 100,000 people in key positions . . . to press the Government for action".

338   **my internationalist politics, G.'s:** Catlin was not a pacifist.

338   **Sir John Hammerton:** A writer and editor (1871–1949), he founded *World Digest* in 1939.

341 **Canon Raven:** A Professor of Theology, Canon Charles Raven (1885–1964) expounded Christian pacifism in several books and was a P.P.U. Sponsor.

341 **Norman Ginsbury, Ibsen's** *An Enemy of the People*: Norman Ginsbury (b. 1902), who adapted the play about political conflict, by the great Norwegian playwright (1828–1906), revised WH's *Take Back Your Freedom* to give it greater force. He is best known for his plays *Viceroy Sarah* and *The First Gentleman*.

341 **Aldous Huxley; Elizabeth Thorneycroft:** The well-known writer (1894–1963), author of *Brave New World*; and a prominent barrister.

342 **Barker:** (Sir) Ernest Barker (1874–1960), Professor of Political Science at Cambridge, published several important books. (Catlin wrote Barker's *DNB* entry.)

342 **Hugh Dalton:** (Edward) Hugh (Baron) Dalton (1887–1962), a well-known politician, was a Labour M.P. 1924–31 and 1935–59, Chancellor of the Exchequer 1945–47 and Minister of Town and Country Planning 1950–51.

342 **Mrs Hamilton:** Mary A. Hamilton (1882–1966), journalist, biographer, Labour M.P. 1929–31, Governor of the BBC 1933–37, L.C.C. Alderman 1937–40.

342 **Gaitskell:** (Sir) Hugh Gaitskell (1906–63), an economist and statesman; he was a Labour M.P. from 1945, Chancellor of the Exchequer 1950–51 and Leader of the Opposition 1955–63.

342 **Dr Eileen Power:** An academic and writer (1889–1940), she was Professor of Economic History at the London School of Economics from 1931.

342 **Denis Browne:** An eminent surgeon, (Sir) Denis Browne (1892–1967); he was at the Hospital for Sick Children, Great Ormond Street, 1928–57. His wife was the novelist Helen Simpson.

342 **William Hillman:** An American journalist (1895–1962), he was a Hearst Press correspondent in Europe.

343 **Horace Shipp:** An art critic and journalist (b. 1891).

343 **Stanley Cursiter:** A painter and engraver (1887–1976), he was Director of the National Gallery of Scotland 1930–48.

345 *Truth Is Not Sober*: A collection of short stories by WH (1934).

345 **Hacha:** President Emile Hacha held office in Moravia and Bohemia (sometimes called Czechia) throughout the War, under German "Protectors".

345 **Dr Schreiber:** A "Czech-Jewish woman dentist whom [Catlin] had met the previous summer on the train from Prague to Vienna"; with VB's help, she came to England and "trained as a maternity nurse under the National Midwives Scheme".

345 **Lord Ponsonby:** Arthur Ponsonby, Lord Ponsonby of Shulbrede (1871–1946), an eminent politician and pacifist, was a Labour M.P. 1922–30 and Leader of the Opposition in the House of Lords 1931–35.

346 **Miss Picton-Turbervill:** A social activist and politician (d. 1960), she was a prominent advocate of women's ordination.

346 **Mrs Hubback, Edith Summerskill:** Prominent feminists: Eva Hubback (1886–1949), an economist and educationalist; (Lady) Edith Summerskill (1901–80), a Labour M.P. 1938–61, Minister of National Insurance 1950 –51.

346 **Bishop of Chichester:** Rt Rev. George Bell (1883–1958), a respected philanthropist; during the war VB worked closely with him in opposition to area-bombing.

346 **H. G. Elvin; Miss Tanner:** Herbert Elvin (1874–1949), lay preacher and trade-union official, social and religious activist; (Dame) Emmelina Tanner (1876–1955), Headmistress of Roedean 1924–47.

347 **Lesser House, Woking:** The home of VB's Aunt Lillie and Uncle Arthur.

347 **Gollancz, attack on Fascism:** As a result of this speech, VB and Victor Gollancz were estranged for several years; but they were reconciled during the War, and in its aftermath worked together to help Europe.

347 **John Barclay:** A devout Christian pacifist, he was National Group Organiser of the P.P.U. 1936–42.

348 **Claud Cockburn:** A Scottish-born socialist, journalist and novelist (1904 –81), he edited *The Week*.

348 **Frank Pakenham:** 7th Earl of Longford (1961), a socialist known for his extreme humanitarianism (b. 1905).

348 **President Lebrun's arrival:** Albert Lebrun, President of France, visited Britain and discussed with Chamberlain the possibility of an alliance with Poland and Russia against Germany.

348 *Take Back Your Freedom*: WH's "anti-dictator" play, written in 1934 and published, as revised by Norman Ginsbury, in 1939.

348 **occupation of Memel:** The Treaty of Versailles had ceded the previously-German Baltic port of Memel to Lithuania.

348 **Brogan:** (Sir) Denis W. Brogan (1900–74), an eminent political scientist.

349 **Hockaday School:** A private school for girls in Dallas, Texas, it was named after its founder and first headmistress.

350 **Howard Lewis:** (Cecil) Howard Lewis, the artist who painted the well-known portrait of WH now in Somerville College, Oxford.

350 **Angela Thirkell:** A prolific English-born novelist (1890–1961), she was a journalist and broadcaster in Australia 1918–30.

350 **Committee of Friends of Africa:** A group founded by WH to campaign for the rights of Africans, especially in South Africa.

351 **Ruth Fry:** (Anne) Ruth Fry (1878–1962); a writer, pacifist and Quaker, she was a prominent social activist.

351 **"Gnädige Frau":** "Gracious lady."

351 **Plowman:** Max Plowman (1883–1941), a poet and critic who edited the *Adelphi* 1938–41, was Secretary of the P.P.U. 1937–38; his book *The Faith Called Pacifism* (1936) was influential, and he became a close friend of VB.

351 **Daladier:** Edouard Daladier (1884–1970), French statesman and Prime Minister 1933–34 and 1938–40.

353 **Jean Monnet:** The eminent French economist (1888–1979); he advocated Anglo-French economic collaboration, and through the Monnet Plan promoted rapid French recovery after the Second World War.

354 **Percy Bartlett, Embassies of Reconciliation:** A pacifist organisation founded in 1936, it sponsored George Lansbury's 1937 European tour (during which he met Hitler and Mussolini); Percy Bartlett, who resigned from the Fellowship of Reconciliation in 1936, was the Secretary.

354 **Lord Stanley:** A Conservative politician, Lord Edward Stanley (1894–1938) was Parliamentary Under-Secretary in the India Office 1937–38.

355 **Albania invaded:** Mussolini's forces occupied Albania on Good Friday 1939; King Zog I fled into exile.

355 **Tunis, Djibouti:** Tunisia and French Somaliland were North African French colonies.

355 **"The better the day . . .":** A saying attributed to Matthew Henry (1662–1714).

356 **Greek pact:** To counter the Italian invasion of Albania, Britain and France offered guarantees of independence to Greece and Romania.

358 **question of future publication:** VB and Gollancz were later reconciled but, partly as a result of their quarrel, only one major later book—*Testament of Experience*—was published by Gollancz. When he was dying, she visited him several times and expressed her gratitude for all he had done as her publisher.

358 **Admiral Drury-Lowe:** Vice-Admiral Sidney Drury-Lowe (1871–1945).

360 **luncheon with Mrs Roosevelt:** During her American lecture tour of 1937, VB was invited to the White House by Eleanor Roosevelt (1884–1962) and also met the President.

362 **negotiations with Russia:** These unsuccessful negotiations lasted from 15 April to 21 August; two days after they ended, a Nazi–Soviet non-aggression pact was signed.

362 **Señor Madariaga:** Don Salvador de Madariaga (1886–1978), a Spanish writer and academic, Professor of Spanish at Oxford 1928–31, Spanish Delegate to the League of Nations 1931–36.

362 **Sir Eric Drummond:** (James) Eric Drummond, 16th Earl of Perth (1876–1951), a Liberal politician, was Secretary General of the League of Nations 1919–33 and British Ambassador to Italy 1933–39.

363 **Ronald Gurner:** As well as *Day Boy* (1924), (Stanley) Ronald Gurner (1890–1939) published books about his First World War experiences.

364 **Sybil Morrison:** A feminist, pacifist and social activist (1893–1984), she was a founding member of the P.P.U. and twice its National Chairman.

364 **Dr Alfred Salter, Andrew Stewart, Maurice Rowntree, Mary Gamble:** All P.P.U. Sponsors: Salter (1878–1945) was a Labour M.P. 1922–45;

Stewart, as Chairman of the Glasgow University Pacifist Society, had worked hard for Dick Sheppard's election as Rector; Rowntree, Treasurer after Mumford, died suddenly during the War; Mary Gamble later became John Middleton Murry's fourth wife.

INDEX

INDEX

(The diary's range and complexity of reference have imposed obvious constraints on this index. Please note the following points:

1. Passing references, unless considered of some importance in the diary, have been excluded.

2. Unless mentioned in the diary, honorific titles have usually been omitted.

3. The entries for Vera Brittain (who is abbreviated within entries as "VB") and Winifred Holtby ("WH") have been firmly focussed; to a lesser extent, so have those for other frequently-mentioned individuals or organisations.

4. Books and plays are listed under their authors unless unattributed in the diary; but Honourable Estate, Inheritance, South Riding, Testament of Friendship *and* Testament of Youth *all have independent entries.*

5. London areas, clubs, halls and meeting-places, hospitals, hotels or hostels and restaurants, libraries, places of worship, shops, and theatres, have been gathered alphabetically under the entry "London".

6. British cities and towns, if visited by VB on holiday or to lecture, appear under the entry "Brittain, Vera".

7. Cities and towns outside Great Britain have usually been gathered under their countries.

And finally: I hope to have pleased the Earl of Stockton—"every good index should have a joke".)